CONCINI, LEONORA GALIGAI, AND MARY DE' MEDICI

FRANCE

BY

M. GUIZOT AND MADAME GUIZOT DE WITT

TRANSLATED BY ROBERT BLACK

Illustrated

WITH A SUPPLEMENTARY CHAPTER OF RECENT EVENTS
BY MAYO W. HAZELTINE

IN EIGHT VOLUMES

VOLUME FOUR

NEW YORK AND LONDON
THE CO-OPERATIVE PUBLICATION SOCIETY

HISTORY OF FRANCE

VOLUME FOUR

TABLE OF CONTENTS—VOL. IV.

THE HISTORY OF FRANCE.

CHAPTER XXXVII.

REGENCY OF MARY DE' MEDICI (1610—1617).

ON the death of Henry IV. there was extreme disquietude as well as grief in France. To judge by appearances, however, there was nothing to justify excessive alarm. The edict of Nantes (April 13, 1598) had put an end, so far as the French were concerned, to religious wars. The treaty of Vervins (May 2, 1598) between France and Spain, the twelve years' truce between Spain and the United Provinces (April 9, 1609), the death of Philip II. (Sept. 13, 1598) and the alliance between France and England seemed to have brought peace to Europe. It might have been thought that there remained no more than secondary questions, such as the possession of the marquisate of Saluzzo and the succession to the duchies of Clèves and Juliers. But the instinct of peoples sees further than the negotiations of diplomats. In the public estimation of Europe Henry IV. was the representative of and the security for order, peace, national and equitable policy, intelligent and practical ideas. So thought Sully when, at the king's death, he went, equally alarmed and disconsolate, and shut himself up in the arsenal; and the people had grounds for being of Sully's opinion. Public confidence was concentrated upon the king's personality. Spectators pardoned, almost with a smile, those tender foibles of his which, nevertheless, his proximity to old age rendered still more shocking. They were pleased at the clear-sighted and strict attention he paid to the education of his son Louis, the dauphin, to whose governess, Madame de Montglas, he wrote: "I am vexed with you for not having sent me word that you have whipped my son, for I do wish and command you to whip him every time he shows obstinacy in anything wrong, knowing well by my own case that there is nothing in the world that does more good than that." And to Mary de' Medici herself he added, "Of one thing I do assure you, and that is that being of the temper I know you to be of, and foreseeing that of your son, you stubborn, not to say headstrong, Madame, and he obstinate, you will verily have many a tussle together."

Henry IV. saw as clearly into his wife's as into his son's character. Persons who were best acquainted with the disposition of Mary de' Medici and were her most indulgent critics said of her, in 1610, when she was now thirty-seven years of age, "that she was courageous, haughty, firm, discreet, vain, obstinate, vindictive and mistrustful, inclined to idleness, caring but little about affairs, and fond of royalty for nothing beyond its pomp and its honors." Henry had no liking for her or confidence in her, and in private had frequent quarrels with her. He had, nevertheless, had her coronation solemnized and had provided by anticipation for the necessities of government. On the king's death and at the imperious instance of the duke of Épernon, who at once introduced the queen and said in open session, as he exhibited his sword; "It is as yet in the scabbard; but it will have to leap therefrom unless this moment there be granted to the queen a title which is her due according to the order of nature and of justice," the Parliament forthwith declared Mary regent of the kingdom. Thanks to Sully's firm administration, there were, after the ordinary annual expenses were paid, at that time in the vaults of the Bastille or in securities easily realizable, forty-one million three hundred and forty-five thousand livres, and there was nothing to suggest that extraordinary and urgent expenses would come to curtail this substantial reserve. The army was disbanded and reduced to from twelve to fifteen thousand men, French or Swiss. For a long time past no power in France had, at its accession, possessed so much material strength and so much moral authority.

But Mary de' Medici had, in her household and in her court, the wherewithal to rapidly dissipate this double treasure. In 1600, at the time of her marriage, she had brought from Florence to Paris her nurse's daughter, Leonora Galigaï, and Leonora's husband, Concino Concini, son of a Florentine notary, both of them full of coarse ambition, covetous, vain and determined to make the best of their new position so as to enrich themselves and exalt themselves beyond measure and at any price. Mary gave them, in that respect, all the facilities they could possibly desire; they were her confidants, her favorites and her instruments, as regarded both her own affairs and theirs. These private and subordinate servants were before long joined by great lords, court folks, ambitious and vain likewise, egotists, mischief-makers, whom the strong and able hand of Henry IV. had kept aloof, but who, at his death, returned upon the scene, thinking of nothing whatever but their own fortunes and their rivalries. They shall just be named here pell-mell, whether members or relatives of the royal family or merely great lords, the Condés, the Contis, the Enghiens, the dukes of Épernon, Guise, Elbeuf, Mayenne, Bouillon and Nevers, great names and pretty characters encountered at every step under the regency of Mary de' Medici and, with their following, forming about her a court-hive, equally restless and useless. Time does justice to some few men and executes justice on the ruck: one must have been of great worth indeed to deserve not to be forgotten. Sully appeared once more at court after his momentary retreat to the arsenal; but, in spite of the show of favor which Mary de' Medici thought it prudent and decent to preserve towards him for some little time, he soon saw that it was no longer the place for him, and that he was of as little use there to the State as to himself; he sent in, one after the other, his resignation of all his important offices and terminated his life in regular retirement at Rosny and Sully-sur-Loire. Du Plessis-Mornay attempted to still exercise a salutary influence over his party. "Let there be no more talk amongst us," said he, "of Huguenots or Papists; those words are prohibited by our edicts. And, though there were no edict at all, still if we are French, if we love our country, our families, and even ourselves, they ought henceforth to be wiped out of our remembrance. Whoso is a good Frenchman, shall be to me a citizen, shall to me be a brother." This meritorious and patriotic language was not entirely without moral effect, but it no longer guided, no longer inspired the government; egotism, intrigue and mediocrity in ideas as well as in feelings had taken the place of Henry IV.

Facts, before long, made evident the sad result of this. All the parties, all the personages who walked the stage and considered themselves of some account believed that the moment had arrived for pushing their pretensions and lost no time about putting them forward. Those persons we will just pass in review without stopping at any one of them. History has no room for all those who throng about her gates without succeeding in getting in and leaving traces of their stay.

The reformers were the party to which the reign of Henry IV. had brought most conquests and which was bound to strive above everything to secure the possession of them by extracting from them every legitimate and practicable consequence. Mary de' Medici, having been declared regent, lost no time about confirming, on the 22nd of May, 1610, the edict of Nantes and proclaiming religious peace as the due of France. "We have nothing to do with the quarrels of the grandees," said the people of Paris; "we have no mind to be mixed up with them." Some of the preachers of repute and of the party's old leaders used the same language. "There must be naught but a scarf any longer between us," Du Plessis-Mornay would say. Two great protestant names were still intact at this epoch: one, the duke of Sully, without engaging in religious polemics, had persisted in abiding by the faith of his fathers, in spite of his king's example and attempts to bring him over to the catholic faith; the other, Du Plessis-Mornay, had always striven and was continuing to strive actively for the protestant cause. These two illustrious champions of the reformed party were in agreement with new principles of national right and with the intelligent instincts of their people, whose confidence they deserved and seemed to possess.

But the passions, the usages and the suspicions of the party were not slow in reappearing. The Protestants were highly displeased to see the catholic worship and practices re-established in Béarn, whence Queen Jeanne of Navarre had banished them; the rights of religious liberty were not yet powerful enough with them to surmount their taste for exclusive domination. As a guarantee for their safety they had been put in possession of several strong places in France; neither the edict of Nantes nor its confirmation by Mary de' Medici appeared to them a sufficient substitute for this guarantee; and they claimed its continuance, which was granted them for five years. After Henry IV.'s conversion to catholicism his European policy had no longer been essentially protestant; he had thrown out feelers and entered into negotiations for catholic alliance; and these, when the king's own liberal and patriotic spirit was no longer there to see that they did not sway his government, became objects of great suspicion and antipathy to the Protestants. Henry had constantly and to good purpose striven against the spirit of religious faction and civil war; anxious, after his death, about their liberty and their political importance, the reformers reassumed a blind confidence in their own strength and a hope of forming a small special State in the midst of the great national State. Their provincial assemblies and their national synods were, from 1611 to 1621, effective promoters of this tendency, which before long became a formal and organized design; at Saumur, at Tonneins, at Privas, at Grenoble, at Loudun, at La Rochelle, the language, the movements, and the acts of the party took more and more the character of armed resistance and, ere long, of civil war; the leaders, old and new, Duke Henry of Rohan as well as the duke of Bouillon, the marquis of La Force as well as the duke of Lesdiguières, more or less timidly urged on the zealous Protestants in that path from which the ancient counsels of Sully and Mornay were not successful in deterring them. On the 10th of May, 1621, in the assembly at La Rochelle, a commission of nine members was charged to present and get adopted a plan of military organization whereby protestant France, Béarn included, was divided into eight circles, having each a special council composed of three deputies at the general assembly, under a chief who had the disposal of all the military forces; with each army-corps there was a minister to preach; the royal monies, talliages, aid and gabel, were to be seized for the wants of the army; the property of the catholic Church was confiscated and the revenues therefrom appropriated to the expenses of war and the pay of the ministers of the religion. It was a protestant republic, organized on the model of the United Provinces, and disposed to act as regarded the French kingship with a large measure of independence. When, after thus preparing for war, they came to actually make it, the Protestants soon discovered their impotence; the duke of Bouillon, sixty-five years of age and crippled with gout, interceded for them in his letters to Louis XIII. but did not go out of Sedan; the duke of Lesdiguières, to whom the assembly had given the command of the Protestants of Burgundy, Provence and Dauphiny, was at that very moment on the point of abjuring their faith and marching with their enemies. Duke Henry of Rohan himself, who was the youngest and seemed to be the most ardent of their new chiefs, was for doing nothing and breaking up. "If you are not disposed to support the assembly," said the marquis of Châteauneuf who had been sent to him to bring him to a decision, "it will be quite able to defend itself without you." "If the assembly," said Rohan, feeling his honor touched, "does take resolutions contrary to my advice, I shall not sever myself from the interest of our churches," and he sacrificed his better judgment to the popular blindness. The dukes of La Trémoille and of Soubise, and the marquises of La Force and of Châtillon followed suit. As M. de Sismondi says, to these five lords and to a small number of towns was the strength reduced of the party which was defying the king of France.

Thus, since the death of Henry IV., the king and court of France were much changed: the great questions and the great personages had disappeared. The last of the real chiefs of the League, the brother of Duke Henry of Guise, the old duke of Mayenne, he on whom Henry, in the hour of victory, would wreak no heavier vengeance than to walk him to a standstill, was dead. Henry IV.'s first wife, the sprightly and too facile Marguerite de Valois, was dead also, after consenting to descend from the throne in order to make way for the mediocre Mary de' Medici. The catholic champion whom Henry IV. felicitated himself upon being able to oppose to Du Plessis-Mornay in the polemical conferences between the two communions, Cardinal de Perron, was at the point of death. The decay was general and the same amongst the Protestants as amongst the Catholics; Sully and Mornay held themselves aloof or were barely listened to. In place of these eminent personages had come intriguing or ambitious subordinates, who were either innocent of or indifferent to anything like a great policy and who had no idea beyond themselves and their fortunes. The husband of Leonora Galigaï, Concini, had amassed a great deal of money and purchased the marquisate of Ancre; nay more, he had been created marshal of France, and he said to the count of Bassompierre: "I have learned to know the world, and I am aware that a man, when he has arrived at a certain pitch of prosperity, comes down with a greater run the higher he has mounted. When I came to France, I was not worth a sou, and I owed more than eight thousand crowns. My marriage and the queen's kind favor has given me much advancement, office and honor; I have worked at making my fortune and I pushed it forward as long as I saw the wind favorable. So soon as I felt it turning, I thought about beating a retreat and enjoying in peace the large property we have acquired. It is my wife who is opposed to this desire. At every crack of the whip we receive from Fortune, I continue to urge her. God knows whether warnings have been wanting. My daughter's death is the last, and, if we do not heed it, our downfall is at hand." Then he quietly made out an abstract of all his property, amounting to eight millions, with which he purposed to buy from the pope the usufruct of the duchy of Ferrara, and leave his son, besides, a fine inheritance. But his wife continued her opposition; it would be cowardly and ungrateful, she said, to abandon the queen: "So that," cried he, "I see myself ruined without any help for it; and, if it were not that I am under so much obligation to my wife, I would leave her and go some whither where neither grandees nor common-folk would come to look after me."

This modest style of language did not prevent Marshal d'Ancre from occasionally having strange fits of domineering arrogance. "By God, sir," he wrote to one of his friends, "I have to complain of you; you treat for peace without me; you have caused the queen to write to me that, for her sake, I must give up the suit I had commenced against M. de Montbazon to get paid what he owes me. In all the devils' names, what do the queen and you take me for? I am devoured to my very bones with rage." In his dread lest influence opposed to his own should be exercised over the young king, he took upon himself to regulate his amusements and his walks, and prohibited him from leaving Paris. Louis XIII. had amongst his personal attendants a young nobleman, Albert de Luynes, clever in training little sporting birds, called *butcher-birds* (*pies grièches* or *shrikes*), then all the rage; and the king made him his falconer and lived on familiar terms with him. Playing at billiards one day, Marshal d'Ancre, putting on his hat, said to the king, "I hope your Majesty will allow me to be covered." The king allowed it; but remained surprised and shocked. His young page, Albert de Luynes, observed his displeasure, and being anxious, himself also, to become a favorite, he took pains to fan it. A domestic plot was set hatching against Marshal d'Ancre. What was its extent and who were the accomplices in it? This is not clear. However it may have been, on the 24th of April, 1617, M. de Vitry, captain of the guard (*capitaine de quartier*) that day in the royal army which was besieging Soissons, ordered some of his officers to provide themselves with a pistol each in their pockets and he himself went to that door of the Louvre by which the king would have to go to the queen-mother's. When Marshal d'Ancre arrived at this door,

"There is the marshal," said one of the officers; and Vitry laid hands upon him, saying, "Marshal, I have the king's orders to arrest you." "Me!" said the marshal in surprise and attempting to resist. The officer fired upon him, and so did several others. It was never known or, at any rate, never told whose shot it was that hit him; but, "Sir," said Colonel d'Ornano, going up to the young king, "you are this minute king of France: Marshal d'Ancre is dead." And the young king, before the assembled court, repeated with the same tone of satisfaction, "Marshal d'Ancre is dead." Baron de Vitry was appointed marshal of France in the room of the favorite whom he had just murdered. The day after the murder, the mob rushed into the church of St. Germain-l'Auxerrois, where the body of Marshal d'Ancre had been interred; they heaved up the slabs, hauled the body from the ground, dragged it over the pavement as far as the Pont-Neuf, where they hanged it by the feet to a gallows; and they afterwards tore it in pieces, which were sold, burnt and thrown into the Seine. The ferocious passions of the populace were satisfied; but court-hatred and court-envy were not; they attacked the marshal's widow, Leonora Galigaï. She resided at the Louvre and, at the first rumor of what had happened, she had sent to demand asylum with the queen-mother. Meeting with a harsh refusal, she had undressed herself in order to protect with her body her jewels which she had concealed in her mattresses. The moment she was discovered, she was taken to the Bastille and brought before the parliament. She began by throwing all the blame upon her husband; it was he, she said, who had prevented her from retiring into Italy and who had made every attempt to push his fortunes farther. When she was sentenced to death, Leonora recovered her courage and pride. "Never," said a contemporary, "was anybody seen of more constant and resolute visage." "What a lot of people to look at one poor creature!" said she at sight of the crowd that thronged upon her passage. There is nothing to show that her firmness at the last earned her more of sympathy than her weaknesses had brought her of compassion. The mob has its seasons of pitilessness. Leonora Galigaï died leaving one child, a son, who was so maltreated that he persisted in refusing all food and, at last, would take nothing but the sweetmeats that the young queen, Anne of Austria, married two years before to Louis XIII., had the kindness to send him.

We encounter, in this very insignificant circumstance, a trace of one of those important events which marked the earliest years of Mary de' Medici's regency and the influence of her earliest favorites. Concini and his wife, both of them, probably, in the secret service of the court of Madrid, had promoted the marriage of Louis XIII. with the Infanta Anne of Austria, eldest daughter of Philip III. king of Spain, and that of Philip, Infante of Spain, who was afterwards Philip IV., with Princess Elizabeth of France, sister of Louis XIII. Henry IV., in his plan for the pacification of Europe, had himself conceived this idea and testified a desire for this double marriage, but without taking any trouble to bring it about. It was after his death that, on the 30th of April, 1612, Villeroi, minister of foreign affairs in France, and Don Inigo de Caderñas, ambassador of the king of Spain, concluded this double union by a formal deed. They signed on the same day, at Fontainebleau, between the king and queen-regent of France on one side and the king of Spain on the other, a treaty of defensive alliance to the effect "that those sovereigns should give one another mutual succor against such as should attempt anything against their kingdoms or revolt against their authority; that they should in such case, send one to the other, at their own expense for six months, a body of six thousand foot and twelve hundred horse; that they should not assist any criminal charged with high treason, and should even give them over into the hands of the ambassadors of the king who claimed them." It is quite certain that Henry IV. would never have let his hands be thus tied by a treaty so contrary to his general policy of alliance with protestant powers, such as England and the United Provinces; he had no notion of servile subjection to his own policy; but he would have taken good care not to abandon it; he was of those, who, under delicate circumstances, remain faithful to their ideas and promises without systematic obstinacy and with a due regard for the varying interests and requirements of their country and their age. The two Spanish marriages were regarded in France as an abandonment of the national policy. France was, in a great majority, catholic, but its Catholicism differed essentially from the Spanish Catholicism: it affirmed the entire separation of the temporal power and the spiritual power and the inviolability of the former by the latter; it refused assent, moreover, to certain articles of the council of Trent. It was Gallican Catholicism, determined to keep a pretty large measure of national independence, political and moral, as opposed to Spanish Catholicism essentially devoted to the cause of the papacy and of absolutist Austria. Under the influence of this public feeling, the two Spanish marriages and the treaty which accompanied them were unfavorably regarded by a great part of France; a remedy was desired, it was hoped that one would be found in the convocation of the States-general of the kingdom, to which the populace always looked expectantly; they were convoked first for the 16th of September, 1614, at Sens; and, afterwards, for the 20th of October following, when the young king, Louis XIII., after the announcement of his majority, himself opened them in state. Amongst the members there were 140 of the clergy, 132 of the noblesse and 192 of the third-estate. The clergy elected for their president Cardinal de Joyeuse who had crowned Mary de' Medici; the noblesse Henry de Bauffremont, baron of Senecey, and the third estate Robert Miron, provost of the tradesmen of Paris.

These elections were not worth much and have left no trace on history. The chief political fact connected with the convocation of the States-general of 1614 was the entry into their ranks of the youthful bishop of Luçon, Armand John du Plessis de Richelieu, marked out by the finger of God to sustain, after the powerful reign of Henry IV. and the incapable regency of Mary de' Medici, the weight of the government of France. He was in two cases elected to the States-general, by the clergy of Loudun and by that of Poitou. As he was born on the 5th of September, 1585, he was but 28 years old in 1614. He had not been destined for the Church and he was pursuing a layman's course of study at the college of Navarre, under the name of the marquis de Chillon, when his elder brother, Alphonse Louis du Plessis de Richelieu, became disgusted with ecclesiastical life, turned Carthusian and resigned the unpretending bishopric of Luçon in favor of his brother Armand, whom Henry IV. nominated to it in 1605, instructing Cardinal du Perron, at that time his chargé d'affaires at Rome, to recommend to Pope Paul V. that election which he had very much at heart. The young prelate betook himself with so much ardor to his theological studies that at twenty years of age he was a doctor and maintained his theses in rochet and camail as bishop-nominate. At Rome some objection was still made to his extreme youth; but he hastened thither and delivered before the pope a Latin harangue which scattered all objections to the wind. After consecration at Rome, in 1607, he returned to

Paris and hastened to take possession of his see of Luçon, "the poorest and the nastiest in France," as he himself said. He could support poverty, but he also set great store by riches, and he was seriously anxious for the expenses of his installation. "Taking after you, that is, being a little vain," he wrote to one of his fair friends, Madame de Bourges, with whom he was on terms of familiar correspondence about his affairs, "I should very much like, being more easy in my circumstances, to make more show; but what can I do? No house; no carriage; furnished apartments are inconvenient; I must borrow a coach, horses, and a coachman, in order to at least arrive at Luçon with a decent turn-out." He purchased second-hand the velvet bed of one Madame de Marconnay, his aunt; he made for himself a muff out of a portion of his uncle the Commander's marten-skins. Silver-plate he was very much concerned about. "I beg you," he wrote to Madame de Bourges, "to send me word what will be the cost of two dozen silver dishes of fair size, as they are made now; I should very much like to get them for five hundred crowns, for my resources are not great. I am quite sure that for a matter of a hundred crowns more, you would not like me to have anything common. I am a beggar, as you know; in such sort that I cannot do much in the way of playing the opulent; but at any rate, when I have silver dishes, my nobility will be considerably enhanced."

He succeeded, no doubt, in getting his silver dishes and his well appointed episcopal mansion; for when, in 1614, he was elected to the states-general he had acquired amongst the clergy and at the court of Louis XIII. sufficent importance to be charged with the duty of speaking in presence of the king on the acceptance of the acts of the council of Trent and on the restitution of certain property belonging to the catholic Church in Béarn. He made skilful use of the occasion for the purpose of still further exalting and improving the question and his own position. He complained that for a long time past ecclesiastics had been too rarely summoned to the sovereign's councils, "as if the honor of serving God," he said, "rendered them incapable of serving the king;" he took care at the same time to make himself pleasant to the mighty ones of the hour; he praised the young king for having, on announcing his majority, asked his mother to continue to watch over France, and "to add to the august title of *mother of the king* that of *mother of the kingdom.*" The post of almoner to the queen-regnant, Anne of Austria, was his reward. He carried still further his ambitious foresight; in Feb., 1615, at the time when the session of the States-general closed, Marshal d'Ancre and Leonora Galigaï were still favorites with the queen-mother; Richelieu laid himself out to be pleasant to them, and received from the marshal in 1616 the post of Secretary of State for war and foreign affairs. Marshal d'Ancre was at that time looking out for supports against his imminent downfall. When, in 1617, he fell and was massacred, people were astonished to find Richelieu on good terms with the marshal's court-rival Albert de Luynes, who pressed him to remain in the council at which he had sat for only five months. To what extent was the bishop of Luçon at that time on terms of understanding with the victor? There is no saying; but to accept the responsibility of the new favorite's accession was a compromising act. Richelieu judged it more prudent to remain bishop of Luçon and to wear the appearance of defeat by following Mary de' Medici to Blois, whither, since the fall of her favorites, she had asked leave to retire. He would there, he said, be more useful to the government of the young king; for, remaining at the side of Mary de' Medici, he would be able to advise her and restrain her. He so completely persuaded Louis XIII. and Albert de Luynes that he received orders to set out for Blois with the queen-mother, which he did on the 4th of May, 1617. The bishop of Luçon, though still young, was already one of the ambitious sort who stake their dignity upon the ultimate success of their fortunes, success gained no matter at what price, by address or by hardihood, by complaisance or by opposition, according to the requirements of facts and times. Dignity apart, the young bishop had accurately measured the expediency of the step he was taking in the interest of his future, high-soaring ambition.

On arriving at Blois with the queen-mother, be began by dividing his life between that petty court in disgrace and his diocese of Luçon. He wished to set Albert de Luynes at rest as to his presence at the court of Mary de' Medici, the devotion he showed her and the counsels he gave her. He had but small success, however. The new favorite was suspicious and anxious. Richelieu appeared to be occupied with nothing but the duties of his office; he presided at conferences; and he published against the Protestants, a treatise entitled: *The Complete Christian (De la perfection du Chrétien)*. Luynes was not disposed to believe in these exclusively religious preoccupations; he urged upon the king that Richelieu should not live constantly in the queen-mother's neighborhood, and in June, 1617, he had orders given him to retire to the countship of Avignon. Pope Paul V. complained that the bishop of Luçon was exiled from his diocese: "What is to be done about residence," said he, "which is due to his bishopric, and what will the world say at seeing him prohibited from going whither his duty binds him to go?" The king answered that he was surprised at the pope's complaint: "An ecclesiastic," said he, "could not possibly be in any better place than Avignon, Church territory; my lord the bishop of Luçon is far from finding time for nothing but the exercises of his profession; I have discovered that he indulged in practices prejudicial to my service. He is one of those spirits that are carried away far beyond their duty, and are very dangerous in times of public disorder."

Richelieu obeyed without making any objection; he passed two years at Avignon, protesting that he would never depart from it without the consent of Luynes and without the hope of serving him. The favor and fortune of the young falconer went on increasing every day. He had, in 1617, married the daughter of the duke of Montbazon and, in 1619, prevailed upon the king to have the estate of Maillé raised for him to a duchy-peerage under the title of Luynes. In 1621 he procured for himself the dignity of constable, to which he had no military claim. Louis XIII. sometimes took a malicious pleasure in making fun of his favorite's cupidity and that of his following. "I never saw," said he, "one person with so many relatives; they come to court by ship-loads and not a single one of them with a silk dress." "See," said he one day to the count of Bassompierre, pointing to Luynes surrounded by a numerous following: "he wants to play the king, but I shall know how to prevent it; I will make him disgorge what he has taken from me." Friends at court warned Luynes of this language; and Luynes replied with a somewhat disdainful impertinence: "It is good for me to cause the king a little vexation from time to time; it revives the affection he feels for me." Richelieu kept himself well-informed of court-rumors and was cautious not to treat them with indifference. He took great pains to make himself pleasant to the young constable: "My lord," he wrote to him in August, 1621, "I am extremely pleased to have an opportunity of testifying to you that I shall never have any possession that I shall not be most happy to employ for the satisfaction of the king and yourself. The queen did me the honor of desiring that I should have the abbey of Redon; but the moment I knew that the king and you, my lord, were desirous of disposing of it otherwise, I gave it up with very good cheer in order that being in your hands you might gratify therewith whomsoever you pleased; assuring you, my lord, that I have more contentment in testifying to you thereby that which you will on every occasion recognize in me than I should have had by an augmentation of 4000 crowns' income. The queen is very well, thank God. I think it will be very meet that from time to time, by means of those who are passing, you should send her news of the king and of you and yours, which will give her great satisfaction" (*Letters of Cardinal Richelieu*, t. i. p. 690).

Whilst Richelieu was thus behaving towards the favorite with complaisance and modesty, Mary de' Medici, whose mouthpiece he appeared to be, assumed a different posture and used different language; she complained bitterly of the slavery and want of money to which she was reduced at Blois; a plot, on the part of both aristocrats and domestics, was contrived by those about her to extricate her; she entered into secret relations with a great, a turbulent, and a malcontent lord, the duke of Épernon; two Florentine servants, Ruccellaï and Vincenti Ludovici, were their go-betweens; and it was agreed that she should escape from Blois and take refuge at Angoulême, a lordship belonging to the duke of Épernon. She at the same time wrote to the king to plead for more liberty. He replied: "Madame, having understood that you have a wish to visit certain places of devotion, I am rejoiced thereat. I shall be still more pleased if you take a resolution to move about and travel henceforward more than you have done in the past; I consider that it will be of great service to your health which is extremely precious to me. If business permitted me to be of the party, I would accompany you with all my heart." Mary replied to him with formal assurances of fidelity and obedience; she promised *before God and His angels* "to have no correspondence which could be prejudicial to the king's service, to warn him of all intrigues, which should come to her knowledge, that were opposed to his will, and to entertain no design of returning to court save when it should please the king to give her orders to do so." There was between the king, the queen-mother, Albert de Luynes, the duke of Épernon and their agents, an exchange of letters and empty promises which deceived scarcely anybody and which destroyed all confidence as well as all truthfulness between them. The duke of Épernon protested that he had no idea of disobeying the king's commands, but that he thought his presence was more necessary for the king's service in Angoumois than at Metz. He complained at the same time that "for two years past he had received from the court only the simple pay of a colonel at ten months for the year, which took it out of his power to live suitably to his rank. He set out for Metz at the end of January, 1619, saying, "I am going to take the boldest step I ever took in my life."

The queen-mother made her exit from Blois on the night between the 21st and 22nd of February, 1619, by her closet window, against which a ladder had been placed for the descent to the terrace, whence a second ladder was to enable her to descend right down. On arriving at the terrace she found herself so fatigued and so agitated that she declared it would be impossible to avail herself of the second ladder; she preferred to have herself let down upon a cloak to the bottom of the terrace which had a slight slant. Her two equerries escorted her along the faubourg to the end of the bridge. Some officers of her household saw her pass without recognizing her and laughed at meeting a woman between two men, at night and with a somewhat agitated air. "They take me for a *bona roba*," said the queen. On arriving at the end of the faubourg of Blois she did not find her carriage, which was to have been waiting for her there. When she had come up with it, there was a casket missing which contained her jewels; there was a hundred thousand crowns' worth in it; the casket had fallen out two hundred paces from the spot; it was recovered, and the queen-mother got into her carriage and took the road to Loches, where the duke of Épernon had been waiting for her since the day before. He came to meet her with a hundred and fifty horsemen. Nobody in the household of Mary de' Medici had observed her departure.

Great were the rumors when her escape became known, and greater still when it was learnt in whose hands she had placed herself. It was civil war, said everybody. At the commencement of the seventeenth century there were still two possible and even probable chances of civil war in France; one between Catholics and Protestants, and the other between what remained of the great feudal or quasi-feudal lords and the kingship. Which of the two wars was about to commence?

Nobody knew; on every side there was hesitation; the most contradictory moves were made. Louis XIII., when he heard of his mother's escape, tried first of all to disconnect her from the duke of Épernon: "I could never have imagined," said he, "that there was any man who, in time of perfect peace, would have had the audacity, I do not say to carry out, but to conceive the resolution of making an attempt upon the mother of his king . . . ; in order to release you from the difficulty you are in, Madame, I have determinedto take up arms to put you in possession of the liberty of which your enemies have deprived you." And he marched troops and cannon to Angoumois. "Many men," says Duke Henry of Rohan, "envied the duke of Épernon his gallant deed, but few were willing to submit themselves to his haughty temper, and everybody, having reason to believe that it would all end in a peace, was careful not to embark in the affair merely to incur the king's hatred and leave to others the honors of the enterprise." The king's troops were well received wherever they showed themselves; the towns opened their gates to them. "It needs," said a contemporary, "mighty strong citadels to make the towns of France obey their governors when they see the latter disobedient to the king's will." Several great lords held themselves carefully aloof: others determined to attempt an arrangement between the king and his mother; it was known what influence over her continued to be preserved by the bishop of Luçon, still in exile at Avignon; he was pressed to return; his confidant, Father Joseph du Tremblay, was of opinion that he should; and Richelieu, accordingly, set out. The governor of Lyons had him arrested at Vienne in Dauphiny, and was much surprised to find him armed with a letter from the king commanding that he should be allowed to pass freely everywhere. Richelieu was prepared to advise a reconciliation between king and queen-mother, and the king was as much disposed to exert himself to that end as the queen-mother's friends. At Limoges the bishop of Luçon was obliged to carefully avoid Count Schomberg, commandant of the royal troops, who was not at all in the secret of the negotiation. When he arrived at Angers a fresh difficulty supervened. The most daring of the queen-mother's domestic advisers, Ruccellaï, had conceived a hatred of the bishop and tried to exclude him from the privy council. Richelieu let be, "Certain," as he said, "that they would soon fall back upon him." He was one of the patient as well as ambitious, who can calculate upon success, even afar off, and wait for it. The duke of Épernon supported him; Ruccellaï, defeated, left the queen-mother, taking with him some of her most warmly attached servants. When the subordinates were gone, recourse was had, accordingly, to Richelieu. On the 10th of August, 1619, he concluded at Angoulême between the king and his mother a treaty, whereby the king promised to consign to oblivion all that had passed since Blois; the queen-mother consented to exchange her government of Touraine against that of Anjou; and the duke of Épernon received from the town of Boulogne fifty thousand crowns in recompense for what he had done, and he wrote to the king to protest his fidelity. The queen-mother still hesitated to see her son; but, at his entreaty, she at last sent off the bishop of Luçon from Angoulême to make preparations for the interview and, five days afterwards, she set out herself, accompanied by the duke of Épernon who halted at the limits of his own government, not caring to come to any closer quarters with so recently reconciled a court. The king received his mother, according to some, in the little town of Cousières, and, according to others, at Tours or Amboise. They embraced, with tears. "God bless me, my boy, how you are grown!" said the queen: "In order to be of more service to you, mother," answered the king. The cheers of the people hailed their reconciliation; not without certain signs of disquietude on the part of the favorite, Albert de Luynes, who was an eye-witness. After the interview, the king set out for Paris again; and Mary de' Medici returned to her government of Anjou to take possession of it, promising, she said, to rejoin her son subsequently at Paris. Du Plessis-Mornay wrote to one of his friends at court: "If you do not get the queen along with you, you have done nothing at all; distrust will increase with absence; the malcontents will multiply; and the honest servants of the king will have no little difficulty in managing to live between them."

How to live between mother and son without being committed to one or the other was indeed the question. A difficult task. For three months the courtiers were equal to it; from May to July, 1619, the court and the government were split in two; the king at Paris or at Tours, the queen-mother at Angers or at Blois. Two eminent men, Richelieu amongst the Catholics and Du Plessis-Mornay amongst the Protestants, advised them strongly and incessantly to unite again, to live and to govern together. "Apply yourself to winning the king's good graces," said Richelieu to the queen-mother: "support on every occasion the interests of the public without speaking of your own; take the side of equity against that of favor, without attacking the favorites and without appearing to envy their influence." Mornay used the same language to the Protestants. "Do not wear out the king's patience," he said to them: "there is no patience without limits." Louis XIII. listened to them without allowing himself to be persuaded by them; the warlike spirit was striving within the young man: he was brave and loved war as war rather than for political reasons. The grand provost of Normandy was advising him one day not to venture in person into his province, saying, "You will find there nothing but revolt and disagreeables." "Though the roads were all paved with arms," answered the king, "I would march over the bellies of my foes, for they have no cause to declare against me who have offended nobody. You shall have the pleasure of seeing it; you served the late king my father too well not to rejoice at it." The queen-mother, on her side, was delighted to see herself surrounded at Angers by a brilliant court; and the dukes of Longueville, of La Trémoille, of Retz, of Rohan, of Mayenne, of Épernon, and of Nemours promised her numerous troops and effectual support. She might, nevertheless, have found many reasons to doubt and wait for proofs. The king moved upon Normandy; and his quarter-masters came to assign quarters at Rouen. "Where have you left the king?" asked the duke of Longueville. "At Pontoise, my lord; but he is by this time far advanced and is to sleep to-night at Magny." "Where do you mean to quarter him here?" asked the duke. "In the house where you are, my lord." It is right that I yield him place," said the duke, and the very same evening took the road back to the district of Caux. It was under this aspect of public feeling that an embassy from the king and a pacific mission from Rome came, without any success, to Angers, and that on the 4th of July, 1619, a fresh civil war between the king and the partisans of the queen-mother was declared.

It was short and not very bloody though pretty vigorously contested. The two armies met at Ponts de Cé; they had not, either of them, any orders or any desire to fight; and pacific negotiations were opened at La Flèche. The queen-mother declared that she had made up her mind to live henceforth at her son's court, and that all she desired was to leave honorably the party with which she was engaged. That was precisely the difficulty. The king also declared himself resolved to receive his mother affectionately; but he required her to abandon the lords of her party, and that was what she could not make up her mind to do. In the unpremeditated conflict that took place at Ponts de Cé, the troops of the queen-mother were beaten. "They had two hundred men killed or drowned," says Bassompierre, "and about as many taken prisoners." This reverse silenced the queen's scruples; there was clearly no imperative cause for war between her and the king, and the queen's partisans could not be blind to the fact that, if the struggle were prolonged, they would be beaten. The kingship had the upper hand in the country, and a consent was given to the desired arrangements. "Assure the king that I will go and see him to-morrow at Brissac," said the queen-mother: "I am perfectly satisfied with him, and all I think of is to please him and pray God for him personally and for the prosperity of his kingdom." A treaty was concluded at Angers on the 10th of August, 1620: the queen-mother returned to Paris; and the civil war at court was evidently, not put an end to never to recur, but stricken with feebleness and postponed.

Two men of mark, Albert de Luynes and Richelieu, came out of this crisis well content. The favorite felicitated himself on the king's victory over the queen-mother, for he might consider the triumph as his own; he had advised and supported the king's steady resistance to his mother's enterprises. Besides, he had gained by it the rank and power of constable; it was at this period that he obtained them, thanks to the retirement of Lesdiguières, who gave them up to assume the title of marshal-general of the king's camps and armies. The royal favor did not stop there for Luynes; the keeper of the seals, Du Vair, died in 1621; and the king handed over the seals to the new constable who thus united the military authority with that of justice, without being either a great warrior or a great lawyer. All he had to do was to wait for an opportunity of displaying his double power. The defaults of the French Protestants soon supplied one. In July, 1567, Henry IV.'s mother, Jeanne d'Albret, on becoming queen of Navarre, had, at the demand of the Estates of Béarn, proclaimed Calvinism as the sole religion of her petty kingdom; all catholic worship was expressly forbidden there; religious liberty, which Protestants everywhere invoked, was proscribed in Béarn; moreover, ecclesiastical property was confiscated there. The Catholics complained loudly; the kings of France were supporters of their plaint; it had been for a long time past repudiated or eluded; but on the 13th of August, 1620, Louis XIII. issued two edicts for the purpose of restoring in Béarn free catholic worship and making restitution of their property to the ecclesiastical establishments. The council of Pau, which had at first repudiated them, hastened to enregister these edicts in the hope of retarding at least their execution; but the king said: "In two days I shall be at Pau; you want me there to assist your weakness." He was asked how he would be received at Pau. "As sovereign of Béarn," said he: "I will dismount first of all at the church, if there be one; but, if not, I want no canopy or ceremonial entry; it would not become me to receive honors in a place where I have never been, before giving thanks to God from whom I hold all my dominions and all my power." Religious liberty was thus re-established at Pau. "It is the king's intention," said the duke of Montmorency to the Protestants of Villeneuve-de-Berg, who asked that they might enjoy the liberty promised them by the edicts, "that all his subjects, catholic or protestant, be equally free in the exercise of their religion; you shall not be hindered in yours, and I will take good care that you do not hinder the Catholics in theirs." The duke of Montmorency did not foresee that the son and successor of the king in whose name he was so energetically proclaiming religious liberty, Louis XIV., would abolish the edict of Nantes whereby his grandfather, Henry IV., had founded it. Justice and iniquity are often all but contemporary.

It has just been said that not only Luynes but Richelieu too had come well content out of the crisis brought about by the struggle between Louis XIII. and the queen-mother. Richelieu's satisfaction was neither so keen nor so speedy as the favorite's. Pope Paul V. had announced, for the 11th of January, 1621, a promotion of ten cardinals. At the news of this the queen-mother sent an express courier to Rome with an urgent demand that the bishop of Luçon should be included in the promotion. The marquis of Cœuvres, ambassador of France at Rome, insisted rather strongly, in the name of the queen-mother and of the duke of Luynes, from whom he showed the pope some very pressing letters. The pope, in surprise, gave him a letter to read in the handwriting of King Louis XIII., saying that he did not at all wish the bishop of Luçon to become cardinal and begging that no notice might be taken of any recommendations which should be forwarded on the subject. The ambassador, greatly surprised in his turn, ceased to insist. It was evidently the doing of the duke of Luynes who, jealous of the bishop of Luçon and dreading his influence, had demanded and obtained from the king this secret measure. It was effectual; and, at the beginning of the year 1621, Richelieu had but a vague hope of the hat. He had no idea, when he heard of this check, that at the end of a few months Luynes would undergo one graver still, would die almost instantaneously after having practised a policy analogous to that which Richelieu was himself projecting, and would leave the road open for him to obtain the cardinal's hat, and once mere enter into the councils of the king, who, however, said to the queen-mother, "I know him better than you, Madame; he is a man of unbounded ambition."

The two victories won in 1620 by the duke of Luynes, one over the Protestants by the re-establishment in Béarn of free worship for the Catholics, and the other over his secret rival Richelieu by preventing him from becoming cardinal, had inspired him with great confidence in his good fortune. He resolved to push it with more boldness than he had yet shown. He purposed to subdue the Protestants as a political party whilst respecting their religious creed, and to reduce them to a condition of subjection in the State whilst leaving them free, as Christians, in the Church. A fundamentally contradictory problem: for the different liberties are closely connected one with another and have need to be security one for another; but, at the commencement of the seventeenth century, people were not so particular in point of consequence, and it was thought possible to give religious liberty its guarantees whilst refusing them to general political liberty. That is what the duke of Luynes attempted to do; to all the towns to which Henry IV. had bound himself by the edict of Nantes he made a promise of preserving to them their religious liberties, and he called upon them at the same time to remain submissive and faithful subjects of the sovereign kingship. La Rochelle, Montauban, Saumur, Sancerre, Charité-sur-Loire, and St. Jean d'Angely were in this category; and it was to Montauban, as one of the most important of those towns, that Louis XIII. first addressed his promise and his appeal, inconsistent one with the other.

Some years previously, in May, 1610, amidst the grief and

anxiety awakened by the assassination of Henry IV. by Ravaillac, the population of Montauban had maintained and testified a pacific and moderate disposition. The synod was in assembly when the news of the king's death arrived there. We read in the report of the town-council, under date of May 19, 1610, "The ecclesiastics (catholic) having come to the council, the consuls gave them every assurance for their persons and property, and took them under the protection and safeguard of the king and the town, without suffering or permitting any hurt, wrong or displeasure to be done them. . . . The ecclesiastics thanked them and protested their desire to live and die in that town, as good townsmen and servants of the king . . ." On the 22nd of May, in a larger council-general, the council gives notice to the Parliament of Toulouse that everything shall remain peaceable . . . . Council Béraud moves that "every one take forthwith the oath of fidelity we owe to his Majesty, and that every one also testify, by acclamation, his wishes and desires for the prosperity and duration of his reign."

Ten years later, in 1620, the disposition of the Protestants was very much changed; distrust and irritation had once more entered into their hearts. Henry IV. was no longer there to appease them or hold them in. The restoration of the freedom of catholic worship in Béarn had alarmed and offended them as a violation of their own exclusive right proclaimed by Jeanne d'Albret. In January, 1621, during an assembly held at La Rochelle, they exclaimed violently against what they called "the woes experienced by their brethren of Béarn." Louis XIII. considered their remonstrances too arrogant to be tolerated. On the 24th of April, 1621, by a formal declaration, he confirmed all the edicts issued in favor of the liberty of Protestants, but with a further announcement that he would put down with all the rigor of the laws those who did not remain submissive and tranquil in the enjoyment of their own rights. This measure produced amongst the Protestants a violent schism. Some submitted, and their chiefs gave up to the king the places they commanded. On the 10th of May, 1621, Saumur opened her gates to him. Others, more hot-tempered and more obstinate, persisted in their remonstrances. La Rochelle, Montauban, and St. Jean d'Angely took that side. Duke Henry of Rohan and the duke of Soubise, his brother, supported them in their resistance. Rohan went to Montauban and, mounting into the pulpit, said to the assembly: "I will not conceal from you that the most certain conjecture which can be formed from the current news is that in a short time the royal army will camp around your walls, since St. Jean d'Angely is surrendered, and all that remains up to here is weakened, broken down, and ready to receive the yoke, through the factions of certain evil spirits. I have no fear lest the consternation and cowardice of the rest should reach by contagion to you. In days past you swore in my presence the union of the churches. Of a surety we will get peace restored to you here. I pray you to have confidence in me that on this occasion I will not desert you, whatever happen. Though there should be but two men left of my religion, I will be one of the two. My houses and my revenues are seized, because I would not bow beneath the proclamation. I have my sword and my life left. Three stout hearts are better than thirty that quail."

The whole assembly vehemently cheered this fiery speech. The premier consul of Mantauban, Dupuy, swore to live and die in the cause of union of the churches. "The duke of Rohan exerted himself to place Montauban in a position to oppose a vigorous resistance to the royal troops. Consul Dupuy, for his part, was at the same time collecting munitions and victuals." It was announced that the king's army was advancing; and reports were spread, with the usual exaggeration, of the deeds of violence it was already committing. "At the news thereof, every nerve is strained to advance the fortifications; there is none that shirks, of whatever age or sex or condition; every other occupation ceases: night serves to render the day's work bigger; the inhabitants are all a-sweat, soiled with dust, laden with earth." Whilst the multitude was thus working pell-mell to put the town substantially in a state of defence, the warlike population, gentlemen and burgesses, were arming and organizing for the struggle. They had chosen for their chief a younger son of Sully's, Baron d'Orval, devoted to the Protestant cause, even to the extent of rebellion, whilst his elder brother, the marquis of Rosny, was serving in the royal army. Their aged father, Sully, went to Montauban to counsel peace; not that he exactly blamed the resistance, but he said that it would be vain and that a peace on good terms was possible. He was listened to with respect, though he was not believed and though the struggle was all the while persisted in. The royal army, with a strength of 20,000 men and commanded by the young duke of Mayenne, son of the great Leaguer, came up on the 18th of August, 1621, to besiege Montauban, with its population of from 15,000 to 20,000. Besiegers and besieged were all of them brave; the former the more obstinate, the latter the more hair-brained and rash. The siege lasted two months and a half with alternate successes and reverses. The people of the town were directed and supported by commissions charged with the duty of collecting meal, preparing quarters for the troops, looking after the sick and wounded and distributing ammunition. "Day and night, from hour to hour, one of the consuls went to inspect these services. All was done without confusion, without a murmur. Ministers of the reformed Church, to the number of thirteen, were charged to keep up the enthusiasm with chants, psalms, and prayers. One of them, the pastor Chamier, was animated by a zealous and bellicose fanaticism; he was never tired of calling to mind the calamities undergone by the towns that had submitted to the royal army; he was incessantly comparing Montauban to Bethulia, Louis XIII. to Nabuchodonosor, the duke of Mayenne to Holofernes, the Montalbanese to the people of God, and the Catholics to the Assyrians. The indecision and diversity of views in the royal camp formed a singular contrast to the firm resolution, enthusiasm, and union which prevailed in the town. On the 16th and 17th of August the king passed his army in review; several captains were urgent in dissuading him from prosecuting the siege; they proposed to build forts around Montauban and leave there the duke of Mayenne "to harass the inhabitants, make them consume both their gunpowder and their tooth-powder and, peradventure bring them to a composition." But the self-respect of the king and of the army was compromised; the duke of Luynes ardently desired to change his name for that of duke of Montauban; there was promise of help from the prince of Condé and the duke of Vendôme, who were commanding, one in Berry and the other in Brittany. These personal interests and sentiments carried the day; the siege was pushed forward with ardor, although without combined effort; the duke of Mayenne was killed there on the 16th of September, 1621; and amongst the insurgents, the preacher Chamier met, on the 17th of October, the same fate. It was in the royal army and the government that fatigue and the desire of putting a stop to a struggle so costly and of such doubtful issue first began to be manifested. And, at the outset, in the form of attempts at negotiation. The duke of Luynes himself had a proposal made to the duke of Rohan, who was in residence at Castres, for an interview, which Rohan accepted, notwithstanding the mistrust of the people of Castres and of the majority of his friends. The conference was held at a league's distance from Montauban. After the proper compliments, Luynes drew Rohan aside into an alley alone, and, "I thank you," he said, "for having put trust in me; you shall not find it misplaced; your safety is as great here as in Castres. Having become connected with you, I desire your welfare; but you deprived me, whilst my favor lasted, of the means of procuring the greatness of your house. You have succored Montauban in the very teeth of your king. It is a great feather in your cap; but you must not make too much of it. It is time to act for yourself and your friends. The king will make no general peace; treat for them who ac knowledge you. Represent to them of Montauban that their ruin is but deferred for a few days; that you have no means of helping them. For Castres and other places in your department ask what you will and you shall obtain it. For your own self, any thing you please (*carte blanche*) is offered you. . . If you will believe me, you will get out of this miserable business with glory, with the good graces of the king and with what you desire for your own fortunes, which I am anxious to promote so as to be a support to mine."

Rohan replied: "I should be my own enemy if I did not desire my king's good graces and your friendship. I will never refuse from my king benefits and honors, or from you the offices of a kind connection. I do well consider the peril in which I stand; but I beg you also to look at yours. You are universally hated, because you alone possess what everybody desires. Wars against them of the religion have often commenced with great disadvantages for them; but the restlessness of the French spirit, the discontent of those not in the government and the influence of foreigners have often retrieved them. If you manage to make the king grant us peace, it will be to his great honor and advantage, for, after having humbled the party, without having received any check and without any appearance of division within or assistance from without, he will have shown that he is not set against the religion, but only against the disobedience it covers, and he will break the neck of other parties without having met with anything disagreeable. But, if you push things to extremity, and the torrent of your successes do not continue—and you are on the eve of seeing it stopped in front of Montauban—every one will recover his as yet flurried senses, and will give you a difficult business to unravel. Bethink you that you have gathered in the harvest of all that promises mingled with threats could enable you to gain, and that the remnant is fighting for the religion in which it believes. For my own part, I have made up my mind to the loss of my property and my posts; if you have retarded the effects thereof on account of our connection, I am obliged to you for it; but I am quite prepared to suffer everything, since my mind is made up, having solemnly promised it and my conscience so bidding me, to hear of nothing but a general peace."

The reply was worthy of a great soul devoted to a great cause, a soul that would not sacrifice to the hopes of fortune either friends or creed. It was a mark of Duke Henry of Rohan's superior character to take account, before everything, of the general interests and the moral sentiments of his party. The chief of the royal party, the duke of Luynes, was, on the contrary, absorbed in the material and momentary success of his own personal policy; he refused to treat for a general peace with the Protestants, and he preferred to submit to a partial and local defeat before Montauban rather than be hampered with the difficulties of national pacification. At a council held on the 26th of October, 1621, it was decided to publicly raise the siege. The king and the royal army departed in November from the precincts of Montauban which they purposed to a tack afresh on the return of spring; the king was in a hurry to go and receive at Toulouse the empty acclamations of the mob, and he ordered Luynes to go and take, on the little town of Monheur, in the neighborhood of Toulouse, a specious revenge for his check before Montauban. Monheur surrendered on the 11th of December, 1621. Another little village in the neighborhood, Négrepelisse, which offered resistance to the royal army, was taken by assault and its population infamously massacred. But in the midst of these insignificant victories, on the 14th of December, 1621, the royal favorite, the constable, interim keeper of the seals, Duke Albert of Luynes, had an attack of malignant fever and died in three days at the camp of Longueville. "What was marvellously surprising and gave a good idea of the world and its vanity," says his contemporary, the marquis of Fontaine Mareuil, "was that this man, so great and so powerful, found himself, nevertheless, to such a degree abandoned and despised that for two days during which he was in agony there was scarcely one of his people who would stay in his room, the door being open all the time and anybody who pleased coming in, as if he had been the most insignificant of men; and when his body was taken to be interred, I suppose, to his duchy of Luynes, instead of priests to pray for him, I saw some of his valets playing piquet on his bier whilst they were having their horses baited."

It was not long before magnificence revisited the favorite's bier. "On the 11th of January, 1622, his mortal remains having arrived at Tours, all the religious bodies went out to receive it; the constable was placed in a chariot drawn by six horses, accompained by pages, Swiss, and gentlemen in mourning. He was finally laid in the cathedral-church, where there took place a service which was attended by Marshal de Lesdiguières, the greatest lords of the court, the judicature, and the corporation. It is a contemporary sheet, the *Mercure Français*, which has preserved to us these details as to the posthumous grandeur of Albert de Luynes after the brutal indifference to which he had been subjected at the moment of his death. His brothers after him held a high historical position, which the family have maintained, through the course of every revolution, to the present day; a position which M. Cousin took pleasure in calling to mind, and which the last duke but one of Luynes made it a point of duty to commemorate by raising to Louis XIII. a massive silver statue almost as large as life, the work of that able sculptor, M. Rudde, which figured at the public exhibition set on foot by Count d'Haussonville in honor of the Alsace-Lorrainers whom the late disasters of France drove off in exile to Algeria.

Richelieu, when he had become cardinal, premier minister of Louis XIII. and of the government of France, passed a just but severe judgment upon Albert de Luynes. "He was a mediocre and timid creature," he said, "faithless, ungenerous, too weak to remain steady against the assault of so great a fortune as that which ruined him incontinently; allowing himself to be borne away by it as by a torrent, without any foothold, unable to set bounds to his ambition, incapable of arresting it and not knowing what he was about, like a man on the top of a tower, whose head goes round and who has no longer any power of discernment. He would fain have been prince of Orange, count of Avignon, duke of Albret, king of Austrasia, and would not have refused more if he had seen his way to it" [*Mémoires de Richelieu*, p. 169, in the Petitot Collection, Series v., t. xxii.].

This brilliant and truthful portrait lacks one feature which was the merit of the constable de Luynes: he saw coming and he anticipated, a long way off and to little purpose but heartily enough, the government of France by a supreme kingship, whilst paying respect, as long as he lived, to religious liberty and showing himself favorable to intellectual and literary liberty though he was opposed to political and national liberty. That was the government which, after him, was practised with a high hand and rendered triumphant by Cardinal Richelieu to the honor, if not the happiness, of France.

CHAPTER XXXVIII.

LOUIS XIII., CARDINAL RICHELIEU, AND THE COURT (1622—1642).

THE characteristic of Louis XIV.'s reign is the uncontested empire of the sovereign over the nation, the authority of the court throughout the country. All intellectual movement proceeded from the court or radiated about it; the whole government, whether for war or peace, was concentrated in its hands. Condé, Turenne, Catinat, Luxembourg, Villars, Vendôme belonged, as well as Louvois or Colbert, to the court; from the court went the governors and administrators of provinces; there was no longer any greatness existing outside of the court; there were no longer any petty private courts. As for the State, the king was it.

For ages past, France had enjoyed the rare good fortune of seeing her throne successively occupied by Charlemagne and Charles V., by St. Louis and Louis XI., by Louis XII., Francis I. and Henry IV., great conquerers or wise administrators, heroic saints or profound politicians, brilliant knights or models of patriot-kings. Such sovereigns had not only governed, but also impressed the imagination of the people; it was to them that the weak, oppressed by the great feudal lords, had little by little learned to apply for support and assistance; since the reign of Francis I., especially, in the midst of the religious struggles which had caused division amongst the noblesse and were threatening to create a state within the State, the personal position of the grandees, and that of their petty private courts, had been constantly diminishing in importance; the wise policy, the bold and prudent courage of Henry IV. and his patriotic foresight had pacified hatred and stayed civil wars; he had caused his people to feel the pleasure and pride of being governed by a man of a superior order. Cardinal Richelieu, more stern than Henry IV., set his face steadily against all the influences of the great lords; he broke them down one after another; he persistently elevated the royal authority; it was the hand of Richelieu which made the court and paved the way for the reign of Louis XIV. The Fronde was but a paltry interlude and a sanguinary game between parties. At Richelieu's death, pure monarchy was founded.

In the month of December, 1622, the work was as yet full of difficulty. There were numerous rivals for the heritage of royal favor that had slipped from the dying hands of Luynes. The prince of Condé, a man of ability and moderation, "a good managing man (*homme de bon ménage*)," as he was afterwards called by the cardinal, was the first to get possession of the mind of the king, at that time away from his mother who was residing at Paris. "It was not so much from dislike that they opposed her," says Richelieu, "as from fear lest, when once established at the king's council, she might wish to introduce me there. They acknowledged in me some force of judgment; they dreaded my wits, fearing lest, if the king were to take special cognizance of me, it might come to his committing to me the principal care of his affairs" (*Mémoires de Richelieu*, t. ii. p. 193). On returning to Paris, the king, nevertheless, could not refuse this gratification to his mother. However, "The prince, who was in the habit of speaking very freely and could not be mum about what he had on his mind, permitted himself to go so far as to say that she had been received into the council on two conditions, one, that she should have cognizance of nothing but what they pleased, and the other, that, though only a portion of affairs was communicated to her, she would serve as authority for all in the minds of the people." (*Mémoires de Richelieu*, t. ii. p. 194). In fact, the queen-mother quite perceived that "she was only shown the articles in the window and did not enter the shop;" but, with all the prudence and patience of an Italian, when she was not carried away by passion, she knew how to practise dissimulation towards the prince of Condé and his allies, Chancellor Sillery and his son Puisieux, secretary of state. She accompanied her son on an expedition against the Huguenots of the South, which she had not advised, "foreseeing quite well, that, if she were separated from the king, she would have no part either in peace or war, and that, if they got on without her for ten months, they would become accustomed to getting on without her." She had the satisfaction of at last seeing the bishop of Luçon promoted to the cardinalship she had often solicited for him in vain; but, at the same time, the king called to the council Cardinal Rochefoucauld, "not through personal esteem for the old cardinal," says Richelieu, "but to cut off from the new one all hope of a place for which he might be supposed to feel some ambition." Nevertheless, in spite of his enemies' intrigues, in spite of a certain instinctive repugnance on the part of the king himself who repeated to his mother, "I know him better than you, Madame; he is a man of unbounded ambition," the "new cardinal" was called to the council at the opening of the year 1624, on the instance of the marquis of La Vieuville, superintendent of finance and chief of the council, who felt himself unsteady in his position and sought to secure the favor of the queen-mother. It was as the protégé and organ of Mary de' Medici that the cardinal wrote to the prince of Condé on the 11th of May, 1624: "The king having done me the honor to place me on his council, I pray God with all my heart to render me worthy of serving him as I desire; and I feel myself bound thereto by every sort of consideration. I cannot sufficiently thank you for the satisfaction that you have been pleased to testify to me thereat. Therefore would I far rather do so in deed by serving you than by bootless words. And in that I cannot fail without failing to follow out the king's intention. I have made known to the queen the assurance you give her by your letter of your affection, for which she feels all the reciprocity you can desire. She is the more ready to flatter herself with the hope of its continuance in that she will be very glad to incite you thereto by all the good offices she has means of rendering you with His Majesty" [*Lettres du cardinal de Richelieu*, t. ii. p. 5]. On the 12th of August, however, M. de la Vieuville fell irretrievably and was confined in the castle of Amboise. A pamphlet of the time had forewarned him of the danger which threatened him when he introduced Richelieu into the council; "You are both of the same temper," it said, "that is, you both desire one and the same thing, which is, to be, each of you, sole governor. That which you believe to be your making will be your undoing."

From that moment the cardinal, in spite of his modest resistance based upon the state of his health, became the veritable chief of the council: "Everybody knew that, amidst the mere private occupations he had hitherto had, it would have been impossible for him to exist with such poor health, unless he took frequent recreation in the country" [*Mémoires de Richelieu*, t. ii. p. 289]. Turning his attention to founding his power and making himself friends, he authorized the recall of Count Schomberg, lately disgraced, and of the duke of Anjou's the king's brother's, governor, Colonel Ornano, imprisoned by the marquis of La Vieuville. He, at the same time, stood out against the danger of concentrating all the power of the government in a single pair of hands: "Your Majesty," he said, "ought not to confide your public business to a single one of your councillors and hide it from the rest; those whom you have chosen ought to live in fellowship and amity in your service, not in partisanship and division. Every time and as many times as a single one wants to do everything himself, he wants to ruin himself; but in ruining himself he will ruin your kingdom and you, and as often as any single one wants to possess your ear and do in secret what should be resolved upon openly, it must necessarily be for the purpose of concealing from Your Majesty either his ignorance or his wickedness" [*Mémoires de Richelieu*, t. ii. p. 349]. Prudent rules and acute remarks, which Richelieu, when he became all powerful, was to forget.

Eighteen months had barely rolled away when Colonel Ornano, lately created a marshal at the duke of Anjou's request, was again arrested and carried off a prisoner "to the very room, where, twenty-four years ago, Marshal Biron had been confined." For some time past "it had been current at court and throughout the kingdom that a great cabal was going on," says Richelieu in his *Mémoires*, "and the cabalists said quite openly that under his ministry, men might cabal with impunity, for he was not a dangerous enemy." If the cabalists had been living in that confidence, they were most wofully deceived. Richelieu was neither meddlesome nor cruel, but he was stern and pitiless towards the suffering as well as the supplications of those who sought to thwart his policy. At this period, he wished to bring about a marriage between the duke of Anjou, then eighteen years old, and Mdlle. de Montpensier, the late duke of Montpensier's daughter, and the richest heiress in France. The young prince did not like it. Madame de Chevreuse, it was said, seeing the king an invalid and childless, was already anticipating his death and the possibility of marrying his widowed queen to his successor. "I should gain too little by the change," said Anne of Austria one day, irritated by the accusations of which she was the object. Divers secret or avowed motives had formed about the duke of Anjou what was called the "aversion" party, who were opposed to his marriage; but the arrest of Colonel Ornano dismayed the accomplices for a while. The duke of Anjou protested his fidelity to his brother, and promised the cardinal to place in the king's hands a written undertaking to submit his wishes and affections to him. The intrigue appeared to have been abandoned. But the "*dreadful (épouvantable) faction*," as the cardinal calls it in his *Mémoires*, conspired to remove the young prince from the court. The duke of Vendôme, son of Henry IV. and Gabrielle d'Estrées, had offered him an asylum in his government of Brittany; but the far-sighted policy of the minister took away this refuge from the heir to the throne, always inclined as he was to put himself at the head of a party. The duke of Vendôme and his brother the Grand Prior, disquieted at the rumors which were current about them, hastened to go and visit the king at Blois. He received them with great marks of affection. "Brother," said he, to the duke of Vendôme, laying his hand upon his shoulder, "I was impatient to see you." Next morning, the 15th of June, the two princes were arrested in bed. "Ah! brother," cried Vendôme, "did not I tell you in Brittany that we should be arrested?" "I wish I were dead and you were there," said the Grand Prior. "I told you, you know, that the castle of Blois was a fatal place for princes," rejoined the duke. They were conducted to Amboise. The king, continually disquieted by the projects of assassination hatched against his minister, gave him a company of musketeers as guards and set off for Nantes, whither the cardinal was not slow to go and join him. In the interval, a fresh accomplice in the plot had been discovered.

This time it was in the king's own household that he had been sought and found. Henry de Talleyrand, count of Chalais, master of the wardrobe, hare-brained and frivolous, had hitherto made himself talked about only for his duels and his successes with women. He had already been drawn into a plot against the cardinal's life; but, under the influence of remorse, he had confessed his criminal intentions to the minister himself. Richelieu appeared touched by the repentance but he did not forget the offence, and his watch over this "unfortunate gentleman," as he himself calls him, made him aware before long that Chalais was compromised in an intrigue which aimed at nothing less, it was said, than to secure the person of the cardinal by means of an ambush, so as to get rid of him at need. Chalais was arrested in his bed on the 8th of July. The marquis of La Valette, son of the duke of Épernon and governor of Metz, who had been asked to give an asylum to Monsieur, in case he decided upon flying from the court, had answered after an embarrassed fashion; the cardinal had his enemies in a trap. He went to call on Monsieur; it was in Richelieu's own house and under pretext of demanding hospitality of him that the conspirators calculated upon striking their blow; "I very much regret," said the cardinal to Gaston, "that your Highness did not warn me that you and your friends meant to do me the honor of coming to sup with me, I would have exerted myself to entertain them and receive them to the best of my ability" [*Journal de Bassompierre*, t. ii.]. Monsieur seemed to be dumbfounded; he still thought of flight, but Madame de Guise had just arrived at Nantes with her daughter, Mdlle. de Montpensier; Madame de Chevreuse had been driven from court; the young prince's friends had been scared or won over; and President le Coigneux, his most honest adviser, counselled him to get the cardinal's support with the king: "That rascal," said the president, "gets so sharp an edge on his wits, that it is necessary to avail oneself of all sorts of means to undo what he does." Monsieur at last gave way and consented to be married, provided that the king would treat it as appanage. Louis XIII., in his turn, hesitated, being attracted by the arguments of certain underlings, "folks ever welcome, as being apparently out of the region of political interests, and seeming to have an eye in everything to their master's person only." They represented to the king that if the duke of Anjou were to have children, he would become of more importance in the country, which would be to the king's detriment. The minister boldly demanded of the king the dismissal of "those petty folks who insolently abused his ear." Louis XIII., in his turn, gave way; and on the 5th of August, 1626, the cardinal himself celebrated the marriage of Gaston, who became duke of Orleans on the occasion, with Mary of Bourbon, Mdlle. de Montpensier. "No viols or music were heard that day, and it was said in the bridegroom's circle that there was no occasion for having Monsieur's marriage stained with blood. This was reported to the king, and to the cardinal who did not at all like it."

When Chalais, in his prison, heard of the marriage, he undoubtedly conceived some hope of a pardon, for he exclaimed, as the cardinal himself says: "That is a mighty sharp trick, to have not only scattered a great faction, but, by removing its object, to have annihilated all hopes of re-uniting it. Only the sagacity of the king and his minister could have made such a hit; it was well done to have caught Monsieur between touch-and-go (*entre bond et volee*). The prince, when he knows of this, will be very vexed, though he do not say so, and the count (of Soissons, nephew of Condé) will weep over it with his mother."

The hopes of Chalais were deceived. He had written to the king to confess his fault: "I was only thirteen days in the faction," he said; but those thirteen days were enough to destroy him. In vain did his friends intercede passionately for him; in vain did his mother write to the king the most touching letter: "I gave him to you, Sir, at eight years of age; he is a grandson of Marshal Montluc and President Jeannin; his family serve you daily, but dare not throw themselves at your feet for fear of displeasing you; nevertheless, they join with me in begging of you the life of this wretch, though he should have to end his days in perpetual imprisonment or in serving you abroad." Chalais was condemned to death on the 18th of August, 1626, by the criminal court established at Nantes for that purpose; all the king's mercy went no further than a remission of the tortures which should have accompanied the execution. He sent one of his friends to assure his mother of his repentance. "Tell him," answered the noble lady, "that I am very glad to have the consolation he gives me of his dying in God; if I did not think that the sight of me would be too much for him, I would go to him and not leave him until his head was severed from his body; but, being unable to be of any help to him in that way I am going to pray God for him." And she returned into the church of the nuns of Sainte-Claire. The friends of Chalais had managed to have the executioner carried off so as to retard his execution; but an inferior criminal, to whom pardon had been granted for the performance of this service, cut off the unfortunate culprit's head in thirty-one strokes [*Mémoires d' un Favori du duc d'Orléans* (*Archives curieuses de l'histoire de France*), 2nd series, t. iii.]. "The sad news was brought to the duke of Orleans, who, was playing *abbot;* he did not leave the game, and went on as if instead of death he had heard of deliverance." An example of cruelty which might well have discouraged the friends of the duke of Orleans "from dying a martyr's death for him" like the unhappy Chalais.

It has been said that Richelieu was neither meddlesome nor cruel, but that he was stern and pitiless; and he gave proof of that the following year, on an occasion when his personal interests were not in any way at stake. At the outset of his ministry, in 1624, he had obtained from the king a severe ordinance against duels, a fatal custom which was at that time decimating the noblesse. Already several noblemen, amongst others M. du Plessis-Praslin, had been deprived of their offices or sent into exile in consequence of their duels, when M. de Bouteville, of the house of Montmorency, who had been previously engaged in twenty-one affairs of honor, came to Paris to fight the marquis of Beuvron on the *Place Royale.* The marquis' second, M. de Bussy d'Amboise, was killed by the count of Chapelles, Bouteville's second. Beuvron fled to England. M. de Bouteville and his comrade had taken post for Lorraine; they were recognized and arrested at Vitry-le-Brûlé and brought back to Paris; and the king immediately ordered Parliament to bring them to trial. The crime was flagrant and the defiance of the king's orders undeniable; but the culprit was connected with the greatest houses in the kingdom; he had given striking proofs of bravery in the king's service; and all the court interceded for him. Parliament, with regret, pronounced condemnation, absolving the memory of Bussy d'Amboise, who was a son of President de Mesmes's wife, and reducing to one-third of their goods the confiscation to which the condemned were sentenced. "Parliament has played the king," was openly said in the queen's ante-chamber; "if things proceed to execution, the king will play Parliament."

"The cardinal was much troubled in spirit," says he himself: "it was impossible to have a noble heart and not pity this poor gentleman whose youth and courage excited so much compassion." However, whilst expounding, according to his practice, to the king the reasons for and against the execution of the culprits, Richelieu let fall this astounding expression: "It is a question of breaking the neck of duels or of your Majesty's edicts."

Louis XIII. did not hesitate: though less stern than his minister, he was more indifferent, and "the love he bore his kingdom prevailed over his compassion for these two gentlemen." Both died with courage: "There was no sign of anything weak in their words or mean in their actions. They received the news that they were to die with the same visage as they would have that of pardon," in such sort that they who had lived like devils were seen dying like saints, and they who had cared for nothing but to foment duels serving towards the extinction of them" [*Mémoires d'un Favori du duc d'Orléans* (*Archives curieuses de l'histoire de France*), t. ii.].

The cardinal had got Chalais condemned as a conspirator; he had let Bouteville be executed as a duellist; the greatest lords bent beneath his authority, but the power that depends on a king's favor is always menaced and tottering. The enemies of Richelieu had not renounced the idea of overthrowing him, their hopes ever went on growing, since for some time past, the queen-mother had been waxing jealous of the all-powerful minister, and no longer made common cause with him. The king had returned in triumph from the siege of La Rochelle; the queen-mother hoped to retain him by her at court; but the cardinal ever on the watch over the movements of Spain, prevailed upon Louis XIII. to support his subject, the duke of Nevers, legitimate heir to Mantua and Montferrat, of which the Spaniards were besieging the capital. The army began to march, but the queen designedly retarded the movements of her son. The cardinal was appointed generalissimo, and the king, who had taken upon himself the occupation of Savoy, was before long obliged by his health to return to Lyons, where he fell seriously ill. The two queens hurried to his bedside; and they were seconded by the keeper of the seals, M. de Marillac, but lately raised to power by Richelieu, as a man on whom he could depend, and now completely devoted to the queen-mother's party.

At the news of the king's danger, the cardinal quitted St. Jean-de-Maurienne for a precipitate journey to Lyons; but he was soon obliged to return to his army. During the king's convalescence the resentment of the queen-mother against the minister, as well as that of Anne of Austria, had free course; and when the royal train took the road slowly back to Paris in the month of October, the ruin of the cardinal had been resolved upon.

What a trip was that descent of the Loire from Roanne to Briare in the same boat and "at very close quarters between the queen-mother and the cardinal!" says Bassompierre.

"She hoped that she would more easily be able to have her will and crush her servant with the more facility, the less he was on his guard against it; she looked at him with a kindly eye, accepted his dutiful attentions and respects as usual, and spoke to him with as much appearance of confidence as if she had wholly given it him" [*Mémoires de Richelieu*, t. iii. pp. 303–305].

The king had requested his mother "to put off for six weeks or two months the grand move against the cardinal, for the sake of the affairs of his kingdom, which were then at a crisis in Italy" [*Mémoires de Bassompierre*, t. iii. p. 276], and she had promised him; but Richelieu "suspected something wrong, and discovered more," and, on the 12th of November, 1630, when mother and son were holding an early conference at the Luxembourg, a fine palace which Mary de' Medici had just finished, "the cardinal arrived there; finding the door of the chamber closed, he entered the gallery and went and knocked at the door of the cabinet, where he obtained no answer. Tired of waiting and knowing the ins and outs of the mansion, he entered by the little chapel, whereat the king was somewhat dismayed and said to the queen in despair, 'Here he is!' thinking, no doubt, that he would blaze forth. The cardinal, who perceived this dismay, said to them, 'I am sure you were speaking about me.' The queen answered, 'We were not.' Whereupon, he having replied, 'Confess it, Madame,' she said *yes* and thereupon conducted herself with great tartness towards him, declaring to the king 'that she would not put up with the cardinal any longer or see in her house either him or any of his relatives and friends, to whom she incontinently gave their dismissal, and not to them only, but even down to the pettiest of her officers who had come to her from his hands'" [*Mémoires de Richelieu*, t. iii. p. 428].

The struggle was begun. Already the courtiers were flocking to the Luxembourg; the keeper of the seals, Marillac, had gone away to sleep at his country-house at Glatigny, quite close to Versailles, where the king was expected; and he was hoping that Louis XIII. would summon him and put the power in his hands. The king was chatting with his favorite St. Simon, and tapping with his finger-tips on the window-pane. "What do you think of all this?" he asked. "Sir," was the reply, "I seem to be in another world, but at any rate you are master." "Yes, I am," answered the king, "and I will make it felt too." He sent for Cardinal la Vallette, son of the duke of Épernon, but devoted to Richelieu: "The cardinal has a good master," he said: "go and make my compliments to him and tell him to come to me without delay" [*Mémoires de Bassompierre*, t. iii. p. 276].

With all his temper and the hesitations born of his melancholy mind Louis XIII. could appreciate and discern the great interests of his kingdom and of his power. The queen had supposed that the king would abandon the cardinal, and "that her private authority as mother, and the pious affection and honor the king showed her as her son, would prevail over the public care which he ought, as king to take of his kingdom and his people. But God who holds in His hand the hearts of princes, disposed things otherwise: his Majesty resolved to defend his servant against the malice of those who prompted the queen to this wicked design" [*Mémoires de Richelieu*]; he conversed a long while with the cardinal, and when the keeper of the seals awoke the next morning it was to learn that the minister was at Versailles with the king, who had lodged him in a room under his own, that His Majesty demanded the seals back and that the exons were at his, Marillac s, door to secure his person.

At the same time was despatched a courier to head-quarters at Foglizzo in Piedmont. The three marshals Schomberg, La Force, and Marillac, had all formed a junction there. Marillac, brother of the keeper of the seals, held the command that day; and he was awaiting with impatience the news, already announced by his brother, of the cardinal's disgrace. Marshal Schomberg opened the despatches; and the first words that met his eye were these, written in the king's own hand: "My dear cousin, you will not fail to arrest Marshal Marillac; it is for the good of my service and for your own exculpation." The marshal was greatly embarrassed; a great part of the troops had come with Marillac from the army of Champagne and were devoted to him. Schomberg determined, on the advice of Marshal la Force, in full council of captains, to show Marillac the postscript. "Sir," answered the marshal, "a subject must not murmur against his master, nor say of him that the things he alleges are false. I can protest with truth that I have done nothing contrary to his service. The truth is that my brother the keeper of the seals and I have always been the servants of the queen-mother; she must have had the worst of it and Cardinal Richelieu has won the day against her and her servants" [*Mémoires de Puy-Ségur.*]

Thus arrested in the very midst of the army he commanded, Marshal Marillac was taken to the castle of St. Menehould and thence to Verdun, where a court of justice extraordinary sat upon his case. It was cleared of any political accusation; the marshal was prosecuted for peculation and extortion, common crimes at that time with many generals and always odious to the nation, which regarded their punishment with favor. "It is a very strange thing," said Marillac, "to prosecute me as they do; my trial is a mere question of hay, straw, wood, stones and lime; there is not case enough for whipping a lacquey." There was case enough for sentencing to death a marshal of France. The proceedings lasted eighteen months; the commission was transferred from Verdun to Ruel, to the very house of the cardinal. Marillac was found guilty by a majority of one only. The execution took place on the 10th of May, 1632. The former keeper of the seals, Michael de Marillac, died of decline at Châteaudun, three months after the death of his brother.

Dupes' Day was over and lost. The queen-mother's attack on Richelieu had failed before the minister's ascendancy and the king's calculating fidelity to a servant he did not like; but Mary de' Medici's anger was not calmed and the struggle remained set between her and the cardinal. The duke of Orleans, who had lost his wife after a year's marriage, had not hitherto joined his mother's party, but all on a sudden, excited by his grievances, he arrived at the cardinal's, on the 30th of January, 1631, with a strong escort, and told him that he would consider it a strange purpose that had brought him there; that, so long as he supposed that the cardinal would serve him, he had been quite willing to show him amity; now, when he saw that he foiled him in everything that he had promised, to such extent that the way in which he, Monsieur, had behaved himself, had served no end but to make the world believe that he had abandoned the queen his mother, he had come to take back the word he had given him to show him affection." On leaving the cardinal's house Monsieur got into his carriage and went off in haste to Orleans, whilst the king, having received notice from Richelieu, was arriving with all despatch from Versailles to assure his minister "of his protection, well knowing that nobody could wish him ill save for the faithful services he rendered him" [*Mémoires de Richelieu*, t. ii. p. 444].

The queen-mother had undoubtedly been aware of the duke

of Orleans' project, for she had given up to him Madame's jewels which he had confided to her; she nevertheless sent her equerry to the king, protesting "that she had been much astonished when she heard of Monsieur's departure, that she had almost fainted on the spot, and that Monsieur had sent her word that he was going away from court because he could no longer tolerate the cardinal's violent proceedings against her."

"When the king signified to her that he considered this withdrawal very strange and let her know that he had much trouble in believing that she knew nothing about it, she took occasion to belch forth fire and flames against the cardinal, and made a fresh attempt to ruin him in the king's estimation, though she had previously bound herself by oath to take no more steps against him" [*Mémoires de Richelieu*, t. ii. p. 465].

The cardinal either had not sworn at all or did not consider himself more bound than the queen by oaths. Their Majesties set out for Compiègne; there the minister brought the affair before the council, explaining with a skilful appearance of indifference the different courses to be taken, and ending by propounding the question of his own retirement or the queen-mother's. "His Majesty, without hesitation, made his own choice, taking the resolution of returning to Paris and of begging the queen-mother to retire for the time being to one of his mansions, particularly recommending Moulins, which she had formerly expressed to the late king a wish to have; and, in order that she might be the better contented with it, he offered her the government of it and of all the province." Next day, February 23, 1631, before the queen-mother was up, her royal son had taken the road back to Paris, leaving Marshal d'Estrées at Compiègne to explain to the queen his departure and to hasten his mother's, a task in which the marshal had but small success, for Mary de' Medici declared that, if they meant to make her depart, they would have to drag her stark naked from her bed. She kept herself shut up in the castle, refusing to go out and complaining of the injury the seclusion did to her health; then she fled by night from Compiègne, attended by one gentleman only, to go and take refuge in Flanders, whence she arrived before long at Brussels.

The cardinal's game was definitively won. Mary de' Medici had lost all empire over her son, whom she was never to see again.

The duke of Orleans, meanwhile, had taken the road to Lorraine, seeking a refuge in the dominions of a prince able, crafty, restless, and hostile to France from inclination as well as policy. Smitten, before long, with the duke's sister, Princess Margaret, Gaston of Orleans married her privately, with a dispensation from the cardinal of Lorraine, all which did not prevent either duke or prince from barefacedly denying the marriage when the king reproached them with having contracted this marriage without his consent. In the month of June, 1632, the duke of Orleans entered France again at the head of some wretched regiments, refuse of the Spanish army, given to him by Don Gonzalvo di Cordova. For the first time, he raised the standard of revolt openly. For him it was of little consequence, accustomed as he was to place himself at the head of parties that he abandoned without shame in the hour of danger; but he dragged along with him in his error a man worthy of another fate and of another chief. Henry, duke of Montmorency, marshal of France and governor of Languedoc, was a godson of Henry IV., who said one day to M. de Villeroy and to President Jeannin, "Look at my son Montmorency, how well made he is; if ever the house of Bourbon came to fail, there is no family in Europe which would so well deserve the crown of France as his, whose great men have always supported it and even added to it at the price of their blood." Shining at court as well as in arms, kind and charitable, beloved of every body and adored by his servants, the duke of Montmorency had steadily remained faithful to the king up to the fatal day when the duke of Orleans entangled him in his hazardous enterprise. Languedoc was displeased with Richelieu, who had robbed it of some of its privileges; the duke had no difficulty in collecting adherents there; and he fancied himself to be already wielding the constable's sword, five times borne by a Montmorency, when Gaston of Orleans entered France and Languedoc sooner than he had been looked for and with a smaller following than he had promised. The eighteen hundred men brought by the king's brother did not suffice to re-establish him, with the queen his mother, in the kingdom; the governor of Languedoc made an appeal to the Estates then assembled at Pézenas; he was supported by the bishop of Alby and by that of Nîmes; the province itself proclaimed revolt. The sums demanded by the king were granted to the duke, whom the deputies prayed to remain faithful to the interests of the province, just as they promised never to abandon his. The archbishop of Narbonne alone opposed this rash act; he left the Estates, where he was president, and the duke marched out to meet

Monsieur as far as Lunel. "Troops were levied throughout the province and the environs as openly as if it had been for the king." But the regiments were slow in forming; the duke of Orleans wished to gain over some of the towns; Narbonne and Montpellier closed their gates. The bishop's influence had been counted upon for making sure of Nîmes, and Montmorency everywhere tried to practise on the Huguenots; "but the reformed ministers of Nîmes, having had advices by letter from His Majesty whereby he represented himself to have been ad vertised that the principal design of Monsieur was to excite them of the religion styled reformed, considered themselves bound in their own defence to do more than the rest for the king's service. They assembled the consistory, resolved to die in obedience to him, went to seek the consuls and requested them to have the town-council assembled, in order that it might be brought to take a similar resolution; which the consuls, gained over by M. de Montmorency, refused" [*Mémoires de Richelieu*, t. iii. p. 160]. Thereupon the ministers sent off in haste to Marshal la Force, who had already taken position at Pont-Saint-Esprit with his army; and, he having despatched some light horse on the 26th of July, the people cried "*Hurrah! for the king!*" the bishop was obliged to fly and the town was kept to its allegiance. "Beaucaire, the governor of which had been won over," made armed resistance. "If we beat the king's army," said the duke of Montmorency on returning to Pézenas after this incident, "we shall have no lack of towns; if not, we shall have to go and make our court at Brussels."

At the news of his brother's revolt, the king, who happened to be on the frontiers of Lorraine, had put himself in motion, but he marched at his ease and by short stages, "thinking that the fire Monsieur would kindle would be only a straw-fire." He hurried his movements when he heard of Montmorency's uprising and left Paris after having put the seals upon the duke's house, who had imprudently left five hundred and fifty thousand livres there; the money was seized and lodged in the royal safe. The princess of Guémené, between whom and Montmorency there were very strong ties, went to see the cardinal, who was in attendance on the king. "Sir," she said to him, "you are going to Languedoc; remember the great marks of attachment that M. de Montmorency showed you not long ago; you cannot forget them without ingratitude." Indeed, when the king believed himself to be dying at Lyons, he had recommended the cardinal to the duke of Montmorency, who had promised to receive him into his government. "Madame," replied Richelieu coldly, "I have not been the first to break off."

Already the parliament of Toulouse, remaining faithful to the king, had annulled the resolutions of the Estates, the letters and commissions of the governor; and the parliament of Paris had just enregistered a resolution against the servants and adherents of the duke of Orleans, as rebels guilty of high treason and disturbers of the common peace. Six weeks were granted the king's brother to put an end to all acts of hostility; else the king was resolved to decree against him, after that interval of delay, "whatsoever he should consider it his duty to do for the preservation of his kingdom, according to the laws of the realm and the example of his predecessors."

It was against Marshal Schomberg that Montmorency was advancing. The latter found himself isolated in his revolt, shut up within the limits of his government, between the two armies of the king, who was marching in person against him. Calculations had been based upon an uprising of several provinces and the adhesion of several governors, amongst others of the aged duke of Épernon, who had sent to Monsieur to say: "I am his very humble servant, let him place himself in a position to be served;" but no one moved, the king every day received fresh protestations of fidelity, and the duke of Épernon had repaired to Montauban to keep that restless city to its duty and to prevent any attempt from being made in the province.

At three leagues' distance from Castelnaudary, Marshal Schomberg was besieging a castle called St. Félix-de-Carmain, which held out for the duke of Orleans. Montmorency advanced to the aid of the place; he had two thousand foot and three thousand horse; and the duke of Orleans accompanied him with a large number of gentlemen. The marshal had won over the defenders of St. Felix, and he was just half a league from Castelnaudary when he encountered the rebel army. The battle began almost at once. Count de Moret, natural son of Henry IV. and Jacqueline de Bueil, fired the first shot. Hearing the noise, Montmorency, who commanded the right wing, takes a squadron of cavalry, and, "urged on by that impetuosity which takes possession of all brave men at the like juncture, he spurs his horse forward, leaps the ditch which was across the road, rides over the musketeers, and, the mishap of finding himself alone causing him to feel more indignation than fear, he makes up his mind to signalize by his resistance a death which he cannot avoid." Only a few gentlemen had followed him, amongst others an old officer named Count de Rieux, who had promised to die at his feet: and he kept his word. In vain had Montmorency called to him his men-at-arms and the regiment of Ventadour; the rest of the cavalry did not budge. Count de Moret had been killed; terror was everywhere taking possession of the men. The duke was engaged with the king's light horse; he had just received two bullets in his mouth. His horse, "a small barb, extremely swift," came down with him; and he fell wounded in seventeen places, alone, without a single squire to help him. A sergeant of a company of the guards saw him fall and carried him into the road; some soldiers who were present burst out crying; they seemed to be lamenting their general's rather than their prisoner's misfortune. Montmorency alone remained as if insensible to the blows of adversity, and testified by the grandeur of his courage that in him it had its seat in a place higher than the heart" [*Journal du duc de Montmorency* (*Archives curieuses de l'histoire de France*), t. iv.].

Whilst the army of the duke of Orleans was retiring, carrying off their dead, nearly all of the highest rank, the king's men were bearing away Montmorency mortally wounded to Castelnaudary. His wife, Mary Felicia des Ursins, daughter of the duke of Bracciano, being ill in bed at Béziers, sent him a doctor together with her equerry to learn the truth about her husband's condition. "Thou'lt tell my wife," said the duke, "the number and greatness of the wounds thou hast seen, and thou'lt assure her that it which I have caused her spirit is incomparably more painful to me than all the others." On passing through the faubourgs of the town, the duke desired that his litter should be opened, "and the serenity that shone through the pallor of his visage moved the feelings of all present and forced tears from the stoutest and the most stolid" [*Journal du duc de Montmorency* (*Archives curieuses l'histoire de France*), t. iv.].

The duke of Orleans did not lack the courage of the soldier; he would fain have rescued Montmorency and sought to rally his forces; but the troops of Languedoc would obey none but the governor; the foreigners mutinied, and the king's brother had no longer an army. "Next day, when it was too late, I says Richelieu, "Monsieur sent a trumpeter to demand battle of Marshal Schomberg, who replied that he would not give it, but that, if he met him, he would try to defend himself against him." Monsieur considered himself absolved from seeking the combat, and henceforth busied himself about nothing but negotiation. Alby, Béziers, and Pézenas hastened to give in their submission. It was necessary for the duchess of Montmorency, ill and in despair, to quicken her departure from Béziers, where she was no longer safe. "As she passed along the streets she heard nothing but a confusion of voices amongst the people, speaking insolently of those who would withdraw in apprehension." The king was already at Lyons.

He was at Pont-Saint-Esprit when he sent a message to his brother, from whom he had already received emissaries on the road. The first demands of Gaston d'Orleans were still proud; he required the release of Montmorency, the rehabilitation of all those who had served his party and his mother's, places of surety and money. The king took no notice; and a second envoy from the prince was put in prison. Meanwhile, the superintendent of finance, M. de Bullion, had reached him from the king, and "found the mind of Monsieur very penitent and well disposed, but not that of all the rest, for Monsieur confessed that he had been ill-advised to behave as he did at the cardinal's house and afterwards leave the court; acknowledging himself to be much obliged to the king for the clemency he had shown to him, in his proclamation, which had touched him to the heart, and that he was bounden therefor to the cardinal, whom he had always liked and esteemed, and believed that he also on his side liked him" [*Mémoires de Richelieu*, t. viii. p. 196].

The duchess of Montmorency knew Monsieur, although she, it was said, had pressed her husband to join him; and all ill as she was, had been following him ever since the battle of Castelnaudary, in the fear lest he should forget her husband in the treaty. She could not, unfortunately, enter Béziers, and it was there that the arrangements were concluded. Monsieur protested his repentance, cursing in particular Father Chanteloube, confessor and confidant of the queen his mother, "whom he wished the king would have hanged; he had given pretty counsel to the queen, causing her to leave the kingdom; for all the great hopes he had led her to conceive, she was reduced to relieve her weariness by praying to God" [*Mémoirés de Richelieu*, t. viii. p. 196]. As for Monsieur, he was ready to give up all intelligence with Spain, Lorraine, and the queen his mother, "who could negotiate her business herself." He bound himself to take no interest "in him or those who had connected themselves with him on these occasions for their own purposes, and he would not complain should the king make them suffer what they had deserved." It is true that he added to these base concessions many entreaties in favor of M. de Montmorency; but M. de Bullion did not permit him to be under any delusion. "It is for Your Highness to choose," he said, "whether or not you prefer to cling to the interests of M. de Montmorency, displease the king and lose his good graces." The prince signed everything; then he set out for Tours, which the king had assigned for his residence, receiving on the way, from town to town, all the honors that would have been paid to His Majesty himself. M. de Montmorency remained in prison.

"He awaited death with a resignation which is inconceivable," says the author of his *Mémoires*, "never did man speak more boldly than he about it; it seemed as if he were recounting another's perils when he described his own to his servants and his guards, who were the only witnesses of such lofty manliness." His sister, the princess of Condé, had a memorial prepared for his defence put before him. He read it carefully, then he tore it up, "having always determined," he said, "not to (*chicaner*) go pettifogging for (or, dispute) his life." "I ought by rights to answer before the Parliament of Paris only," said he to the commission of the Parliament of Toulouse instructed to conduct his trial, "but I give up with all my heart this privilege and all others that might delay my sentence."

There was not long to wait for the decree. On arriving at Toulouse, October 27, at noon, the duke had asked for a confessor. "Father," said he to the priest, "I pray you to put me this moment in the shortest and most certain path to heaven that you can, having nothing more to hope or wish for but God." All his family had hurried up, but without being able to obtain the favor of seeing the king. "His Majesty had strengthened himself in the resolution he had taken from the first to make in the case of the said Sieur de Montmorency a just example for all the grandees of his kingdom in the future, as the late king his father had done in the person of Marshal Biron," says Richelieu in his *Mémoires*. The princess of Condé could not gain admittance to His Majesty, who lent no ear to the supplications of his oldest servants, represented by the aged duke of Épernon, who accused himself by his own mouth of having but lately committed the same crime as the duke of Montmorency. "You can retire, duke," was all that Louis

XIII. deigned to reply. "I should not be a king, if I had the feelings of private persons," said he to Marshal Châtillon who pointed out to him the downcast looks and swollen eyes of all his court.

It was the 30th of October, early; and the duke of Montmorency was sleeping peacefully. His confessor came and awoke him. "*Surgite, eamus* (*Rise, let us be going*)," he said, as he awoke; and when his surgeon would have dressed his wounds, "Now is the time to heal all my wounds with a single one," he said, and he had himself dressed in the clothes of white linen he had ordered to be made at Lectoure for the day of execution. When the last questions were put to him by the judges, he answered by a complete confession; and, when the decree was made known to him: "I thank you, gentlemen," said he to the commissioners, "and I beg you to tell all them of your body from me that I hold this decree of the king's justice for a decree of God's mercy." He walked to the scaffold with the same tranquillity, saluting right and left those whom he knew, to take leave of them; then, having with difficulty placed himself upon the block, so much did his wounds still cause him to suffer, he said out loud: "*Domine Jesu, accipe spiritum meum* (*Lord Jesus, receive my spirit*)*!*" As his head fell the people rushed forward to catch his blood and dip their handkerchiefs in it.

Henry de Montmorency was the last of the ducal branch of his house and was only thirty-seven.

It was a fine opportunity for Monsieur to once more break his engagements. Shame and anxiety drove him equally. He was universally reproached with Montmorency's death; and he was by no means easy on the subject of his marriage, of which no mention had been made in the arrangements. He quitted Tours and withdrew to Flanders, writing to the king to complain of the duke's execution, saying that the life of the latter had been the tacit condition of his agreement, and that, his promise being thus not binding, he was about to seek a secure retreat out of the kingdom. "Everybody knows in what plight you were, brother, and whether you could have done anything else," replied the king.

"What think you, gentlemen, was it that lost the duke of Montmorency his head?" said Cardinal Zapata to Bautru and Barrault, envoys of France, whom he met in the antechamber of the king of Spain. "His crimes," replied Bautru. "No," said the cardinal, "but the clemency of His Majesty's predecessors." Louis XIII. and Cardinal Richelieu have assuredly not merited that reproach in history.

So many and such terrible examples were at last to win the all-powerful minister some years of repose. Once only, in 1636, a new plot on the part of Monsieur and the count of Soissons threatened not only his power but his life. The king's headquarters were established at the castle of Demuin; and the princes, urged on by Montrésor and Saint-Ibal, had resolved to compass the cardinal's death. The blow was to be struck at the exit from the council. Richelieu conducted the king back to the bottom of the staircase. The two gentlemen were awaiting the signal; but Monsieur did not budge and retired without saying a word. The count of Soissons dared not go any further, and the cardinal mounted quietly to his own rooms, without dreaming of the extreme peril he had run. Richelieu was rather lofty than proud, and too clear-sighted to mistake the king's feelings towards him. Never did he feel any confidence in his position; and never did he depart from his jealous and sometimes petty watchfulness. Any influence foreign to his own disquieted him in proximity to a master whose affairs he governed altogether, without ever having been able to get the mastery over his melancholy and singular mind.

Women filled but a small space in the life of Louis XIII. Twice, however, in that interval of ten years which separated the plot of Montmorency from that of Cinq-Mars, did the minister believe himself to be threatened by feminine influence; and twice he used artifice to win the monarch's heart and confidence from two young girls of his court, Louise de la Fayette and Marie d'Hautefort. Both were maids of honor to the queen. Mdlle. d'Hautefort was fourteen years old when, in 1630, at Lyons, in the languors of convalescence, the king first remarked her blooming and at the same time severe beauty, and her air of nobility and modesty; and it was not long before the whole court knew that he had remarked her, for his first care, at the sermon, was to send the young maid of honor the velvet-cushion on which he knelt for her to sit upon. Mdlle. d'Hautefort declined it, and remained seated, like her companions, on the ground; but henceforth the courtiers' eyes were riveted on her movements, on the interminable conversations in which she was detained by the king, on his jealousies, his tiffs and his reconciliations. After their quarrels, the king would pass the greater part of the day in writing out what he had said to Mdlle. d'Hautefort and what she had replied to him. At his death, his desk was found full of these singular reports of the most innocent, but also most stormy and most troublesome love-affair that ever was. The king was especially jealous of Mdlle. d'Hautefort's passionate devotion to the queen her mistress, Anne of Austria: "You love an ingrate," he said, "and you will see how she will repay your services." Richelieu had been unable to win Mdlle. d'Hautefort; and he did his best to embitter the tiff which separated her from the king in 1635. But Louis XIII. had learnt the charm of confidence and intimacy; and he turned to Louise de la Fayette, a charming girl of seventeen, who was as virtuous as Mdlle. d'Hautefort, but more gentle and tender than she, and who gave her heart in all guilelessness to that king so powerful, so a-weary, and so melancholy at the very climax of his reign. Happily for Richelieu he had a means, more certain than even Mdlle. d'Hautefort's pride, of separating her from Louis XIII.; Mdlle. de la Fayette, whilst quite a child, had serious ideas of becoming a nun; and scruples about being false to her vocation troubled her at court and even in those conversations, in which she reproached herself with taking too much pleasure. Father Coussin, her confessor, who was also the king's, sought to quiet her conscience; he hoped much from the influence she could exercise over the king; but Mdlle. de la Fayette, feeling herself troubled and perplexed, was urgent. When the Jesuit reported to Louis XIII. the state of his fair young friend's feelings, the king, with tears in his eyes, replied: "Though I am very sorry she is going away, nevertheless I have no desire to be an obstacle to her vocation; only let her wait until I have left for the army." She did not wait, however. Their last interview took place at the queen's, who had no liking for Mdlle. de la Fayette; and, as the king's carriage went out of the court-yard, the young girl, leaning against the window, turned to one of her companions and said, "Alas! I shall never see him again!" But she did see him again often for some time. He went to see her in her convent, and "remained so long glued to her grating," says Madame de Motteville, "that Cardinal Richelieu, falling a prey to fresh terrors, recommenced his intrigues to tear him from her entirely. And he succeeded." The king's affection for Mdlle. d'Hautefort awoke again. She had just rendered the queen an important service. Anne of Austria was secretly corresponding with her two brothers, King Philip

IV. and the Cardinal Infante, a correspondence which might well make the king and his minister uneasy, since it was carried on through Madame de Chevreuse and there was war at the time with Spain. The queen employed for this intercourse a valet named Laporte, who was arrested and thrown into prison. The chancellor removed to Val-de-Grâce, whither the queen frequently retired; he questioned the nuns and rummaged Anne of Austria's cell. She was in mortal anxiety, not knowing what Laporte might say or how to unloose his tongue so as to keep due pace with her own confessions to the king and the cardinal. Mdlle. d'Hautefort disguised herself as a servant, went straight to the Bastille and got a letter delivered to Laporte, thanks to the agency of Commander de Jars, her friend, then in prison. The confessions of mistress and agent being thus set in accord, the queen obtained her pardon, but not without having to put up with reproaches and conditions of stern supervision. Madame de Chevreuse took fright and went to seek refuge in Spain. The king's inclination towards Mdlle. d'Hautefort revived, without her having an idea of turning it to profit on her own account. "She had so much loftiness of spirit that she could never have brought herself to ask anything for herself and her family; and all that could be wrung from her was to accept what the king and queen were pleased to give her."

Richelieu had never forgotten Mdlle. d'Hautefort's airs: he feared her and accused her to the king of being concerned in Monsieur's continual intrigues. Louis XIII.'s growing affection for young Cinq-Mars, son of Marshal d'Effiat, was beginning to occupy the gloomy monarch; and he the more easily sacrificed Mdlle. d'Hautefort. The cardinal merely asked him to send her away for a fortnight. She insisted upon hearing the order from the king's own mouth. "The fortnight will last all the rest of my life," she said: "and so I take leave of Your Majesty for ever." She went accompanied by the regrets and tears of Anne of Austria and leaving the field opened to the new favorite, the king's "rattle," as the cardinal called him.

M. de Cinq-Mars was only nineteen when he was made master of the wardrobe and grand equerry of France. Brilliant and witty, he amused the king and occupied the leisure which peace gave him. The passion Louis XIII. felt for his favorite was jealous and capricious. He upbraided the young man for his flights to Paris to see his friends and the elegant society of the Marais, and sometimes also Mary di Gonzaga, daughter of the duke of Mantua, wooed but lately by the duke of Orleans, and not indifferent, it was said, to the vows of M. le Grand, as Cinq-Mars was called. The complaints were detailed to Richelieu by the king himself in a strange correspondence, which reminds one of the "reports" of his quarrels with Mdlle. d'Hautefort. "I am very sorry," wrote Louis XIII. on the 4th of January, 1641, "to trouble you about the ill tempers of M. le Grand. I upbraided him with his heedlessness; he answered that for that matter he could not change, and that he should do no better than he had done. I said that, considering his obligations to me, he ought not to address me in that manner. He answered in his usual way: that he didn't want my kindness, that he could do very well without it, and that he would be quite as well content to be Cinq-Mars as M. le Grand, but, as for changing his ways and his life, he couldn't do it. And so, he continually knagging at me and I at him, we came as far as the court-yard, when I said to him that, being in the temper he was in, he would do me the pleasure of not coming to see me. I have not seen him since. Signed LOUIS." This time the cardinal reconciled the king and the favorite, whom he had himself placed near him but whose constant attendance upon the king his master he was beginning to find sometimes very troublesome. "One day he sent word to him not to be for the future so continually at his heels, and treated him even to his face with so much tartness and imperiousness as if he had been the lowest of the valets." Cinq-Mars began to lend an ear to those who were egging him on against the cardinal.

Then began a series of negotiations and intrigues; the duke of Orleans had come back to Paris, the king was ill and the cardinal more so than he; thence arose conjectures and insensate hopes; the duke of Bouillon, being sent for by the king who confided to him the command of the army of Italy, was at the same time drawn into the plot which was beginning to be woven against the minister; the duke of Orleans and the queen were in it; and the town of Sedan, of which Bouillon was prince-sovereign, was wanted to serve the authors of the conspiracy as an asylum in case of reverse. Sedan alone was not sufficient; there was need of an army. Whence was it to come? Thoughts naturally turned towards Spain.

For so perilous a treaty a negotiator was required, and the grand equerry proposed his friend, Viscount de Fontrailles, a man of wit, who detested the cardinal, and who would have considered it a simpler plan to assassinate him; he consented, however, to take charge of the negotiation, and he set out for Madrid, where his treaty was soon concluded, in the name of the duke of Orleans. The Spaniards were to furnish 12,000 foot and 5000 horse, 400,000 crowns down, 12,000 crowns' pay a month, and 300,000 livres to fortify the frontier-town which was promised by the duke. Sedan, Cinq-Mars and the duke of Bouillon were only mentioned in a separate instrument.

The king was then at Narbonne, on his way to his army which was besieging Perpignan, the grand equerry was with him. Fontrailles went to call upon him: "I do not intend to be seen by anybody," said he, "but to make speedily for England, as I do not think I am strong enough to undergo the torture the cardinal might put me to in his own room on the least suspicion." On the 21st of April, the cardinal was dangerously ill, and the king left him at Narbonne a prey to violent fever, with an abscess on the arm which prevented him from writing, whilst Cinq-Mars, ever present and ever at work, was doing his best to insinuate into his master's mind suspicion of the minister and the hopes founded upon his disgrace or death. The king listened, as he subsequently avowed, in order to discover his favorite's wicked thoughts and make him tell all he had in his heart. "The king was tacitly the head of this conspiracy," says Madame de Motteville: "the grand equerry was the soul of it; the name made use of was that of the duke of Orleans, the king's only brother; and their council was the duke of Bouillon, who joined with them because, having belonged to the party of M. de Soissons, he was in very ill odor at court. They all formed fine projects touching the change that was to take place to the advantage of their aggrandizement and fortunes, persuading themselves that the cardinal could not live above a few days, during which he would not be able to set himself right with the king." Such were their projects and their hopes when the *Gazette de France* on the 21st of June, 1642, gave these two pieces of news both together: "The cardinal-duke, after remaining two days at Arles, embarked on the 11th of this month for Tarascon, his health becoming better and better. The king has ordered under arrest Marquis de Cinq-Mars, grand equerry of France."

Great was the surprise and still greater was the dismay amongst the friends of Cinq-Mars. "Your grand designs are as well known at Paris as that the Seine flows under the Pont Neuf," wrote Mary di Gonzaga to him a few days previously.

Those grand designs so imprudently divulged caused a presentiment of great peril. When left alone with his young favorite and suddenly overwhelmed, amidst his army, with cares and business of which his minister usually relieved him, the king had too much wit not to perceive the frivolous insignificance of Cinq-Mars compared with the mighty capability of the cardinal. "I love you more than ever," he wrote to Richelieu: "we have been too long together to be ever separated, as I wish everybody to understand." In reply, the cardinal had sent him a copy of the treaty between Cinq-Mars and Spain.

The king could not believe his eyes; and his wrath equalled his astonishment. Together with that of the grand equerry he ordered the immediate arrest of M. de Thou, his intimate friend; and the order went out to secure the duke of Bouillon, then at the head of the army of Italy. He, caught like Marshal Marillac in the midst of his troops, had vainly attempted to conceal himself; but he was taken and conducted to the castle of Pignerol. Fontrailles had seen the blow coming. He went to visit the grand equerry, and, "Sir," said he, "you are a fine figure; if you were shorter by the whole head, you would not cease to be very tall; as for me, who am already very short, nothing could be taken off me without inconveniencing me and making me cut the poorest figure in the world; you will be good enough, if you please, to let me get out of the way of edged tools." And he set out for Spain, whence he had hardly returned.

What had become of the most guilty, if not the most dangerous, of all the accomplices? Monsieur, "the king's only (*unique*) brother," as Madame de Motteville calls him, had come as far as Moulins and had sent to ask the grand equerry to appoint a place of meeting, when he heard of his accomplice's arrest and, before long, that of the duke of Bouillon. Frightened to death as he was, he saw that treachery was safer than flight, and, just as the king had joined the all but dying cardinal at Tarascon, there arrived an emissary from the duke of Orleans bringing letters from him. He assured the king of his fidelity; he intreated Chavigny, the minister's confidant, to give him "means of seeing his Eminence before he saw the king, in which case all would go well." He appealed to the cardinal's generosity, begging him to keep his letter as an eternal reproach, if he were not thenceforth the most faithful and devoted of his friends.

Abbé de la Rivière, who was charged to implore pardon for

his master, was worthy of such a commission: he confessed everything, he signed everything, though he "all but died of terror," and, at the cardinal's demand, he soon brought all those poltrooneries written out in the duke of Orleans' own hand. The prince was all but obliged to appear at the trial and deliver up his accomplices in the face of the whole world. The respect, however, of Chancellor Séguier for his rank spared him this crowning disgrace. The king's orders to his brother, after being submitted to the cardinal, bore this note in the minister's hand: "Monsieur will have in his place of exile 12,000 crowns a month, the same sum that the king of Spain had promised to give him."

"Paralysis of the arm did not prevent the head from acting:" the dying cardinal had dictated to the king stretched on a couch at his side, in a chamber of his house at Monfrin, near Tarascon, those last commands which completed the dishonor of the duke of Orleans and the ruin of the favorite. Louis XIII. slowly took the road back to Fontainebleau in the cardinal's litter, which the latter had lent him. The prisoners were left in the minister's keeping, who ordered them before long to Lyons, whither be was himself removed. The grand equerry coming from Montpellier, M. de Thou from Tarascon, in a boat towed by that of the cardinal, and the duke of Bouillon from Pignerol, were all three lodged in the castle of Pierre-Encise. Their examination was put off until the arrival of such magistrates "as should be capable of philosophizing and perpetually thinking of the means they must use for arriving at their ends." That was useless, inasmuch as the grand equerry "never ceased to say quite openly that he had done nothing to which the king had not consented."

Louis XIII. was, no doubt, affected by such language; for, scarcely had he arrived at Fontainebleau, whither he had been preceded by news of the end of the queen, his mother, who had died at Cologne in exile and poverty, when he wrote to all the parliaments of his kingdom, to the governors of the provinces, and to the ambassadors at foreign courts, to give his own account of the arrest of the guilty and the part he himself had played in the matter. "The notable and visible change which had for the last year appeared in the conduct of Sieur de Cinq-Mars, our grand equerry, made us resolve, as soon as we perceived it, to carefully keep watch on his actions and his words, in order to fathom them and discover what could be the cause. To this end, we resolved to let him act and speak with us more freely than heretofore." And in a letter written straight to the chancellor, the king exclaims in wrath: "It is true that having seen me sometimes dissatisfied with the cardinal, whether from the apprehension I felt lest he should hinder me from going to the siege of Perpignan or induce me to leave it, for fear lest my health might suffer, or from any other like reason, the said Sieur de Cinq-Mars left nothing undone to chafe me against my said cousin, which I put up with so long as his evil offices were confined within the bounds of moderation. But when he went so far as to suggest to me that the cardinal must be got rid of and offered to carry it out himself, I conceived a horror of his evil thoughts and held them in detestation. Although I have only to say so for you to believe it, there is nobody who can deem but that it must have been so; for, otherwise, what motive would he have had for joining himself to Spain against me, if I had approved of what he desired?"

The trial was a foregone conclusion; the king and his brother made common cause in order to overwhelm the accused, "an earnest of a peace which was not such as God announced with good will to man on Christmas-day," writes Madame de Motteville, "but such as may exist at court and amongst brothers of royal blood."

The cardinal did not think it necessary to wait for the sentence. He had arrived at his house at Lyons, in a sort of square chamber, covered with red damask, and borne on the shoulders of eighteen guards; there, stretched upon his couch, a table covered with papers beside him, he worked and chattered with whomsoever of his servants he had been pleased to have as his companion on the road. It was in the same equipage that he left Lyons to gain the Loire and return to Paris. On his passage, it was necessary to pull down lumps of wall and throw bridges over the fosses to make way for this vast litter and the indomitable man that lay dying within it.

It was on the 12th of September, 1642, that the accused appeared before the commission; there were now but two of them; the duke of Bouillon had made his private arrangement with the cardinal, confessing everything, and requesting "to have his life spared in order that he might employ it to preserve to the Catholic Church five little children whom his death would leave to persons of the opposite religion." In consideration of this pardon, a demand was made upon him to give up Sedan to the king, "though it were easy to gain possession of it by investment." The duke consented to all, and he awaited in his dungeon at Pierre-Encise the execution of his accomplices who had no town to surrender. Their death was to be the signal of his liberation.

The two accused denied nothing: M. de Thou merely maintained that he had not been in any way mixed up with the conspiracy, proving that he had blamed the treaty with Spain and that his only crime was not having revealed it. "He believed me to be his friend, his one faithful friend," said he, speaking of Cinq-Mars, "and I had no mind to betray him." The grand equerry told in detail the story of the plot, his connection with the duke of Orleans, who had missed no opportunity of paying court to him, the resolutions taken in concert with the duke of Bouillon, and the treaty concluded with Spain, "confessing that he had erred and had no hope but in the clemency of the king, and of the cardinal whose generosity would be so much the more shown in asking pardon for him as he was the less bound to do so." There was not long to wait for the decree; the votes were unanimous against the grand equerry, a single one of the judges pronouncing in favor of M. de Thou. The latter turned towards Cinq-Mars, and said: "Ah! well, sir; humanly speaking I might complain of you; you have placed me in the dock, and you are the cause of my death; but God knows how I love you. Let us die, sir, let us die courageously and win paradise."

The decree against Cinq-Mars sentenced him to undergo the question in order to get a more complete revelation of his accomplices. "It had been resolved not to put him to it," says Tallemant des Réaux: "but it was exhibited to him nevertheless; it gave him a turn, but it did not make him do anything to belie himself, and he was just taking off his doublet, when he was told to raise his hand in sign of telling the truth."

The execution was not destined to be long deferred; the very day on which the sentence was delivered saw the execution of it. "The grand equerry showed a never changing and very resolute firmness to the death, together with admirable calmness and the constancy and devoutness of a Christian," wrote M. du Marca, councillor of State, to the secretary of State Brionne; and Tallemant des Réaux adds: "he died with astoundingly great courage and did not waste time in speechifying; he would not have his eyes bandaged, and kept them open when the blow was struck." M. de Thou said not a word save to God, repeating the *Credo* even to the very scaffold, with a fervor of devotion that touched all present. "We have seen," says a report of the time, "the favorite of the greatest and most just of kings lose his head upon the scaffold at the age of twenty-two, but with a firmness which has scarcely its parallel in our histories. We have seen a councillor of state die like a saint after a crime which men cannot justly pardon. There is nobody in the world who, knowing of their conspiracy against the State, does not think them worthy of death, and there will be few who, having knowledge of their rank and their fine natural qualities, will not mourn their sad fate."

"Now that I make not a single step which does not lead me to death, I am more capable than anybody else of estimating the value of the things of the world," wrote Cinq-Mars to his mother, the wife of Marshal d'Effiat. "Enough of this world; away to Paradise!" said M. de Thou, as he marched to the scaffold. Châlais and Montmorency had used the same language. At the last hour, and at the bottom of their hearts, the frivolous courtier and the hare-brained conspirator as well as the great soldier and the grave magistrate had recovered their faith in God.

CHAPTER XXXIX.

LOUIS XIII., CARDINAL RICHELIEU AND THE PROVINCES.

THE story has been told of the conspiracies at court and the repeated checks suffered by the great lords in their attempts against Cardinal Richelieu. With the exception of Languedoc, under the influence of its governor the duke of Montmorency, the provinces took no part in these enterprises; their opposition was of another sort; and it is amongst the parliaments chiefly that we must look for it.

"The king's cabinet and his bed-time business (*petit coucher*) cause me more embarrassment than the whole of Europe causes me," said the cardinal in the days of the *great storms at court;* he would often have had less trouble in managing the parliaments and the parliament of Paris in particular, if the latter had not felt itself supported by a party at court. For a long time past a pretention had been put forward by that great body to give the king advice, and to replace towards him the vanished States-general. "We hold the place in council of the princes and barons, who from time immemorial were near the person of the kings," was the language used, in 1615, in the representations of the parliament, which had dared, without the royal order, to summon the princes, dukes, peers, and officers of the crown to deliberate upon what was to be done for the service of the king, the good of the State, and the relief of the people.

This pretention on the part of the parliaments was what Cardinal Richelieu was continually fighting against. He would not allow the intervention of the magistrates in the government of the State. When he took the power into his hands, nine parliaments sat in France—Paris, Toulouse, Grenoble, Bordeaux, Dijon, Rouen, Aix, Rennes, and Pau: he created but one, that of Metz, in 1633, to sever in a definitive manner the bonds which still attached the three bishoprics to the Germanic Empire. Trials at that time were carried in the last resort to Spires.

Throughout the history of France we find the parliament of Paris bolder and more enterprising than all the rest: and it did not belie its character in the very teeth of Richelieu. When, after *Dupes' Day* was over, Louis XIII. declared all the companions of his brother's escape guilty of high treason, the parliament of Dijon, to which the decree was presented by the king himself, enregistered it without making any difficulty. All the other parliaments followed the example; that of Paris alone resisted, and its decision on the 25th of April contained a bitter censure upon the cardinal's administration. On the 12th of May, the decision of that parliament was quashed by a decree of the royal council, and all its members were summoned to the Louvre: on their knees they had to hear the severe reprimand by Châteauneuf, keeper of the seals; and one president and three counsellors were at the same time dismissed. When the parliament, still indomitable, would have had those magistrates sit in defiance of the royal order, they were not to be found in their houses; the soldiery had carried them off.

The trial of Marshal Marillac, before a commission, twice modified during the course of proceedings, of the Parliament of Dijon, was the occasion of a fresh reclamation on the part of the parliament of Paris; and the king's ill-humor against the magistrates burst forth on the occasion of a commission constituted at the Arsenal to take cognizance of the crime of coining. The parliament made some formal objections; the king, who was at that time at Metz with his troops, summoned President Séguier and several counsellors. He quashed the decree of the parliament. "You are only constituted," said he, "to judge between Master Peter and Master John (between *John Doe* and *Richard Roe*); if you go on as at present, I will pare your nails so close that you'll be sorry for it." Five counsellors were interdicted and had great trouble in obtaining authority to sit again.

So many and such frequent squabbles, whether about points of jurisdiction or about the registration of edicts respecting finances, which the parliament claimed to have the right of looking into, caused between the king, inspired by his minister, and the parliament of Paris an irritation which reached its height during the trial of the duke of La Valette, third son of the duke of Épernon, accused, not without grounds, of having caused the failure of the siege of Fontarabia from jealousy towards the prince of Condé. The affair was called on before a commission composed of dukes and peers, some councillors of State and some members of the parliament, which demanded that the duke should be removed to its jurisdiction. "I will not have it," answered the king; "you are always making difficulties; it seems as if you wanted to keep me in leading-strings; but I am master and shall know how to make myself obeyed. It is a gross error to suppose that I have not a right to bring to judgment whom I think proper and where I please." The king himself asked the judges for their opinion [*Isambert, Recueil des anciennes lois Françaises*, t. xvi.]. "Sir," replied Counsellor Pinon, dean of the grand chamber, "for fifty years I have been in the parliament, and I never saw anything of this sort; M. de la Valette had the honor of wedding a natural sister of your Majesty, and he is, besides, a peer of France; I implore you to remove him to the jurisdiction of the parliament." "Your opinion!" said the king curtly. "I am of opinion that the duke of La Valette be removed to be tried before the parliament." "I will not have that; it is no opinion." "Sir, removal is a legitimate opinion." "Your opinion on the case!" rejoined the king, who was beginning to be angry; "if not, I know what I must do." President Bellièvre was even bolder: "It is a strange thing," said he to Louis XIII.'s face, "to see a king giving his vote at the criminal trial of one of his subjects; hitherto kings have reserved to themselves the rights of grace and have removed to their officers' province the sentencing of culprits. Could your Majesty bear to see in the dock a nobleman, who might leave your presence only for the scaffold? It is incompatible with kingly majesty." "Your opinion on the case!" bade the king. "Sir, I have no other opinion." The duke of La Valette had taken refuge in England: he was condemned and executed in effigy. The attorney-general, Matthew Molé, "did not consider it his business to carry out an execution of that sort:" and recourse was obliged to be had to the lieut.-governor of convicts at the Châtelet of Paris.

The cup had overflowed, and the cardinal resolved to put an end to an opposition which was the more irritating inasmuch as it was sometimes legitimate. A notification of the king's, published in 1641, prohibited the parliament from any interference in affairs of state and administration. The whole of Richelieu's home-policy is summed up in the preamble to that instrument, a formal declaration of absolute power concentrated in the hands of the king. "It seemeth that, the institution of monarchies having its foundation in the government of a single one, that rank is as it were the soul which animates them and inspires them with as much force and vigor as they can have short of perfection. But as this absolute authority raises States to the highest pinnacle of their glory, so, when it happens to be enfeebled, they are observed, in a short time, to fall from their high estate. There is no need to go out of France to find instances of this truth. . . . The fatal disorders and divisions of the League, which ought to be buried in eternal oblivion, owed their origin and growth to disregard of the kingly authority. . . . Henry the Great, in whom God had put the most excellent virtues of a great prince, on succeeding to the crown of Henry III., restored by his valor the kingly authority which had been as it were cast down and trampled under foot. France recovered her pristine vigor and let all Europe see that power concentrated in the person of the sovereign is the source of the glory and greatness of monarchies, and the foundation upon which their preservation rests. . . . We, then, have thought it necessary to regulate the administration of justice and to make known to our parliaments what is the legitimate usage of the authority which the kings, our predecessors, and we have deposited with them, in order that a thing which was established for the good of the people may not produce contrary effects, as would happen if the officers, instead of contenting themselves with that power which makes them judges in matters of life and death and touching the fortunes of our subjects, would fain meddle in the government of the State which appertains to the prince only."

The cardinal had gained the victory; parliament bowed the head; its attempts at independence during the Fronde were but a flash, and the yoke of Louis XIV. became the more heavy for it. The pretensions of the magistrates were often foundationless, the restlessness and meddlesome character of their assemblies did harm to their remonstrances; but for a long while they maintained, in the teeth of more and more absolute kingly power, the country's rights in the government, and they had perceived the dangers of that sovereign monarchy which certainly sometimes raises States to the highest pinnacle of their glory, but only to let them sink before long to a condition of the most grievous abasement.

Though always first in the breach, the parliament of Paris was not alone in its opposition to the cardinal. The parliament of Dijon protested against the sentence of Marshal Marillac, and refused, to its shame, to bear its share of the expenses for the defence of Burgundy against the duke of Lorraine, in 1636, a refusal which cost it the suspension of its premier president. The parliament of Brittany, in defence of its jurisdictional privileges, refused to enregister the decree which had for object the foundation of a company trading with the Indies "for the general trade between the West and the East," a grand idea of Richelieu's, the seat of which was to be in the roads of Morbihan; the company, already formed, was disheartened, thanks to the delays caused by the parliament, and the enterprise failed. The parliament of Grenoble, fearing a dearth of corn in Dauphiny, quashed the treaties of supply for the army of Italy, at the time of the second expedition to Mantua; it went so far as to have the dealers' granaries thrown open and the superintendent of finance, D'Émery, was obliged to come to terms with the deputies of Dauphiny, "in order that they of the parliament of Grenoble, who said they had no interests but those of the province, might have no reason to prevent for the future the transport of corn," says Richelieu himself in his *Mémoires*.

The parliament of Rouen had always passed for one of the most recalcitrant. The province of Normandy was rich and, consequently, overwhelmed with imposts; and several times the parliament refused to enregister financial edicts which still further aggravated the distress of the people. In 1637, the king threatened to go in person to Rouen and bring the parliament to submission, whereat it took fright and enregistered decrees for twenty-two millions. It was, no doubt, this augmentation of imposts that brought about the revolt of the *Nu-pieds* (*Barefoots*) in 1639. Before now, in 1624 and in 1637, in Périgord and Rouergue, two popular risings of the same sort, under the name of *Croquants* (*Paupers*), had disquieted the authorities, and the governor of the province had found some trouble in putting them down. The *Nu-pieds* were more numerous and more violent still; from Rouen to Avrances all the country was ablaze. At Coutances and at Vire, several *monopoliers* and *gabeleurs*, as the fiscal officers were called, were massacred; a great number of houses were burnt, and most of the receiving-offices were pulled down or pillaged. Everywhere the *army of suffering* (*armée de souffrance*), the name given by the revolters to themselves, made appeal to violent passions; popular rhymes were circulated from hand to hand, in the name of General *Nu-pieds* (*Barefoot*), an imaginary personage whom nobody ever saw. Some of these verses are fair enough:—

To Normandy.

"Dear land of mine, thou canst no more:
What boots it to have served so well?
For, see! thy faithful service bore
This bitter fruit—the cursed gabelle.
Is that the guerdon earn'd by those
Who succour'd France against her foes,
Who saved her kings, upheld her crown,
And raised the lilies trodden down,
In spite of all the foe could do,
In spite of Spain and England too?

"Recall thy generous blood and show—
That all posterity may know—
Duke William's breed still lives at need:
Show that thou hast a heavier hand
Than erst came forth from Northern land;
A hand so strong, a heart so high,
These tyrants all shall beaten cry:
'From Normans and the Norman race,
Deliver us, O God of grace!'"

The tumult was more violent at Rouen than anywhere else, and the parliament energetically resisted the mob. It had sent two counsellors as a deputation to Paris to inform the king about the state of affairs. "You may signify to the gentlemen of the parliament of Rouen," said Chancellor Séguier in answer to the delegates, "that I thank them for the trouble they have taken on this occasion; I will let the king know how they have behaved in this affair. I beg them to go on as they have begun. I know that the parliament did very good service there."

In fact, several counsellors, on foot in the street and in the very midst of the revolters, had, at the peril of their lives, defended Le Tellier de Tourneville, receiver-general of gabels, and his officers, whilst the whole parliament, in their robes, with the premier president at their head, perambulated Rouen, amidst the angry mob, repairing at once to the points most threatened, insomuch that the presidents and counsellors were "in great danger and fear for their skins" [*Histoire du Parlement de Normandie*, by M. Floquet, t. iv.]. It was this terror, born of tumults and the sight of an infuriated populace, which, at a later period retarded the parliament in dealing out justice and brought down upon it the wrath of the king and of the cardinal.

Meanwhile the insurrection was gaining ground, and the local authorities were powerless to repress it. There was hesitation at the king's council in choosing between Marshal Rantzau and M. de Gassion to command the forces ordered to march into Normandy. "That country yields no wine," said the king: "that will not do for Rantzau, or be good quarters for him." And they sent Colonel Gassion, not so heavy a drinker as Rantzau, a good soldier and an inflexible character. First at Caen, then at Avranches, where there was fighting to be done, at Coutances and at Elbeuf, Gassion's soldiery everywhere left the country behind them in subjection, in ruin and in despair. They entered Rouen on the 31st of December, 1639, and on the 2nd of January, 1640, the chancellor himself arrived to do justice on the rebels heaped up in the prisons, whom the parliament dared not bring up for judgment. "I come to Rouen," he said on entering the town, "not to deliberate but to declare and execute the matters on which my mind is made up." And he forbade all intervention on the part of the archbishop, Francis de Harlay, who was disposed, in accordance with his office of love as well as the parliamentary name he bore, to implore pity for the culprits and to excuse the backward judges. The chancellor did not give himself the trouble to draw up sentences. "The decree is at the tip of my staff," replied Picot, captain of his guards, when he was asked to show his orders. The executions were numerous in Higher and Lower Normandy, and the parliament received the wages of its tardiness. All the members of the body, even the most aged and infirm, were obliged to leave Rouen. A commission of fifteen councillors of the parliament of Paris came to replace provisionally the interdicted parliament of Normandy; and, when the magistrates were empowered at last to resume their sitting, it was only a *six months' term:* that is, the parliament henceforth found itself divided into two fragments perfect strangers one to the other, which were to sit alternately for six months. "A veritable thunderbolt for that sovereign court, for by the *six months' term,*" says M. Floquet, "there was no longer any parliament properly speaking, but two phantoms of parliament, making war on each other, whilst the government had the field open to carve and cut without control."

"All obedience is now from fear," wrote Grotius to Oxenstiern, chancellor of Sweden; "the idea is to exorcise and annihilate hatred by means of terror." "This year," wrote an inhabitant of Rouen, "there have been no New Year's presents [*étrennes*], no singing of 'the king's drinking-song' [*le roi boit*], in any house. Little children will be able to tell tales of it when they have attained to man's estate; for never, these fifty years past, so far as I can learn, has it been so" [*Journal de l'Abbé de la Rue*]. The heaviest imposts weighed upon the whole province, which thus expiated the crime of an insignificant portion of its inhabitants. "The king shall not lose the value of this handkerchief that I hold," said the superintendent Bullion, on arriving at Rouen. And he kept his word: Rouen alone had to pay more than three millions. The province and its parliament were henceforth reduced to submission.

It was not only the parliaments that resisted the efforts of Cardinal Richelieu to concentrate all the power of the government in the hands of the king. From the time that the sovereigns had given up convoking the states-general, the states-provincial had alone preserved the right of bringing to the foot of the throne the plaints and petitions of subjects. Unhappily few provinces enjoyed this privilege; Languedoc, Brittany, Burgundy, Provence, Dauphiny, and the countship of Pau alone were *states-districts*, that is to say, allowed to tax themselves independently and govern themselves to a certain extent. Normandy, though an *elections-district*, and, as such, subject to the royal agents in respect of finance, had states which continued to meet even in 1666. The states-provincial were always convoked by the king, who fixed the place and duration of assembly.

The composition of the states-provincial varied a great deal, according to the districts. In Brittany all noblemen settled in the province had the right of sitting, whilst the third estate were represented by only forty deputies. In Languedoc, on the contrary, the nobility had but twenty-three representatives, and the class of the third estate numbered sixty-eight deputies. Hence, no doubt, the divergences of conduct to be remarked in those two provinces between the parliament and the states-provincial. In Languedoc, even during Montmorency's insurrection, the parliament remained faithful to the king and submissive to the cardinal, whilst the states declared in favor of the revolt: in Brittany, the parliament thwarted Richelieu's efforts in favor of trade, which had been enthusiastically welcomed by the states.

In Languedoc as well as in Dauphiny the cardinal's energy was constantly directed towards reducing the privileges which put the imposts and, consequently, the royal revenues at the discretion of the states. Montmorency's insurrection cost Languedoc a great portion of its liberties, which had already been jeoparded, in 1629, on the occasion of the Huguenots' rising; and those of Dauphiny were completely lost: the states were suppressed in 1628.

The states of Burgundy ordinarily assembled every three years, but they were accustomed, on separating, to appoint "a chamber of states-general," whereat the nobility, clergy, and third estate were represented, and which was charged to watch over the interests of the province in the interval between the sessions. When, in 1629, Richelieu proposed to create, as in Languedoc, a body of "elect" to arrange with the fiscal agents for the rating of imposts without the concurrence of the states, the assembly proclaimed that "it was all over with the liberties of the province if the edict passed," and in the chamber of the nobility, two gentlemen were observed to draw their swords. But, spite of the disturbance which took place at Dijon, in 1630, on occasion of an impost on wines, and which was called, from the title of a popular ditty, *la Sédition de Lanturlu*, the province preserved its liberties and remained a states-district.

It was the same subject that excited in Provence the revolt of the *Cascaveous*, or bell-bearers. Whenever there was any question of elections or "elect," the conspirators sounded their bells as a rallying signal, and so numerous was the body of adherents that the bells were heard tinkling everywhere. The prince of Condé was obliged to march against the revolters, and the states assembled at Tarascon found themselves forced to vote a subsidy of 1,500,000 livres. At this cost the privileges of Provence were respected.

The states of Brittany, on the contrary, lent the cardinal faithful support, when he repaired thither with the king, in 1626, at the time of the conspiracy of Châlais; the duke of Vendôme, governor of Brittany, had just been arrested; the states requested the king "never to give them a governor issue of the old dukes, and to destroy the fortifications of the towns and castles which were of no use for the defence of the country." The petty noblemen, a majority in the states, thus delivered over the province to the kingly power, from jealousy of the great lords. The ordinance, dated from Nantes on the 31st of July, 1626, rendered the measure general throughout France. The battlements of the castles fell beneath the axe of the demolishers, and the masses of the district welcomed enthusiastically the downfall of those old reminiscences of feudal oppression.

As a sequel to the systematic humiliation of the great lords, even when provincial governors, and to the gradual enfeeblement of provincial institutions, Richelieu had to create in all parts of France, still so diverse in organization as well as in manners, representatives of the kingly power, of too modest and feeble a type to do without him, but capable of applying his measures and making his wishes respected. Before now the kings of France had several times over perceived the necessity of keeping up a supervision over the conduct of their officers in the provinces. The *inquisitors* (*enquesteurs*) of St. Louis, the *ridings of the revising-masters* (*chevauchées des maîtres des requêtes*), the *departmental commissioners* (*commissaires départis*) of Charles IX., were so many temporary and travelling inspectors, whose duty it was to inform the king of the state of affairs throughout the kingdom. Richelieu substituted for these shifting commissions a fixed and regular institution, and in 1637 he established in all provinces overseers of *justice, police, and finance*, who were chosen for the most part from amongst the burgesses and who before long concentrated in their hands the whole administration and maintained the struggle of the kingly power against the governors, the sovereign courts and the states-provincial.

At the time when the overseers of provinces were instituted, the battle of pure monarchy was gained; Richelieu had no further need of allies, he wanted mere subjects; but at the beginning of his ministry he had felt the need of throwing himself sometimes for support on the nation, and this great foe of the states-general had twice convoked the *assembly of notables.* The first took place at Fontainebleau, in 1625–6. The cardinal was at that time at loggerheads with the court of Rome: "If the Most Christian King," said he, "is bound to watch over the interests of the Catholic Church, he has first of all to maintain his own reputation in the world. What use would it be for a State to have power, riches, and popular government, if it had not character enough to bring other people to form alliance with it?" These few words summed up the great minister's foreign policy, to protect the Catholic Church whilst keeping up protestant alliances. The notables understood the wisdom of this conduct, and Richelieu received their adhesion.

It was just the same the following year, the day after the conspiracy of Châlais; the cardinal convoked the assembly of notables. "We do protest before the living God," said the letters of convocation, "that we have no other aim and intention but His honor and the welfare of our subjects; that is why we do conjure in His name those whom we convoke and do most expressly command them, without fear or desire of displeasing or pleasing any, to give us in all frankness and sincerity the counsels they shall judge on their consciences to be the most salutary and convenient for the welfare of the commonwealth." The assembly so solemnly convoked opened its sittings at the palace of the Tuileries on the 2nd of December, 1626. The state of the finances was what chiefly occupied those present; and the cardinal himself pointed out the general principles of the reform he calculated upon establishing. "It is impossible," he said, "to meddle with the expenses necessary for the preservatian of the State; it were a crime to think of such a thing. The retrenchment, therefore, must be in the case of useless expenses. The most stringent rules are and appear to be, even to the most ill regulated minds, comparatively mild, when they have, in deed as well as in appearance, no object but the public good and the safety of the State. To restore the State to its pristine splendor, we need not many ordinances but a great deal of practical performance."

The performance appertained to Richelieu, and he readily dispensed with many ordinances. The assembly was favorable to his measures; but amongst those that it rejected was the proposal to substitute loss of offices and confiscation for the penalty of death in matters of rebellion and conspiracy. "Better a moderate but certain penalty," said the cardinal, "than a punishment too severe to be always inflicted." It was the notables who preserved in the hands of the inflexible minister the terrible weapon of which he availed himself so often. The assembly separated on the 24th of February, 1627, the last that was convoked before the revolution of 1789. It was in answer to its demands, as well as to those of the states of 1614, that the keeper of the seals, Michael Marillac, drew up, in 1629, the important administrative ordinance which has preserved from its author's name the title of *Code Michau.*

The cardinal had propounded to the notables a question which he had greatly at heart, the foundation of a navy. Already, when disposing, some weeks previously, of the government of Brittany, which had been taken away from the duke of Vendôme, he had separated from the office that of admiral of Brittany; already he was in a position to purchase from M. de Montmorency his office of grand admiral of France, so as to suppress it and substitute for it that of grand master of navigation, which was personally conferred upon Richelieu by an edict enregistered on the 18th of March, 1627.

"Of the power which it has seemed agreeable to His Majesty that I should hold," he wrote on the 20th of January, 1627, "I can say with truth that it is so moderate that it could not be more so to be an appreciable service, seeing that I have desired no wage or salary so as not to be a charge to the State, and I can add without vanity that the proposal to take no wage came from me, and that His Majesty made a difficulty about letting it be so."

The notables had thanked the king for the intention he had "of being pleased to give the kingdom the treasures of the sea which nature had so liberally proffered it, for without [keeping] the sea one cannot profit by the sea nor maintain war." Harbors repaired and fortified, arsenals established at various points on the coast, organization of marine regiments, foundation of pilot-schools, in fact, the creation of a powerful marine which, in 1642, numbered 63 vessels and 22 galleys, that left the roads of Barcelona after the rejoicings for the capture of Perpignan and arrived the same evening at Toulon—such were the fruits of Richelieu's administration of naval affairs. "Instead," said the bailiff of Forbin, "of having a handful of rebels forcing us, as of late, to compose our naval forces of foreigners and implore succor from Spain, England, Malta, and Holland, we are at present in a condition to do as much for them if they continue in alliance with us, or to beat them when they fall off from us."

So much progress on every point, so many efforts in all directions, 85 vessels afloat, a hundred regiments of infantry, and 300 troops of cavalry, almost constantly on a war-footing, naturally entailed enormous expenses and terrible burthens on the people. It was Richelieu's great fault to be more concerned about his object than scrupulous as to the means he employed for arriving at it. His principles were as harsh as his conduct. "Reason does not admit of exempting the people from all burdens," said he, "because in such case, on losing the mark of their subjection, they would also lose remembrance of their condition, and, if they were free from tribute, would think that they were from obedience also." Cruel words those, and singularly destitute of regard for Christian charity and human dignity, beside which, however, must be placed these: "If the subsidies imposed on the people were not to be kept within moderate bounds, even when they were needed for the service of the country, they would not cease to be unjust." The strong common-sense of this great mind did not allow him to depart for long from a certain hard equity. Posterity has preserved the memory of his equity less than of his hardiness: men want sympathy more than justice.

CHAPTER XL.

LOUIS XIII., CARDINAL RICHELIEU, THE CATHOLICS AND THE PROTESTANTS.

CARDINAL RICHELIEU has often been accused of indifference towards the catholic Church; the ultramontanes called him the *Huguenots' cardinal;* in so speaking there was either a mistake or a desire to mislead; Richelieu was all his life profoundly and sincerely catholic; not only did no doubt as to the fundamental doctrines of his Church trouble his mind, but he also gave his mind to her security and her aggrandisement. He was a believer on conviction, without religious emotions and without the mystic's zeal; he labored for catholicism whilst securing for himself protestant alliances, and if the independence of his mind caused him to feel the necessity for a reformation, it was still in the Church and by the Church that he would have had it accomplished.

Spirits more fervent and minds more pious than Richelieu's felt the same need. On emerging from the violent struggles of the religious wars, the catholic Church had not lost her faith, but she had neglected sweetness and light. King Henry IV.'s conversion had secured to her the victory in France, but she was threatened with letting it escape from her hands by her own fault. God raised up for her some great servants who preserved her from this danger.

The oratorical and political brilliancy of the catholic Church in the reign of Louis XIV. has caused men to forget the great religious movement in the reign of Louis XIII. Learned and mystic in the hands of Cardinal Bérulle, humane and charitable with St. Vincent de Paul, bold and saintly with M. de Saint-Cyran, the Church underwent from all quarters quickening influences which roused her from her dangerous lethargy. The effort was attempted at all points at once. The priests had sunk into an ignorance as perilous as their lukewarmness. Mid all the diplomatic negotiations which he undertook in Richelieu's name and the intrigues he, with the queen-mother, often hatched against him, Cardinal Bérulle founded the congregation of the Oratory, designed to train up well-informed and pious young priests with a capacity for devoting themselves to the education of children as well as the edification of the people. "It is a body," said Bossuet, "in which everybody obeys and nobody commands." No vow fettered the members of this celebrated congregation which gave to the world Mallebranche and Massillon. It was, again, under the inspiration of Cardinal Bérulle, renowned for the pious direction of souls, that the order of Carmelites, hitherto confined to Spain, was founded in France. The convent in Rue St. Jacques soon numbered amongst its penitents women of the hightest rank.

The labors of Mgr. de Bérulle tended especially to the salvation of individual souls; those of St. Vincent de Paul embraced a vaster field and one offering more scope to Christian humanity. Some time before, in 1610, St. Francis de Sales had founded, under the direction of Madame de Chantal, the order of *Visitation*, whose duty was the care of the sick and poor; he had left the direction of his new institution to *M. Vincent*, as was at that time the appellation of the poor priest without birth and without fortune who was one day to be celebrated throughout the world under the name of St. Vincent de Paul. This direction was not enough to satisfy his zeal for charity; children and sick, the ignorant and the convict, all those who suffered in body or spirit, seemed to summon M. Vincent to their aid; he founded in 1617, in a small parish of Bresse, the charitable society of Servants of the poor, which became in 1633, at Paris, under the direction of Madame Legras, niece of the keeper of the seals Marillac, the sisterhood of Servants of the sick poor and the cradle of the Sisters of Charity. "They shall not have, as a regular rule," said St. Vincent, "any monastery but the houses of the sick, any chapel but their parish-church, any cloister but the streets of the town and the rooms of the hospitals, any enclosure but obedience, any 'grating' but the fear of God, or any veil but the holiest and most perfect modesty." Eighteen thousand daughters of St. Vincent de Paul, of whom fourteen thousand are French, still testify at this day to the far-sighted wisdom of their founder; his regulations have endured like his work and the necessities of the poor.

It was to the daughters of Charity that M. Vincent confided the work in connection with foundlings, when his charitable impulses led him, in 1638, to take up the cause of the poor little abandoned things who were perishing by heaps at that time in Paris. Appealing for help, on their account, to the women of the world, one evening when he was in want of money, he exclaimed at the house of the duchess of Aiguillon, Cardinal Richelieu's niece, "Come now, ladies; compassion and charity have made you adopt these little creatures as your own children; you have been their mothers according to grace, since their mothers according to nature have abandoned them. Consider, then, whether you too will abandon them; their life and their death are in your hands; it is time to pronounce their sentence and know whether you will any longer have pity upon them. They will live, if you continue to take a charitable care of them; they will die and perish infallibly, if you abandon them." St. Vincent de Paul had confidence in human nature and everywhere on his path sprang up good works in response to his appeals; the foundation of Mission-priests or Lazarists, designed originally to spread about in the rural districts the knowledge of God, still testifies in the East, whither they carry at one and the same time the Gospel and the name of France, to that great awakening of Christian charity which signalized the reign of Louis XIII. The same inspiration created the seminary of St. Sulpice, by means of M. Olier's solicitude, the brethren of Christian Doctrine and the Ursulines, devoted to the education of childhood, and so many other charitable or pious establishments, noble fruits of devoutness and Christian sacrifice.

Nowhere was this fructuating idea of the sacrifice, the immolation of man for God and of the present in prospect of eternity, more rigorously understood and practised than amongst the disciples of John du Vergier de Hauranne, abbot of St. Cyran. More bold in his conceptions than Cardinal Bérulle and St. Vincent de Paul, of a nature more austere and at the same time ardent, he had early devoted himself to the study of theology. Connected in his youth with a Fleming, Jansen, known under the name of Jansenius and afterwards created bishop of Yprès, he adopted with fervor the doctrines as to the grace of God which his friend had inbibed in the school of St. Augustin, and employing in the direction of souls that zealous ardor which makes conquerors, he set himself to work to regenerate the Church by penance, sanctity and sacrifice; God supreme, reigning over hearts subdued, that was his ultimate object, and he marched towards it without troubling himself about revolts and sufferings, certain that he would be triumphant with God and for Him.

Victories gained over souls are from their very nature of a silent sort: but M. de St. Cyran was not content with them. He wrote also, and his book, "*Petrus Aurelius*," published under the veil of the anonymous, excited a great stir by its defence of the rights of the bishops against the monks and even against the pope. The Gallican bishops welcomed at that time with lively satisfaction its eloquent pleadings in favor of their cause. But, at a later period, the French clergy discovered in St. Cyran's book free-thinking concealed under dogmatic forms. "In case of heresy any Christian may become judge," said Petrus Aurelius. Who, then, should be commissioned to define heresy? So M. de St. Cyran was condemned.

He had been already by an enemy more formidable than the assemblies of the clergy of France. Cardinal Richelieu, naturally attracted towards greatness as he was at a later period towards the infant prodigy of the Pascals, had been desirous of attaching St. Cyran to himself. "Gentlemen," said he one day as he led back the simple priest into the midst of a throng of his courtiers, "here you see the most learned man in Europe." But the abbot of St. Cyran would accept no yoke but God's: he remained independent and perhaps hostile, pursuing, without troubling himself about the cardinal, the great task he had undertaken. Having had, for two years past, the spiritual direction of the convent of Port Royal, he had found in Mother Angelica Arnauld, the superior and reformer of the monastery, in her sister, Mother Agnes, and in the nuns of their order, souls worthy of him and capable of tolerating his austere instructions.

Before long he had seen forming, beside Port Royal and in the solitude of the fields, a nucleus of penitents, emulous of the hermits of the desert. M. le Maître, Mother Angelica's nephew, a celebrated advocate in the parliament of Paris, had quitted all "to have no speech but with God." A *howling* (*rugissant*) penitent, he had drawn after him his brothers, MM. de Sacy and de Séricourt, and, ere long, young Lancelot, the learned author of *Greek roots:* all steeped in the rigors of penitential life, all blindly submissive to M. de St. Cyran and his saintly requirements. The director's power over so many eminent minds became too great. Richelieu had comprehended better than the bishops the tendency of M. de St. Cyran's ideas and writings. "He continued to publish many opinions, new and leading to dangerous conclusions," says Father Joseph in his *Mémoires*, "in such sort that the king being advertised, commanded him to be kept a prisoner in the Bois de Vincennes." "That man is worse than six armies," said Cardinal Richelieu; "if Luther and Calvin had been shut up when they began to dogmatize, States would have been spared a great deal of trouble.

The consciences of men and the ardor of their souls are not so easily stifled by prison or exile. The abbot of St. Cyran, in spite of the entreaties of his powerful friends, remained at Vincennes up to the death of Cardinal Richelieu; the seclusionists of Port Royal were driven from their retreat and obliged to disperse; but neither the severities of Richelieu nor, at a later period, those of Louis XIV. were the true cause of the ultimate powerlessness of Jansenism to bring about that profound reformation of the Church which had been the dream of the abbot of St. Cyran. He had wished to immolate sinful man to God, and he regarded sanctity as the complete sacrifice of human nature corrupt to its innermost core. Human conscience could not accept this cruel yoke; its liberty revolted against so narrow a prison; and the protestant reformation, with a doctrine as austere as that of M. de St. Cyran, but more true and more simple in its practical application, offered strong minds the satisfaction of direct and personal relations between God and man; it saw the way to satisfy them without crushing them; and that is why the kingly power in France succeeded in stifling Jansenism without having ever been able to destroy the protestant faith.

Cardinal Richelieu dreaded the doctrines of M. de St. Cyran, and still more those of the reformation, which went directly to the emancipation of souls; but he had the wit to resist ecclesiastical encroachments, and, for all his being a cardinal, never did minister maintain more openly the independence of the civil power. "The king, in things temporal, recognizes no sovereign save God." That had always been the theory of the Gallican Church. "The Church of France is in the kingdom, and not the kingdom in the Church," said the jurisconsult Loyseau, thus subjecting ecclesiastics to the common law of all citizens.

The French clergy did not understand it so; they had recourse to the liberties of the Gallican Church in order to keep up a certain measure of independence as regarded Rome, but they would not give up their ancient privileges, and especially the right of taking an independent share in the public necessities without being taxed as a matter of law and obligation. Here it was that Cardinal Richelieu withstood them: he maintained that, the ecclesiastics and the brotherhoods not having the right to hold property in France by mort-main, the king tolerated their possession, of his grace, but he exacted the payment of seignorial dues. The clergy at that time possessed more than a quarter of the property in France; the tax to be paid amounted, it is said, to eighty millions. The subsidies further demanded reached a total of eight millions six hundred livres.

The clergy in dismay wished to convoke an assembly to determine their conduct; and after a great deal of difficulty it was authorized by the cardinal. Before long he intimated to the five prelates who were most hostile to him that they must quit the assembly and retire to their dioceses. "There are," said the bishop of Autun, who was entirely devoted to Richelieu, "some who show great delicacy about agreeing to all that the king demands, as if they had a doubt whether all the property of the Church belonged to him or not, and whether His Majesty, leaving the ecclesiastics wherewithal to provide for their subsistence and a moderate establishment, could not take all the surplus." That sort of doctrine would never do for the clergy; still they consented to pay five millions and a half, the sum to which the minister lowered his pretensions. "The wants of the State," said Richelieu, "are real; those of the Church are fanciful and arbitrary; if the king's armies had not repulsed the enemy, the clergy would have suffered far more."

Whilst the cardinal imposed upon the French clergy the obligations common to all subjects, he defended the kingly power and majesty against the ultramontanes, and especially against the Jesuits. Several of their pamphlets had already been censured by his order when Father Sanctarel published a treatise *on heresy and schism*, clothed with the pope's approbation and containing, amongst other dangerous propositions, the following: "The pope can depose emperor and kings for their iniquities or for personal incompetence, seeing that he has a sovereign, supreme and absolute power." The work was referred to the parliament, who ordered it to be burnt in Place de Grève; there was talk of nothing less than the banishment of the entire order.

Father Cotton, superior of the French Jesuits, was summoned to appear before the council; he gave up Father Sanctarel unreservedly, making what excuse he best could for the approbation of the pope and of the general of the Jesuits. The condemnation of the work was demanded, and it was signed by sixteen French fathers. The parliament was disposed to push the matter farther, when Richelieu, always as prudent as he was firm in his relations with this celebrated order, represented to the king that there are "certain abuses which are more easily put down by passing them over than by resolving to destroy them openly, and that it was time to take care lest proceedings should be carried to a point which might be as prejudicial to his service as past action had been serviceable to it." The Jesuits remained in France, and their college at Clermont was not closed; but they published no more pamphlets against the cardinal. They even defended him at need.

Richelieu's grand quarrel with the clergy was nearing its end when the climax was reached of a disagreement with the court of Rome, dating from some time back. The pope had never forgiven the cardinal for not having accepted his mediation in the affair with Spain on the subject of the Valteline; he would not accede to the desire which Richelieu manifested to become legate of the Holy See in France as Cardinal d'Amboise had been; and when Marshal d'Estrées arrived as ambassador at Rome, his resolute behavior brought the misunderstanding to a head: the pope refused the customary funeral honors to Cardinal la Valette, who had died in battle, without dispensation, at the head of the king's army in Piedmont. Richelieu preserved appearances no longer; the king refused to receive the pope's nuncio and prohibited the bishops from any communication with him. The quarrel was envenomed by a pamphlet called *Optatus Gallus.* The cardinal's enemies represented him as a new Luther ready to excite a schism and found a patriarchate in France. Father Rabardeau, of the Jesuits' order, maintained in reply that the act would not be schismatical, and that the consent of Rome would be no more necessary to create a patriarchate in France than it had been to establish those of Constantinople and Jerusalem.

Urban VIII. took fright; he sent to France Julius Mazarin, at that time vice-legate, and already frequently employed in the negotiations between the court of Rome and Cardinal Richelieu, who had taken a great fancy to him. The French clergy had just obtained authority to vote the subsidy in an assembly; and the pope contented himself with this feeble concession. Mazarin put the finishing touch to the reconciliation and received as recompense the cardinal's hat. In fact, the victory of the civil power was complete, and the independence of the crown clearly established. "His Holiness," said the cardinal, "ought to commend the zeal shown by His Majesty for the welfare of the Church and to remain satisfied with the respect shown him by an appeal to his authority which His Majesty might have dispensed with in this matter, having his parliaments to fall back upon for the chastisement of those who lived evilly in his kingdom." In principle, the supreme question between the court of Rome and the kingly power remained undecided, and it showed wisdom on the part of Urban VIII. as well as of Cardinal Richelieu never to fix fundamentally and within their exact limits the rights and pretensions of the Church or the crown.

Cardinal Richelieu had another battle to deliver and another victory, which was to be more decisive, to gain. During his exile at Avignon, he had written against the reformers, violently attacking their doctrines and their precepts; he was, therefore, personally engaged in the theological strife and more hotly than has been made out; but he was above everything a great politician, and the rebellion of the reformers, their irregular political assemblies, their alliances with the foreigner, occupied him far more than their ministers' preaching. It was State within State that the reformers were seeking to found, and that the cardinal wished to upset. Seconded by the prince of Condé, the king had put an end to the war which cost the life of the constable De Luynes, but the peace concluded at Montpellier on the 19th of November, 1622, had already received many a blow; pacific counsels amongst the reformers were little by little dying out together with the old servants of Henry IV.; Du Plessis-Mornay had lately died (Nov. 11, 1623) at his castle of Forêt-sur-Sèvres, and the direction of the party fell entirely into the hands of the duke of Rohan, a fiery temper and soured by misfortunes as well as by continual efforts made on the part of his brother the duke of Soubise, more restless and less earnest than he. Hostilities broke out afresh at the beginning of the year 1625. The reformers complained that, instead of demolishing Fort Louis which commanded La Rochelle, all haste was being made to complete the ramparts they had hoped to see razed to the ground: a small royal fleet mustered quietly at Le Blavet and threatened to close the sea against the Rochellese. The peace of Montpellier had left the protestants only two surety-places, Montauban and La Rochelle; and they clung to them with desperation. On the 6th of January, 1625, Soubise suddenly entered the harbor of Le Blavet with twelve vessels, and seizing without a blow the royal ships, towed them off in triumph to La Rochelle, a fatal success which was to cost that town dear.

The royal marine had hardly an existence; after the capture made by Soubise, help had to be requested from England and Holland; the marriage of Henrietta of France, daughter of Henry IV., with the prince of Wales who was soon to become Charles I., was concluded; the English promised eight ships; the treaties with the United Provinces obliged the Hollanders to supply twenty, which they would gladly have refused to send against their brethren, if they could; the cardinal even required that the ships should be commanded by French captains: "One lubber may ruin a whole fleet," said he, "and a captain of a ship, if assured by the enemy of payment for his vessel, may undertake to burn the whole armament, and that the more easily inasmuch as he would think he was making a grand sacrifice to God, for the sake of his religion."

Meanwhile, Soubise had broken through the feeble obstacles opposed to him by the duke of Vendôme, and, making himself master of all the trading-vessels he encountered, soon took possession of the islands of Ré and Oléron and effected descents even into Médoc, whilst the duke of Rohan, leaving the duchess his wife, Sully's daughter, at Castres, where he had established the seat of his government, was scouring Lower Languedoc and the Cévennes to rally his partisans. The insurrection was very undecided and the movement very irregular. Nîmes, Uzès and Alais closed their gates; even Montauban hesitated a long while before declaring itself. The duke of Épernon ravaged the outskirts of that place. "At night," writes his secretary, "might be seen a thousand fires. Wheat, fruit-trees, vines and houses were the food that fed the flames." Marshal Thémine did the same all round Castres, defended by the duchess of Rohan.

There were negotiations, nevertheless, already. Rohan and Soubise demanded to be employed against Spain in the Valteline, claiming the destruction of Fort Louis; parleys mitigated hostilities; the duke of Soubise obtained a suspension of arms from the Dutch admiral Haustein, and then, profiting by a favorable gust of wind, approached the fleet, set fire to the admiral's ship and captured five vessels, which he towed off to the island of Ré. But he paid dear for his treachery: the Hollanders in their fury seconded with more zeal the efforts of the duke of Montmorency who had just taken the command of the squadron; the island of Ré was retaken and Soubise obliged to retreat in a shallop to Oléron, leaving for "pledge his sword and his hat which dropped off in his flight." Nor was the naval fight more advantageous for Soubise: "The battle was fierce, but the enemy had the worst," says Richelieu in his *Mémoires:* "night coming on was favorable to their designs; nevertheless, they were so hotly pursued that on the morrow, at daybreak, eight of their vessels were taken." Soubise sailed away to England with the rest of his fleet, and the island of Oléron surrendered.

The moment seemed to have come for crushing La Rochelle, deprived of the naval forces that protected it; but the cardinal, still at grips with Spain in the Valteline, was not sure of his allies before La Rochelle. In Holland all the churches echoed with reproaches hurled by the preachers against States that gave help against their own brethren to catholics; at Amsterdam the mob had besieged the house of Admiral Haustein; and the Dutch fleet had to be recalled. The English protestants were not less zealous; the duke of Soubise had been welcomed with enthusiasm, and, though Charles I., now king of England and married, had refused to admit the fugitive to his presence, he would not restore to Louis XIII. the vessels, captured from that king and his subjects, which Soubise had brought over to Portsmouth.

The game was not yet safe; and Richelieu did not allow himself to be led astray by the anger of fanatics who dubbed him *State-cardinal.* "The cardinal alone, to whom God gave the blessedness of serving the king and restoring to his kingdom its ancient lustre and to his person the power and authority meet for royal Majesty which is the next Majesty after the divine, saw in his mind the means of undoing all those tangles, clearing away all those mists and emerging to the honor of his master from all those confusions" [*Mémoires de Richelieu,* t. iv. p. 2].

Marshal Bassompierre was returning from his embassy to Switzerland, having secured the alliance of the Thirteen Cantons in the affair of the Valteline, when it was noised abroad that peace with Spain was signed. Count du Fargis, it was said, had, in an excess of zeal, taken upon himself to conclude without waiting for orders from Paris. Bassompierre was preparing a grand speech against this unexpected peace, but during the night he reflected that the cardinal had perhaps been not so much astonished as he would have made out. "I gave up my speech," says he, "and betook myself to my jubilee."

The Huguenots on their side yielded at the entreaties of the ambassadors who had been sent by the English to France, "with orders to beg the Rochellese to accept the peace which the king had offered them, and who omitted neither arguments nor threats in order to arrive at that conclusion; whence it came to pass that, by a course of conduct full of unwonted dexterity, the Huguenots were brought to consent to peace for fear of that with Spain, and the Spaniards to make peace for fear of that with the Huguenots.

"The greatest difficulty the cardinal had to surmount was in the king's council; he was not ignorant that by getting peace made with the Huguenots, and showing them that he was somewhat inclined to favor their cause with the king, he might expose himself to the chance of getting into bad odor at Rome. But in no other way could he arrive at His Majesty's ends. His cloth made him suspected by the Huguenots; it was necessary, therefore, to behave so that they should think him favorable to them, for by so doing he found means of waiting more conveniently for an opportunity of reducing them to the terms to which all subjects ought to be reduced in a State, that is to say, inability to form any separate body, and liability to accept their sovereign's wishes.

"It was a grievous thing for him to bear, to see himself so unjustly suspected at the court of Rome, and by those who affected the name of zealous Catholics, but he resolved to take patiently the rumors that were current about him, apprehending that if he had determined to clear himself of them effectually he might not find that course of advantage to his master or the public."

The cardinal, in fact, took it patiently, revising and then confirming the treaty with Spain, and imposing on the Huguenots a peace so hard that they would never have accepted it but for the hope of obtaining at a later period some assuagements, with the help of England, which refused formally to help them to carry on the war. At the first parleys the king had said, "I am disposed enough toward peace; I am willing to grant it to Languedoc and the other provinces. As for La Rochelle, that is another thing" [*Mémoires de Richelieu*, t. iii.]. It was ultimately La Rochelle that paid the expenses of the war, biding the time when the proud city, which had resisted eight kings in succession, would have to succumb before Louis XIII. and his all-powerful minister. Already her independence was threatened on all sides; the bastions and new fortifications had to be demolished; no armed vessel of war might be stationed in her harbor. "The way was at last open," said the cardinal, "to the extermination of the Huguenot party, which, for a hundred years past, had divided the kingdom" [*Mémoires de Richelieu*, t. iii. p. 17].

The peace of 1626, then, was but a preliminary to war. Richelieu was preparing for it by land and sea; vessels of war were being built, troops were being levied; and the temper of England furnished a pretext for commencing the struggle. King Charles I., at the instigation of his favorite the duke of Buckingham, had suddenly and unfeelingly dismissed the French servants of the queen his wife, without giving her even time to say good-bye to them, insomuch that "the poor princess, hearing their voices in the courtyard, dashed to the window and, breaking the glass with her head, clung with her hands to the bars to show herself to her women and take the last look at them. The king indignantly dragged her back with so great an effort that he tore her hands right away." Louis XIII. had sent Marshal Bassompierre to England to complain of the insult done to his sister; the duke of Buckingham wished to go in person to France to arrange the difference, but the cardinal refused. "Has Buckingham ever undertaken any foreign commission without going away dissatisfied and offended with the princes to whom he was sent?" said Cardinal Richelieu to the king. So the favorite of Charles I. resolved to go to France "in other style and with other attendants than he had as yet done; having determined to win back the good graces of the parliament and the people of England by the succor he was about to carry to the oppressed protestant Churches," he pledged his property; he sold the trading-vessels captured on the coasts of France; and on the 17th of July, 1627, he set sail with a hundred and twenty vessels, heading for La Rochelle. Soubise was on board his ship; and the duke of Rohan, notified of the enterprise, had promised to declare himself the moment the English set foot in France. Already he was preparing his manifesto to the Churches, avowing that he had summoned the English to his legitimate defence, and that, since the king had but lately been justified in employing the arms of the Hollanders to defeat them, much more reasonably might he appeal to those of the English their brethren for protection against him.

This time the cardinal was ready; he had concluded an alliance with Spain against England, "declaring merely to the king of Spain that he was already at open war with England, and that he would put in practice with all the power of his forces against his own States all sorts of hostilities permissible in honorable warfare, which His Majesty also promised to do by the month of June, 1628, at the latest." The king set out to go and take in person the command of the army intended to give the English their reception. He had gone out ill from the parliament, where he had been to have some edicts enregistered. "I did nothing but tremble all the time I was holding my bed of justice," he said to Bassompierre. "It is there, however, that you make others tremble," replied the Marshal. Louis XIII. was obliged to halt at Villeroy, where the cardinal remained with him, "being all day at his side, and most frequently not leaving him at night; he, nevertheless, had his mind constantly occupied with giving orders, taking care above everything to let it appear before the king that he had no fear; he preferred to put himself in peril of being blamed or ruined in well-doing rather than, in order to secure himself, to do anything which might be a cause of illness to His Majesty." In point of fact Richelieu was not without anxiety, for Sieur de Toiras, a young favorite of the king's, to whom he had entrusted the command in the island of Ré, had not provided for the defence of that place so well as had been expected; Buckingham had succeeded in effecting his descent. The French were shut up in the fort of St. Martin, scarcely finished as it was, and ill-provisioned. The cardinal "saw to it directly, sending of his own money because that of the king was not to be quickly got at, and because he had at that time none to spare; he despatched Abbé Marcillac, who was in his confidence, to see that everything was done punctually and no opportunity lost. He did not trouble himself to make reports of all the despatches that passed, and all the orders that were within less than a fortnight given on the subject of this business during the king's illness, in order to provide for everything that was necessary, and to prepare all things in such wise that the king and France might reap from them the fruit which was shortly afterwards gathered in."

Meanwhile, La Rochelle had closed her gates to the English, and the old duchess of Rohan had been obliged to leave the town in order to bring Soubise in with her. "Before taking any resolution," replied the Rochellese authorities to the entreaties of the duke who was pressing them to lend assistance to the English, "we must consult the whole body of the religion, of which La Rochelle is only one member." An assembly was already convoked to that end at Uzès; and when it met, on the 11th of September, the duke of Rohan communicated to the deputies from the churches the letter of the inhabitants of La Rochelle, "not such an one," he said, "as he could have desired, but such as he must make the best of." The king of England had granted his aid and promised not to relax until the reformers had firm repose and solid contentment, provided that they seconded his efforts. "I bid you thereto in God's name," he added, "and for my part, were I alone, abandoned of all, I am determined to prosecute this sacred cause even to the last drop of my blood and to the last gasp of my life." The assembly fully approved of their chief's behavior, accepting "with gratitude the king of England's powerful intervention, without, however, loosing themselves from the humble and inviolable submission which they owed to their king." The consuls of the town of Milhau were bolder in their reservations: "We have at divers time experienced," they wrote to the duke of Rohan, whilst refusing to join the movement, "that violence is no certain means of obtaining observation of our edicts, for force extorts many promises, but the hatred it engenders prevents them from taking effect." The duke was obliged to force an entrance into this small place. La Rochelle had just renounced her neutrality and taken sides with the English, "flattering ourselves," they said in their proclamation, "that, having good men for our witnesses and God for our judge, we shall experience the same assistance from His goodness as our fathers had aforetime."

M. de la Millière, the agent of the Rochellese, wrote to one of his friends at the duke of Rohan's quarters: "Sir, I am arrived from Villeroy, where the English are not held as they are at Paris to be a mere chimera. Only I am very apprehensive of the September-tides and lest the new grapes should kill us off more English than the enemy will. I am much vexed to hear nothing from your quarter to second the exploits of the English, being unable to see without shame foreigners showing more care for our welfare than we ourselves show. I know that it will not be M. de Rohan's fault nor yours that nothing good is done.

"I forgot to tell you that the cardinal is very glad that he is no longer a bishop, for he has put so many rings in pawn to send munitions to the islands that he has nothing remaining wherewith to give the episcopal benediction. The most zealous amongst us pray God that the sea may swallow up his person as it has swallowed his goods. As for me, I am not of that number, for I belong to those who offer incense to the powers that be." It was as yet a time when the religious fatherland was dearer than the political; the French Huguenots naturally appealed for aid to all protestant nations. It was even now an advance in national ideas to call the English who had come to the aid of La Rochelle *foreigners.*

Toiras, meanwhile, still held out in the fort of St. Martin, and Buckingham was beginning to "abate somewhat of the absolute confidence he had felt about making himself master of it, having been so ill advised as to write to the king his master that he would answer for it." The proof of this was that a burgess of La Rochelle, named Laleu, went to see the king with authority from the duke of Angoulême, who commanded the army in His Majesty's absence, and that "he proposed that the English should retire provided that the king would have Fort Louis dismantled. The duke of Angoulême was inclined to accept this proposal, but the cardinal forcibly represented all the reasons against it: 'It will be said perhaps that if the island of Ré be lost, it will be very difficult to recover it;' this he allowed, but he put forward, to counterbalance this consideration, another, that, if honor were lost, it would never be recovered, and that, if the island of Ré were lost, he considered that His Majesty was bound to stick to the blockade of Rochelle, and that he might do so with success. Upon this, His Majesty resolved to push the siege of Rochelle vigorously and to give the command to Mylord his brother;" but Monsieur was tardy as usual, not wanting to serve under the king when the health of His Majesty might permit him to return to his army, so that the cardinal wrote to President le Coigneux, one of the favorite counsellors of the duke of Orleans, to say that "if imaginary *hydras* of that sort were often taking shape in the mind of Monsieur, he had nothing more to say than that there would be neither pleasure nor profit in being mixed up with his affairs. As for himself, he would always do his duty." Monsieur at last made up his mind to join the army, and it was resolved to give aid to the forts in the island of Ré.

It was a bold enterprise that was about to be attempted: "to hold La Rochelle invested and not quit it, and, nevertheless, to send the flower of the force to succor a citadel considered to be half-lost; to make a descent upon an island blockaded by a large naval armament; to expose the best part of the army to the mercy of the winds and the waves of the sea, and of the English cannons and vessels, in a place where there was no landing in order and under arms" [*Mémoires de Richelieu*, t. iii. p. 361]; but it had to be resolved upon or the island of Ré lost. Toiras had already sent to ask the duke of Buckingham if he would receive him to terms.

On the 8th of October, at eight a.m., the duke of Buckingham was preparing to send a reply to the fort, and he was already rejoicing "to see his felicity and the crowning of his labors," when, on nearing the citadel, "there were exhibited to him at the ends of pikes lots of bottles of wine, capons, turkeys, hams, ox-tongues and other provisions, and his vessels were saluted with lots of cannonades, they having come too near in the belief that those inside had no more powder." During the night, the fleet which was assembled at Oléron and had been at sea for two days past had succeeded in landing close to the fort, bringing up reinforcements of troops, provisions and munitions. At the same time the king and the cardinal had just arrived at the camp before La Rochelle.

Before long the English could not harbor a doubt but that the king's army had recovered its real heads; a grand expedition was preparing to attack them in the island of Ré, and the cardinal had gone in person to Oléron and to Le Brouage in order to see to the embarcation of the troops. "The nobility of the court came up in crowds to take leave of His Majesty, and their looks were so gay that it must be allowed that to no nation but the French is it given to march so freely to death for the service of their king or for their own honor as to make it impossible to remark any difference between him that inflicts it and him that receives" [*Mémoires de Richelieu*, t. iii. p. 398]. Marshal Schomberg took the road to Marennes, whence he sent to the cardinal for boats to carry over all his troops. "This took him greatly by surprise, and as his judgments are always followed by the effect he intended, he thought that this great following of nobility might hinder the said sir marshal from executing his design so promptly. However, by showing admirable diligence, doubling both his vessels and his provisions, he found sufficient to embark the whole" [*Siége de La Rochelle. Archives curieuses de l'Histoire de France*, t. iii. p. 76]. By this time the king's troops, in considerable numbers, had arrived in the island without the English being able to prevent their disembarcation; the enemy therefore took the resolution of setting sail, in spite of the entreaties which the duke of Soubise sent them on the part of the Rochellese, those latter promising great assistance in men and provisions, more than they could afford. To satisfy them, the duke of Buckingham determined to deliver a general assault before he departed.

The assault was delivered on the 5th and 6th of November, and everywhere repulsed, exhausted as the besieged were. "Those who were sick and laid up in their huts appeared on the bastions. There were some of them so weak that, unable to fight, they loaded their comrades' muskets; and others, having fought beyond their strength, being able to do no more, said to their comrades, 'Friend, here are my arms for thee; prithee, make my grave; and, thither retiring, there they died.'" The duke of Buckingham wrote to M. de Fiesque, who was holding Fort la Prée, that he was going to embark, without waiting for any more men to make their descent upon the island; but the king, who trusted not his enemies and least of all the English, from whom, even when friends, he had received so many proofs of faithlessness and falsehood, besides that he knew Buckingham for a man who, from not having the force of character to decide on such an occasion, did not know whether to fight or to fly, continued in his first determination to transport promptly all those who remained, in order to encounter the enemy on land, fight them, and make them for the future quake with fear if it were proposed to them to try another descent upon his dominions.

Marshal Schomberg, thwarted by bad weather, had just rallied his troops which had been cast by the winds on different parts of the coast, when it was perceived that the enemy had sheered off. M. de Toiras, issuing from his fortress to meet the marshal, would have pursued them at once to give them battle, but Schomberg refused, saying, "I ought to make them a bridge of gold rather than a barrier of iron;" and he contented himself with following the English, who retreated to a narrow causeway which led to the little island of Oie. There, a furious charge of French cavalry broke the ranks of the enemy, disorder spread amongst them, and when night came to put an end to the combat, forty flags remained in the hands of the king's troops; and he sent them at once to Notre-Dame, by Claude de St. Simon, together with a quantity of prisoners, of whom the king made a present to his sister the queen of England.

"Such," says the duke of Rohan in his *Mémoires*, "was the success of the duke of Buckingham's expedition, wherein he ruined the reputation of his nation and his own, consumed a portion of the provisions of the Rochellese. and reduced to despair the party for whose sake he had come to France. The duke of Rohan first learnt this bad news by the bonfires which all the Roman Catholics lighted for it all through the countship of Foix, and, later on, by a despatch from the duke of Soubise, who exhorted him not to lose courage, saying, that he hoped to come back next spring in condition to efface the affront received." This latter prince had not covered himself with glory in the expedition. "As recompense and consolation for all their losses," says the cardinal, "they carried off Soubise to England. He has not been mentioned all through this siege, because, whenever there was any question of negotiation, no one would apply to him but only to Buckingham. When there was nothing for it but to fight, he would not hear of it. On the day the English made their descent, he was at La Rochelle; nobody knows where he was at the time of the assault, but he was one of the first and most forward in the rout."

Soubise had already been pronounced guilty of high-treason by decree of the parliament of Toulouse, but the duke of Rohan had been degraded from his dignities, and "a title offered to those who would assassinate him, which created an inclination in three or four wretches to undertake it, who had but a rope or the wheel for recompense, it not being in any human power to prolong or shorten any man's life without the permission of God." The prince of Condé had been commissioned to fight the valiant chief of the Huguenots, "for that he was their sworn enemy," says the cardinal. In the eyes of fervent Catholics the name of Condé had many wrongs for which to obtain pardon.

The English were ignominiously defeated; the king was now confronted by none but his revolted subjects; he resolved to blockade the place at all points, so that it could not be entered by land or sea, and, to this end, he claimed from Spain the fleet which had been promised him and which did not arrive. "The whole difficulty of this enterprise," said the cardinal to the king, "lies in this, that the majority will only labor therein in a perfunctory manner."

His ordinary penetration did not deceive him; the great lords entrusted with commands saw with anxiety the increasing power of Richelieu. "You will see," said Bassompierre, "that we shall be mad enough to take La Rochelle." "His Majesty had just then many of his own kingdom and all his allies sworn together against him, and so much the more dangerously in that it was secretly. England at open war, and with all her maritime power but lately on our coasts; the king of Spain apparently united to his Majesty, yet, in fact, not only giving him empty words but, under cover of the emperor's name, making a diversion against him in the direction of Germany. Nevertheless the king held firm to his resolve; and then the siege of La Rochelle was undertaken with a will."

The old duchess of Rohan (Catherine de Parthenay Larchevêque) had shut herself up in La Rochelle with her daughter Anne de Rohan, as pious and as courageous as her mother, and of rare erudition into the bargain: she had hitherto refused to leave the town; but, when the blockade commenced, she asked leave to retire with two hundred women. The town had already been refused permission to get rid of useless mouths. "All the Rochellese shall go out together," was the answer returned to Madame de Rohan. She determined to undergo with her brethren in the faith all the rigors of the siege. "Secure peace, complete victory or honorable death," she wrote to her son the duke of Rohan: the old device of Jeanne d'Albret which had never been forgotten by the brave chief of the Huguenots.

At the head of the burgesses of La Rochelle, as determined as the duchess of Rohan to secure their liberties or perish, was the president of the board of marine, soon afterwards mayor of the town, John Guiton, a rich merchant, whom the misfortunes of the times had wrenched away from his business to become a skilful admiral, an intrepid soldier, accustomed for years past to scour the seas as a corsair. "He had at his house," says a narrative of those days, "a great number of flags which he used to show one after another, indicating the princes from whom he had taken them." When he was appointed mayor, he drew his poniard and threw it upon the council-table: "I accept," he said, "the honor you have done me, but on condition that yonder poniard shall serve to pierce the heart of whoever dares to speak of surrender, mine first of all, if I were ever wretch enough to condescend to such cowardice." Of indomitable nature, of passionate and proud character, Guiton, in fact, rejected all proposals of peace: "My friend, tell the cardinal that I am his very humble servant," was his answer to insinuating speeches as well as to threats; and he prepared with tranquil coolness for defence to the uttermost. Two municipal councillors, two burgesses and a clergyman were commissioned to judge and to punish spies and traitors; attention was concentrated upon getting provisions into the town; the country was already devastated, but reliance was placed upon promises of help from England; and religious exercises were everywhere multiplied. "We will hold out to the last day," reiterated the burgesses.

It was the month of December; bad weather interfered with the siege-works; the king was having a line of circumvallation pushed forward to close the approaches to the city on the land side; the cardinal was having a mole of stone-work, occupying the whole breadth of the roads, constructed; the king's little fleet, commanded by M. de Guise, had been ordered up to protect the laborers; Spain had sent twenty-eight vessels in such bad condition that those which were rolled into the sea laden with stones were of more value; "They were employed Spanish-fashion," says Richelieu, "that is, to make an appearance so as to astound the Rochellese by the union of the two crowns." A few days after their arrival, at the rumor of assistance coming from England, the Spanish admiral, who had secret orders to make no effort for France, demanded permission to withdraw his ships. "It was very shameful of them, but it was thought good to let them go without the king's consent, making believe that he had given them their dismissal and desired them to go and set about preparing, one way or another, a large armament by the spring." The Rochellese were rejoicing over the treaty they had just concluded with the king of England, who promised "to aid them by land and sea, to the best of his kingly power, until he should have brought about a fair and secure peace." The mole was every moment being washed away by the sea; and, "whilst the cardinal was employing all the wits which God had given him to bring to a successful issue the siege of La Rochelle to the glory of God and the welfare of the State, and was laboring to that end more than the bodily strength granted to him by God seemed to permit, one would have said that the sea and the winds favoring the English and the islands, were up in opposition and thwarting his designs."

The king was growing tired and wished to go to Paris; but this was not the advice of the cardinal, and "the truths he uttered were so displeasing to the king that he fell somehow into disgrace. The dislike the king conceived for him was such that he found fault with him about everything." The king at last took his departure, and the cardinal who had attended him "without daring, out of respect, to take his sunshade to protect him against the heat of the sun which was very great that day," was on his return taken ill with fever. "I am so down-hearted that I cannot express the regret I feel at quitting the cardinal, fearing lest some accident may happen to him," the king had said to one of his servants: "tell him from me to take care of himself, to think what a state my affairs would be in if I were to lose him." When the king returned to La Rochelle on the 10th of April, he found his army strengthened, the line of circumvallation finished, and the mole well advanced into the sea; the assault was becoming possible, and the king summoned the place to surrender [*Siége de La Rochelle. Archives curieuses de l'Histoire de France,* t. iii. p. 102]. "We recognize no other sheriffs and governors than ourselves," answered the sergeant on guard to the improvised herald sent by the king; "nobody will listen to you; away at once!" It was at last announced that the reinforcements so impatiently expected were coming from England. "The cardinal, who knew that there was nothing so dangerous as to have no fear of one's enemy, had a long while before set everything in order as if the English might arrive any day." Their fleet was signalled at sea; it numbered thirty vessels and had a convoy of twenty barques laden with provisions and munitions, and it was commanded by the earl of Denbigh, Buckingham's brother-in-law. The Rochellese, transported with joy, "had planted a host of flags on the prominent points of their town." The English came and cast anchor at the tip of the island of Ré. The cannon of La Rochelle gave them a royal salute. A little boat with an English captain on board found means of breaking the blockade; and "Open a passage," said the envoy to the Rochellese, "as you sent notice to us in England, and we will deliver you." But the progress made in the works of the mole rendered the enterprise difficult; the besieged could not attempt anything; they waited and waited for Lord Denbigh to bring on an engagement; on the 19th of May, all the English ships got under sail and approached the roads. The besieged hurried on to the ramparts, there was the thunder of one broadside, and one only; and then the vessels tacked and crowded sail for England, followed by the gaze "of the king's army, who returned to make good cheer without any fear of the enemy and with great hopes of soon taking the town."

Great was the despair in La Rochelle: "This shameful retreat of the English, and their aid which had only been received by faith as they do in the Eucharist," wrote Cardinal Richelieu, "astounded the Rochellese so mightily that they would readily have made up their minds to surrender, if Madame de Rohan, the mother, whose hopes for her children were all centred in the preservation of this town, and the minister Salbert, a very seditious fellow, had not regaled them with imaginary succor which they made them hope for." The cardinal, when he wrote these words, knew nothing of the wicked proposals made to Guiton and to Salbert: "Couldn't the cardinal be got rid of by the deed of one determined man?" it was asked: but the mayor refused; and "It is not in such a way that God willeth our deliverance," said Salbert, "it would be too offensive to His holiness." And they suffered on.

Meanwhile, on the 24th of May, the posterns were observed to open, and the women to issue forth one after another with their children and the old men; they came gliding towards the king's encampment, but "he ordered them to be driven back by force; and further, knowing that they had sown beans near the counterscarps of their town, a detachment was sent out to cut them down as soon as they began to come up, and likewise a little corn that they had sown in some dry spots of their marshes." Louis the Just fought the Rochellese in other fashion than that in which Henry the Great had fought the Parisians.

The misery in the place became frightful; the poor died of hunger, or were cut down by the soldiery when they ventured upon shore at low tide to look for cockles; the price of provisions were such that the richest alone could get a little meat to eat; a cow fetched 2000 livres, and a bushel of wheat 800 livres. Madame de Rohan had been the first to have her horses killed, but this resource was exhausted, and her cook at last "left the town and allowed himself to be taken, saying that he would rather be hanged than return to die of hunger." A rising even took place amongst the inhabitants who were clamorous to surrender, but Guiton had the revolters hanged. "I am ready," said he, "to cast lots with anybody else which shall live or be killed to feed his comrade with his flesh. As long as there is one left to keep the gates shut, it is enough." The mutineers were seized with terror, and men died without daring to speak.

"We have been waiting three months for the effect of the excellent letters we received from the king of Great Britain," wrote Guiton on the 24th of August, to the deputies from La Rochelle who were in London, "and, meanwhile, we cannot see by what disasters it happens that we remain here in misery without seeing any sign of succor; our men can do no more, our inhabitants are dying of hunger in the streets, and all our families are in a fearful state from mourning, want, and perplexity; nevertheless we will hold out to the last day, but in God's name delay no longer, for we perish."

This letter never reached its destination; the watchmaker, Marc Biron, who had offered to convey it to England, was arrested whilst attempting to pass the royal lines, and was immediately hanged. La Rochelle, however, still held out. "Their rabid fury," says the cardinal, "gave them new strength, or rather the avenging wrath of God caused them to be supplied therewith in extraordinary measure by his evil spirit in order to prolong their woes; they were already almost at the end thereof and misery found upon them no more substance whereon it could feed and support itself; they were skeletons, empty shadows, breathing corpses rather than living men." At the bottom of his heart, and in spite of the ill temper their resistance caused in him, the heroism of the Rochellese excited the cardinal's admiration. Buckingham had just been assassinated: "The king could not have lost a more bitter or a more idiotic enemy; his unreasoning enterprises ended unluckily, but they, nevertheless, did not fail to put us in great peril and cause us much mischief," says Richelieu: "the idiotic madness of an enemy being more to be feared than his wisdom, inasmuch as the idiot does not act on any principle common to other men, he attempts everything and anything, violates his own interests and is restrained by impossibility alone."

It was this impossibility of any aid that the cardinal attempted to impress upon the Rochellese by means of letters which he managed to get into the town, representing to them that Buckingham, their protector, was dead and that they were allowing themselves to be unjustly tyrannized over by a small number amongst them who, being rich, had wheat to eat, whereas, if they were good citizens, they would take their share of the general misery. These manœuvres did not remain without effect: the besieged resolved to treat and a deputation was just about to leave the town, when a burgess who had broken through the lines arrived in hot haste, on his return from England; he had seen, he said, the armament all ready to set out to save them or perish; it must arrive within a week; the public body of La Rochelle had promised not to treat without the king of England's participation; he was not abandoning his allies; and so the deputies returned home and there was more waiting still.

On the 29th of September the English flag appeared before St. Martin de Ré; it was commanded by the earl of Lindsay and was composed of a hundred and forty vessels, which carried six thousand soldiers, besides the crews; the French who were of the *religion* were in the van, commanded by the duke of Soubise and the count of Laval, brother of the duke of La

Trémoille who had lately renounced his faith in front of La Rochelle, being convinced of his errors by a single lesson from the cardinal. "This armament was England's utmost effort, for the Parliament which was then being holden had granted six millions of livres to fit it out to avenge the affronts and ignominy which the English nation had encountered on the island of Ré and afterwards by the shameful retreat of their armament in the month of May." But it was too late coming; the mole was finished and the opening in it defended by two forts; and a floating palisade blocked the passage as well. The English sent some petards against this construction, but they produced no effect; and when, next day, they attacked the royal fleet, the French crews lost but twenty-eight men: the fire-ships were turned aside "by men who feared fire as little as water." Lord Lindsay retired with his squadron to the shelter of the island of Aix, sending to the king "Lord Montagu to propose some terms of accommodation. He demanded pardon for the Rochellese, freedom of conscience, and quarter for the English garrison in La Rochelle; the answer was "that the Rochellese were subjects of the king who knew quite well what he had to do with them, and that the King of England had no right to interfere. As for the English, they should meet with the same treatment as was received by the French whom they held prisoners." Montagu set out for England to obtain further orders from the king his master.

All hope of effectual aid was gone, and the Rochellese felt it; the French who were on board the English fleet had taken, like them, a resolution to treat; and they had already sent to the cardinal when, on the 29th of October, the deputies from La Rochelle arrived at the camp: "Your fellows who were in the English army have already obtained grace," said the cardinal to them; and when they were disposed not to believe it, the cardinal sent for the pastors Vincent and Gobert, late delegates to King Charles I.; "they embraced with tears in their eyes, not daring to speak of business, as they had been forbidden to do so on pain of death."

The demands of the Rochellese were more haughty than befitted their extreme case: "Though they were but shadows of living men and their life rested solely on the king's mercy, they actually dared, nevertheless, to propose to the cardinal a general treaty on behalf of all those of their party, including Madame de Rohan and Monsieur de Soubise, the maintenance of their privileges, of their governor, and of their mayor, together with the right of those bearing arms to march out with beat of drum and lighted match" [with the honors of war].

The cardinal was amused at their impudence, he writes in his *Mémoires*, and told them that they had no right to expect anything more than pardon, which, moreover, they did not deserve. "He was nevertheless anxious to conclude, wishing that Montagu should find peace made, and that the English fleet should see it made without their consent, which would render the rest of the king's business easier, whether as regarded England or Spain, or the interior of the kingdom." On the 28th the treaty or rather the grace was accordingly signed, "the king granting life and property to those of the inhabitants of the town who were then in it, and the exercise of the religion within La Rochelle." These articles bore the signature of a brigadier-general, M. de Marillac, the king not having thought proper to put his name at the bottom of a convention made with his subjects.

Next day, twelve deputies issued from the town, making a request for horses to Marshal de Bassompierre, whose quarters were close by, for they had not strength to walk. They dismounted on approaching the king's quarters, and the cardinal presented them to his Majesty: "Sir," said they, "we do acknowledge our crimes and rebellions and demand mercy; promising to remain faithful for the future, if your Majesty deign to remember the services we were able to render to the king your father."

The king gazed upon these suppliants kneeling at his feet, deputies from the proud city which had kept him more than a year at her gates; fleshless, almost fainting, they still bore on their features the traces of the haughty past. They had kept the lilies of France on their walls, refusing to the last to give themselves to England. "Better surrender to a king who could take Rochelle, than to one who couldn't succor her," said the mayor John Guiton, who was asked if he would not become an English subject. "I know that you have always been malignants," said the king at last, "and that you have done all you could to shake off the yoke of obedience to me; I forgive you, nevertheless, your rebellions and will be a good prince to you, if your actions conform to your protestations." Thereupon he dismissed them, not without giving them a dinner, and sent victuals into the town; without which, all that remained would have been dead of hunger within two days.

The fighting men marched out, "the officers and gentlemen wearing their swords and the soldiery with bare (white) staff in hand," according to the conventions; as they passed they were regarded with amazement, there not being more than sixty-four Frenchmen and ninety English: all the rest had been killed in sorties or had died of want. The cardinal at the same time entered this city which he had subdued by sheer perseverance; Guiton came to meet him with six archers; he had not appeared during the negotiations, saying that his duty detained him in the town. "Away with you!" said the cardinal, "and at once dismiss your archers, taking care not to style yourself mayor any more on pain of death." Guiton made no reply and went his way quietly to his house, a magnificent dwelling till lately, but now lying desolate amidst the general ruin. He was not destined to reside there long; the heroic defender of La Rochelle was obliged to leave the town and retire to Tournay-Boutonne. He returned to La Rochelle to die, in 1656.

The king made his entry into the subjugated town on the 1st of November, 1628: it was full of corpses in the chambers, the houses, the public thoroughfares; for those who still survived were so weak that they had not been able to bury the dead. Madame de Rohan and her daughter, who had not been included in the treaty, were not admitted to the honor of seeing his Majesty. "For having been the brand that had consumed this people," they were sent to prison at Niort; "there kept captive, without exercise of their religion, and so strictly that they had but one domestic to wait upon them, all which, however, did not take from them their courage or wonted zeal for the good of their party. The mother sent word to the duke of Rohan, her son, that he was to put no faith in her letters, since she might be made to write them by force, and that no consideration of her pitiable condition should make her flinch to the prejudice of her party, whatever harm she might be made to suffer" (*Mémoires du duc de Rohan*, t. i. p. 395). Worn out by so much suffering, the old duchess of Rohan died in 1631 at her castle Du Parc: she had been released from captivity by the pacification of the South.

With La Rochelle fell the last bulwark of religious liberties. Single-handed, duke Henry of Rohan now resisted at the head of a handful of resolute men. But he was about to be crushed in his turn. The capture of La Rochelle had raised the cardinal's power to its height; it had, simultaneously, been the death-blow to the Huguenot party and to the factions of the grandees. "One of them was bold enough to say," on seeing that La Rochelle was lost, "now we may well say that we are all lost" (*Mémoires de Richelieu*).

Upper Languedoc had hitherto refused to take part in the rising, and the prince of Condé was advancing on Toulouse when the duke of Rohan attempted a bold enterprise against Montpellier. He believed that he was sure of his communications with the interior of the town; but when the detachment of the advance-guard got a footing on the draw-bridge the ropes that held it were cut, and "the soldiers fell into a ditch, where they were shot down with arquebuses, at the same time that musketry played upon them from without." The lieutenant fell back in all haste upon the division of the duke of Rohan, who retreated "to the best villages between Montpellier and Lunel, without ever a man from Montpellier going out to follow and see whither he went." The war was wasting Languedoc, Viverais and Rouergue; the dukes of Montmorency and Ventadour, under the orders of the prince of Condé, were pursuing the troops of Rohan in every direction; the burgesses of Montauban had declared for the reformers, and were ravaging the lands of their catholic neighbors in return for the frightful ruin everywhere caused by the royal troops. The wretched peasantry laid the blame on the duke of Rohan, "for one of the greatest misfortunes connected with the position of party-chiefs is this necessity they lie under of accounting for all their actions to the people, that is, to a monster composed of numberless heads, amongst which there is scarcely one open to reason" (*Mémoires de Montmorency*). "Whoso has to do with a people that considers nothing difficult to undertake and, as for the execution, makes no sort of provision, is apt to be much hampered," writes the duke of Rohan in his *Mémoires* (t. i. p. 376). It was this extreme embarrassment that landed him in crime. One of his emissaries, returning from Piedmont where he had been admitted to an interview with the ambassador of Spain, made overtures to him on behalf of that power "which had an interest, he said, in a prolongation of the hostilities in France, so as to be able to peaceably achieve its designs in Italy. The great want of money in which the said duke then found himself, the country being unable to furnish more and the towns being unwilling to do anything further, there being nothing to hope from England, and nothing but words without deeds having been obtained from the duke of Savoy, absolutely constrained him to find some means of raising it in order to subsist." And so, in the following year, the duke of Rohan treated with the king of Spain, who promised to allow him annually three hundred thousand ducats for the keep of his troops and forty thousand for himself. In return the duke, who looked forward to "the time when he and his might make themselves sufficiently strong to canton themselves and form a separate State," promised, in that State, freedom and enjoyment of their property to all Catholics. A piece of strange and culpable blindness for which Rohan was to pay right dearly.

It was in the midst of this cruel partisan war that the duke heard of the fall of La Rochelle; he could not find fault "with folks so attenuated by famine that the majority of them could not support themselves without a stick, for having sought safety in capitulation;" but to the continual anxiety felt by him for the fate of his mother and sister was added disquietude as to the effect that this news might produce on his troops. "The people, weary of and ruined by the war, and naturally disposed to be very easily cast down by adversity; the tradesmen annoyed at having no more chance of turning a penny; the burgesses seeing their possessions in ruins and uncultivated; all were inclined for peace at any price whatever." The prince of Condé, whilst cruelly maltreating the countries in revolt, had elsewhere had the prudence to observe some gentle measures towards the peaceable reformers in the hope of thus producing submission. He made this quite clear himself when writing to the duke of Rohan: "Sir, the king's express commands to maintain them of the religion styled reformed in entire liberty of conscience have caused me to hitherto preserve those who remain in due obedience to his Majesty in all catholic places, countries as well as towns, in entire liberty. Justice has run its free course, the worship continues everywhere, save in two or three spots where it served not for the exercise of religion but to pave the way for rebellion. The officers who came out of rebel cities have kept their commissions: in a word, the treatment of so-styled reformers, when obedient, has been the same as that of catholics faithful to the king . . ." To which Henry de Rohan replied: "I confess to have once taken up arms unadvisedly, in so far as it was not on behalf of the affairs of our religion, but of those of yourself personally, who promised to obtain us reparation for the infractions of our treaties, and you did nothing of the kind, having had thoughts of peace before receiving news from the general assembly. Since that time everybody knows that I have had arms in my hands only from sheer necessity in order to defend our properties, our lives, and the freedom of our consciences. I seek my repose in Heaven, and God will give me grace to always find that of my conscience on earth. They say that in this war you have not made a bad thing of it. This gives me some assurance that you will leave our poor Cévennes at peace, seeing that there are more hard knocks than pistoles to be got there." The prince of Condé avenged himself for this stinging reply by taking possession, in Brittany, of all the duke of Rohan's property, which had been confiscated, and of which the king had made him a present. There were more pistoles to be picked up on the duke's estates than in the Cévennes.

The king was in Italy, and the reformers hoped that his affairs would detain him there a long while; but "God, who had disposed it otherwise, breathed upon all those projects," and the arms of Louis XIII. were everywhere victorious; peace was concluded with Piedmont and England, without the latter treaty making any mention of the Huguenots. The king then turned his eyes towards Languedoc, and, summoning to him the dukes of Montmorency and Schomberg, he laid siege to Privas. The cardinal soon joined him there, and it was on the day of his arrival that the treaty with England was proclaimed by heralds beneath the walls. The besieged thus learnt that their powerful ally had abandoned them without reserve; at the first assault the inhabitants fled into the country, the garrison retired within the forts, and the king's soldiers, penetrating into the deserted streets, were able without resistance to deliver up the town to pillage and flames. When the affrighted inhabitants came back by little and little within their walls, they found the houses confiscated to the benefit of the king, who invited a new population to inhabit Privas.

Town after town, "fortified Huguenot-wise," surrendered, opening to the royal armies the passage to the Cévennes. The duke of Rohan, who had at first taken position at Nîmes, repaired to Anduze for the defence of the mountains, the real fortress of the reformation in Languedoc. Alais itself had just opened its gates. Rohan saw that he could no longer impose the duty of resistance upon a people weary of suffering, "easily believing ill of good folks and readily agreeing with those whiners who blame everything and do nothing." He sent "to the king, begging to be received to mercy, thinking it better to resolve on peace, whilst he could still make some show of being able to help it, than to be forced, after a longer resistance, to surrender to the king with a rope round his neck." The cardinal advised the king to show the duke grace, "well knowing that, together with him individually, the other cities whether they wished it or not, would be obliged to do the like, there being but little resolution and constancy in people deprived of leaders, especially when they are threatened with immediate harm and see no door of escape open."

The general assembly of the reformers, which was then in meeting at Nîmes, removed to Anduze to deliberate with the duke of Rohan; a wish was expressed to have the opinion of the province of the Cévennes, and all the deputies repaired to the king's presence. No more surety-towns; fortifications everywhere raised, at the expense and by the hands of the reformers; the catholic worship re-established in all the churches of the reformed towns; and, at this price, an amnesty granted for all acts of rebellion, and religious liberties confirmed anew —such were the conditions of the peace signed at Alais on the 28th of June, 1629, and made public the following month at Nîmes under the name of *Edict of grace.* Montauban alone refused to submit to them.

The duke of Rohan left France and retired to Venice, where his wife and daughter were awaiting him. He had been appointed by the Venetian senate generalissimo of the forces of the republic, when the cardinal, who had no doubt preserved some regard for his military talents, sent him an offer of the command of the king's troops in the Valteline. There he for several years maintained the honor of France, being at one time abandoned and at another supported by the cardinal, who ultimately left him to bear the odium of the last reverse. Meeting with no response from the court, cut off from every resource, he brought back into the district of Gex the French troops driven out by the Grisons themselves, and then retired to Geneva. Being threatened with the king's wrath, he set out for the camp of his friend Duke Bernard of Saxe-Weimar; and it was whilst fighting at his side against the imperialists that he received the wound of which he died in Switzerland on the 16th of April, 1638. His body was removed to Geneva amidst public mourning. A man of distinguished mind and noble character, often wild in his views and hopes, and so deeply absorbed in the interests of his party and of his Church, that he had sometimes the misfortune to forget those of his country.

Meanwhile the king had set out for Paris, and the cardinal was marching on Montauban. Being obliged to halt at Pézenas because he had a fever, he there received a deputation from Montauban, asking to have its fortifications preserved. On the minister's formal refusal, supported by a movement in advance on the part of Marshal Bassompierre with the army, the town submitted unreservedly. "Knowing that the cardinal had made up his mind to enter in force, they found this so bitter a pill that they could scarcely swallow it;" they, nevertheless, offered the dais to the minister as they had been accustomed to do to the governor, but he refused it, and would not suffer the consuls to walk on foot beside his horse. Bassompierre set guards at the doors of the meeting-house, that things might be done without interruption or scandal; it was ascertained that the parliament of Toulouse, "habitually intractable in all that concerned religion," had enregistered the Edict without difficulty; the gentlemen of the neighborhood came up in crowds, the Reformers to make their submission and the Catholics to congratulate the cardinal; on the day of his departure the pickaxe was laid to the fortifications of Montauban; those of Castres were already beginning to fall; and the Huguenot party in France was dead. Deprived of the political guarantees which had been granted them by Henry IV., the reformers had nothing for it but to retire into private life. This was the commencement of their material prosperity; they henceforth transferred to commerce and industry all the intelligence, courage and spirit of enterprise that they had but lately displayed in the service of their cause, on the battle-field or in the cabinets of kings.

"From that time," says Cardinal Richelieu, "difference in religion never prevented me from rendering the Huguenots all sorts of good offices, and I made no distinction between Frenchmen but in respect of fidelity." A grand assertion, true at bottom, in spite of the frequent grievances that the reformers had often to make the best of; the cardinal was more tolerant than his age and his servants; what he had wanted to destroy was the political party; he did not want to drive the reformers to extremity, nor force them to fly the country; happy had it been if Louis XIV. could have listened to and borne in mind the instructions given by Richelieu to Count de Sault, commissioned to see after the application in Dauphiny of the Edicts of pacification: "I hold that, as there is no need to extend in favor of them of the religion styled reformed that which is provided by the edicts, so there is no ground for cutting down the favors granted them thereby: even now, when, by the grace of God, peace is so firmly established in the kingdom, too much precaution cannot be used for the prevention of all these discontents amongst the people. I do assure you that the king's veritable intention is to have all his subjects living peaceably in the observation of his edicts, and that those who have authority in the provinces will do him service by conforming thereto." The era of liberty passed away with Henry IV.; that of tolerance, for the reformers, began with Richelieu, pending the advent with Louis XIV. of the day of persecution.

CHAPTER XLI.

LOUIS XIII., CARDINAL RICHELIEU, AND FOREIGN AFFAIRS.

France was reduced to submission; six years of power had sufficed for Richelieu to obtain the mastery; from that moment he directed his ceaseless energy towards Europe; "He feared the repose of peace," said the ambassador Nani in his letters to Venice; "and, thinking himself more safe amidst the bustle of arms, he was the originator of so many wars and of such long-continued and heavy calamities, he caused so much blood and so many tears to flow within and without the kingdom, that there is nothing to be astonished at, if many people have represented him as faithless, atrocious in his hatred, and inflexible in his vengeance. But no one, nevertheless, can deny him the gifts that this world is accustomed to attribute to its greatest men, and his most determined enemies are forced to confess that he had so many and such great ones that he would have carried with him power and prosperity wherever he might have had the direction of affairs. We may say that, having brought back unity to divided France, having succored Italy, upset the Empire, confounded England and enfeebled Spain, he was the instrument chosen by divine Providence to direct the great events of Europe."

The Venetian's independent and penetrating mind did not mislead him; everywhere in Europe were marks of Richelieu's handiwork. "There must be no end to negotiations near and far," was his saying: he had found negotiations succeed in France; he extended his views; numerous treaties had already marked the early years of the cardinal's power; and, after 1630, his activity abroad was redoubled. Between 1623 and 1642 seventy-four treaties were concluded by Richelieu: four with England; twelve with the United Provinces; fifteen with the princes of Germany; six with Sweden; twelve with Savoy; six with the Republic of Venice; three with the pope; three with the emperor; two with Spain; four with Lorraine; one with the Grey Leagues of Switzerland; one with Portugal; two with the revolters of Catalonia and Roussillon; one with Russia; two with the emperor of Morocco; such was the immense network of diplomatic negotiations whereof the cardinal held the threads during nineteen years.

An enumeration of the alliances would serve, without further comment, to prove this: that the foreign policy of Richelieu was a continuation of that of Henry IV.; it was to protestant alliances that he looked for their support in order to maintain the struggle against the House of Austria, whether the German or the Spanish branch. In order to give his views full swing, he waited till he had conquered the Huguenots at home; nearly all his treaties with protestant powers are posterior to 1630. So soon as he was secure that no political discussions in France itself would come to thwart his foreign designs, he marched with a firm step towards that *enfeeblement* of Spain and that *upsetting* of the empire of which Nani speaks; Henry IV. and Queen Elizabeth, pursuing the same end, had sought and found the same allies; Richelieu had the good fortune, beyond theirs, to meet, for the execution of his designs, with Gustavus Adolphus, king of Sweden.

Richelieu had not yet entered the king's council (1624), when the breaking off of the long negotiations between England and Spain, on the subject of the marriage of the prince of Wales with the Infanta, was officially declared to Parliament. At the very moment when Prince Charles, with the duke of Buckingham, was going post-haste to Madrid to see the Infanta Mary Anne of Spain, they were already thinking at Paris of marrying him to Henrietta of France, the king's young sister, scarcely fourteen years of age. King James I. was at that time obstinately bent upon his plan of alliance with Spain; when it failed, his son and his favorite forced his hand to bring him round to France. His envoys at Paris, the

Earl of Carlisle and Lord Holland, found themselves confronted by Cardinal Richelieu, commissioned, together with some of his colleagues, to negotiate the affair. M. Guizot, in his *Projet de mariage royal* (1 vol. 18mo: 1863; Paris, Hachette et C[ie]), has said that the marriage of Henry IV.'s daughter with the prince of Wales was, in Richelieu's eyes, one of the essential acts of a policy necessary to the greatness of the kingship and of France. He obtained the best conditions possible for the various interests involved, but without any stickling and without favor for such and such a one of these interests, skilfully adapting words and appearance but determined upon attaining his end.

The tarryings and miscarriages of Spanish policy had warned Richelieu to make haste. "In less than nine moons," says James I.'s private secretary, James Howell, "this great matter was proposed, prosecuted and accomplished, whereas the sun might, for as many years, have run his course from one extremity of the zodiac to the other, before the court of Spain would have arrived at any resolution and conclusion. That gives a good idea of the difference between the two nations, the leaden step of the one and the quick-silver movements of the other. It is also shows that the Frenchman is more noble in his proceedings, less full of scruple, reserve and distrust, and that he acts more chivalrously."

In France meanwhile, as well as in Spain, the question of religion was the rock of offence. Richelieu confined himself to demanding in a general way that, in this matter, the king of England should grant, in order to obtain the sister of the king of France, all that he had promised in order to obtain the king of Spain's. "So much was required," he said, "by the equality of the two crowns."

The English negotiators were much embarrassed; the protestant feelings of Parliament had shown themselves very strongly on the subject of the Spanish marriage. "As to public freedom for the catholic religion," says the cardinal, "they would not so much as hear of it, declaring that it was a design, under cover of alliance, to destroy their constitution even to ask such a thing of them." "You want to conclude the marriage," said Lord Holland to the queen-mother, "and yet you enter on the same paths that the Spaniards took to break it off; which causes all sorts of doubts and mistrusts, the effect whereof the premier minister of Spain, Count Olivarez, is very careful to aggravate by saying that, if the pope granted a dispensation for the marriage with France, the king his master would march to Rome with an army and give it up to sack." "We will soon stop *that*," answered Mary de' Medici quickly, "we will cut out work for him elsewhere." At last it was agreed that King James and his son should sign a private engagement, not inserted in the contract of marriage, "securing to the English Catholics more liberty and freedom in all that concerns their religion than they would have obtained by virtue of any articles whatsoever accorded by the marriage-treaty with Spain, provided that they made sparing use of them, rendering to the king of England the obedience owed by good and true subjects, the which king, of his benevolence, would not bind them by any oath contrary to their religion." The promises were vague and the securities anything but substantial; still the vanity as well as the fears of King James were appeased, and Richelieu had secured, simultaneously with his own ascendancy, the policy of France. Nothing remained but to send to Rome for the purpose of obtaining the dispensation. The ordinary ambassador, Count de Béthune, did not suffice for so delicate a negotiation; Richelieu sent Father Bérulle.

Father Bérulle, founder of the brotherhood of the Oratory, patron of the Carmelites and the intimate friend of Francis de Sales, though devoid of personal ambition, had been clever enough to keep himself on good terms with Cardinal Richelieu, whose political views he did not share, and with the court of Rome, whose most faithful allies, the Jesuits, he had often thwarted. He was devoted to Queen Mary de' Medici and willingly promoted her desires in the matter of her daughter's marriage. He found the court of Rome in confusion and much exercised by Spanish intrigue. "This court," he wrote to the cardinal, "is, in conduct and in principles, very different from what one would suppose before having tried it for oneself; for my part, I confess to having learnt more of it in a few hours, since I have been on the spot, than I knew by all the talk that I have heard. The dial constantly observed in this country is the balance existing between France, Italy and Spain." "The king my master," said Count de Béthune, quite openly, "has obtained from England all he could; it is no use to wait for more ample conditions, or to measure them by the Spanish ell; I have orders against sending off any courier save to give notice of concession of the dispensation; otherwise there would be nothing but asking one thing after another." "If we determine to act like Spain, we, like her, shall lose everything," said Father Bérulle. Some weeks later, on the 6th of January, 1625, Bérulle wrote to the cardinal: "For a month I have been on the point of starting, but we have been obliged to take so much trouble and have so many meetings, on the subject of transcripts and missives as well as the kernel of the business . . . I will merely tell you that the dispensation is *pure and simple.*"

King James I. had died on the 6th of April, 1625; and so it was King Charles I. and not the prince of Wales whom the duke of Chevreuse represented at Paris on the 11th of May, 1625, at the espousals of Princess Henrietta Maria. She set out on the 2nd of June for England, escorted by the duke of Buckingham, who had been sent by the king to fetch her and who had gladly prolonged his stay in France, smitten as he was by the young queen Anne of Austria. Charles I. went to Dover to meet his wife, showing himself very amiable and attentive to her. Though she little knew how fatal they would be to her, the king of England's palaces look bare and deserted to the new queen, accustomed as she was to French elegance; she, however, appeared contented. "How can your Majesty reconcile yourself to a Huguenot for a husband?" asked one of her suite, indiscreetly. "Why not?" she replied with spirit: "was not my father one?"

By this speech Henrietta Maria expressed, undoubtedly without realizing all its grandeur, the idea which had suggested her marriage and been prominent in France during the whole negotiations. It was the policy of Henry IV. that Henry IV.'s daughter was bringing to a triumphant issue. The marriage between Henrietta Maria and Charles I., negotiated and concluded by Cardinal Richelieu, was the open declaration of the fact that the style of Protestant or Catholic was not the supreme law of policy in Christian Europe, and that the interests of nations should not remain subservient to the religious faith of the reigning or governing personages,

Unhappily the policy of Henry IV., carried on by Cardinal Richelieu, found no Queen Elizabeth any longer on the throne of England to comprehend it and maintain it. Charles I. tossed about between the haughty caprices of his favorite Buckingham and the religious or political passions of his people, did not long remain attached to the great idea which had predominated in the alliance of the two crowns. Proud and timid, imperious and awkward, all at the same time, he did not succeed, in the first instance, in gaining the affections of his young wife, and early infractions of the treaty of marriage, the dismissal of all the queen's French servants, hostilities between the merchant navies of the two nations had for some time been paving the way for open war, when the Duke of Buckingham, in the hope of winning back to him the House of Commons (June, 1626), madly attempted the expedition against the island of Ré. What was the success of it, as well as of the two attempts that followed it, has already been shown Three years later, on the 24th of April, 1629, the king of England concluded peace with France without making any stipulation in favor of the reformers whom hope of aid from him had drawn into rebellion. "I declare," says the duke of Rohan, "that I would have suffered any sort of extremity rather than be false to the many sacred oaths we had given him not to listen to any treaty without him, who had many times assured us that he would never make peace without including us in it." The English accepted the peace "as the king had desired, not wanting the king of Great Britain to meddle with his rebellious Huguenot subjects any more than he would want to meddle with his catholic subjects if they were to rebel against him." [*Mémoires de Richelieu*, t. iv. p. 421]. The subjects of Charles I. were soon to rebel against him: and France kept her word and did not interfere.

The Hollanders, with more prudence and ability than distinguished Buckingham and Charles I. had done better service to the protestant cause without ever becoming entangled in the quarrels that divided France; natural enemies as they were of Spain and the House of Austria, they readily seconded Richelieu in the struggle he maintained against them; besides, the United Provinces were as yet poor, and the cardinal always managed to find money for his allies; nearly all the treaties he concluded with Holland were treaties of alliance and subsidy; those of 1641 and 1642 secured to them twelve hundred thousand livres a year out of the coffers of France. Once only the Hollanders were faithless to their engagements: it was during the siege of Rochelle, when the national feeling would not admit of war being made on the French Huguenots. All the forces of Protestantism readily united against Spain; Richelieu had but to direct them. She, in fact, was the great enemy, and her humiliation was always the ultimate aim of the cardinal's foreign policy; the struggle, power to power, between France and Spain explains, during that period, nearly all the political and military complications in Europe. There was no lack of pretexts for bringing it on. The first was the question of the Valteline, a lovely and fertile valley, which, extending from the Lake of Como to the Tyrol, thus serves as a natural communication between Italy and Germany. Possessed but lately, as it was, by the Grey Leagues of the protestant Swiss, the Valteline, a catholic district, had revolted at the instigation of Spain in 1620; the emperor, Savoy and Spain had wanted to divide the spoil between them; when France, the old ally of the Grisons, had interfered, and, in 1623, the forts of the Valteline had been entrusted on deposit to the pope, Urban VIII. He still retained them in 1624, when the Grison lords, seconded by a French reinforcement under the orders of the marquis of Cœuvres, attacked the feeble garrison of the Valteline; in a few days they were masters of all the places in the canton; the pope sent his nephew, Cardinal Barberini, to Paris to complain of French aggression and with a proposal to take the sovereignty of the Valteline from the Grisons; that was, to give it to Spain. "Besides," said Cardinal Richelieu, "the precedent and consequences of it would be perilous for kings in whose dominions it hath pleased God to permit diversity of religion." The legate could obtain nothing. The assembly of notables, convoked by Richelieu in 1625, approved of the king's conduct, and war was resolved upon. The siege of La Rochelle retarded it for two years; Richelieu wanted to have his hands free; he concluded a specious peace with Spain, and the Valteline remained for the time being in the hands of the Grisons, who were one day themselves to drive the French out of it.

Whilst the cardinal was holding La Rochelle besieged, the duke of Mantua had died in Italy, and his natural heir, Charles di Gonzaga, who was settled in France with the title of Duke of Nevers, had hastened to put himself in possession of his dominions. Meanwhile the duke of Savoy claimed the marquisate of Montferrat; the Spaniards supported him; they entered the dominions of the duke of Mantua and laid siege to Casale. When La Rochelle succumbed, Casale was still holding out; but the duke of Savoy had already made himself master of the greater part of Montferrat; the duke of Mantua claimed the assistance of the king of France whose subject he was; here was a fresh battle-field against Spain; and, scarcely had he been victorious over the Rochellese, when the king was on the march for Italy. The duke of Savoy refused a passage to the royal army, which found the defile of Suza Pass fortified with three barricades. Marshal Bassompierre went to the king, who was a hundred paces behind the storming-party, ahead of his regiment of guards. "'Sir,' said he, 'the company is ready, the violins have come in and the masks are at the door; when your Majesty pleases, we will commence the ballet.' 'The king came up to me and said to me angrily, "Do you know, pray, that we have but five hundred pounds of lead in the park of artillery?"' I said to him, 'It is a pretty time to think of that. Must the ballet not dance, for lack of one mask that is not ready? Leave it to us, sir, and all will go well.' 'Do you answer for it?' said he to me. 'Sir,' replied the cardinal, 'by the marshal's looks I prophesy that all will be well, rest assured of it'" [*Mémoires de Bassompierre*]. The French dashed forward, the marshals with the storming-party, and the barricades were soon carried. The duke of Savoy and his son had hardly time to fly. "Gentlemen," cried the duke to some Frenchmen who happened to be in his service, "gentlemen, allow me to pass; your countrymen are in a temper."

With the same dash, on debouching from the mountains, the king's troops entered Suza. The prince of Piedmont soon arrived to ask for peace; he gave up all pretensions to Montferrat and promised to negotiate with the Spanish general to get the siege of Casale raised; and the effect was that, on the 18th of March, Casale, delivered "by the mere wind of the renown gained by the king's arms, saw, with tears of joy, the Spaniards retiring desolate, showing no longer that pride which they had been wont to wear on their faces, looking constantly behind them, not so much from regret for what they were leaving as for fear lest the king's vengeful sword should follow after them and come to strike their death-blow" [*Mémoires de Richelieu*, t. iv. p. 370].

The Spaniards remained, however, in Milaness, ready to burst again upon the duke of Mantua. The king was in a hurry to return to France in order to finish the subjugation of the reformers in the south, commanded by the duke of Rohan. The cardinal placed little or no reliance upon the duke of Savoy, whose "mind could get no rest, and going more swiftly than the rapid movements of the heavens, made every day more than twice the circuit of the world, thinking how to set by the ears all kings, princes and potentates, one with another, so that he alone might reap advantage from their divisions" [*Mémoires de Richelieu*, t. iv. p. 375]. A league, however, was formed between France, the republic of Venice, the duke of

Mantua, and the duke of Savoy, for the defence of Italy in case of fresh aggression on the part of the Spaniards; and the king, who had just concluded peace with England, took the road back to France. Scarcely had the cardinal joined him before Privas when an Imperialist army advanced into the Grisons and, supported by the celebrated Spanish general Spinola, laid siege to Mantua. Richelieu did not hesitate: he entered Piedmont in the month of March, 1630, to march before long on Pignerol, an important place commanding the passage of the Alps; it, as well as the citadel, was carried in a few days; the governor having asked for time to "do his Easter" (take the sacrament), Marshal Créqui, who was afraid of seeing aid arrive from the duke of Savoy, had all the clocks in the town put on, to such purpose that the governor had departed and the place was in the hands of the French when the reinforcements came up. The duke of Savoy was furious and had the soldiers who surrendered Pignerol cut in pieces.

The king had put himself in motion to join his army. "The French noblesse," said Spinola, "are very fortunate in seeing themselves honored by the presence of the king their master amongst their armies; I have nothing to regret in my life but never to have seen the like on the part of mine." This great general had resumed the siege of Casale when Louis XIII. entered Savoy; the inhabitants of Chambéry opened their gates to him; Annecy and Montmélian succumbed after a few days' siege; Maurienne in its entirety made its submission and the king fixed his quarters there whilst the cardinal pushed forward to Casale with the main body of the army. Rejoicings were still going on for a success gained before Veillane over the troops of the duke of Savoy, when news arrived of the capture of Mantua by the Imperialists. This was the finishing blow to the ambitious and restless spirit of the duke of Savoy. He saw Mantua in the hands of the Spaniards "who never give back aught of what falls into their power, whatever justice and the interests of alliance may make binding on them;" it was all hope lost of an exchange which might have given him back Savoy; he took to his bed and died on the 26th of July, 1630, telling his son that peace must be made on any terms whatever. "By just punishment of God, he who, during forty or fifty years of his reign, had constantly tried to set his neighbors a-blaze, died amidst the flames of his own dominions which he had lost by his own obstinacy against the advice of his friends and his allies."

The king of France, in ill health, had just set out for Lyons; and thither the cardinal was soon summoned, for Louis XIII. appeared to be dying. When he reached convalescence, the truce suspending hostilities since the death of the duke of Savoy was about to expire; Marshal Schomberg was preparing to march on the enemy, when there was brought to him a treaty signed at Ratisbonne between the emperor and the ambassador of France, assisted by Francis du Tremblay, now known as Father Joseph, perhaps the only friend and certainly the most intimate confidant of the cardinal, who always employed him on delicate or secret business. But Marshal Schomberg was fighting against Spain; he did not allow himself to be stopped by a treaty concluded with the emperor, and speedily found himself in front of Casale. The two armies were already face to face, when there was seen coming out of the intrenchments an officer in the pope's service who waved a white handkerchief; he came up to Marshal Schomberg and was recognized as Captain Giulio Mazarini, often employed on the nuncio's affairs; he brought word that the Spaniards would consent to leave the city, if at the same time, the French would evacuate the citadel. Spinola was no longer there to make a good stand before the place; he had died a month previously, complaining loudly that his honor had been filched from him, and, determined not to yield up his last breath in a town which would have to be abandoned, he had caused himself to be removed out of Casale to go and die in a neighboring castle.

Casale evacuated, the cardinal broke out violently against the negotiators of Ratisbonne, saying that they had exceeded their powers and declaring that the king regarded the treaty as null and void; there was accordingly a recommencement of negotiations with the emperor as well as the Spaniards.

It was only in the month of September, 1631, that the States of Savoy and Mantua were finally evacuated by the hostile troops, Pignerol had been given up to the new duke of Savoy, but a secret agreement had been entered into between that prince and France; French soldiers remained concealed in Pignerol; and they retook possession of the place in the name of the king, who had purchased the town and its territory, to secure himself a passage into Italy. "The Spaniards, when they had news of it, made so much the more uproar as they had the less foreseen it and as it cut the thread of all the enterprises they were meditating against Christendom. The affairs of the emperor in Germany were in too bad a state for him to kindle war, and France kept Pignerol.

The House of Austria, in fact, was threatened mortally. For two years Cardinal Richelieu had been laboring to carry war into its very heart. Ferdinand II. had displeased many electors of the empire, who began to be disquieted at the advances made by his power. "It is, no doubt, a great affliction for the Christian commonwealth," said the cardinal to the German princes, "that none but the Protestants should dare to oppose such pernicious designs; they must not be aided in their enterprises against religion, but they must be made use of in order to maintain Germany in the enjoyment of her liberties." The catholic league in Germany, habitually allied as it was with the House of Austria, did not offer any leader to take the field against her. The king of Denmark, after a long period of hostilities, had just made peace with the emperor; and "in their need, all these offended and despoiled princes looked, as sailors look to the North," towards the king of Sweden, Gustavus Adolphus.

"The king of Sweden was a new rising-sun, who, having been at war with all his neighbors, had wrested from them several provinces; he was young but of great reputation, and already incensed against the emperor, not so much on account of any real injuries he had received from him as because he was his neighbor. His Majesty had kept an eye upon him with a view of attempting to make use of him in order to draw off in course of time the main body of the emperor's forces and give him work to do in his own dominions" [*Mémoires de Richelieu*, t. v. p. 119]. Through Richelieu's good offices, Gustavus Adolphus had just concluded a long truce with the Poles, with whom he had been for some time at war: the cardinal's envoy, M. de Charnacé, at once made certain propositions to the king of Sweden, promising the aid of France if he would take up the cause of the German princes; but Gustavus turned a cold ear to these overtures, "not seeing in any quarter any great encouragement to undertake the war, either in England, peace with the Spaniards being there as good as determined upon, or in Holland, for the same reason, or in the Hanseatic towns, which were all exhausted of wealth, or in Denmark, which had lost heart and was daily disarming, or in France whence he got not a word on which he could place certain reliance." The emperor, on his side, was seeking to make peace with Sweden, "and the people of that country were not disinclined to listen to him."

God, for the accomplishment of His will, sets at naught the designs and intentions of men. Gustavus Adolphus was the instrument chosen by Providence to finish the work of Henry IV. and Richelieu. Negotiations continued to be carried on between the two parties, but, before his alliance with France was concluded, the king of Sweden, taking a sudden resolution, set out for Germany, on the 30th of May, 1630, with fifteen thousand men, "having told Charnacé that he would not continue the war beyond that year, if he did not agree upon terms of treaty with the king; so much does passion blind us," adds the cardinal, "that he thought it to be in his power to put an end to so great a war as that, just as it had been in his power to commence it."

By this time Gustavus Adolphus was in Pomerania, the duke whereof, maltreated by the Emperor, admitted him on the 10th of July into Stettin, after a show of resistance. The Imperialists, in their fury, put to a cruel death all the inhabitants of the said city who happened to be in their hands and gave up all its territory to fire and sword. "The king of Sweden, on the contrary, had his army in such discipline that it seemed as if every one of them were living at home and not amongst strangers, for in the actions of this king there was nothing to be seen but inexorable severity towards the smallest excesses on the part of his men, extraordinary gentleness towards the populations and strict justice on every occasion, all which conciliated the affections of all, and so much the more in that the emperor's army, unruly, insolent, disobedient to its leaders, and full of outrage against the people, made their enemy's virtues shine forth the brighter" [*Mémoires de Richelieu*, t. vi. p. 419].

Gustavus Adolphus had left Sweden under the impulse of love for those glorious enterprises which make great generals, but still more of a desire to maintain the protestant cause, which he regarded as that of God. He had assembled the estates of Sweden in the castle of Stockholm, presenting to them his daughter Christina, four years old, whom he confided to their faithful care. "I have hopes," he said to them, "of ending by bringing triumph to the cause of the oppressed; but, as the pitcher that goes often to the well gets broken, so I fear it may be 'my fate. I who have exposed my life amidst so many dangers, who have so often spilt my blood for the country without, thanks to God, having been wounded to death, must in the end make a sacrifice of myself; for that reason I bid you farewell, hoping to see you again in a better world." He continued advancing into Germany. "This snow-king will go on melting as he comes south," said the emperor, Ferdinand, on hearing that Gustavus Adolphus had disembarked; but Mecklenburg was already in his hands, and the elector of Brandenburg had just declared in his favor; he everywhere made proclamation, "that the inhabitants were to come forward and join him to take the part of their princes, whom he was coming to replace in possession." He was investing all parts of Austria, whose hereditary dominions he had not yet attacked; it was in the name of the empire that he fought against the emperor.

The diet was terminating at Ratisbonne, and it had just struck a fatal blow at the imperial cause. The electors, catholic and protestant, jealous of the power as well as of the glory of the celebrated Wallenstein, creator and commander-in-chief of the emperor's army, who had made him duke of Friedland and endowed him with the duchies of Mecklenburg, had obliged Ferdinand II. to withdraw from him the command of the forces. At this price he had hoped to obtain their votes to designate his son king of the Romans; the first step towards hereditary empire had failed, thanks to the ability of Father Joseph. "This poor Capuchin has disarmed me with his chaplet," said the emperor, "and for all that his cowl is so narrow he has managed to get six electoral hats into it." The treaty he had concluded, disavowed by France, did not for an instant hinder the progress of the king of Sweden; and the cardinal lost no time in letting him know that "the king's intention was in no wise to abandon him but to assist him more than ever, insomuch as he deemed it absolutely necessary in order to thwart the designs of those who had no end in view but their own augmentation to the prejudice of all the other princes of Europe." On the 25th of January, 1631, at Bernwald, the treaty of alliance between France and Sweden was finally signed. Baron Charnacé had inserted in the draft of the treaty the term *protection* as between France and Gustavus Adolphus: "Our master asks for no protection but that of heaven," said the Swedish plenipotentiaries; "after God, His Majesty holds himself indebted only to his sword and his wisdom for any advantages he may gain." Charnacé did not insist; and the victories of Gustavus Adolphus were an answer to any difficulties.

The king of Sweden bound himself to furnish soldiers, thirty thousand men at the least; France was to pay by way of subsidy four hundred thousand crowns a year, and to give a hundred thousand crowns to cover past expenses. Gustavus Adolphus promised to maintain the existing religion in such countries as he might conquer, "though he said laughingly that there was no possibility of promising about that, except in the fashion of him who sold the bear's skin;" he likewise guaranteed neutrality to the princes of the catholic league, provided that they observed it towards him. The treaty was made public at once through the exertions of Gustavus Adolphus, though Cardinal Richelieu had charged Charnacé to keep it secret for a time.

Torquato Conti, one of the emperor's generals, who had taken Wallenstein's place, wished to break off warfare during the long frosts. "My men do not recognize winter," answered Gustavus Adolphus. "This prince, who did not take to war as a pastime, but made it in order to conquer," marched with giant-strides across Germany, reducing everything as he went. He had arrived, by the end of April, before Frankfurt-on-the-Oder which he took; and he was preparing to succor Magdeburg, which had early pronounced for him and which Tilly, the emperor's general, kept besieged. The elector of Saxony hesitated to take sides; he refused Gustavus Adolphus a passage over the bridge of Dessau on the Elbe. On the 20th of May Magdeburg fell, and Tilly gave over the place to the soldiery; thirty thousand persons were massacred and the houses committed to the flames. "Nothing like it has been seen since the taking of Troy and of Jerusalem," said Tilly in his savage joy. The protestant princes, who had just been reconstituting the Evangelical Union in the diet they had held in February at Leipzig, revolted openly, ordering levies of soldiers to protect their territories; the Catholic League, renouncing neutrality, flew to arms on their side; the question became nothing less than that of restoring to the Protestants all that had been granted them by the peace of Passau. The soldiery of Tilly were already let loose on electoral Saxony; the elector, constrained by necessity, entrusted his soldiers to Gustavus Adolphus, who had just received reinforcements from Sweden; and the king marched against Tilly, still encamped before Leipzig, which he had forced to capitulate.

The Saxons gave way at the first shock of the imperial troops, but the king of Sweden had dashed forward, and nothing could withstand him; Tilly himself, hitherto proof against lead and steel, fell wounded in three places; five thousand dead were left on the field of battle; and Gustavus Adolphus dragged at his heels seven thousand prisoners. "Never did the grace of God pull me out of so bad a scrape," said the conqueror. He halted some time at Mayence, which had just opened its gates to him. Axel Oxenstiern, his most faithful servant and oldest friend, whose intimacy with his royal master reminds one of that between Henry IV. and Sully, came to join him in Germany; he had hitherto been commissioned to hold the government of the conquests won from the Poles. He did not approve of the tactics of Gustavus Adolphus, who was attacking the catholic league, and meanwhile leaving to the elector of Saxony the charge of carrying the war into the hereditary dominions of Austria . . . "Sir," said he, "I should have liked to offer you my felicitations on your victories not at Mayence but at Vienna." "If, after the battle of Leipzig, the king of Sweden had gone straight to attack the emperor in his hereditary provinces, it had been all over with the House of Austria," says Cardinal Richelieu; "but either God did not will the certain destruction of that house, which would perhaps have been too prejudicial to the catholic religion, and He turned him aside from the counsel which would have been more advantageous for him to take, or the same God, who giveth not all to any, but distributeth His gifts diversely to each, had given to this king as to Hannibal, the knowledge how to conquer but not how to use victory."

Gustavus Adolphus had resumed his course of success: he came up with Tilly again on the Leck, April 10, 1632, and crushed his army; the general was mortally wounded, and the king of Sweden, entering Augsburg in triumph, proclaimed religious liberty there. He had moved forward in front of Ingolstadt and was making a reconnoissance in person. "A king is not worthy of his crown who makes any difficulty about carrying it wherever a simple soldier can go," he said. A cannon-ball carried off the hind quarters of his horse and threw him down. He picked himself up, all covered with blood and mud. "The fruit is not yet ripe," he cried, with that strange mixture of courage and fatalism which so often characterizes great warriors; and he marched to Munich, on which he imposed a heavy war-contribution. The elector of Bavaria, strongly favored by France, sought to treat in the name of the catholic league; but Gustavus Adolphus required complete restitution of all territories wrested from the protestant princes, the withdrawal of the troops occupying the dominions of the evangelicals, and the absolute neutrality of the catholic princes. "These conditions smacked rather of your victorious prince, who would lay down and not accept the law." He summoned to him all the inhabitants of the countries he traversed in conqueror's style: "*Surgite à mortuis*," he said to the Bavarians, "*et venite ad judicium*" (*Rise from the dead, and come to judgment*). Protestant Suabia had declared for him, and Duke Bernard of Saxe-Weimar, one of his ablest lieutenants, carried the Swedish arms to the very banks of the Lake of Constance. The Lutheran countries of Upper Austria had taken up arms; and Switzerland had permitted the king of Sweden to recruit on her territory. "Italy began to tremble," says Cardinal Richelieu; "the Genevese themselves were fortifying their town, and to see them doing so, it seemed as if the king of Sweden were at their gates; but God had disposed it otherwise."

The Emperor Ferdinand had recalled the only general capable of making a stand against Gustavus Adolphus. Wallenstein, deeply offended, had for a long while held out; but, being assured of the supreme command over the fresh army which Ferdinand was raising in all directions, he took the field at the end of April, 1632. Wallenstein effected a junction with the elector of Bavaria, forcing Gustavus Adolphus back, little by little, on Nuremberg. "I mean to show the king of Sweden a new way of making war," said the German general. The sufferings of his army in an intrenched camp soon became intolerable to Gustavus Adolphus. In spite of inferiority of forces, he attacked the enemy's redoubts and was repulsed; the king revictualled Nuremberg and fell back upon Bavaria. Wallenstein at first followed him, and then flung himself upon Saxony and took Leipzig; Gustavus Adolphus advanced to succor his ally, and the two armies met near the little town of Lützen, on the 16th of November, 1632.

There was a thick fog. Gustavus Adolphus, rising before daybreak, would not put on his breast-plate, his old wounds hurting him under harness: "God is my breast-plate," he said. When somebody came and asked him for the watchword, he answered, "God with us;" and it was Luther's hymn, "Ein feste Burg ist unser Gott" (Our God is a strong tower), that the Swedes sang as they advanced towards the enemy. The king had given orders to march straight on Lützen. "He animated his men to the fight," says Richelieu, "with words that he had at command, whilst Wallenstein, by his mere presence and the sternness of his silence, seemed to let his men understand that, as he had been wont to do, he would reward them or chastise them, according as they did well or ill on that great day."

It was ten a.m. and the fog had just lifted; six batteries of cannon and two large ditches defended the Imperialists; the artillery from the ramparts of Lützen played upon the king's army, the balls came whizzing about him; Bernard of Saxe-Weimar was the first to attack, pushing forward on Lützen, which was soon taken, Gustavus Adolphus marched on to the enemy's intrenchments; for an instant the Swedish infantry seemed to waver; the king seized a pike and flung himself amidst the ranks; "After crossing so many rivers, scaling so many walls and storming so many places, if you have not courage enough to defend yourselves, at least turn your heads to see me die," he shouted to the soldiers. They rallied: the king remounted his horse, bearing along with him a regiment of Smalandaise cavalry. "You will behave like good fellows, all of you," he said to them, as he dashed over the two ditches, carrying, as he went, two batteries of the enemy's cannon. "He took off his hat and rendered thanks to God for the victory He was giving him."

Two regiments of Imperial cuirassiers rode up to meet him; the king charged them at the head of his Swedes; he was in the thickest of the fight; his horse received a ball through the neck; Gustavus had his arm broken; the bone came through the sleeve of his coat; he wanted to have it attended to, and begged the duke of Saxe-Altenburg to assist him in leaving the battle-field; at that very moment, Falkenberg, lieutenant-colonel in the Imperial army, galloped his horse on to the king and shot him, point-blank, in the back with a pistol. The king fell from his horse; and Falkenberg took to flight, pursued by one of the king's squires, who killed him. Gustavus Adolphus was left alone with a German page, who tried to raise him; the king could no longer speak; three Austrian cuirassiers surrounded him, asking the page the name of the wounded man; the youngster would not say, and fell riddled with wounds on his master's body; the Austrians sent one more pistol-shot into the dying man's temple and stripped him of his clothes, leaving him only his shirt. The melley recommenced, and successive charges of cavalry passed over the hero's corpse; there were counted nine open wounds and thirteen scars on his body when it was recovered towards the evening.

One of the king's officers, who had been unable to quit the fight in time to succor him, went and announced his fall to Duke Bernard of Saxe-Weimar. To him a retreat was suggested; but, "We mustn't think of that," said he, "but of death or victory." A lieutenant-colonel of a cavalry regiment made some difficulty about resuming the attack: the duke passed his sword through his body, and, putting himself at the head of the troops, led them back upon the enemy's intrenchments which he carried and lost three times. At last he succeeded in turning the cannon upon the enemy, and "that gave the turn to the victory, which, nevertheless, was disputed till night." "It was one of the most horrible ever heard of," says Cardinal Richelieu; "six thousand dead or dying were left on the field of battle, where Duke Bernard encamped till morning."

When day came, he led the troops off to Weisenfeld. The army knew nothing yet of the king's death. The duke of Saxe-Weimar had the body brought to the front: "I will no longer conceal from you," he said, "the misfortune that has befallen us; in the name of the glory that you have won in following this great prince, help me to exact vengeance for it and to let all the world see that he commanded soldiers who rendered him invincible and, even after his death, the terror of his enemies." A shout arose from the host: "We will follow you whither you will, even to the end of the earth."

"Those who look for spots on the sun and find something reprehensible even in virtue itself, blame this king," says Cardinal Richelieu, "for having died like a trooper; but they do not reflect that all conqueror-princes are obliged to do not only the duty of captain but of simple soldier and to be the first in peril in order to lead thereto the soldiers who would not run the risk without them. It was the case with Cæsar and with Alexander, and the Swede died so much the more gloriously than either the one or the other, in that it is more becoming the condition of a great captain and a conqueror to die sword in hand, making a tomb for his body of his enemies on the field of battle, then to be hated of his own and poniarded by the hands of his nearest and dearest, or to die of poison or of drowning in a wine-butt."

Just like Napoleon in Egypt and Italy, Gustavus Adolphus

had performed the prelude, by numerous wars against his neighbors, to the grand enterprise which was to render his name illustrious. Vanquished in his struggle with Denmark in 1613, he had carried war into Muscovy, conquered towns and provinces, and as early as 1617 he had effected the removal of the Russians from the shores of the Baltic. The Poles made a pretence of setting their own king, Sigismund, upon the throne of Sweden; and for eighteen years Gustavus Adolphus had bravely defended his rights, and protected and extended his kingdom up to the truce of Altenmarket, concluded in 1629 through the intervention of Richelieu, who had need of the young king of Sweden in order to oppose the Emperor Ferdinand and the dangerous power of the House of Austria. Summoned to Germany by the protestant princes who were being oppressed and despoiled, and assured of assistance and subsidies from the king of France, Gustavus Adolphus had, no doubt, ideas of a glorious destiny, which have been flippantly taxed with egotistical ambition. Perhaps, in the noble joy of victory, when he "was marching on without fighting," seeing provinces submit, one after another, without his being hardly at the pains to draw his sword, might he have sometimes dreamed of a protestant empire and the imperial crown upon his head; but, assuredly, such was not the aim of his enterprise and of his life. "I must in the end make a sacrifice of myself," he had said on bidding farewell to the Estates of Sweden; and it was to the cause of Protestantism in Europe that he made this sacrifice. Sincerely religious in heart, Gustavus Adolphus was not ignorant that his principal political strength was in the hands of the protestant princes; and he put at their service the incomparable splendor of his military genius. In two years the power of the House of Austria, a work of so many efforts and so many years, was shaken to its very foundations. The evangelical union of protestant princes was reforming in Germany and treating, as equal with equal, with the emperor; Ferdinand was trembling in Vienna, and the Spaniards, uneasy even in Italy, were collecting their forces to make head against the irresistible conqueror, when the battle-field of Lützen saw the fall, at thirty years of age, of the "hero of the North, the bulwark of Protestantism," as he was called by his contemporaries, astounded at his greatness. God sometimes thus cuts off His noblest champions in order to make men see that He is master and He alone accomplishes His great designs; but to them whom He deigns to thus employ He accords the glory of leaving their imprint upon the times they have gone through and the events to which they have contributed. Two years of victory in Germany at the head of Protestantism sufficed to make the name of Gustavus Adolphus illustrious for ever.

Richelieu had continued the work of Henry IV.; and Chancellor Oxenstiern did not leave to perish that of his master and friend. Scarcely was Gustavus Adolphus dead when Oxenstiern convoked at Erfurt the deputies from the protestant towns and made them swear the maintenance of the union. He afterwards summoned to Heilbronn all the protestant princes; the four circles of Upper Germany (Franconia, Suabia, the Palatinate and the Upper Rhine), and the elector of Brandenburg alone sent their representatives; but Richelieu had delegated M. de Feuquières, who quietly brought his weight to bear on the decision of the assembly and got Oxenstiern appointed to direct the protestant party, the elector of Saxony, who laid claim to his honor, was already leaning towards the treason which he was to consummate in the following year; France at the same time renewed her treaty with Sweden and Holland; the great general of the armies of the Empire, Wallenstein, displeased with his master, was making secret advances to the cardinal and to Oxenstiern; wherever he did not appear in person the Imperial armies were beaten. The emperor was just having his eyes opened, when Wallenstein, summoning around him at Pilsen his generals and his lieutenants, made them take an oath of confederacy for the defence of his person and of the army, and, begging Bernard of Saxe-Weimar and the Saxon generals to join him in Bohemia, he wrote to Feuquières to accept the king's secret offers.

Amongst the generals assembled at Pilsen there happened to be Max Piccolomini, in whom Wallenstein had great confidence: he at once revealed to the emperor his generalissimo's guilty intrigues. Wallenstein fell, assassinated by three of his officers, on the 15th of February, 1634; and the young king of Hungary, the emperor's eldest son, took the command-in-chief of the army under the direction of the veteran generals of the Empire. On the 6th of September, by one of those reversals which disconcert all human foresight, Bernard of Saxe-Weimar and the Swedish marshal, Horn, coming up to the aid of Nordlingen, which was being besieged by the Austrian army, were completely beaten in front of that place; and their army retired in disorder, leaving Suabia to the conqueror. Protestant Germany was in consternation; all eyes were turned towards France.

Cardinal Richelieu was ready; the frequent treasons of Duke Charles of Lorraine had recently furnished him with an opportunity, whilst directing the king's arms against him, of taking possession, partly by negotiation and partly by force, first of the town of Nancy and then of the duchy of Bar; the duke had abdicated in favor of the cardinal, his brother, who, renouncing his ecclesiastical dignity, espoused his cousin, Princess Claude of Lorraine, and took refuge with her at Florence, whilst Charles led into Germany, to the emperor, all the forces he had remaining. The king's armies were coming to provisionally take possession of all the places in Lothringen, where the Swedes, beaten in front of Nördlingen, being obliged to abandon the left bank of the upper Rhine, placed in the hands of the French the town of Philipsburg, which they had but lately taken from the Spaniards. The Rhinegrave Otto, who was commanding in Elsass for the confederates, in the same way effected his retreat, delivering over to Marshal La Force Colmar, Schlestadt and many small places; the bishop of Basle and the free city of Mülhausen likewise claimed French protection.

On the 1st of November, the ambassadors of Sweden and of the protestant League signed at Paris a treaty of alliance, soon afterwards ratified by the diet at Worms, and the French army, entering Germany, under Marshals La Force and Brézé, caused the siege of Heidelberg to be raised on the 23rd of December. Richelieu was in treaty at the same time with the United Provinces for the invasion of the catholic Low Countries. It was in the name of their ancient liberties that the cardinal, in alliance with the heretics of Holland, summoned the ancient Flanders to revolt against Spain; if they refused to listen to this appeal, the confederates were under mutual promises to divide their conquest between them. France confined herself to stipulating for the maintenance of the catholic religion in the territory that devolved to Holland. The army destined for this enterprise was already in preparation and the king was setting out to visit it, when, in April, 1635, he was informed of Chancellor Oxenstiern's arrival. Louis XIII. awaited him at Compiègne. The chancellor was accompanied by a numerous following, worthy of the man who held the command of a sovereign over the princes of the protestant

League; he had at his side the famous Hugo Grotius, but lately exiled from his country on account of religious disputes, and now accredited as ambassador to the king of France from the little queen, Christina of Sweden. It was Grotius who acted as interpreter between the king and the chancellor of Sweden. A rare and grand spectacle was this interview between, on the one side, the Swede and the Hollander, both of them great political philosophers in theory or practice, and, on the other, the all-powerful minister of the king of France, in presence of that king himself. When Oxenstiern and Richelieu conferred alone together, the two ministers had recourse to Latin, that common tongue of the cultivated minds of their time, and nobody was present at their conversation. Oxenstiern soon departed for Holland, laden with attentions and presents: he carried away with him a new treaty of alliance between Sweden and France and the assurance that the king was about to declare war against Spain.

And it broke out, accordingly, on the 19th of May, 1635. The violation of the electorate of Trèves by the Cardinal Infante, and the carrying-off of the elector-archbishop served as pretext; and Louis XIII. declared himself protector of a feeble prince who had placed in his hands the custody of several places. Alençon, herald-at-arms of France, appeared at Brussels, proclamation of war in hand; and, not being able to obtain an interview with the Cardinal Infante, he hurled it at the feet of the Belgian herald-at-arms commissioned to receive him, and he affixed a copy of it to a post he set up in the ground in the last Flemish village, near the frontier. On the 6th of June, a proclamation of the king's summoned the Spanish Low Countries to revolt. A victory had already been gained in Luxembourg, close to the little town of Avein, over Prince Thomas of Savoy, the duke-regnant's brother, who was embroiled with him, and whom Spain had just taken into her service. The campaign of 1635 appeared to be commencing under happy auspices. These hopes were deceived; the Low Countries did not respond to the summons of the king and of his confederates; there was no rising anywhere against the Spanish yoke; traditional jealousy of the heretics of Holland prevented the Flanders from declaring for France; it was necessary to undertake a conquest instead of fomenting an insurrection. The prince of Orange was advancing slowly into Germany; the elector of Saxony had treated with the emperor, and several towns were accepting the peace concluded between them at Prague; Bernard of Saxe-Weimar, supported by Cardinal Valette, at the head of French troops, had been forced to fall back to Metz in order to protect Lothringen and Elsass. In order to attach this great general to himself for ever, the king had just ceded to Duke Bernard the landgravate of Elsass, hereditary possession, as it was, of the House of Austria. The prince of Condé was attacking Franche-Comté; the siege of Dôle was dragging its slow length along, when the emperor's most celebrated lieutenants, John van Weert and Piccolomini, who had formed a junction in Belgium, all at once rallied the troops of Prince Thomas, and, advancing rapidly towards Picardy, invaded French soil at the commencement of July, 1636. La Capelle and Le Catelet were taken by assault, and the Imperialists laid siege to Corbie, a little town on the Somme, four leagues from Amiens.

Great was the terror at Paris, and, besides the terror, the rage; the cardinal was accused of having brought ruin upon France; for a moment the excitement against him was so violent that his friends were disquieted by it: he alone was unmoved. The king quitted St. Germain and returned to Paris, whilst Richelieu, alone, without escort, and with his horses at a walk, had himself driven to the Hôtel de Ville right through the mob in their fury. "Then was seen," says Fontenay-Mareuil, "what can be done by a great heart (*vertu*), and how it is revered even of the basest souls, for the streets were so full of folks that there was hardly room to pass, and all so excited that they spoke of nothing but killing him: as soon as they saw him approaching, they all held their peace or prayed God to give him good speed, that he might be able to remedy the evil which was apprehended."

On the 15th of August, Corbie surrendered to the Spaniards, who crossed the Somme, wasting the country behind them; but already alarm had given place to ardent desire for vengeance; the cardinal had thought of everything and provided for everything: the bodies corporate, from the parliament to the trade-syndicates, had offered the king considerable sums; all the gentlemen and soldiers unemployed had been put on the active list of the army: and the burgesses of Paris, mounting in throngs the steps of the Hôtel de Ville, went and shook hands with the veteran Marshal La Force, saying, "Marshal, we want to make war with you." They were ordered to form the nucleus of the reserve army which was to protect Paris. The duke of Orleans took the command of the army assembled at Compiègne, at the head of which the count of Soissons already was; the two princes advanced slowly; they halted two days to recover the little fortress of Roze; the Imperialists fell back; they retired into Artois; they were not followed, and the French army encamped before Corbie.

Winter was approaching; nobody dared to attack the town; the cardinal had no confidence in either the duke of Orleans or the count of Soissons. He went to Amiens, whilst the king established his head-quarters at the castle of Demuin, closer to Corbie. Richelieu determined to attack the town by assault; the trenches were opened on the 5th of November; on the 10th the garrison parleyed; on the 14th the place was surrendered. "I am very pleased to send you word that we have recovered Corbie," wrote Voiture to one of his friends, very hostile to the cardinal [*Œuvres de Voiture*, p. 175]: "the news will astonish you, no doubt, as well as all Europe; nevertheless, we are masters of it. Reflect, I beg you, what has been the end of this expedition which has made so much noise. Spain and Germany had made for the purpose their supremest efforts. The emperor had sent his best captains and his best cavalry. The army of Flanders had given its best troops. Out of that is formed an army of twenty-five thousand horse, fifteen thousand foot and forty cannon. This cloud, big with thunder and lightning, comes bursting over Picardy, which it finds unsheltered, our arms being occupied elsewhere. They take, first of all, La Capelle and Le Catelet; they attack and, in nine days, take Corbie; and so they are masters of the river; they cross it, and they lay waste all that lies between the Somme and the Oise. And so long as there is no resistance, they valiantly hold the country, they slay our peasants and burn our villages; but, at the first rumor that reaches them to the effect that Monsieur is advancing with an army, and that the king is following close behind him, they intrench themselves behind Corbie; and, when they learn that there is no halting, and that the march against them is going on merrily, our conquerors abandon their intrenchments. And these determined gentry, who were to pierce France even to the Pyrenees, who threatened to pillage Paris, and recover there, even in Notre-Dame, the flags of the battle of Avein, permit us to effect the circumvallation of a place which is of so much importance to them, give us leisure to construct forts, and, after that, let us attack and take it by assault before their very eyes. Such is the end of the bravadoes of Piccolomini, who sent us word by his trumpeters to say, at one time, that he wished we had some powder, and, at another, that we had some cavalry coming, and, when we had both one and the other, he took very good care to wait for us. In such sort, sir, that, except La Capelle and Le Catelet, which are of no consideration, all the flash made by this grand and victorious army has been the capture of Corbie, only to give it up again and replace it in the king's hands, together with a counterscarp, three bastions and three demilunes, which it did not possess. If they had taken ten more of our places with similar success, our frontier would be in all the better condition for it, and they would have fortified it better than those who hitherto have had the charge of it. . . . Was it not said that we should expend before this place many millions of gold and many millions of men with a chance of taking it, perhaps, in three years? Yet, when the resolution was taken to attack it by assault, the month of November being well advanced, there was not a soul but cried out. The best intentioned avowed that it showed blindness, and the rest said that we must be afraid lest our soldiers should not die soon enough of misery and hunger, and must wish to drown them in their own trenches. As for me, though I knew the inconveniencies which necessarily attend sieges undertaken at this season, I suspended my judgment; for, sooth to say, we have often seen the cardinal out in matters that he has had done by others, but we have never yet seen him fail in enterprises that he has been pleased to carry out in person and that he has supported by his presence. I believed, then, that he would surmount all difficulties; and that he who had taken La Rochelle in spite of Ocean would certainly take Corbie too in spite of Winter's rains. . . . You will tell me, that it is luck which has made him take fortresses without ever having conducted a siege before, which has made him, without any experience, command armies successfully, which has always led him, as it were, by the hand, and preserved him amidst precipices into which he had thrown himself, and which, in fact, has often made him appear bold, wise, and far-sighted: let us look at him, then, in misfortune, and see if he had less boldness, wisdom and far-sightedness. Affairs were not going over well in Italy, and we had met with scarcely more success before Dôle. When it was known that the enemy had entered Picardy, that all is a-flame to the very banks of the Oise, everybody takes fright, and the chief city of the realm is in consternation. On top of that come advices from Burgundy that the siege of Dôle is raised, and from Saintonge that there are fifteen thousand peasants revolted, and that there is fear lest Poitou and Guienne may follow this example. Bad news comes thickly, the sky is overcast on all sides, the tempest beats upon us in all directions and from no quarter whatever does a single ray of good fortune shine upon us. Amidst all this darkness, did the cardinal see less clearly? Did he lose his head during all this tempest? Did he not still hold the helm in one hand, and the compass in the other? Did he throw himself into the boat to save his life? Nay, if the great ship he commanded were to be lost, did he not show that he was ready to die before all the rest? Was it luck that drew him out of this labyrinth, or was it his own prudence, steadiness and magnanimity? Our enemies are fifteen leagues from Paris, and his are inside it. Every day come advices that they are intriguing there to ruin him. France and Spain, so to speak, have conspired against him alone. What countenance was kept amidst all this by the man who they said would be dumbfounded at the least ill-success, and who had caused Le Havre to be fortified in order to throw himself into it at the first misfortune? He did not make a single step backward all the same. He thought of the perils of the State, and not of his own; and the only change observed in him all through was that, whereas he had not been wont to go out but with an escort of two hundred guards, he walked about, every day, attended by merely five or six gentlemen. It must be owned that adversity borne with so good a grace, and such force of character is worth more than a great deal of prosperity and victory. To me he did not seem so great and so victorious on the day he entered La Rochelle as then; and the journeys he made from his house to the arsenal seem to me more glorious for him than those which he made beyond the mountains, and from which he returned with the triumphs of Pignerol and Suza."

This was Cardinal Richelieu's distinction, that all his contemporaries, in the same way as Voiture, identified the mishaps and the successes of their country with his own fortunes, and that upon him alone were fixed the eyes of Europe, whether friendly or hostile, when it supported or when it fought against France.

For four years the war was carried on with desperation by land and sea in the Low Countries, in Germany and in Italy, with alternations of success and reverse. The actors disappeared one after another from the scene; the emperor, Ferdinand II., had died on the 15th of February, 1637; the election of his son, Ferdinand III., had not been recognized by France and Sweden; Bernard of Saxe-Weimar succumbed, at thirty-four years of age, on the 15th of July, 1639, after having beaten, in the preceding year, the celebrated John van Weert, whom he sent a prisoner to Paris. At his death the landgravate of Elsass reverted to France, together with the town of Brisach which he had won from the Imperialists.

The duke of Savoy had died in 1637; his widow, Christine of France, daughter of Henry IV., was, so far as her brother's cause in Italy was concerned, but a poor support; but Count d'Harcourt, having succeeded, as head of the army, Cardinal Valette, who died in 1638, had retaken Turin and Casale from the Imperialists in the campaign of 1640; two years later, in the month of June, 1642, the Princes Thomas and Maurice, brothers-in-law of the Duchess Christine, wearied out by the maladdress and haughtiness of the Spaniards, attached themselves definitively to the interests of France, drove out the Spanish garrisons from Nice and Ivrea, in concert with the duke of Longueville, and retook the fortress of Tortona as well as all Milaness to the south of the Po. Perpignan, besieged for more than two years past by the king's armies, capitulated at the same moment. Spain, hard pressed at home by the insurrection of the Catalans and the revolt of Portugal at the same time, both supported by Richelieu, saw Arras fall into the hands of France (August 9, 1640), and the plot contrived with the duke of Bouillon and the count of Soissons fail at the battle of La Marfée, where this latter prince was killed on the 16th of July, 1641. In Germany, Marshal Guébriant and the Swedish general Torstenson, so paralyzed that he had himself carried in a litter to the head of his army, had just won back from the empire Silesia, Moravia, and nearly all Saxony; the chances of war were everywhere favorable to France, a just recompense for the indomitable perseverance of Cardinal Richelieu through good and evil fortune. "The great tree of the House of Austria was shaken to its very roots, and he had all but felled that trunk which with its two branches covers the North and the West, and throws a shadow over the rest of the earth" [*Lettres de Malherbe*, t. iv.]. The king, for a moment shaken in his fidelity towards his minister by the intrigues of Cinq-Mars, had returned to the cardinal with all the impetus of the indignation caused by the guilty treaty made by his favorite with Spain. All Europe thought as the young captain in the guards, afterwards Marshal Fabert, who, when the king said to him, "I know that my army is divided into two factions, royalists and cardinalists, which are you for?" answered, "Cardinalists, sir, for the cardinal's party is yours." The cardinal and France were triumphing together, but the conqueror was dying; Cardinal Richelieu had just been removed from Ruel to Paris.

For several months past, the cardinal's health, always precarious, had taken a serious turn; it was from his sick-bed that he, a prey to cruel agonies, directed the movements of the army and, at the same time, the prosecution of Cinq-Mars. All at once his chest was attacked; and the cardinal felt that he was dying. On the 2nd of December, 1642, public prayers were ordered in all the churches; the king went from St. Germain to see his minister. The cardinal was quite prepared. "I have this satisfaction," he said, "that I have never deserted the king and that I leave his kingdom exalted and all his enemies abased." He commended his relatives to his Majesty, "who on their behalf will remember my services;" then, naming the two secretaries of state, Chavigny and De Noyers, he added: "Your Majesty has Cardinal Mazarin; I believe him to be capable of serving the king." And he handed to Louis XIII. a proclamation which he had just prepared for the purpose of excluding the duke of Orleans from any right to the regency in case of the king's death. The preamble called to mind that the king had five times already pardoned his brother, recently engaged in a new plot against him.

The king had left the cardinal, but without returning to St. Germain. He remained at the Louvre. Richelieu had in vain questioned the physicians as to how long he had to live. One, only, dared to go beyond common-place hopes: "Monsignor," he said, "in twenty-four hours you will be dead or cured." "That is the way to speak!" said the cardinal; and he sent for the priest of St. Eustache, his parish. As they were bringing into his chamber the Holy Eucharist, he stretched out his hand, and, "There," said he, "is my Judge before whom I shall soon appear; I pray Him with all my heart to condemn me if I have ever had any other aim than the welfare of religion and of the State." The priest would have omitted certain customary questions, but "Treat me as the commonest of Christians," said the cardinal. And when he was asked to pardon his enemies, "I never had any but those of the State," answered the dying man.

The cardinal's family surrounded his bed; and the attendance was numerous. The bishop of Lisieux, Cospéan, a man of small wits but of sincere devoutness, listened attentively to the firm speech, the calm declarations of the expiring minister. "So much self-confidence appals me," he said, below his breath. Richelieu died as he had lived, without scruples and without delicacies of conscience, absorbed by his great aim and but little concerned about the means he had employed to arrive at it. "I believe absolutely, all the truths taught by the Church," he had said to his confessor, and this faith sufficed for his repose. The memory of the scaffolds he had caused to be erected did not so much as recur to his mind. "I have loved justice and not vengeance. I have been severe towards some in order to be kind towards all," he had said in his will written in Latin. He thought just the same on his death-bed.

The king left him, not without emotion and regret. The cardinal begged Madame d'Aiguillon, his niece, to withdraw. "She is the one whom I have loved most," he said. Those around him were convulsed with weeping. A Carmelite whom he had sent for turned to those present, and "Le. those," he said, "who cannot refrain from showing the excess of their weeping and their lamentation leave the room; let us pray for this soul." In presence of the majesty of death and eternity human grandeur disappears irrevocably; the all-powerful minister was at that moment only *this soul*. A last gasp announced his departure: Cardinal Richelieu was dead.

He was dead, but his work survived him. On the very evening of the 3rd of December, Louis XIII. called to his council Cardinal Mazarin; and next day he wrote to the parliament and governors of provinces: "God having been pleased to take to Himself the Cardinal de Richelieu, I have resolved to preserve and keep up all establishments ordained during his ministry, to follow out all projects arranged with him for affairs abroad and at home, in such sort that there shall not be any change. I have continued in my councils the same persons as served me then, and I have called thereto Cardinal Mazarin, of whose capacity and devotion to my service I have had proof, and of whom I feel no less sure than if he had been born amongst my subjects." Scarcely had the most powerful kings yielded up their last breath, when their wishes had been at once forgotten: Cardinal Richelieu still governed in his grave.

The king had distributed amongst his minister's relatives the offices and dignities which he had left vacant; the fortune that came to them was enormous; the legacies left to mere domestics amounted to more than three hundred thousand livres. During his lifetime Richelieu had given to the Crown "my grand hôtel, which I built, and called Palais-de-Cardinal, my chapel (or chapel-service) of gold, enriched with diamonds, my grand buffet of chased silver, and a large diamond that I bought of Lopez." In his will he adds: "I most humbly beseech His Majesty to think proper to have placed in his hands, out of the coined gold and silver that I have at my decease, the sum of fifteen hundred thousand livres, of which sum I can truly say that I made very good use for the great affairs of his kingdom, in such sort, that if I had not had this money at my disposal, certain matters which have turned out well would have, to all appearances, turned out ill; which gives me ground for daring to beseech His Majesty to destine this sum, that I leave him, to be employed on divers occasions which cannot abide the tardiness of financial forms."

The minister and priest who had destroyed the power of the grandees in France had, nevertheless, the true instinct respecting the perpetuation of families: "Inasmuch as it hath pleased God," he says in his will, "to bless my labors, and make them considered by the king, my kind master, showing recognition of them by his royal munificence, beyond what I could hope for, I have esteemed it a duty to bind my heirs to preserve the estate in my family, in such sort that it may maintain itself for a long while in the dignity and splendor which it hath pleased the king to confer upon it, in order that posterity may know that, as I served him faithfully, he, by virtue of a complete kingliness, knew what love to show me, and how to load me with his benefits."

The cardinal had taken pleasure in embellishing the estate of Richelieu, in Touraine, where he was born, and which the king had raised to a duchy-peerage. Mdlle. de Montpensier, in her *Mémoires*, gives an account of a visit she paid to it in her youth. "I passed," she says, "along a very fine street of the town, all the houses of which are in the best style of building, one like another and quite newly made, which is not to be wondered at. MM. de Richelieu, though gentlemen of good standing, had never built a town; they had been content with their village and with a mediocre house. At the present time it is the most beautiful and most magnificent castle you could possibly see, and all the ornament that could be given to a house is found there. This will not be difficult to believe if one considers that it is the work of the most ambitious and most ostentatious man in the world, premier minister of State too, who for a long while possessed absolute authority over affairs. It is, nevertheless, inconceivable that the apartments should correspond so ill in size with the beauty of the outside: I hear that this arose from the fact that the cardinal wished to have the chamber preserved in which he was born. To adjust the house of a simple gentleman to the grand ideas of the most powerful favorite there has ever been in France, you will observe that the architect must have been hampered; accordingly he did not see his way to planning any but very small quarters, which, by way of recompense, as regards gilding or painting, lack no embellishment inside.

"Amidst all that modern invention has employed to embellish it, there are to be seen, on the chimney-piece in a drawing-room the arms of Cardinal Richelieu, just as they were during the lifetime of his father, which the cardinal desired to leave there, because they comprise a collar of the Holy Ghost, in order to prove to those who are wont to misrepresent the origin of favorites that he was born a gentleman of a good house. In this point, he imposed upon nobody."

The castle of Richelieu is well-nigh destroyed; his family, after falling into poverty, is extinct; the Palais-Cardinal has assumed the name of Palais-Royal; and pure monarchy, the aim of all his efforts and the work of his whole life, has been swept away by the blast of revolution. Of the cardinal there remains nothing but the great memory of his power and of the services he rendered his country. Evil has been spoken, with good reason, of glory; it lasts, however, more durably than material successes even when they rest on the best security. Richelieu had no conception of that noblest ambition on which a human soul can feed, that of governing a free country, but he was one of the greatest, the most effective and the boldest as well as the most prudent servants that France ever had.

Cardinal Richelieu gave his age, whether admirers or adversaries, the idea which Malherbe expressed in a letter to one of his friends: "You know that my humor is neither to flatter nor to lie; but I swear to you that there is in this man a something which surpasses humanity, and that if our bark is ever to outride the tempests, it will be whilst this glorious hand holds the rudder. Other pilots diminish my fear, this one makes me unconscious of it. Hitherto, when we had to build anew or repair some ruin, plaster alone was put in requisition. Now we see nothing but marble used; and, whilst the counsels are judicious and faithful, the execution is diligent and magnanimous. Wits, judgment and courage never existed in any man to the degree that they do in him. As for interest, he knows none but that of the public. To that he clings with a passion so unbridled, if I may dare so to speak, that the visible injury it does his constitution is not capable of detaching him from it. Sees he anything useful to the king's service, he goes at it without looking to one side or the other. Obstacles tempt him, resistance piques him, and nothing that is put in his way diverts him; the disregard he shows of self, and of all that touches himself, as if he knew no sort of health or disease but the health or disease of the State, causes all good men to fear that his life will not be long enough for him to see the fruit of what he plants; and moreover, it is quite evident that what he leaves undone can never be completed by any man that holds his place. Why, man, he does a thing because it has to be done! The space between the Rhine and the Pyrenees seems to him not field enough for the lilies of France. He would have them occupy the two shores of the Mediterranean, and waft their odors thence to the extremest countries of the Orient. Measure by the extent of his designs the extent of his courage." [Letters to Racan and to M. de Mentin. *Œuvres de Malherbe*, t. iv.]

The cardinal had been barely four months reposing in that chapel of the Sorbonne which he had himself repaired for the purpose, and already King Louis XIII. was sinking into the tomb. The minister had died at fifty-seven, the king was not yet forty-two; but his always languishing health seemed unable to bear the burden of affairs which had been but lately borne by Richelieu alone. The king had permitted his brother to appear again at court. "Monsieur supped with me," says Mdlle. de Montpensier, "and we had the twenty-four violins; he was as gay as if MM. Cinq-Mars and De Thou had not tarried by the way. I confess that I could not see him without thinking of them, and that in my joy I felt that his gave me a pang." The prisoners and exiles, by degrees, received their pardon; the duke of Vendôme, Bassompierre, and Marshal Vitry had been empowered to return to their castles, the duchess of Chevreuse and the ex-keeper of the seals, Châteauneuf, were alone excepted from this favor. "After the peace," said the declaration touching the regency, which the king got enregistered by the Parliament on the 23rd of April. The little dauphin, who had merely been sprinkled, had just received baptism in the chapel of the castle of St. Germain. The king asked him, next day, if he knew what his name was. "My name is Louis XIV.," answered the child. "Not yet, my son, not yet," said the king softly.

Louis the XIII. did not cling to life: it had been sad and burthensome to him by the mere fact of his own melancholy and singular character, not that God had denied him prosperity or success. He had the windows opened of his chamber in the new castle of St. Germain looking towards the abbey of St. Denis, where he had, at last, just laid the body of the queen his mother, hitherto resting at Cologne. "Let me see my last resting-place," he said to his servants. The crowd of courtiers thronged to the old castle, inhabited by the queen; visits were made to the new castle to see the king, who still worked with his ministers; when he was alone, "he was seen nearly always with his eyes open towards heaven, as if he talked with God heart to heart." [*Mémoires sur la mort de Louis XIII.*, by his valet-de-chambre Dubois; *Archives curieuses*, t. v. p. 428.] On the 23rd of April, it was believed that the last moment had arrived: the king received extreme unction; a dispute arose about the government of Brittany, given by the king to the duke of La Meilleraye and claimed by the duke of Vendôme; the two claimants summoned their friends; the queen took fright, and, being obliged to repair to the king, committed the imprudence of confiding her children to the duke of Beaufort, Vendôme's eldest son, a young scatter-brain who made a great noise about this favor. The king rallied and appeared to regain strength. He was sometimes irritated at sight of the courtiers who filled his chamber. "Those gentry," he said to his most confidential servants, "come to see how soon I shall die. If I recover, I will make them pay dearly for their desire to have me die." The austere nature of Louis XIII. was awakened again with the transitory return of his powers; the severities of his reign were his own as much as Cardinal Richelieu's.

He was, nevertheless, dying, asking God for deliverance. It was Thursday, May 14. "Friday has always been my lucky day," said Louis XIII.: "on that day I have undertaken assaults that I have carried; I have even gained battles: I should have liked to die on a Friday." His doctors told him that they could find no more pulse; he raised his eyes to heaven and said out loud, "My God, receive me to mercy!" and, addressing himself to all, he added, "Let us pray!" Then, fixing his eyes upon the bishop of Meaux, he said, "You will, of course, see when the time comes for reading the agony-prayers, I have marked them all." Everybody was praying and weeping; the queen and all the court were kneeling in the king's chamber. At three o'clock, he softly breathed his last, on the same day and almost at the same moment at which his father had died beneath the dagger of Ravaillac, thirty-three years before.

France owed to Louis XIII. eighteen years of Cardinal Richelieu's government; and that is a service which she can never forget. "The minister made his sovereign play the second part in the monarchy and the first in Europe," said Montesquieu: "he abased the king, but he exalted the reign." It is to the honor of Louis XIII. that he understood and accepted the position designed for him by Providence in the government of his kingdom, and that he upheld with dogged fidelity a power which often galled him all the while that it was serving him.

CHAPTER XLII.

LOUIS XIII., RICHELIEU AND LITERATURE.

Cardinal Richelieu was dead and "his works followed him," to use the words of Holy Writ. At home and abroad, in France and in Europe, he had to a great extent continued the reign of Henry IV., and had completely cleared the way for that of Louis XIV. "Such was the strength and superiority of his genius that he knew all the depths and all the mysteries of government," said La Bruyère in his admission-speech before the French Academy; "he was regardful of foreign countries, he kept in hand crowned heads, he knew what weight to attach to their alliance; with allies he hedged himself against the enemy. . . . And, can you believe it, gentlemen? this practical and austere soul, formidable to the enemies of the State, inexorable to the factious, overwhelmed in negotiations, occupied at one time in weakening the party of heresy, at another in breaking up a league, and at another in meditating a conquest, found time for literary culture, and was fond of literature and of those who made it their profession!" From inclination and from personal interest therein this indefatigable and powerful mind had courted literature; he had foreseen its nascent power; he had divined in the literary circle he got about him a means of acting upon the whole nation; he had no idea of neglecting them; he did not attempt to subjugate them openly; he brought them near to him and protected them. It is one of Richelieu's triumphs to have founded the French Academy.

We must turn back for a moment and cast a glance at the intellectual condition which prevailed at the issue of the Renaissance and the Reformation.

For sixty years a momentous crisis had been exercising language and literature as well as society in France. They yearned to get out of it. Robust intellectual culture had ceased to be the privilege of the erudite only; it began to gain a footing on the common domain; people no longer wrote in Latin, like Erasmus; the Reformation and the Renaissance spoke French. In order to suffice for this change, the language was taking form; everybody had lent a hand to the work: Calvin with his *Christian Institutes* (*Institution Chrétienne*) at the same time as Rabelais with his learned and buffoonish romance, Ramus with his *Dialectics*, and Bodine with his *Republic*, Henry Estienne with his essays in French philology, as well as Ronsard and his friends by their classical crusade. Simultaneously with the language there was being created a public, intelligent, inquiring and eager. Scarcely had the translation of Plutarch by Amyot appeared, when it at once became, as Montaigne says, "the breviary of women and of ignoramuses." "God's life, my love," wrote Henry IV. to Mary de' Medici, "you could not have sent me any more agreeable news than of the pleasure you have taken in reading. Plutarch has a smile for me of never failing freshness; to love him is to love me, for he was during a long while the instructor of my tender age; my good mother, to whom I owe everything and who set so great store on my good deportment, and did not want me to be (that is what she used to say) an illustrious ignoramus, put that book into my hands, though I was then little more than a child at the breast. It has been like my conscience to me, and has whispered into my ear many good hints and excellent maxims for my behavior and for the government of my affairs."

Thanks to Amyot, Plutarch "had become a Frenchman:" Montaigne would not have been able to read him easily in Greek. Indifferent to the Reformation, which was too severe and too affirmative for him, Montaigne, "to whom Latin had been presented as his mother-tongue," rejoiced in the Renaissance without becoming a slave to it, or intoxicated with it like

Rabelais or Ronsard. "The ideas I had naturally formed for myself about man," he says, "I confirmed and fortified by the authority of others and by the sound examples of the ancients, with whom I found my judgment in conformity." Born in 1533, at the castle of Montaigne in Périgord, and carefully brought up by "the good father God had given him," Michael de Montaigne was, in his childhood, "so heavy, lazy and sleepy, that he could not be roused from sloth, even for the sake of play." He passed several years in the parliament of Bordeaux, but "he had never taken a liking to jurisprudence, though his father had steeped him in it, when quite a child, to his very lips, and he was always asking himself why common language, so easy for every other purpose, becomes obscure and unintelligible in a contract or will, which made him fancy that the men of law had muddled everything in order to render themselves necessary." He had lost the only man he had ever really loved, Stephen de la Boétie, an amiable and noble philosopher, counsellor in the parliament of Bordeaux. "If I am pressed to declare why I loved him," Montaigne used to say, "I feel that it can only be expressed by answering: because he was he, and I was I." Montaigne gave up the parliament, and travelled in Switzerland and Italy, often stopping at Paris, and gladly returning to his castle of Montaigne, where he wrote down what he had seen, "hungering for self-knowledge," inquiring, indolent, without ardor for work, an enemy of all constraint, he was at the same time frank and subtle, gentle, humane, and moderate. As an inquiring spectator, without personal ambition, he had taken for his life's motto, "Who knows? (Que sais-je?)" Amidst the wars of religion he remained without political or religious passion. "I am disgusted by novelty, whatever aspect it may assume, and with good reason," he would say, "for I have seen some very disastrous effects of it." Outside as well as within himself, Montaigne studied mankind without regard to order and without premeditated plan. "I have no drill-sergeant to arrange my pieces (of writing) save hap-hazard only," he writes; "just as my ideas present themselves, I heap them together; sometimes they come rushing in a throng, sometimes they straggle single file. I like to be seen at my natural and ordinary pace, all a-hobble though it be; I let myself go, just as it happens. The parlance I like is a simple and natural parlance, the same on paper as in the mouth, a succulent and a nervous parlance, short and compact, not so much refined and finished to a hair as impetuous and brusque, difficult rather than wearisome, devoid of affectation, irregular, disconnected and bold, not pedant-like, not preacher-like, not pleader-like." That fixity which Montaigne could not give to his irresolute and doubtful mind he stamped upon the tongue; it came out in his *Essays* supple, free and bold; he had made the first decisive step towards the formation of the language, pending the advent of Descartes and the great literature of France.

The sixteenth century began everything, attempted everything; it accomplished and finished nothing; its great men opened the road of the future to France; but they died without having brought their work well through, without foreseeing that it was going to be completed. The Reformation itself did not escape this misappreciation and discouragement of its age; and nowhere do they crop out in a more striking manner than in Montaigne. At the beginning of the sixteenth century, Rabelais is a satirist and a cynic, he is no sceptic; there is felt circulating through his book a glowing sap of confidence and hope; fifty years later, Montaigne, on the contrary, expresses, in spite of his happy nature, in vivid, picturesque, exuberant language, only the lassitude of an antiquated age. Henry IV. was still disputing his throne with the League and Spain. Several times, amidst his embarrassments and his wars, the king had manifested his desire to see Montaigne; but the latter was ill, and felt "death nipping him continually in the throat or the reins." And he died, in fact, at his own house, on the 13th of September, 1592, without having had the good fortune to see Henry IV. in peaceable possession of the kingdom which was destined to receive from him, together with stability and peace, a return of generous hope. All the writers of mark in the reign of Henry IV. bear the same imprint; they all yearn to get free from the chaos of those ideas and sentiments which the sixteenth century left still bubbling up. In literature as well as in the State, one and the same need of discipline and unity, one universal thirst for order and peace was bringing together all the intellects and all the forces which were but lately clashing against and hampering one another; in literature, as well as in the State, the impulse, everywhere great and effective, proceeded from the king, without pressure or effort: "Make known to Monsieur de Genève," said Henry IV. to one of the friends of St. Francis de Sales, "that I desire of him a work to serve as a manual for all persons of the court and the great world, without excepting kings and princes, to fit them for living Christianly each according to their condition. I want this manual to be accurate, judicious, and such as any one can make use of." St. Francis de Sales published, in 1608, the *Introduction to a Devout Life*, a delightful and charming manual of devotion, more stern and firm in spirit than in form, a true Christian regimen softened by the tact of a delicate and acute intellect, knowing the world and its ways. "The book has surpassed my hope," said Henry IV. The style is as supple, the fancy as rich, as Montaigne's; but scepticism has given place to Christianism; St. Francis de Sales does not doubt, he believes; ingenious and moderate withal, he escapes out of the controversies of the violent and the incertitudes of the sceptics. The step is firm, the march is onward towards the seventeenth century, towards the reign of order, rule and *method*. The vigorous language and the beautiful arrangement in the style of the magistrates had already prepared the way for its advent. Descartes was the first master of it and its great exponent.

Never was any mind more independent in voluntary submission to an inexorable logic. René Descartes, who was born at La Haye, near Tours, in 1596, and died at Stockholm in 1650, escaped the influence of Richelieu by the isolation to which he condemned himself as well as by the proud and somewhat uncouth independence of his character. Engaging as a volunteer, at one and twenty, in the Dutch army, he marched over Germany in the service of several princes, returned to France, where he sold his property, travelled through the whole of Italy, and ended, in 1629, by settling himself in Holland, seeking everywhere solitude and room for his thoughts. "In this great city of Amsterdam, where I am now," he wrote to Balzac, "and where there is not a soul, except myself, that does not follow some commercial pursuit, everybody is so attentive to his gains, that I might live there all my life without being noticed by anybody. I go walking every day amidst the confusion of a great people with as much freedom and quiet as you could do in your forest-alleys, and I pay no more attention to the people who pass before my eyes than I should do to the trees that are in your forests and to the animals that feed there. Even the noise of traffic does not interrupt my reveries any more than would that of some rivulet." Having devoted himself for a long time past to the study of geometry and astronomy, he composed in Holland his *Treatise on the World* (*Traité du Monde*); "I had intended to send you my *World* for your New Year's gift," he wrote to the learned Minime, Father Mersenne, who was his best friend; "but I must tell you that, having had inquiries made, lately, at Leyden and at Amsterdam, whether Galileo's system of the world was to be obtained there, word was sent me that all the copies of it had been burnt at Rome, and the author condemned to some fine, which astounded me so mightily that I almost resolved to burn all my papers, or at least not let them be seen by anybody. I confess that if the notion of the earth's motion is false, all the foundations of my philosophy are too, since it is clearly demonstrated by them. It is so connected with all parts of my treatise that I could not detach it without rendering the remainder wholly defective. But as I would not, for anything in the world, that there should proceed from me a discourse in which there was to be found the least word which might be disapproved of by the Church, so would I rather suppress it altogether than let it appear mutilated.

Descartes' independence of thought did not tend to revolt, as he had proved: in publishing his *Discourse on Method* he halted at the threshold of Christianism without laying his hand upon the sanctuary. Making a clean sweep of all he had learnt, and tearing himself free by a supreme effort from the whole tradition of humanity, he resolved "never to accept anything as true until he recognized it to be clearly so, and not to comprise amongst his opinions anything but what presented itself so clearly and distinctly to his mind that he could have no occasion to hold it in doubt." In this absolute isolation of his mind, without past and without future, Descartes, first of all assured of his own personal existence by that famous axiom, "*Cogito, ergo sum*" (*I think, therefore I am*), drew from it as a necessary consequence the fact of the separate existence of soul and of body; passing on by a sort of internal revelation which he called *innate ideas*, he came to the pinnacle of his edifice, concluding for the existence of a God from the notion of the infinite impressed on the human soul. A laborious reconstruction of a primitive and simple truth which the philosopher could not, for a single moment, have banished from his mind all the while that he was laboring painfully to demonstrate it.

By a tacit avowal of the weakness of the human mind, the speculations of Descartes stopped short at death. He had hopes, however, of retarding the moment of it. "I felt myself alive," he said, at forty years of age, "and, examining myself with as much care as if I were a rich old man, I fancied I was even farther from death than I had been in my youth." He had yielded to the entreaties of Queen Christina of Sweden, who had promised him an observatory, like that of Tycho-Brahé. He was delicate, and accustomed to follow a regimen adapted to his studies. "O flesh!" he wrote to Gassendi, whose philosophy contradicted his own: "O idea!" answered Gassendi. The climate of Stockholm was severe; Descartes caught inflammation of the lungs; he insisted upon doctoring himself, and died on the 11th of February, 1650. "He didn't want to resist death," said his friends, not admitting that their master's will could be vanquished by death itself. His influence remained for a long while supreme over his age: Bossuet and Fénelon were Cartesians. "I think, therefore I am," wrote Madame de Sévigné to her daughter: "I think of you tenderly, therefore I love you; I think only of you in that manner, therefore I love you only." Pascal alone, though adopting to a certain extent Descartes' form of reasoning, foresaw the excess to which other minds less upright and less firm would push the system of the great philosopher: "I cannot forgive Descartes," he said: "he would have liked throughout his philosophy to be able to do without God, but he could not help making Him give just a flick to set the world in motion; after that he didn't know what to do with God." A severe, but a true saying; Descartes had required everything of pure reason, he had felt a foreshadowing of the infinite and the unknown without daring to venture into them. In the name of reason, others have denied the infinite and the unknown. Pascal was wiser and bolder when, with St. Augustine, he found in reason itself a step towards faith: "Reason would never give in if she were not of opinion that there are occasions when she ought to give in."

By his philosophical method, powerful and logical, as well as by the clear, strong, and concise style he made use of to expound it, Descartes accomplished the transition from the sixteenth century to the seventeenth; he was the first of the great prose-writers of that incomparable epoch, which laid for ever the foundations of the language. At the same moment the great Corneille was rendering poetry the same service.

It had come out of the sixteenth century more disturbed and less formed then prose; Ronsard and his friends had received it, from the hands of Marot, quite young, unsophisticated and undecided; they attempted, at the first effort, to raise it to the level of the great classic models of which their minds were full. The attempt was bold, and the Pleiad did not pretend to consult the taste of the vulgar. "The obscurity of Ronsard," says M. Guizot in his *Corneille et son Temps*, "is not that of a subtle mind torturing itself to make something out of nothing, it is the obscurity of a full and a powerful mind, which is embarrassed by its own riches, and has not learnt to regulate the use of them. Furnished, by his reading of the ancients, with that which was wanting in our poetry, Ronsard thought he could perceive in his lofty and really poetical imagination what was needed to supply it; he cast his eyes in all directions with the view of enriching the domain of poetry: 'Thou wilt do well to pick dexterously,' he says in his abridgment of the art of French poetry, 'and adopt to thy work the most expressive words in the dialects of our own France; there is no need to care whether the vocables are Gascon, or Poitevin, or Norman, or Mancese, or Lyonnese, or of other districts, provided that they are good and properly express what thou wouldst say." Ronsard was too bold in extending his conquests over the classical languages; it was that exuberance of ideas, that effervescence of a genius not sufficiently master over its conceptions which brought down upon him in after-times the contempt of the writers who, in the seventeenth century, followed with more wisdom and taste the road which he had contributed to open. 'He is not,' said Balzac, 'quite a poet; he has the first beginnings and the making of a poet; we see in his works nascent and half-animated portions of a body which is in formation, but which does not care to arrive at completion.'"

This body is that of French poetry; Ronsard traced out its first lineaments, full of elevation, play of fancy, images and a poetic fire unknown before him. He was the first to comprehend the dignity which befits grand subjects, and which earned him in his day the title of *Prince of poets*. He lived in stormy times, not much adapted for poetry, and steeped in the most cruel tragedies; he felt deeply the misfortunes of his country rent by civil war, when he wrote:

"A cry of dread, a din, a thundering sound
Of men and clashing harness roars around;
Peoples 'gainst peoples furiously rage;
Cities with cities deadly battle wage;
Temples and towns—one heap of ashes lie;
Justice and equity fade out and die;
Uncheck'd the soldier's wicked will is done;
With human blood the outraged churches run;
Bedridden Age disbedded perisheth,
And over all grins the pale face of Death."

There was something pregnant, noble and brilliant about Ronsard, in spite of exaggerations of style and faults of taste; his friends and disciples imitated and carried to an extreme his defects without possessing his talent; the unruliness was such as to call for reform. Peace revived with Henry IV., and the court, henceforth in accord with the nation, resumed that empire over taste, manners and ideas, which it was destined to exercise so long and so supremely under Louis XIV. Malherbe became the poet of the court, whose business it was to please it, to adopt for it that literature which had but lately been reserved for the feasts of the learned. "He used often to say, and chiefly when he was reproached with not following the meaning of the authors he translated or paraphrased, that he did not dress his meat for cooks, as if he had meant to infer that he cared very little to be praised by the literary folks who understood the books he had translated, provided that he was by the court-folks." A complete revolution in in the opposite direction to that which Ronsard attempted appeared to have taken place, but the human mind never loses all the ground it has once won; in the verses of Malherbe, often bearing the imprint of beauties borrowed from the ancients, the language preserved, in consequence of the character given to it by Ronsard, a dignity, a richness of style, of which the times of Marot showed no conception, and it was falling, moreover, under the chastening influence of an elegant correctness. It was for the court that Malherbe made verses, striving, as he said, to *degasconnise* it, seeking there his public and the source of honor as well as profit. As passionate an admirer of Richelieu as of Henry IV., naturally devoted to the service of the order established in the State as well as in poetry, he, under the regency of Mary de' Medici, favored the taste which was beginning to show itself for intellectual things, for refined pleasures and elegant occupations. It was not around the queen that this honorable and agreeable society gathered; it was at the Hôtel Rambouillet, around Catherine de Vivonne, in Rue St. Thomas du Louvre. Literature was there represented by Malherbe and Racan, afterwards by Balzac and Voiture, Gombault and Chapelain, who constantly met there, in company with Princess de Condé and her daughter, subsequently duchess of Longueville, Mademoiselle du Vigean, Madame and Mdlle. d'Épernon, and the bishop of Luçon himself, quite young as yet, but already famous. "All the wits were received at the Hôtel Rambouillet, whatever their condition," says M. Cousin: "all that was asked of them was to have good manners; but the aristocratic tone was established there without any effort, the majority of the guests at the house being very great lords, and the mistress being at one and the same time Rambouillet and Vivonne. The wits were courted and honored, but they did not hold the dominion." At that great period which witnessed the growth of Richelieu's power and of the action he universally exercised upon French society, at the outcome from the moral licentiousness which Henry IV.'s example had encouraged in his court and after a certain roughness, the fruit of long civil wars, a lesson was taught at Madame de Rambouillet's of modesty, grace and lofty politeness, together with the art of forming good ideas and giving them good expression, sometimes with rather too much of far-fetched and affected cleverness, always in good company, and with much sweetness and self-possession on the part of the mistress of the house. In 1627, Cardinal Richelieu, having become minister, sent the Marquis of Rambouillet as ambassador to Spain. He wanted to be repaid for this favor. One of his friends went to call upon Madame de Rambouillet. At the first hint of what was expected from her: "I do not believe that there are any intrigues between Cardinal Valette and the princess," said she, "and, even if there were, I should not be the proper person for the office it is intended to put upon me. Besides, everybody is so convinced of the consideration and friendship I have for his Eminence that nobody would dare to speak ill of him in my presence; I cannot, therefore, ever have an opportunity of rendering him the services you ask of me."

The cardinal did not persist, and remained well-disposed towards Hôtel Rambouillet. Completely occupied in laying solidly the foundations of his power, in checkmating and punishing conspiracies at court and in breaking down the party of the Huguenots, he had no leisure just yet to think of literature and the literary. He had, nevertheless, in 1626, begun removing the ruins of the Sorbonne, with a view of reconstructing the buildings on a new plan and at his own expense. He wrote, in 1627, to M. Saintôt: "I thank him for the care he has taken of the Sorbonne, begging him to continue it, assuring him that, though I have many expenses on my hands, I am as desirous of continuing to build up that house as of contributing, to the best of my little ability, to pull down the fortifications of La Rochelle." The works were not completely finished at the death of the cardinal, who provided therefor by his will.

At the same time that he was repairing and enriching the Sorbonne, the cardinal was helping Guy de la Brosse, the king's physician, to create the Botanic Gardens (*Le Jardin des plantes*), he was defending the independence of the College of France against the pretensions of the University of Paris, and gave it for its Grand Almoner his brother, the archbishop of Lyons. He was preparing the foundation of the King's Press (*Imprimerie royale*), definitively created in 1640; and he gave the *Academy* or *King's College* (*collége royal*) of his town of Richelieu a regulation-code of studies which bears the imprint of his lofty and strong mind. He prescribed a deep study of the French tongue. "It often happens unfortunately that the difficulties which must be surmounted and the long time which is employed in learning the dead languages before any knowledge of the sciences can be arrived at have the effect, at the outset, of making young gentlemen disgusted and hasten to betake themselves to the exercise of arms without having been sufficiently instructed in good literature, though it is the fairest ornament of their profession. . . . It has, therefore, been thought necessary to establish a royal academy at which discipline suitable to their condition may be taught them in the French tongue, in order that they may exercise themselves therein, and that even foreigners, who are curious about it, may learn to know its riches and the graces it hath in unfolding the secrets of the highest discipline." Herein is revealed the founder of the French Academy, skilful as he was in divining the wants of his day, and always ready to profit by new means of action and to make them his own whilst doing them service.

Associations of the literary were not unknown in France; Ronsard and his friends, at first under the name of the *brigade* and then under that of the *Pleiad*, often met to read together their joint productions and to discuss literary questions; and the same thing was done, subsequently, in Malherbe's rooms. "Now let us speak at our ease," Balzac would say, when the sitting was over, "and without fear of committing solecisms." When Malherbe was dead and Balzac had retired to his country-house on the borders of the Charente, some friends, "men of letters and of merits very much above the average," says Pellisson in his *Histoire de l'Académie Française*, "finding that nothing was more inconvenient in this great city than to go often and often to call upon one another without finding anybody at home, resolved to meet one day in the week at the house of one of them. They used to assemble at M. Conrart's, who happened to be most conveniently quartered for receiving them and in the very heart of the city (Rue St. Martin). There they conversed familiarly as they would have on an ordinary visit, and upon all sorts of things, business, news and literature. If any one of the company had a work done, as often happened, he readily communicated its contents to all the others, who freely gave him their opinion of it, and their conferences were followed sometimes by a walk and sometimes by a collation which they took together. Thus they continued for three or four years, as I have heard many amongst them say; it was an extreme pleasure and an incredible gain, insomuch that, when they speak nowadays of that time and of those early days of the Academy, they speak of it as a golden age during the which, without bustle and without show, and without any other laws but those of friendship, they enjoyed all that is sweetest and most charming in the intercourse of intellects and in rational life."

Even after the intervention and regulationizing of Cardinal Richelieu, the French Academy still preserved something of that sweetness and that polished familiarity in their relations which caused the regrets of its earliest founders. [They were MM. Godeau, afterwards bishop of Grasse, Conrart and Gombault who were Huguenots, Chapelain, Giry, Habert, Abbé de Cérisy, his brother, M. de Sérizay and M. de Maleville.] The secret of the little gatherings was not so well kept but that Bois-Robert, the cardinal's accredited gossip, ever on the alert for news to divert his patron, heard of them and begged before long to be present at them. "There was no probability of his being refused, for, besides that he was on friendly terms with many of these gentlemen, the very favor he enjoyed gave him some sort of authority and added to his consequence. He was full of delight and admiration at what he saw and did not fail to give the cardinal a favorable account of the little assembly, insomuch that the cardinal, who had a mind naturally inclined towards great things and who loved the French language which he himself wrote extremely well, asked if those persons would not be disposed to form a body and assemble regularly and under public authority." Bois-Robert was entrusted with the proposal.

Great was the consternation in the little voluntary and friendly Academy. There was scarcely one of these gentlemen who did not testify displeasure: MM. de Sérizay and de

Maleville, who were attached to the households of the duke of La Rochefoucauld and Marshal Bassompierre, one in retirement on his estates and the other a prisoner in the Bastille, were for refusing and excusing themselves as best they might to the cardinal. Chapelain, who had a pension from his Eminence, represented that "in good truth he could have been well pleased to dispense with having their conferences thus bruited abroad, but in the position to which things were reduced it was not open to them to follow the more agreeable of the two courses; they had to do with a man who willed in no half-hearted way whatever he willed, and who was not accustomed to meet resistance or to suffer it with impunity; he would consider as an insult the disregard shown for his protection, and might visit his resentment upon each individual; he could, at any rate, easily prohibit their assemblies, breaking up by that means a society which every one of them desired to be eternal."

The arguments were strong, the members yielded; Bois-Robert was charged to thank his Eminence very humbly for the honor he did them, assuring him that they were all resolved to follow his wishes. "I wish to be of that assembly the protector and the father," said Richelieu, giving at once divers proofs that he took a great interest in that establishment, a fact which soon brought the Academy solicitations from those who were most intimate with the cardinal, and who, being in some sort of repute for wit, gloried in being admitted to a body which he regarded with favor.

In making of this little private gathering a great national institution, Cardinal Richelieu yielded to his natural yearning for government and dominion; he protected literature as a minister and as an admirer; the admirer's inclination was supported by the minister's influence. At the same time, and perhaps without being aware of it, he was giving French literature a centre of discipline and union whilst securing for the independence and dignity of writers a supporting-point which they had hitherto lacked. Whilst recompensing them by favors nearly always conferred in the name of the State, he was preparing for them afar off the means of withdrawing themselves from that private dependence the yoke of which they nearly always had to bear. Set free at his death from the weight of their obligations to him, they became the servants of the State; ere long the French Academy had no other protector but the king.

Order and rule everywhere accompanied Cardinal Richelieu; the Academy drew up its statutes, chose a director, a chancellor and a perpetual secretary: Conrart was the first to be called to that honor; the number of Academicians was set down at forty by letters patent from the king: "As soon as God had called us to the conduct of this realm, we had for aim, not only to apply a remedy to the disorders which the civil wars had introduced into it, but also to enrich it with all ornaments suitable for the most illustrious and the most ancient of the monarchies that are at this day in the world. Although we have labored without ceasing at the execution of this design, it hath been impossible for us hitherto to see the entire fulfilment thereof. The disturbances so often excited in the greater part of our provinces and the assistance we have been obliged to give to many of our allies have diverted us from any other thought but that of war, and have hindered us for a long while from enjoying the repose we procured for others. . . . Our very dear and very much beloved cousin, the cardinal-duke of Richelieu, who hath had the part that everybody knows in all these things, hath represented to us that one of the most glorious signs of the happiness of a kingdom was that the sciences and arts should flourish there, and that letters should be in honor there as well as arms; that, after having performed so many memorable exploits, we had nothing further to do but to add agreeable things to the necessary, and ornament to utility; and he was of opinion that we could not begin better than with the most noble of all the arts, which is eloquence; that the French tongue, which up to the present hath only too keenly felt the neglect of those who might have rendered it the most perfect of the day, is more than ever capable of becoming so, seeing the number of persons who have knowledge of the advantages it possesses; it is to establish fixed rules for it that he hath ordained an assembly whose propositions were satisfactory to him. For these reasons and in order to secure the said conferences, we will that they continue henceforth, in our good city of Paris, under the name of *French Academy*, and that letters patent be enregistered to that end by our gentry of the parliament of Paris."

The parliament was not disposed to fulfil the formality of enregistration. The cardinal had compressed it, stifled it, but he had never mastered it; the Academy was a new institution, it was regarded as his work; on that ground it inspired great distrust in the public as well as the magistrates. "The people, to whom everything that came from this minister looked suspicious, knew not whether, beneath these flowers, there were not a serpent concealed, and were apprehensive that this establishment was, at the very least, a new prop to support his domination, that it was but a batch of folks in his pay, hired to maintain all that he did and to observe the actions and sentiments of others. It went about that he cut down the scavenging expenses of Paris by eighty thousand livres in order to give them a pension of two thousand livres apiece; the vulgar were so frightened, without attempting to account for their terror, that a tradesman of Paris, who had taken a house that suited him admirably in Rue *Cinq Diamants*, where the Academy then used to meet at M. Chapelain's, broke off his bargain on no other ground but that he did not want to live in a street where a '*Cademy of Conspirators* (*une Cadémie de Manopoleurs*) met every week." The wits, like St. Évremond, in his comedy of the *Académistes*, turned into ridicule a body which, as it was said, claimed to subject the language of the public to its decisions:

"So I, with hoary head, to school
Must, like a child, go day by day;
And learn my parts of speech, poor fool,
When Death is taking speech away!"

said Maynard, who, nevertheless, was one of the forty.

The letters patent for establishment of the French Academy had been sent to the parliament in 1635; they were not enregistered until 1637 at the express instance of the cardinal, who wrote to the premier President to assure him that "the foundation of the Academy was useful and necessary to the public, and the purpose of the Academicians was quite different from what it had been possible to make people believe hitherto." The decree of verification, when it at length appeared, bore traces of the jealous prejudices of the parliament. "They of the said assembly and academy," it ran, "shall not be empowered to take cognizance of anything but the ornamentation, embellishment and augmentation of the French language, and of the books that shall be made by them and by other persons who shall desire it and want it."

The French Academy was founded; it was already commencing its Dictionary in accordance with the suggestion enunciated by Chapelain at the second meeting; the cardinal was here carrying out that great moral idea of literature which he had expressed but lately in a letter to Balzac: "The conceptions in your letters," said he, "are forcible and as far removed from ordinary imaginations as they are in conformity with the common sense of those who have superior judgment. Truth has this advantage, that it forces those who have eyes and mind sufficiently clear to discern what it is to represent it without disguise." Neither Balzac and his friends, nor the protection of Cardinal Richelieu, sufficed as yet to give lustre to the Academy; great minds and great writers alone could make the glory of their society. The principle of the association of men of letters was, however, established: men of the world, friendly to literature, were already preparing to mingle with them; the literary, but lately servitors of the great, had henceforth at their disposal a privilege envied and sought after by courtiers; their independence grew by it and their dignity gained by it. The French Academy became an institution and took its place amongst the glories of France. It had this piece of good fortune, that Cardinal Richelieu died without being able to carry out the project he had conceived. He had intended to open on the site of the horse-market, near Porte St. Honoré and behind the Palais-Cardinal, "a great *Place* which he would have called *Ducale* in imitation of the *Royale*, which is at the other end of the city," says Pellisson; he had placed in the hands of M. de la Mesnardière a memorandum drawn up by himself for the plan of a college "which he was meditating for all the noble sciences and in which he designed to employ all that was most telling for the cause of literature in Europe. He had an idea of making the members of the Academy directors and as it were arbiters of this great establishment, and aspired, with a feeling worthy of the immortality with which he was so much in love, to set up the French Academy there in the most distinguished position in the world, and to offer an honorable and pleasant repose to all persons of that class who had deserved it by their labors." It was a noble and a liberal idea, worthy of the great mind which had conceived it; but it would have stifled the fertile germ of independence and liberty which he had unconsciously buried in the womb of the French Academy. Pensioned and barracked, the Academicians would have remained men of letters, shut off from society and the world. The Academy grew up alone, favored indeed but never reduced to servitude; it alone has withstood the cruel shocks which have for so long a time agitated France; in a country where nothing lasts, it has lasted, with its traditions, its primitive statutes, its reminiscences, its respect for the past. It has preserved its courteous and modest dignity, its habits of polite neutrality, the suavity and equality of the relations between its members. It was said just now that Richelieu's work no longer existed save in history, and that revolutions have left him nothing but his glory; but that was a mistake: the French Academy is still standing, stronger and freer than at its birth, and it was founded by Richelieu and has never forgotten him.

Amongst the earliest members of the Academy the cardinal had placed his most habitual and most intimate literary servants, Bois-Robert, Desmarets, Colletet, all writers for the theatre, employed by Richelieu in his own dramatic attempts. Theatrical representations were the only pleasure the minister enjoyed, in accord with the public of his day. He had everywhere encouraged this taste, supporting with marked favor Hardy and the *Théâtre parisien.* With his mind constantly exercised by the wants of the government, he soon sought in the theatre a means of acting upon the masses. He had already foreseen the power of the press; he had laid hands on Doctor Renaudot's *Gazette de France;* King Louis XIII. often wrote articles in it; the manuscript exists in the National Library, with some corrections which appear to be Richelieu's. As for the theatre, the cardinal aspired to try his own hand at the work; his literary labors were nearly all political pieces; his tragedy of *Mirame*, to which he attached so much value, and which he had represented at such great expense for the opening of his theatre in the Palais-Cardinal, is nothing but one continual allusion, often bold even to insolence, to Buckingham's feelings towards Anne of Austria. The comedy, in heroic style, of *Europe*, which appeared in the name of Desmarets after the cardinal's death, is a political allegory touching the condition of the world. *Francion* and *Ibère* contend together for the favors of Europe, not without, at the same time, paying court to the Princess Austrasia (Lorraine). All the cardinal's foreign policy, his alliances with Protestants, are there described in verses which do not lack a certain force: *Germanique* (the emperor) pleads the cause of Ibère with Europe:

"No longer can he brook to gaze on such as these,
Destroyers of the shrines, foes of the Deities.
By Francion evoked from out the Frozen Main,*
That he might cope with us and equal war maintain.

* The Swedes.

EUROPE.

Oh! call not by those names th' indomitable race,
Who 'midst my champions hold honorable place.
Unlike to us, they own no shrine, no sacrifice;
But still, unlike Ibère, they use no artifice;
About the Gods they speak their mind as seemeth best,
Whilst he, with pious air, still keepeth me opprest:
Through them I hold mine own, from harm and insult free,
Their errors I deplore, their valor pleases me.
What was that noble king,* that puissant conqueror,
Who through thy regions, like a mighty torrent, tore?
Who march'd with giant strides along the path of fame,
And, in the hour of death, left vict'ry with his name?
What are those gallant chiefs, who from his ashes rose,
Whom still, methinks, his shade assists against their foes?
What was that Saxon heart,† so full of noble rage,
He, whom thine own decrees drove from his heritage?
Who, with his gallant few, full many a deed hath done
Within thine own domains, and many a laurel won?
Who, wasting not his strength in strife with granite walls,
Routs thee in open field, and lo! the fortress falls?
Who, taking just revenge for loss of all his own,
Compress'd thy boundaries, and cut thy frontiers down.
How many virtues in that prince's ‡ heart reside
Who leads yon free-set § people's armies in their pride,
People who boldly spurn'd Ibère and all his laws,
Bravely shook off his yoke and bravely left his cause?
Francion, without such aid, thou say'st would helpless be;
What were Ibère without thy provinces and thee?

GERMANIQUE.

But I am of his blood:—own self-same Deities.

EUROPE.

All they are of my blood:—gaze on the self-same skies;
Do all your hosts adore the Deities we own?
Nay from your very midst come errors widely sown.
Ibère for chief support on erring men relies:
Yet, what himself may do, to others he denies.
What! Francion favor error! This is idle prate:
He who from irreligion thoroughly purged the State!
Who brought the worship back to altars in decay;
Who built the temples up that in their ashes lay;
True son of them, who, spite of all thy fathers' feats,
Replaced my reverend priests upon their holy seats!
'Twixt Francion and Ibère this difference remains:
One sets them in their seats, and one in iron chains."

Already, in *Mirame*, Richelieu had celebrated the fall of Rochelle and of the Huguenot party, bringing upon the scene the king of Bithynia who is taking arms

"To tame a rebel slave,
Perch'd proudly on his rock wash'd by the ocean-wave."

---

* Gustavus Adolphus.
† Bernard of Saxe-Weimar.
‡ Prince of Orange.
§ The Hollanders.

As epigraph to *Europe* there were these lines:

"All friends of France to this my work will friendly be;
And all unfriends of her will say the author ill;
Yet shall I be content, say, reader, what you will;
The joy of some, the rage of others, pleases me."

The enemies of France did not wait for the comedy, in heroic style, of *Europe* in order to frequently say ill of Cardinal Richelieu.

Occupied as he was in governing the affairs of France and of Europe otherwise than in verse, the cardinal chose out work-fellows; there were five of them, to whom he gave his ideas and the plan of his piece; he entrusted to each the duty of writing an act and "by this means finished a comedy a month," says Pellisson. Thus was composed the comedy of the *Tuileries* and the *Aveugle de Smyrne*, which were printed in 1638; Richelieu had likewise taken part in the composition of the *Visionnaires* of Desmarets, and supported in a rather remarkable scene the rule of the three unities against its detractors. A new comedy, the *Grande Pastorale*, was in hand. "When he was purposing to publish it," says the History of the Academy, "he desired M. Chapelain to look over it and make careful observations upon it. These observations were brought to him by M. de Bois-Robert and, though they were written with much discretion and respect, they shocked and nettled him to such a degree either by their number or by the consciousness they caused him of his faults that, without reading them through, he tore them up. But on the following night, when he was in bed and all his household asleep, having thought over the anger he had shown, he did a thing incomparably more estimable than the best comedy in the world, that is to say, he listened to reason, for he gave orders to collect and glue together the pieces of that torn paper, and, having read it from one end to the other and given great thought to it, he sent and awakened M. de Bois-Robert to tell him that he saw quite well that the Gentlemen of the Academy were better informed about such matters than he, and that there must be nothing more said about that paper and print."

The cardinal ended by permitting the liberties taken in literary matters by Chapelain and even Colletet. His courtiers were complimenting him about some success or other obtained by the king's arms, saying that nothing could withstand his Eminence: "You are mistaken," he answered, laughing; "and I find even in Paris persons who withstand me. There's Colletet, who, after having fought with me yesterday over a word, does not give in yet; look at this long letter that he has just written me!" He counted, at any rate, in the number of his five work-fellows one mind too independent to be subservient for long to the ideas and wishes of another, though it were Cardinal Richelieu and the premier minister. In conjunction with Colletet, Bois-Robert, De l'Etoile and Rotrou, Peter Corneille worked at his Eminence's tragedies and comedies. He handled according to his fancy the act entrusted to him, with so much freedom that the cardinal was shocked and said that he lacked, in his opinion, "the follower-spirit" (*l'esprit de suite*). Corneille did not appeal from this judgment; he quietly took the road to Rouen, leaving henceforth to his four work-fellows the glory of putting into form the ideas of the all-powerful minister; he worked alone, for his own hand, for the glory of France and of the human mind.

Peter Corneille, born at Rouen on the 6th of June, 1606, in a family of lawyers, had been destined for the bar from his infancy; he was a briefless barrister; his father had purchased him two government posts, but his heart was otherwise set than "on jurisprudence"; in 1635, when he quietly renounced the honor of writing for the cardinal, Corneille had already had several comedies played. He himself said of the first, *Mélite*, which he wrote at three and twenty: "It was my first attempt, and it has no pretence of being according to the rules, for I did not know then that there were any. I had for guide nothing but a little common sense together with the models of the late Hardy, whose vein was rather fertile than polished." "The comedies of Corneille had met with success; praised as he was by his competitors in the career of the theatre, he was as yet in their eyes but one of the supports of that literary glory which was common to them all. Tranquil in their possession of bad taste, they were far from foreseeing the revolution which was about to overthrow its sway and their own" [*Corneille et son temps*, by M. Guizot].

Corneille made his first appearance in tragedy, in 1633, with a *Médée*. "Here are verses which proclaim Corneille," said Voltaire:

> "After so many boons, to leave me can he bear?
> After so many sins, to leave me can he dare?"

They proclaimed tragedy; it had appeared at last to Corneille: its features, roughly sketched, were nevertheless recognizable. He was already studying Spanish with an old friend of his family, and was working at the *Cid*, when he brought out his *Illusion comique*, a mediocre piece, Corneille's last sacrifice to the taste of his day. Towards the end of the year 1636, the *Cid* was played for the first time at Paris. There was a burst of enthusiasm forthwith. "I wish you were here," wrote the celebrated comedian Mondory to Balzac, on the 18th of January, 1637, "to enjoy amongst other pleasures that of the beautiful comedies that are being played and especially a *Cid* who has charmed all Paris. So beautiful is he that he has smitten with love all the most virtuous ladies, whose passion has many times blazed out in the public theatre. Seated in a body on the benches of the boxes have been seen those who are commonly seen only in gilded chamber and on the seat with the fleurs-de-lis. So great has been the throng at our doors and our place has turned out so small, that the corners of the theatre which served at other times as niches for the page-boys have been given as a favor to blue ribands, and the scene has been embellished, ordinarily, with the crosses of knights of the order." "It is difficult," says Pellisson, "to imagine with what approbation this piece was received by court and people." It was impossible to tire of seeing it, nothing else was talked of in company; everybody knew some portion by heart; it was taught to children, and in many parts of France it had passed into a proverb to say: *Beautiful as the Cid.* Criticism itself was silenced for a while; carried along in the general whirl, bewildered by its success, the rivals of Corneille appeared to join the throng of his admirers; but they soon recovered their breath, and their first sign of life was an effort of resistance to the torrent which threatened to carry them away; with the exception of Rotrou, who was worthy to comprehend and enjoy Corneille, the revolt was unanimous. The malcontents and the envious had found in Richelieu an eager and a powerful auxiliary.

Many attempts have been made to fathom the causes of the cardinal's animosity to the *Cid.* It was a Spanish piece, and represented in a favorable light the traditional enemies of France and of Richelieu; it was all in honor of the duel, which the cardinal had prosecuted with such rigorous justice; it depicted a king simple, patriarchal, genial in the exercise of his power, contrary to all the views cherished by the minister touching royal majesty; all these reasons might have contributed to his wrath, but there was something more personal and petty in its bitterness. In tacit disdain for the work that had been entrusted to him, Corneille had abandoned Richelieu's pieces; he had retired to Rouen; far away from the court, he had only his successes to set against the perfidious insinuations of his rivals. The triumph of the *Cid* seemed to the resentful spirit of a neglected and irritated patron a sort of insult. Therewith was mingled a certain shade of author's jealousy. Richelieu saw in the fame of Corneille the success of a rebel. Egged on by base and malicious influences, he attempted to crush him as he had crushed the House of Austria and the Huguenots.

The cabal of bad taste enlisted to a man in this new war. Scudéry was standard-bearer; astounded that "such fantastic beauties should have seduced knowledge as well as ignorance and the court as well as the cit, and conjuring decent folks to suspend judgment for a while and not condemn without a hearing, *Sophonisbe*, *César*, *Cléopâtre*, *Hercule*, *Marianne*, *Cléomédon*, and so many other illustrious heroes who had charmed them on the stage." Corneille might have been satisfied; his adversaries themselves recognized his great popularity and success.

A singular mixture of haughtiness and timidity, of vigorous imagination and simplicity of judgment! It was by his triumphs that Corneille had become informed of his talents; but, when once aware, he had accepted the conviction thereof as that of those truths which one does not arrive at by one's self, absolutely, without explanation, without modification.

"I know my worth, and well believe men's rede of it;
I have no need of leagues, to make myself admired;
Few voices may be raised for me, but none is hired;
To swell th' applause, my just ambition seeks no *claque*,
Nor out of holes and corners hunts the hireling pack,
Upon the boards, quite self-supported, mount my plays,
And every one is free to censure or to praise;
There, though no friends expound their views or preach my cause,
It hath been many a time my lot to win applause;
There, pleased with the success by modest merit won,
With brilliant critics' laws I seek to dazzle none;
To court and people both I give the same delight,
Mine only partisans the verses that I write;
To them alone I owe the credit of my pen,
To my own self alone the fame I win of men;
And if, when rivals meet, I claim equality,
Methinks I do no wrong to whosoe'er it be."

"Let him rise on the wings of composition," said La Bruyère, "and he is not below Augustus, Pompey, Nicodemus, Sertorius; he is a king and a great king; he is a politician, he is a philosopher." M dest and bashful in what concerns himself, when it has nothing to do with his works and his talents, Corneille, who does not disdain to receive a pension from Cardinal Richelieu or, in writing to Scudéry, to call him "your master and mine," becomes quite another creature when he defends his genius:

> "Leaving full oft the earth, soon as he leaves the goal,
> With lofty flight he soars into the upper air,
> Looks down on envious men and smiles at their despair."

The contest was becoming fierce and bitter; much was written for and against the *Cid;* the public remained faithful to it; the cardinal determined to submit it to the judgment of the Academy, thus exacting from that body an act of complaisance towards himself as well as an act of independence and authority in the teeth of predominant opinion. At his instigation, Scudéry wrote to the Academy to make them the judges in the dispute. "The cardinal's desire was plain to see," says Pellisson; "but the most judicious amongst that body testified a great deal of repugnance to this design. They said that the Academy, which was only in its cradle, ought not to incur odium by a judgment which might perhaps displease both parties, and which could not fail to cause umbrage to one at least, that is to say, to a great part of France; that they were scarcely tolerated from the mere fancy which prevailed that they pretended to some authority over the French tongue; what would be the case if they proved to have exercised it in respect of a work which had pleased the majority and won the approbation of the people? M. Corneille did not ask for this judgment, and, by the statutes of the Academy, they could only sit in judgment upon a work with the consent and at the entreaty of the author." Corneille did not facilitate the task of the Academicians: he excused himself modestly, protesting that such occupation was not worthy of such a body, that a mere piece (*un libelle*) did not deserve their judgment. . . . "At length, under pressure from M. de Bois-Robert, who gave him pretty plainly to understand what was his master's desire, this answer slipped from him: 'The gentlemen of the Academy can do as they please: since you write me word that My Lord would like to see their judgment and it would divert his Eminence, I have nothing further to say.'"

These expressions were taken as a formal consent, and as

the Academy still excused themselves: "Let those gentlemen know," said the cardinal, at last, "that I desire it, and that I shall love them as they love me."

There was nothing for it but to obey. Whilst Bois-Robert was amusing his master by representing before him a parody of the *Cid*, played by his lacqueys and scullions, the Academy was at work drawing up their *sentiments* respecting the *Cid*. Thrice submitted to the cardinal, who thrice sent it back with some strong remarks appended, the judgment of the Academicians did not succeed in satisfying the minister. "What was wanted was the complaisance of submission, what was obtained was only that of gratitude." "I know quite well," says Pellisson, "that His eminence would have wished to have the *Cid* more roughly handled, if he had not been adroitly made to understand that a judge must not speak like a party to a suit, and that, in proportion as he showed passion, he would lose authority."

Balzac, still in retirement at his country-place, made no mistake as to the state of mind either in the Academy or in the world when he wrote to Scudéry, who had sent him his *Observations sur le Cid:* "Reflect, sir, that all France takes sides with M. Corneille, and that there is not one perhaps of the judges with whom it is rumored that you have come to an agreement who has not praised that which you desire him to condemn; so that, though your arguments were incontrovertible and your adversary should acquiesce therein, he would still have the wherewith to give himself glorious consolation for the loss of his case, and be able to tell you that it is something more to have delighted a whole kingdom than to have written a piece according to regulation. This being so, I doubt not that the gentlemen of the Academy will find themselves much hampered in delivering a judgment on your case, and that, on the one hand, your arguments will stagger them, whilst, on the other, the public approbation will keep them in check. You have the best of it in the closet; he has the advantage on the stage. If the *Cid* be guilty, it is of a crime which has met with reward; if he be punished, it will be after having triumphed; if Plato must banish him from his republic, he must crown him with flowers whilst banishing him and not treat him worse than he formerly treated Homer."

The *Sentiments de l'Académie* at last saw the light in the month of December, 1637, and, as Chapelain had foreseen, they did not completely satisfy either the cardinal or Scudéry. in spite of the thanks which the latter considered himself bound to express to that body, or Corneille, who testified bitter displeasure: "The Academy proceeds against me with so much violence and employs so supreme an authority to close my mouth, that all the satisfaction I have is to think that this famous production, at which so many fine intellects have been working for six months, may no doubt be esteemed the opinion of the French Academy, but will probably not be the opinion of the rest of Paris. I wrote the *Cid* for my diversion and that of decent folks who like comedy. All the favor that the opinion of the Academy can hope for is to make as much way; at any rate, I have had my account settled before them, and I am not at all sure that they can wait for theirs."

Corneille did not care to carry his resentment higher than the Academy. At the end of December, 1637, when writing to Bois-Robert a letter of thanks for getting him his pension, which he calls "the liberalities of my Lord," he adds: "As you advise me not to reply to the *Sentiments de l'Académie*, seeing what personages are concerned therein, there is no need of interpreters to understand that; I am somewhat more of this world than Heliodorus was, who preferred to lose his bishopric rather than his book, and I prefer my master's good graces to all the reputations on earth. I shall be mum, then, not from disdain, but from respect."

The great Corneille made no further defence; he had become a servitor again; but the public, less docile, persisted in their opinion:

"In vain against the Cid a minister makes league;
All Paris gazing on Chimène, thinks with Rodrigue;
In vain to censure her th' Academy aspires;
The stubborn populace revolts and still admires;"

said Boileau, subsequently.

The dispute was ended; and, in spite of the judgment of the Academy, the cardinal did not come out of it victorious; his anger, however, had ceased: the duchess of Aiguillon, his niece, accepted the dedication of the *Cid;* when *Horace* appeared, in 1639, the dedicatory epistle addressed to the cardinal proved that Corneille read his works to him beforehand; the cabal appeared for a while on the point of making head again: "Horace, condemned by the decemvirs, was acquitted by the people," said Corneille. The same year *Cinna* came to give the finishing touch to the reputation of the great poet:

"To the persecuted *Cid* the *Cinna* owed its birth."

Corneille had withdrawn to the obscurity which suited the

simplicity of his habits; the cardinal, it was said, had helped him to get married; he had no longer to defend his works, their fame was amply sufficient. "Henceforth, Corneille walks freely by himself and in the strength of his own powers; the circle of his ideas grows larger, his style grows loftier and stronger, together with his thoughts, and purer, perhaps, without his dreaming of it; a more correct, a more precise expression comes to him, evoked by greater clearness in idea, greater fixity of sentiment; genius, with the mastery of means, seeks new outlets. Corneille writes *Polyeucte*" [*Corneille et son temps*, by M. Guizot].

It was a second revolution accomplished for the upsetting of received ideas, at a time when paganism was to such an extent master of the theatre that in the midst of an allegory of the seventeenth century, alluding to Gustavus Adolphus and the wars of religion, Richelieu and Desmarets, in the heroic comedy of *Europe*, dared not mention the name of God save in the plural. Corneille read his piece at the Hôtel Rambouillet. "It was applauded to the extent demanded by propriety and the reputation already achieved by the author," says Fontenelle; "but, some days afterwards, M. de Voiture went to call upon M. Corneille and took a very delicate way of telling him that *Polyeucte* had not been so successful as he supposed, that the Christianism had been extremely displeasing." "The story is," adds Voltaire, "that all the Hôtel Rambouillet and especially the bishop of Vence, Godeau condemned the attempt of *Polyeucte* to overthrow idols." Corneille in alarm, would have withdrawn the piece from the hands of the comedians, who were learning it, and he only left it on the assurance of one of the comedians who did not play in it because he was too bad an actor. Posterity has justified the poor comedian against the Hôtel Rambouillet; amongst so many of Corneille's master-pieces it has ever given a place apart to *Polyeucte;* neither the *Saint-Genest* of Rotrou, nor the *Zaïre* of Voltaire, in spite of their various beauties, have dethroned *Polyeucte;* in fame as well as in date it remains the first of the few pieces in which Christianism appeared, to gain applause, upon the French classic stage.

Richelieu was no longer there to lay his commands upon the court and upon the world: he was dead, without having been forgiven by Corneille:—

> "Of our great cardinal let men speak as they will,
> By me, in prose or verse, they shall not be withstood:
> He did me too much good for me to say him ill,
> He did me too much ill for me to say him good!"

The great literary movement of the seventeenth century had begun; it had no longer any need of a protector; it was destined to grow up alone during twenty years, amidst troubles at home and wars abroad, to flourish all at once, with incomparable splendor, under the reign and around the throne of Louis XIV. Cardinal Richelieu, however, had the honor of protecting its birth; he had taken personal pleasure in it; he had comprehended its importance and beauty; he had desired to serve it whilst taking the direction of it. Let us end, as we began, with the judgment of La Bruyère: "Compare yourselves, if you dare, with the great Richelieu, you men devoted to fortune, you, who say that you know nothing, that you have read nothing, that you will read nothing. Learn that Cardinal Richelieu did know, did read; I say not that he had no estrangement from men of letters, but that he loved them, caressed them, favored them, that he contrived privileges for them, that he appointed pensions for them, that he united them in a celebrated body, and that he made of them the French Academy."

The Academy, the Sorbonne, the Botanic Gardens (Jardin des Plantes), the King's Press have endured; the theatre has grown and been enriched by many master-pieces, the press has become the most dreaded of powers; all the new forces that Richelieu created or foresaw have become developed without him, frequently in opposition to him and to the work of his whole life; his name has remained connected with the commencement of all these wonders, beneficial or disastrous, which he had grasped and presaged, in a future happily concealed from his ken.

CHAPTER XLIII.

LOUIS XIV., THE FRONDE AND THE GOVERNMENT OF CARDINAL MAZARIN (1643—1661).

Louis XIII. had never felt confidence in the queen his wife; and Cardinal Richelieu had fostered that sentiment which promoted his views. When M. de Chavigny came, on Anne of Austria's behalf, to assure the dying king that she had never had any part in the conspiracy of Chalais, or dreamt of espousing Monsieur in case she was left a widow, Louis XIII. answered, "Considering the state I am in, I am bound to forgive her, but not to believe her." He did not believe her, he never had believed her, and his declaration touching the Regency was entirely directed towards counteracting by anticipation the power entrusted to his wife and his brother. The queen's regency and the duke of Orleans' lieutenant-generalship were in some sort subordinated to a council composed of the prince of Condé, Cardinal Mazarin, Chancellor Séguier, Superintendent Bouthillier, and Secretary of State Chavigny, "with a prohibition against introducing any change therein, for any cause or on any occasion whatsoever." The queen and the duke of Orleans had signed and sworn the declaration.

King Louis XIII. was not yet in his grave when his last wishes were violated; before his death the queen had made terms with the ministers; the course to be followed had been decided. On the 18th of May, 1643, the queen, having brought back the little king to Paris, conducted him in great state to the parliament of Paris to hold his bed of justice there. The boy sat down and said with a good grace that he had come to the parliament to testify his good will to it, and that his chancellor would say the rest. The duke of Orleans then addressed the queen: "The honor of the regency is the due altogether of your Majesty," said he, "not only in your capacity of mother, but also for your merits and virtues; the regency having been confided to you by the deceased king and by the consent of all the grandees of the realm, I desire no other part in affairs than that which it may please your Majesty to give me, and I do not claim to take any advantage from the special clauses contained in the declaration." The prince of Condé said much the same thing, but with less earnestness, and on the evening of the same day the queen regent, having sole charge of the administration of affairs, and modifying the council at her pleasure, announced to the astounded court that she should retain by her Cardinal Mazarin. Not a word had been said about him at the parliament, the courtiers believed that he was on the point of leaving France; but the able Italian, attractive as he was subtle, had already found a way to please the queen. She retained as chief of her council the heir to the traditions of Richelieu, and deceived the hopes of the party of Importants, those meddlers of the court at whose head marched the duke of Beaufort, all puffed up with the confidence lately shown to him by her Majesty. Potier, bishop of Beauvais, the queen's confidant during her troubles, "expected to be all-powerful in the State; he sought out the duke of Orleans and the prince of Condé, promising them governorship of places and, generally, anything they might desire. He thought he could set the affairs of State going as easily as he could his parish-priests; but the poor prelate came down from his high hopes when he saw that the cardinal was advancing more and more in the queen's confidence, and that, for him, too much was already thought to have been done in according him admittance to the council, whilst flattering him with a hope of the purple" [*Mémoires de Brienne*, ii. 37]. Cardinal Mazarin soon sent him off to his diocese. Continuing to humor all parties, and displaying foresight and prudence, the new minister was even now master. Louis XIII., without any personal liking, had been faithful to Richelieu to the death; with different feelings, Anne of Austria was to testify the same constancy toward Mazarin.

A stroke of fortune came at the very first to strengthen the regent's position. Since the death of Cardinal Richelieu, the Spaniards, but recently overwhelmed at the close of 1642, had recovered courage and boldness; new counsels prevailed at the court of Philip IV. who had dismissed Olivarez; the House of Austria vigorously resumed the offensive; at the moment of Louis XIII.'s death, Don Francisco de Mello, governor of the Low Countries, had just invaded French territory by way of the Ardennes, and laid siege to Rocroi, on the 12th of May. The French army was commanded by the young duke of Enghien, the prince of Condé's son, scarcely twenty-two years old; Louis XIII. had given him as his lieutenant and director the veteran Marshal de l'Hôpital; and the latter feared to give battle. The duke of Enghien, who "was dying with impatience to enter the enemy's country, resolved to accomplish by address what he could not carry by authority. He opened his heart to Gassion alone. As he was a man who saw nothing but what was easy even in the most dangerous deeds, he had very soon brought matters to the point that the prince desired. Marshal de l'Hôpital found himself imperceptibly so near the Spaniards that it was impossible for him any longer to hinder an engagement" [*Relation de M. de la Moussaye*]. The army was in front of Rocroi, and out of the dangerous defile which led to the place, without any idea on the part of the marshal and the army that Louis XIII. was dead. The duke of Enghien, who had received the news, had kept it secret. He had merely said in the tone of a master "that he meant to fight and would answer for the issue. His orders given, he passed along the ranks of his army with an air which communicated to it the same impatience that he himself felt to see the night over in order to begin the battle. He passed the whole of it at the camp fire of the officers of Picardy." In the morning "it was necessary to rouse from deep slumber this second Alexander. Mark him as he flies to victory or death! As soon as he had kindled from rank to rank the ardor with which he was animated, he was seen, in almost the same moment, driving in the enemy's right, supporting ours that wavered, rallying the half-beaten French, putting to flight the victorious Spaniards, striking terror everywhere, and dumbfounding with his flashing looks those who escaped from his blows. There remained that dread infantry of the army of Spain, whose huge battalions, in close order, like so many towers, but towers that could repair their breaches, remained unshaken amidst all the rest of the rout, and delivered their fire on all sides. Thrice the young conqueror tried to break these fearless warriors; thrice he was driven back by the valiant count of Fuentès, who was seen carried about in his chair, and, in spite of his infirmities, showing that a warrior's soul is mistress of the body it animates. But yield they must: in vain through the woods, with his cavalry all fresh, does Beck rush down to fall upon our exhausted men: the prince has been beforehand with him; the broken battalions cry for quarter, but the victory is to be more terrible than the fight for the duke of Enghien. Whilst with easy mien he advances to receive the parole of these brave fellows, they, watchful still, apprehend the surprise of a fresh attack; their terrible volley drives our men mad; there is nothing to be seen but slaughter; the soldier is drunk with blood, till that great prince, who could not bear to see such lions butchered like so many sheep, calmed excited passions and to the pleasure of victory joined that of mercy. He would willingly have saved the life of the brave count of Fuentès, but found him lying amidst thousands of the dead whose loss is still felt by Spain. The prince bends the knee and, on the field of battle, renders thanks to the God of armies for the victory He hath given him. Then were there rejoicings over Rocroi delivered, the threats of a dread enemy converted to their shame, the regency strengthened, France at rest, and a reign, which was to be so noble, commenced with such happy augury" [Bossuet, *Oraison funèbre de Louis de*

Bourbon, prince de Condé]. *Victory or death*, below the cross of Burgundy, was borne upon most of the standards taken from the imperialists; and "indeed," says the *Gazette de France*, "the most part were found dead in the ranks where they had been posted. Which was nobly brought home by one of the prisoners to our captains when, being asked how many there had been of them, he replied, *Count the dead.*" Condé was worthy to fight such enemies, and Bossuet to recount their defeat. '"The prince was a born captain," said Cardinal de Retz. And all France said so with him, on hearing of the victory of Rocroi.

The delight was all the keener in the queen's circle, because the house of Condé openly supported Cardinal Mazarin, bitterly attacked as he was by the Importants, who accused him of reviving the tyranny of Richelieu.

A ditty on the subject was current in the streets of Paris:—

" He is not dead, he is but changed of age,
The cardinal, at whom men gird with rage,
But all his household make thereat great cheer;
It pleaseth not full many a chevalier;
They fain had brought him to the lowest stage.
Beneath his wing came all his lineage,
By the same art whereof he made usage:
And, by my faith, 'tis still their day, I fear.
He is not dead.

" Hush! we are mum, because we dread the cage;
For he's at court—this eminent personage,
There to remain of years to come a score.
Ask those Importants, would you fain know more,
And they will say in dolorous language:
'He is not dead.' "

And indeed, on pretext offered by a feminine quarrel between the young duchess of Longueville, daughter of the prince of Condé, and the duchess of Montbazon, the duke of Beaufort and some of his friends resolved to assassinate the cardinal. The attempt was a failure, but the duke of Beaufort, who was arrested on the 2nd of September, was taken to the castle of Vincennes. Madame de Chevreuse, recently returned to court where she would fain have exacted from the queen the reward for her services and her past sufferings, was sent into exile as well as the duke of Vendôme. Madame d'Hautefort, but lately summoned by Anne of Austria to be near her, was soon involved in the same disgrace. Proud and compassionate, without any liking for Mazarin, she was daring enough, during a trip to Vincennes, to ask pardon for the duke of Beaufort,

"The queen made no answer, and, the collation being served, Madame d'Hautefort, whose heart was full, ate nothing; when she was asked why, she declared that she could not enjoy anything in such close proximity to that poor boy." The queen could not put up with reproaches; and she behaved with extreme coldness to Madame d'Hautefort. One day, at bedtime, her ill temper showed itself so plainly that the old favorite could no longer be in doubt about the queen's sentiments. As she softly closed the curtains, "I do assure you, Madame," she said, "that if I had served God with as much attachment and devotion as I have your Majesty all my life, I should be a great saint." And, raising her eyes to the crucifix, she added, "Thou knowest, Lord, what I have done for her." The queen let her go—to the convent where Mademoiselle de la Fayette had taken refuge ten years before. Madame d'Hautefort left it ere long to become the wife of Marshal Schomberg, but the party of the Importants was dead, and the power of Cardinal Mazarin seemed to be firmly established. "It was not the thing just then for any decent man to be on bad terms with the court," says Cardinal de Retz.

Negotiations for a general peace, the preliminaries whereof had been signed by King Louis XIII. in 1641, had been going on since 1644 at Münster and at Osnabrück, without having produced any result; the duke of Enghien, who became prince of Condé in 1646, was keeping up the war in Flanders and Germany, with the co-operation of Viscount Turenne, younger brother of the duke of Bouillon, and, since Rocroi, a marshal of France. The capture of Thionville and of Dunkerque, the victories of Friburg and Nördlingen, the skilful opening effected in Germany as far as Augsburg by the French and the Swedes, had raised so high the reputation of the two generals, that the prince of Condé, who was haughty and ambitious, began to cause great umbrage to Mazarin. Fear of having him unoccupied deterred the cardinal from peace and made all the harder the conditions he presumed to impose upon the Spaniards. Meanwhile the United Provinces, weary of a war which fettered their commerce, and skilfully courted by their old masters, had just concluded a private treaty with Spain; the emperor was trying, but to no purpose, to detach the Swedes likewise from the French alliance, when the victory of Lens, gained on the 20th of August, 1648, over Archduke Leopold and General Beck, came to throw into the balance the weight of a success as splendid as it was unexpected; one more campaign, and Turenne might be threatening Vienna whilst Condé entered Brussels; the emperor saw there was no help for it and bent his head. The House of Austria split in two; Spain still refused to treat with France, but the whole of Germany clamored for peace; the conditions of it were at last drawn up at Münster by MM. Servien and de Lionne; M. d'Avaux, the most able diplomatist that France possessed, had been recalled to Paris at the beginning of the year. On the 24th of October, 1648, after four years of negotiation, France at last had secured to her Elsass and the three bishoprics of Metz, Toul, and Verdun; Sweden gained Western Pomerania, including Stettin, the isle of Rugen, the three mouths of the Oder and the bishoprics of Bremen and Werden, thus becoming a German power: as for Germany, she had won liberty of conscience and political liberty; the rights of the Lutheran or reformed Protestants were equalized with those of Catholics; henceforth the consent of a free assembly of all the Estates of the empire was necessary to make laws, raise soldiers, impose taxes, and decide peace or war. The peace of Westphalia put an end at one and the same time to the Thirty Years' War and to the supremacy of the House of Austria in Germany.

So much glory and so many military or diplomatic successes cost dear; France was crushed by imposts, and the finances were discovered to be in utter disorder; the superintendent, D'Emery, an able and experienced man, was so justly discredited that his measures were, as a foregone conclusion, unpopular; an edict laying octroi or tariff on the entry of provisions into the city of Paris irritated the burgesses, and parliament refused to enregister it. For some time past the parliament, which had been kept down by the iron hand of Richelieu, had perceived that it had to do with nothing more than an able man and not a master; it began to hold up its head again; a union was proposed between the four sovereign courts of Paris, to wit, the parliament, the grand council, the chamber of exchequer, and the court of aids or indirect taxes; the queen quashed the deed of union; the magistrates set her at naught; the queen yielded, authorizing the delegates to deliberate in the chamber of St. Louis at the Palace of Justice; the pretensions of the parliament were exorbitant and aimed at nothing short of resuming, in the affairs of the State, the position from which Richelieu had deposed it; the concessions which Cardinal Mazarin with difficulty wrung from the queen augmented the parliament's demands. Anne of Austria was beginning to lose patience, when the news of the victory of Lens restored courage to the court. "Parliament will be very sorry," said the little king, on hearing of the prince of Condé's success. The grave assemblage, on the 26th of August, was issuing from Notre Dame, where a *Te Deum* had just been sung, when Councillor Broussel and President Blancmesnil were arrested in their houses and taken one to St. Germain and the other to Vincennes. This was a familiar proceeding on the part of royal authority in its disagreements with the parliament. Anne of Austria herself had practised it four years before.

It was a mistake on the part of Anne of Austria and Cardinal Mazarin not to have considered the different condition of the public mind. A suppressed excitement had for some months been hatching in Paris and in the provinces. "The parliament growled over the tariff-edict," says Cardinal de Retz; "and no sooner had it muttered than everybody awoke. People went groping as it were after the laws; they were no longer to be found. Under the influence of this agitation the people entered the sanctuary and lifted the veil that ought always to conceal whatever can be said about the right of peoples and that of kings which never accord so well as in silence." The arrest of Broussel, an old man in high esteem, very keen in his opposition to the court, was like fire to flax. "There was a blaze at once, a sensation, a rush, an outcry and a shutting up of shops." Paul de Godi, known afterwards as Cardinal de Retz, was at that time coadjutor of the Archbishop of Paris, his uncle; witty, debauched, bold and restless, lately compromised in the plots of the count of Soissons against Cardinal Richelieu, he owed his office to the queen, and "did not hesitate," he says; "to repair to her, that he might stick to his duty above all things." There was already a great tumult in the streets when he arrived at the Palais-Royal: the people were shouting, "Broussel! Broussel!" The coadjutor was accompanied by Marshal la Meilleraye; and both of them reported the excitement amongst the people. The queen grew angry: "There is revolt in imagining that there can be revolt," she said: "these are the ridiculous stories of those who desire it; the king's authority will soon restore order." Then, as old M. de Guitaut, who had just come in, supported the coadjutor and said that he did not understand how anybody could sleep in the state in which things were, the cardinal asked him, with some slight irony, "Well, M. de Guitaut, and what is your advice?" "My advice," said Guitaut, "is to give up that old rascal of a Broussel, dead or alive." "The former," replied the coadjutor, "would not accord with either the queen's piety or her prudence; the latter might stop the tumult." At this word the queen blushed and exclaimed: "I understand you, Mr. Coadjutor, you would have me set Broussel at liberty. I would strangle him with these hands first!" "And, as she finished the last syllable, she put them close to my face," says De Retz, "adding, 'and those who . . . .' The cardinal advanced and whispered in her ear." Advices of a more and more threatening character continued to arrive; and, at last, it was resolved to promise that Broussel should be set at liberty, provided that the people dispersed and ceased to demand it tumultuously. The coadjutor was charged to proclaim this concession throughout Paris; he asked for a regular order, but was not listened to. "The queen had retired to her little grey room. Monsignor pushed me very gently with his two hands, saying, 'Restore the peace of the realm.' Marshal Meilleraye drew me along, and so I went out with my rochet and camail, bestowing benedictions right and left, but this occupation did not prevent me from making all the reflections suitable to the difficulty in which I found myself. The impetuosity of Marshal Meilleraye did not give me opportunity to weigh my expressions; he advanced sword in hand, shouting with all his might: 'Hurrah! for the king! Liberation for Broussel!' As he was seen by many more folks than heard him, he provoked with his sword far more people than he appeased with his voice." The tumult increased; there was a rush to arms on all sides; the coadjutor was felled to the ground by a blow from a stone. He had just picked himself up, when a burgess put his musket to his head. "Though I did not know him a bit," says Retz, "I thought it would not be well to let him suppose so at such a moment; on the contrary, I said to him, 'Ah! wretch, if thy father saw thee!' He thought I was the best friend of his father, on whom, however, I had never set eyes." The coadjutor was recognized, and the crowd pressed round him, dragging him to the market-place. He kept repeating everywhere that "the queen promised to restore Broussel." The frippers laid down their arms, and thirty or forty thousand men accompanied him to the Palais-Royal. "Madame," said Marshal Meilleraye as he entered, "here is he to whom I owe my life, and your Majesty the safety of the Palais-Royal." The queen began to smile. "The marshal flew into a passion and said with an oath: 'Madame, no proper man can venture to flatter you in the state in which things are; and if you do not this very day set Broussel at liberty, to-morrow there will not be left one stone upon another in Paris.' I wished to speak in support of what the marshal said, but the queen cut me short, saying with an air of raillery, 'Go and rest yourself, sir; you have worked very hard.'"

The coadjutor left the Palais-Royal "in what is called a rage;" and he was in a greater one in the evening, when his friends came and told him that he was being made fun of at the queen's supper-table; that she was convinced that he had done all he could to increase the tumult; that he would be the first to be made a great example of; and that the parliament was about to be interdicted. Paul de Gondi had not waited for their information to think of revolt. "I did not reflect as to what I could do," says he, "for I was quite certain of that; I reflected only as to what I ought to do, and I was perplexed." The jests and the threats of the court appeared to him to be sufficient justification. "What effectually stopped my scruples was the advantage I imagined I had in distinguishing myself from those of my profession by a state of life in which there was something of all professions. In disorderly times, things lead to a confusion of species, and the vices of an archbishop may, in an infinity of conjunctures, be the virtues of a party-leader." The coadjutor recalled his friends: "We are not in such bad case as you supposed, gentlemen," he said to them: "there is an intention of crushing the public; it is for me to defend it from oppression; to-morrow before mid-day I shall be master of Paris."

For some time past the coadjutor had been laboring to make himself popular in Paris; the general excitement was only waiting to break out, and when the chancellor's carriage appeared in the streets in the morning, on the way to the Palace of Justice, the people, secretly worked upon during the night, all at once took up arms again. The chancellor had scarcely time to seek refuge in the Hôtel de Luynes; the mob rushed in after him, pillaging and destroying the furniture, whilst the chancellor, flying for refuge into a small chamber and believing his last hour had come, was confessing to his brother, the bishop of Meaux. He was not discovered, and the crowd moved off in another direction. "It was like a sudden and violent conflagration lighted up from the Pont Neuf over the whole city. Everybody without exception took up arms. Children of five and six years of age were seen dagger in hand;

and the mothers themselves carried them. In less than two hours there were in Paris more than two hundred barricades, bordered with flags and all the arms that the League had left entire. Everybody cried: 'Hurrah! for the king!' but echo answered: 'None of your Mazarin!'"

The coadjutor kept himself shut up at home, protesting his powerlessness; the parliament had met at an early hour; the Palace of Justice was surrounded by an immense crowd, shouting "Broussel! Broussel!" The parliament resolved to go in a body and demand of the queen the release of their members arrested the day before. "We set out in full court," says the premier president Molé, "without sending, as the custom is, to ask the queen to appoint a time, the ushers in front, with their square caps and a-foot; from this spot as far as the Trahoir cross we found the people in arms and barricades thrown up at every hundred paces" [*Mémoires de Matthieu Molé*, iii. p. 255].

"If it were not blasphemy to say that there was any one in our age more intrepid than the great Gustavus and the Prince, I should say it was M. Molé, premier president," writes Cardinal de Retz. Sincerely devoted to the public weal and a magistrate to the very bottom of his soul, Molé, nevertheless, inclined towards the side of power, and understood better than his brethren the danger of factions. He represented to the queen the extreme danger the sedition was causing to Paris and to France. "She, who feared nothing because she knew but little, flew into a passion and answered furiously, 'I am quite aware that there is disturbance in the city, but you shall answer to me for it, gentlemen of the parliament, you, your wives and your children.'" "The queen was pleased," says Molé, in his dignified language, "to signify in terms of wrath that the magisterial body should be answerable for the evils which might ensue and which the king, on reaching his majority, would remember."

The queen had retired to her room, slamming the door violently; the parliament turned back to the Palace of Justice; the angry mob thronged about the magistrates; when they arrived at Rue St. Honoré, just as they were about to turn on to the Pont Neuf, a band of armed men fell upon them, "and a cookshop-lad, advancing at the head of two hundred men, thrust his halbert against the premier president's stomach, saying, 'Turn, traitor, and, if thou wouldst not thyself be slain, give up to us Broussel, or Mazarin and the chancellor as hostages.'" Matthew Molé quietly put the weapon aside, and, "You forget yourself," he said, "and are oblivious of the respect you owe to my office." "Thrice an effort was made to thrust me into a private house," says his account in his *Mémoires*, "but I still kept my place, and, attempts having been made with swords and pistols on all sides of me to make an end of me, God would not permit it, some of the *members* (*Messieurs*) and some true friends having placed themselves in front of me. I told President de Mesmes that there was no other plan but to return to the Palais-Royal and thither take back the body, which was much diminished in numbers, five of the presidents having dropped away, and also many of the members on whom the people had inflicted unworthy treatment." "Thus having given himself time to rally as many as he could of the body, and still preserving the dignity of the magistracy both in his words and in his movements, the premier president returned at a slow pace to the Palais-Royal, amidst a running fire of insults, threats, execrations and blasphemies" [*Mémoires de Retz*].

The whole court had assembled in the gallery: Molé spoke first. "This man," says Retz, "had a sort of eloquence peculiar to himself. He knew nothing of apostrophes, he was not correct in his language, but he spoke with a force which made up for all that, and he was naturally so bold that he never spoke so well as in the midst of peril. Monsieur made as if he would throw himself on his knees before the queen, who remained inflexible; four or five princesses, who were trembling with fear, did throw themselves at her feet; the queen of England, who had come that day from St. Germain, represented that the troubles had never been so serious at their commencement in England, nor the feelings so heated or united" [*Histoire du temps*, 1647–48. (*Archives curieuses*, vi., p. 162)]. At last the cardinal made up his mind; "he had been roughly handled in the queen's presence by the presidents and councillors in their speeches, some of them telling him, in mockery, that he had only to give himself the trouble of going as far as the Pont Neuf to see for himself the state in which things were," and he joined with all those present in entreating Anne of Austria; finally, the release of Broussel was extorted from her, "not without a deep sigh which showed what violence she did her feelings in the struggle."

"We returned in full court by the same road," says Matthew Molé, "and the people demanding with confused clamor of voices, whether M. Broussel were at liberty, we gave them assurances thereof, and entered by the back-door of my lodging; before crossing the threshold, I took leave of Presidents De Mesmes and Le Coigneux and waited until the members had passed, testifying my sentiments of gratitude for that they had been unwilling to separate until they had seen to the security of my person, which I had not at all deserved, but such was their good pleasure. After this business, which had lasted from six in the morning until seven o'clock, there was need of rest, seeing that the mind had been agitated amidst so many incidents, and not a morsel had been tasted" [*Mémoires de Matthieu Molé*, t. iii. p. 265].

Broussel had taken his seat in the parliament again. The prince of Condé had just arrived in Paris; he did not like the cardinal, but he was angry with the parliament, which he considered imprudent and insolent. "They are going ahead," said he: "If I were to go ahead with them, I should perhaps do better for my own interests, but my name is Louis de Bourbon, and I do not wish to shake the throne; these devils of square-caps, are they mad about bringing me either to commence a civil war before long or to put a rope round their own necks, and place over their heads and over my own an adventurer from Sicily, who will be the ruin of us all in the end? I will let the parliament plainly see that they are not where they suppose, and that it would not be a hard matter to bring them to reason." The coadjutor, to whom he thus expressed himself, answered that "the cardinal might possibly be mistaken in his measures, and that Paris would be a hard nut to crack." Whereupon the prince rejoined angrily: "It will not be taken, like Dunkerque, by mining and assaults, but if the bread of Gonesse were to fail them for a week . . ." The coadjutor took the rest as said. Some days afterwards, during the night between the 5th and 6th of January, 1649, the queen, with the little king and the whole court, set out at four a.m. from Paris for the castle of St. Germain, empty, unfurnished, as was then the custom in the king's absence, where the courtiers had great difficulty in finding a bundle of straw. "The queen had scarcely a bed to lie upon," says Mdlle. de Montpensier, "but never did I see any creature so gay as she was that day; had she won a battle, taken Paris, and had all who had displeased her hanged, she could not have been more so, and nevertheless she was very far from all that."

Paris was left to the malcontents; everybody was singing—

> "A Fronde-ly wind
> Got up to-day,
> 'Gainst Mazarin
> It howls, they say."

On the 8th of January the parliament of Paris, all the chambers in assembly, issued a decree whereby Cardinal Mazarin was declared an enemy to the king and the State, and a disturber of the public peace, and injunctions were laid upon all subjects of the king to hunt him down; war was declared.

Scarcely had it begun, when the greatest lords came flocking to the popular side. On the departure of the court for St. Germain, the duchess of Longueville had remained in Paris, her husband and her brother the prince of Conti were not slow in coming to look after her; and already the duke of Elbeuf, of the House of Lorraine, had offered his services to the parliament. Levies of troops were beginning in the city, and the command of the forces was offered to the prince of Conti; the dukes of Bouillon and Beaufort and Marshal de la Mothe likewise embraced the party of revolt; the duchesses of Longueville and Bouillon established themselves with their children at the Hôtel de Ville as hostages given by the Fronde of princes to the Fronde of the people; the parliaments of Aix and Rouen made common cause with that of Paris; a decree ordered the seizure, in all the exchequers of the kingdom, of the royal moneys, in order that they might be employed for the general defence. Every evening Paris wore a festive air; there was dancing at the Hôtel de Ville, and the gentlemen who had been skirmishing during the day around the walls came for recreation in the society of the princesses. "This commingling of blue scarves, of ladies, of cuirasses, of violins in the hall and of trumpets in the square, offered a spectacle which is oftener seen in romances than elsewhere" [*Mémoires du Cardinal de Retz*, t. i.]. Affairs of gallantry were mixed up with the most serious resolves; Madame de Longueville was of the Fronde because she was in love with M. de Marsillac (afterwards duke of La Rochefoucauld) and he was on bad terms with Cardinal Mazarin.

Meanwhile war was rumbling round Paris; the post of Charenton, fortified by the Frondeurs, had been carried by the prince of Condé at the head of the king's troops; the parliament was beginning to perceive its mistake and desired to have peace again, but the great lords engaged in the contest aspired to turn it to account; they had already caused the gates of Paris to be closed against a herald sent by the queen to recall her subjects to their duty; they were awaiting the army of Germany, commanded by M. de Turenne, whom his brother, the duke of Bouillon, had drawn into his culpable enterprise; nay more, they had begun to negotiate with Spain, and they brought up to the parliament a pretended envoy from Archduke Leopold, but the court refused to receive him; "What! sir," said President de Mesmes, turning to the prince of Conti, "is it possible that a prince of the blood of France should propose to give a seat upon the fleurs-de-lis to a deputy from the most cruel enemy of the fleurs-de-lis?"

The parliament sent a deputation to the queen, and conferences were opened at Ruel on the 4th of March; the great lords of the Fronde took no part in it, "they contented themselves with having at St. Germain low-voiced (*à basses notes*—secret) agents," says Madame de Motteville, "commissioned to negotiate in their favor." Paris was beginning to lack bread; it was festival-time, and want began to make itself felt; a "complaint of the Carnival" was current amongst the people:

"In my extreme affliction, yet
I can this consolation get,
That, at his hands, my enemy,
Old Lent, will fare the same as I;
That, at the times when people eat,
We both shall equal worship meet.
Thus, joining with the whole of France
In war against him *à outrance*,
Grim Lent and festive Carnival,
Will fight against the cardinal."

It was against the cardinal, in fact, that all attacks were directed, but the queen remained immovable in her fidelity: "I should be afraid," she said to Madame de Motteville, "that, if I were to let him fall, the same thing would happen to me that happened to the king of England (Charles I. had just been executed), and that, after he had been driven out, my turn would come." Grain had found its way into Paris during the truce; and when, on the 13th of March, the premier president, Molé, and the other negotiators, returned to Paris, bringing the peace which they had signed at Ruel, they were greeted with furious shouts: "None of your peace! None of your Mazarin! We must go to St. Germain to seek our good king! We must fling into the river all the Mazarins!" A rioter had just laid his hand on the premier president's arm. "When you have killed me," said the latter calmly, "I shall only want six feet of earth;" and, when he was advised to get back into his house by way of the record-offices, "The court never hides itself," he said; "if I were certain to perish, I would not commit this poltroonery, which, moreover, would but serve to give courage to the rioters. They would, of course, come after me to my house if they thought that I shrank from them here." The deputies of the parliament were sent back to Ruel, taking a statement of the claims of the great lords: "according to their memorials, they demanded the whole of France" [*Mémoires de Madame de Motteville*, t. iii. p. 247].

Whilst Paris was in disorder, and the agitation, through its example, was spreading over almost the whole of France, M. de Turenne, obliged to fly from his army, was taking refuge, he and five others, with the landgrave of Hesse; his troops had refused to follow him in revolt; the last hope of the Frondeurs was slipping from them.

They found themselves obliged to accept peace, not without obtaining some favors from the court.

There was a general amnesty; and the parliament preserved all its rights. "The king will have the honor of it, and we the profit," said Guy-Patin. The great lords reappeared one after another at St. Germain. "It is the way of our nation to return to their duty with the same airiness with which they depart from it, and to pass in a single instant from rebellion to obedience" [*La Rochefoucauld*]. The return to rebellion was not to be long delayed. The queen had gone back to Paris, and the prince of Condé with her; he, proud of having beaten the parliamentary Fronde, affected the conqueror's airs, and the throng of his courtiers, the "petit maîtres," as they were called, spoke very slightingly of the cardinal. Condé, reconciled with the duchess of Longueville, his sister, and his brother, the prince of Conti, assumed to have the lion's share in the government, and claimed all the favors for himself or his friends; the Frondeurs made skilful use of the ill-humor which this conduct excited in Cardinal Mazarin; the minister responded to their advances; the coadjutor was secretly summoned to the Louvre; the dowager-princess of Condé felt some apprehensions; but, "What have I to fear?" her son said to her, "the cardinal is my friend." "I doubt it," she answered. "You are wrong; I rely upon him as much as upon you." "Please God you may not be mistaken!"

replied the princess, who was setting out for the Palais-Royal to see the queen, said to be indisposed that day.

Anne of Austria was upon her bed; word was brought to her that the council was waiting; this was the moment agreed upon; she dismissed the princess, shut herself up in her oratory with the little king, to whom she gave an account of what was going to be done for his service; then, making him kneel down, she joined him in praying to God for the success of this great enterprise. As the prince of Condé arrived in the grand gallery, he saw Guitaut, captain of the guards, coming towards him; at the same instant, through a door at the bottom, out went the cardinal, taking with him Abbé de la Rivière, who was the usual confidant of the duke of Orleans, but from whom his master had concealed the great secret. The prince supposed that Guitaut was coming to ask him some favor; the captain of the guards said in his ear: "My lord, what I want to say is, that I have orders to arrest you—you, the prince of Conti your brother, and M. de Longueville." "Me, M. Guitaut, arrest me?" Then, reflecting for a moment, "In God's name," he said, "go back to the queen and tell her that I entreat her to let me have speech of her!" Guitaut went to her, whilst the prince, returning to those who were waiting for him, said, "Gentlemen, the queen orders my arrest, and yours too, brother, and yours too, M. de Longueville; I confess that I am astonished, I who have always served the king so well and believed myself secure of the cardinal's friendship." The chancellor, who was not in the secret, declared that it was Guitaut's pleasantry. "Go and seek the queen then," said the prince, "and tell her of the pleasantry that is going on; as for me, I hold it to be very certain that I am arrested." The chancellor went out, and did not return. M. Servien, who had gone to speak to the cardinal, likewise did not appear again. M. de Guitaut entered alone: "The queen cannot see you, my lord," he said. "Very well, I am content; let us obey:" answered the prince: "but whither are you going to take us? I pray you let it be to a warm place." "We are going to the wood of Vincennes, my lord," said Guitaut. The prince turned to the company and took his leave without uneasiness and with the calmest countenance: as he was embracing M. de Brienne, secretary of State, he said to him, "Sir, as I have often received from you marks of your friendship and generosity, I flatter myself that you will some day tell the king the services I have rendered him." The princes went out; and, as they descended the staircase, Condé leant towards Comminges, who commanded the detachment of guards, saying, "Comminges, you are a man of honor and a gentleman, have I anything to fear?" Comminges assured him he had not, and that the orders were merely to escort him to the wood of Vincennes. The carriage upset on the way; as soon as it was righted, Comminges ordered the driver to urge on his horses. The prince burst out laughing: "Don't be afraid, Comminges," he said; "there is nobody to come to my assistance; I swear to you that I had not taken any precautions against this trip." On arriving at the castle of Vincennes, there were no beds to be found, and the three princes passed the night playing at cards; the princess of Condé and the dowager-princess received orders to retire to their estates; the duchess of Longueville, fearing with good cause that she would be arrested, had taken with all speed the road to Normandy, whither she went and took refuge at Dieppe, in her husband's government.

The State-stroke had succeeded; Mazarin's skill and prudence once more checkmated all the intrigues concocted against him; when the news was told to Chavigny, in spite of all his reasons for bearing malice against the cardinal, who had driven him from the council and kept him for some time in prison, he exclaimed: "That is a great misfortune for the prince and his friends; but the truth must be told: the cardinal has done quite right; without it he would have been ruined." The contest was begun between Mazarin and the great Condé, and it was not with the prince that the victory was to remain.

Already hostilities were commencing; Mazarin had done everything for the Frondeurs who remained faithful to him, but the house of Condé was rallying all its partisans; the dukes of Bouillon and La Rochefoucauld had thrown themselves into Bordeaux, which was in revolt against the royal authority, represented by the duke of Épernon. The princess of Condé and her young son left Chantilly to join them; Madame de Longueville occupied Stenay, a strong place belonging to the prince of Condé: she had there found Turenne; on the other hand, the queen had just been through Normandy; all the towns had opened their gates to her; it was just the same in Burgundy; the princess of Condé's able agent, Lenet, could not obtain a declaration from the parliament of Dijon in her favor. Bordeaux was the focus of the insurrection; the people, passionately devoted to "the dukes," as the saying was, were forcing the hand of the parliament; riots were frequent in the town; the little king, with the queen and the cardinal, marched in person upon Bordeaux; one of the faubourgs was attacked, the dukes negotiated and obtained a general amnesty, but no mention was made of the princes' release.

The parliament of Paris took the matter up. The premier president spoke in so bitter a tone of the *unhappy policy* of the minister, that the little king, feeling hurt, told his mother that, if he had thought it would not displease her, he would have made the premier president hold his tongue and would have dismissed him. On the 30th of January, Anne of Austria sent word to the parliament that she would consent to grant the release of the princes, "provided that the armaments of Stenay and of M. de Turenne might be discontinued."

But it was too late; the duke of Orleans had made a treaty with the princes. England served as pretext. Mazarin compared the parliament to the House of Commons, and the coadjutor to Cromwell. Monsieur took the matter up for his friends, and was angry. He openly declared that he would not set foot again in the Palais-Royal as long as he was liable to meet the cardinal there, and joined the parliament in demanding the removal of Mazarin. The queen replied that nobody had a right to interfere in the choice of ministers. By way of answer, the parliament laid injunctions upon all the officers of the crown to obey none but the duke of Orleans, lieutenant-general of the kingdom. A meeting of the noblesse, at a tumultuous assembly in the house of the duke of Nemours, expressed themselves in the same sense. It was the 6th of February, 1651: during the night, Cardinal Mazarin set out for St. Germain; a rumor spread in Paris that the queen was preparing to follow him with the king; a rush was made to the Palais-Royal: the king was in his bed. Next day, Anne of Austria complained to the parliament: "The prince is at liberty," said the premier president, "and the king, the king our master, is a prisoner." "Monsieur, who felt no fear," says Retz, "because he had been more cheered in the streets and the hall of the palace than he had ever been," answered with vivacity; "The king was a prisoner in the hands of Mazarin; but, thank God, he is not any longer." The premier president was right, the king was a prisoner to the Parisians; patrols of burgesses were moving incessantly round the Palais

Royal; one night the queen was obliged to let the people into her chamber; the king was asleep; and two officers of the town-guard watched for some hours at his pillow. The yoke of Richelieu and the omnipotence of Mazarin were less hard for royalty to bear than the capricious and jealous tyranny of the populace.

The cardinal saw that he was beaten; he made up his mind, and, anticipating the queen's officers, he hurried to Le Havre to release the prisoners himself; he entered the castle alone, the governor having refused entrance to the guards who attended him. "The prince told me," says Mdlle. de Montpensier, "that, when they were dining together, Cardinal Mazarin was not so much in the humor to laugh as he himself was, and that he was very much embarrassed. Liberty to be gone had more charms for the prince than the cardinal's company. He said that he felt marvellous delight at finding himself outside Le Havre, with his sword at his side; and he might well be pleased to wear it, he is a pretty good hand at using it. As he went out he turned to the cardinal and said: 'Farewell, Cardinal Mazarin,' who kissed 'the tip of sleeve' to him."

The cardinal had slowly taken the road to exile, summoning to him his nieces, Mdlles. Mancini and Martinozzi, whom he had, a short time since, sent for to court; he crossed from Normandy into Picardy, made some stay at Doullens, and, impelled by his enemies' hatred, he finally crossed the frontier on the 12th of March. The parliament had just issued orders for his arrest in any part of France. On the 6th of April, he fixed his quarters at Brühl, a little town belonging to the electorate of Cologne, in the same territory which had but lately sheltered the last days of Mary de' Medici.

The Frondeurs, old and new, had gained the day; but even now there was disorder in their camp. Condé had returned to and court "like a raging lion, seeking to devour everybody, and, in revenge for his imprisonment, to set fire to the four corners of the realm" [*Mémoires de Montglat*]. After a moment's reconciliation with the queen he began to show himself more and more haughty towards her in his demands every day; he required the dismissal of the ministers Le Tellier, Servien and Lionne, all three creatures of the cardinal and in correspondence with him at Brühl; as Anne of Austria refused, the prince retired to St. Maur; he was already in negotiation with Spain, being inveigled into treason by the influence of his sister,

Madame de Longueville, who would not leave the duke of La Rochefoucauld or return into Normandy to her husband. Fatal results of a guilty passion which enlisted against his country the arms of the hero of Rocroi! When he returned to Paris, the queen had, in fact, dismissed her ministers, but she had formed a fresh alliance with the coadjutor, and, on the 17th of August, in the presence of an assembly convoked for that purpose at the Palais-Royal, she openly denounced the intrigues of the prince with Spain, accusing him of being in correspondence with the archduke. Next day Condé brought the matter before the parliament.

The coadjutor quite expected the struggle, and had brought supporters; the queen had sent some soldiers; the prince arrived with a numerous attendance. On entering, he said to the company, that he could not sufficiently express his astonishment at the condition in which he found the palace, which seemed to him more like a camp than a temple of justice, and that it was not seemly that there could be found in the kingdom people insolent enough to presume to dispute (superiority) the pavement (*disputer le pavé*) with him. "I made him a deep obeisance," says Retz, "and said that I very humbly begged His Highness to pardon me if I told him that I did not believe that there was anybody in the kingdom insolent enough to dispute the wall (*le haut du pavé*) with him, but I was persuaded that there were some who could not and ought not, for their dignity's sake, to yield the pavement (*quitter le pavé*) to any but the king. The prince replied that he would make me yield it. I said that that would not be easy." The dispute grew warm; the presidents flung themselves between the disputants; Condé yielded to their entreaties, and begged the duke of La Rochefoucauld to go and tell his friends to withdraw. The coadjutor went out to make the same request to his friends. "When he would have returned into the ushers' little court," writes Mdlle. de Montpensier, "he met at the door the duke of La Rochefoucauld, who shut it in his face, just keeping it ajar to see who accompanied the coadjutor; he, seeing the door ajar, gave it a good push, but he could not pass quite through, and remained as it were jammed between the two folds, unable to get in or out. The duke of La Rochefoucauld had fastened the door with an iron catch, keeping it so to prevent its opening any wider. The coadjutor was in an ugly position, for he could not help fearing lest a dagger should pop out and take his life from behind. A complaint was made to the grand chamber, and Champlâtreux, son of the premier president, went out and, by his authority, had the door opened, in spite of the duke of La Rochefoucauld." The coadjutor protested, and the duke of Brissac, his relative, threatened the duke of La Rochefoucauld; whereupon the latter said that, if he had them outside, he would strangle them both; to which the coadjutor replied; "My dear La Franchise (the duke's nickname), do not act the bully; you are a poltroon and I am a priest; we shall not do one another much harm." There was no fighting, and the parliament, supported by the duke of Orleans, obtained from the queen a declaration of the innocence of the prince of Condé, and at the same time a formal disavowal of Mazarin's policy, and a promise never to recall him. Anne of Austria yielded everything; the king's majority was approaching, and she flattered herself that under cover of his name she would be able to withdraw the concessions which she felt obliged to make as regent. Her declaration, nevertheless, deeply wounded Mazarin, who was still taking refuge at Brühl, whence he wrote incessantly to the queen, who did not neglect his counsels: "Ten times I have taken up my pen to write to you," he said on the 26th of September, 1651 [*Lettres du Cardinal Mazarin à la reine*, pp. 292, 293], "but could not, and I am so beside myself at the mortal wound I have just received, that I am not sure whether anything I could say to you would have rhyme or reason. The king and the queen, by an authentic deed, have declared me a traitor, a public robber, an incapable, and an enemy to the repose of Christendom after I had served them with so many signs of my devotion to the advancement of peace: it is no longer a question of property, repose, or whatever else there may be of the sort. I demand the honor which has been taken from me, and that I be let alone, renouncing very heartily the cardinalate and the benefices, whereof I send in my resignation joyfully, consenting willingly to have given up to France twenty-three years of the best of my life, all my pains and my little of wealth, and merely to withdraw with the honor which I had when I began to serve her." The persistent hopes of the adroit Italian appeared once more in the postscript of the letter: "I had forgotten to tell you that it was not the way to set me right in the eyes of the people to impress upon their mind that I am the cause of all the evils they suffer, and of all the disorders of the realm, in such sort that my ministry will be held in horror forever."

Condé did not permit himself to be caught by the queen's

declarations; of all the princes he alone was missing at the ceremony of the bed of justice whereat the youthful Louis XIV., when entering his fourteenth year, announced, on the 7th of September, "to his people that, according to the laws of his realm, he intended himself to assume the government, hoping of God's goodness that it would be with piety and justice." The prince had retired to Chantilly, on the pretext that the new minister, the president of the council, Châteauneuf, and the keeper of the seals, Matthew Molé, were not friends of his. The duchess of Longueville at last carried the day; Condé was resolved upon civil war. "You would have it," he said to his sister on repelling the envoy, who had followed him to Bourges, from the queen and the duke of Orleans; "remember that I draw the sword in spite of myself, but I will be the last to sheathe it." And he kept his word.

A great disappointment awaited the rebels; they had counted upon the duke of Bouillon and M. de Turenne, but neither of them would join the faction. The relations between the two great generals had not been without rubs; Turenne had, moreover, felt some remorse because he, being a general in the king's army, had but lately declared against the court, "doing thereby a deed at which Le Balafré and Admiral de Coligny would have hesitated," says Cardinal de Retz. The two brothers went, before long, and offered their services to the queen.

Meanwhile, Condé had arrived at Bordeaux: a part of Guienne, Saintonge and Périgord had declared in his favor; Count d'Harcourt, at the head of the royal troops, marched against La Rochelle, which he took from the revolters under the very beard of the prince, who had come from Bordeaux to the assistance of the place, whilst the king and the queen, resolutely quitting Paris, advanced from town to town as far as Poitiers, keeping the centre of France to its allegiance by their mere presence. The treaty of the prince of Condé with Spain was concluded: eight Spanish vessels, having money and troops on board, entered the Gironde. Condé delivered over to them the castle and harbor of Talmont. The queen had commissioned the cardinal to raise levies in Germany; and he had already entered the country of Liège, embodying troops and forming alliances. On the 17th of November, Anne of Austria finally wrote to Mazarin to return to the king's assistance. In the presence of Condé's rebellion she had no more appearances to keep up with anybody; and it was already in the master's tone that Mazarin wrote to the queen, on the 30th of October, to put her on her guard against the duke of Orleans: "The power committed to his Royal Highness and the neutrality permitted to him, being as he is wholly devoted to the prince, surrounded by his partisans and adhering blindly to their counsels, are matters highly prejudicial to the king's service, and, for my part, I do not see how one can be a servant of the king's, with ever so little judgment and knowledge of affairs, and yet dispute these truths. The queen, then, must bide her time to remedy all this."

The cardinal's penetration had not deceived him; the duke of Orleans was working away in Paris, where the queen had been obliged to leave him, on the prince of Condé's side. The parliament had assembled to enregister against the princes the proclamation of high treason despatched from Bourges by the court; Gaston demanded that it should be sent back, threatened as they were, he said, with a still greater danger than the rebellion of the princes in the return of Mazarin, who was even now advancing to the frontier; but the premier president took no notice, and put the proclamation to the vote in these words: "It is a great misfortune when princes of the blood give occasion for such proclamations, but this is a common and ordinary misfortune in the kingdom, and, for five or six centuries past, it may be said that they have been the scourges of the people and the enemies of the monarchy." The decree passed by a hundred votes to forty

On the 24th of December, the cardinal crossed the frontier with a large body of troops, and was received at Sedan by lieutenant-general Fabert, faithful to his fortunes even in exile. The parliament was furious and voted, almost unanimously, that the cardinal and his adherents were guilty of high treason; ordering the communes to hound him down, and promising, from the proceeds of his furniture and library which were about to be sold, a sum of 500,000 livres to whoever should take him dead or alive. At once began the sale of the magnificent library which the cardinal had liberally opened to the public. The dispersion of the books was happily stopped in time to still leave a nucleus for the Mazarin Library.

Meanwhile, Mazarin had not allowed himself to be frightened by parliamentary decrees or by dread of assassins. Re-entering France, with six thousand men, he forced the passage of Pont-sur-Yonne, in spite of the two councillors of the parliaments who were commissioned to have him arrested; the duke of Beaufort, at the head of Monsieur's troops, did not even attempt to impede his march, and, on the 28th of January, the cardinal entered Poitiers, at once resuming his place beside the king, who had come to meet him a league from the town. The court took leisurely the road to Paris.

The coadjutor had received the price of his services in the royal cause; he was a cardinal "sooner," said he, "than Mazarin would have had him;" and so the new prince of the Church considered himself released from any gratitude to the court, and sought to form a third party at the head of which was to be placed the duke of Orleans as nominal head. Monsieur, harried by intrigues in all directions, remained in a state of inaction, and made a pretension of keeping Paris neutral; his daughter, Mdlle. de Montpensier, who detested Anne of Austria and Mazarin and would have liked to marry the king, had boldly taken the side of the princes; the court had just arrived at Blois, on the 27th of March, 1652; the keeper of the seals, Molé, presented himself in front of Orleans to summon the town to open its gates to the king; at that very moment arrived Mdlle., the *great Mdlle.*, as she was then called; and she claimed possession of Orleans in her father's name. "It was the appanage of Monsieur; but the gates were shut and barricaded. After they had been told that it was I," writes Mdlle., "they did not open; and I was there three hours. The governor sent me some sweetmeats, and what appeared to me rather funny was that he gave me to understand that he had no influence. At the window of the sentry-box was the marquis d'Halluys, who watched me walking up and down by the fosse. The rampart was fringed with people who shouted incessantly, 'Hurrah, for the king! hurrah, for the princes! None of your Mazarin!' I could not help calling out to them: 'Go to the Hôtel de Ville and get the gate opened to me!' The captain made signs that he had not the keys. I said to him; 'It must be burst open, and you owe me more allegiance than to the gentlemen of the town, seeing that I am your master's daughter.' The boatmen offered to break open for me a gate which was close by there. I told them to make haste, and I mounted upon a pretty high mound of earth overlooking that gate. I thought but little about any nice way of getting thither; I climbed like a cat; I held on to briars and thorns, and I leapt all the hedges without hurting myself at all; two boats were brought up to serve me for a bridge, and in the second was placed a ladder by which I mounted. The gate was burst at last. Two planks had been forced out of the middle; signs were made to me to advance;

and as there was a great deal of mud a footman took me up, carried me along and put me through this hole, through which I had no sooner passed my head than the drums began beating. I gave my hand to the captain and said to him, 'You will be very glad that you can boast of having managed to get me in.'" The keeper of the seals was obliged to return to Blois, and Mdlle. kept Orleans, but without being able to effect an entrance for the troops of the dukes of Nemours and Beaufort, who had just tried a surprise against the court. Had it not been for the aid of Turenne, who had defended the bridge of Jargeau, the king might have fallen into the hands of his revolted subjects. The queen rested at Gien, whilst the princes went on as far as Montargis, thus cutting off the communications of the Court with Paris. Turenne was preparing to fall upon his incapable adversaries when the situation suddenly changed: the prince of Condé, weary of the bad state of his affairs in Guienne, where the veteran soldiers of the count of Harcourt had the advantage everywhere over the new levies, had traversed France in disguise, and forming a junction, on the 1st of April, with the dukes of Nemours and Beaufort, threw himself upon the quarters of Marshal d'Hocquincourt, defeated him, burnt his camp, and drove him back to Bléneau; a rapid march, on the part of Turenne, coming to the aid of his colleague, forced Condé to fall back upon Châtillon; on the 11th of April he was in Paris.

The princes had relied upon the irritation caused by the return of Mazarin to draw Paris into the revolt, but they were only half successful; the parliament would scarcely give Condé admittance; President de Bailleul, who occupied the chair in the absence of Molé, declared that the body always considered it an honor to see the prince in their midst, but that they would have preferred not to see him there in the state in which he was at the time, with his hands still bloody from the defeat of the king's troops. Amelot, premier president of the Court of Aids, said to the prince's face, "that it was a matter of astonishment, after many battles delivered or sustained against His Majesty's troops, to see him not only returning to Paris without having obtained letters of amnesty, but still appearing amongst the sovereign bodies as if he gloried in the spoils of His Majesty's subjects, and causing the drum to be beaten for levying troops, to be paid by money coming from Spain, in the capital of the realm, the most loyal city possessed by the king." The city of Paris resolved not to make "common cause or furnish money to assist the princes against the king under pretext of its being against Mazarin." The populace alone were favorable to the princes' party.

Meanwhile, Turenne had easy work with the secondary generals remaining at the head of the factious army; by his able manœuvres he had covered the march of the court, which established itself at St. Germain.

Condé assembled his forces encamped around Paris: he intended to fortify himself at the confluence of the Seine and the Marne, hoping to be supported by the little army which had just been brought up by Duke Charles of Lorraine, as capricious and adventurous as ever. Turenne and the main body of his troops barred the passage. Condé threw himself back upon Faubourg St. Antoine and there intrenched himself, at the outlet of the three principal streets which abutted upon Porte St. Antoine (now Place de la Bastille). Turenne had meant to wait for reinforcements and artillery, but the whole court had flocked upon the heights of Charonne to see the fight; pressure was put upon him, and the marshal gave the word to attack. The army of the Fronde fought with fury. "I did not see *a* prince of Condé," Turenne used to say; "I saw more than a dozen." The king's soldiers had entered the houses, thus turning the barricades; Marshal Ferté had just arrived with the artillery and was sweeping Rue St. Antoine. The princes' army was about to be driven back to the foot of the walls of Paris, when the cannon of the Bastille, replying all on a sudden to the volleys of the royal troops, came like a thunderbolt on M. de Turenne; the Porte St. Antoine opened, and the Parisians, under arms, fringing the streets, protected the return of the rebel army. Mdlle. de Montpensier had taken the command of the city of Paris.

For a week past the Duke of Orleans had been ill or pretended to be; he refused to give any order. When the prince began his movement, on the 2nd of July, early, he sent to beg Mdlle. not to desert him. "I ran to the Luxembourg," she says, "and I found Monsieur at the top of the stairs. 'I thought I should find you in bed,' said I; 'Count Fiesque told me that you didn't feel well.' He answered, 'I am not ill enough for that, but enough not to go out.' I begged him to ride out to the aid of the prince, or, at any rate, to go to bed and assume to be ill; but I could get nothing from him. I went so far as to say, 'Short of having a treaty with the court in your pocket, I cannot understand how you can take things so easily; but can you really have one to sacrifice the prince to Cardinal Mazarin?' He made no reply: all I said lasted quite an hour, during which every friend we had might have been killed, and the prince as well as another, without anybody's caring; nay there were people of Monsieur's in high spirits, hoping that the prince would perish; they were friends of Cardinal de Retz. At last Monsieur gave me a letter for the gentlemen of the Hôtel, leaving it to me to tell them his intention. I was there in a moment, assuring those present that, if ill luck would have it that the enemy should beat the prince, no more quarter would be shown to Paris than to the men who bore arms. Marshal de l'Hôpital, governor of Paris for the king, said to me, 'You are aware, Mdlle., that if your troops had not approached this city, those of the king would not have come thither and that they only came to drive them away.' Madame de Nemours did not like this, and began to argue the point. I broke off their altercation. 'Consider, sir, that, whilst time is being wasted in discussing useless matters, the prince is in danger in your faubourgs.'" She carried with her the aid of the duke of Orleans' troops and immediately moved forwards, meeting everywhere on her road her friends wounded or dying. "When I was near the gate, I went into the house of an exchequer-master (*maître des comptes*). As soon as I was there, the prince came thither to see me; he was in a pitiable state; he had two fingers' breadth of dust on his face, and his hair all matted; his collar and his shirt were covered with blood, although he was not wounded; his breastplate was riddled all over; and he held his sword bare in his hand, having lost the scabbard. He said to me, 'You see a man in despair; I have lost all my friends; MM. de Nemours, de la Rochefoucauld, and Clinchamps are wounded to death.' I consoled him a little by telling him that they were in better case than he supposed. Then I went off to the Bastille where I made them load the cannon which was trained right upon the city; and I gave orders to fire as soon as I had gone. I went thence to the Porte St. Antoine. The soldiers shouted, 'Let us do something that will astonish them; our retreat is secure; here is Mdlle. at the gate, and she will have it opened for us, if we are hard pressed.' The prince gave orders to march back into the city; he seemed to me quite different from what he had been early in the day, though he had not changed at all; he paid me a thousand compliments and thanks for the great service he considered that I had rendered him. I said to him, 'I have a favor to ask of you: that is, not to say anything to Monsieur about the laches he has displayed towards you.' At this very moment up came Monsieur, who embraced the prince with as gay an air as if he had not left him at all in the lurch. The prince confessed that he had never been in so dangerous a position."

The fight at Porte St. Antoine had not sufficiently compromised the Parisians, wh began to demand peace at any price. The mob, devoted to the princes, set themselves to insult in the street all those who did not wear in their hats a tuft of straw, the rallying sign of the faction. On the 4th of July, at the general assembly of the city, when the king's attorney-general proposed to conjure His Majesty to return to Paris without Cardinal Mazarin, the princes, who demanded the union of the Parisians with themselves, rose up and went out, leaving the assembly to the tender mercies of the crowd assembled on the Place de Grève. "Down on the Mazarins!" was the cry; "there are none but Mazarins any longer at the Hôtel de Ville!" Fire was applied to the doors defended by the archers; all the outlets were guarded by men beside themselves; more than thirty burgesses of note were massacred; many died of their wounds, the Hôtel de Ville was pillaged, Marshal de l'Hôpital escaped with great difficulty and the provost of tradesmen yielded up his office to Councillor Broussel. Terror reigned in Paris: it was necessary to drag the magistrates to the Palace of Justice to decree, on the 10th of July, by seventy-four votes against sixty-nine, that the duke of Orleans should be appointed "lieutenant-general of the kingdom, and the prince of Condé commandant of all the armies." The usurpation of the royal authority was flagrant, the city-assembly voted subsidies, and Paris wrote to all the good towns of France to announce to them her resolution. Chancellor Séguier had the poltroonery to accept the presidency of the council, offered him by the duke of Orleans; he thus avenged himself for the preference the queen had but lately shown for Molé by confiding the seals to him. At the same time the Spaniards were entering France; for all the strong places were dismantled or disgarrisoned. The king, obliged to confront civil war, had abandoned his frontiers; Gravelines had fallen on the 18th of May, and the archduke had undertaken the siege of Dunkerque. At Condé's instance, he detached a body of troops, which he sent, under the orders of Count Fuendalsagna, to join the duke of Lorraine, who had again approached Paris. Everywhere the fortune of arms appeared to be against the king. "This year we lost Barcelona, Catalonia, and Casale, the key of Italy," says Cardinal de Retz. "We saw Brisach in revolt, on the point of falling once more into the hands of the House of Austria. We saw the flags and standards of Spain fluttering on the Pont Neuf, the yellow scarves of Lorraine appeared in Paris as freely as the isabels and the blues." Dissension, ambition, and poltroonery were delivering France over to the foreigner.

The evil passions of men, under the control of God, help sometimes to destroy and sometimes to preserve them. The interests of the Spaniards and of the prince of Condé were not identical. He desired to become the master of France, and to command in the king's name; the enemy were laboring to humiliate France and to prolong the war indefinitely. The archduke recalled Count Fuendalsagna to Dunkerque; and Turenne, withstanding the terrors of the court which would fain have fled first into Normandy and then to Lyons, prevailed upon the queen to establish herself at Pontoise, whilst the army occupied Compiègne. At every point cutting off the passage of the duke of Lorraine, who had been reinforced by a body of Spaniards, Turenne held the enemy in check for three weeks, and prevented them from marching on Paris. All parties began to tire of hostilities.

Cardinal Mazarin took his line, and loudly demanded of the king permission to withdraw, in order, by his departure, to restore peace to the kingdom. The queen refused: "There is no consideration shown," she said, "for my son's honor and my own; we will not suffer him to go away." But the cardinal insisted. Prudent and far-sighted as he was, he knew that to depart was the only way of remaining. He departed on the 19th of August, but without leaving the frontier: he took up his quarters at Bouillon. The queen had summoned the parliament to her at Pontoise. A small number of magistrates responded to her summons, enough, however, to give the queen the right to proclaim rebellious the parliament remaining at Paris. Chancellor Séguier made his escape in order to go and rejoin the court. Nobody really believed in the cardinal's withdrawal; men are fond of yielding to appearances in order to excuse in their own eyes a change in their own purposes. Disorder went on increasing in Paris; the great lords, in their discontent, were quarrelling one with another; the prince of Condé struck M. de Rieux, who returned the blow; the duke of Nemours was killed in a duel by M. de Beaufort; the burgesses were growing weary of so much anarchy; a public display of feeling in favor of peace took place on the 24th of September in the garden of the Palais-Royal; those present stuck in their hats pieces of white paper in opposition to the Frondeurs' tufts of straw. People fought in the streets on behalf of these tokens.

For some weeks past Cardinal de Retz had remained inactive, and his friends pressed him to move. "You see quite well," they said, "that Mazarin is but a sort of jack-in-the-box, out of sight to-day and popping up to-morrow; but you also see that, whether he be in or out, the spring that sends him up or down is that of the royal authority, the which will not, apparently, be so very soon broken by the means taken to break it. The obligation you are under towards Monsieur, and even towards the public, as regards Mazarin, does not allow you to work for his restoration; he is no longer here, and, though his absence may be nothing but a mockery and a delusion, it nevertheless gives you an opportunity for taking certain steps which naturally lead to that which is for your good." Retz lost no time in going to Compiègne, where the king had installed himself after Mazarin's departure; he took with him a deputation of the clergy, and received in due form the cardinal's hat. He was the bearer of proposals for an accommodation from the duke of Orleans, but the queen cut him short. The court perceived its strength, and the instructions of Cardinal Mazarin were precise. The ruin of De Retz was from that moment resolved upon.

The prince of Condé was ill; he had left the command of his troops to M. de Tavannes; during the night between the 5th and 6th of October, Turenne struck his camp at Villeneuve-St.-Georges, crossed the Seine at Corbeil, the Marne at Meaux, without its being in the enemy's power to stop him, and established himself in the neighborhood of Dammartin. Condé was furious: "Tavannes and Vallon ought to wear bridles," he said, "they are asses;" he left his house, and placed himself once more at the head of his army, at first following after Turenne, and soon to sever himself completely from that Paris which was slipping away from him. "He would find himself more at home at the head of four squadrons in the Ardennes than commanding a dozen millions of such fellows as we have here, without excepting President Charton," said the duke of Orleans. "The prince was wasting away with sheer disgust; he was so weary of hearing all the talk about parliament, court of aids, chambers in assembly and Hôtel de Ville, that he would often declare that his grandfather had never been more fatigued by the parsons of La Rochelle." The great Condé was athirst for the thrilling emotions of war; and the crime he committed was to indulge at any price that boundless passion. Ever victorious at the head of French armies, he was about to make experience of defeat in the service of the foreigner.

The king had proclaimed a general amnesty on the 18th of October; and on the 21st he set out in state for Paris. The duke of Orleans still wavered. "You wanted peace," said Madame, "when it depended but on you to make war; you now want war when you can make neither war nor peace. It is of no use to think any longer of anything but going with a good grace to meet the king." At these words he exclaimed aloud, as if it had been proposed to him to go and throw himself in the river. "And where the devil should I go?" he answered. He remained at the Luxembourg. On drawing near Paris, the king sent word to his uncle that he would have to leave the city. Gaston replied in the following letter:

"Monseigneur,—Having understood from my cousin the duke of Danville and from Sieur d'Aligre the respect that your Majesty would have me pay you, I most humbly beseech your Majesty to allow me to assure you by these lines that I do not propose to remain in Paris longer than till to-morrow, and that I will go my way to my house at Limours, having no more passionate desire than to testify by my perfect obedience that I am, with submission,

"Monseigneur,

"Your most humble and most obedient servant and subject,

"GASTON."

The duke of Orleans retired before long to his castle at Blois, where he died in 1660, deserted, towards the end of his life, by all the friends he had successively abandoned and betrayed. "He had, with the exception of courage, all that was necessary to make an honorable man," says Cardinal de Retz, "but weakness was predominant in his heart through fear, and in his mind through irresolution; it disfigured the whole course of his life. He engaged in everything because he had not strength to resist those who drew him on, and he always came out disgracefully, because he had not the courage to support them." He was a prey to fear, fear of his friends as well as of his enemies.

The Fronde was all over, that of the gentry of the long robe as well as that of the gentry of the sword. The Parliament of Paris was once more falling in the State to the rank which had been assigned to it by Richelieu, and from which it had wanted to emerge by a supreme effort. The attempt had been the same in France as in England, however different had been the success. It was the same yearnings of patriotism and freedom, the same desire on the part of the country to take an active part in its own government, which had inspired the opposition of the Parliament of England to the despotism of Charles I., and the opposition of the French parliaments to Richelieu as well as to Mazarin. It was England's good fortune to have but one parliament of politicians instead of ten parliaments of magistrates, the latter more fit for the theory than the practice of public affairs; and the Reformation had, beforehand, accustomed its people to discussion as well as to liberty. Its great lords and its gentlemen placed themselves from the first at the head of the national movement, demanding nothing and expecting nothing for themselves from the advantages they claimed for their country. The remnant of the feudal system had succumbed with the duke of Montmorency under Richelieu; France knew not the way to profit by the elements of courage, disinterestedness and patriotism offered her by her magistracy; she had the misfortune to be delivered over to noisy factions of princes and great lords, ambitious or envious, greedy of honors and riches, as ready to fight the court as to be on terms with it, and thinking far more of their own personal interests than of the public service. Without any unity of action or aim, and by turns excited and dismayed by the examples that came to them from England, the Frondeurs had to guide them no Hampden or Cromwell; they had at their backs neither people nor army; the English had been able to accomplish a revolution; the Fronde failed before the dexterous prudence of Mazarin and the queen's fidelity to her minister. In vain did the coadjutor aspire to take his place; Anne of Austria had not forgotten the earl of Strafford.

Cardinal de Retz learnt before long the hollowness of his hopes. On the 19th of December, 1652, as he was repairing to the Louvre, he was arrested by M. de Villequier, captain of the guards on duty, and taken the same evening to the Bois de Vincennes; there was a great display of force in the street and around the carriage; but nobody moved, "whether it were," says Retz, "that the dejection of the people was too great, or that those who were well-inclined towards me lost courage on seeing nobody at their head." People were tired of raising barricades and hounding down the king's soldiers.

"I was taken into a large room where there were neither hangings nor bed; that which was brought in about eleven o'clock at night was of Chinese taffeta, not at all the thing for winter furniture. I slept very well, which must not be attributed to stout-heartedness, because misfortune has naturally that effect upon me. I have on more than one occasion discovered that it wakes me in the morning and sends me to sleep at night. I was obliged to get up the next day without a fire, because there was no wood to make one, and the three exons who had been posted near me had the kindness to assure me that I should not be without it the next day. He who remained alone on guard over me took it for himself, and I was a whole fortnight, at Christmas, in a room as big as a church, without warming myself. I do not believe that there could be found under heaven another man like this exon. He stole my linen, my clothes, my boots, and I was sometimes obliged to stay in bed eight or ten days for lack of anything to put on. I could not believe that I was subjected to such treatment without orders from some superior, and without some mad notion of making me die of vexation. I fortified myself against that notion, and I resolved at any rate not to die that kind of death. At last I got him into the habit of not tormenting me any more, by dint of letting him see that I did not torment myself at all. In point of fact, I had risen pretty nearly superior to all these ruses, for which I had a supreme contempt; but I could not assume the same loftiness of spirit in respect of the prison's entity (*substance*), if one may use the term, and the sight of myself, every morning when I awoke, in the hands of my enemies made me perceive that I was anything rather than a stoic." The archbishop of Paris had just died, and the dignity passed to his coadjutor; as the price of his release, Mazarin demanded his resignation. The clergy of Paris were highly indignant; Cardinal de Retz was removed to the castle of Nantes, whence he managed to make his escape in August, 1653; for nine years he lived abroad, in Spain, Italy and Germany, everywhere mingling in the affairs of Europe, engaged in intrigue, and not without influence; when at last he returned to France, in 1662, he resigned the archbishopric of Paris and established himself in the principality of Commercy, which belonged to him, occupied up to the day of his death in paying his debts, doing good to his friends and servants, writing his memoirs, and making his peace with God. This was in those days a solicitude which never left the most worldly: the prince of Conti had died very devout, and Madame de Longueville had just expired at the Carmelites', after twenty-five years' penance, when Cardinal de Retz died on the 24th of August, 1679. At the time of his arrest, it was a common saying of the people in the street that together with "Cardinal de Retz it would have been a very good thing to imprison Cardinal Mazarin as well, in order to teach them of the clergy not to meddle for the future in the things of this world." Language which was unjust to the grand government of Cardinal Richelieu, unjust even to Cardinal Mazarin. The latter was returning with greater power than ever at the moment when Cardinal de Retz, losing forever the hope of supplanting him in power, was beginning that life of imprisonment and exile which was ultimately to give him time to put retirement and repentance between himself and death.

Cardinal Mazarin had once more entered France, but he had not returned to Paris. The prince of Condé, soured by the ill-success of the Fronde and demented by illimitable pride, had not been ashamed to accept the title of generalissimo of the Spanish armies; Turenne had succeeded in hurling him back into Luxembourg, and it was in front of Bar, besieged, that Mazarin, with a body of four thousand men, joined the French army; Bar was taken, and the campaign of 1652, disastrous at nearly every point, had just finished with this success, when the cardinal re-entered Paris at the end of January, 1653. Six months later, at the end of July, the insurrection in Guienne becoming extinguished by a series of private conventions; the king's armies were entering Bordeaux; the revolted princes received their pardon, waiting, meanwhile, for the prince of Conti to marry, as he did next year, Mdlle. Martinozzi, one of Mazarin's nieces; Madame de Longueville retired to Moulins into the convent where her aunt, Madame de Montmorency, had for the last twenty years been mourning for her husband; Condé was the only rebel left, more dangerous, for France, than all the hostile armies he commanded.

Cardinal Mazarin was henceforth all-powerful; whatever may have been the nature of the ties which united him to the queen, he had proved their fidelity and strength too fully to always avoid the temptation of adopting the tone of a master; the young king's confidence in his minister, who had brought him up, equalled that of his mother; the merits as well as the faults of Mazarin were accordingly free to crop out: he was neither vindictive nor cruel towards even his most inveterate enemies, whom he could not manage, as Richelieu did, to confound with those of the State; the excesses of the factions had sufficed to destroy them; "Time is an able fellow," the cardinal would frequently say; if people often complained of being badly compensated for their services, Mazarin could excuse himself on the ground of the deplorable condition of the finances. He nevertheless feathered his own nest inordinately, taking care, however, not to rob the people, it was said. He confined himself to selling everything at a profit to himself, even the offices of the royal household, without making, as Richelieu had made, any "advance out of his own money to the State, when there was none in the treasury." The power had been honestly won, if the fortune were of a doubtful kind. M. Mignet has said with his manly precision of language: "Amidst those unreasonable disturbances which upset for a while the judgment of the great Turenne, which, in the case of the great Condé, turned the sword of Rocroi against France, and which led Cardinal Retz to make so poor a use of his talent, there was but one firm will, and that was Anne of Austria's; but one man of good sense, and that was Mazarin" [*Introduction aux négociations pour la succession d'Espagne*].

From 1653 to 1657, Turenne, seconded by Marshal La Ferté and sometimes by Cardinal Mazarin in person, constantly kept the Spaniards and the prince of Condé in check, recovering the places but lately taken from France and relieving the besieged towns; without ever engaging in pitched battles, he almost always had the advantage. Mazarin resolved to strike a decisive blow. It was now three years since, after long negotiations, the cardinal had concluded with Cromwell, Protector of the Commonwealth of England, a treaty of peace and commerce, the prelude and first fruits of a closer alliance which the able minister of Anne of Austria had not ceased to wish for and pave the way for. On the 23rd of March, 1657, the parleys ended at last in a treaty of alliance offensive and defensive; it was concluded at Paris between France and England. Cromwell promised that a body of six thousand English, supported by a fleet prepared to victual and aid them along the coasts, should go and join the French army, twenty thousand strong, to make war on the Spanish Low Countries, and especially to besiege the three forts of Gravelines, Mardyk and Dunkerque, the last of which was to be placed in the hands of the English and remain in their possession. Six weeks after the conclusion of the treaty, the English troops disembarked at Boulogne; they were regiments formed and trained in the long struggles of the civil war, drilled to the most perfect discipline, of austere manners, and of resolute and stern courage; the king came in person to receive them on their arrival; Mardyk was soon taken and placed as pledge in the hands of the English. Cromwell sent two fresh regiments for the siege of Dunkerque. In the spring of 1658, Turenne invested the place. Louis XIV. and Mazarin went to Calais to be present at this great enterprise.

"At Brussels," says M. Guizot in his *Histoire de la République d'Angleterre et de Cromwell,* "neither Don Juan nor the marquis of Carracena would believe that Dunkerque was in danger; being at the same time indolent and proud, they disdained the counsel, at one time of vigilant activity and at another of prudent reserve, which was constantly given them by Condé; they would not have anybody come and rouse them during their siesta if any unforeseen incident occurred, nor allow any doubt of their success when once they were up and on horseback. They hurried away to the defence of Dunkerque, leaving behind them their artillery and a portion of their cavalry. Condé conjured them to intrench themselves whilst awaiting them; Don Juan, on the contrary, was for advancing on to the 'dunes' and marching to meet the French army. 'You don't reflect,' said Condé: 'that ground is fit only for infantry, and that of the French is more numerous and has seen more service.' 'I am persuaded,' replied Don Juan, 'that they will not even dare to look His Most Catholic Majesty's army in the face.' 'Ah! you don't know M. de Turenne; no mistake is made with impunity in the presence of such a man as that.' Don Juan persisted, and, in fact, made his way on to the 'dunes.' Next day, the 13th of June, Condé, more and more convinced of the danger, made fresh efforts to make him retire. 'Retire!' cried Don Juan: 'if the French dare fight, this will be the finest day that ever shone on the arms of His Most Catholic Majesty.' 'Very fine, certainly,' answered Condé, 'if you give orders to retire.' Turenne put an end to this disagreement in the enemy's camp. Having made up his mind to give battle on the 14th, at daybreak, he sent word to the English general, Lockhart, by one of his officers who wanted at the same time to explain the commander-in-chief's plan and his grounds for it: 'All right,' answered Lockhart: 'I leave it to M. de Turenne; he shall tell me his reasons after the battle, if he likes.' A striking contrast between the manly discipline of English good sense and the silly blindness of Spanish pride. Condé was not mistaken: the issue of a battle, begun under such auspices, could not be doubtful. 'My lord,' said he to the young duke of Gloucester, who was serving in the Spanish army by the side of his brother, the duke of York, 'did you ever see a battle?' 'No, prince.' 'Well, then you are going to see one lost.' The battle of the Dunes was, in fact, totally lost by the Spaniards after four hours' very hard fighting, during which the English regiments carried bravely and with heavy losses the most difficult and the best defended position; all the officers of Lockhart's regiment, except two, were killed or wounded before the end of the day; the Spanish army retired in disorder, leaving four thousand prisoners in the hands of the conqueror. 'The enemy came to meet us,' wrote Turenne in the evening to his wife; 'they were beaten, God be praised! I have worked rather hard all day; I wish you good night, and am going to bed.' Ten days afterwards, on the 23rd of June, 1658, the garrison of Dunkerque was exhausted; the aged governor, the marquis of Leyden, had been mortally wounded in a sortie; the place surrendered, and, the next day but one, Louis XIV. entered it, but merely to hand it over at once to the English. 'Though the court and the army are in despair at the notion of letting go what he calls a rather nice morsel,' wrote Lockhart the day before to Secretary Thurloe, 'nevertheless the cardinal is staunch to his promises, and seems as well satisfied at giving up this place to His Highness as I am to take it. The king also is extremely polite and obliging, and he has in his soul more honesty than I had supposed.'"

The surrender of Dunkerque was soon followed by that of Gravelines and several other towns; the great blow against the Spanish arms had been struck; negotiations were beginning; tranquillity reigned everywhere in France; the parliament had caused no talk since the 20th of March, 1655, when, they having refused to enregister certain financial edicts, *for want of liberty of suffrage*, the king, setting out from the castle of Vincennes, "had arrived early at the Palace of Justice, in scarlet jacket and gray hat, attended by all his court in the same costume, as if he were going to hunt the stag, which was unwonted up to that day. When he was in his bed of justice, he prohibited the parliament from assembling, and, after having said a word or two, he rose and went out without listening to any address." [*Mémoires de Montglat*, t. ii.] The sovereign courts had learnt to improve upon the old maxim of Matthew Molé: "I am going to court; I shall tell the truth; after which the king must be obeyed." Not a tongue wagged, and obedience at length was rendered to Cardinal Mazarin as it had but lately been to Cardinal Richelieu.

The court was taking its diversion. "There were plenty of fine comedies and ballets going on. The king, who danced very well, liked them extremely," says Mdlle. de Montpensier, at that time exiled from Paris; "all this did not affect me at all; I thought that I should see enough of it on my return; but my ladies were different, and nothing could equal their vexation at not being in all these gayeties." It was still worse when announcement was made of the arrival of Queen Christina of Sweden, that celebrated princess who had reigned from the time she was six years old, and had lately abdicated, in 1654, in favor of her cousin, Charles Gustavus, in order to regain her liberty, she said, but perhaps also because she found herself confronted by the ever-increasing opposition of the grandees of her kingdom, hostile to the foreign fashions favored by the queen as well as to the design that was attributed to her of becoming converted to Catholicism. When Christina arrived at Paris, in 1656, she had already accomplished her abjuration at Brussels, without assigning her motives for it to anybody. "Those who talk of them know nothing about them," she would say, "and she who knows something about them has never talked of them." There was great curiosity at Paris to see this queen. The king sent the duke of Guise to meet her, and he wrote to one of his friends as follows:—"She is not tall, she has a good arm, a hand white and well made, but rather a man's than a woman's, a high shoulder, a defect which she so well conceals by the singularity of her dress, her walk and her gestures that you might make a bet about it. Her face is large without being defective, all her features are the same and strongly marked, a pretty tolerable turn of countenance, set off by a very singular head-dress, that is, a man's wig, very big and very much raised in front; the top of the head is a tissue of hair, and the back has something of a woman's style of head-dress. Sometimes she also wears a hat; her bodice laced behind, crosswise, is made something like our doublets, her chemise bulging out all around her petticoat, which she wears rather badly fastened and not over-straight. She is always very much powdered, with a good deal of pomade, and almost never puts on gloves. She has at the very least as much swagger and haughtiness as the great Gustavus, her father, can have had; she is mighty civil and coaxing, speaks eight languages, and principally French, as if she had been born in Paris. She knows as much about it as all our Academy and the Sorbonne put together, has an admirable knowledge of painting as well as of everything else, and knows all the intrigues of our court better than I. In fact, she is quite an extraordinary person." "The king, though very timid at that time," says Madame de Motteville, "and not at all well informed, got on so well with this bold, well-informed and haughty princess, that, from the first moment, they associated together with much freedom and pleasure on both sides. It was difficult, when you had once had a good opportunity of seeing her, and above all of listening to her, not to forgive all her irregularities, though some of them were highly blamable." All the court and all Paris made a great fuss about this queen who insisted upon going everywhere, even to the French Academy, where no woman had ever been admitted. Patru thus relates to one of his friends the story of her visit: "No notice was given until about eight or nine in the morning of this princess's purpose, so that some of our body could not receive information in time. M. de Gombault came without having been advertised, but, as soon as he knew of the queen's purpose, he went away again, for thou must know that he is wrath with her because, he having written some verses in which he praised the great Gustavus, she did not write to him, she who, as thou knowest, has written to a hundred impertinent apes. I might complain with far more reason; but, so long as kings, queens, princes, and princesses do me only that sort of harm, I shall never complain. The chancellor [Séguier at whose house the Academy met] had forgotten to have the portrait of this princess, which she had given to the society, placed in the room; which, in my opinion, ought not to have been forgotten. Word was brought that the carriage was entering the court-yard. The chancellor, followed by the whole body, went to receive the princess. . . . As soon as she entered the room, she went off-hand, according to her habit, and sat down in her chair; and at the same moment, without any order given us, we also sat down. The princess, seeing that we were at some little distance from the table, told us that we could draw up close to it. There was some little drawing up, but not as if it were a dinner-party. . . . Several pieces were read; and then the director, who was M. de la Chambre, told the queen that the ordinary exercise of the society was to work at the Dictionary, and that, if it were agreeable to Her Majesty, a sheet should be read. 'By all means,' said she. M. de Mézeray, accordingly, read the word *Jeux*, under which, amongst other proverbial expressions, there was: '*Jeux de princes, qui ne plaisent qu'à ceux qui les font*' (*Princes' jokes, which amuse only those who make them*). She burst out laughing. The word, which was in fair copy, was finished. It would have been better to read a word which had to be weeded, because then we should all have spoken; but people were taken by surprise—the French always are. . . . After about an hour, the princess rose, made a courtesy to the company, and went away as she had come. Here is really what passed at this famous interview which, no doubt, does great honor to the Academy. The duke of Anjou talks of coming to it, and the zealous are quite transported with this bit of glory" [*Œuvres diverses de Patru*, t. ii. p. 512].

Queen Christina returned the next year and passed some time at Fontainebleau. It was there, in a gallery that King Louis Philippe caused to be turned into apartments, which M. Guizot at one time occupied, that she had her first equerry, Monaldeschi, whom she accused of having betrayed her, assassinated almost before her own eyes; and she considered it astonishing and very bad taste that the court of France should be shocked at such an execution. "This barbarous princess," says Madame de Motteville, "after so cruel an action as that, remained in her room laughing and chatting as easily as if she had done something of no consequence or very praiseworthy. The queen-mother, a perfect Christian, who had met with so many enemies whom she might have punished but who had received from her nothing but marks of kindness, was scandalized by it. The king and Monsieur blamed her, and the minister, who was not a cruel man, was astounded."

The queen-mother had other reasons for being less satisfied than she had been at the first trip of Queen Christina of Sweden. The young king testified much inclination for Mary de Mancini, Cardinal Mazarin's niece, a bold and impassioned creature, whose sister Olympia had already found favor in his eyes before her marriage with the count of Soissons. The eldest of all had married the duke of Mercœur, son of the duke of Vendôme; the other two were destined to be united, at a later period, to the dukes of Bouillon and la Meilleraye; the hopes of Mary went still higher; relying on the love of young Louis XIV. she dared to dream of the throne; and the Queen of Sweden encouraged her. "The right thing is to marry one's love," she told the king. No time was lost in letting Christina understand that she could not remain long in France; the cardinal, "with a moderation for which he cannot be sufficiently commended," says Madame de Motteville, "himself put obstacles in the way of his niece's ambitious designs; he sent her to the convent of Brouage, threatening, if that exile were not sufficient, to leave France and take his niece with him."

"No power," he said to the king, "can wrest from me the free authority of disposal which God and the laws give me over my family." "You are king; you weep; and yet I am going away!" said the young girl to her royal lover, who let her go. Mary de Mancini was mistaken; he was not yet *King.*

Cardinal Mazarin and the queen had other views regarding the marriage of Louis XIV.; for a long time past the object of their labors had been to terminate the war by an alliance with Spain. The Infanta, Maria Theresa, was no longer heiress to the crown, for King Philip at last had a son; Spain was exhausted by long-continued efforts and dismayed by the checks received in the campaign of 1658; the alliance of the Rhine, recently concluded at Frankfurt between the two leagues, catholic and protestant, confirmed immutably the advantages which the treaty of Westphalia had secured to France. The electors had just raised to the head of the Empire young Leopold I., on the death of his father Ferdinand III., and they proposed their mediation between France and Spain. Whilst King Philip IV. was still hesitating, Mazarin took a step in another direction; the king set out for Lyons, accompanied by his mother and his minister, to go and see Princess Margaret of Savoy, who had been proposed to him a long time ago as his wife. He was pleased with her, and negotiations were already pretty far advanced, to the great displeasure of the queen-mother, when the cardinal, on the 29th of November, 1659, in the evening, entered Anne of Austria's room. "He found her pensive and melancholy, but he was all smiles. 'Good news, Madame,' said he. 'Ah!' cried the queen, 'is it to be peace?' 'More than that, Madame; I bring your Majesty both peace and the Infanta.'" The Spaniards had become uneasy; and Don Antonio de Pimentel had arrived at Lyons at the same time with the court of Savoy, bearing a letter from Philip IV. for the queen his sister. The duchess of Savoy had to depart and take her daughter with her, disappointed of her hopes; all the consolation she obtained was a written promise that the king would marry Princess Margaret, if the marriage with the Infanta were not accomplished within a year.

The year had not yet rolled away, and the duchess of Savoy had already lost every atom of illusion. Since the 13th of August, Cardinal Mazarin had been officially negotiating with Don Louis de Haro representing Philip IV. The ministers had held a meeting in the middle of the Bidassoa, on the Island of Pheasants, where a pavilion had been erected on the boundary-line between the two States. On the 7th of November, the peace of the Pyrenees was signed at last; it put an end to a war which had continued for twenty-three years, often internecine, always burdensome, and which had ruined the finances of the two countries. France was the gainer of Artois and Roussillon, and of several places in Flanders, Hainault and Luxembourg; and the peace of Westphalia was recognized by Spain, to whom France restored all that she held in Catalonia and in Franche-Comté. Philip IV. had refused to include Portugal in the treaty. The Infanta received as dowry 500,000 gold crowns, and renounced all her rights to the throne of Spain; the prince of Condé was taken back to favor by the king, and declared that he would fain redeem with his blood all the hostilities he had committed in and out of France. The king restored him to all his honors and dignities, gave him the government of Burgundy, and bestowed on his son, the duke of Enghien, the office of Grand Master of France. The honor of the king of Spain was saved, he did not abandon his allies, and he made a great match for his daughter. But the eyes of Europe were not blinded; it was France that triumphed, the policy of Cardinal Richelieu and of Cardinal Mazarin was everywhere successful. The work of Henry IV. was completed, the House of Austria was humiliated and vanquished in both its branches; the man who had concluded the peace of Westphalia and the peace of the Pyrenees had a right to say, "I am more French in heart than in speech."

The prince of Condé returned to court, "as if he had never gone away," says Mdlle. de Montpensier (*Mémoires*, t. iii. p. 451). "The king talked familiarly with him of all that he had done both in France and in Flanders, and that with as much gusto as if all those things had taken place for his service."

"The prince discovered him to be so great in every point that, from the first moment at which he could approach him, he comprehended, as it appeared, that the time had come to humble himself. That genius for sovereignty and command which God had implanted in the king, and which was beginning to show itself, persuaded the prince of Condé that all which remained of the previous reign was about to be annihilated" [*Mémoires de Madame de Motteville*, t. v. p. 39]. From that day King Louis XIV. had no more submissive subject than the great Condé.

The court was in the South, travelling from town to town, pending the arrival of the dispensations from Rome. On the 3rd of June, 1660, Don Louis de Haro, in the name of the king of France, espoused the Infanta in the church of Fontarabia. Mdlle. de Montpensier made up her mind to be present, unknown to anybody, at the ceremony. When it was over, the new queen, knowing that the king's cousin was there, went up to her, saying, "I should like to embrace this fair unknown," and led her away to her room, chatting about everything, but pretending not to know her. The queen-mother and King Philip IV. met next day, on the Island of Pheasants, after forty-five years' separation. The king had come privately to have a view of the Infanta, and he watched her, through a door ajar, towering a whole head above the courtiers. "May I ask my niece what she thinks of this unknown?" said Anne of Austria to her brother. "It will be time when she has passed that door," replied the king. Young *Monsieur*, the king's brother, leaned forward towards his sister-in-law, and "What does your Majesty think of this door?" he whispered. "I think it very nice and handsome," answered the young queen. The king had thought her handsome, "despite the ugliness of her head-dress and of her clothes, which had at first taken him by surprise." King Philip IV. kept looking at M. de Turenne, who had accompanied the king. "That man has given me dreadful times," he repeated twice or thrice. "You can judge whether M. de Turenne felt himself offended," says Mdlle. de Montpensier. The definitive marriage took place at Saint-Jean-de-Luz on the 9th of June, and the court took the road leisurely back to Vincennes. Scarcely had the arrival taken place, when all the sovereign bodies sent a solemn deputation to pay their respects to Cardinal Mazarin and thank him for the peace he had just concluded. It was an unprecedented honor, paid to a minister upon whose head the parliament had but lately set a price. The cardinal's triumph was as complete at home as abroad; all foes had been reduced to submission or silence, Paris and France rejoicing over the peace and the king's marriage; but, like Cardinal Richelieu, Mazarin succumbed at the very pinnacle of his glory and power; the gout, to which he was subject, flew to his stomach, and he suffered excruciating agonies. One day when the king came to get his advice upon a certain matter: "Sir," said the cardinal, "you are asking counsel of a man who no longer has his reason and who raves." He saw the approach of death calmly but not unregretfully. Concealed, one day, behind a curtain in the new apartments of the Mazarin Palace (now the National Library), young Brienne heard the cardinal coming. "He dragged his slippers along like a man very languid and just recovering from some serious illness. He paused at every step, for he was very feeble; he fixed his gaze first on one side and then on the other, and letting his eyes wander over the magnificent objects of art he had been all his life collecting, he said, 'All that must be left behind!' And turning round, he added, 'And that too! what trouble I have had to obtain all these things! I shall never see them more where I am going.'" He had himself removed to Vincennes of which he was governor. There he continued to regulate all the affairs of State, striving to initiate the young king in the government. "Nobody," Turenne used to say, "works so much as the cardinal or discovers so many expedients with great clearness of mind for the terminating of much business of different sorts." The dying minister recommended to the king MM. Le Tellier and de Lionne, and he added: "Sir, to you I owe everything; but I consider that I to some extent acquit myself of my obligation to your Majesty by giving you M. Colbert." The cardinal, uneasy about the large possessions he left, had found a way of securing them to his heirs by making, during his lifetime, a gift of the whole of them to the king. Louis XIV. at once returned it. The minister had lately placed his two nieces, the princess of Conti and the countess of Soissons, at the head of the household of two queens; he had married his niece, Hortensia Mancini, to the duke of La Meilleraye, who took the title of duke of Mazarin. The father of this duke was the relative and protégé of Cardinal Richelieu, for whom Mazarin had always preserved a feeling of great gratitude. It was to him and his wife that he left the remainder of his vast possessions, after having distributed amongst all his relatives liberal bequests to an enormous amount. The pictures and jewels went to the king, to Monsieur and to the queens. A considerable sum was employed for the foundation and endowment of the Collége des Quatre Nations (now the Palais de l'Institut), intended for the education of sixty children of the four provinces reunited to France by the treaties of Westphalia and the Pyrenees, Alsace, Roussillon, Artois and Pignerol. The cardinal's fortune was estimated at fifty millions.

Mazarin had scarcely finished making his final dispositions when his malady increased to a violent pitch. "On the 5th of March, forty hours' public prayers were ordered in all the churches of Paris, which is not generally done except in the case of kings," says Madame de Motteville. The cardinal had sent for M. Joly, parish-priest of St. Nicholas des Champs, a man of great reputation for piety, and begged him not to leave him. "I have misgivings about not being sufficiently afraid of death," he said to his confessor. He felt his own pulse himself, muttering quite low, "I shall have a great deal more to suffer." The king had left him on the 7th of March, in the evening. He did not see him again and sent to summon the ministers. Already the living was taking the place of the dying, with a commencement of pomp and circumstance which excited wonder at the changes of the world. "On the 9th, between two and three in the morning, Mazarin raised himself slightly in his bed, praying to God and suffering greatly: then he said aloud, 'Ah! holy Virgin, have pity upon me; receive my soul,' and so he expired, showing a fair front to death up to the last moment." The queen-mother had left her room for the last two days, because it was too near that of the dying man. "She wept less than the king," says Madame de Motteville, "being more disgusted with the creatures of his making by reason of the knowledge she had of their imperfections, insomuch that it was soon easy to see that the defects of the dead man would before long appear to her greater than they had yet been in her eyes, for he did not content himself with exercising sovereign power over the whole realm, but he exercised it over the sovereigns themselves who had given it him, not leaving them liberty to dispose of anything of any consequence" [*Mémoires de Madame de Motteville*, t. v. p. 103].

Louis XIV. was about to reign with a splendor and puissance without precedent; his subjects were submissive and Europe at peace: he was reaping the fruits of the labors of his grandfather Henry IV., of Cardinal Richelieu and of Cardinal Mazarin. Whilst continuing the work of Henry IV. Richelieu had rendered possible the government of Mazarin; he had set the kingly authority on foundations so strong that the princes of the blood themselves could not shake it. Mazarin had destroyed party and secured to France a glorious peace. Great minister had succeeded great king and able man great minister; Italian prudence, dexterity and finesse had replaced the indomitable will, the incomparable judgment and the grandeur of view of the French priest and nobleman. Richelieu and Mazarin had accomplished their patriotic work: the King's turn had come.

CHAPTER XLIV.

LOUIS XIV., HIS WARS AND HIS CONQUESTS, 1661–1697.

CARDINAL MAZARIN on his deathbed had given the young king this advice: "Manage your affairs yourself, Sir, and raise no more premier ministers to where your bounties have placed me; I have discovered, by what I might have done against your service, how dangerous it is for a king to put his servants in such a position." Mazarin knew thoroughly the king whose birth he had seen. "He has in him the making of four kings and one honest man," he used to say. Scarcely was the minister dead, when Louis XIV. sent to summon his council: Chancellor Séguier, Superintendent Fouquet and Secretaries of State Le Tellier, de Lionne, Brienne, Duplessis-Guénéguaud, and La Vrillière. Then, addressing the chancellor: "Sir," said he, "I have had you assembled together with my ministers and my Secretaries of State to tell you that until now I have been well pleased to leave my affairs to be governed by the late cardinal: it is time that I should govern them myself; you will aid me with your counsels when I ask for them. Beyond the general business of the seal, in which I do not intend to make any alteration, I beg and command you, Mr. Chancellor, to put the seal of authority to nothing without my orders and without having spoken to me thereof, unless a Secretary of State shall bring them to you on my behalf. . . . And for you, gentlemen," addressing the Secretaries of State,

I warn you not to sign anything, even a safety-warrant or passport, without my command, to report every day to me personally, and to favor nobody in your monthly rolls. Mr. Superintendent, I have explained to you my intentions; I beg that you will employ the services of M. Colbert, whom the late cardinal recommended to me."

The king's councillors were men of experience; and they all recognized the master's tone. From timidity or respect, Louis XIV. had tolerated the yoke of Mazarin, not, however, without impatience and in expectation of his own turn [Portraits de la Cour, *Archives curieuses*, t. viii. p. 371]: "The cardinal," said he one day, "does just as he pleases, and I put up with it because of the good service he has rendered me, but I shall be master in my turn;" and he added, "the king my grandfather did great things and left some to do; if God gives me grace to live twenty years longer, perhaps I may do as much or more." God was to grant Louis XIV. more time and power than he asked for, but it was Henry IV.'s good fortune to maintain his greatness at the sword's point, without ever having leisure to become intoxicated with it. Absolute power is in its nature so unwholesome and dangerous that the strongest mind cannot always withstand it. It was Louis XIV.'s misfortune to be king for seventy-two years, and to reign fifty-six years as sovereign master.

"Many people made up their minds," says the king in his *Mémoires* [t. ii. p. 392], "that my assiduity in work was but a heat which would soon cool; but time showed them what to think of it, for they saw me constantly going on in the same way, wishing to be informed of all that took place, listening to the prayers and complaints of my meanest subjects, knowing the number of my troops and the condition of my fortresses, treating directly with foreign ministers, receiving despatches, making in person part of the replies and giving my secretaries the substance of the others, regulating the receipts and expenditure of my kingdom, having reports made to myself in person by those who were in important offices, keeping my affairs secret, distributing graces according to my own choice, reserving to myself alone all my authority, and confining those who served me to a modest position very far from the elevation of premier ministers."

The young king, from the first, regulated his life and his time: "I laid it down as a law to myself," he says in his *Instructions au dauphin*, "to work regularly twice a day. I cannot tell you what fruit I reaped immediately after this resolution. I felt myself rising as it were both in mind and courage; I found myself quite another being; I discovered in myself what I had no idea of and I joyfully reproached myself for having been so long ignorant of it. Then it dawned upon me that I was king and was born to be."

A taste for order and regularity was natural to Louis XIV., and he soon made it apparent in his councils. "Under Cardinal Mazarin, there was literally nothing but disorder and confusion; he had the council held whilst he was being shaved and dressed, without ever giving anybody a seat, not even the chancellor or Marshal Villeroy, and he was often chattering with his linnet and his monkey all the time he was being talked to about business. After Mazarin's death the king's council assumed a more decent form. The king alone was seated, all the others remained standing, the chancellor leaned against the bedrail, and M. de Lionne upon the edge of the chimney-piece. He who was making a report placed himself opposite the king and, if he had to write, sat down on a stool which was at the end of the table where there was a writing-desk and paper" [*Histoire de France*, by Le P. Daniel, t. xvi. p. 89]. "I will settle this matter with your Majesty's ministers," said the Portuguese ambassador one day to the young king. "I have no ministers, Mr. Ambassador," replied Louis XIV.: "you mean to say my men of business."

Long habituation to the office of king was not destined to wear out, to exhaust the youthful ardor of King Louis XIV. He had been for a long while governing, when he wrote: "You must not imagine, my son, that affairs of State are like those obscure and thorny passages in the sciences which you will perhaps have found fatiguing, at which the mind strives to raise itself, by an effort, beyond itself, and which repel us quite as much by their, at any rate apparent, uselessness as by their difficulty. The function of kings consists principally in leaving good sense to act, which always acts naturally without any trouble. All that is most necessary in this kind of work is at the same time agreeable; for it is, in a word, my son, to keep an open eye over all the world, to be continually learning news from all the provinces and all nations, the secrets of all courts, the temper and the foible of all foreign princes and ministers, to be informed about an infinite number of things of which we are supposed to be ignorant, to see in our own circle that which is most carefully hidden from us, to discover the most distant views of our own courtiers and their most darkly cherished interests which come to us through contrary interests, and, in fact, I know not what other pleasure we would not give up for this, even if it were curiosity alone that caused us to feel it" [*Mémoires de Louis XIV.*, t. ii. p. 428].

At twenty-two years of age, no more than during the rest of his life, was Louis XIV. disposed to sacrifice business to pleasure, but he did not sacrifice pleasure to business. It was on a taste so natural to a young prince, for the first time free to do as he pleased, that Superintendent Fouquet counted to increase his influence and probably his power with the king. "The attorney-general [Fouquet was attorney-general in the parliament of Paris], though a great thief, will remain master of the others," the queen-mother had said to Madame de Motteville at the time of Mazarin's death. Fouquet's hopes led him to think of nothing less than to take the minister's place.

Fouquet, who was born in 1615, and had been superintendent of finance in conjunction with Servien since 1655, had been in sole possession of that office since the death of his colleague in 1659. He had faithfully served Cardinal Mazarin through the troubles of the Fronde. The latter had kept him in power in spite of numerous accusations of malversation and extravagance. Fouquet, however, was not certain of the cardinal's good faith: he bought Belle-Ile to secure for himself a retreat, and prepared, for his personal defence, a mad project which was destined subsequently to be his ruin. From the commencement of his reign, the counsels of Mazarin on his death-bed, the suggestions of Colbert, the first observations made by the king himself irrevocably ruined Fouquet in the mind of the young monarch. Whilst the superintendent was dreaming of the ministry and his friends calling him *the Future*, when he was preparing, in his castle of Vaux-le-Vicomte, an entertainment in the king's honor at a cost of 40,000 crowns, Louis XIV., in concert with Colbert, had resolved upon his ruin. The form of trial was decided upon. The king did not want to have any trouble with the parliament, and Colbert suggested to Fouquet the idea of ridding himself of his office of attorney-general. Achille de Harlay bought it for fourteen hundred thousand livres; a million in ready money was remitted to the king for his Majesty's urgent necessities; the superintendent was buying up everybody, even the king.

On the 17th of August, 1661, the whole court thronged the gardens of Vaux, designed by Le Nôtre; the king, whilst admiring the pictures of Le Brun, the *Fâcheux* of Molière represented that day for the first time, and the gold and silver plate which encumbered the tables, felt his inward wrath redoubled; "Ah! Madame," he said to the queen his mother, "shall not we make all these fellows disgorge?" He would have had the superintendent arrested in the very midst of those festivities, the very splendor of which was an accusation against him. Anne of Austria, inclined in her heart to be indulgent towards Fouquet, restrained him: "Such a deed would scarcely be to your honor, my son," she said, "everybody can see that this poor man is ruining himself to give you good cheer, and you would have him arrested in his own house!"

"I put off the execution of my design," says Louis XIV. in his *Mémoires*, "which caused me incredible pain, for I saw that during that time he was practising new devices to rob me. You can imagine that at the age I then was it required my reason to make a great effort against my feelings in order to act with so much self-control. All France commended especially the secrecy with which I had for three or four months kept a resolution of that sort, particularly as it concerned a man who had such special access to me, who had dealings with all that approached me, who received information from within and from without the kingdom, and who, of himself, must have been led by the voice of his own conscience to apprehend everything." Fouquet apprehended and became reassured by turns; the king, he said, had forgiven him all the disorder which the troubles of the times and the absolute will of Mazarin had possibly caused in the finances. However, he was anxious when he followed Louis XIV. to Nantes, the king being about to hold an assembly of the states of Brittany. "Nantes, Belle-Ile! Nantes, Belle-Ile!" he kept repeating. On arriving, Fouquet was ill and trembled as if he had the ague; he did not present himself to the king.

On the 5th of September, in the evening, the king himself wrote to the queen-mother: "My dear mother, I wrote you word this morning about the execution of the orders I had given to have the superintendent arrested; you know that I have had this matter for a long while on my mind, but it was impossible to act sooner, because I wanted him first of all to have thirty thousand crowns paid in for the marine, and because, moreover, it was necessary to see to various matters which could not be done in a day; and you cannot imagine the difficulty I had in merely finding means of speaking in private to D'Artagnan. I felt the greatest impatience in the world to get it over, there being nothing else to detain me in this district. At last, this morning, the superintendent having come to work with me as usual, I talked to him first of one matter and then of another, and made a show of searching for papers, until, out of the window of my closet, I saw D'Artagnan in the castle-yard; and then I dismissed the superintendent, who, after chatting a little while at the bottom of the staircase with La Feuillade, disappeared during the time he was paying his respects to M. Le Tellier, so that poor D'Artagnan thought he had missed him, and sent me word by Maupertuis that he suspected that somebody had given him warning to look to his safety; but he caught him again in the place where the great church stands and arrested him for me about mid-day. They put the superintendent into one of my carriages followed by my musketeers, to escort him to the castle of Angers, whilst his wife, by my orders, is off to Limoges. . . . I have told those gentlemen who are here with me that I would have no more superintendents, but myself take the work of finance in conjunction with faithful persons who will do nothing without me, knowing that this is the true way to place myself in affluence and relieve my people. During the little attention I have as yet given thereto I observed some important matters which I did not at all understand. You will have no difficulty in believing that there have been many people placed in a great fix; but I am very glad for them to see that I am not such a dupe as they supposed and that the best plan is to hold to me."

Three years were to roll by before the end of Fouquet's trial. In vain had one of the superintendent's valets, getting the start of all the king's couriers, shown sense enough to give timely warning to his distracted friends; Fouquet's papers were seized, and very compromising they were for him as well as for a great number of court-personages, of both sexes. Colbert prosecuted the matter with a rigorous justice that looked very like hate; the king's self-esteem was personally involved in procuring the condemnation of a minister guilty of great extravagances and much irregularity rather than of intentional want of integrity. Public feeling was at first so greatly against the superintendent that the peasants shouted to the musketeers told off to escort him from Angers to the Bastille: "No fear of his escaping; we would hang him with our own hands." But the length and the harshness of the proceedings, the efforts of Fouquet's family and friends, the wrath of the parliament out of whose hands the case had been taken in favor of carefully chosen commissioners, brought about a great change; of the two prosecuting counsel (*conseillers rapporteurs*) one, M. de Sainte-Hélène, was inclined towards severity; the other, Oliver d'Ormesson, a man of integrity and courage, thought of nothing but justice, and treated with contempt the hints that reached him from the court. Colbert took the trouble one day to go and call upon old M. d'Ormesson, the counsel's father, to complain of the delays that the son, as he said, was causing in the trial: "It is very extraordinary," said the minister, "that a great king, feared throughout Europe, cannot finish a case against one of his own subjects." "I am sorry," answered the old gentleman, "that the king is not satisfied with my son's conduct; I know that he practises what I have always taught him: to fear God, serve the king and render justice without respect of persons. The delay in the matter does not depend upon him; he works at it night and day without wasting a moment." Oliver d'Ormesson lost the stewardship of Soissonness to which he had the titular right, but he did not allow himself to be diverted from his scrupulous integrity. Nay, he grew wroth at the continual attacks of Chancellor Séguier, more of a courtier than ever in his old age and anxious to finish the matter to the satisfaction of the court. "I told many of the Chamber," he writes, "that I did not like to have the whip applied to me every morning, and that the chancellor was a sort of chastiser I would not put up with" [*Journal d'Oliver d'Ormesson*, t. ii. p. 88].

Fouquet, who claimed the jurisdiction of the parliament, had at first refused to answer the interrogatory; it was determined to conduct his case "as if he were dumb," but his friends had him advised not to persist in his silence. The courage and presence of mind of the accused more than once embarrassed his judges. The ridiculous scheme which had been discovered behind a looking-glass in Fouquet's country house was read; the instructions given to his friends in case of his arrest seemed to foreshadow a rebellion; Fouquet listened, with his eyes bent upon the crucifix. "You cannot be ignorant that this is a State-crime," said the chancellor. "I confess that it is outrageous, sir," replied the accused, "but it is not a State-crime. I entreat these gentlemen," turning to the judges, "to kindly allow me to explain what a State-crime is. It is when you hold a chief office, when you are in the secrets of your prince, and when, all at once, you range yourself on the side of his enemies, enlist all your family in the same interest, cause the passes to be given up by your son-in-law, and the gates to be opened to a foreign army so as to introduce it into the heart of the kingdom. That, gentlemen, is what is called a State-crime.'' The chancellor could not protest; nobody had forgotten his conduct during the Fronde. M. d'Ormesson summed up for banishment and confiscation of all the property of the accused; it was all that the friends of Fouquet could hope for. M. de Sainte-Hélène summed up for beheadal. "The only proper punishment for him would be rope and gallows," exclaimed M. Pussort, the most violent of the whole court against the accused; "but, in consideration of the offices he has held, and the distinguished relatives he has, I relent so far as to accept the opinion of M. de Sainte-Hélène." "What say you to this moderation?" writes Madame de Sévigné to M. de Pomponne, like herself, a faithful friend of Fouquet's: "it is because he is Colbert's uncle and was objected to that he was inclined for such handsome treatment. As for me, I am beside myself when I think of such infamy. . . . You must know that M. Colbert is in such a rage that there is apprehension of some atrocity and injustice which will drive us all to despair. If it were not for that, my poor dear sir, in the position in which we now are, we might hope to see our friend, although very unfortunate, at any rate with his life safe, which is a great matter."

"Pray much to your God and entreat your judges," was the message sent to Mesdames Fouquet by the queen-mother, "for, so far as the king is concerned, there is nothing to be expected." "If he is sentenced, I shall leave him to die," proclaimed Louis XIV. Fouquet was not sentenced, the court declared for the view of Oliver d'Ormesson. "Praise God, sir, and thank Him," wrote Madame de Sévigné, on the 20th of December, 1664, "our poor friend is saved; it was thirteen for M. d'Ormesson's summing-up and nine for Saint-Hélene's. It will be a long while before I recover from my joy; it is really too overwhelming, I can hardly restrain it. The king changes exile into imprisonment and refuses him permission to see his wife, which is against all usage; but take care not to abate one jot of your joy, mine is increased thereby and makes me see more clearly the greatness of our victory." Fouquet was taken to Pignerol, and all his family were removed from Paris. He died piously in his prison, in 1680, a year before his venerable mother Marie Maupeou, who was so deeply concerned about her son's soul at the very pinnacle of greatness that she threw herself upon her knees on hearing of his arrest and exclaimed, "I thank Thee, O God; I have always prayed for his salvation, and here is the way to it!" Fouquet was guilty; the bitterness of his enemies and the severities of the king have failed to procure his acquittal from history any more than from his judges.

Even those who, like Louis XIV. and Colbert, saw the canker in the State, deceived themselves as to the resources at their disposal for the cure of it; the punishment of the superintendent and the ruin of the farmers of taxes (*traitants*) might put a stop for a while to extravagances; the powerful hand of Colbert might re-establish order in the finances, found new manufactures, restore the marine and protect commerce, but the order was but momentary and the prosperity superficial, as long as the sovereign's will was the sole law of the State. Master as he was over the maintenance of peace in Europe after so many and such long periods of hostility, young Louis XIV. was only waiting for an opportunity of recommencing war. "The resolutions I had in my mind seemed to me very worthy of execution," he says: "my natural activity, the ardor of my age and the violent desire I felt to augment my reputation made me very impatient to be up and doing; but I found at this moment that love of glory has the same niceties and, if I may say so, the same timidities as the most tender passions; for, the more ardent I was to distinguish myself, the more apprehensive I was of failing, and, regarding as a great misfortune the shame which follows the slightest errors, I intended, in my conduct, to take the most extreme precautions."

The day of reverses was further off from Louis XIV. than that of errors. God has vouchsafed him incomparable instruments for the accomplishment of his designs. Whilst Colbert was replenishing the exchequer, all the while diminishing the imposts, a younger man than the king himself, the marquis of Louvois, son of Michael Le Tellier, admitted to the council at twenty years of age, was eagerly preparing the way for those wars which were nearly always successful so long as he lived, however insufficient were the reasons for them, however unjust was their aim.

Foreign affairs were in no worse hands than the administration of finance and of war. M. de Lionne was an able diplomatist, broken in for a long time past to important affairs, shrewd and sensible, more celebrated amongst his contemporaries than in history, always falling into the second rank, behind Mazarin or Louis XIV., "who have appropriated his fame," says M. Mignet. The negotiations conducted by M. de Lionne were of a delicate nature. Louis XIV. had never renounced the rights of the queen to the succession in Spain; King Philip IV. had not paid his daughter's dowry, he said; the French ambassador at Madrid, the archbishop of Embrun, was secretly negotiating to obtain a revocation of Maria Theresa's renunciation or at the very least a recognition of the right of *devolution* over the catholic Low Countries. This strange custom of Hainault secured to the children of the first marriage succession to the paternal property to the exclusion of the offspring of the second marriage. Louis XIV. claimed the application of it to the advantage of the queen his wife, daughter of Elizabeth of France. "It is absolutely necessary that justice should sooner or later be done the queen as regards the rights that may belong to her or that I should try to exact it myself," wrote Louis XIV. to the archbishop of Embrun. This justice and these rights were, sooth to say, the pivot of all the negotiations and all the wars of King Louis XIV. "I cannot, all in a moment, change from white to black all the ancient maxims of this crown," said the king. He obtained no encouragement from Spain, and he began to make preparations, in anticipation, for war.

In this view and with these prospects, he needed the alliance of the Hollanders. Shattered as it had been by the behavior of the United Provinces at the congress of Münster and by their separate peace with Spain, the friendship between the States-general and France had been re-soldered by the far-sighted policy of John van Witt, grand pensionary of Holland and preponderant, with good right, in the policy of his country. Bold and prudent, courageous and wise, he had known better than anybody how to estimate the true interests of Holland and how to maintain them everywhere against Cromwell as well as Mazarin, with high-spirited moderation. His great and cool judgment had inclined him towards France, the most useful ally Holland could have. In spite of the difficulties put in the way of their friendly relations by Colbert's commercial measures, a new treaty was concluded between Louis XIV. and the United Provinces. "I am informed from a good quarter," says a letter to John van Witt from his ambassador at Paris, Boreel, June 8, 1662, "that His Majesty makes quite a special case of the new alliance between him and their High Mightinesses, which he regards as his own particular work. He expects great advantages from it as regards the security of his kingdom and that of the United Provinces which, he says, he knows to have been very affectionately looked upon by Henry the Great; and he desires that, if their High Mightinesses looked upon his ancestor as a father, they should love him from this moment as a son, taking him for their best friend and principal ally." A secret negotiation was at the same time going on between John van Witt and Count d'Estrades, French ambassador in Holland, for the formation and protection of a catholic republic in the Low Countries, according to Richelieu's old plan, or for partition between France and the United Provinces. John van Witt was anxious to act; but Louis XIV. seemed to be keeping himself hedged in view of the king of Spain's death, feeling it impossible, he said, with *propriety and honor*, to go contrary to the faith of the treaties which united him to his father-in-law. "That which can be kept secret for some time cannot be forever, nor be concealed from posterity," he said to Count d'Estrades in a private letter: "any how, there are certain, things which are good to do and bad to commit to writing." An understanding was come to without any writing. Louis XIV. well understood the noble heart and great mind with which he had to deal, when he wrote to Count d'Estrades, April 20th, 1663: "It is clear that God caused M. de Witt to be born [in 1632] for great things, seeing that at his age he has already for many years deservedly been the most considerable person in his State; and I believe too that my having obtained so good a friend in him was not a simple result of chance but of Divine Providence, who is thus early arranging the instruments of which He is pleased to make use for the glory of this crown and for the advantage of the United Provinces. The only complaint I make of him is that, having so much esteem and affection as I have for his person, he will not be kind enough to let me have the means of giving him some substantial tokens of it, which I would do with very great joy." Louis XIV. was not accustomed to meet at foreign courts with the high-spirited disinterestedness of the burgess patrician who since the age of five and twenty, had been governing the United Provinces.

Thus, then, it was a case of strict partnership between France and Holland, and Louis XIV. had remained faithful to the policy of Henry IV. and Richelieu when Philip IV. died on the 17th of September, 1665. Almost at the same time the dissension between England and Holland, after a period of tacit hostility, broke out into action. The United Provinces claimed the aid of France.

Close ties at that time united France and England. Monsieur, the king's only brother, had married Henrietta of England, sister of Charles II. The king of England, poor and debauched, had scarcely been restored to the throne when he sold Dunkerque to France for five millions of livres, to the great scandal of Cromwell's old friends, who had but lately helped Turenne to wrest it from the Spaniards. "I knew without doubt that the aggression was on the part of England," writes Louis XIV. in his *Mémoires*, "and I resolved to act with good faith towards the Hollanders, according to the terms of my treaty; but as I purposed to terminate the war on the first opportunity, I resolved to act towards the English as handsomely as could be, and I begged the queen of England, who happened to be at that time in Paris, to signify to her son that, with the singular regard I had for him, I could not without sorrow form the resolution which I considered myself bound by the obligation of my promise to take; for, at the origin of this war, I was persuaded that he had been carried away by the wishes of his subjects farther than he would have been by his own, insomuch that, between ourselves, I thought I had less reason to complain of him than for him. It is certain that this subordination which places the sovereign under the necessity of receiving the law from his people is the worst calamity that can happen to a man of our rank. I have pointed out to you elsewhere, my son, the miserable condition of princes who commit their people and their own dignity to the management of a premier minister; but it is little beside the misery of those who are left to the indiscretion of a popular assembly; the more you grant, the more they claim; the more you caress, the more they despise; and that which is once in their possession is held by so many arms that it cannot be wrenched away without an extreme amount of violence." In his compassion for the misery of the king of a free country, Louis XIV. contented himself with looking on at the desperate engagements between the English and the Dutch fleets. Twice the English destroyed the Dutch fleet under the orders of Admiral van Tromp. John van Witt placed himself at the head of the squadron. "Tromp has courage enough to fight," he said, "but not sufficient prudence to conduct a great action. The heat of battle is liable to carry officers away, confuse them and not leave them enough independence of judgment to bring matters to a successful issue. That is why I consider myself bound by all the duties of manhood and conscience to be myself on the watch, in order to set bounds to the impetuosity of valor when it would fain go too far." The resolution of the grand pensionary and the skill of Admiral Ruyter, who was on his return from an expedition in Africa, restored the fortunes of the Hollanders; their vessels went and offered the English battle at the very mouth of the Thames. The French squadron did not leave the Channel. It was only against the bishop of Münster, who had just invaded the Dutch territory, that Louis XIV. gave his allies effectual aid; M. de Turenne marched against the troops of the bishop, who was forced to retire, in the month of April, 1666. Peace was concluded, at Bréda, between England and Holland, in the month of July, 1667. Louis XIV. had not waited for that moment to enter Flanders.

Everything, in fact, was ready for this great enterprise: the regent of Spain, Mary Anne of Austria, a feeble creature under the thumb of one Father Nithard, a Jesuit, had allowed herself to be sent to sleep by the skilful manœuvres of the archbishop of Embrun; she had refused to make a treaty of alliance with England and to recognize Portugal, to which Louis XIV. had just given a French queen by marrying Mdlle. de Nemours to King Alphonso VI. The League of the Rhine secured to him the neutrality, at the least, of Germany; the emperor was not prepared for war; Europe, divided between fear and favor, saw with astonishment Louis XIV. take the field in the month of May, 1667. "It is not," said the manifesto sent by the king to the court of Spain, "either the ambition of possessing new States or the desire of winning glory by arms which inspires the Most Christian King with the design of maintaining the rights of the queen his wife; but would it not be shame for a king to allow all the privileges of blood and of law to be violated in the persons of himself, his wife and his son? As king, he feels himself obliged to prevent this injustice; as master, to oppose this usurpation; and, as father, to secure the patrimony to his son. He has no desire to employ force to open the gates, but he wishes to enter as a beneficent sun by the rays of his love, and to scatter everywhere in country, towns and private houses the gentle influences of abundance and peace which follow in his train." To secure the *gentle influences of peace*, Louis XIV. had collected an army of fifty thousand men, carefully armed and equipped under the supervision of Turenne, to whom Louvois as yet rendered docile obedience. There was none too much of this fine army for recovering the queen's rights over the duchy of Brabant, the marquisate of Antwerp, Limburg, Hainault, the countship of Namur and other territories. "Heaven not having ordained any tribunal on earth at which the kings of France can demand justice, the Most Christian King has only his own arms to look to for it," said the manifesto. Louis XIV. set out with M. de Turenne. Marshal Créqui had orders to observe Germany.

The Spaniards were taken unprepared; Armentières, Charleroi, Douai and Tournay had but insufficient garrisons, and they fell almost without striking a blow. Whilst the army was busy with the siege of Courtray, Louis XIV. returned to Compiègne to fetch the queen. The whole court followed him to the camp. "All that you have read about the magnificence of Solomon and the grandeur of the king of Persia, is not to be compared with the pomp that attends the king in his expedition," says a letter to Bussy-Rabutin from the count of Coligny. "You see passing along the streets nothing but plumes, gold-laced uniforms, chariots, mules superbly harnessed, parade-horses, housings with embroidery of fine gold." "I took the queen to Flanders," says Louis XIV., "to show her to the peoples of that country, who received her, in point of fact, with all the delight imaginable, testifying their sorrow at not having had more time to make preparations for receiving her more befittingly." The queen's quarters were at Courtrai. Marshal Turenne had moved on Dendermonde, but the Flemings had opened their sluices; the country was inundated; it was necessary to fall back on Audenarde; the town was taken in two days; and the king, still attended by the court, laid siege to Lille. Vauban, already celebrated as an engineer, traced out the lines of circumvallation; the army of M. de Créqui formed a junction with that of Turenne; there was expectation of an attempt on the part of the governor of the Low Countries to relieve the place; the Spanish force sent for that purpose arrived too late and was beaten on its retreat; the burgesses of Lille had forced the garrison to capitulate; and Louis XIV. entered it on the 27th of August after ten days' open trenches. On the 2nd of September, the king took the road back to St. Germain; but Turenne still found time to carry the town of Alost before taking up his winter-quarters.

Louis XIV.'s first campaign had been nothing but playing at

war, almost entirely without danger or bloodshed; it had, nevertheless, been sufficient to alarm Europe. Scarcely had peace been concluded at Bréda, when another negotiation was secretly entered upon between England, Holland and Sweden. It was in vain that King Charles II. leant personally towards an alliance with France; his people had their eyes opened to the dangers incurred by Europe from the arms of Louis XIV. "Certain persons of the greatest influence in Parliament come sometimes to see me, without any lights and muffled in a cloak in order not to be recognized," says a letter of September 26, 1669, from the marquis of Ruvigny to M. de Lionne; "they give me to understand that common sense and the public security forbid them to see, without raising a finger, the whole of the Low Countries taken, and that they are bound in good policy to oppose the purposes of this conquest if his Majesty intend to take all for himself." On the 23rd of January, 1668, the celebrated treaty of the Triple Alliance was signed at the Hague. The three powers demanded of the king of France that he should grant the Low Countries a truce up to the month of May, in order to give time for treating with Spain and obtaining from her, as France demanded, the definitive cession of the conquered places or Franche-Comté in exchange. At bottom, the Triple Alliance was resolved to protect helpless Spain against France; a secret article bound the three allies to take up arms to restrain Louis XIV. and to bring him back, if possible, to the peace of the Pyrenees. At the same moment, Portugal was making peace with Spain who recognized her independence.

The king refused the long armistice demanded of him: "I will grant it up to the 31st of March," he had said, "being unwilling to miss the first opportunity of taking the field." The Marquis of Castel-Rodriguo made merry over this proposal: "I am content," said he, "with the suspension of arms that winter imposes upon the king of France." The governor of the Low Countries made a mistake: Louis XIV. was about to prove that his soldiers, like those of Gustavus Adolphus, did not recognize winter. He had entrusted the command of his new army to the prince of Condé, amnestied for the last nine years, but, up to that time, a stranger to the royal favor. Condé expressed his gratitude with more fervor than loftiness when he wrote to the king on the 20th of December' 1667: "My birth binds me more than any other to your Majesty's service, but the kindnesses and the confidence you deign to show me after I have so little deserved them bind me still more than my birth. Do me the honor to believe, Sir, that I hold neither property nor life but to cheerfully sacrifice them for your glory and for the preservation of your person, which is a thousand times dearer to me than all the things of the world."

"On pretence of being in Burgundy at the states," writes Oliver d'Ormesson, the prosecutor of Fouquet, "the prince had obtained perfect knowledge that Franche-Comté was without troops and without apprehension, because they had no doubt that the king would accord them neutrality as in the last war, the inhabitants having sent to him to ask it of him. He kept them amused. Meanwhile the king had set his army in motion without disclosing his plan, and the inhabitants of Franche-Comté found themselves attacked without having known that they were to be. Besançon and Salins surrendered at sight of the troops. The king, on arriving, went to Dôle, and superintended an affair of counterscarps and some demilunes, whereat there were killed some four or five hundred men. The inhabitants, astounded and finding themselves without troops or hope of succor, surrendered on Shrove Tuesday, February 14. The king at the same time marched to Gray. The governor made some show of defending himself, but the Marquis of Yenne, governor-general under Castel-Rodriguo, who belongs to the district and has all his property there, came and surrendered to the king and then, having gone to Gray, persuaded the governor to surrender. Accordingly, the king entered it on Sunday, February 19, and had a *Te Deum* sung there, having at his right the governor-general and at his left the special governor of the town; and, the same day, he set out on his return. And so, within twenty-two days of the month of February, he had set out from St. Germain, been in Franche-Comté, taken it entirely and returned to St. Germain. This is a great and wonderful conquest from every point of view. Having paid a visit to the prince to make my compliments, I said that the glory he had won had cost him dear as he had lost his shoes; he replied, laughing, that it had been said so, but the truth was that, happening to be at the guards' attack, somebody came and told him that the king had pushed forward to M. de Gadaignes' attack, that he had ridden up full gallop to bring back the king who had put himself in too great peril, and that, having dismounted at a very moist spot, his shoe had come off and he had been obliged to re shoe himself in the king's presence" [*Journal d'Oliver d'Ormesson*, t. ii. p. 542].

Louis XIV. had good reason to "push forward to the attack and put himself in too great peril;" a rumor had circulated that, having run the same risk at the siege of Lille, he had let a moment's hesitation appear; the old duke of Charost, captain of his guards, had come up to him, and "Sir," he had whispered in the young king's ear, "the wine is drawn and it must be drunk." Louis XIV. had finished his reconnoissance, not without a feeling of gratitude towards Charost for preferring before his life that honor which ended by becoming his idol.

The king was back at St. Germain, preparing enormous armaments for the month of April. He had given the prince of Condé the government of Franche-Comté. "I had always esteemed your father," he said to the young duke of Enghien, "but I had never loved him; now I love him as much as I esteem him." Young Louvois, already in high favor with the king, as well as his father, Michael Le Tellier, had contributed a great deal towards getting the prince's services appreciated; they still smarted under the reproaches of M. de Turenne touching the deficiency of supplies for the troops before Lille in 1667.

War seemed to be imminent; the last days of the armistice were at hand. "The opinion prevailing in France as to peace is a disease which is beginning to spread very much," wrote Louvois in the middle of March, "but we shall soon find a cure for it, as here is the time approaching for taking the field. You must publish almost everywhere that it is the Spaniards who do not want peace." Louvois lied brazen-facedly; the Spaniards were without resources, ut they had even less of spirit than of resources; they consented to the abandonment of all the places won in the Low Countries during 1667. A congress was opened at Aix-la-Chapelle, presided over by the nuncio of the new pope Clement IX., as favorable to France as his predecessor, Innocent X., had been to Spain. "A phantom arbiter between phantom plenipotentiaries," says Voltaire, in the *Siècle de Louis XIV.* The real negotiations were going on at St. Germain. "I did not look merely," writes Louis XIV., "to profit by the present conjuncture, but also to put myself in a position to turn to my advantage those which might probably arrive. In view of the great increments that my fortune might receive nothing seemed to me more necessary than to establish for myself amongst my smaller neighbors such a character for moderation and probity as might assuage in them those emotions of dread which everybody naturally experiences at sight of too great a power. I was bound not to lack means of breaking with Spain, when I pleased; Franche-Comté, which I gave up, might become reduced to such a condition that I should be master of it at any moment, and my new conquests, well secured, would open for me a surer entrance into the Low Countries." Determined by these wise motives, the king gave orders to sign the peace. "M. de Turenne appeared yesterday like a man who had received a blow from a club," writes Michael Le Tellier to his son: "when Don Juan arrives, matters will change; he says that, meanwhile, all must go on just the same, and he repeated it more than a dozen times, which made the prince laugh." Don Juan did not protest, and on the 2nd of May, 1668, the peace of Aix-la-Chapelle was concluded. Before giving up Franche-Comté, the king issued orders for demolishing the fortifications of Dôle and Gray; he at the same time commissioned Vauban to fortify Ath, Lille and Tournay. The Triple Alliance was triumphant, the Hollanders at the head. "I cannot tell your Excellency all that these beer brewers write to our traders," said a letter to M. de Lionne from one of his correspondents: "as there is just now nothing further to hope for, in respect of the Low Countries, I vent all my feelings upon the Hollanders, whom I hold at this day to be our most formidable enemies, and I exhort your Excellency, as well for your own reputation as for the public satisfaction, to omit from your policy nothing that may tend to the discovery of means to abase this great power which exalts itself too much."

Louis XIV. held the same views as M. de Lionne's correspondent, not merely from resentment against the Hollanders, who had stopped him in his career of success, but because he quite saw that the key to the barrier between the catholic Low Countries and himself remained in the hands of the United Provinces. He had relied upon his traditional influence in the Estates as well as on the influence of John van Witt; but the latter's position had been shaken. "I learnt from a good quarter that there are great cabals forming against the authority of M. de Witt, and for the purpose of ousting him from it," writes M. de Lionne on the 30th of March, 1668; Louis XIV. resolved to have recourse to arms in order to humiliate this insolent republic which had dared to hamper his designs. For four years, every effort of his diplomacy tended solely to make Holland isolated in Europe.

It was to England that France would naturally first turn her eyes. The sentiments of King Charles II. and of his people, as regarded Holland, were not the same. Charles had not forgiven the Estates for having driven him from their territory at the request of Cromwell; the simple and austere manners of the republican patricians did not accord with his taste for luxury and debauchery; the English people, on the contrary, despite of that rivalry in trade and on the seas which had been the source of so much ancient and recent hostility between the two nations, esteemed the Hollanders and leaned towards an alliance with them. Louis XIV., in the eyes of the English Parliament, was the representative of Catholicism and absolute monarchy, two enemies which it had vanquished but still feared. The king's proceedings with Charles II. had, therefore, necessarily to be kept secret; the ministers of the king of England were themselves divided; the duke of Buckingham, as mad and as prodigal as his father, was favorable to France; the earl of Arlington had married a Hollander, and persisted in the Triple Alliance. Louis XIV. employed in this negotiation his sister-in-law, Madame Henriette, who was much attached to her brother the king of England, and was intelligent and adroit; she was on her return from a trip to London, which she had with great difficulty snatched from the jealous susceptibilities of Monsieur, when she died suddenly at Versailles on the 30th of June, 1670. "It were impossible to praise sufficiently the incredible dexterity of this princess in treating the most delicate matters, in finding a remedy for those hidden suspicions which often keep them in suspense and in terminating all difficulties in such a manner as to conciliate the most opposite interests; this was the subject of all talk, when on a sudden resounded, like a clap of thunder, that astounding news: Madame is dying! Madame is dead! And there, in spite of that great heart, is this princess, so admired and so beloved; there, as death has made her for us!" [*Bossuet*, *Oraison funèbre d'Henriette d'Angleterre.*]

Madame's work was nevertheless accomplished and her death was not destined to interrupt it. The treaty of alliance was secretly concluded, signed by only the catholic councillors of Charles II.; it bore that the king of England was resolved to publicly declare his return to the catholic Church; the king of France was to aid him towards the execution of this project with assistance to the amount of two millions of livres of Tours; the two princes bound themselves to remain faithful to the peace of Aix-la-Chapelle as regarded Spain, and to declare war together against the United Provinces; the king of France would have to supply to his brother of England, for this war, a subsidy of three million livres of Tours every year. When the protestant ministers were admitted to share the secret, silence was kept as to the declaration of catholicity, which was put off till after the war in Holland; Parliament had granted the king thirteen hundred thousand pounds sterling to pay his debts, and eight hundred thousand pounds to "equip in the ensuing spring" a fleet of fifty vessels, in order that he might take the part he considered most expedient for the glory of his kingdom and the welfare of his subjects. "The government of our country is like a great bell which you cannot stop when it is once set going," said King Charles II., anxious to commence the war in order to handle the subsidies the sooner; he was, nevertheless, obliged to wait. Louis XIV. had succeeded in dragging him into an enterprise contrary to the real interests of his country as well as of his national policy; in order to arrive at his ends he had set at work all the evil passions which divided the court of England; he had bought up the king, his mistresses and his ministers; he had dangled before the fanaticism of the duke of York the spectacle of England converted to Catholicism; but his work was not finished in Europe; he wished to assure himself of the neutrality of Germany in the great duel he was meditating with the republic of the United Provinces.

As long ago as 1667 Louis XIV. had practically paved the way towards the neutrality of the empire by a secret treaty regulating the eventual partition of the Spanish monarchy. In case the little king of Spain died without children, France was to receive the Low Countries, Franche-Comté, Navarre, Naples and Sicily; Austria was to keep Spain and Milaness. The Emperor Leopold therefore turned a deaf ear to the entreaties of the Hollanders who would fain have bound him down to the Triple Alliance; a new convention between France and the empire, secretly signed on the 1st of November, 1670, made it reciprocally obligatory on the two princes not to aid their enemies. The German princes were more difficult to win over; they were beginning to feel alarm at the pretensions of France. The electors of Trèves and of Mayence had already collected some troops on the Rhine; the duke of Lorraine seemed disposed to lend them assistance; Louis XIV. seized the pretext of the restoration of certain fortifications contrary to the treaty of Marsal; on the 23rd of August, 1675, he ordered Marshal Créqui to enter Lorraine; at the commencement of September, the whole duchy was reduced and the duke a fugitive. "The king had at first been disposed to give up Lorraine to some one of the princes of that house," writes Louvois; "but, just now, he no longer considers that province to be a country which he ought to quit so soon, and it appears likely that, as he sees more and more every day how useful that conquest will be for the unification of his kingdom, he will seek the means of preserving it for himself." In point of fact, the king, in answer to the emperor's protests replied that he did not want to turn Lorraine to account for his own profit, but that he would not give it up at the solicitations of anybody. Brandenburg and Saxony alone refused point blank to observe neutrality; France had renounced protestant alliances in Germany, and the protestant electors comprehended the danger that threatened them.

Sweden also comprehended it, but Gustavus Adolphus and Oxenstiern were no longer there; there remained nothing but the remembrance of old alliances with France; the Swedish senators gave themselves up to the buyer one after another. "When you have made some stay at Stockholm," wrote Courtin, the French ambassador in Sweden, to M. de Pomponne, "and seen the vanity of the Gascons of the North, the little honesty there is in their conduct, the cabals which prevail in the Senate, and the feebleness and inertness of those who compose it, you cannot be surprised at the delays and changes which take place. If the Senate of Rome had shown as little inclination as that of Sweden at the present time for war, the Roman empire would not have been of so great an extent." The treaty, however, was signed on the 14th of April, 1672; in consideration of an annual subsidy of six hundred thousand livres Sweden engaged to oppose by arms those princes of the empire who should determine to support the United Provinces. The gap was forming round Holland.

In spite of the secrecy which enveloped the negotiations of Louis XIV., Van Witt was filled with disquietude; favorable as ever to the French alliance, he had sought to calm the irritation of France which set down the Triple Alliance to the account of Holland. "I remarked," says a letter, in 1669, from M. de Pomponne, French ambassador at the Hague, "that it seemed to me a strange thing that, whereas this republic had two kings for its associates in the Triple Alliance, it affected in some sort to put itself at their head so as to do all the speaking and that it was willing to become the seat of all the manœuvres that were going on against France, which was very likely to render it suspected of some prepossession in favor of Spain." John Van Witt defended his country with dignified modesty: "I know not whether to regard as a blessing or a curse," said he, "the incidents which have for several years past brought it about that the most important affairs of Europe have been transacted in Holland. It must no doubt be attributed to the situation and condition of this State which, whilst putting it after all the crowned heads, caused it to be readily agreed to as a place without consequence; but, as for the prepossession of which we are suspected in favor of Spain, it cannot surely be forgotten what aversion we have as it were sucked in with our milk towards that nation, the remnants that still remain of a hatred fed by so much blood and such long wars, which make it impossible, for my part, that my inclinations should ever turn towards that crown."

Hatred to Spain was not so general in Holland as Van Witt represented; and internal dissensions amongst the Estates, sedulously fanned by France, were slowly ruining the authority of the aristocratic and republican party, only to increase the influence of those who favored the House of Nassau. In his far-sighted and sagacious patriotism, John van Witt had for a long time past foreseen the defeat of his cause, and he had carefully trained up the heir of the stadtholders, William of Nassau, the natural head of his adversaries. It was this young prince whom the policy of Louis XIV. at that time opposed to Van Witt in the councils of the United Provinces, thus strengthening in advance the indomitable foe who was to triumph over all his greatness and vanquish him by dint of defeats. The despatch of an ambassador to Spain, to form there an alliance offensive and defensive, was decided upon. "M. de Beverninck, who has charge of this mission, is without doubt a man of strength and ability," said M. de Pomponne, "and there are many who put him on a par with M. de Witt; it is true that he is not on a par with the other the whole day long, and that with the sobriety of morning he often loses the desert and capacity that were his up to dinner-time." The Spaniards at first gave but a cool reception to the overtures of the Hollanders. "They look at their monarchy through the spectacles of Philip II.," said Beverninck, "and they take a pleasure in deceiving themselves whilst they flatter their vanity." Fear of the encroachments of France carried the day, however; "They consider," wrote M. de Lionne, "that, if they left the United Provinces to ruin, they would themselves have but the favor granted by the Cyclops, to be eaten last," a defensive league was concluded between Spain and Holland, and all the efforts of France could not succeed in breaking it.

John van Witt was negotiating in every direction. The treaty of Charles II. with France had remained a profound secret, and the Hollanders believed that they might calculate upon the good-will of the English nation. The arms of England were effaced from the *Royal Charles*, a vessel taken by Van Tromp in 1667, and a curtain was put over a picture, in the town-hall of Dordrecht, of the victory at Chatham, representing the ruart [inspector of dykes] Cornelius van Witt leaning on a cannon. These concessions to the pride of England were not made without a struggle. "Some," says M. de Pomponne, "thought it a piece of baseness to despoil themselves during peace of tokens of the glory they had won in the war; others, less sensitive on this point of delicacy and more affected by the danger of disobliging a crown which formed the first and at this date the most necessary of their connections, preferred the less spirited but safer to the honorable but more dangerous counsels." Charles II. played with Boreel, ambassador of the United Provinces at the court of London; taking advantage of the Estates' necessity in order to serve his nephew the prince of Orange, he demanded for him the office of captain-general which had been filled by his ancestors. Already the prince had been recognized as premier noble of Zealand, and he had obtained entrance to the council; John van Witt raised against him the vote of the Estates of Holland, still preponderant in the republic: "The grand pensionary soon appeased the murmurs and complaints that were being raised against him," writes M. de Pomponne. "He prefers the greatest dangers to the re-establishment of the prince of Orange, and to his re-establishment on the recommendation of the king of England; he would consider that the republic accepted a double yoke, both in the person of a chief who, from the post of captain-general, might rise to all those which his fathers had filled, and in accepting him at the instance of a suspected crown." The grand pensionary did not err. In the spring of 1672, in spite of the loss of M. de Lionne, who died September 1, 1671, all the negotiations of Louis XIV. had succeeded; his armaments were completed; he was at last about to crush that little power which had for so long a time past presented an obstacle to his designs. "The true way of arriving at the conquest of the Spanish Low Countries is to abase the Hollanders and annihilate them if it be possible," said Louvois to the prince of Condé on the 1st of November, 1671; and the king wrote in an unpublished memorandum: "In the midst of all my successes during my campaign of 1667, neither England nor the Empire, convinced as they were of the justice of my cause, whatever interest they may have had in checking the rapidity of my conquests, offered any opposition. I found in my path only my good, faithful and old friends the Hollanders who, instead of interesting themselves in my fortune as the foundation of their dominion, wanted to impose laws upon me and oblige me to make peace, and even dared to use threats in case I refused to accept their mediation. I confess that their insolence touched me to the quick and that, at the risk of whatever might happen to my conquests in the Spanish Low Countries, I was very near turning all my forces against this proud and ungrateful nation; but, having summoned prudence to my aid, and considered that I had neither number of troops nor quality of allies requisite for such an enterprise, I dissimulated, I concluded peace on honorable conditions, resolved to put off the punishment of such perfidy to another time." The time had come; to the last attempt towards conciliation, made by Van Groot, son of the celebrated Grotius, in the name of the States-general, the king replied with threatening haughtiness: "When I discovered that the United Provinces were trying to debauch my allies and were soliciting kings, my relatives, to enter into offensive leagues against me, I made up my mind to put myself in a position to defend myself and I levied some troops; but I intend to have more by the spring and I shall make use of them at that time in the manner I shall consider most proper for the welfare of my dominions and for my own glory."

"The king starts to-morrow, my dear daughter," writes Madame de Sévigné to Madame de Grignan on the 27th of April: "there will be a hundred thousand men out of Paris;

the two armies will form a junction; the king will command Monsieur, Monsieur the prince, the prince M. de Turenne, and M. de Turenne the two marshals and even the army of Marshal Créqui. The king spoke to M. de Bellefonds and told him that his desire was that he should obey M. de Turenne without any fuss. The marshal, without asking for time (that was his mistake), said that he should not be worthy of the honor his Majesty had done him if he dishonored himself by an obedience without precedent. Marshal d'Humières and Marshal Créqui said much the same. M. de la Rochefoucauld says that Bellefonds has spoilt everything because he has no joints in his mind. Marshal Créqui said to the king, 'Sir, take from me my bâton, for are you not master? Let me serve this campaign as marquis of Créqui; perhaps I may deserve that your Majesty give me back the bâton at the end of the war.' The king was touched, but the result is that they have all three been at their houses in the country planting cabbages (have ceased to serve)." "You will permit me to tell you that there is nothing for it but to obey a master who says that he means to be obeyed," wrote Louvois to M. de Créqui. The king wanted to have order and one sole command in his army; and he was right.

The prince of Orange, who had at last been appointed captain-general for a single campaign, possessed neither the same forces nor the same authority; the violence of party-struggles had blinded patriotic sentiment and was hampering the preparations for defence. Out of 64,000 troops inscribed on the registers of the Dutch army, a great number neglected the summons; in the towns, the burgesses rose up against the magistrates, refusing to allow the faubourgs to be pulled down, and the peasants threatened to defend the dikes and close the sluices. "When word was sent yesterday to the peasants to come and work on the Rhine at the redoubts and at piercing the dikes, not a man presented himself," says a letter of June 28, from John van Witt to his brother Cornelius; "all is disorder and confusion here." "I hope that, for the moment, we shall not lack gunpowder," said Beverninck; "but as for gun-carriages there is no help for it; a fortnight hence we shall not have more than seven." Louvois had conceived the audacious idea of purchasing in Holland itself the supplies of powder and ball necessary for the French army; and the commercial instincts of the Hollanders had prevailed over patriotic sentiment. Ruyter was short of munitions in the contest already commenced against the French and English fleet. "Out of thirty-two battles I have been in I never saw any like it," said the Dutch admiral after the battle of Soultbay (Solebay) on the 7th of June. "Ruyter is admiral, captain, pilot, sailor and soldier all in one," exclaimed the English. Cornelius van Witt, in the capacity of commissioner of the Estates had remained seated on the deck of the admiral's vessel during the fight, indifferent to the bullets that rained around him. The issue of the battle was indecisive; Count D'Estrées, at the head of the French flotilla, had taken little part in the action.

It was not at sea and by the agency of his lieutenants that Louis XIV. aspired to gain the victory; he had already arrived at the banks of the Rhine, marching straight into the very heart of Holland. "I thought it more advantageous for my designs and less common on the score of glory," he wrote to Colbert on the 31st of May, "to attack four places at once on the Rhine and to take the actual command in person at all four sieges. . . . I chose, for that purpose, Rheinberg, Wesel, Burick and Orsoy, and I hope that there will be no complaint of my having deceived public expectation." The four places did not hold out four days. On the 12th of June, the king and the prince of Condé appeared unexpectedly on the right bank of the intermediary branch of the Rhine, between the Wahal and the Yssel. The Hollanders were expecting the enemy at the ford of the Yssel, being more easy to pass; they were taken by surprise; the king's cuirassier regiment dashed into the river and crossed it partly by fording and partly by swimming; the resistance was brief; meanwhile the duke of Longueville was killed and the prince of Condé was wounded for the first time in his life. "I was present at the passage, which was bold, vigorous, full of brilliancy and glorious for the nation," writes Louis XIV. Arnh im and Deventer had just surrendered to Turenne and Luxembourg; Duisbourg resisted the king for a few days; Monsieur was besieging Zutphen. John van Witt was for evacuating the Hague and removing to Amsterdam the centre of government and resistance; the prince of Orange had just abandoned the province of Utrecht, which was immediately occupied by the French; the defensive efforts were concentrated upon the province of Holland; already Naarden, three leagues from Amsterdam, was in the king's hands; "We learn the surrender of towns before we have heard of their investment," wrote Van Witt. A deputation from the States was sent on the 22nd of June to the king's head-quarters to demand peace. Louis XIV. had just entered Utrecht, which, finding itself abandoned, opened its gates to him. On the same day, John van Witt received in a street of the Hague four stabs with a dagger from the hand of an assassin, whilst the city of Amsterdam, but lately resolved to surrender and prepared to send its magistrates as delegates to Louis XIV., suddenly decided upon resistance to the bitter end. "If we must perish, let us at any rate be the last to fall," exclaimed the town-councillor Walkernier, "and let us not submit to the yoke it is desired to impose upon us until there remain no means of securing ourselves against it." All the sluices were opened and the dikes cut. Amsterdam floated amidst the waters. "I thus found myself under the necessity of limiting my conquests, as regarded the province of Holland, to Naarden, Utrecht and Werden," writes Louis XIV. in his unpublished *Mémoire* touching the campaign of 1672, and he adds with rare impartiality: "the resolution to place the whole country under water was somewhat violent; but what would not one do to save one's self from foreign domination? I cannot help admiring and commending the zeal and stoutheartedness of those who broke off the negotiation of Amsterdam, though their decision, salutary as it was for their country, was very prejudicial to my service; the proposals made to me by the deputies from the States-general were very advantageous, but I could never prevail upon myself to accept them."

Louis XIV. was as yet ignorant what can be done amongst a proud people by patriotism driven to despair; the States-general offered him Maestricht, the places on the Rhine, Brabant and Dutch Flanders, with a war-indemnity of ten millions; it was an open door to the Spanish Low Countries, which became a patch enclosed by French possessions; but the king wanted to annihilate the Hollanders; he demanded southern Gueldres, the island of Bonmel, twenty-four millions, the restoration of Catholic worship, and, every year, an embassy commissioned to thank the king for having a second time given peace to the United Provinces. This was rather too much; and, whilst the deputies were negotiating with heavy hearts, the people of Holland had risen in wrath.

From the commencement of the war, the party of the House of Nassau had never ceased to gain ground. John van Witt was accused of all the misfortunes of the State; the people demanded with loud outcries the restoration of the stadtholderate, but lately abolished by a law voted by the States under the presumptuous title of *perpetual edict*. Dordrecht, the native place of the Van Witts, gave the signal of insurrection. Cornelius van Witt, who was confined to his house by illness, yielded to the prayers of his wife and children and signed the municipal act which destroyed his brother's work; the contagion spread from town to town, from province to province; on the 4th of July, the States-general appointed William of Orange stadtholder, captain-general and admiral of the Union; the national instinct had divined the saviour of the country and with tumultuous acclamations placed in his hands the reins of the State.

William of Orange was barely two and twenty when the fate of revolutions suddenly put him at the head of a country invaded, devastated, half conquered; but his mind as well as his spirit were up to the level of his task. He loftily rejected at the assembly of the Estates the proposals brought forward in the king's name of Peter van Groot. "To subscribe them would be suicide," he said: "even to discuss them is dangerous; but, if the majority of this assembly decide otherwise, there remains but one course for the friends of Protestantism and liberty, and that is to retire to the colonies in the West Indies, and there found a new country where their consciences and their persons will be beyond the reach of tyranny and despotism." The States-general decided to "reject the hard and intolerable conditions proposed by their lordships the kings of France and Great Britain, and to defend this State and its inhabitants with all their might." The province of Holland in its entirety followed the example of Amsterdam; the dikes were everywhere broken down, at the same time that the troops of the electors of Brandenburg and Saxony were advancing to the aid of the United Provinces, and that the emperor was signing with those two princes a defensive alliance for the maintenance of the treaties of Westphalia, the Pyrenees and Aix-la-Chapelle.

Louis XIV. could no longer fly from conquest to conquest; henceforth his troops had to remain on observation; care for his pleasures recalled him to France; he left the command-in-chief of his army to M. de Turenne and set out for St. Germain, where he arrived on the 1st of August. Before leaving Holland, he had sent home almost without ransom twenty thousand prisoners of war who before long entered the service of the States again. "It was an excess of clemency of which

I had reason afterwards to repent," says the king himself. His mistake was that he did not understand either Holland or the new chief she had chosen.

Dispirited and beaten, like his country, John van Witt had just given in his resignation as councillor pensionary of Holland. He wrote to Ruyter on the 5th of August, as follows: "The capture of the towns on the Rhine in so short a time, the irruption of the enemy as far as the banks of the Yssel and the total loss of the provinces of Gueldres, Utrecht and Over-Yssel, almost without resistance and through unheard-of poltroonery, if not treason, on the part of certain people, have more and more convinced me of the truth of what was in olden times applied to the Roman republic: *Successes are claimed by everybody, reverses are put down to one* (*Prospera omnes sibi vindicant, adversa uni imputantur*). That is my own experience. The people of Holland have not only laid at my door all the disasters and calamities that have befallen our republic; they have not been content to see me fall unarmed and defenceless into the hands of four individuals whose design was to murder me; but when, by the agency of Divine Providence, I escaped the assassins' blows and had recovered from my wounds, they conceived a violent hatred against such of their magistrates as they believed to have most to do with the direction of public affairs; it is against me chiefly that this hatred has manifested itself, although I was nothing but a servant of the State; it is this that has obliged me to demand my discharge from the office of councillor-pensionary." He was at once succeeded by Gaspard van Fagel, passionately devoted to the prince of Orange.

Popular passion is as unjust as it is violent in its excesses. Cornelius van Witt, but lately sharing with his brother the public confidence, had just been dragged, as a criminal, to the Hague accused by a wretched barber of having planned the assassination of the prince of Orange. In vain did the magistrates of the town of Dordrecht claim their right of jurisdiction over their fellow-citizen. Cornelius van Witt was put to the torture to make him confess his crime. "You will not force me to confess a thing I never even thought of," he said, whilst the pulleys were dislocating his limbs. His baffled judges heard him repeating Horace's ode: *Justum et tenacem propositi virum.* . . . At the end of three hours he was carried back to his cell, broken but indomitable. The court condemned him to banishment; his accuser, Tichelaer, was not satisfied.

Before long, at his instigation, the mob collected about the prison, uttering imprecations against the judges and their clemency. "They are traitors," cried Tichelaer, "but let us first take vengeance on those whom we have." John van Witt had been brought to the prison by a message supposed to have come from the ruart. In vain had his daughter conjured him not to respond to it. "What are you come here for?" exclaimed Cornelius, on seeing his brother enter. "Did you not send for me?" "No, certainly not." "Then we are lost," said John van Witt, calmly. The shouts of the crowd redoubled; a body of cavalry still preserved order; a rumor suddenly spread that the peasants from the environs were marching on the Hague to plunder it; the States of Holland sent orders to the count of Tilly to move against them; the brave soldier demanded a written order. "I will obey," he said, "but the two brothers are lost."

The troops had scarcely withdrawn, and already the doors of the prison were forced; the ruart, exhausted by the torture, was stretched upon his bed, whilst his brother sat by his side reading the Bible aloud; the madmen rushed into the chamber, crying, "Traitors, prepare yourselves, you are going to die." Cornelius van Witt started up, joining his hands in prayer; the blows aimed at him did not reach him. John was wounded. They were both dragged forth; they embraced one another; Cornelius, struck from behind, rolled to the bottom of the staircase; his brother would have defended him; as he went out into the street, he received a pike-thrust in the face; the ruart was dead already; the murderers vented their fury on John van Witt; he had lost nothing of his courage or his coolness, and, lifting his arms towards heaven, he was opening his mouth in prayer to God, when a last pistol-shot stretched him upon his back: "There's the perpetual edict floored!" shouted the assassins, lavishing upon the two corpses insults and imprecations. It was only at night and after having with difficulty recognized them, so disfigured had they been, that poor Jacob van Witt was able to have his sons' bodies removed; he was before long to rejoin them in everlasting rest.

William of Orange arrived next day at the Hague, too late for his fame and for the punishment of the obscure assassins whom he allowed to escape. The compassers of the plot obtained before long appointments and rewards. "He one day assured me," says Gourville, "that it was quite true he had not given any orders to have the Witts killed, but that, having heard of their death without having contributed to it, he had certainly felt a little relieved." History and the human heart have mysteries which it is not well to probe to the bottom.

For twenty years John van Witt had been the most noble exponent of his country's traditional policy. Long faithful to the French alliance, he had desired to arrest Louis XIV. in his dangerous career of triumph; foreseeing the peril to come, he had forgotten the peril at hand; he had believed too much and too long in the influence of negotiations and the possibility of regaining the friendship of France. He died unhappy, in spite of his pious submission to the will of God; what he had desired for his country was slipping from him abroad as well as at home; Holland was crushed by France, and the aristocratic republic was vanquished by monarchical democracy. With the weakness characteristic of human views, he could not open his eyes to a vision of constitutional monarchy freely chosen, preserving to his country the independence, prosperity and order which he had labored to secure for her. A politician as bold as and more far-sighted than Admiral Coligny, twice struck down, like him, by assassins, John van Witt remained in history the unique model of a great republican chief, virtuous and able, proud and modest, up to the day at which other United Provinces, fighting like Holland for their liberty, presented a rival to the purity of his fame when they chose for their governor General Washington.

For all their brutal ingratitude, the instinct of the people of Holland saw clearly into the situation. John van Witt would have failed in the struggle against France; William of Orange, prince, politician and soldier, saved his country and Europe from the yoke of Louis XIV.

On quitting his army, the king had inscribed in his note-book: "My departure.—I do not mean to have anything more done." The temperature favored his designs; it did not freeze, the country remained inundated and the towns unapproachable; the troops of the elector of Brandenburg, together with a corps sent by the emperor, had put themselves in motion towards the Rhine; Turenne kept them in check in Germany. Condé covered Alsace; the duke of Luxembourg, remaining in Holland, confined himself to burning two large villages, Bodegrave and Saammerdam. "There was a grill of all the Hollanders who were in those burghs," wrote the marshal to the prince of Condé, "not one of whom was let out of the houses. This morning we were visited by two of the enemy's drummers who came to claim a colonel of great note amongst them (I have him in cinders at this moment), as well as several officers that we have not and that are demanded of us, who, I suppose, were killed at the approaches to the villages, where I saw some rather pretty little heaps." The attempts of the prince of Orange on Charleroi had failed as well as those of Luxembourg on the Hague; the Swedes had offered their mediation, and negotiations were beginning at Cologne; on the 10th of June, 1673, Louis XIV. laid siege to Maestricht; Condé was commanding in Holland, with Luxembourg under his orders; Turenne was observing Germany. The king was alone with Vauban. Maestricht held out three weeks. "M. de Vauban, in this siege as in many others, saved a number of lives by his ingenuity," wrote a young subaltern, the count of Alligny. "In times past it was sheer butchery in the trenches, now he makes them in such a manner that one is as safe as if one were at home." "I don't know whether it ought to be called swagger, vanity, or carelessness the way we have of showing ourselves unadvisedly and without cover," Vauban used to say, "but it is an original sin of which the French will never purge themselves if God, who is all-powerful, do not reform the whole race." Maestricht taken, the king repaired to Elsass, where skilful negotiations delivered into his hands the towns that had remained independent; it was time to consolidate past conquests; the coalition of Europe was forming against France; the Hollanders held the sea against the hostile fleets; after three desperate fights, Ruyter had prevented all landing in Holland; the States no longer entertained the proposals they had but lately submitted to the king at Utrecht; the prince of Orange had recovered Naarden and just carried Bonn with the aid of the Imperialists, commanded by Montecuculli; Luxembourg had already received orders to evacuate the province of Utrecht; at the end of the campaign of 1673, Gueldres and Over-Yssel were likewise delivered from the enemies who had oppressed and plundered them; Spain had come forth from her lethargy; and the emperor, resuming the political direction of Germany, had drawn nearly all the princes after him into the league against France. The protestant qualms of the English Parliament had not yielded to the influence of the marquis of Ruvigny, a man of note amongst the French Reformers and at this time ambassador of France in London; the nation desired peace with the Hollanders; and Charles II. yielded, in appearance at least, to the wishes of his people. On the 21st of February, 1674, he repaired to Parliament to announce to the two Houses that he had concluded with the United Provinces "a prompt peace, as they had prayed, honorable and, as he hoped, durable." He at the same time wrote to Louis XIV. to beg to be condoled with rather than upbraided for a consent which had been wrung from him. The regiments of English and Irish auxiliaries remained quietly in the service of France; and the king did not withdraw his subsidies from his royal pensioner.

Thus was being undone, link by link, the chain of alliances which Louis XIV. had but lately twisted round Holland; France, in her turn, was finding herself alone, with all Europe against her, scared, and consequently active and resolute; the congress of Cologne had broken up; not one of the belligerents desired peace; the Hollanders had just settled the heredity of the stadtholderate in the House of Orange. Louis XIV. saw the danger. "So many enemies," says he in his *Mémoires*, "obliged me to take care of myself and think what I must do to maintain the reputation of my arms, the advantage of my dominions and my personal glory." It was in Franche-Comté that Louis XIV. went to seek these advantages. The whole province was reduced to submission in the month of June, 1674. Turenne had kept the Rhine against the Imperialists; the marshal alone escaped the tyranny of the king and Louvois, and presumed to conduct the campaign in his own way; when Louis XIV. sent him instructions, he was by this time careful to add: "You will not bind yourself down to what I send you hereby as to my intentions save when you think that the good of my service will permit you, and you will give me of your news the oftenest you find it possible." (30th of March, 1674.) Turenne did not always write, and it sometimes happened that he did not obey.

This redounded to his honor in the campaign of 1674. Condé had gained on the 11th of August at the bloody victory of Seneffe over the prince of Orange and the allied generals; the four squadrons of the king's household, posted within range of the fire, had remained for eight hours in order of battle without any movement but that of closing up as the men fell. Madame de Sévigné, to whom her son, standard-bearer in the Dauphin's gendarmes, had told the story, wrote to M. de Bussy-Rabutin, "But for the *Te Deum* and some flags brought to Notre-Dame we should have thought we had lost the battle." The prince of Orange, ever indomitable in his cold courage, had attacked Audenarde on the 15th of September, but he was not in force, and the approach of Condé had obliged him to raise the siege; to make up, he had taken Grave, spite of the heroic resistance made by the marquis of Chemilly, who had held out ninety-three days. Advantages remained balanced in Flanders; the result of the Campaign depended on Turenne, who commanded on the Rhine. "If the king had taken the most important place in Flanders," he wrote to Louvois, "and the emperor were master of Alsace, even without Philipsburg or Brisach, I think the king's affairs would be in the worst plight in the world; we should see what armies we should have in Lorraine, in the Bishoprics and in Champagne. I do assure you that, if I had the honor of commanding in Flanders, I would speak as I do." On the 16th of June, he engaged in battle at Sinzheim with the duke of Lorraine, who was coming up with the advance-guard. "I never saw a more obstinate fight," said Turenne: "those old regiments of the emperor's did mighty well." He subsequently entered the Palatinate, quartering his troops upon it, whilst the superintendents sent by Louvois were burning and plundering the country, crushed as it was under war-contributions. The king and Louvois were disquieted by the movement of the enemy's troops, and wanted to get Turenne back into Lothringen. "An army like that of the enemy," wrote the marshal to Louvois, on the 13th of September, "and at the season it is now, cannot have any idea but that of driving the king's army from Alsace, having neither provisions nor means of getting into Lorraine unless I be driven from the country." On the 20th of September, the burgesses of the free city of Strasburg delivered up the bridge over the Rhine to the imperialists who were in the heart of Elsass. The victory of Ensheim, the fights of Mülhausen and Turckheim, sufficed to drive them back; but it was only on the 22nd of January, 1675, that Turenne was at last enabled to leave Elsass reconquered. "There is no longer in France an enemy that is not a prisoner," he wrote to the king whose thanks embarrassed him. "Everybody has remarked that M. de Turenne is a little more bashful than he was wont to be," said Pellisson.

The coalition was proceeding slowly; the prince of Orange was ill; the king made himself master of the citadel of Liège and some small places. Limburg surrendered to the prince of Condé, without the allies having been able to relieve it; Turenne was posted with the Rhine in his rear, keeping Montecuculli in his front; he was preparing to hem him in and hurl him back upon Black Mountain. His army was thirty thousand strong. "I never saw so many fine fellows," Turenne would say, "nor better intentioned." Spite of his modest reserve, he felt sure of victory. "This time I have them," he kept saying: "they cannot escape me."

On the 27th of June, 1675, in the morning, Turenne ordered an attack on the village of Salzbach. The young count of St. Hilaire found him at the head of his infantry, seated at the foot of a tree into which he had ordered an old soldier to climb in order to have a better view of the enemy's manœuvres. The count of Roye sent to conjure him to reconnoitre in person the German column that was advancing. "I shall remain where I am," said Turenne, "unless something important occur;" and he sent off reinforcements to M. de Roye; the latter repeated his entreaties; the marshal asked for his horse and, at a hand-gallop, reached the right of the army, along a hollow, in order to be under cover from two small pieces of cannon which kept up an incessant fire: "I don't at all want to be killed to-day," he kept saying. He perceived M. de St. Hilaire, the father, coming to meet him, and asked him what column it was on account of which he had been sent for. "My father was pointing it out to him," writes young St. Hilaire, "when, unhappily, the two little pieces fired: a ball, passing over the quarters of my father's horse, carried away his left arm and the horse's neck and struck M. de Turenne in the left side; he still went forward about twenty paces on his horse's neck and fell dead. I ran to my father who was down and raised him up: 'No need to weep for me,' he said; 'it is the death of that great man; you may perhaps lose your father, but neither your country nor you will ever have a general like that again. O poor army, what is to become of you?' Tears fell from his eyes; then, suddenly recovering himself: 'Go, my son, and leave me,' he said: 'with me it will be as God pleases; time presses, go and do your duty'" [*Mémoires du marquis de St. Hilaire*, t. i. p. 205]. They threw a cloak over the corpse of the great general and bore it away. "The soldiers raised a cry that was heard two leagues off," writes Madame de Sévigné; "no consideration could restrain them; they roared to be led to battle, they wanted to avenge the death of their father; with him they had feared nothing, but they would show how to avenge him, let it be left to them, they were frantic, let them be led to battle." Montecuculli had for a moment halted: "To-day a man has fallen who did honor to man," said he, as he uncovered respectfully. He threw himself, however, on the rear-guard of the French army, which was falling back upon Elsass, and re-crossed the Rhine at Altenheim. The death of Turenne was equivalent to a defeat.

The Emperor Napoleon said of Turenne, "He is the only general whom experience ever made more daring." He had been fighting for forty years and his fame was still increasing without effort or ostentation on his part. "M. de Turenne, from his youth up, possessed all good qualities," wrote Cardinal de Retz, who knew him well, "and the great he acquired full early. He lacked none but those that he did not think about. He possessed nearly all virtues as it were by nature; he never possessed the glitter of any. He was believed to be more fitted for the head of an army than of a party, and so I think, because he was not naturally enterprising: but, however, who knows? He always had in everything, just as in his speech, certain obscurities which were never cleared up save by circumstances, but never save to his glory." He had said, when he set out, to this same Cardinal de Retz, then in retirement at Commercy: "Sir, I am no *talker* (*diseur*), but I beg you to believe that, if it were not for this business in which perhaps I may be required, I would go into retirement as you have gone, and I give you my word that, if I come back, I, like you, will put some space between life and death." God did not leave him time. He summoned suddenly to Him this noble, grand and simple soul. "I see that cannon loaded with all eternity," says Madame de Sévigné: "I see all that leads M. de Turenne thither, and I see therein nothing gloomy for him. What does he lack? He dies in the meridian of his fame. Sometimes, by living on, the star pales. It is safer to cut to the quick, especially in the case of heroes whose actions are all so watched. M. de Turenne did not feel death: count you that for nothing?" Turenne was sixty-four; he had become a convert to Catholicism in 1668, seriously and sincerely, as he did everything. For him Bossuet had written his Exposition of faith. Heroic souls are rare, and those that are heroic and modest are rarer still: that was the distinctive feature of M. de Turenne. "When a man boasts that he has never made mistakes in war, he convinces me that he has not been long at it," he would say. At his death, France considered herself lost. "The premier president of the court of aids has an estate in Champagne, and the farmer of it came the other day to demand to have the contract dissolved; he was asked why; he answered that in M. de Turenne's time one could gather in with safety and count upon the lands in that district, but that, since his death, everybody was going away, believing that the enemy was about to enter Champagne" [*Lettres de Madame de Sévigné*]. "I should very much like to have only two hours' talk with the shade of M. de Turenne," said the prince of Condé, on setting out to take command of the army of the Rhine, after a check received by Marshal Créqui. "I would take the consequences of his plans if I could only get at his views and make myself master of the knowledge he had of the country and of Montecuculli's tricks of feint." "God preserves you for the sake of France, my lord," people said to him; but the prince made no reply beyond a shrug of the shoulders.

It was his last campaign. The king had made eight marshals, "change for a Turenne." Créqui began by getting beaten before Trèves, which surrendered to the enemy. "Why did the marshal give battle?" asked a courtier. The king turned round quickly: "I have heard," said he, "that the duke of Weimar, after the death of the great Gustavus, commanded the Swedish allies of France; one Parabère, an old blue riband, said to him, speaking of the last battle, which he had lost, 'Sir, why did you give it?' 'Sir,' answered Weimar, 'because I thought I should win it.' Then, leaning over towards somebody else, he asked, 'Who is that fool with the blue riband?'" The Germans retired. Condé returned to Chantilly once more, never to go out of it again. Montecuculli, old and ill, refused to serve any longer. "A man who has had the honor of fighting against Mahomet Coprogli, against the prince, and against M. de Turenne, ought not to compromise his glory against people who are only just beginning to command armies," said the veteran general to the emperor on taking his retirement. The chiefs were disappearing from the scene, the heroic period of the war was over.

Europe demanded a general peace; England and Holland desired it passionately. "I am as anxious as you for an end to be put to the war," said the prince of Orange to the deputies from the Estates, "provided that I get out of it with honor." He refused obstinately to separate from his allies. "It is not astonishing that the prince of Orange does not at once give way even to things which he considers reasonable," said Charles

II.: "he is the son of a father and mother whose obstinacy was carried to extremes; and he resembles them in that." Meanwhile, William had just married (November 15, 1677), the Princess Mary, eldest daughter of the duke of York and Anne Hyde. An alliance offensive and defensive between England and Holland was the price of this union, which struck Louis XIV. an unexpected blow. He had lately made a proposal to the prince of Orange to marry one of his natural daughters. "The first notice I had of the marriage," wrote the king, "was through the bonfires lighted in London." "The loss of a decisive battle could not have scared the king of France more," said the English ambassador, Lord Montagu. For more than a year past negotiations had been going on at Nimeguen; Louis XIV. resolved to deal one more great blow.

The campaign of 1676 had been insignificant, save at sea. John Bart, a corsair of Dunkerque, scoured the seas and made foreign commerce tremble; he took ships by boarding, and killed with his own hands the Dutch captain of the *Neptune*, who offered resistance. Messina, in revolt against the Spaniards, had given herself up to France; the duke of Vivonne, brother of Madame de Montespan, who had been sent thither as governor, had extended his conquests; Duquesne, quite young still, had triumphantly maintained the glory of France against the great Ruyter, who had been mortally wounded off Catana on the 21st of April. But already the possession of Sicily was becoming precarious, and these distant successes had paled before the brilliant campaign of 1677; the capture of Valenciennes, Cambrai, and St. Omer, the defence of Lorraine, the victory of Cassel gained over the prince of Orange, had confirmed the king in his intentions. "We have done all that we were able and bound to do," wrote William of Orange to the Estates on the 13th of April, 1677, "and we are very sorry to be obliged to tell your High Mightinesses that it has not pleased God to bless on this occasion the arms of the State under our guidance."

"I was all impatience," says Louis XIV. in his *Mémoires*, "to commence the campaign of 1678, and greatly desirous of doing something therein as glorious as and more useful than what had already been done; but it was no easy matter to come by it and to surpass the lustre conferred by the capture of three large places and the winning of a battle. I examined what was feasible, and Ghent being the most important of all I could attack, I fixed upon it to besiege." The place was invested on the 1st of March and capitulated on the 11th; Ypres in its turn succumbed on the 25th after a vigorous resistance. On the 7th of April the king returned to St. Germain, "pretty content with what I had done," he says, "and purposing to do better in the future if the promise I had given not to undertake anything for two months were not followed by the conclusion of peace." Louis XIV. sent his *ultimatum* to Nimeguen.

Holland had weight in congress as well as in war, and her influence was now enlisted on the side of peace. "Not only is it desired," said the grand pensionary Fagel, "but it is absolutely indispensable, and I would not answer for it that the States-general, if driven to extremity by the sluggishness of their allies, will not make a separate peace with France. I know nobody in Holland who is not of the same opinion." The prince of Orange flew out at such language: "Well then, *I* know somebody," said he, "and that is myself; I will oppose it to the best of my ability; but," he added more slowly, upon reflection, "if I were not here, I know quite well that peace would be concluded within twenty-four hours."

One man alone, though it were the prince of Orange, cannot long withstand the wishes of a free people. The republican party, for a while cast down by the death of John van Witt, had taken courage again, and Louis XIV. secretly encouraged it. William of Orange had let out his desire of becoming duke of Gueldres and count of Zutphen; these foreshadowings of sovereignty had scared the province of Holland, which refused its consent; the influence of the stadtholder was weakened thereby; the Estates pronounced for peace, spite of the entreaties of the prince of Orange; "I am always ready to obey the orders of the State," said he, "but do not require me to give my assent to a peace which appears to me not only ruinous but shameful as well." Two deputies from the United Provinces set out for Brussels.

"It is better to throw one's self out of the window than from the top of the roof," said the Spanish plenipotentiary to the nuncio when he had cognizance of the French proposals, and he accepted the treaty offered him. "The duke of Villa Hermosa says that he will accept the conditions; for ourselves, we will do the same," said the prince of Orange, bitterly, "and so here is peace made, if France continues to desire it on this footing, which I very much doubt."

At one moment, in fact, Louis XIV. raised fresh pretensions. He wished to keep the places on the Meuse until the Swedes, almost invariably unfortunate in their hostilities with Denmark and Brandenburg, should have been enabled to win back what they had lost. This was to postpone peace indefinitely. The English parliament and Holland were disquieted and concluded a new alliance. The Spaniards were preparing to take up arms again. The king, who had returned to the army, all at once cut the knot. "The day I arrived at the camp," writes Louis XIV., "I received news from London apprising me that the king of England would bind himself to join me in forcing my enemies to make peace, if I consented to add something to the conditions he had already proposed. I had a battle over this proposal, but the public good, joined to the glory of gaining a victory over myself, prevailed over the advantage I might have hoped for from war. I replied to the king of England that I was quite willing to make the treaty he proposed to me, and, at the same time, I wrote to the States-general a letter stronger than the first, being convinced that, since they were wavering, they ought not to have time given them to take counsel upon the subject of peace with their allies who did not want it." Beverninck went to visit the king at Ghent; and he showed so much ability that the special peace concluded by his pains received in Holland the name of Beverninck's peace. "I settled more business in an hour with M. de Beverninck than the plenipotentiaries would have been able to conclude in several days," said Louis XIV.: "the care I had taken to detach the allies one from another overwhelmed them to such an extent, that they were constrained to submit to the conditions of which I had declared myself in favor at the commencement of my negotiations. I had resolved to make peace, but I wished to conclude one that would be glorious for me and advantageous for my kingdom. I wished to recompense myself, by means of the places that were essential, for the probable conquests I was losing, and to console myself for the conclusion of a war which I was carrying on with pleasure and success. Amidst such turmoil, then, I was quite tranquil and saw nothing but advantage for myself, whether the war went on or peace were made."

All difficulties were smoothed away: Sweden had given up all stipulations for her advantage; the firm will of France had triumphed over the vacillations of Charles II. and the allies. "The behavior of the French in all this was admirable," says Sir W. Temple, an experienced diplomatist, long versed in all the affairs of Europe, "whilst our own counsels and behavior resembled those floating islands which winds and tide drive from one side to the other."

On the 10th of August, in the evening, the special peace between Holland and France was signed after twenty-four hours' conference. The prince of Orange had concentrated all his forces near Mons, confronting Marshal Luxembourg, who occupied the plateau of Casteau; he had no official news as yet from Nimeguen, and, on the 14th, he began the engagement outside the abbey of St. Denis. The affair was a very murderous one and remained indecisive: it did more honor to the military skill of the prince of Orange than to his loyalty. Holland had not lost an inch of her territory during this war, so long, so desperate, and notoriously undertaken in order to destroy her; she had spent much money, she had lost many men, she had shaken the confidence of her allies by treating alone and being the first to treat, but she had furnished a chief to the European coalition, and she had shown an example of indomitable resistance; the States-general and the prince of Orange alone, besides Louis XIV., came the greater out of the struggle. The king of England had lost all consideration both at home and abroad, and Spain paid all the expenses of the war.

Peace was concluded on the 17th of September, thanks to the energetic intervention of the Hollanders. The king restored Courtray, Audenarde, Ath, and Charleroi, which had been given him by the treaty of Aix-la-Chapelle, Ghent, Limburg and St. Ghislain; but he kept by definitive right St. Omer, Cassel, Aire, Ypres, Cambray, Bouchain, Valenciennes, and all Franche-Comté; henceforth he possessed in the north of France a line of places extending from Dunkerque to the Meuse; the Spanish monarchy was disarmed.

It still required a successful campaign under Marshal Créqui to bring the emperor and the German princes over to peace; exchanges of territory and indemnities re-established the treaty of Westphalia on all essential points. The duke of Lorraine refused the conditions on which the king proposed to restore to him his duchy; so Louis XIV. kept Lorraine.

The king of France was at the pinnacle of his greatness and power. "Singly against all," as Louvois said, he had maintained the struggle against Europe, and he came out of it victorious; everywhere, with good reason, was displayed his proud device, *Nec pluribus impar*. "My will alone," says Louis XIV. in his *Mémoires*, "concluded this peace, so much desired by those on whom it did not depend; for, as to my enemies, they feared it as much as the public good made me desire it, and that prevailed on this occasion over the gain and personal glory I was likely to find in the continuation of the war. . . . . I was in full enjoyment of my good fortune and the fruits of my good conduct, which had caused me to profit by all the occasions I had met with for extending the borders of my kingdom at the expense of my enemies."

"Here is peace made," wrote Madame de Sévigné to the count of Bussy. "The king thought it handsomer to grant it this year to Spain and Holland than to take the rest of Flanders; he is keeping that for another time."

The prince of Orange thought as Madame de Sévigné: he regarded the peace of Nimeguen as a truce, and a truce fraught with danger to Europe. For that reason did he soon seek to form alliances in order to secure the repose of the world against the insatiable ambition of King Louis XIV. Intoxicated by his successes and the adulation of his court, the king of France no longer brooked any objections to his will or any limits to his desires. The poison of absolute power had done its work: Louis XIV. considered the "office of king" grand, noble, delightful, "for he felt himself worthy of acquitting himself well in all matters in which he engaged." "The ardor we feel for glory," he used to say, "is not one of those feeble passions which grow dull by possession; its favors, which are never to be obtained without effort, never on the other hand cause disgust, and whoever can do without longing for fresh ones is unworthy of all he has received."

Standing at the king's side and exciting his pride and ambition, Louvois had little by little absorbed all the functions of prime minister without bearing the title. Colbert alone resisted him, and he, weary of the struggle, was about to succumb before long (1683), driven to desperation by the burdens that the wars and the king's luxury caused to weigh heavily upon France. Peace had not yet led to disarmament; an army of a hundred and forty thousand men remained standing, ever ready to uphold the rights of France during the long discussions over the regulation of the frontiers. In old papers ancient titles were found, and by degrees the villages, burghs, and even principalities, claimed by King Louis XIV., were reunited quietly to France; King Charles XI. was thus alienated, in consequence of the seizure of the countship of Deux-Ponts, to which Sweden laid claim. Strasburg was taken by a surprise.

This free city had several times violated neutrality during the war; Louvois had kept up communications inside the place; suddenly he had the approaches and the passage over the Rhine occupied by thirty-five thousand men on the night between the 16th and 17th of September, 1681; the burgesses sent up to ask aid from the emperor, but the messengers were arrested; on the 30th, Strasburg capitulated, and Louis XIV. made his triumphant entry there on the 24th of October. "Nobody," says a letter of the day, "can recover from the consternation caused by the fact that the French have taken Strasburg without firing a single shot; everybody says it is one of the wheels of the chariot to be used for a drive into the empire, and that the door of Elsass is shut from this moment."

The very day of the surrender of Strasburg (September 30, 1681), Catinat, with a corps of French troops, entered Casale, sold to Louis XIV. by the duke of Mantua. The king thought to make sure of Piedmont by marrying his niece, Monsieur's daughter, to the duke of Savoy, Victor-Amadeo, quite a boy, delicate and taciturn, at loggerheads with his mother and with her favorites. Marie Louise d'Orléans, elder sister of the young duchess of Savoy, had married the king of Spain, Charles II., a sickly creature of weak intellect. Louis XIV. felt the necessity of forming new alliances; the old supports of France had all gone over to the enemy. Sweden and Holland were already allied to the empire; the German princes joined the coalition. The prince of Orange, with an ever vigilant eye on the frequent infractions of the treaties which France permitted herself to commit, was quietly negotiating with his allies and ready to take up arms to meet the common danger. "He was," says Massillon, "a prince profound in his views, skilful in forming leagues and banding spirits together, more successful in exciting wars than on the battle-field, more to be feared in the privacy of the closet than at the head of armies, a prince and an enemy whom hatred of the French name rendered capable of conceiving great things and of executing them, one of those geniuses who seem born to move at their will both peoples and sovereigns." French diplomacy was not in a condition to struggle with the prince of Orange. M. de Pomponne had succeeded Lionne; he was disgraced in 1679: "I order his recall," said the king, "because all that passes through his hands loses the grandeur and force which ought to be shown in executing the orders of a king who is no poor creature." Colbert de Croissy, the minister's brother, was from that time employed to manage with foreign countries all the business which Louvois did not reserve to himself.

Duquesne had bombarded Algiers in 1682; in 1684, he destroyed several districts of Genoa, which was accused of having failed in neutrality between France and Spain; and at the same time Marshals Humières and Créqui occupied Audenarde, Courtray and Dixmude, and made themselves masters of Luxembourg; the king reproached Spain with its delays in the regulation of the frontiers and claimed to occupy the Low Countries pacifically; the diet of Ratisbonne intervened; the emperor, with the aid of Sobieski, king of Poland, was occupied in repelling the invasions of the Turks; a truce was concluded for twenty-four years; the empire and Spain acquiesced in the king's new conquests. "It seemed to be established," said the marquis de la Fare, "that the empire of France was an evil not to be avoided by other nations." Nobody was more convinced of this than King Louis XIV.

He was himself about to deal his own kingdom a blow more fatal than all those of foreign wars and of the European coalition. Intoxicated by so much success and so many victories, he fancied that consciences were to be bent like States, and he set about bringing all his subjects back to the Catholic faith. Himself returning to a regular life, under the influence of age and of Madame de Maintenon, he thought it a fine thing to establish in his kingdom that unity of religion which Henry IV. and Richelieu had not been able to bring about. He set at nought all the rights consecrated by edicts, and the long patience of those Protestants whom Mazarin called "the faithful flock;" in vain had persecution been tried for several years past; tyranny interfered, and the edict of Nantes was revoked on the 13th of October, 1685. Some years later, the reformers, by hundreds of thousands, carried into foreign lands their industries, their wealth and their bitter resentments. Protestant Europe, indignant, opened her doors to these martyrs to conscience, living witnesses of the injustice and arbitrary power of Louis XIV. All the princes felt themselves at the same time insulted and threatened in respect of their faith as well as of their puissance. In the early months of 1686, the league of Augsburg united all the German princes, Holland and Sweden; Spain and the duke of Savoy were not slow to join it. In 1687, the diet of Ratisbonne refused to convert the twenty years' truce into a definitive peace. By his haughty pretensions the king gave to the coalition the support of Pope Innocent XI.

Louis XIV. was once more single-handed against all, when he invaded the electorate of Cologne in the month of August, 1686. Philipsburg, lost by France in 1676, was recovered on the 29th of October; at the end of the campaign, the king's armies were masters of the Palatinate. In the month of January, 1689, war was officially declared against Holland, the emperor and the empire. The command-in-chief of the French forces was entrusted to the Dauphin, then twenty-six years of age. "I give you an opportunity of making your merit known," said Louis XIV. to his son: "exhibit it to all Europe, so that when I come to die it shall not be perceived that the king is dead."

The Dauphin was already tasting the pleasures of conquest, and the coalition had not stirred. They were awaiting their chief: William of Orange was fighting for them in the very act of taking possession of the kingdom of England. Weary of the narrow-minded and cruel tyranny of their king James II., disquieted at his blind zeal for the Catholic religion, the English nation had summoned to their aid the champion of Protestantism; it was in the name of the political liberties and the religious creed of England that the prince of Orange set sail on the 11th of November, 1688: on the flags of his vessels was inscribed the proud device of his house: *I will maintain;* below were the words, *Pro libertate et Protestante religione.* William landed without obstacle at Torbay, on the 15th of November; on the 4th of January King James, abandoned by everybody, arrived in France, whither he had been preceded by his wife, Mary of Modena, and the little prince of Wales; the convention of the two Houses in England proclaimed William and Mary *kings* (*rois*—? king and queen); the prince of Orange had declined the modest part of mere husband of the queen: "I will never be tied to a woman's apron-strings," he had said.

By his personal qualities as well as by the defects and errors of his mind, Louis XIV. was a predestined acquisition to the cause of James II.; he regarded the revolution in England as an insolent attack by the people upon the kingly majesty, and William of Orange was the most dangerous enemy of the crown of France. The king gave the fallen monarch a magnificent reception. "The king acts towards these majesties of England quite divinely," writes Madame de Sévigné, on the 10th of January, 1689: "for is it not to be the image of the Almighty to support a king out-driven, betrayed, abandoned as he is? The king's noble soul is delighted to play such a part as this. He went to meet the queen of England with all his household and a hundred six-horse carriages; he escorted her to St. Germain, where she found herself supplied like the queen with all sorts of knick-knacks, amongst which was a very rich casket with six thousand louis d'or. The next day the king of England arrived late at St. Germain; the king was there waiting for him and went to the end of the Guards' hall to meet him; the king of England bent down very low, as if he meant to embrace his knees; the king prevented him and embraced him three or four times over, very cordially. At parting, his Majesty would not be escorted back, but said to the king of England, 'This is your house; when I come hither you shall do me the honors of it, as I will do you when you come to Versailles.' The king subsequently sent the king of England ten thousand louis. The latter looked aged and worn, the queen thin and with eyes that have wept, but beautiful black ones; a fine complexion, rather pale, a large mouth, fine teeth, a fine figure and plenty of wits: all that makes up a very pleasing person. All she says is quite just and full of good sense. Her husband is not the same; he has plenty of spirit but a common mind which relates all that has passed in England with a want of feeling which causes the same towards him. It is so extraordinary to have this court here that it is the subject of conversation incessantly. Attempts are being made to regulate ranks and prepare for permanently living with people so far from their restoration."

In his pride and his kingly illusions, Louis XIV. had undertaken a burden which was to weigh heavily upon him to the very end of his reign.

Catholic Ireland had not acquiesced in the elevation of William of Orange to the throne of England; she invited over King James. Personally brave and blinded by his hopes he set out from St. Germain on the 25th of February, 1689. "Brother," said the king to him on taking leave, "the best I can wish you is not to see you back." He took with him a corps of French troops commanded by M. de Rosen, and the count of Avaux as adviser. "It will be no easy matter to keep any secret with the king of England," wrote Avaux to Louis XIV.: "he has said before the sailors of the *St. Michael* what he ought to have reserved for his greatest confidants. Another thing which may cause us trouble is his indecision, for he has frequent changes of opinion and does not always determine upon the best. He lays great stress on little things over which he spends all his time and passes lightly by the most essential. Besides, he listens to everybody, and as much time has to be spent in destroying the impressions which bad advice has produced upon him as in inspiring him with good. It is said here that the Protestants of the North will intrench themselves in Londonderry, which is a pretty strong town for Ireland, and that it is a business which will possibly last some days."

The siege of Londonderry lasted a hundred and five days; most of the French officers fell there; the place had to be abandoned; the English army had just landed at Carrickfergus (August 25), under the orders of Marshal Schomberg. Like their leader a portion of Schomberg's men were French Protestants who had left their native country after the revocation of the edict of Nantes; they fought to the bitter end against the French regiments of Rosen. The Irish parliament was beginning to have doubts about James II.: "Too English," it was said, "to render full justice to Ireland." There was disorder everywhere, in the Government as well as in the military operations; Schomberg held the Irish and French in check; at last William III. appeared.

He landed on the 14th of June, and at once took the road to Belfast; the protestant opposition was cantoned in the province of Ulster, peopled to a great extent by Cromwell's Scotch colonists; three parts of Ireland were still in the hands of the Catholics and King James. "I haven't come hither to let the grass grow under my feet," said William to those who counselled prudence. He had brought with him his old Dutch and German regiments and numbered under his orders thirty-five thousand men; representatives from all the Protestant churches of Europe were there in arms against the enemies of their liberties.

The forces of King James were scarcely inferior to those of his son-in-law; Louis XIV. had sent him a reinforcement of eight thousand men under the orders of the duke of Lauzun. On the 1st of July the two armies met on the banks of the Boyne, near the town of Drogheda. William had been slightly wounded in the shoulder the evening before during a reconnoissance. "There's no harm done," said he at once to his terrified friends, "but as it was, the ball struck quite high enough." He was on horseback at the head of his troops; at daybreak the whole army plunged into the river; Marshal Schomberg commanded a division; he saw that the Huguenot regiments were staggered by the death of their leader, M. de

Caillemotte, younger brother of the marquis of Ruvigny. He rushed his horse into the river, shouting, "Forward, gentlemen, yonder are your persecutors." He was killed, in his turn, as he touched the bank. King William himself had just entered the Boyne; his horse had taken to swimming, and he had difficulty in guiding it with his wounded arm; a ball struck his boot, another came and hit against the butt of his pistol; the Irish infantry, ignorant and undisciplined, everywhere took flight. "We were not beaten," said a letter to Louvois from M. de la Hoguette, a French officer, "but the enemy drove the Irish troops, like sheep, before them, without their having attempted to fire a single musket-shot." All the burden of the contest fell upon the troops of Louis XIV. and upon the Irish gentlemen, who fought furiously; William rallied around him the Protestants of Enniskillen and led them back to the charge; the Irish gave way on all sides; King James had prudently remained at a distance, watching the battle from afar; he turned bridle and hastily took the road back to Dublin. On the 3rd of July he embarked at Waterford, himself carrying to St. Germain the news of his defeat. "Those who love the king of England must be very glad to see him in safety," wrote Marshal Luxembourg to Louvois; "but those who love his glory have good reason to deplore the figure he made." "I was in trouble to know what had become of the king my father," wrote Queen Mary to William III.; "I dared not ask anybody but Lord Nottingham, and I had the satisfaction of learning that he was safe and sound. I know that I need not beg you to spare him, but to your tenderness add this, that for my sake the world may know that you would not have any harm happen to him. You will forgive me this." The rumor had spread at Paris that King William was dead; the populace lighted bonfires in the streets; and the governor of the Bastille fired a salute. The anger and hatred of a people are perspicacious.

The insensate pride of king and nation were to be put to other trials; the campaign of 1689 had been without advantage or honor to the king's arms. Disembarrassed of the great Condé, of Turenne and even of Marshal Luxembourg, who was compromised in some distressing law proceedings, Louvois exercised undisputed command over generals and armies; his harsh and violent genius encountered no more obstacles. He had planned a defensive war which was to tire out the allies, all the while ravaging their territories. The Palatinate underwent all its horrors. Manheim, Heidelberg, Spires, Worms, Bingen, were destroyed and burnt. "I don't think," wrote the count of Tessé to Louvois, "that for a week past my heart has been in its usual place. I take the liberty of speaking to you naturally, but I did not foresee that it would cost so much to personally look to the burning of a town with a population, in proportion, like that of Orleans. You may rely upon it that nothing at all remains of the superb castle of Heidelberg. There were yesterday at noon, besides the castle, four hundred and thirty-two houses burnt; and the fire was still going on. I merely caused to be set apart the family pictures of the Palatine House; that is, the fathers, mothers, grandmothers and relatives of Madame; intending, if you order me or advise me so, to make her a present of them and have them sent to her when she is somewhat distracted from the desolation of her native country; for, except herself, who can take any interest in them? Of the whole lot there is not a single copy worth a dozen livres." The poor Princess Palatine, Monsieur's second wife, was not yet *distracted from her native country*, and she wrote in March, 1689: "Should it cost me my life, it is impossible for me not to regret, not to deplore having been, so to speak, the pretext for the destruction of my country. I cannot look on in cold blood and see the ruin at a single blow, in poor Manheim, of all that cost so much pains and trouble to the late prince-elector, my father. When I think of all the explosions that have taken place, I am so full of horror that every night, the moment I begin to go to sleep, I fancy myself at Heidelberg or Manheim and an eye-witness of the ravages committed. I picture to myself how it all was in my time and to what condition it has been reduced now, and I cannot refrain from weeping hot tears. What distresses me above all is that the king waited to reveal his orders until the very moment of my intercession in favor of Heidelberg and Manheim. And yet it is thought bad taste for me to be afflicted!"

The elector of Bavaria, an able prince and a good soldier, had roused Germany to avenge his wrongs; France had just been placed under the ban of the empire; and the *grand alliance* was forming. All the German princes joined it; the United Provinces, England and Spain combined for the restoration of the treaties of Westphalia and of the Pyrenees. Europe had mistaken hopes of forcing Louis XIV. to give up all his conquests. Twenty years of wars and reverses were not to suffice for that. Fortune, however, was tiring of being favorable to

France; Marshals Duras and Humières were unable to hamper the movements of the duke of Lorraine, Charles V., and of the elector of Bavaria; the French garrisons of Mayence and of Bonn were obliged to capitulate after a heroic defence: their munitions failed. The king recalled Marshal Luxembourg to the head of his armies. The able courtier had managed to get reconciled with Louvois. "You know, sir," he wrote to him on the 9th of May, 1690, "with what pleasure I shall seek after such things as will possibly find favor with the king and give you satisfaction. I am too well aware how far my small authority extends to suppose that I can withdraw any man from any place without having written to you previously. It is with some repugnance that I resolve to put before you what comes into my head, knowing well that all that is good can come only from you, and looking upon anything I conceive as merely simple ideas produced by the indolence in which we are living here."

The wary indolence and the observations of Luxembourg were not long in giving place to activity. The marshal crossed the Sambre on the 29th of June, entered Charleroi and Namur, and on the 2nd of July attacked the prince of Waldeck near the rivulet of Fleurus. A considerable body of troops had made a forced march of seven leagues during the night and came up to take the enemy in the rear; it was a complete success, but devoid of result, like the victory of Stafarde, gained by Catinat over the duke of Savoy, Victor-Amadeo, who had openly joined the coalition. The triumphant naval battle delivered by Tourville to the English and Dutch fleets off Beachy Head was a great humiliation for the maritime powers. "I cannot express to you," wrote William III. to the grand pensionary Heinsius, holding in his absence the government of the United Provinces, "how distressed I am at the disasters of the fleet; I am so much the more deeply affected as I have been informed that my ships did not properly support those of the Estates and left them in the lurch." William had said, when he left Holland: "The republic must lead off the dance." The moment had come when England was going to take her part in it.

In the month of January, 1691, William III. arrived in Holland. "I am languishing for that moment," he wrote six months before to Heinsius. All the allies had sent their ambassadors thither. "It is no longer the time for deliberation, but for action," said the king of England to the congress: "the king of France has made himself master of all the fortresses which bordered on his kingdom; if he be not opposed, he will take all the rest. The interest of each is bound up in the general interest of all. It is with the sword that we must wrest from his grasp the liberties of Europe, which he aims at stifling, or we must submit forever to the yoke of servitude. As for me, I will spare for that purpose neither my influence, nor my forces, nor my person, and in the spring I will come, at the head of my troops, to conquer or die with my allies."

The spring had not yet come, and already (March 15) Mons was invested by the French army. The secret had been carefully kept. On the 21st, the king arrived in person with the Dauphin; William of Orange collected his troops in all haste, but he did not come up in time: Mons capitulated on the 8th of April; five days later Nice, besieged by Catinat, surrendered like Mons; Louis XIV. returned to Versailles, according to his custom after a brilliant stroke. Louvois was pushing on the war furiously; the naturally fierce temper of the minister was soured by excess of work and by his decline in the king's favor; he felt his position towards the king shaken by the influence of Madame de Maintenon; venting his wrath on the enemy, he was giving orders everywhere for conflagration and bombardment, when on the 17th of July, 1691, after working with the king, Louvois complained of pain; Louis XIV. sent him to his rooms; on reaching his chamber he fell down fainting; the people ran to fetch his third son, M. de Barbezieux; Madame de Louvois was not at Versailles, and his two elder sons were in the field; he arrived too late, his father was dead.

"So he is dead, this great minister, this man of such importance, whose *egotism* (*le moi*), as M. Nicole says, was so extensive, who was the centre of so many things! What business, what designs, what projects, what secrets, what interests to unfold, what wars begun, what intrigues, what beautiful moves-in-check to make and to superintend! Ah! my God, grant me a little while, I would fain give check to the duke of Savoy and mate to the prince of Orange! No, no, thou shalt not have one, one single moment!" Thus wrote Madame de Sévigné to her daughter Madame de Grignan. Louis XIV., in whose service Louvois had spent his life was less troubled at his death. "Tell the king of England that I have lost a good minister," was the answer he sent to the complimentary condolence of King James, "but that his affairs and mine will go on none the worse,"

In his secret heart and beneath the veil of his majestic observance of the proprieties, the king thought that his business as well as the agreeableness of his life would probably gain from being no longer subject to the tempers and the roughnesses of Louvois. The *Grand Monarque* considered that he had trained (*instruit*) his minister, but he felt that the pupil had got away from him. He appointed Barbezieux secretary for war. "I will form you," said he. No human hand had formed Louvois, not even that of his father, the able and prudent Michael le Tellier; he had received straight from God the strong qualities, resolution, indomitable will, ardor for work, the instinct of organization and command, which had made of him a minister without equal for the warlike and ambitious purposes of his master. Power had spoilt him, his faults had prevailed over his other qualities without destroying them; violent, fierce, without principle and without scruple in the execution of his designs, he had egged the king on to incessant wars, treating with disdain the internal miseries of the kingdom as well as any idea of pity for the vanquished; he had desired to do everything, order everything, grasp everything, and he died at fifty-three, dreaded by all, hated by a great many, and leaving in the government of the country a void which the king felt, all the time that he was angrily seeking to fill it up.

Louvois was no more; negotiations were beginning to be whispered about, but the war continued by land and sea; the campaign of 1691 had completely destroyed the hopes of James II. in Ireland; it was decided to attempt a descent upon England; a plot was being hatched to support the invasion. Tourville was commissioned to cover the landing. He received orders to fight, whatever might be the numbers of the enemy. The wind prevented his departure from Brest; the Dutch fleet had found time to join the English. Tourville wanted to wait for the squadrons of Estrées and Rochefort; Pontchartrain had been minister of finance and marine since the death of Seignelay, Colbert's son, in 1690; he replied from Versailles to the experienced sailor, familiar with battle from the age of fourteen: "It is not for you to discuss the king's orders, it is for you to execute them and enter the Channel; if you are not ready to do it, the king will put in your place somebody more obedient and less discreet than you." Tourville went out and encountered the enemy's squadrons between the headlands of La Hogue and Barfleur; he had forty-four vessels against ninety-nine, the number of English and Dutch together. Tourville assembled his council of war, and all the officers were for withdrawing; but the king's orders were peremptory, and the admiral joined battle. After three days' desperate resistance, backed up by the most skilful manœuvres, Tourville was obliged to withdraw beneath the forts of La Hogue in hopes of running his ships ashore; but in this King James and Marshal Bellefonds opposed him. Tourville remained at sea, and lost a dozen vessels. The consternation in France was profound; the nation had grown accustomed to victory; on the 20th of June the capture of Namur raised their hopes again; this time again William III. had been unable to succor his allies; he determined to revenge himself on Luxembourg, whom he surprised on the 31st of August, between Enghien and Steinkirk; the ground was narrow and uneven, and the king of England counted upon thus paralyzing the brilliant French cavalry. M. de Luxembourg, ill of fever as he was, would fain have dismounted to lead to the charge the brigades of the French guards and of the Swiss, but he was prevented; the duke of Bourbon, the prince of Conti, the duke of Chartres, and the duke of Vendôme, placed themselves at the head of the infantry and, sword in hand, led it against the enemy; a fortunate movement on the part of Marshal Boufflers, resulted in rendering the victory decisive. Next year at Neerwinden (29th of July, 1693) the success of the day was likewise due to the infantry. On that day the French guards had exhausted their ammunition; putting the bayonet at the end of their pieces, they broke the enemy's battalions; this was the first charge of the kind in the French armies. The king's household troops had remained motionless for four hours under the fire of the allies; William III. thought for a moment that his gunners made bad practice, he ran up to the batteries; the French squadrons did not move except to close up the ranks as the files were carried off; the king of England could not help an exclamation of anger and admiration, "Insolent nation!" he cried. The victory of Neerwinden ended in nothing but the capture of Charleroi; the successes of Catinat at Marsaglia, in Piedmont, had washed out the shame of the duke of Savoy's incursion into Dauphiny in 1692. Tourville had remained with the advantage in several maritime engagements off Cape St. Vincent and burnt the English vessels in the very roads of Cadiz. On every sea the corsairs of St. Malo and Dunkerque, John Bart and Duguay-Trouin, now enrolled in the king's navy, towed at their sterns numerous prizes; the king and France, for a long time carried away by a common passion, had arrived at that point at which victories no longer suffice in the place of solid and definitive success. The nation was at last tiring of its glory. "People were dying of want to the sound of the *Te Deum*," says Voltaire in the *Siècle de Louis XIV.*; everywhere there was weariness equal to the suffering. Madame de Maintenon and some of her friends at that time, sincerely devoted to the public good, rather Christians than warriors, Fénélon, the dukes of Beauvilliers and Chevreuse, were laboring to bring the king over to pacific views; he saw generals as well as ministers falling one after another; Marshal Luxembourg, exhausted by the fatigues of war and the pleasures of the court, died on the 4th of January, 1695, at sixty-seven years of age. An able general, a worthy pupil of the great Condé, a courtier of much wits and no shame, he was more corrupt than his age, and his private life was injurious to his fame; he died, however, as people did die in his time, turning to God at the last day. "I haven't lived like M. de Luxembourg," said Bourdaloue, "but I should like to die like him." History has forgotten Marshal Luxembourg's death and remembered his life.

Louis XIV. had lost Condé and Turenne, Luxembourg, Colbert, Louvois and Seignelay; with the exception of Vauban, he had exhausted the first rank; Catinat alone remained in the second: the king was about to be reduced to the third: sad fruits of a long reign, of an incessant and devouring activity, which had speedily used up men and was beginning to tire out fortune; grievous result of mistakes long hidden by glory, but glaring out at last before the eyes most blinded by prejudice! "The whole of France is no longer anything but one vast hospital," wrote Fénelon to the king under the veil of the anonymous: "The people who so loved you are beginning to lose affection, confidence, and even respect; the allies prefer carrying on war with loss to concluding a peace which would not be observed. Even those who have not dared to declare openly against you are nevertheless impatiently desiring your enfeeblement and your humiliation as the only resource for liberty and for the repose of all Christian nations. Everybody knows it, and none dares tell you so. Whilst you in some fierce conflict are taking the battle-field and the cannon of the enemy, whilst you are storming strong places, you do not reflect that you are fighting on ground which is sinking beneath your feet, and that you are about to have a fall in spite of your victories. It is time to humble yourself beneath the mighty hand of God, you must ask peace, and by that shame expiate all the glory of which you have made your idol; finally, you must give up, the soonest possible, to your enemies, in order to save the State, conquests that you cannot retain without injustice. For a long time past God has had His arm raised over you, but He is slow to smite you because He has pity upon a prince who has all his life been beset by flatterers." Noble and strong language, the cruel truth of which the king did not as yet comprehend, misled as he was by his pride, by the splendor of his successes, and by the concert of praises which his people as well as his court had so long made to reverberate in his ears.

Louis XIV. had led France on to the brink of a precipice, and he had in his turn been led on by her; king and people had given themselves up unreservedly to the passion for glory and to the intoxication of success; the day of awakening was at hand.

Louis XIV. was not so blind as Fénelon supposed; he saw the danger at the very moment when his kingly pride refused to admit it. The king of England had just retaken Namur, without Villeroi, who had succeeded Marshal Luxembourg, having been able to relieve the place. Louis XIV. had already let out that he "should not pretend to avail himself of any special conventions until the prince of Orange was satisfied as regarded his person and the crown of England." This was a great step towards that *humiliation* recommended by Fénelon. The secret negotiations with the duke of Savoy were not less significant. After William III., Victor Amadeo was the most active and most devoted, as well as the most able and most stubborn of the allied princes. In the month of June, 1696, the treaty was officially declared: Victor Amadeo would recover Savoy, Suza, the countship of Nice and Pignerol dismantled; his eldest daughter, Princess Mary Adelaide, was to marry the duke of Burgundy, eldest son of the Dauphin, and the ambassadors of Piedmont henceforth took rank with those of crowned heads. In return for so many concessions, Victor Amadeo guaranteed to the king the neutrality of Italy and promised to close the entry of his dominions against the Protestants of Dauphiny who came thither for refuge. If Italy refused her neutrality, the duke of Savoy was to unite his forces to those of the king and command the combined army.

Victory would not have been more advantageous for Victor Amadeo than his constant defeats were; but, by detaching him from the coalition, Louis XIV. had struck a fatal blow at the great alliance; the campaign of 1696, in Germany and in Flanders, had resolved itself into mere observations and insignificant engagements; Holland and England were exhausted, and their commerce was ruined; in vain did Parliament vote fresh and enormous supplies: "I should want ready money," wrote William III. to Heinsius, "and my poverty is really incredible."

There was no less cruel want in France. "I calculate that in these latter days more than a tenth part of the people," said Vauban, "are reduced to beggary and in fact beg." Sweden had for a long time been proffering mediation: conferences began on the 9th of May, 1697, at Nieuburg, a castle belonging to William III., near the village of Ryswick. Three great halls opened one into another; the French and the plenipotentiaries of the coalition of princes occupied the two wings, the mediators sat in the centre. Before arriving at Ryswick, the most important points of the treaty between France and William III. were already settled.

Louis XIV. had at last consented to recognize the king that England had adopted; William demanded the expulsion of James II. from France; Louis XIV. formally refused his consent: "I will engage not to support the enemies of King William directly or indirectly," said he: "it would not comport with my honor to have the name of King James mentioned in the treaty." William contented himself with the concession and merely desired that it should be reciprocal. "All Europe has sufficient confidence in the obedience and submission of my people," said Louis XIV., "and, when it is my pleasure to prevent my subjects from assisting the king of England, there are no grounds for fearing lest he should find any assistance in my kingdom. There can be no occasion for reciprocity, I have neither sedition nor faction to fear." Language too haughty for a king who had passed his infancy in the midst of the troubles of the Fronde, but language explained by the patience and fidelity of the nation towards the sovereign who had so long lavished upon it the intoxicating pleasures of success.

France offered restitution of Strasburg, Luxembourg, Mons, Charleroi and Dinant, restoration of the House of Lorraine, with the conditions proposed at Nimeguen, and recognition of the king of England. "We have no equivalent to claim," said the French plenipotentiaries haughtily; "your masters have never taken anything from ours."

On the 27th of July a preliminary deed was signed between Marshal Boufflers and Bentinck, earl of Portland, the intimate friend of King William; the latter left the army and retired to his castle of Loo; there it was that he heard of the capture of Barcelona by the duke of Vendôme; Spain, which had hitherto refused to take part in the negotiations, lost all courage and loudly demanded peace, but France withdrew her concessions on the subject of Strasburg, and proposed to give as equivalent Friburg in Brisgau and Brisach. William III. did not hesitate. Heinsius signed the peace in the name of the States-general on the 20th of September at midnight; the English and Spanish plenipotentiaries did the same; the emperor and the empire were alone in still holding out; the emperor Leopold made pretensions to regulate in advance the Spanish succession, and the Protestant princes refused to accept the maintenance of the Catholic worship in all the places in which Louis XIV. had restored it.

Here again the will of William III. prevailed over the irresolution of his allies. "The prince of Orange is sole arbiter of Europe," Pope Innocent XII. had said to Lord Perth, who had a commission to him from James II.; "peoples and kings are his slaves; they will do nothing which might displease him."

"I ask," said William, "where anybody can see a probability of making France give up a succession for which she would maintain, at need, a twenty years' war; and God knows if we are in a position to dictate laws to France." The emperor yielded, despite the ill humor of the Protestant princes. For the ease of their consciences they joined England and Holland in making a move on behalf of the French reformers. Louis XIV. refused to discuss the matter, saying, "It is my business, which concerns none but me." Up to this day the refugees had preserved some hope, henceforth their country was lost to them; many got themselves naturalized in the countries which had given them asylum.

The revolution of 1789 alone was to reopen to their children the gates of France.

For the first time since Cardinal Richelieu, France moved back her frontiers by the signature of a treaty. She had gained the important place of Strasburg, but she lost nearly all she had won by the treaty of Nimeguen in the Low Countries and in Germany; she kept Franche-Comté, but she gave up Lothringen. Louis XIV. had wanted to aggrandize himself at any price and at any risk; he was now obliged to precipitately break up the grand alliance, for King Charles II. was slowly dying at Madrid, and the Spanish Succession was about to open. Ignorant of the supreme evils and sorrows which awaited him on this fatal path, the king of France began to forget, in this distant prospect of fresh aggrandizement and war, the checks that his glory and his policy had just met with.

CHAPTER XLV.

LOUIS XIV., HIS WARS AND HIS REVERSES (1697—1713).

FRANCE was breathing again after nine years of a desperate war, but she was breathing uneasily, and as it were in expectation of fresh efforts. Everywhere the memorials of the superintendents repeated the same complaints: "War, the mortality of 1693, the constant quarterings and movements of soldiery, military service, the heavy dues and the withdrawal of the Huguenots have ruined the country." "The people," said the superintendent of Rouen, "are reduced to a state of want which moves compassion. Out of seven hundred and fifty thousand souls of which the public is composed, if this number remain, it may be taken for certain that there are not fifty thousand who have bread to eat when they want it and anything to lie upon but straw." Agriculture suffered for lack of money and hands; commerce was ruined; the manufactures established by Colbert no longer existed; the population had diminished more than a quarter since the palmy days of the king's reign; Pontchartrain, secretary of finance, was reduced to all sorts of expedients for raising money; he was anxious to rid himself of this heavy burden and became chancellor in 1699; the king took for his substitute Chamillard, already comptroller of finance, honest and hard-working, incapable and docile; Louis XIV. counted upon the inexhaustible resources of France and closed his ears to the grievances of the financiers. "What is not spoken of is supposed to be put an end to," said Madame de Maintenon. The camp at Compiègne, in 1698, surpassed in splendor all that had till then been seen; the enemies of Louis XIV. in Europe called him "the king of reviews."

Meanwhile, the king of Spain, Charles II., dying as he was, was regularly besieged at Madrid by the queen, his second wife,

Mary Anne of Neuburg, sister of the empress, as well as by his minister, Cardinal Porto-Carrero. The competitors for the succession were numerous; the king of France and the emperor claimed their rights in the name of their mothers and wives, daughters of Philip III. and Philip IV.; the elector of Bavaria put up the claims of his son by right of his mother, Mary Antoinette of Austria, daughter of the emperor; for a short time Charles II. had adopted this young prince; the child died suddenly at Madrid in 1699. For a long time past King Louis XIV. had been secretly negotiating for the partition of the king of Spain's dominions, not with the emperor who still hoped to obtain from Charles II. a will in favor of his second son, the Archduke Charles, but with England and Holland, deeply interested as they were in maintaining the equilibrium between the two kingly houses which divided Europe. William III. considered himself certain to obtain the acceptance by the emperor of the conditions subscribed by his allies. On the 13th and 15th of May, 1700, after long hesitation and a stubborn resistance on the part of the city of Amsterdam, the treaty of partition was signed in London and at the Hague. "King William is honorable in all this business," said a letter to the king from his embassador, Count de Tallard; "his conduct is sincere; he is proud, none can be more so than he, but he has a modest manner, though none can be more jealous in all that concerns his rank."

The treaty of partition secured to the Dauphin all the possessions of Spain in Italy, save Milaness, which was to indemnify the duke of Lorraine, whose duchy passed to France; Spain, the Indies and the Low Countries were to belong to Archduke Charles.

Great was the wrath at Vienna when it was known that the treaty was signed. "Happily," said the minister, Von Kaunitz, to the marquis of Villars, ambassador of France, "there is One on high who will work for us in these partitions." "That One," replied M. de Villars, "will approve of their justice." "It is something new, however, for the king of England and for Holland to partition the monarchy of Spain," continued the count. "Allow me," replied M. de Villars, "to excuse them in your eyes; those two powers have quite recently come out of a war which cost them a great deal and the emperor nothing; for, in fact, you have been at no expense but against the Turks. You had some troops in Italy, and in the empire two regiments only of hussars which were not on its pay-list; England and

Holland alone bore all the burden." William III. was still negotiating with the emperor and the German princes to make them accept the treaty of partition, when it all at once became known in Europe that Charles II. had breathed his last at Madrid on the 1st of November, 1700, and that by a will dated October 2nd he disposed of the Spanish monarchy in favor of the duke of Anjou, grandson of Louis XIV.

This will was the work of the council of Spain, at the head of which sat Cardinal Porto-Carrero. "The national party," says M. Mignet in his *Introduction aux documents relatifs à la succession d'Espagne,* "detested the Austrians because they had been so long in Spain . . . .; it liked the French because they were no longer there. The former had been there time enough to weary by their dominion, whilst the latter were served by the mere fact of their removal." Single-handed, Louis XIV. appeared powerful enough to maintain the integrity of the Spanish monarchy before the face and in the teeth of all the competitors. "The king of Spain was beginning to see the things of this world by the light alone of that awful torch which is lighted to lighten the dying" [*Mémoires de St. Simon,* t. iii. p. 16]; wavering, irresolute, distracted within himself, he asked the advice of Pope Innocent XII. who was favorable to France. The hopes of Louis XIV. had not soared so high; on the 9th of November, 1700, he heard at one and the same time of Charles II.'s death and the contents of his will.

It was a solemn situation. The acceptance by France of the king of Spain's will meant war; the refusal did not make peace certain; in default of a French prince, the crown was to go to Archduke Charles; neither Spain nor Austria would hear of dismemberment; could they be forced to accept the treaty of partition which they had hitherto rejected angrily? The king's council was divided: Louis XIV. listened in silence to the arguments of the Dauphin and of the ministers; for a moment the resolution was taken of holding by the treaty of partition; next day the king again assembled his council without as yet making known his decision; on Tuesday, November 16th, the whole court thronged into the galleries of Versailles; it was known that several couriers had arrived from Madrid; the king sent for the Spanish ambassador into his closet; "The duke of Anjou had repaired thither by the back way," says the duke of St. Simon in his *Mémoires;* the king, introducing him to him, told him he might salute him as his king. The instant afterwards the king, contrary to all custom, had the folding-doors thrown open and ordered everybody who was there—and there was a crowd—to come in; then, casting his eyes majestically over the numerous company: "Gentlemen," he said, introducing the duke of Anjou, "here is the king of Spain. His birth called him to that crown; the last king gave it him by his will; the grandees desired him and have demanded him of me urgently; it is the will of Heaven, and I have yielded with pleasure." And, turning to his grandson: "Be a good Spaniard," he said: "that is from this moment your first duty; but remember that you are French born in order to keep up the union between the two nations; that is the way to render them happy and to preserve the peace of Europe." Three weeks later the young king was on the road to Spain. "There are no longer any Pyrenees," said Louis XIV. as he embraced his grandson. The rights of Philip V. to the crown of France had been carefully reserved by a formal act of the king's.

Great were the surprise and wrath in Europe; William III. felt himself personally affronted: "I have no doubt," he wrote to Heinsius, "that this unheard-of proceeding on the part of France has caused you as much surprise as it has me; I never had much confidence in engagements contracted with France, but I confess I never could have supposed that that court would have gone so far as to break, in the face of Europe, so solemn a treaty before it had even received the finishing stroke. Granted that we have been dupes; but when, beforehand, you are resolved to hold your word of no account, it is not very difficult to overreach your man. I shall be blamed perhaps for having relied upon France, I who ought to have known by the experience of the past that no treaty has ever bound her! Would to God I might be quit for the blame, but I have only too many grounds for fearing that the fatal consequences of it will make themselves felt shortly. I groan in the very depths of my spirit to see that in this country the majority rejoice to find the will preferred by France to the maintenance of the treaty of partition, and that too on the ground that the will is more advantageous for England and Europe. This opinion is founded partly on the youth of the duke of Anjou: 'He is a child,' they say; 'he will be brought up in Spain; he will be indoctrinated with the principles of that monarchy, and he will be governed by the council of Spain;' but these are surmises which it is impossible for me to entertain, and I fear that we shall before long find out how erroneous they are. Would it not seem as if this profound indifference with which, in this country, they look upon everything that takes place outside of this island, were a punishment from Heaven? Meanwhile, are not our causes for apprehension and our interests the same as those of the peoples of the continent?"

William III. was a more far-sighted politician than his subjects either in England or Holland. The States-general took the same view as the English. "Public funds and shares have undergone a rise at Amsterdam," wrote Heinsius to the king of England: "and although this rests on nothing solid, your Majesty is aware how much influence such a fact has."

Louis XIV. had lost no time in explaining to the powers the grounds of his acceptance. "The king of Spain's will," he said in his manifesto, "establishes the peace of Europe on solid bases." "Tallard did not utter a single word on handing me his sovereign's letter, the contents of which are the same as of that which the States have received," wrote William to Heinsius. "I said to him that perhaps I had testified too eager a desire for the preservation of peace, but that, nevertheless, my inclination in that respect had not changed. Whereupon he replied: 'The king my master, by accepting the will, considers that he gives a similar proof of his desire to maintain peace.' Thereupon he made me a bow and withdrew."

William of Orange had not deceived himself in thinking that Louis XIV. would govern Spain in his grandson's name. Nowhere are the old king's experience and judgment more strikingly displayed than in his letters to Philip V. "I very much wish," he wrote to him, "that you were as sure of your own subjects as you ought to be of mine in the posts in which they may be employed; but do not be astounded at the disorder you find amongst your troops, and at the little confidence you are able to place in them; it needs a long reign and great pains to restore order and secure the fidelity of different peoples accustomed to obey a house hostile to yours. If you thought it would be very easy and very pleasant to be a king, you were very much mistaken." A sad confession for that powerful monarch, who in his youth found "the vocation of king, beautiful, noble and delightful."

"The eighteenth century opened with a fulness of glory and unheard-of prosperity;" but Louis XIV. did not suffer himself to be lulled to sleep by the apparent indifference with which Europe, the empire excepted, received the elevation of Philip V. to the throne of Spain. On the 6th of February, 1701, the seven barrier towns of the Spanish Low Countries, which were occupied by Dutch garrisons in virtue of the peace of Ryswick, opened their gates to the French on an order from the king of Spain. "The instructions which the elector of Bavaria, governor of the Low Countries, had given to the various governors of the places, were so well executed," says M. de Vault in his account of the campaign in Flanders, "that we entered without any hindrance. Some of the officers of the Dutch troops grumbled and would have complained, but the French general officers who had led the troops pacified them, declaring that they did not come as enemies, and that all they wanted was to live in good understanding with them."

The twenty-two Dutch battalions took the road back before long to their own country, and became the nucleus of the army which William of Orange was quietly getting ready in Holland as well as in England; his peoples were beginning to open their eyes; the States-general, deprived of the barrier towns, had opened the dikes; the meadows were flooded. On the 7th of September, 1701, England and Holland signed for the second time with the emperor a *Grand Alliance*, engaging not to lay down arms until they had reduced the possessions of King Philip V. to Spain and the Indies, restored the barrier of Holland, and secured an indemnity to Austria, and the definitive severance of the two crowns of France and Spain. In the month of June the Austrian army had entered Italy under the orders of Prince Eugène of Savoy-Carignano, son of the count of Soissons and Olympia Mancini, conqueror of the Turks and revolted Hungarians, and passionately hostile to Louis XIV., who, in his youth, had refused to employ him. He had already crossed the Adige and the Mincio, driving the French back behind the Oglio. Marshal Catinat, a man of prudence and far-sightedness, but discouraged by the bad condition of his troops, coldly looked upon at court, and disquieted by the aspect of things in Italy, was acting supinely; the king sent Marshal Villeroi to supersede him; Catinat, as modest as he was warmly devoted to the glory of his country, finished the campaign as a simple volunteer.

The king of France and the emperor were looking up allies. The princes of the North were absorbed by the war which was being waged against his neighbors of Russia and Poland by the young king of Sweden, Charles XII., a hero of eighteen, as irresistible as Gustavus Adolphus in his impetuous bravery, without possessing the rare qualities of authority and judgment which had distinguished the *Lion of the North.* He joined the Grand Alliance, as did Denmark and Poland, whose new king, the elector of Saxony, had been supported by the emperor in his candidature and in his abjuration of Protestantism. The elector of Brandenburg, recently recognized as king of Prussia under the name of Frederic I., and the new elector of Hanover, were eager to serve Leopold, who had aided them in their elevation. In Germany, only Maximilian, elector of Bavaria, governor of the Low Countries, and his brother, the elector of Cologne, embraced the side of France. The duke of Savoy, generalissimo of the king's forces in Italy, had taken the command of the army: "But in that country," wrote the count of Tessé, "there is no reliance to be placed on places, or troops, or officers, or people. I have had another interview with this incomprehensible prince, who received me with every manifestation of kindness, of outward sincerity, and, if he were capable of it, I would say of friendship for him of whom his Majesty made use but lately in the work of peace in Italy. 'The king is master of my person, of my dominions,' he said to me, 'he has only to give his commands, but I suppose that he still desires my welfare and my aggrandizement.' 'As for your aggrandizement, Monseigneur,' said I, 'in truth I do not see much material for it just at present; as for your welfare, we must be allowed to see your intentions a little more clearly first, and I take the liberty of repeating to you that my prescience does not extend so far.' I do him the justice to believe that he really feels the greater part of all that he expresses for your Majesty; but that horrid habit of indecision and putting off till to-morrow what he might do to-day is not eradicated and never will be."

The duke of Savoy was not so undecided as M. de Tessé supposed; he managed to turn to good account the mystery which hung habitually over all his resolutions. A year had not rolled by, and he was openly engaged in the Grand Alliance, pursuing, against France, the cause of that aggrandizement which he had but lately hoped to obtain from her, and which, by the treaty of Utrecht, was worth the title of *king* to him. Pending the time to declare himself he had married his second daughter, Princess Marie Louise Gabrielle, to the young king of Spain, Philip V.

"Never had the tranquillity of Europe been so unstable as it was at the commencement of 1702," says the correspondence of Chamillard published by General Pelet; "it was but a phantom of peace that was enjoyed, and it was clear, from whatever side matters were regarded, that we were on the eve of a war which could not but be of long duration, unless, by some unforeseen accident, the houses of Bourbon and Austria should come to an arrangement which would allow them to set themselves in accord touching the Spanish succession; but there was no appearance of conciliation."

Louis XIV. had just done a deed which destroyed the last faint hopes of peace. King James II. was dying at St. Germain, and the king went to see him. The sick man opened his eyes for a moment when he was told that the king was there [*Mémoires de Dangeau*, t. viii. p. 192], and closed them again immediately. The king told him that he had come to assure him that he might die in peace as regarded the prince of Wales, and that he would recognize him as king of England, Ireland, and Scotland. All the English who were in the room fell upon their knees and cried, "God save the king!" James II. expired a week later, on the 16th of September, 1701, saying to his son as his last advice: "I am about to leave this world, which has been to me nothing but a sea of tempests and storms. The Omnipotent has thought right to visit me with great afflictions; serve Him with all your heart and never place the crown of England in the balance with your eternal salvation." James II. was justified in giving his son this supreme advice; the solitary ray of greatness in his life and in his soul had proceeded from his religious faith and his unwavering resolution to remain loyal to it at any price and at any risk.

"On returning to Marly," says St. Simon, "the king told the whole court what he had just done. There was nothing but acclamations and praises. It was a fine field for them; but reflections too were not less prompt, if they were less public. The king still flattered himself that he would hinder Holland and England, the former of which was so completely dependent, from breaking with him in favor of the house of Austria; he relied upon that to terminate before long the war in Italy as well as the whole affair of the succession in Spain and its vast dependencies, which the emperor could not dispute with his own forces only or even with those of the empire. Nothing, therefore, could be more incompatible with this position and with the solemn recognition he had given, at the peace of Ryswick, of the prince of Orange as king of England. It was to hurt him personally in the most sensitive spot, all England with him and Holland into the bargain, without giving the prince of Wales, by recognition, any solid support in his own case."

William III. was at table in his castle of Dieren in Holland when he received this news. He did not utter a word, but he colored, crushed his hat over his head, and could not command his countenance. The earl of Manchester, English ambassador, left Paris without taking leave of the king otherwise than by this note to M. de Torcy:

"Sir,

"The king my master, being informed that his Most Christian Majesty has recognized another king of Great Britain, does not consider that his dignity and his service will permit him to any longer keep an ambassador at the court of the king your master, and he has sent me orders to withdraw at once, of which I do myself the honor to advertise you by this note."

"All the English," says Torcy in his *Mémoires*, "unanimously regard it as a mortal affront on the part of France that she should pretend to arrogate to herself the right of giving them a king, to the prejudice of him whom they had themselves invited and recognized for many years past."

Voltaire declares, in the *Siècle de Louis XIV.*, that M. de Torcy attributed the recognition of the prince of Wales by Louis XIV. to the influence of Madame de Maintenon, who was touched by the tears of the queen, Mary of Modena. "He had not," he said, "inserted the fact in his *Mémoires*, because he did not think it to his master's honor that two women should have made him change a resolution to the contrary taken in his council." Perhaps the deplorable state of William III.'s health and the inclination supposed to be felt by Princess Anne of Denmark to restore the Stuarts to the throne, since she herself had lost the Duke of Gloucester, the last survivor of her seventeen children, might have influenced the unfortunate resolution of Louis XIV. His kingly magnanimity and illusions might have bound him to support James II., dethroned and fugitive; but no obligation of that sort existed in the case of a prince who had left England at his nurse's breast and who had grown up in exile. In the *Athalie* of Racine, Joad (Jehoida) invokes upon the impious queen:—

"That spirit of infatuation and error
The fatal avant-courier of the fall of kings."

The recognition of the prince of Wales as king of England, was, in the case of Louis XIV., the most indisputable token of that fatal blindness.

William III. had paid dear for the honor of being called to the throne of England. More than once he had been on the point of abandoning the ungrateful nation which so ill requited his great services; he had thought of returning to live in the midst of his Hollanders, affectionately attached to his family as well as to his person. The insult of the king of France restored to his already dying adversary all the popularity he had lost. When William returned from Holland to open a new parliament, on the 10th of January, 1702, manifestations of sympathy were lavished upon him on all sides of the house. "I have no doubt," said he, "that the late proceedings of his Most Christian Majesty and the dangers which threaten all the powers of Europe have excited your most lively resentment. All the world have their eyes fixed upon England; there is still time, she may save her religion and her liberty, but let her profit by every moment, let her arm by land and sea, let her lend her allies all the assistance in her power, and swear to show her enemies, the foes of her religion, her liberty, her government and the king of her choice, all the hatred they deserve!"

This speech, more impassioned than the utterances of William III. generally were, met with an eager echo from his people; the houses voted a levy of forty thousand sailors and fifty thousand soldiers; Holland had promised ninety thousand men; but the health of the king of England went on declining; he had fallen from his horse on the 4th of March and broken his collar-bone; this accident hastened the progress of the malady which was pulling him down; when his friend Keppel, whom he had made earl of Albermarle, returned on the 18th of March, from Holland, William received him with these words: "I am drawing towards my end."

He had received the consolations of religion from the bishops and had communicated with great self-possession; he scarcely spoke now, and breathed with difficulty. "Can this last long?" he asked the physician, who made a sign in the negative. He had sent for the earl of Portland, Bentinck, his oldest and most faithful friend; when he arrived, the king took his hand and held it between both his own upon his heart. Thus he remained for a few moments, then he yielded up his great spirit to God, on the 19th (8th) of March, 1702, at eight in the morning. He was not yet fifty-two.

In a greater degree perhaps than any other period the eighteenth century was rich in men of the first order. But never did more of the spirit of policy, never did loftier and broader views, never did steadier courage animate and sustain a weaker body than in the case of William of Orange. Saviour of Holland at the age of twenty-two in the war against Louis XIV., protector of the liberties of England against the tyranny of James II., defender of the independence of the European States against the unbridled ambition of the king of France, he became the head of Europe by the proper and free ascendancy of his genius; cold and reserved, more capable of feeling than of testifying sympathy, often ill, always unfortunate in war, he managed to make his will triumph, in England despite Jacobite plots and the jealous suspicions of the English parliaments, in Holland despite the constant efforts of the republican and aristocratic party, in Europe despite envy and the waverings of the allied sovereigns. Intrepid, spite of his bad health, to the extent of being ready, if need were, to die in the last ditch, of idomitable obstinacy in his resolutions and of rare ability in the manipulation of affairs, he was one of those who are born masters of men, no matter what may at the outset be their condition and their destiny. In vain had Cromwell required of Holland the abolition of the stadtholderate in the house of Nassau, in vain had John van Witt obtained the voting of the perpetual edict, William of Orange lived and died stadtholder of Holland and king of that England which had wanted to close against him forever the approaches to the throne of his own native country. When God has created a man to play a part and hold a place in this world, all efforts and all counsels to the contrary are but so many stalks of straw under his feet. William of Orange at his death had accomplished his work: Europe had risen against Louis XIV.

The campaigns of 1702 and 1703 presented an alternation of successes and reverses favorable on the whole to France. Marshal Villeroi had failed in Italy against Prince Eugene. He was susperseded by the duke of Vendôme, grandson of Henry IV. and captor of Barcelona, indolent, debauched, free in tone and in conduct, but able, bold, beloved by the soldiers and strongly supported at court. Catinat had returned to France, and went to Versailles at the commencement of the year 1702. "M. de Chamillard had told him the day before from the king that his Majesty had resolved to give him the command of the army in Germany; he excused himself for some time from accepting this employment; the king ended by saying: 'Now we are in a position for you to explain to me, and open your heart about all that took place in Italy during the last campaign.' The marshal answered: 'Sir, those things are all past; the details I could give you thereof would be of no good to the service of your Majesty, and would serve merely, perhaps, to keep up eternal heartburnings; and so I entreat you to be pleased to let me preserve a profound silence as to all that. I will only justify myself, Sir, by thinking how I may serve you still better, if I can, in Germany than I did in Italy.'" Worn out and disgusted, Catinat failed in Germany as he had in Italy; he took his retirement, and never left his castle of St. Gratien any more; it was the marquis of Villars, lately ambassador at Vienna, who defeated the imperialists at Friedlingen on the 14th of August, 1702; a month later Tallard retook the town of Landau. The perfidious manœuvres of the duke of Savoy had just come to light. The king ordered Vendôme to disarm the five thousand Piedmontese who were serving in his army. That operation effected, the prince sent Victor Amadeo this note written by Louis XIV.'s own hand.

"Sir,

"As religion, honor and your own signature count for nothing between us, I send my cousin, the duke of Vendôme, to explain to you my wishes. He will give you twenty-four hours to decide."

The mind of the duke of Savoy was made up; from this day forth the father of the duchess of Burgundy and of the queen of Spain took rank amongst the declared enemies of France and Spain.

Whilst Louis XIV. was facing Europe, in coalition against him, with generals of the second and third order, the allies were discovering in the duke of Marlborough a worthy rival of Prince Eugene. A covetous and able courtier, openly disgraced by William III. in consequence of his perfidious intrigues with the court of St. Germain, he had found his fortunes suddenly retrieved by the accession of Queen Anne, over whom his wife had for a long time held the sway of a haughty and powerful favorite. The campaigns of 1702 and 1703 had shown him to be a prudent and a bold soldier, fertile in resources and novel conceptions; and those had earned him the thanks of Parliament and the title of duke. The campaign of 1704 established his glory upon the misfortunes of France. Marshals Tallard and Marsin were commanding in Germany together with the elector of Bavaria; the emperor, threatened with a fresh insurrection in Hungary, recalled Prince Eugene from Italy; Marlborough effected a junction with him by a rapid march, which Marshal Villeroi would fain have hindered but to no purpose; on the 13th of August, 1704, the hostile armies met between Blenheim and Hochstett, near the Danube; the forces were about equal, but on the French side the counsels were divided, the various corps acted independently. Tallard sustained single-handed the attack of the English and the Dutch commanded by Marlborough; he was made prisoner, his son was killed at his side; the cavalry having lost their leader and being pressed by the enemy took to flight in the direction of the Danube; many officers and soldiers perished in the river; the slaughter was awful. Marsin and the elector, who had repulsed five successive charges of Prince Eugene, succeeded in effecting their retreat; but the electorates of Bavaria and Cologne were lost, Landau was recovered by the allies after a siege of two months, the French army recrossed the Rhine, Elsass was uncovered and Germany evacuated. In Spain the English had just made themselves masters of Gibraltar. "This shows clearly, Sir," wrote Tallard to Chamillard after the defeat, "what is the effect of such diversity of counsel, which makes public all that one intends to do, and it is a severe lesson never to have more than one man at the head of an army. It is a great misfortune to have to deal with a prince of such a temper as the elector of Bavaria." Villars was of the same opinion; it had been his fate in the campaign of 1703 to come to open loggerheads with the elector. "The king's army will march to-morrow as I have had the honor to tell your Highness," he had declared. "At these words," says Villars, "the blood mounted to his face; he threw his hat and wig on the table in a rage. 'I commanded,' said he, 'the emperor's army in conjunction with the duke of Lorraine; he was a tolerably great general, and he never treated me in this manner.' 'The duke of Lorraine,' answered I, 'was a great prince and a great general; but, for myself, I am responsible to the king for his army and I will not expose it to destruction through the evil counsels so obstinately persisted in. Thereupon I went out of the room.'" Complete swaggerer as he was, Villars had more wits and resolution than the majority of the generals left to Louis XIV., but in 1704 he was occupied in putting down the insurrection of the Camisards in the south of France: neither Tallard nor Marsin had been able to impose their will upon the elector. In 1705, Villars succeeded in checking the movement of Marlborough on Lothringen and Champagne. "He flattered himself he would swallow me like a grain of salt," wrote the marshal. The English fell back, hampered in their adventurous plans by the prudence of the Hollanders, controlled from a distance by the grand pensionary Heinsius. The imperialists were threatening Elsass; the weather was fearful; letters had been written to Chamillard to say that the inundations alone would be enough to prevent the enemy from investing Fort Louis. "There is nothing so nice as a map," replied Villars: "with a little green and blue one puts under water all that one wishes; but a general who goes and examines it, as I have done, finds in divers places distances of a mile where these little rivers, which are supposed to inundate the country, are quite snug in their natural bed, larger than usual, but not enough to hinder the enemy in any way in the world from making bridges." Fort Louis was surrounded, and Villars found himself obliged to retire upon Strasburg whence he protected Elsass during the whole campaign of 1706.

The defeat of Hochstett in 1704 had been the first step down the ladder; the defeat of Ramilies on the 23rd of May, 1706, was the second and the fatal rung. The king's personal attachment to Marshal Villeroi blinded him as to his military talents. Beaten in Italy by Prince Eugene, Villeroi, as presumptuous as he was incapable, hoped to retrieve himself against Marlborough. "The whole army breathed nothing but battle; I know it was your Majesty's own feeling," wrote Villeroi to the king after the defeat: "could I help committing myself to a course which I considered expedient?" The marshal had deceived himself as regarded his advantages as well as the confidence of his troops; there had been eight hours' fighting at Hochstett, inflicting much damage upon the enemy; at Ramilies, the Bavarians took to their heels at the end of an hour; the French, who felt that they were badly commanded, followed their example; the rout was terrible and the disorder inexpressible: Villeroi kept recoiling before the enemy, Marlborough kept advancing; two thirds of Belgium and sixteen strong places were lost, when Louis XIV. sent Chamillard into the Low Countries; it was no longer the time when Louvois made armies spring from the very soil, and when Vauban prepared the defence of Dunkerque. The king recalled Villeroi, showing him to the last unwavering kindness. "There is no more luck at our age, marshal," was all he said to Villeroi on his arrival at Versailles. "He was nothing more than an old wrinkled balloon out of which all the gas that inflated it has gone," says St. Simon: "he went off to Paris and to Villeroi, having lost all the varnish that made him glitter and having nothing more to show but the under-stratum."

The king summoned Vendôme, to place him at the head of the army of Flanders, "in hopes of restoring to it the spirit of vigor and audacity natural to the French nation," as he himself says. For two years past, amidst a great deal of ill-success, Vendôme had managed to keep in check Victor Amadeo and Prince Eugene, in spite of the embarrassment caused him by his brother the grand prior, the duke of La Feuillade, Chamillard's son-in-law, and the orders which reached him directly from the king; he had gained during his two campaigns the name of *taker of towns*, and had just beaten the Austrians in the battle of Cascinato. Prince Eugene had, however, crossed the Adige and the Po when Vendôme left Italy.

"Everybody here is ready to take off his hat when Marlborough's name is mentioned," he wrote to Chamillard on arriving in Flanders. The English and Dutch army occupied all the country from Ostend to Maestricht.

The duke of Orleans, nephew of the king, had succeeded the duke of Vendôme. He found the army in great disorder, the generals divided and insubordinate, Turin besieged according to the plans of La Feuillade, against the advice of Vauban who had offered "to put his marshal's bâton behind the door and confine himself to giving his counsels for the direction of the siege;" the prince, in his irritation, resigned his powers into the hands of Marshal Marsin; Prince Eugene, who had effected his junction with Victor Amadeo, encountered the French army between the rivers Doria and Stora. The soldiers remembered the duke of Orleans at Steinkirk and Neerwinden; they asked him if he would grudge them his sword. He yielded and was severely wounded at the battle of Turin on the 7th of September, 1706; Marsin was killed, discouragement spread amongst the generals and the troops, and the siege of Turin was raised; before the end of the year, nearly all the places were lost, and Dauphiny was threatened. Victor Amadeo refused to listen to a special peace; in the month of March, 1707, the prince of Vaudemont, governor of Milaness for the king of Spain, signed a capitulation at Mantua and led back to

France the troops which still remained to him. The imperialists were masters of Naples. Spain no longer had any possessions in Italy.

Philip V. had been threatened with the loss of Spain as well as of Italy. For two years past Archduke Charles, under the title of Charles III., had, with the support of England and Portugal, been disputing the crown with the young king. Philip V. had lost Catalonia and had just failed in his attempts to retake Barcelona; the road to Madrid was cut off, the army was obliged to make its way by Roussillon and Béarn to resume the campaign; the king threw himself in person into his capital, whither he was escorted by Marshal Berwick, a natural son of James II., a Frenchman by choice, full of courage and resolution, "but a great stick of an Englishman who hadn't a word to say," and who was distasteful to the young queen Marie-Louise. Philip V. could not remain at Madrid, which was threatened by the enemy: he removed to Burgos; the English entered the capital and there proclaimed Charles III.

This was too much; Spain could not let herself submit to have an Austrian king imposed upon her by heretics and Portuguese; the old military energy appeared again amongst that people besotted by priests and ceremonials; war broke out all at once at every point; the foreign soldiers were everywhere attacked openly or secretly murdered; the towns rose; a few horsemen sufficed for Berwick to recover possession of Madrid; the king entered it once more on the 4th of October amidst the cheers of his people, whilst Berwick was pursuing the enemy whom he had *cornered (rencogné)*, he says, in the mountains of Valencia. Charles III. had no longer anything left in Spain but Aragon and Catalonia. The French garrisons, set free by the evacuation of Italy, went to the aid of the Spaniards. "Your enemies ought not to hope for success," wrote Louis XIV. to his grandson, "since their progress has served only to bring out the courage and fidelity of a nation always equally brave and firmly attached to its masters. I am told that your people cannot be distinguished from regular troops. We have not been fortunate in Flanders, but we must submit to the judgment of God." He had already let his grandson understand that a great sacrifice would be necessary to obtain peace, which he considered himself bound to procure before long for his people. The Hollanders refused their mediation. "The three men who rule in Europe, to wit the grand pensionary Heinsius, the duke of Marlborough and Prince Eugene, desire war for their own interests," was the saying in France. The campaign of 1707 was signalized in Spain by the victory of Almanza gained on the 13th of April by Marshal Berwick over the Anglo-Portuguese army, and by the capture of Lérida, which capitulated on the 11th of November into the hands of the duke of Orleans. In Germany, Villars drove back the enemy from the banks of the Rhine, advanced into Suabia and ravaged the Palatinate, crushing the country with requisitions, of which he openly reserved a portion for himself. "Marshal Villars is doing very well for himself," said somebody one day to the king. "Yes," answered his Majesty, "and for me too." "I wrote to the king that I really must *fat my calf*," said Villars.

The inexhaustible elasticity and marvellous resources of France were enough to restore some hope in 1707. The invasion of Provence by Victor Amadeo and Prince Eugene, their check before Toulon and their retreat precipitated by the rising of the peasants had irritated the allies; the attempts at negotiation which the king had entered upon at the Hague remained without result; the duke of Burgundy took the command of the armies of Flanders with Vendôme for his second; it was hoped that the lieutenant's boldness, his geniality towards the troops, and his consummate knowledge of war could counterbalance the excessive gravity, austerity and inexperience of the young prince so virtuous and capable, but reserved, cold and unaccustomed to command; discord arose amongst the courtiers; on the 5th of July, Ghent was surprised; Vendôme had intelligence inside the place, the Belgians were weary of their new masters: "The States have dealt so badly with this country," said Marlborough, "that all the towns are ready to play us the same trick as Ghent the moment they have the opportunity." Bruges opened its gates to the French. Prince Eugene advanced to second Marlborough, but he was late in starting; the troops of the elector of Bavaria harassed his march. "I shouldn't like to say a word against Prince Eugene," said Marlborough, "but he will arrive at the appointed spot on the Moselle ten days too late." The English were by themselves when they encountered the French army in front of Audernarde. The engagement began. Vendôme, who commanded the right wing, sent word to the duke of Burgundy. The latter hesitated and delayed; the generals about him did not approve of Vendôme's movement. He fought single-handed, and was beaten. The excess of confidence of one leader and the inertness of the other caused failure in all the operations of the campaign; Prince Eugene and the duke of Marlborough laid siege to Lille, which was defended by old Marshal Boufflers, the bravest and the most respected of all the king's servants. Lille was not relieved and fell on the 25th of October; the citadel held out until the 9th of December; the king heaped rewards on Marshal Boufflers; at the march out from Lille, Prince Eugene had ordered all his army to pay him the same honors as to himself. Ghent and Bruges were abandoned to the imperialists. "We had made blunder upon blunder in this campaign," says Marshal Berwick in his *Mémoires*, "and, in spite of all that, if somebody had not made the last in giving up Ghent and Bruges, there would have been a fine game the year after." The Low Countries were lost and the French frontier was encroached upon by the capture of Lille. For the first time, in a letter addressed to Marshal Berwick, Marlborough let a glimpse be seen of a desire to make peace; the king still hoped for the mediation of Holland, and he neglected the overtures of Marlborough: "the army of the allies is without doubt in evil plight," said Chamillard.

The campaign in Spain had not been successful; the duke of Orleans, weary of his powerlessness and under suspicion at the court of Philip V., had given up the command of the troops; the English admiral, Leake, had taken possession of Sardinia, of the island of Minorca and of Port Mahon; the archduke was master of the isles and of the sea. The destitution in France was fearful, and the winter so severe that the poor were in want of everything; riots multiplied in the towns; the king sent his plate to the Mint, and put his jewels in pawn; he likewise took a resolution which cost him even more, he determined to ask for peace.

"Although his courage appeared at every trial," says the Marquis of Torcy, "he felt within him just sorrow for a war whereof the weight overwhelmed his subjects. More concerned for their woes than for his own glory, he employed, to terminate them, means which might have induced France to submit to the hardest conditions before obtaining a peace that had become necessary, if God, protecting the king, had not, after humiliating him, struck his foes with blindness."

There are regions to which superior minds alone ascend, and which are not attained by the men, however distinguished, who succeed them. William III. was no longer at the head of affairs in Europe; and the *triumvirate* of Heinsius, Marlborough and Prince Eugene did not view the aggregate of things from a sufficiently calm height to free themselves from the hatreds and bitternesses of the strife, when the proposals of Louis XIV. arrived at the Hague. "Amidst the sufferings caused to commerce by the war, there was room to hope," says Torcy, "that the grand pensionary, thinking chiefly of his country's interest, would desire the end of a war of which he felt all the burdensomeness. Clothed with authority in his own republic, he had no reason to fear either secret design or cabals to displace him from a post which he filled to the satisfaction of his masters and in which he conducted himself with moderation. Up to that time the United Provinces had borne the principal burden of the war. The emperor alone reaped the fruit of it. One would have said that the Hollanders kept the temple of peace and that they had the keys of it in their hands."

The king offered the Hollanders a very extended barrier in the Low Countries and all the facilities they had long been asking for their commerce. He accepted the abandonment of Spain to the archduke and merely claimed to reserve to his grandson Naples, Sardinia and Sicily. This was what was secured to him by the second treaty of partition lately concluded between England, the United Provinces and France; he did not even demand Lothringen. President Rouillé, formerly French envoy to Lisbon, arrived disguised in Holland; conferences were opened secretly at Bodegraven.

The treaties of partition negotiated by William of Orange, as well as the wars which he had sustained against Louis XIV. with such persistent obstinacy, had but one sole end, the maintenance of the European equilibrium between the houses of Bourbon and Austria, which were alone powerful enough to serve as mutual counterpoise. To despoil one to the profit of the other, to throw all at once into the balance on the side of the empire all the weight of the Spanish succession, was to destroy the work of William III.'s far-sighted wisdom. Heinsius did not see it; but led on by his fidelity to the allies, distrustful and suspicious as regarded France, burning to avenge the wrongs put upon the republic, he, in concert with Marlborough and Prince Eugene, required conditions so hard that the French agent scarcely dared transmit them to Versailles. What was demanded was the abdication pure and simple of Philip V.; Holland merely promised her good offices to obtain in his favor Naples and Sicily; England claimed Dunkerque; Germany wanted Strasburg and the renewal of the peace of Westphalia; Victor Amadeo aspired to recover Nice and Savoy; to the Dutch barrier stipulated for at Ryswick were to be added Lille, Condé and Tournay. In vain was the matter discussed article by article; Rouillé for some time believed that he had gained Lille: "You misinterpreted our intentions," said the deputies of the States-general; "we let you believe what you pleased; at the commencement of April, Lille was still in a bad condition; we had reason to fear that the French had a design of taking advantage of that; it was a matter of prudence to let you believe that it would be restored to you by the peace; Lille is at the present moment in a state of security; do not count any longer on its restitution." "Probably," said the States' delegate to Marlborough, "the king will break off negotiations rather than entertain such hard conditions." "So much the worse for France," rejoined the English general, "for when the campaign is once begun, things will go farther than the king thinks. The allies will never unsay their preliminary demands." And he set out for England without even waiting for a favorable wind to cross.

Louis XIV. assembled his council, the same which, in 1700, had decided upon acceptance of the crown of Spain. "The king felt all these calamities so much the more keenly," says Torcy, "in that he had experienced nothing of the sort ever since he had taken into his own hands the government of a flourishing kingdom. It was a terrible humiliation for a monarch accustomed to conquer, belauded for his victories, his triumphs, his moderation when he granted peace and prescribed its laws, to see himself now obliged to ask it of his enemies, to offer them to no purpose, in order to obtain it, the restitution of a portion of his conquests, the monarchy of Spain, the abandonment of his allies, and forced, in order to get such offers accepted, to apply to that same republic whose principal provinces he had conquered in the year 1692, and whose submission he had rejected when she entreated him to grant her peace on such terms as he should be pleased to dictate. The king bore so sensible a change with the firmness of a hero, and with a Christian's complete submission to the decrees of Providence, being less affected by his own inward pangs than by the suffering of his people, and being ever concerned about the means of relieving it, and terminating the war. It was scarcely perceived that he did himself some violence in order to conceal his own feelings from the public; indeed they were so little known that it was pretty generally believed that, thinking more of his own glory than of the woes of his kingdom, he preferred to the blessing of peace the keeping of certain places he had taken in person. This unjust opinion had crept in even amongst the council."

The reading of the Dutch proposals tore away every veil; "the necessity of obtaining peace, whatever price it might cost, was felt so much the more." The king gave orders to Rouillé to resume the conferences, demanding clear and precise explanations. "If the worst come to the worst," said he, "I will give up Lille to the Hollanders, Strasburg dismantled to the Empire, and I will content myself with Naples without Sicily for my grandson. You will be astounded at the orders contained in this despatch, so different from those that I have given you hitherto and that I considered, as it was, too liberal, but I have always submitted to the Divine will, and the evils with which He is pleased to afflict my kingdom do not permit me any longer to doubt of the sacrifice He requires me to make to Him of all that might touch me most nearly. I waive, therefore, my glory." The marquis of Torcy, secretary of state for foreign affairs, followed close after the despatch; he had offered the king to go and treat personally with Heinsius.

"The grand pensionary appeared surprised when he heard that his Majesty was sending one of his ministers to Holland. He had been placed at that post by the prince of Orange, who put entire confidence in him. Heinsius had not long before been sent to France to confer with Louvois and, in the discharge of that commission, he had experienced the bad temper of a minister more accustomed to speak harshly to military officers than to treat with foreigners: he had not forgotten that the minister had threatened to have him put in the Bastille. Consummate master of affairs, of which he had a long experience, he was the soul of the league with Prince Eugene and the duke of Marlborough; but the pensionary was not accused either of being so much in love with the importance given him by continuance of the war as to desire its prolongation or of any personally interested view. His externals were simple, there was no ostentation in his household; his address was cold without any sort of rudeness, his conversation was polished, he rarely grew warm in discussion." Torcy could not obtain anything from Heinsius, any more than from Marlborough and Prince Eugene who had both arrived at the Hague; the prince remained cold and stern, he had not forgotten the king's behavior towards his house. "That's a splendid post in France, that of colonel general," said he one day; "my father held it; at his death we hoped that my brother might get it; the king thought it better to give it to one of his natural sons. He is master, but all the same is one not sorry sometimes to find one's self in a position to make slights repented of." "Marlborough displayed courtesy, insisting upon seeing in the affairs of the coalition the finger of God, who had permitted eight nations to think and act like one man." The concessions extorted from France were no longer sufficient; M. de Torcy gave up Sicily, and then Naples; a demand was made for Elsass, and certain places in Dauphiny and Provence; lastly, the allies required that the conditions of peace should be carried out at short notice, during the two months' truce it was agreed to grant, and that Louis XIV. should forthwith put into the hands of the Hollanders three places by way of guarantee, in case Philip V. should refuse to abdicate. This was to despoil himself prematurely and gratuitously, for it was impossible to execute the definitive treaty of peace at the time fixed. "The king did not hesitate about the only course there was for him to take, not only for his own glory but for the welfare of his kingdom," says Torcy; he recalled his envoys and wrote to the governors of the provinces and towns:—

"Sir,

"The hope of an imminent peace was so generally diffused throughout my kingdom, that I consider it due to the fidelity which my people have shown during the course of my reign to give them the consolation of informing them of the reasons which still prevent them from enjoying the repose I had intended to procure for them. I would, to restore it, have accepted conditions much opposed to the security of my frontier provinces, but the more readiness and desire I displayed to dissipate the suspicions which my enemies affect to retain of my power and my designs, the more did they multiply their pretensions, refusing to enter into any undertaking beyond putting a stop to all acts of hostility until the first of the month of August, reserving to themselves the liberty of then acting by way of arms if the king of Spain, my grandson, persisted in his resolution to defend the crown which God has given him; such a suspension was more dangerous than war for my people, for it secured to the enemy more important advantages than they could hope for from their troops. As I place my trust in the protection of God and hope that the purity of my intentions will bring down His blessing on my arms, I wish my people to know that they would enjoy peace if it had depended only on my will to procure them a boon which they reasonably desire, but which must be won by fresh efforts, since the immense conditions I would have granted are useless for the restoration of the public peace.

"Signed LOUIS."

In spite of all the mistakes due to his past arrogance, the king had a right to make use of such language. In their short-sighted resentment the allies had overstepped reason. The young king of Spain felt this when he wrote to his grandfather: "I am transfixed at the chimerical and insolent pretensions of the English and Dutch regarding the preliminaries of peace; never was seen the like. I am beside myself at the idea that anybody could have so much as supposed that I should be forced to leave Spain as long as I have a drop of blood in my veins. I will use all my efforts to maintain myself upon a throne on which God has placed me and on which you, after Him, have set me, and nothing but death shall wrench me from it or make me yield it." War recommenced on all sides. The king had just consented at last to give Chamillard his discharge. "Sir, I shall die over the job," had for a long time been the complaint of the minister worn out with fatigue. "Ah! well, we will die together," had been the king's rejoiner.

France was dying, and Chamillard was by no means a stranger to the cause. Louis XIV. put in his place Voysin, former superintendent of Hainault, entirely devoted to Madame de Maintenon. He loaded with benefits the minister from whom he was parting, the only one whom he had really loved. The troops were destitute of everything. On assuming the command of the army of the Low Countries, Villars wrote in despair: "Imagine the horror of seeing an army without bread! There was none delivered to-day until the evening and very late. Yesterday, to have bread to serve out to the brigades I had ordered to march, I made those fast that remained behind. On these occasions I pass along the ranks, I coax the soldier, I speak to him in such a way as to make him have patience, and I have had the consolation of hearing several of them say, 'The marshal is quite right; we must suffer sometimes.' '*Panem nostrum quotidianum da nobis hodie* (*give us this day our daily bread*),' the men say to me as I go through the ranks; it is a miracle how we subsist, and it is a marvel to see the steadiness and fortitude of the soldier in enduring hunger; habit is everything: I fancy, however, that the habit of not eating is not easy to acquire."

In spite of such privations and sufferings, Villars found the army in excellent spirits, and urged the king to permit him to give battle. "M. de Turenne used to say that he who means to altogether avoid battle gives up his country to him who appears to seek for it," the marshal assured him; the king was afraid of losing his last army; the dukes of Harcourt and Berwick were covering the Rhine and the Alps; Marlborough and Prince Eugene, who had just made themselves masters of Tournay, marched against Villars, whom they encountered on the 11th of September, 1709, near the hamlet of Malplaquet. Marshal Boufflers had just reached the army to serve as a volunteer. Villars had intrenched himself in front of the woods; his men were so anxious to get under fire that they threw away the rations of bread just served out; the allies looked sulkily at the works: "We are going to fight moles again," they said.

There was a thick fog, as at Lützen; the fighting went on from seven in the morning till mid-day. Villars had yielded the right wing, by way of respect, to Boufflers as his senior, says the allies' account, but the general command nevertheless devolved entirely upon him. "At the hottest of the engagement, the marshal galloped furiously to the centre attacked by Prince Eugene. It was a sort of jaws of hell, a pit of fire, sulphur and saltpetre, which it seemed impossible to approach and live. One shot and my horse fell," says Villars: "I jumped up, and a second broke my knee; I had it bandaged on the spot and myself placed in a chair to continue giving my orders, but the pain caused a fainting-fit which lasted long enough for me to be carried off without consciousness to Quesnoy." The prince of Hesse, with the imperial cavalry, had just turned the intrenchments which the Dutch infantry had attacked to no purpose; Marshal Boufflers was obliged to order a retreat, which was executed as on parade. "The allies had lost more than twenty thousand men," according to their official account. "It was too much for this victory which did not entail the advantage of entirely defeating the enemy, and the whole fruits of which were to end with the taking of Mons." Always a braggart, in spite of his real courage and indisputable military talent, Villars wrote from his bed to the king, on sending him the flags taken from the enemy: "If God give us grace to lose such another battle, your Majesty may reckon that your enemies are annihilated." Boufflers was more proud and at the same time more modest when he said: "The series of disasters that have for some years past befallen your Majesty's arms, had so humiliated the French nation that one scarcely dared avow one's self a Frenchman. I dare assure you, Sir, that the French name was never in so great esteem, and was never perhaps more feared than it is at present in the army of the allies."

Louis XIV. was no longer in a position to delude himself and to celebrate a defeat, even a glorious one, as a victory. Negotiations recommenced. Heinsius had held to his last proposals. It was on this sorry basis that Marshall d'Huxelles and Abbé de Polignac began the parleys, at Gertruydenberg, a small fortress of Mardyk. They lasted from March 9th to July 25th, 1710; the king consented to give some fortresses as guarantee, and promised to recommend his grandson to abdicate; in case of refusal, he engaged not only to support him no longer but to furnish the allies into the bargain with a monthly subsidy of a million, whilst granting a passage through French territory; he accepted the cession of Elsass to Lothringen, the return of the three bishoprics to the empire; the Hollanders, commissioned to negotiate in the name of the coalition, were not yet satisfied. "The desire of the allies," they said, "is that the king should undertake, himself alone and by his own forces, either to persuade or to oblige the king of Spain to give up all his monarchy. Neither money nor the co-operation of the French troops suit their purpose; if the preliminary artiticles be not complied with in the space of two months, the truce is broken off, war will recommence, even though on the part of the king the other conditions should have been wholly fulfilled. The sole means of obtaining peace is to receive from the king's hands Spain and the Indies."

The French plenipotentiaries had been recommended to have patience. Marshal d'Huxelles was a courtier as smooth as he was clever; Abbé de Polignac was shrewd and supple, yet he could not contain his indignation: "It is evident that you have not been accustomed to conquer!" said he haughtily to the Dutch delegates. When the allies' *ultimatum* reached the king, the pride of the sovereign and the affection of the father rose up at last in revolt: "Since war there must be," said he, "I would rather wage it against my enemies than against my grandson," and he withdrew all the concessions which had reduced Philip V. to despair. The allies had already invaded Artois; at the end of the campaign they were masters of Douai, St. Venant, Béthune and Aire; France was threatened everywhere, the king could no longer protect the king of Spain; he confined himself to sending him Vendôme. Philip V., sustained by the indomitable courage of his young wife, refused absolutely to abdicate. "Whatever misfortunes may await me," he wrote to the king, "I still prefer the course of submission to whatever it may please God to decide for me by fighting to that of deciding for myself by consenting to an arrangement which would force me to abandon the people on whom my reverses have hitherto produced no other effect than to increase their zeal and affection for me."

It was, therefore, with none but the forces of Spain that Philip V., at the outset of the campaign of 1710, found himself confronting the English and Portuguese armies. The Emperor Joseph, brother of Archduke Charles, had sent him a body of troops commanded by a distinguished general, Count von Stahrenberg. Going from defeat to defeat, the young king found himself forced, as in 1706, to abandon his capital; he removed the seat of government to Valladolid and departed, accompanied by more than thirty thousand persons of every rank, resolved to share his fortunes. The archduke entered Madrid: "I have orders from Queen Anne and the allies to escort King Charles to Madrid," said the English general, Lord Stanhope; "when he is once there, God or the devil keep him in or turn him out; it matters little to me; that is no affair of mine."

Stanhope was in the right not to pledge himself; the hostility of the population of Madrid did not permit the archduke to reside there long; after running the risk of being carried off in his palace on the Prado, he removed to Toledo; Vendôme blocked the road against the Portuguese; the Archduke left the town and withdrew into Catalonia; Stahrenberg followed him on the 22nd of November, harassed on his march by the Spanish guerillas rising everywhere upon his route; every straggler, every wounded man, was infallibly murdered by the peasants; Stanhope, who commanded the rearguard, found himself invested by Vendôme in the town of Brihuega; the Spaniards scarcely gave the artillery time to open a breach, the town was taken by assault and the English made prisoners.

Stahrenberg retraced his steps; on the 10th of December fighting began near Villaviciosa; the advantage was for a long time undecided and disputed; night came, the Austrian general spiked his guns and retreated by forced marches; the Spaniards bivouacked on the battle-field, the king slept on a bed made of the enemy's flags; the allies had taken refuge in Catalonia; Spain had won back her independence and her king. There was great joy at Versailles, greater than in the kingdom; the sole aspiration was for peace.

An unexpected assistance was at hand. Queen Anne, wearied with the cupidity and haughtiness of the duke and duchess of Marlborough, had given them notice to quit; the friends of the duke had shared his fall, and the Tories succeeded the Whigs in power. The chancellor of the exchequer, Harley, soon afterwards earl of Oxford, and the secretary of state, St. John, who became Lord Bolingbroke, were inclined to peace. Advances were made to France. A French priest, Abbé Gautier, living in obscurity in England, arrived in Paris during January, 1711; he went to see M. de Torcy at Versailles. "Do you want peace?" said he. "I have come to bring you the means of treating for it and concluding independently of the Hollanders, unworthy of the king's kindnesses and of the honor he has so often done them of applying to them to pacificate Europe." "To ask just then one of his Majesty's ministers if he desired peace," says Torcy, "was to ask a sick man suffering from a long and dangerous disease if he wants to be cured." Negotiations were secretly opened with the English cabinet. The Emperor Joseph had just died (April 17, 1711). He left none but daughters. From that moment Archduke Charles inherited the domains of the House of Austria and aspired to the imperial crown; by giving him Spain Europe re-established the monarchy of Charles V.; she saw the dangers into which she was being drawn by the resentments or shortsighted ambition of the *triumvirate;* she fell back upon the wise projects of William III. Holland had abandoned them; to England fell the honor of making them triumphant. She has often made war upon the Continent, with indomitable obstinacy and perseverance; but at bottom and by the very force of circumstances England remains, as regards the affairs of Europe, an essentially pacific power. War brings her no advantage; she cannot pretend to any territorial aggrandisement in Europe; it is the equilibrium between the continental powers that makes her strength, and her first interest was always to maintain it.

The campaign of 1711 was everywhere insignificant. Negotiations were still going on with England, secretly and through subordinate agents: Ménager, member of the Board of Trade, for France; and, for England, the poet Prior, strongly attached to Harley. On the 29th of January, 1712, the general conferences were opened at Utrecht. The French had been anxious to avoid the Hague, dreading the obstinacy of Heinsius in favor of his former proposals. Preliminary points were already settled with England; enormous advantages were secured in America to English commerce, to which was ceded Newfoundland and all that France still possessed in Arcadia; the general proposals had been accepted by Queen Anne and her ministers. In vain had the Hollanders and Prince Eugene made great efforts to modify them; St. John had dryly remarked that England had borne the greatest part in the burden of the war and it was but just that she should direct the negotiations for peace. For five years past the United Provinces, exhausted by the length of hostilities, had constantly been defaulters in their engagements; it was proved to Prince Eugene that the imperial army had not been increased by two regiments in consequence of the war; the emperor's ambassador, M. de Galas, displayed impertinence; he was forbidden to come to the court; in spite of the reserve imposed upon the English ministers by the strife of parties in a free country, their desire for peace was evident. The queen had just ordered the creation of new peers in order to secure a majority of the upper house in favor of a pacific policy.

The bolts of Heaven were falling one after another upon the royal family of France. On the 14th of April, 1711, Louis XIV. had lost by small-pox his son, the grand dauphin, a mediocre and submissive creature, ever the most humble subject of the king, at just fifty years of age. His eldest son, the duke of Burgundy, devout, austere and capable, the hope of good men and the terror of intriguers, had taken the rank of dauphin and was seriously commencing his apprenticeship in government, when he was carried off on the 18th of February, 1712, by spotted fever (*rougeole pourprée*), six days after his wife, the charming Mary Adelaide of Savoy, the idol of the whole court, supremely beloved by the king, and by Madame de Maintenon who had brought her up; their son, the duke of Brittany, four years old, died on the 8th of March; a child in the cradle, weakly and ill, the little duke of Anjou, remained the only shoot of the elder branch of the Bourbons.

Dismay seized upon all France; poison was spoken of; the duke of Orleans was accused; it was necessary to have a post mortem examination; only the hand of God had left its traces. Europe in its turn was excited. If the little duke of Anjou were to die, the crown of France reverted to Philip V. The Hollanders and the ambassadors of the emperor Charles VI., recently crowned at Frankfurt, insisted on the necessity of a formal renunciation. In accord with the English ministers, Louis XIV. wrote to his grandson:—

"You will be told what England proposes, that you should renounce your birth-right, retaining the monarchy of Spain and the Indies, or renounce the monarchy of Spain, retaining your rights to the succession in France and receiving in exchange for the crown of Spain the kingdoms of Sicily and Naples, the States of the duke of Savoy, Montferrat and the Mantuan, the said duke of Savoy succeeding you in Spain; I confess to you that, notwithstanding the disproportion in the dominions, I have been sensibly affected by the thought that you would continue to reign, that I might still regard you as my successor, sure, if the dauphin lives, of a regent accustomed to command, capable of maintaining order in my kingdom and stifling its cabals. If this child were to die, as his weakly complexion gives too much reason to suppose, you would enjoy the succession to me following the order of your birth and I should have the consolation of leaving to my people a virtuous king, capable of commanding them, and one who, on succeeding me, would unite to the crown States so considerable as Naples, Savoy, Piedmont and Montferrat. If gratitude and affection towards your subjects are to you pressing reasons for remaining with them, I may say that you owe me the same sentiments; you owe them to your own house, to your own country, before Spain. All that I can do for you is to leave you once more the choice, the necessity for concluding peace becoming every day more urgent."

The choice of Philip V. was made; he had already written to his grandfather to say that he would renounce all his rights of succession to the throne of France rather than give up the crown of Spain. This decision was solemnly enregistered by the Cortes. The English required that the dukes of Berry and Orleans should likewise make renunciation of their rights to the crown of Spain. Negotiations began again, but war began again at the same time as the negotiations.

The king had given Villars the command of the army of

Flanders. The marshal went to Marly to receive his last orders. "You see my plight, marshal," said Louis XIV. "There are few examples of what is my fate—to lose in the same week a grandson, a grandson's wife and their son, all of very great promise and very tenderly beloved. God is punishing me; I have well deserved it. But suspend we my griefs at my own domestic woes and look we to what may be done to prevent those of the kingdom. If anything were to happen to the army you command, what would be your idea of the course I should adopt as regards my person?" The marshal hesitated. The king resumed: "This is what I think; you shall tell me your opinion afterwards. I know the courtiers' line of argument; they nearly all wish me to retire to Blois and not wait for the enemy's army to approach Paris, as it might do if mine were beaten. For my part, I am aware that armies so considerable are never defeated to such an extent as to prevent the greater part of mine from retiring upon the Somme. I know that river, it is very difficult to cross; there are forts, too, which could be made strong. I should count upon getting to Péronne or St. Quentin and there massing all the troops I had, making a last effort with you, and falling together or saving the kingdom; I will never consent to let the enemy approach my capital [*Mémoires de Villars*, t. ii. p. 362]."

God was to spare Louis XIV. that crowning disaster reserved for other times; in spite of all his defaults and the culpable errors of his life and reign, Providence had given this old man overwhelmed by so many reverses and sorrows a truly royal soul and that regard for his own greatness which set him higher as a king than he would have been as a man. "He had too proud a soul to descend lower than his misfortunes had brought him," says Montesquieu, "and he well knew that courage may right a crown and that infamy never does." On the 25th of May, the king secretly informed his plenipotentiaries as well as his generals that the English were proposing to him a suspension of hostilities, and he added: "It is no longer a time for flattering the pride of the Hollanders, but, whilst we treat with them in good faith, it must be with the dignity that becomes me." "A style different from that of the conferences at the Hague and Gertruydenberg," is the remark made by M. de Torcy. That which the king's pride refused to the ill will of the Hollanders he granted to the good will of England. The day of the commencement of the armistice Dunkerque was put as guarantee into the hands of the English, who recalled their native regiments from the army of Prince Eugene; the king complained that they left him the auxiliary troops; the English ministers proposed to prolong the truce, promising to treat separately with France if the allies refused assent to the peace. The news received by Louis XIV. gave him assurance of better conditions than any one had dared to hope for.

Villars had not been able to prevent Prince Eugene from becoming master of Quesnoy on the 3rd of July; the imperialists were already making preparations to invade France; in their army the causeway which connected Marchiennes with Landrecies was called the *Paris road.* The marshal resolved to relieve Landrecies, and, having had bridges thrown over the Scheldt, he on the 23rd of July, 1712, crossed the river between Bouchain and Denain; the latter little place was defended by the duke of Albemarle, son of General Monk, with seventeen battalions of auxiliary troops in the pay of the allies; Lieutenant-general Albergotti, an experienced soldier, considered the undertaking perilous. "Go and lie down for an hour or two, M. d'Albergotti," said Villars; "to-morrow by three in the morning you shall know whether the enemy's intrenchments are as strong as you suppose." Prince Eugene was coming up by forced marches to relieve Denain, by falling on the rearguard of the French army. It was proposed to Villars to make fascines to fill up the fosses of Denain. "Do you suppose," said he pointing to the enemy's army in the distance, "that those gentry will give us the time? Our fascines shall be the bodies of the first of our men who fall in the fosse."

"There was not an instant, not a minute to lose," says the marshal in his *Mémoires.* "I made my infantry march on four lines in the most beautiful order; as I entered the intrenchment at the head of the troops, I had not gone twenty paces when the duke of Albemarle and six or seven of the emperor's lieutenant-generals were at my horse's feet. I begged them to excuse me if present matters did not permit me to show them all the politeness I ought, but that the first of all was to provide for the safety of their persons." The enemy thought of nothing but flight; the bridges over the Scheldt broke down under the multitude of vehicles and horses; nearly all the defenders of Denain were taken or killed. Prince Eugene could not cross the river, watched as it was by French troops; he did not succeed in saving Marchiennes, which the count of Broglie had been ordered to invest in the very middle of the action in front of Denain;

the imperialists raised the siege of Landrecies, but without daring to attack Villars, reënforced by a few garrisons; the marshal immediately invested Douai; on the 27th of August, the emperor's troops who were defending one of the forts demanded a capitulation; the officers who went out asked for a delay of four days so as to receive orders from Prince Eugene; the marshal, who was in the trenches, called his grenadiers. "This is my council on such occasions," said he to the astonished imperialists. "My friends, these captains demand four days' time to receive orders from their general; what do you think?" "Leave it to us, marshal," replied the grenadiers: "in a quarter of an hour we will slit their wind-pipes." "Gentlemen," said I to the officers, "they will do as they have said, so take your own course." The garrison surrendered at discretion. Douai capitulated on the 8th of September; Le Quesnoy was taken on the 4th of October, and Bouchain on the 18th; Prince Eugene had not been able to attempt anything, he fell back under the walls of Brussels. On the Rhine, on the Alps, in Spain, the French and Spanish armies had held the enemy in check. The French plenipotentiaries at Utrecht had recovered their courage. "We put on the face the Hollanders had at Gertruydenberg and they put on ours," wrote Cardinal de Polignac from Utrecht: "it is a complete turning of the tables." "Gentlemen, peace will be treated for amongst you, for you and without you," was the remark made to the Hollanders. Hereditary adversary of the Van Witts and their party, Heinsius had pursued the policy of William III. without the foresight and lofty views of William III.; he had not seen his way in 1709 to shaking off the yoke of Marlborough and Prince Eugene in order to take the initiative in a peace necessary for Europe; in 1712, he submitted to the will of Harley and St. John, thus losing the advantages of the powerful mediatorial position which the United Provinces had owed to the eminent men successively entrusted with their government. Henceforth Holland remained a free and prosperous country, respected and worthy of her independence, but her political influence and importance in Europe were at an end. Under God's hand great men make great destinies and great positions for their country as well as for themselves.

The battle of Denain and its happy consequences hastened the conclusion of the negotiations; the German princes themselves began to split up; the king of Prussia, Frederic William I., who had recently succeeded his father, was the first to escape from the emperor's yoke. Lord Bolingbroke put the finishing stroke at Versailles to the conditions of a general peace; the month of April was the extreme limit fixed by England for her allies; on the 11th peace was signed between France, England, the United Provinces, Portugal, the king of Prussia and the duke of Savoy. Louis XIV. recovered Lille, Aire, Béthune and St. Venant, he strengthened with a few places the barrier of the Hollanders, he likewise granted to the duke of Savoy a barrier on the Italian slope of the Alps, he recognized Queen Anne, at the same time exiling from France the Pretender James III. whom he had but lately proclaimed with so much flourish of trumpets, and he razed the fortifications of Dunkerque. England kept Gibraltar and Minorca; Sicily was assigned to the duke of Savoy. France recognized the king of Prussia. The peace was an honorable and unexpected one, after so many disasters; the king of Spain held out for some time, he wanted to set up an independent principality for the Princess des Ursins, *camerera mayor* to the queen his wife, an able, courageous and clever intriguer, all-powerful at court, who had done good service to the interests of France; he could not obtain any dismemberment of the United Provinces; and at last Philip V. in his turn signed. The emperor and the empire alone remained aloof from the general peace. War recommenced in Germany and on the Rhine. Villars carried Spires and Kaiserlautern. He laid siege to Landau. His lieutenants were uneasy. "Gentlemen," said Villars, "I have heard the prince of Condé say that the enemy should be feared at a distance and despised at close quarters." Landau capitulated on the 20th of August; on the 30th of September Villars entered Friburg; the citadel surrendered on the 13th of November; the imperialists began to make pacific overtures; the two generals, Villars and Prince Eugene, were charged with the negotiations.

"I arrived at Rastadt on the 26th of November in the afternoon," writes Villars in his *Mémoires*, "and the prince of Savoy half an hour after me. The moment I knew he was in the court-yard, I went to the top of the steps to meet him, apologizing to him on the ground that a lame man could not go down; we embraced with the feelings of an old and true friendship which long wars and various engagements had not altered." The two plenipotentiaries were headstrong in their discussions. "If we begin war again," said Villars, ' where will you find money?" "It is true that we haven't any," rejoined the prince: "but there is still some in the empire." "Poor States of the empire!" I exclaimed: "your advice is not asked about beginning the dance; yet you must of course follow the leaders." Peace was at last signed on the 6th of March, 1714; France kept Landau and Fort Louis, she restored Spires, Brisach and Friburg. The emperor refused to recognize Philip V., but he accepted the *status quo;* the crown of Spain remained definitely with the house of Bourbon; it had cost men and millions enough; for an instant the very foundations of order in Europe had seemed to be upset; the old French monarchy had been threatened; it had recovered of itself and by its own resources, sustaining single-handed the struggle which was pulling down all Europe in coalition against it; it had obtained conditions which restored its frontiers to the limits of the peace of Ryswick: but it was exhausted, gasping at wit's end for men and money; absolute power had obtained from national pride the last possible efforts, but it had played itself out in the struggle; the confidence of the country was shaken; it had been seen what dangers the will of a single man had made the nation incur; the tempest was already gathering within men's souls. The habit of respect, the memory of past glories, the personal majesty of Louis XIV. still kept up about the aged king the deceitful appearances of uncontested power and sovereign authority; the long decadence of his great-grandson's reign was destined to complete its ruin.

"I loved war too much," was Louis XIV.'s confession on his death-bed. He had loved it madly and exclusively, but this fatal passion which had ruined and corrupted France had not at any rate remained infructuose. Louis XIV. had the good fortune to profit by the efforts of his predecessors as well as of his own servants: Richelieu and Mazarin, Condé and Turenne, Luxembourg, Catinat, Vauban, Villars and Louvois all toiled at the same work; under his reign France was intoxicated with excess of the pride of conquest, but she did not lose all its fruits; she witnessed the conclusion of five peaces, mostly glorious, the last sadly honorable; all tended to consolidate the unity and power of the kingdom; it is to the treaties of the Pyrenees, of Westphalia, of Nimeguen, of Ryswick and of Utrecht, all signed with the name of Louis XIV., that France owed Roussillon, Artois, Alsace, Flanders and Franche-Comté. Her glory has more than once cost her dear, it has never been worth so much and such solid increment to her territory.

CHAPTER XLVI.

LOUIS XIV. AND HOME ADMINISTRATION.

IT is King Louis XIV.'s distinction and heavy burthen in the eyes of history that it is impossible to tell of anything in his reign without constantly recurring to himself. He had two ministers of the higher order, Colbert and Louvois; several of good capacity, such as Seignelay and Torcy; others incompetent, like Chamillard; he remained as much master of the administrators of the first rank as if they had been insignificant clerks; the home government of France, from 1661 to 1715, is summed up in the king's relations with his ministers.

"I resolved from the first not to have any premier minister," says Louis XIV. in his *Mémoires*, "and not to leave to another the functions of king whilst I had nothing but the title. But, on the contrary, I made up my mind to share the execution of my orders amongst several persons, in order to concentrate their authority in my own alone. I might have cast my eyes upon people of higher consideration than those I selected, but they seemed to me competent to execute, under me, the matters with which I purposed to entrust them. I did not think it was to my interest to look for men of higher standing, because, as I wanted above all things to establish my own reputation, it was important that the public should know, from the rank of those of whom I made use, that I had no intention of sharing my authority with them, and that they themselves, knowing what they were, should not conceive higher hopes than I wished to give them."

It has been said already that the court governed France in the reign of Louis XIV.; and what was, in fact, the court? The men who lived about the king, depending on his favor, the source or arbiter of their fortunes. The great lords served in the army, with lustre, when they bore the names of Condé, Turenne or Luxembourg; but they never had any place amongst the king's confidential servants. "Luck, in spite of us, has as much to do as wisdom—and more—with the choice of our ministers," he says in his *Mémoires*, "and, in respect of what wisdom may have to do therewith, genius is far more effectual than counsel." It was their genius which made the fortunes and the power of Louis XIV.'s two great ministers, Colbert and Louvois.

In advance, and on the faith of Cardinal Mazarin, the king knew the worth of Colbert. "I had all possible confidence in him," says he, "because I knew that he had a great deal of application, intelligence and probity." Rough, reserved, taciturn, indefatigable in work, passionately devoted to the cause of order, public welfare and the peaceable aggrandizement of France, Colbert, on becoming the comptroller of finance in 1661, brought to the service of the State superior views, consummate experience and indomitable perseverence. The position of affairs required no fewer virtues. "Disorder reigned everywhere," says the king; "on casting over the various portions of my kingdom not eyes of indifference but the eyes of a master, I was sensibly affected not to see a single one which did not deserve and did not press to be taken in hand. The destitution of the lower orders was extreme, and the finances, which give movement and activity to all this great framework of the monarchy, were entirely exhausted and in such plight that there was scarcely any resource to be seen; the affluent, to be seen only amongst official people, on the one hand cloaked all their malversations by divers kinds of artifices and uncloaked them on the other by their insolent and audacious extravagance, as if they were afraid to leave me in ignorance of them."

The punishment of the tax-collectors (*traitants*), prosecuted at the same time as superintendent Fouquet, the arbitrary redemption of *rentes* (annuities) on the city of Paris or on certain branches of the taxes did not suffice to alleviate the extreme suffering of the people. The talliages from which the nobility and the clergy were nearly everywhere exempt pressed upon the people with the most cruel inequality. "The poor are reduced to eating grass and roots in our meadows like cattle," said a letter from Blaisois; "those who can find dead carcases devour them, and, unless God have pity upon them, they will soon be eating one another." Normandy, generally so prosperous, was reduced to the uttermost distress. "The great number of poor has exhausted charity and the power of those who were accustomed to relieve them," says a letter to Colbert from the superintendent of Caen: "in 1662, the town was obliged to throw open the doors of the great hospital, having no longer any means of furnishing subsistence to those who were in it. I can assure you that there are persons in this town who have gone for whole days without anything to eat. The country, which ought to supply bread for the towns, is crying for mercy's sake to be supplied therewith itself." The peasants, wasted with hunger, could no longer till their fields; their cattle had been seized for taxes. Colbert proposed to the king to remit the arrears of talliages, and devoted all his efforts to reducing them, whilst regulating their collection. His desire was to arrive at the establishment everywhere of *real* talliages, on landed property, &c., instead of *personal* talliages, variable imposts, depending upon the supposed means or social position of the inhabitants. He was only very partially successful, without, however, allowing himself to be repelled by the difficulties presented by differences of legislation and customs in the provinces. "Perhaps," he wrote to the superintendent of Aix, in 1681, "on getting to the bottom of the matter and considering it in detail, you will not discover in it all the impossibilities you have pictured to yourself." Colbert died without having completed his work; the talliages, however, had been reduced by eight millions of livres within the first two years of his administration. "All the imposts of the kingdom," he writes, in 1662, to the superintendent of Tours, who is complaining of the destitution of the people, "are, as regards the talliages, but about thirty-seven millions, and, for forty or fifty years past, they have always been between forty and fifty millions, except after the peace, when his Majesty reduced them to thirty-two, thirty-three, and thirty-four millions."

Peace was of short duration in the reign of Louis XIV. and often so precarious that it did not permit of disarmament. At the very period when the able minister was trying to make the people feel the importance of the diminution in the talliages, he wrote to the king: "I entreat your Majesty to read these few lines attentively. I confess to your Majesty that the last time you were graciously pleased to speak to me about the state of the finances, my respect, the boundless desire I have always had to please you and serve you to your satisfaction, without making any difficulty or causing any hitch, and still more your natural eloquence which succeeds in bringing conviction of whatever you please, deprived me of courage to insist and dwell somewhat upon the condition of your finances, for the which I see no other remedy but increase of receipts and decrease of expenses; wherefore, though this is no concern at all of mine, I merely entreat your Majesty to permit me to say that in war as well as in peace you have never consulted your finances for the purpose of determining your expenditure, which is a thing so extraordinary that assuredly there is no example thereof. For the past twenty years during which I have had the honor of serving your Majesty, though the receipts have greatly increased, you would find that the expenses have much exceeded the receipts, which might perhaps induce you to moderate and retrench such as are excessive. I am aware, Sir, that the figure I present herein is not an agreeable one; but in your Majesty's service there are different functions: some entail nothing but agreeables whereof the expenses are the foundation; that with which your Majesty honors me entails this misfortune that it can with difficulty produce anything agreeable, since the proposals for expenses have no limit; but one must console oneself by constantly laboring to do one's best."

Louis XIV. did not "moderate or retrench his expenses." Colbert labored to increase the receipts; the new imposts excited insurrections in Angoumois, in Guyenne, in Brittany. Bordeaux rose in 1695 with shouts of "*Hurrah! for the king without gabel!*" Marshal d'Albret ventured into the streets in the district of St. Michel; he was accosted by one of the ringleaders: "Well, my friend," said the marshal, "with whom is thy business? Dost wish to speak to me?" "Yes," replied the townsman, "I am deputed by the people of St. Michel to tell you that they are good servants of the king, but that they do not mean to have any gabel, or marks on pewter or tobacco, or stamped papers, or *greffe d'arbitrage* (arbitration-clerk's fee)." It was not until a year afterwards that the taxes could be established in Gascony; troops had to be sent to Rennes to impose the stamp-tax upon the Bretons. "Soldiers are more likely to be wanted in Lower Brittany than in any other spot," said a letter to Colbert from the lieutenant-general, M. de Lavardin; "it is a rough and wild country which breeds inhabitants who resemble it. They understand French but slightly and reason not much better. The parliament is at the back of all this." Riots were frequent and were put down with great severity. "The poor Low-Bretons collect by forty or fifty in the fields," writes Madame de Sévigné on the 24th of September, 1675: "as soon as they see soldiers, they throw themselves on their knees, saying, *Mea culpa!* all the French they know. . . ." "The severities are abating," she adds on the 3rd of November: "after the hangings there will be no more hanging." All these fresh imposts which had cost so much suffering and severity brought in but 2,500,000 livres at Colbert's death. The indirect taxes, which were at that time called *fermes générales* (farmings-general), amounted to 37,000,000 during the first two years of Colbert's administration, and rose to 64,000,000 at the time of his death. "I should be apprehensive of going too far and that the prodigious augmentations of the *fermes* (farmings) would be very burdensome to the people," wrote Louis XIV. in 1680. The expenses of recovering the taxes, which had but lately led to great abuses, were diminished by half. "The bailiffs generally and especially those who are set over the recovery of talliages, are such terrible brutes that, by way of exterminating a good number of these, you could not do anything more worthy of you than suppress those," wrote Colbert to the criminal-magistrate of Orleans. "I am at this moment promoting two suits against the collectors of talliages, in which I expect at present to get ten thousand crowns' damages, without counting another against an assessor's officer, who wounded one Grimault, the which had one of his daughters killed before his eyes, his wife, another of his daughters and his female-servant wounded with swords and sticks, the writ of distrainment being executed whilst the poor creature was being buried." The bailiffs were suppressed, and the king's justice let loose not only against the fiscal officers who abused their power, but also against tyrannical nobles. Masters of requests and members of the parliament of Paris went to Auvergne and Velay and held temporary courts of justice which were called *grands jours*. Several lords were found guilty; Sieur de la Mothe actually died upon the scaffold for having unjustly despoiled and maltreated the people on his estates. "He was not one of the worst," says Fléchier, in his *Journal des grands jours d'Auvergne*. The duke of Bouillon, governor of the province, had too long favored the guilty: "I resolved," says the king in his *Mémoires*, "to prevent the people from being subjected to thousands and thousands of tyrants instead of one lawful king, whose indulgence alone it is that causes all this disorder." The puissance of the provincial governors, already curtailed by Richelieu, suffered from fresh attacks under Louis XIV. Everywhere the power passed into the hands of the superintendents, themselves subjected in their turn to inspection by the masters of requests. "Acting on the information I had that in many provinces the people were plagued by certain folks who abused their title of governors in order to make unjust requisitions," says the king in his *Mémoires*, "I posted men in all quarters for the express purpose of keeping myself more surely informed of such exactions, in order to punish them as they deserved." Order was restored in all parts of France. "The Auvergnats," said a letter to Colbert from President de Novion, "never knew so certainly that they had a king as they do now."

"A useless banquet at a cost of a thousand crowns causes me incredible pain," said Colbert to Louis XIV., "and yet, when it is a question of millions of gold for Poland, I would sell all my property, I would pawn my wife and children and I would go a-foot all my life to provide for it if necessary. Your Majesty, if it please you, will forgive me this little transport. I begin to doubt whether the liberty I take is agreeable to your Majesty; it has seemed to me that you were beginning to prefer your pleasures and your diversions to everything else; at the very time when your Majesty told me at St. Germain that the morsel must be taken from one's mouth to provide for the increment of the naval armament you spent 200,000 livres down for a trip to Versailles, to wit, 13,000 pistoles for your gambling expenses and the queen's, and 50,000 livres for extraordinary banquets; you have likewise so intermingled your diversions with the war on land that it is difficult to separate the two, and, if your Majesty will be graciously pleased to examine in detail the amount of useless expenditure you have incurred, you will plainly see that, if it were all deducted, you would not be reduced to your present necessity. The right thing to do, Sir, is to grudge five sous for unnecessary things and to throw millions about when it is for your glory."

Colbert knew, in fact, how to "throw millions about" when it was for endowing France with new manufactures and industries. "One of the most important works of peace," he used to say, "is the re-establishment of every kind of trade in this kingdom and to put it in a position to do without having recourse to foreigners for the things necessary for the use and comfort of the subjects." "We have no need of anybody and our neighbors have need of us;" such was the maxim laid down in a document of that date, which has often been attributed to Colbert, and which he certainly put incessantly into practice. The cloth manufacturers were dying out, they received encouragement; a protestant Hollander, Van Robais, attracted over to Abbeville by Colbert, there introduced the making of fine cloths; at Beauvais and in the Gobelins establishment at Paris, under the direction of the great painter Lebrun, the French tapestries soon threw into the shade the reputation of the tapestries of Flanders; Venice had to yield up her secrets and her workmen for the glass manufactories of St. Gobain and Tourlaville. The great lords and ladies were obliged to give up the Venetian point with which their dresses had been trimmed; the importation of it was forbidden, and lace manufactories were everywhere established in France; there was even a strike amongst the women at Alençon against the new lace which it was desired to force them to make. "There are more than 80,000 persons working at lace in Alençon, Seez, Argentan, Falaise and the circumjacent parishes," said a letter to Colbert from the superintendent of Alençon, "and I can assure you, my lord, that it is manna and a blessing from heaven over all this district, where even little children of seven years of age find means of earning a livelihood; the little shepherd-girls from the fields work, like the rest, at it; they say they will never be able to make such fine point as this and that one wants to take away their bread and their means of paying their talliage." Point d'Alençon won the battle, and the making of lace spread all over Normandy. Manufacturers of soap, tin, arms, silk, gave work to a multitude of laborers; the home trade of France at the same time received development; the bad state of the roads "were a dreadful hindrance to traffic;" Colbert ordered them to be everywhere improved. "The superintendents have done wonders, and we are never tired of singing their praises," writes Madame de Sévigné to her daughter during one of her trips; "it is quite extraordinary what beautiful roads there are; there is not a single moment's stoppage: there are malls and walks everywhere." The magnificent canal of Languedoc, due to the generous initiative of Riquet, united the Ocean to the Mediterranean; the canal of Orleans completed the canal of Briare, commenced by Henry IV. The inland custom-houses which shackled the traffic between province and province were suppressed at divers points; many provinces demurred to the admission of this innovation, declaring that, to set their affairs right, "there was need of nothing but order, order, order." Colbert also wanted order, but his views were higher and broader than those of Breton or Gascon merchants; in spite of his desire to "put the kingdom in a position to do without having recourse to foreigners for things necessary for the use and comfort of the French," he had too lofty and too judicious a mind to neglect the extension of trade; like Richelieu, he was for founding great trading companies; he had five, for the East and West Indies, the Levant, the North, and Africa; just as with Richelieu, they were with difficulty established and lasted but a little while; it was necessary to levy subscriptions on the members of the sovereign corporations; "M. de Bercy put down his name for a thousand livres," says the journal of Oliver d'Ormesson: "M. de Colbert laughed at him and said that it could not be for his pocket's sake; and the end of it was that he put down three thousand livres." Colbert could not get over the mortifying success of the company of the Dutch Indies. "I cannot believe that they pay forty per cent.," said he. It was with the Dutch that he most frequently had commercial difficulties. The United Provinces produced but little and their merchant navy was exclusively engaged in the business of transport; the charge of fifty sous per ton on merchandise carried in foreign vessels caused so much ill humor amongst the Hollanders that it was partly the origin of their rupture with France and of the treaty of the Triple Alliance. Colbert made great efforts to develop the French navy, both the fighting and the merchant: "The sea-traffic of all the world," he wrote in 1669 to M. de Pomponne, then ambassador to Holland, "is done with twenty thousand vessels or thereabouts. In the natural order of things, each nation should have its own share thereof in proportion to its power, population and sea-board. The Hollanders have fifteen or sixteen thousand out of this number, and the French perhaps four or five hundred at most. The king is employing all sorts of means which he thinks useful in order to approach a little more nearly to the number his subjects ought naturally to have." Colbert's efforts were not useless; at his death, the maritime trade of France had developed itself and French merchants were effectually protected at sea by ships of war. "It is necessary," said Colbert in his instructions to Seignelay, "that my son should be as keenly alive to all the disorders that may occur in trade and all the losses that may be incurred by every trader as if they were his own." In 1692, the royal navy numbered a hundred and eighty-six vessels; a hundred and sixty thousand sailors were down on the books; the works at the ports of Toulon, Brest and Rochefort were in full activity; Louis XIV. was in a position to refuse the salute of the flag which the English had up to that time exacted in the Channel from all nations. "The king my brother and those of whom he takes counsel do not quite know me yet," wrote the king to his ambassador in London, "when they adopt towards me a tone of haughtiness and a certain sturdiness which has a savor of menace. I know of no power under heaven that can make me move a step by that sort of way; evil may come to me, of course, but no sensation of fear. The king of England and his chancellor may, of course, see pretty well what my strength is, but they do not see my heart; I, who feel and know full well both one and the other, desire that, for sole reply to so haughty a declaration, they learn from your mouth that I neither seek nor ask for any accommodation in the matter of the flag, because I shall know quite well how to maintain my right whatever may happen. I intend before long to place my maritime forces on such a footing that the English shall consider it a favor if it be my good pleasure then to listen to modifications touching a right which is due to me more legitimately than to them." Duquesne and Tourville, Duguay-Trouin and John Bart permitted the king to make good on the seas such proud words. From 1685 to 1712 the French fleets could everywhere hold their own against the allied squadrons of England and Holland.

So many and such sustained efforts in all directions, so many vast projects and of so great promise suited the mind of Louis XIV. as well as that of his minister. "I tell you what I think," wrote Louis XIV. to Colbert in 1674; "but, after all, I end as I began, by placing myself entirely in your hands, being certain that you will do what is most advantageous for my service." Colbert's zeal for his master's service merited this confidence. "Oh!" he exclaimed one day, "that I could render this country happy and that, far from the court, without favor, without influence, the grass might grow in my very courts!"

Louis XIV. was the victim of three passions which hampered and in the long-run destroyed the accord between king and minister: that for war, whetted and indulged by Louvois; that for kingly and courtly extravagance; and that for building and costly fancies. Colbert likewise loved "buildments" (*les bâtiments*), as the phrase then was; he urged the king to complete the Louvre, plans for which were requested of Bernini, who went to Paris for the purpose; after two years' infructuous feelers and compliments, the Italian returned to Rome, and the work was entrusted to Perrault, whose plan for the beautiful colonnade still existing had always pleased Colbert. The completion of the castle of St. Germain, the works at Fontainebleau and at Chambord, the triumphal arches of St. Denis and St. Martin, the laying out of the Tuileries, the construction of the Observatory, and even that of the Palais des Invalides, which was Louvois' idea, found the comptroller of the finances well disposed if not eager. Versailles was a constant source of vexation to him: "Your Majesty is coming back from Versailles," he wrote to the king on the 28th of September, 1685. "I entreat that you will permit me to say two words about the reflections I often make upon this subject and forgive me, if it please you, for my zeal. That mansion appertains far more to your Majesty's pleasure and diversion than to your glory; if you would be graciously pleased to search all over Versailles for the 500,000 crowns spent within two years, you would assuredly have a difficulty in finding them. If your majesty thinks upon it, you will reflect that it will appear forever in the accounts of the treasurers of your buildments that, whilst you were expending such great sums on this mansion, you neglected the Louvre, which is assuredly the most superb palace in the world and the most worthy of your Majesty's grandeur. You are aware that, in default of splendid deeds of arms, there is nothing which denotes the grandeur and spirit of princes more plainly than buildments do, and all posterity measures them by the ell of those superb mansions which they have erected during their lives. O what pity it were that the greatest king and the most virtuous in that true virtue which makes the greatest princes should be measured by the ell of Versailles! And, nevertheless, there is room to fear this misfortune. For my part, I confess to your Majesty that, notwithstanding the repugnance you feel to increase the cash-orders [*comptants*], if I could have foreseen that this expenditure would be so large, I should have advised the employment of cash-orders, in order to hide the knowledge thereof forever. [The cash-orders (*ordonnances au comptant*) did not indicate their object and were not revised. The king merely wrote: *Pay cash; I know the object of this expenditure* (*Bon au comptant je: sais l' objet de cette dépense*).]

Colbert was mistaken in his fears for Louis XIV.'s glory; if the expenses of Versailles surpassed his most gloomy apprehensions, the palace which rose upon the site of Louis XIV.'s former hunting-box was worthy of the king who had made it in his own image and who managed to retain all his court around him there, by the mere fact of his will and of his royal presence.

Colbert was dead before Versailles was completed; the bills amounted then to one hundred and sixteen millions; the castle of Marly, now destroyed, cost more than four millions; money was everywhere becoming scarce; the temper of the comptroller of finances went on getting worse. "Whereas formerly it had been noticed that he set to his work rubbing his hands with joy," says his secretary Perrault, brother of the celebrated architect, "he no longer worked but with an air of vexation and even with sighs. From the good-natured and easy-going creature he had been, he became difficult to deal with, and there was not so much business, by a great deal, got through as in the early years of his administration." "I do not mean to build any more, Mansard; I meet with too many mortifications," the king would say to his favorite architect. He still went on building, however; but he quarrelled with Colbert over the cost of the great railings of Versailles. "There's swindling here," said Louis XIV. "Sir," rejoined Colbert, "I flatter myself at any rate that that word does not apply to me?" "No," said the king: "but more attention should have been shown. If you want to know what economy is, go to Flanders, you will see how little those fortifications of the conquered places cost."

It was Vauban whose praise the king thus sang, and Vauban, devoted to Louvois, had for a long time past been embroiled with Colbert. The minister felt himself beaten in the contest he had so long maintained against Michael Le Tellier and his son. In 1664, at the death of Chancellor Séguier, Colbert had opposed the elevation of Le Tellier to this office, "telling the king that, if he came in, he, Colbert could not serve his Majesty, as he would have him thwarting everything he wanted to do." On leaving the council, Le Tellier said to Brienne: "You see what a tone M. Colbert takes up; he will have to be settled with." The antagonism had been perpetuated between Colbert and Louvois; their rivalry in the State had been augmented by the contrary dispositions of the two ministers. Both were passionately devoted to their work, laborious, indefatigable, honest in money-matters, and both of fierce and domineering temper; but Louvois was more violent, more bold, less scrupulous as to ways and means of attaining his end, cruel in the exercise of his will and his wrath, less concerned about the sufferings of the people, more exclusively absorbed by one fixed idea; both rendered great service to the king, but Colbert performing for the prince and the State only useful offices in the way of order, economy, wise and far-sighted administration, courageous and steady opposition; Louvois ever urging the king on according to his bent, as haughty and more impassioned than he, entangling him and encouraging him in wars which rendered his own services necessary, without pity for the woes he entailed upon the nation. It was the misfortune and the great fault of Louis XIV. that he preferred the counsels of Louvois to those of Colbert and that he allowed all the functions so faithfully exercised by the dying minister to drop into the hands of his enemy and rival.

At sixty-four years of age Colbert succumbed to excess of labor and of cares. That man, so cold and reserved, whom Madame de Sévigné called *North*, and Guy-Patin the *Man of Marble* (*Virmarmoreus*), felt that disgust for the things of life which appears so strikingly in the seventeenth century amongst those who were most ardently engaged in the affairs of the world. He was suffering from stone; the king sent to inquire after him and wrote to him. The dying man had his eyes closed; he did not open them: "I do not want to hear anything more about him," said he, when the king's letter was brought to him: "now, at any rate, let him leave me alone." His thoughts were occupied with his soul's salvation. Madame de Maintenon used to accuse him of always thinking about his finances and very little about religion. He repeated bitterly, as the dying Cardinal Wolsey had previously said in the case of Henry: "If I had done for God what I have done for that man, I had been saved twice over; and now I know not what will become of me." He expired on the 6th of September, 1683; and, on the 10th, Madame de Maintenon wrote to Madame de St. Géran: "The king is very well, he feels no more now than a slight sorrow. The death of M. de Colbert afflicted him, and a great many people rejoiced at that affliction. It is all stuff about the pernicious designs he had; and the king very cordially forgave him for having determined to die without reading his letter, in order to be better able to give his thoughts to God. M. de Seignelay was anxious to step into all his posts, and has not obtained a single one; he has plenty of cleverness, but little moral conduct. His pleasures always have precedence of his duties. He has so exaggerated his father's talents and services, that he has convinced everybody how unworthy and incapable he is of succeeding him." The influence of Louvois and the king's ill humor against the Colberts peep out in the injustice of Madame de Maintenon. Seignelay had received from Louis XIV. the reversion of the navy; his father had prepared him for it with anxious strictness, and he had exercised the functions since 1676. Well informed, clever, magnificent, Seignelay drove business and pleasure as a pair. In 1685 he gave the king a splendid entertainment in his castle of Sceaux; in 1686, he set off for Genoa bombarded by Duquesne; in 1689 he, in person, organized the fleet of Tourville at Brest. "He was general in everything," says Madame de la Fayette; "even when he did not give the word, he had the exterior and air of it." "He is devoured by ambition," Madame de Maintenon had lately said: in 1689 she writes: "*Anxious* (*L'Inquiet, i.e.*, Louvois) hangs but by a thread; he is very much shocked at having the direction of the affairs of Ireland taken from him; he blames me for it. He counted on making immense profits; M. de Seignelay counts on nothing but perils and labors. He will succeed, if he do not carry things with too high a hand. The king would have no better servant, if he could rid himself a little of his temperament. He admits as much himself; and yet he does not mend." Seignelay died on the 3rd of November, 1690, at the age of thirty-nine. "He had all the parts of a great minister of State," says St. Simon, "and he was the despair of M. de Louvois whom he often placed in the position of having not a word of reply to say in the king's presence. His defects corresponded with his great qualities. As a hater and a friend he had no peer but Louvois." "How young! How fortunate! How great a position!" wrote Madame de Sévigné, on hearing of the death of M. de Seignelay: "it seems as if splendor itself were dead."

Seignelay had spent freely, but he left at his death more than 400,000 livres a year. Colbert's fortune amounted to ten millions, legitimate proceeds of his high offices and the king's liberalities. He was born of a family of merchants at Rheims, ennobled in the sixteenth century, but he was fond of connecting it with the Colberts of Scotland. The great minister would often tell his children to reflect "what their birth would have done for them if God had not blessed his labors, and if those labors had not been extreme." He had married his daughters to the dukes of Beauvilliers, Chevreuse, and Mortemart; Seignelay had wedded Mdlle. de Matignon, whose grandmother was an Orleans-Longueville. "Thus," said Mdlle. de Montpensier, "they have the honor of being as closely related as M. le Prince to the king; Marie de Bourbon was cousin-germain to the king my grandfather. That lends a grand air to M. de Seignelay, who had by nature sufficient vanity." Colbert had no need to seek out genealogies, and great alliances were naturally attracted to his power and the favor he was in. He had in himself that title which comes of superior merit and which nothing can make up for, nothing can equal; he might have said as Marshal Lannes said to the marquis of Montesquieu, who was exhibiting a coat taken out of his ancestors' drawers, "I am an ancestor myself."

Louvois remained henceforth alone, without rival and without check. The work he had undertaken for the reorganization of the army was pretty nearly completed; he had concentrated in his own hands the whole direction of the military service, the burden and the honor of which were both borne by him. He had subjected to the same rules and the same discipline all corps and all grades; the general as well as the colonel obeyed him blindly. M. de Turenne alone had managed to escape from the administrative level. "I see quite clearly," he wrote to Louvois on the 9th of September, 1673, "what are the king's wishes, and I will do all I can to conform to them, but you will permit me to tell you that I do not think that it would be to his Majesty's service to give precise orders, at such a distance, to the most incapable man in France." Turenne had not lost the habit of command; Louvois, who had for a long while been under his orders, bowed to the will of the king who required apparent accord between the marshal and the minister, but he never forgave Turenne for his cool and proud independence. The prince of Condé more than once turned to advantage this latent antagonism. After the death of Louvois and of Turenne, after the retirement of Condé, when the central power fell into the hands of Chamillard or of Voysin, the pretence of directing war from the king's closet at Versailles produced the most fatal effects. "If M. de Chamillard thinks that I know nothing about war," wrote Villars to Madame de Maintenon, "he will oblige me by finding somebody else in the kingdom who is better acquainted with it." "If your Majesty," he said again, "orders me to shut myself up in Bavaria, and if you want to see your army lost, I will get myself killed at the first opportunity rather than live to see such a mishap." The king's orders, transmitted through a docile minister, ignorant of war, had a great deal to do with the military disasters of Louis XIV.'s later years.

Meanwhile order reigned in the army, and supplies were regular. Louvois received the nickname of great *Victualler* (*Vivrier*). The wounded were tended in hospitals devoted to their use. "When a soldier is once down, he never gets up again," had but lately been the saying. "Had I been at my mother's, in her own house, I could not have been better treated," wrote M. D'Alligny on the contrary, when he came out of one of the hospitals created by Louvois. He conceived the grand idea of the Hôtel des Invalides. "It were very reasonable," says the preamble of the king's edict which founded the establishment, "that they who have freely exposed their lives and lavished their blood for the defence and maintenance of this monarchy, who have so materially contributed to the winning of the battles we have gained over our enemies and who have often reduced them to asking peace of us, should enjoy the repose they have secured for our other subjects and should pass the remainder of their days in tranquillity." Up to his death Louvois insisted upon managing the Hôtel des Invalides himself.

Never had the officers of the army been under such strict and minute supervision; promotion went by seniority, by "the order on the list," as the phrase then was, without any favor for rank or birth; commanders were obliged to attend to their corps. "Sir," said Louvois one day to M. de Nogaret, "your company is in a very bad state." "Sir," answered Nogaret, "I was not aware of it." "You ought to be aware," said M. de Louvois: "have you inspected it?" "No, sir," said Nogaret. "You ought to have inspected it, sir!" "Sir, I will give orders about it." "You ought to have given them: a man ought to make up his mind, sir, either to openly profess himself a courtier or to devote himself to his duty when he is an officer." Education in the schools for *cadets*, regularity in service, obligation to keep the companies full instead of pocketing a portion of the pay in the name of imaginary soldiers who appeared only on the registers and who were called *dummies* (*passe-volants*), the necessity of wearing uniform, introduced into the army customs to which the French nobility, as undisciplined as they were brave, had hitherto been utter strangers.

Artillery and engineering were developed under the influence of Vauban, "the first of his own time and one of the first of all times" in the great art of besieging, fortifying and defending places. Louvois had singled out Vauban at the sieges of Lille, Tournay and Douai, which he had directed in chief under the king's own eye. He ordered him to render the places he had just taken impregnable. "This is no child's play," said Vauban on setting about the fortifications of Dunkerque, "and I would rather lose my life than hear said of me some day what I hear said of the men who have preceded me." Louvois' admiration was unmixed when he went to examine the works. "The achievements of the Romans which have earned them so much fame show nothing comparable to what has been done here," he exclaimed: "they formerly levelled mountains in order to make high-roads, but here more than four hundred have been swept away; in the place where all those sandbanks were there is now to be seen nothing but one great meadow. The English and the Dutch often send people hither to see if all they have been told is true; they all go back full of admiration at the success of the work and the greatness of the master who took it in hand." It was this admiration and this dangerous greatness which suggested to the English their demands touching Dunkerque during the negotiations for the peace of Utrecht.

The honesty and moral worth of Vauban equalled his genius; he was as high-minded as he was modest; evil reports had been spread about concerning the contractors for the fortifications of Lille; Vauban demanded an inquiry: "You are quite right in thinking, my lord," he wrote to Louvois to whom he was united by a sincere and faithful friendship, "that, if you do not examine into this affair, you cannot do me justice, and, if you do it me not, that would be compelling me to seek means of doing it myself and of giving up forever fortification and all its concomitants. Examine, then, boldly and severely; away with all tender feeling, for I dare plainly tell you that in a question of strictest honesty and sincere fidelity I fear neither the king, nor you, nor all the human race together. Fortune had me born the poorest gentleman in France, but in requital she honored me with an honest heart, so free from all sorts of swindles that it cannot bear even the thought of them without a shudder." It was not until eight years after the death of Louvois, in 1699, when Vauban had directed fifty-three sieges, constructed the fortifications of thirty-three places, and repaired those of three hundred towns, that he was made a marshal, an honor that no engineer had yet obtained; "The king fancied he was giving himself the bâton," it was said, "so often had he had Vauban under his orders in besieging places."

The leisure of peace was more propitious to Vauban's fame than to his favor. Generous and sincere as he was, a patriot more far-sighted than his contemporaries, he had the courage to present to the king a memorial advising the recall of the fugitive Huguenots and the renewal, pure and simple, of the edict of Nantes. He had just directed the siege of Brisach and the defence of Dunkerque when he published a great economical work entitled *la Dîme royale*, the fruit of the reflections of his whole life, fully depicting the misery of the people and the system of imposts he thought adapted to relieve it. The king was offended; he gave the marshal a cold reception and had the work seized. Vauban received his death-blow from this disgrace: the royal edict was dated March 19, 1707; the great engineer died on the 30th; he was not quite seventy-four. The king testified no regret at the loss of so illustrious a servant, with whom he had lived on terms of close intimacy. Vauban had appeared to impugn his supreme authority; this was one of the crimes that Louis XIV. never forgave.

In 1683, at Colbert's death, Vauban was enjoying the royal favor, which he attributed entirely to Louvois. The latter reigned without any one to contest his influence with the master. It had been found necessary to bury Colbert by night to avoid the insults of the people who imputed to him the imposts which crushed them. What an unjust and odious mistake of popular opinion which accused Colbert of the evils which he had fought against and at the same time suffered under to the last day! All Colbert's offices, except the navy, fell to Louvois or his creatures; Claude Lepelletier, a relative of Le Tellier, became comptroller of finance; he entered the council; M. de Blainville, Colbert's second son, was obliged to resign in Louvois' favor the superintendence of buildments, of which the king had previously promised him the reversion. All business passed into the hands of Louvois. Le Tellier had been chancellor since 1677; peace still reigned; the all-powerful minister occupied himself in building Trianon, bringing the river Eure to Versailles and establishing unity of religion in France. "The counsel of constraining the Huguenots by violent means to become Catholics was given and carried out by the marquis of Louvois," says an anonymous letter of the time: "he thought he could manage consciences and control religion by those harsh measures which, in spite of his wisdom, his violent nature suggests to him almost in everything." Louvois was the inventor of the *dragonnades*; it was his father, Michael le Tellier, who put the seals to the revocation of the edict of Nantes; and, a few days before he died, full of joy at his last work, he piously sang the canticle of Simeon. Louis XIV. and his ministers believed in good faith that Protestantism was stamped out. "The king," wrote Madame de Maintenon, "is very pleased to have put the last touch to the great work of the reunion of the heretics with the Church. Father la Chaise, the king's confessor, promised that it would not cost a drop of blood, and M. de Louvois said the same thing." Emigration in mass, the revolt of the Camisards and the long-continued punishments were a painful surprise for the courtiers accustomed to bend beneath the will of Louis XIV.: they did not understand that "anybody should obstinately remain of a religion which was displeasing to the king." The Huguenots paid the penalty for their obstinacy. The intelligent and acute biographer of Louvois, M. Camille Rousset, could not defend him from the charge of violence in their case. On the 10th of June, 1686, he wrote to the superintendent of Languedoc: "On my representation to the king of the little heed paid by the women of the district in which you are to the penalties ordained against those who are found at assemblies, his Majesty orders that those who are not *demoiselles* (that is, noble) shall be sentenced by M. de Bâville to be whipped and branded with the fleur-de-lys." He adds on the 22nd of July: "The king having thought proper to have a declaration sent out on the 15th of this month, whereby his Majesty orders that all those who are henceforth found at such assemblies shall be punished by death, M. de Bâville will take no notice of the decree I sent you relating to the women, as it becomes useless by reason of this declaration." The king's declaration was carried out, as the sentences of the victims prove: "condemned to the galleys, or condemned to death—for the *crime of assemblies.*" This was the language of the Roman emperors. Seventeen centuries of Christianity had not sufficed to make men comprehend the sacred rights of conscience. The refined and moderate mind of Madame de Sévigné did not prevent her from writing to M. de Bussy on the 28th of October, 1685: "You have, no doubt, seen the edict by which the king revokes that of Nantes; nothing can be more beautiful than its contents, and never did or will any king do anything more memorable." The noble libertine and freethinker replied to her: "I admire the steps taken by the king to reunite the Huguenots; the war made upon them in former times and the St. Bartholomew gave vigor to this sect; his Majesty has sapped it little by little, and the edict he has just issued, supported by dragoons and Bourdaloues, has given it the finishing stroke."

It was the honorable distinction of the French Protestants to proclaim during more than two centuries by their courageous resistance the rights and duties which were ignored all around them.

Whilst the reformers were undergoing conversion, exile or death, war was recommencing in Europe, with more determination than ever on the part of the Protestant nations, indignant and disquieted as they were. Louvois began to forget all about the obstinacy of the religionists and prepared for the siege of Philipsburg, and the capture of Manheim and Coblentz. "The king has seen with pleasure," he wrote to Marshal Boufflers, "that, after well burning Coblentz and doing all the harm possible to the elector's palace, you were to march back to Mayence." The haughtiness of the king and the violence of the minister went on increasing with the success of their arms; they treated the pope's rights almost as lightly as those of the Protestants; the pamphleteers of the day had reason to write: "It is clearly seen that the religion of the court of France is a pure matter of interest; the king does nothing but what is for that which he calls his glory and grandeur; Catholics and heretics, Holy Pontiff, Church and anything you please, is sacrificed to his great pride; everything must be reduced to powder beneath his feet; we in France are on the high road to putting the sacred rights of the Holy See on the same footing as the privileges granted to Calvinists; all ecclesiastical authority is annihilated. Nobody knows anything of canons, popes, councils; everything is swallowed up in the authority of one man." "The king willeth it;" France had no other law any longer; and William III. saved Europe from the same enslavement.

The Palatinate was in flames; Louvois was urging on the generals and armies everywhere, sending despatch after despatch, orders upon orders. "I am a thousand times more impatient to finish this business than you can be," was the spirited reply he received from M. de la Hoguette who commanded in Italy in the environs of Cuneo; "besides the reasons of duty which I have always before my eyes, I beg you to believe that the last letters I received from you were quite strong enough to prevent negligence of anything that must be done to prevent similar ones and to deserve a little more confidence; but the most willing man can do nothing against roads encumbered with ice and snow." Louvois did not admit this excuse; he wanted soldiers to be able to cross the defiles of mountains in the depths of winter just as he would have orange-trees travel in the month of February. "I received orders to send off to Versailles from La Meilleraye the orange-trees which the duke of Mazarin gave the king," writes Superintendent Foucauld in his journal. "M. Louvois, in spite of the representations I made him, would have them sent by carriage through the snow and ice; they arrived leafless at Versailles, and several are dead. I had sent him word that the king could take towns in winter, but could not make orange-trees bear removal from their hothouses." The nature and the consciences of the Protestants were all that withstood Louis XIV. and Louvois. On the 16th of July, 1691, death suddenly removed the minister, fallen in royal favor, detested and dreaded in France, universally hated in Europe, leaving, however, the king, France and Europe with the feeling that a great power had fallen, a great deal of merit disappeared. "I doubt not," wrote Louis XIV. to Marshal Boufflers, "that, as you are very zealous for my service, you will be sorry for the death of a man who served me well." "Louvois," said the marquis of La Fare, "should never have been born or should have lived longer." The public feeling was expressed in an anonymous epitaph:

> "Here lieth he who to his will
> Bent every one, knew everything:
> Louvois, beloved by no one, still
> Leaves everybody sorrowing."

The king felt his loss, but did not regret the minister whose tyranny and violence were beginning to be oppressive to him: he felt himself to be more than ever master in the presence of the young or inexperienced men to whom he henceforth entrusted his affairs. Louvois' son, Barbezieux, had the reversion of the war-department; Pontchartrain, who had been comptroller of finance ever since the retirement of Lepelletier, had been appointed to the navy in 1690 at the death of Seignelay. "M. de Pontchartrain had begged the king not to give him the navy," says Dangeau ingenuously, "because he knew nothing at all about it, but the king's will was absolute that he should take it. He now has all that M. de Colbert had, except the buildments." What mattered the inexperience of ministers? The king thought that he alone sufficed for all.

God had left it to time to undeceive the all-powerful monarch; he alone held out amidst the ruins: after the fathers the sons were falling around him, Seignelay had followed Colbert to the tomb; Louvois was dead after Michael Le Tellier; Barbezieux died in his turn in 1701. "This secretary of state had naturally good wits, lively and ready conception, and great mastery of details in which his father had trained him early," writes the marquis of Argenson. He had been spoilt in youth by everybody but his father. He was obliged to put himself at the mercy of his officials, but he always kept up his position over them, for the son of M. de Louvois, their creator so to speak, could not fail to inspire them with respect, veneration and even attachment. Louis XIV., who knew the defects of M. de Barbezieux, complained to him and sometimes rated him in private, but he left him his place, because he felt the importance of preserving in the administration of war the spirit and the principles of Louvois. "Take him for all in all," says St. Simon, "he had the making of a great minister in him, but wonderfully dangerous; the best and most useful friend in the world so long as he was one, and the most terrible, the most inveterate, the most implacable and naturally ferocious enemy; he was a man who would not brook opposition in anything and whose audacity was extreme." A worthy son of Louvois, as devoted to pleasure as he was zealous in business, he was carried off in five days at the age of thirty-three. The king, who had just put Chamillard into the place of Pontchartrain, made chancellor at the death of Boucherat, gave him the war department in succession to Barbezieux, "thus loading such weak shoulders with two burdens of which either was sufficient to break down the strongest."

Louis XIV. had been faithfully and mightily served by Colbert and Louvois; he had felt confidence in them, though he had never had any liking for them personally; their striking merits, the independence of their character which peeped out in spite of affected expressions of submission and deference, the spirited opposition of the one and the passionate outbursts of the other often hurt the master's pride and always made him uncomfortable; Colbert had preceded him in the government, and Louvois, whom he believed himself to have trained, had surpassed him in knowledge of affairs as well as aptitude for work; Chamillard was the first, the only one of his ministers whom the king had ever loved. "His capacity was nil," says St. Simon, who had very friendly feelings towards Chamillard, "and he believed that he knew everything and of every sort; this was the more pitiable in that it had got into his head with his promotions and was less presumption than stupidity, and still less vanity, of which he had none. The joke is that the mainspring of the king's great affection for him was this very incapacity. He confessed it to the king at every step, and the king was delighted to direct and instruct him; in such sort that he grew jealous for his success as if it were his own and made every excuse for him."

The king loved Chamillard; the court bore with him because he was easy and good-natured, but the affairs of the State were imperilled in his hands; Pontchartrain had already had recourse to the most objectionable proceedings in order to obtain money; the mental resources of Colbert himself had failed in presence of financial embarrassments and increasing estimates. It is said that, during the war with Holland, Louvois induced the king to contract a loan; the premier-president, Lamoignon, supported the measure. "You are triumphant," said Colbert, who had vigorously opposed it; "you think you have done the deed of a good man; what! did not I know as well as you that the king could get money by borrowing? But I was careful not to say so. And so the borrowing road is opened. What means will remain henceforth of checking the king in his expenditure? After the loans, taxes will be wanted to pay them; and, if the loans have no limit, the taxes will have none either." At the king's death the loans amounted to more than two milliards and a half, the deficit was getting worse and worse every day, there was no more money to be had, and the income from property went on diminishing, "I have only some dirty acres which are turning to stones instead of being bread," wrote Madame de Sévigné. Trade was languishing, the manufactures founded by Colbert were dropping away one after another; the revocation of the edict of Nantes and the emigration of Protestants had drained France of the most industrious and most skilful workmen; many of the reformers had carried away a great deal of capital; the roads, everywhere neglected, were becoming impracticable. "The tradesmen are obliged to put four horses instead of two to their wagons," said a letter to Barbezieux from the superintendent of Flanders, "which has completely ruined the traffic." The administration of the provinces was no longer under supervision. "Formerly," says Villars, "the inspectors would pass whole winters on the frontiers; now they are good for nothing but to take the height and measure of the men and send a fine list to the court." The soldiers were without victuals, the officers were not paid, the abuses but lately put down by the strong hand of Colbert and Louvois were cropping up again in all directions; the king at last determined to listen to the general cry and dismiss Chamillard.

"The dukes of Beauvilliers and Chevreuse were entrusted with this unpleasant commission, as well as with the king's assurance of his affection and esteem for Chamillard, and with the announcement of the marks thereof he intended to bestow upon him. They entered Chamillard's presence with such an air of consternation as may be easily imagined, they having always been very great friends of his. By their manner the unhappy minister saw at once that there was something extraordinary, and, without giving them time to speak, 'What is the matter, gentlemen?' he said with a calm and serene countenance. 'If what you have to say concerns me only you can speak out, I have been prepared a long while for anything.' They could scarcely tell what brought them. Chamillard heard them without changing a muscle, and with the same air and tone with which he had put his first question, he answered: 'The king is master. I have done my best to serve him; I hope another may do it more to his satisfaction and more successfully. It is much to be able to count upon his kindness and to receive so many marks of it.' Then he asked whether he might write to him, and whether they would do him the favor of taking charge of his letter. He wrote the king, with the same coolness, a page and a half of thanks and regards, which he read out to them at once just as he had at once written it in their presence. He handed it to the two dukes, together with the memorandum which the king had asked him for in the morning, and which he had just finished, sent word orally to his wife to come after him to L'Étang, whither he was going, without telling her why, sorted out his papers, and gave up his keys to be handed to his successor. All this was done without the slightest excitement; without a sigh, a regret, a reproach, a complaint escaping him, he went down his staircase, got into his carriage and started off to L'Étang, alone with his son, just as if nothing had happened to him, without anybody's knowing anything about it at Versailles until long afterwards" [*Mémoires de St. Simon*, t. iii. p. 233].

Desmarets in the finance and Voysin in the war department, both superintendents of finance, the former a nephew of Colbert's and initiated into business by his uncle, both of them capable and assiduous, succumbed, like their predecessors, beneath the weight of the burdens which were overwhelming and ruining France. "I know the state of my finances," Louis XIV. had said to Desmarets, "I do not ask you to do impossibilities; if you succeed, you will render me a great service: if you are not successful, I shall not hold you to blame for circumstances." Desmarets succeeded better than could have been expected without being able to rehabilitate the finances of the State. Pontchartrain had exhausted the resource of creating new offices. "Every time your Majesty creates a new post, a fool is bound to buy it," he had said to the king. Desmarets had recourse to the bankers; and the king seconded him by the gracious favor with which he received at Versailles the greatest of the collectors (*traitants*), Samuel Bernard. "By this means everything was provided for up to the time of the general peace," says M. de Argenson. France kept up the contest to the end. When the treaty of Utrecht was signed, the fleet was ruined and destroyed, the trade diminished by two thirds, the colonies lost or devastated by the war, the destitution in the country so frightful that orders had to be given to sow seed in the fields; the exportation of grain was forbidden on pain of death; meanwhile the peasantry were reduced to browse upon the grass in the roads and to tear the bark off the trees and eat it. Thirty years had rolled by since the death of Colbert, twenty-two since that of Louvois; everything was going to perdition simultaneously; reverses in war and distress at home were uniting to overwhelm the aged king, alone upstanding amidst so many dead and so much ruin. "Fifty years' sway and glory had inspired Louis XIV. with the presumptuous belief that he could not only choose his ministers well but also instruct them and teach them their craft," says M. D'Argenson. His mistake was to think that the title of king supplied all the endowments of nature or experience; he was no financier, no soldier, no administrator, yet he would everywhere and always remain supreme master; he had believed that it was he who governed with Colbert and Louvois; those two great ministers had scarcely been equal to the task imposed upon them by war and peace, by armies, buildments and royal extravagance; their successors gave way thereunder and illusions vanished; the king's hand was powerless to sustain the weight of affairs becoming more and more disastrous; the gloom that pervaded the later years of Louis XIV.'s reign veiled from his people's eyes the splendor of that reign which had so long been brilliant and prosperous, though always lying heavy on the nation, even when they forgot their sufferings in the intoxication of glory and success.

It is the misfortune of men, even of the greatest, to fall short of their destiny. Louis XIV. had wanted to exceed his and to bear a burden too heavy for human shoulders. Arbiter, for a while, of the affairs of all Europe, ever absolute master in his own dominions, he bent at last beneath the load that was borne without flinching by princes less powerful, less fortunate, less adored, but sustained by the strong institutions of free countries. William III. had not to serve him a Condé, a Turenne, a Colbert, a Louvois; he had governed from afar his own country and he had always remained a foreigner in the kingdom which had called him to the throne; but, despite the dislikes, the bitternesses, the fierce contests of parties, he had strengthened the foundations of parliamentary government in England and maintained freedom in Holland, whilst the ancient monarchy of France, which reached under Louis XIV. the pinnacle of glory and power, was slowly but surely going down to perdition beneath the internal and secret malady of absolute power, without limit and without restraint.

CHAPTER XLVII.

LOUIS XIV. AND RELIGION.

INDEPENDENTLY of simple submission to the Catholic Church, there were three great tendencies which divided serious minds amongst them during the reign of Louis XIV.; three noble passions held possession of pious souls; liberty, faith, and love were, respectively, the groundwork as well as the banner of Protestantism, Jansenism, and Quietism. It was in the name of the fundamental and innate liberty of the soul, its personal responsibility and its direct relations with God that the Reformation had sprung up and reached growth in France, even more than in Germany and in England. M. de St. Cyran, the head and founder of Jansenism, abandoned the human soul unreservedly to the supreme will of God; his faith soared triumphant over flesh and blood, and his disciples, disdaining the joys and the ties of earth, lived only for eternity. Madame

Guyon and Fénelon, less ardent and less austere, discovered in the tender mysticism of *pure love* that secret of God's which is sought by all pious souls; in the name of divine love, the Quietists renounced all will of their own, just as the Jansenists in the name of faith.

Jansenism is dead after having for a long while brooded in the depths of the most noble souls; Quietism, as a sect, did not survive its illustrious founders; faith and love have withstood the excess of zeal and the erroneous tendencies which had separated them from the aggregate of Christian virtues and doctrines; they have come back again into the pious treasury of the universal Church. Neither time nor persecutions have been able to destroy in France the strong and independent groundwork of Protestantism. Faithful to its fundamental principle, it has triumphed over exile, the scaffold and indifference, without other head than God himself and God alone.

Richelieu had slain the political hydra of Huguenots in France; from that time the reformers had lived in modest retirement. "I have no complaint to make of the little flock," Mazarin would say: "if they eat bad grass, at any rate they do not stray." During the troubles of the Fronde, the Protestants had resumed, in the popular vocabulary, their old nickname of *Tant s'en fault* (*Far from it*), which had been given them at the time of the League. "Faithful to the king in those hard times when most Frenchmen were wavering and continually looking to see which way the wind would blow, the Huguenots had been called *Tant s'en fault*, as being removed from and beyond all suspicion of the League or of conspiracy against the State. And so were they rightly designated, inasmuch as to the cry 'Qui vive?' (Whom are you for?) instead of answering 'Vive Guise!' or 'Vive la Ligue!' they would answer, 'Tant s'en fault, vive le Roi!' So that, when one Leaguer would ask another, pointing to a Huguenot, 'Is that one of ours?' '*Tant s'en fault*,' would be the reply, 'it is one of the new religion.'" Condé had represented to Cromwell all the reformers of France as ready to rise in his favor; the agent sent by the Protector assured him it was quite the contrary; and the bearing of the Protestants decided Cromwell to refuse all assistance to the princes. La Rochelle packed off its governor, who was favorable to the Fronde; St. Jean d'Angely equipped soldiers for the king; Montauban, to resist the Frondeurs, repaired the fortifications thrown down by Richelieu. "The crown was tottering upon the king's head," said Count d'Harcourt to the pastors of Guienne, "but you have made it secure." The royal declaration of 1652, confirming and ratifying the edict of Nantes, was a recompense for the services and fidelity of the Huguenots. They did not enjoy it long; an edict of 1656 annulled, at the same time explaining, the favorable declaration of 1652; in 1660, the last national synod was held at Loudun. "His Majesty has resolved," said M. de la Magdelaine, deputed from the king to the synod, "that there shall be no more such assemblies but when he considers it expedient." Fifteen years had rolled by since the synod of Charenton in 1645. "We are only too firmly persuaded of the usefulness of our synods and how entirely necessary they are for our churches, after having been so long without them," sorrowfully exclaimed the moderator, Peter Daillé. For two hundred and twelve years the reformed Church of France was deprived of its synods. God at last restored to it this corner-stone of its interior constitution.

The suppression of the edict-chambers instituted by Henry IV. in all the parliaments for the purpose of taking cognizance of the affairs of the reformers followed close upon the abolition of national synods. Peter du Bosq, pastor of the church of Cæn, an accomplished gentleman and celebrated preacher, was commissioned to set before the king the representations of the Protestants. Louis XIV. listened to him kindly. "That is the finest speaker in my kingdom," he said to his courtiers after the minister's address. The edict-chambers were, nevertheless, suppressed in 1669; the half-and-half (*mi-partie*) chambers, composed of reformed and catholic councillors, underwent the same fate in 1679, and the Protestants found themselves delivered over to the intolerance and religious prejudices of the parliaments, which were almost everywhere harsher, as regarded them, than the governors and superintendents of provinces.

"It seemed to me, my son," wrote Louis XIV. in his *Mémoires* of the year 1661, "that those who were for employing violent remedies against the religion styled reformed did not understand the nature of this malady, caused partly by heated feelings which should be passed over unnoticed and allowed to die out insensibly instead of being inflamed afresh by equally strong contradiction, which, moreover, is always useless, when the taint is not confined to a certain known number but spread throughout the State. I thought, therefore, that the best way of reducing the Huguenots of my kingdom little by little was, in the first place, not to put any pressure upon them by any fresh rigor against them, to see to the observance of all that they had obtained from my predecessors, but to grant them nothing further and even to confine the performance thereof within the narrowest limits that justice and propriety would permit. But as to graces that depended upon me alone, I have resolved, and I have pretty regularly kept my resolution ever since, not to do them any, and that from kindness, not from bitterness, in order to force them in that way to reflect from time to time of themselves and without violence whether it were for any good reason that they deprived themselves voluntarily of advantages which might be shared by them in common with all my other subjects."

These prudent measures "quite in kindness and not in bitterness" were not enough to satisfy the fresh zeal with which the king had been inspired. All powerful in his own kingdom and triumphant everywhere in Europe, he was quite shocked at the silent obstinacy of those Huguenots who held his favor and graces cheap in comparison with a quiet conscience; his kingly pride and his ignorant piety both equally urged him on to that enterprise which was demanded by the zeal of a portion of the clergy. The system of purchasing conversions had been commenced; and Pellisson, himself originally a Protestant, had charge of the payments, a source of fraud and hypocrisies of every sort. A declaration of 1679 condemned the *relapsed* to *honorable amends* (public recantation, &c.), to confiscation and to banishment. The doors of all employments were closed against Huguenots; they could no longer sit in the courts or parliaments, or administer the finances, or become medical practitioners, barristers or notaries; infants of seven years of age were empowered to change their religion against their parents' will; a word, a gesture, a look were sufficient to certify that a child intended to abjure; its parents, however, were bound to bring it up according to its condition, which often facilitated confiscation of property. Pastors were forbidden to enter the houses of their flocks, save to perform some act of their ministry; every chapel into which a new convert had been admitted was to be pulled down and the pastor was to be banished. It was found necessary to set a guard at the doors of the places of worship to drive away the poor wretches who repented of a moment's weakness; the number of "places of exercise," as the phrase then was, received a gradual reduction; "a single minister had the charge of six, eight, and ten thousand persons," says Elias Benoît, author of the *Histoire de l'Édit de Nantes*, making it impossible for him to visit and assist the families, scattered sometimes over a distance of thirty leagues round his own residence. The wish was to reduce the ministers to give up altogether from despair of discharging their functions. The chancellor had expressly said: "If you are reduced to the impossible, so much the worse for you, we shall gain by it." Oppression was not sufficient to break down the reformers. There was great difficulty in checking emigration, by this time increasing in numbers. Louvois proposed stronger measures. The population was crushed under the burden of military billets. Louvois wrote to Marillac, superintendent of Poitou: "His Majesty has learnt with much joy the number of people who continue to become converts in your department. He desires you to go on paying attention thereto; he will think it a good idea to have most of the cavalry and officers quartered upon Protestants; if, according to the regular proportion, the religionists should receive ten, you can make them take twenty." The dragoons took up their quarters in peaceable families, ruining the more well-to-do, maltreating old men, women and children, striking them with their sticks or the flat of their swords, hauling off Protestants in the churches by the hair of their heads, harnessing laborers to their own plows and goading them like oxen. Conversions became numerous in Poitou. Those who could fly left France, at the risk of being hanged if the attempt happened to fail. "Pray lay out advantageously the money you are going to have," wrote Madame de Maintenon to her brother, M. d'Aubigné: "land in Poitou is to be had for nothing, and the desolation amongst the Protestants will cause more sales still. You may easily settle in grand style in that province." "We are treated like enemies of the Christian denomination," wrote, in 1662, a minister named Jurieu, already a refugee in Holland. "We are forbidden to go near the children that come into the world, we are banished from the bars and the faculties; we are forbidden the use of all the means which might save us from hunger, we are abandoned to the hatred of the mob, we are deprived of that precious liberty which we purchased with so many services; we are robbed of our children, who are a part of ourselves. . . . Are we Turks? Are we infidels? We believe in Jesus Christ, *we* do; we believe Him to be the Eternal Son of God, the Redeemer of the world; the maxims of our morality are of so great purity that none dare gainsay them; we respect the king, we are good subjects, good citizens; we are Frenchmen as much as we are reformed Christians."

Jurieu had a right to speak of the respect for the king which animated the French Reformers; there was no trace left of that political leaven which formerly animated the old Huguenots and made Duke Henry de Rohan say, "You are all republicans; I would rather have to do with a pack of wolves than an assembly of parsons." "The king is hoodwinked," the Protestants declared: and all their efforts were to get at him and tell his Majesty of their sufferings. The army remained open to them, though without hope of promotion; and the gentlemen showed alacrity in serving the king. "What a position is ours!" they would say; "if we make any resistance, we are treated as rebels; if we are obedient, they pretend we are converted, and they hoodwink the king by means of our very submission."

The misfortunes were redoubling. From Poitou the persecution had extended through all the provinces. Superintendent Foucauld obtained the conversion in mass of the province of Béarn. "He egged on the soldiers to torture the inhabitants of the houses they were quartered in, commanding them to keep awake all those who would not give in to other tortures. The dragoons relieved one another so as not to succumb themselves to the punishment they were making others undergo. Beating of drums, blasphemies, shouts, the crash of furniture which they hurled from side to side, commotion in which they kept these poor people in order to force them to be on their feet and hold their eyes open, were the means they employed to deprive them of rest. To pinch, prick, and haul them about, to lay them upon burning coals, and a hundred other cruelties were the sport of these butchers; all they thought most about was how to find tortures which should be painful without being deadly, reducing their hosts thereby to such a state that they knew not what they were doing and promised anything that was wanted of them in order to escape from those barbarous hands." Languedoc, Guienne, Angoumois, Saintonge, all the provinces in which the reformers were numerous, underwent the same fate. The self-restraining character of the Norman people, their respect for law were manifested even amidst persecution; the children were torn away from Protestant families and the chapels were demolished by act of parliament; the soldiery were less violent than elsewhere, but the magistrates were more inveterate. "God has not judged us unworthy to suffer ignominy for His name," said the ministers condemned by the parliament for having performed the offices of their ministry. "The king has taken no cognizance of the case," exclaimed one of the accused, Legendre, pastor of Rouen; "he has relied upon the judges; it is not his Majesty who shall give account before God, you shall be responsible and you alone; you who, convinced as you are of our innocence, have nevertheless condemned us and branded us." "The parliament of Normandy has just broken the ties which held us bound to our churches," said Peter du Bosq. The banished ministers took the road to Holland. The seaboard provinces were beginning to be dispeopled. A momentary disturbance, which led to belief in a rising of the reformers in the Cévennes and the Vivarais, served as pretext for redoubled rigor. Dauphiny and Languedoc were given up to the soldiery; murder was no longer forbidden them, it was merely punishing rebels; several pastors were sentenced to death; Homel, minister of Soyon in the Vivarais, seventy-five years of age, was broken alive on the wheel. Abjurations multiplied through terror. "There have been sixty thousand conversions in the jurisdiction of Bordeaux and twenty thousand in that of Montauban," wrote Louvois to his father in the first part of September, 1685: "the rapidity with which this goes on is such that, before the end of the month, there will not remain ten thousand religionists in the district of Bordeaux, in which there were a hundred and fifty thousand on the 15th of last month." "The towns of Nîmes, Alais, Uzès, Villeneuve and some others are entirely converted," writes the duke of Noailles to Louvois in the month of October, 1685; "those of most note in Nîmes made abjuration in church the day after our arrival. There was then a lukewarmness, but matters were put in good train again by means of some billets that I had put into the houses of the most obstinate. I am making arrangements for going and scouring the Cévennes with the seven companies of Barbezieux, and my head shall answer for it that before the 25th of November not a Huguenot shall be left there." And a few days later, at Alais, "I no longer know what to do with the troops, for the places in which I had meant to post them get converted all in a body, and this goes on so quickly that all the men can do is to sleep for a night at the localities to which I send them. It is certain that you may add very nearly a third to the estimate given you of the people of the religion, amounting to the number of a hundred and eighty-two thousand men, and, when I asked you to give me until the 25th of next month for their complete conversion, I took too long a term, for I believe that by the end of the month all will be settled. I will not, however, omit to tell you that all we have done in these conversions will be nothing but useless, if the king do not oblige the bishops to send good priests to instruct the people who want to hear the Gospel preached. But I fear that the king will be worse obeyed in that respect by the priests than by the religionists. I do not tell you this without grounds." "There is not a courier who does not bring the king great causes for joy," writes Madame de Maintenon, "that is to say, conversions by thousands. I can quite believe that all these conversions are not sincere, but God makes use of all ways of bringing back heretics. Their children, at any rate, will be Catholics, their outward re-union places them within reach of the truth; pray God to enlighten them all; there is nothing the king has more at heart."

In the month of August, 1684, she said: "The king has a design for laboring for the entire conversion of the heretics; he often has conferences about it with M. Le Tellier and M. de Châteauneuf, whereat I was given to understand that I should not be one too many. M. de Châteauneuf proposed measures which are not expedient. There must be no precipitation; it must be conversion, not persecution. M. de Louvois was for gentleness, which is not in accordance with his nature and his eagerness to see matters ended. The king is ready to do what is thought most likely to conduce to the good of religion. Such an achievement will cover him with glory before God and before men. He will have brought back all his subjects into the bosom of the Church and will have destroyed the heresy which his predecessors could not vanquish."

The king's glory was about to be complete: the *gentleness* of Louvois had prevailed; he had found himself obliged to moderate the zeal of his superintendents; "nothing remained but to weed out the religionists of the small towns and villages;" by stretching a point the process had been carried into the principality of Orange, which still belonged to the House of Nassau, on the pretext that the people of that district had received in their chapels the king's subjects. The count of Tessé, who had charge of the expedition, wrote to Louvois: "Not only, on one and the same day, did the whole town of Orange become converted, but the State took the same resolution, and the members of the parliament, who were minded to distinguish themselves by a little more stubbornness, adopted the same course twenty-four hours afterwards. All this was done gently, without violence or disorder. There is only a parson named Chambrun, patriarch of the district, who persists in refusing to listen to reason; for the president, who did aspire to the honor of martyrdom, would, as well as the rest of the parliament, have turned Mohammedan, if I had desired it. You would not believe how infatuated all these people were and are still about the prince of Orange, his authority, Holland, England, and the Protestants of Germany. I should never end if I were to recount all the foolish and impertinent proposals they have made to me." M. de Tessé did not tell Louvois that he was obliged to have the pastors of Orange seized and carried off; they were kept twelve years in prison at Pierre-Encise, none but M. de Chambrun, who had been taken to Valence, managed to escape and take refuge in Holland, bemoaning to the end of his days a moment's weakness. "I was quite exhausted by torture, and I let fall this unhappy expression: 'Very well, then, I will be reconciled.' This sin has brought me down at it were into hell itself, and I have looked upon myself as a dastardly soldier who turned his back on the day of battle and as an unfaithful servant who betrayed the interests of his master."

The king assembled his council: the lists of converts were so long that there could scarcely remain in the kingdom more than a few thousand recalcitrants. "His Majesty proposed to take an ultimate resolution as regarded the Edict of Nantes," writes the duke of Burgundy in a memorandum found amongst his papers: "Monseigneur represented that, according to an anonymous letter he had received the day before, the Huguenots had some expectation of what was coming upon them, that there was perhaps some reason to fear that they would take up arms, relying upon the protection of the princes of their religion, and that, supposing they dared not do so, a great number would leave the kingdom, which would be injurious to commerce and agriculture and, for that same reason, would weaken the State. The king replied that he had foreseen all for some time past and had provided for all; that nothing in the world would be more painful to him than to shed a single drop of the blood of his subjects, but that he had armies and good generals whom he would employ in case of need against rebels who courted their own destruction. As for calculations of interest, he thought them worthy of but little consideration in comparison with the advantages of a measure which would restore to religion its splendor, to the State its tranquillity and to authority all its rights. A resolution was carried unanimously for the suppression of the Edict of Nantes." The declaration, drawn up by Chancellor Le Tellier and Châteauneuf, was signed by the king on the 15th of October, 1685; it was despatched on the 17th to all the superintendents. The edict of pacification, that great work of the liberal and prudent genius of Henry IV., respected and confirmed in its most important particulars by Cardinal Richelieu, recognized over and over again by Louis XIV. himself, disappeared at a single stroke, carrying with it all hope of liberty, repose and justice for fifteen hundred thousand subjects of the king. "Our pains," said the preamble of the Edict, "have had the end we had proposed, seeing that the better and the greater part of our subjects of the religion styled reformed have embraced the catholic; the execution of the Edict of Nantes, consequently remaining useless, we have considered that we could not do better, for the purpose of effacing entirely the memory of the evils which this false religion has caused in our kingdom, than revoke entirely the aforesaid Edict of Nantes and all that has been done in favor of the said religion."

The Edict of October 15, 1685, supposed the religion styled reformed to be already destroyed and abolished. It ordered the demolition of all the chapels that remained standing and interdicted any assembly or worship; *recalcitrant* (*opiniâtres*) ministers were ordered to leave the kingdom within fifteen days; the schools were closed; all new-born babies were to be baptized by the parish-priests; religionists were forbidden to leave the kingdom on pain of the galleys for the men and confiscation of person and property for the women. "The will of the king," said Superintendent Marillac at Rouen, "is that there be no more than one religion in this kingdom; it is for the glory of God and the well-being of the State." Two hours were allowed the reformers of Rouen for making their abjuration.

One clause, at the end of the edict of October 15, seemed to extenuate its effect: "Those of our subjects of the religion styled reformed who shall persist in their errors, pending the time when it may please God to enlighten them like the rest, shall be allowed to remain in the kingdom, country and lands which obey the king, there to continue their trade and enjoy their property without being liable to be vexed or hindered on pretext of prayer or worship of the said religion of whatsoever nature they may be." "Never was there illusion more cruel than that which this clause caused people," says Benoît in his *Histoire dé l'Édit de Nantes :* "it was believed that the king meant only to forbid special exercises, but that he intended to leave conscience free, since he granted this grace to all those who were still reformers, pending the time when it should please God to enlighten them. Many gave up the measures they had taken for leaving the country with their families, many voluntarily returned from the retreats where they had hitherto been fortunate enough to lie hid. The most mistrustful dared not suppose that so solemn a promise was only made to be broken on the morrow. They were all, nevertheless, mistaken; and those who were imprudent enough to return to their homes were only just in time to receive the dragoons there." A letter from Louvois to the duke of Noailles put a stop to all illusion. "I have no doubt," he wrote, "that some rather heavy billets upon the few amongst the nobility and third estate still remaining of the religionists will undeceive them as to the mistake they are under about the Edict M. de Châteauneuf drew up for us; his Majesty desires that you should explain yourself very sternly and that extreme severity should be employed against those who are not willing to become of his religion; those who have the silly vanity to glory in holding out to the last must be driven to extremity." The pride of Louis XIV. was engaged in the struggle; those of his subjects who refused to sacrifice their religion to him were disobedient, rebellious and besotted with *silly vanity.* "It will be quite ridiculous before long to be of that religion," wrote Madame de Maintenon.

Even in his court and amongst his most useful servants the king encountered unexpected opposition. Marshal Schomberg with great difficulty obtained authority to leave the kingdom; Duquesne was refused. The illustrious old man, whom the Algerian corsairs called "the old French captain, whose bride is the sea and whom the angel of death has forgotten," received permission to reside in France without being troubled about his religion. "For sixty years I have rendered to Cæsar that which was Cæsar's," said the sailor proudly, "it is time to render unto God that which is God's." And, when the king regretted that his religion prevented him from properly recognizing his glorious career: "Sir," said Duquesne,

"I am a Protestant, but I always thought that my services were catholic." Duquesne's children went abroad. When he died, 1688, his body was refused to them. His sons raised a monument to him at Aubonne, in the canton of Berne, with this inscription: "This tomb awaits the remains of Duquesne. Passer, should you ask why the Hollanders have raised a superb monument to Ruyter vanquished, and why the French have refused a tomb to Ruyter's vanquisher, the fear and respect inspired by a monarch whose power extends afar do not allow me to answer."

Of the rest, only the marquis of Ruvigny and the princess of Tarento, daughter-in-law of the duke of La Trémoille and issue of the House of Hesse, obtained authority to leave France. All ports were closed, all frontiers watched. The great lords gave way, one after another; accustomed to enjoy royal favors, attaching to them excessive value, living at court, close to Paris which was spared a great deal during the persecution, they, without much effort, renounced a faith which closed to them henceforth the door to all officers and all honors. The gentlemen of the provinces were more resolute; many realized as much as they could of their property and went abroad, braving all dangers, even that of the galleys in case of arrest. The duke of La Force had abjured, then repented of his abjuration, only to relapse again; one of his cousins, seventy-five years of age, was taken to the galleys: he had for his companion Louis de Marolles, late king's councillor. "I live just now all alone," wrote the latter to his wife: "my meals are brought from outside; if you saw me in my beautiful convict-dress, you would be charmed. The iron I wear on my leg, though it weighs only three pounds, inconvenienced me at first far more than that which you saw me in at La Tournelle." Files of Protestant galley-convicts were halted in the towns, in the hope of inspiring the obstinate with a salutary terror.

The error which had been fallen into, however, was perceived at court. The stand made by Protestants astounded the superintendents as well as Louvois himself. Everywhere men said as they said at Dieppe: "We will not change our religion for anybody; the king has power over our persons and our property, but he has no power over our consciences." There was fleeing in all directions. The governors grew weary of watching the coasts and the frontiers. "The way to make only a few go," said Louvois, "is to leave them liberty to do so without letting them know it." Any way was good enough to escape from such oppression. "Two days ago," wrote M. de Tessé, who commanded at Grenoble, "a woman, to get safe away, hit upon an invention which deserves to be known. She made a bargain with a Savoyard, an ironmonger, and had herself packed up in a load of iron rods, the ends of which showed; it was carried to the custom house, and the tradesman paid on the weight of the iron which was weighed together with the woman, who was not unpacked until she was six leagues from the frontier." "For a long time," says M. Floquet, "there was talk in Normandy of the count of Marancé, who, in the middle of a severe winter, flying with thirty-nine others on board a fishing-smack, encountered a tempest and remained a long time at sea, without provisions, dying of hunger, he, the countess and all the passengers, amongst whom were pregnant women, mothers with infants at the breast, without resources of any sort, reduced for lack of everything to a little melted snow with which they moistened the parched lips of the dying babes." It were impossible to estimate precisely the number of emigrations; it was probably between three and four hundred thousand. "To speak only of our own province," writes M. Floquet in his *Histoire du Parlement de Normandie*, "about 184,000 religionists went away; more than 26,000 habitations were deserted; in Rouen there were counted no more than 60,000 men instead of the 80,000 that were to be seen there a few years before. Almost all trade was stopped there as well as in the rest of Normandy. The little amount of manufacture that was possible rotted away on the spot for want of transport to foreign countries, whence vessels were no longer found to come; Rouen, Darnetal, Elbeuf, Louviers, Caudebec, Le Havre, Pont-Audemer, Cæn, St. Lô, Alençon and Bayeux were falling into decay, the different branches of trade and industry which had but lately been seen flourishing there having perished through the emigration of the masters whom their skilled workmen followed in shoals." The Norman emigration had been very numerous, thanks to the extent of its coasts and to the habitual communication between Normandy, England and Holland; Vauban, however, remained very far from the truth when he deplored, in 1688, "the desertion of 100,000 men, the withdrawal from the kingdom of sixty millions of livres, the enemy's fleets swelled by 9000 sailors, the best in the kingdom, and the enemy's armies by

600 officers and 12,000 soldiers, who had seen service." It is a natural but a striking fact that the reformers who left France and were received with open arms in Brandenburg, Holland, England and Switzerland carried in their hearts a profound hatred for the king who drove them away from their country and everywhere took service against him, whilst the Protestants who remained in France, bound to the soil by a thousand indissoluble ties, continued at the same time to be submissive and faithful. "It is right," said Chanlay in a *Mémoire* addressed to the king, "whilst we condemn the conduct of the new converts, fugitives, who have borne arms against France since the commencement of this war up to the present, it is right, say I, to give those who have stayed in France the praise and credit they deserve. Indeed, if we except a few disturbances of little consequence which have taken place in Languedoc, we have, besides the fact of their remaining faithful to the king in the provinces and especially in Dauphiny, even whilst the confederated armies of the emperor, of Spain and of the duke of Savoy were in the heart of that province, in greater strength than the forces of the king, to note that those who were fit to bear arms have enlisted amongst the troops of his Majesty and done good service." In 1745, after sixty years' persecution, consequent upon the revocation of the Edict of Nantes, Matthew Désubas, a young pastor accused before the superintendent of Languedoc, Lenain, said with high-spirited modesty: "The ministers preach nothing but patience and fidelity to the king." "I am aware of it, sir," answered the superintendent. The pastors were hanged or burned, the faithful flock dragged to the galleys and the tower of Constance; prayers for the king, nevertheless, were sent up from the proscribed assemblies in the desert, whilst the pulpit of Saurin at the Hague resounded with his anathemas against Louis XIV. and the regiments of emigrant Huguenots were marching against the king's troops, under the flags of England or Holland.

The peace of Ryswick had not brought the Protestants the hoped for alleviation of their woes. Louis XIV. haughtily rejected the petition of the English and Dutch plenipotentiaries on behalf of "those in affliction who ought to have their share in the happiness of Europe." The persecution everywhere continued, with determination and legality in the North, with violence and passion in the South, abandoned to the tyranny of M. de Lamoignon de Bâville, a crafty and coldbloodedly cruel politician, without the excuse of any zealous religious conviction. The execution of several ministers who had remained in hiding in the Cévennes or had returned from exile to instruct and comfort their flocks raised to the highest pitch the enthusiasm of the reformers of Languedoc. Deprived of their highly prized assemblies and of their pastors' guidance, men and women, greybeards and children, all at once fancied themselves animated by the spirit of prophecy. Young girls had celestial visions; the little peasant-lasses poured out their utterances in French, sometimes in the language and with the sublime eloquence of the Bible, sole source of their religious knowledge; the rumor of these marvels ran from village to village; meetings were held to hear the inspired maidens, in contempt of edicts, the galleys and the stake; a gentleman glass-worker, named Abraham de la Serre, was as it were the Samuel of this new school of prophets. In vain did M. de Bâville have three hundred children imprisoned at Uzès, and then send them to the galleys; the religious contagion was too strong for the punishments; "women found themselves in a single day husbandless, childless, houseless and penniless," says Court: they remained immovable in their pious ecstasy; the assemblies multiplied; the troops which had so long occupied Languedoc had been summoned away by the war of succession in Spain; the militia could no longer restrain the reformers growing every day more enthusiastic through the prophetic hopes which were born of their long sufferings. The arch-priest of the Cévennes, Abbé du Chayla, a tyrannical and cruel man, had undertaken a mission at the head of the Capuchins; his house was crammed with condemned Protestants; the breath of revolt passed over the mountains: on the night of July 27, 1702, the castle of the arch-priest was surrounded by Huguenots in arms, who demanded the surrender of the prisoners. Du Chayla refused: the gates were forced, the condemned released, the priests who happened to be in the house killed or dispersed: the arch-priest had let himself down by a window, he broke his thigh: he was found hiding in a bush; the castle was in flames. "No mercy, no mercy," shouted the madmen: "the Spirit willeth that he die." Every one of the Huguenots stabbed the poor wretch with their poniards: "That's for my father broken on the wheel; that's for my brother sent to the galleys; that's for my mother who died of grief; that's for my relations in exile!" He received fifty-two wounds. Next day the Cévennes were everywhere in revolt: a prophet named

Séguier was at the head of the insurrection. He was soon made prisoner. "How dost thou expect me to treat thee?" asked his judge. "As I would have treated thee, had I caught thee," answered the prophet. He was burned alive in the public square of Pont-de-Montvert, a mountain-burgh. "Where do you live?" he had been asked at his examination. "In the desert," he replied "and soon in Heaven." He exhorted the people from the midst of the flames; the insurrection went on spreading. "Say not: what can we do? we are so few, we have no arms!" said another prophet named Laporte: "The Lord of hosts is our strength! We will intone the battle-psalms, and, from the Lozère to the sea, Israel shall arise! And, as for arms, have we not our axes? They will beget muskets!" The plain rose like the mountain; Baron St. Cômes, an early convert and colonel of the militia, was assassinated near Vauvert; murders multiplied: the priests were especially the object of the revolters' vengeance. They assembled under the name of Children of God, and marched under the command of two chiefs, one, named Roland, who formerly served under Catinat, and the other a young man, whiles a baker and whiles a shepherd, who was born in the neighborhood of Anduze and whose name has remained famous: John Cavalier was barely eighteen, when M. de Bâville launched his brother-in-law, the count of Broglie, with a few troops upon the revolted Cévénols. The catholic peasants called them *Camisards*, the origin of which name has never been clearly ascertained. M. de Broglie was beaten; the insurrection, which was entirely confined to the populace, disappeared all at once in the woods and rocks of the country, to burst once more unexpectedly upon the troops of the king. The great name of Lamoignon shielded Bâville; Chamillard had for a long while concealed from Louis XIV. the rising in the Cévennes. He never did know all its gravity. "It is useless," said Madame de Maintenon, "for the king to trouble himself with all the circumstances of this war; it would not cure the mischief and would do him much injury." "Take care," wrote Chamillard to Bâville, on superseding the count of Broglie by Marshal Montrevel, "not to give this business the appearance of a serious war." The rumor of the insurrection in Languedoc, however, began to spread in Europe; conflagrations, murders, executions in cold blood or in the heat of passion, crimes on the part of the insurgents as well as cruelties on the part of judges and generals, succeeded one another uninterruptedly, without the military authorities being able to crush a revolt that it was impossible to put down by terror or punishments. "I take it for a fact," said a letter to Chamillard from M. de Julien, an able captain of irregulars, lately sent into Languedoc to aid the count of Broglie, "that there are not in this district forty who are real converts and are not entirely on the side of the Camisards: I include in that number females as well as males, and the mothers and daughters would give the more striking proofs of their fury if they had the strength of the men. . . . . I will say but one word more, which is, that the children who were in their cradles at the time of the general conversions, as well as those who were four or five years old, are now more Huguenot than the fathers; nobody, however, has set eyes upon any minister: how, then, comes it that they are so Huguenot? Because the fathers and mothers brought them up in those sentiments all the time they were going to mass. You may rely upon it that this will continue for many generations." M. de Julien came to the conclusion that the proper way was to put to the sword all the Protestants of the country districts and burn all the villages. M. de Bâville protested: "It is not a question of exterminating these people," he said, "but of reducing them, of forcing them to fidelity; the king must have industrious people and flourishing districts preserved to him." The opinion of the generals prevailed; the Cévénols were proclaimed outlaws and the pope decreed a crusade against them. The military and religious enthusiasm of the Camisards went on increasing. Cavalier, young and enterprising, divided his time between the boldest attempts at surprise and mystical ecstasies during which he singled out traitors who would have assassinated him or sinners who were not worthy to take part in the Lord's supper. The king's troops ravaged the country, the Camisards by way of reprisal burned the Catholic villages; everywhere the war was becoming horrible; the peaceable inhabitants, Catholic or Protestant, were incessantly changing from wrath to terror. Cavalier, naturally sensible and humane, sometimes sank into despondency. He would fling himself on his knees, crying, "Lord, turn aside the king from following the counsels of the wicked!" and then he would set off again upon a new expedition. The struggle had been going on for two years and Languedoc was a scene of fire and bloodshed. Marshal Montrevel had gained great advantages when the king ordered Villars to put an end to the revolt. "I made up my mind," writes Villars in his *Mémoires*, "to try everything, to employ all sorts of ways except that of ruining one of the finest provinces in the kingdom, and that, if I could bring back the offenders without punishing them, I should preserve the best soldiers there are in the kingdom. They are, said I to myself, Frenchmen, very brave and very strong, three qualities to be considered." "I shall always," he adds, "have two ears for two sides."

"We have to do here with a very extraordinary people," wrote the marshal to Chamillard, soon after his arrival; "It is a people unlike anything I ever knew, all alive, turbulent, hasty, susceptible of light as well as deep impressions, tenacious in its opinions. Add thereto zeal for religion which is as ardent amongst heretics as Catholics, and you will no longer be surprised that we should be often very much embarrassed. There are three sorts of Camisards: the first with whom we might arrange matters by reason of their being weary of the miseries of war. The second, stark mad on the subject of religion, absolutely intractable on that point: the first little boy or little girl that falls a-trembling and declares that the Holy Spirit is speaking to it, all the people believe it, and, if God with all His angels were to come and speak to them, they would not believe them more; people, moreover, on whom the penalty of death makes not the least impression; in battle they thank those who inflict it upon them; they walk to execution singing the praises of God and exhorting those present, insomuch that it has often been necessary to surround the criminals with drums to prevent the pernicious effect of their speeches. Finally, the third: people without religion, accustomed to pillage, to murder, to quarter themselves upon the peasants; a rascalry furious, fanatical and swarming with prophetesses."

Villars had arrived in Languedoc the day after the checks encountered by the Camisards. The despondency and suffering were extreme; and the marshal had Cavalier sounded. "What do you want to lay down your arms?" said the envoy. "Three things," replied the Cévénol chief: "liberty of conscience, the release of our brethren detained in the prisons and the galleys, and, if these demands are refused, permission to quit France with ten thousand persons." The negotiators were entrusted with the most flattering offers for Cavalier. Sensible and yet vain, moved by his country's woes and flattered by the idea of commanding a king's regiment, the young Camisard allowed himself to be won. He repaired formally to Nîmes for an interview with the marshal. "He is a peasant of the lowest grade," wrote Villars to Chamillard, "who is not twenty-two and does not look eighteen; short and with no imposing air, qualities essential for the lower orders, but surprising good sense and firmness. I asked him yesterday how he managed to keep his fellows under: 'Is it possible,' said I, 'that, at your age and not being long used to command, you found no difficulty in often offering to death your own men?' 'No, sir,' said he, 'when it seemed to me just.' 'But whom did you employ to inflict it?' 'The first whom I ordered, and nobody ever hesitated to follow my orders.' I fancy, sir, that you will consider this rather surprising; furthermore, he shows great method in the matter of his supplies and he disposes his troops for an engagement as well as very experienced officers could do. It is a piece of luck if I get such a man away from them."

Cavalier's *fellows* began to escape from his sway; they had hoped for a while that they would get back that liberty for which they had shed their blood. "They are permitted to have public prayer and chant their psalms. No sooner was that known all round," writes Villars, "than behold my madmen rushing up from burghs and castles in the neighborhood, not to surrender but to chant with the rest. The gates were closed; they leap the walls and force the guards. It is published abroad that I have indefinitely granted free exercise of the religion." The bishops let the marshal be. "Stuff we our ears," said the bishop of Narbonne, "and make we an end." The Camisards refused to listen to Cavalier. "Thou'rt mad," said Roland, "thou hast betrayed thy brethren; thou shouldst die of shame. Go tell the marshal that I am resolved to remain sword in hand until the entire and complete restoration of the Edict of Nantes!" The Cévénols thought themselves certain of aid from England; only a handful followed Cavalier, who remained faithful to his engagements; he was ordered with his troops to Elsass; he slipped away from his watchers and threw himself into Switzerland. At the head of a regiment of refugees he served successively the duke of Savoy, the States-general and England; he died at Chelsea in 1740, the only one amongst the Camisards to leave a name in the world.

The insurrection still went on in Languedoc under the orders of Roland, who was more fanatical and more disinterested than Cavalier: he was betrayed and surrounded in the castle of Castelnau on the 16th of August, 1704. Roland just had time to leap out of bed and mount his horse; he was taking to flight with his men by a back door when a detachment of dragoons came up with him; the Camisard chief put his back against an old olive and sold his life dearly. When he fell. his lieutenants let themselves be taken "like lambs" beside his corpse. "They were destined to serve as examples," writes Villars, "but the manner in which they met death was more calculated to confirm their religious spirit in these wrong-heads than to destroy it. Lieutenant Maillé was a fine young man of wits above the common. He heard his sentence with a smile, passed through the town of Nîmes with the same air, begging the priest not to plague him; the blows dealt him did not alter this air in the least and did not elicit a single exclamation. His arms broken, he still had strength to make signs to the priest to be off, and, as long as he could speak, he encouraged the others. That made me think that the quickest death is always best with these fellows and that their sentence should above all things bear reference to their obstinacy in revolt rather than in religion." Villars did not carry executions to excess, even in the case of the most stubborn; little by little the chiefs were killed off in petty engagements or died in obscurity of their wounds; provisions were becoming scarce; the country was wasted; submission became more frequent every day. The principals all demanded leave to quit France. "There are left none but a few brigands in the Upper Cévennes," says Villars. Some partial risings alone recalled, up to 1709, the fact that the old leaven still existed; the war of the Camisards was over. It was the sole attempt in history on the part of French Protestantism since Richelieu, a strange and dangerous effort made by an ignorant and savage people, roused to enthusiasm by persecution, believing itself called upon by the spirit of God to win, sword in hand, the freedom of its creed under the leadership of two shepherd-soldiers and prophets. Only the Scottish Cameronians have presented the same mixture of warlike ardor and pious enthusiasm, more gloomy and fierce with the men of the North, more poetical and prophetical with the Cévénols, flowing in Scotland as in Languedoc from religious oppression and from constant reading of the Holy Scriptures. The silence of death succeeded everywhere in France to the plaints of the reformers and to the crash of arms; Louis XIV. might well suppose that Protestantism in his dominions was dead.

It was a little before the time when the last of the Camisards,

Abraham Mazel and Claris, perished near Uzès (in 1710), that the king struck the last blow at Jansenism by destroying its earliest nest and its last refuge, the house of the nuns of Port-Royal des Champs. With truces and intervals of apparent repose, the struggle had lasted more than sixty years between the Jesuits and Jansenism. M. de St. Cyran, who left the Bastille a few months after the death of Richelieu, had dedicated the last days of his life to writing against Protestantism, being so much the more scared by the heresy in that, perhaps, he felt himself attracted thereto by a secret affinity. He was already dying when there appeared the book *Fréquente Communion*, by M. Arnauld, youngest son and twentieth child of that illustrious family of Arnaulds in whom Jansenism seemed to be personified. The author was immediately accused at Rome and buried himself for twenty years in retirement. M. de St. Cyran was still working, dictating Christian thoughts and points touching death. *Stantem mori oportet* (*One should die in harness*), he would say. On the 3rd of Oct., 1643, he succumbed suddenly, in the arms of his friends. "I cast my eyes upon the body which was still in the same posture in which death had left it," writes Lancelot, "and I thought it so full of majesty and of mien so dignified that I could not tire of admiring it, and I fancied that he would still have been capable, in the state in which he was, of striking with awe the most passionate of his foes, had they seen him." It was the most cruel blow that could have fallen upon the pious nuns of Port-Royal. "*Dominus in cœlo! (Lord in Heaven!)*" was all that was said by Mother Angelica Arnauld, who, like M. de St. Cyran himself, centred all her thoughts and all her affections upon eternity.

With his dying breath M. de St. Cryan had said to M. Guérin, physician to the college of Jesuits: "Sir, tell your Fathers, when I am dead, not to triumph, and that I leave behind me a dozen stronger than I." With all his penetration the director of consciences was mistaken: none of those he left behind him would have done his work; he had inspired with the same ardor and the same constancy the strong and the weak, the violent and the pacific; he had breathed his mighty faith into the most diverse souls, fired with the same zeal penitents and nuns, men rescued from the scorching furnace of life in the world and women brought up from infancy in the shade of the cloister. M. Arnauld was a great theologian, an indefatigable controversialist, the oracle and guide of his friends in their struggle against the Jesuits; M. de Sacy and M. Singlin were wise and able directors, as austere as M. de St. Cyran in their requirements, less domineering and less rough than he: but M. de St. Cyran alone was and could be the head of Jansenism; he alone could have inspired that idea of immolation of the whole being to the sovereign will of God, as to the truth which resides in Him alone. Once assured of this point, M. de St. Cyran became immovable. Mother Angelica pressed him to appear before the archbishop's council, which was to pronounce upon his book *Théologie familière.* "It is always good to humble one's self," she said. "As for you," he replied, "who are in that disposition and would not in any respect compromise the honor of the truth, you could do it, but as for me, I should break down before the eyes of God if I consented thereto; the weak are more to be feared sometimes than the wicked."

Mother Angelica Arnauld, to whom these lines were addressed, was the most perfect image and the most accomplished disciple of M. de St. Cyran. More gentle and more human than he, she was quite as strong and quite as zealous. "It is necessary to be dead to everything, and after that to await everything;" such was the motto of her inward life and of the constant effort made by this impassioned soul, susceptible of all tender affections, to detach herself violently and irrevocably from earth. The instinct of command, loftiness and breadth of views find their place with the holy priest and with the nun; the mind of M. de St. Cyran was less practical and his judgment less simple than that of the abbess, habituated as she had been from childhood to govern the lives of her nuns as their conscience. A reformer of more than one convent since the day when she had closed the gates of Port-Royal against her father, M. Arnauld, in order to restore the strictness of the cloister, Mother Angelica carried rule along with her, for she carried within herself the government, rigid no doubt, for it was life in a convent, but characterized by generous largeness of heart, which caused the yoke to be easily borne. "To be perfect, there is no need to do singular things," she would often repeat, after St. Francis de Sales: "what is needed is to do common things singularly well!" She carried the same zeal from convent to convent, from Port-Royal des Champs to Port-Royal de Paris; from Maubuisson, whither her superiors sent her to establish a reformation, to St. Sacrement, to establish union between the two orders; ever devoted to religion, without having chosen her vocation; attracting around her all that were hers; her mother, a wife at twelve years of age, and astonished to find herself obeying after having commanded her twenty children for fifty years; five of her sisters, nieces and cousins; and in "the Desert," beside Port-Royal des Champs, her brothers, her nephews, her friends, steeped like herself in penitence. Before her, St. Bernard had "dispeopled the world" of those whom he loved, by an error common to zealous souls and exclusive spirits, solely occupied with thoughts of salvation. Even in solitude Mother Angelica had not found rest. "I am not fit to live on earth," she would say: "I know not why I am still there; I can no longer bear either myself or others, there is none that seeketh after God." She was piously unjust towards her age and still more towards her friends; it was the honorable distinction of M. de St. Cyran and his disciples that they did seek after God and holiness, at every cost and every risk.

Mother Angelica was nearing the repose of eternity, the only repose admitted by her brother M. Arnauld, when the storm of persecution burst upon the monastery. The *Augustinus* of Jansenius, bishop of Ypres, a friend of M. de St. Cyran's, had just been condemned at Rome. Five propositions concerning grace were pronounced heretical. "The pope has a right to condemn them," said the Jansenists, "if they are to be found in the *Augustinus*, but, *in fact*, they are not to be found there." The dispute waxed hot; M. Arnauld threw himself into it passionately. He, in his turn, was condemned by the Sorbonne. "This is the very day," he wrote to his sister, Mother Angelica, "when I am to be wiped out from the number of the doctors; I hope of God's goodness that He will not on that account wipe me out from the number of His servants. That is the only title I desire to preserve." M. Arnauld's friends pressed him to protest agains this condemnation. "Would you let yourself be crushed like a child?" they said. He wrote in the theologian's vein lengthily and bitterly; his friends listened in silence. Arnauld understood them: "I see quite well that you do not consider this document a good one for its purpose," said he, "and I think you are right; but you who are young," and he turned towards Pascal, who had a short time since retired to Port-Royal, "you ought to do something." This was the origin of the *Lettres Provinciales*. For the first time Pascal wrote something other than a treatise on physics. He revealed himself all at once and entirely. The recluses of Port-Royal were obliged to close their schools; they had to disperse. Arnauld concealed himself with his friend Nicole. "I am having search made everywhere for M. Arnauld," said Louis XIV. to Boileau, who was supposed to be much attached to the Jansenists; "Your Majesty always was lucky," replied Boileau: "you will not find him."

The nuns' turn had come; orders were given to send away the pensioners (pupils); Mother Angelica set out for the house at Paris, "where was the battle-ground" [*Mémoires pour servir à l'Histoire de Port-Royal*, t. ii. p. 127]. As she was leaving the house in the fields, which was so dear to her, she met in the court-yard M. d'Andilly, her brother, who was waiting to say good-bye to her. When he came up to her she said to him, "Good-bye, my dear brother; be of good courage, whatever happens." "Fear nothing, my dear sister, I am perfectly so." But she replied, "Brother, brother, let us be humble. Let us remember that humility without fortitude is cowardice; but that fortitude without humility is presumption." "When she arrived at the convent in Paris she found us for the most part very sad," writes her niece, Mother Angelica de St. Jean, "and some were in tears. She, looking at us with an open and confident countenance, said, 'Why, I believe there is weeping here! Come, my children, what is all this? Have you no faith? And at what are you dismayed? What if men do rage? Eh? Are you afraid of that? They are but flies. You hope in God, and yet fear anything! Fear but Him, and, trust me, all will be well;' and to Madame de Chevreuse, who came to fetch her daughters, 'Madame, when there is no God I shall lose courage; but, so long as God is God, I shall hope in Him.'" She succumbed, however, beneath the burden; and the terror she had always felt of death aggravated her sufferings. "Believe me, my children," she would say to the nuns; "believe what I tell you. People do not know what death is and do not think about it. As for me I have apprehended it all my life, and have always been thinking about it. But all I have imagined is less than nothing in comparison with what it is, with what I feel, and with what I comprehend at this moment. It would need but such thought to detach us from everything." M. Singlin, being obliged to conceal himself, came secretly to see her; she would not have her nephew, M. de Sacy, run the same risk. "I shall never see him more," she said: "it is God's will, I do not vex myself about it. My nephew without God could be of no use to me, and God without my nephew will be all in all to me." The grand-vicar of the archbishop of Paris went to Port-Royal to make sure that the pensioners had gone. He sat down beside Mother Angelica's bed. "So you are ill, mother," said he: "pray, what is your complaint?" "I am dropsical, sir," she replied. "Jesus! my dear mother, you say that as if it were nothing at all. Does not such a complaint dismay you?" "No, sir," she replied: "I am incomparably more dismayed at what I see happening in our house. For, indeed, I came hither to die here, but I did not come to see all that I now see, and I had no reason to expect the kind of treatment we are having. Sir, sir, this is man's day: God's day will come, who will reveal many things and avenge everything." She died on the 6th of August, 1661, murmuring over and over again: "Good-bye; good-bye!" And, when she was asked why she said that, she replied simply, "Because I am going away, my children." She had given instructions to bury her in the *préau* (court-yard), and not to have any *nonsense* (*badineries*) after her death. "I am your Jonas," she said to the nuns: "when I am thrown into the whale's belly the tempest will cease." She was mistaken; the tempest was scarcely beginning.

Cardinal de Retz was still titular archbishop of Paris, and rather favorable to Jansenism. It was, therefore, the grand-vicars who prepared the exhortation to the faithful calling upon them to accept the papal decision touching Jansen's book. There was drawn up a formula or *formulary* of adhesion, "turned with some skill," says Madame Périer in her biography of Jacqueline Pascal, and in such a way that subscription did not bind the conscience, as theologians most scrupulous about the truth affirmed; the nuns of Port-Royal, however, refused to subscribe. "What hinders us," said a letter to Mother Angelica de St. Jean from Jacqueline Pascal, Sister St. Euphemia in religion, "what hinders all the ecclesiastics who recognize the truth, to reply, when the formulary is presented to them to subscribe: 'I know the respect I owe the bishops, but my conscience does not permit me to subscribe that a thing is in a book in which I have not seen it,' and after that wait for what will happen? What have we to fear? Banishment and dispersion for the nuns, seizure of temporalities, imprisonment and death, if you will; but is not that our glory, and should it not be our joy? Let us renounce the Gospel or follow the maxims of the Gospel, and deem ourselves happy to suffer somewhat for righteousness' sake. I know that it is not for daughters to defend the truth, though one might say, unfortunately, that since the bishops have the courage of daughters, the daughters must have the courage of bishops; but, if it is not for us to defend the truth, it is for us to die for the truth and suffer everything rather than abandon it."

Jacqueline subscribed, divided between her instinctive repugnance and her desire to show herself a "humble daughter of the Catholic Church." "It is all we can concede," she said: "for the rest, come what may, poverty, dispersion, imprisonment, death, all this seems to me nothing in comparison with the anguish in which I should pass the remainder of my life if I had been wretch enough to make a covenant with death on so excellent an occasion of paying to God the vows of fidelity which our lips have pronounced." "Her health was so shaken by the shock which all this business caused her," writes Madame Périer, "that she fell dangerously ill and died soon after." "Think not, I beg of you, my father, she wrote to M. Arnauld, "firm as I may appear, that nature does not greatly apprehend all the consequences of this, but I hope that grace will sustain me, and it seems to me as if I feel it." "The king does all he wills," Madame de Guémenée had said to M. Le Tellier, whom she was trying to soften towards Port-Royal; "he makes princes of the blood, he makes archbishops and bishops, and he will make martyrs likewise." Jacqueline Pascal was "the first victim" of the formulary.

She was not the only one. "It will not stop there," said the king, to whom it was announced that the daughters of Port-Royal consented to sign the formulary on condition only of giving an explanation of their conduct. Cardinal de Retz had at last sent in his resignation. M. du Marca, archbishop designate in succession to him, died three days after receiving the bulls from Rome; Hardouin de Péréfix had just been nominated in his place. He repaired to Port-Royal. The days of grace were over, the nuns remained indomitable. "What is the use of all your prayers?" said he to Sister Christine Brisquet: "what ground for God to listen to you? You go to Him and say: 'My God, give me Thy spirit and Thy grace; but, my God, I do not mean to subscribe; I will take good care not to do that for all that may be said.' After that, what ground for God to hearken to you?" He forbade the nuns the sacraments. "They are pure as angels and proud as demons," repeated the archbishop angrily as he left the convent. On the 25th of August he returned to Port-Royal, accompanied by a numerous escort of ecclesiastics and exons. "When I say a thing, so it must be," he said as he entered; "I will not eat my words." He picked out twelve nuns, who were immediately taken away and dispersed in different monasteries. M. d'Andilly was at the gate, receiving in his carriage his sister, Mother Agnes, aged and infirm, and his three daughters doomed to exile. "I had borne up all day without weeping and without inclination thereto," writes Mother Angelica de St. Jean on arrival at the *Annonciades bleues;* "but when night came and, after finishing all my prayers, I thought to lay me down and take some rest, I felt myself all in a moment bruised and lacerated in every part by the separations I had just gone through; I then found sensibly that, to escape weakness in the hour of deep affliction, there must be no dropping of the eyes that have been lifted to the mountains." Ten months later the exiled nuns returned, without having subscribed, to Port-Royal des Champs, a little before the moment when M. de Saci, who had become their secret director since the death of M. Singlin, was arrested together with his secretary, Fontaine, at six in the morning, in front of the Bastille. "As he had for two years past been expecting imprisonment, he had got the epistles of St. Paul bound up together so as to always carry them about with him. 'Let them do with me what they please,' he was wont to say; 'wherever they put me, provided that I have my St. Paul with me, I fear nothing.'" On the 13th of May, 1666, the day of his arrest, M. de Saci had for once happened to forget his book. He was put into the Bastille, after an examination "which revealed a man of much wit and worth," said the king himself. Fontaine remained separated from him for three months. "Liberty, for me, is to be with M. de Saci," said the faithful secretary; "open the door of his room and that of the Bastille and you will see to which of the two I shall run. Without him everything will be prison to me; I shall be free wherever I see him." At last he had the joy of recovering his well-beloved master, strictly watched and still deprived of the sacraments. Like Luther at Wartburg, he was finishing the revisal of his translation of the Bible, when his cousins, MM. de Pomponne and Arnauld, entered his room on the 31st of October, 1668. They chatted a while without any appearance of impatience on the part of M. de Saci. "You are free," said his friends at last, who had wanted to prove him, "and they showed him the king's order, which he read," says Abbé Arnauld, "without any change of countenance and as little affected by joy as he had been a moment before by the longinquity of his release."

He lived fifteen years longer, occupied during the interval of rest which the *Peace of the Church* restored to Port-Royal in directing and fortifying souls. He published one after another the volumes of his translation of the Bible with *expositions* (*éclaircissements*) which had been required by the examiners. In 1679, the renewal of the king's severities compelled him to retire completely to Pomponne. On the 3rd of January, 1684, at seventy-one years of age, he felt ill and went to bed; he died next day without being taken by surprise, as regarded either his affairs or his soul, by so speedy an end. "O blessed flames of purgatory!" he said as he breathed his last. He had requested to be buried at Port-Royal des Champs; he was borne thither at night; the cold was intense; and the roads were covered with snow; the carriages were escorted by men carrying torches. The nuns looked a moment upon the face of the saintly director whom they had not seen for so many years; and then he was lowered into his grave. "Needs hide in earth what is but earth," said Mother Angelica de St. Jean in deep accents and a lowly voice, "and return to nothingness what in itself is but nothing." She was, nevertheless, heartbroken, and tarried only for this pious duty to pass away in her turn. "It is time to give up my veil to him from whom I received it," said she. A fortnight after the death of M. de Saci, she expired at Port-Royal, just preceding to the tomb her brother M. de Luzancy, who breathed his last at Pomponne, where he had lived with M. de Saci. "I confess," said the inconsolable Fontaine, "that when I saw this brother and sister stricken with death by that of M. de Saci, I blushed, I who thought I had always loved him, not to follow him like them, and I became consequently exasperated with myself for loving so little in comparison with those persons whose love had been strong as death." The human heart avenges itself for the tortures men pretentiously inflict upon it: the disciples of St. Cyran thought to stifle in their souls all earthly affections, and they died of grief on losing those they loved. "Their life ebbed away in those depths of tears," as M. Vinet has said.

The great Port-Royal was dead with M. de Saci and Mother Angelica de St. Jean, faithful and modest imitators of their illustrious predecessors. The austere virtue and the pious severance from the world existed still in the house in the Fields under the direction of Duguet; the persecution too continued, persistent and noiseless; the king had given the direction of his conscience to the Jesuits; from Father La Chaise, moderate and prudent, he had passed to Father Le Tellier, violent and perfidious; furthermore, the long persistence of the Jansenists in their obstinacy, their freedom of thought which infringed the unity so dear to Louis XIV., displeased the monarch, absolute even in his hour of humiliation and defeat. The property of Port-Royal was seized, and Cardinal de Noailles, well disposed at bottom towards the Jansenists, but so feeble in character that determination disgusted him as if it were a personal insult, ended by once more forbidding the nuns the sacraments; the house in the Fields was suppressed and its title merged in that of Port-Royal in Paris, for some time past replenished with submissive nuns. Madame de Château-Renaud, the new abbess, went to take possession; the daughters of Mother Angelica protested, but without violence, as she would have done in their place; "On the 29th of October, 1709, after prime, Father Letellier having told the king that Madame de Château-Renaud dared not to go to Port-Royal des Champs, being convinced that those headstrong, disobedient and rebellious daughters would laugh at the king's decree, and that, unless his Majesty would be pleased to give precise orders to disperse them, it would never be possible to carry it out, the king, being pressed in this way, sent his orders to M. d'Argenson, lieutenant of police." He appeared at Port-Royal with a commissary and two exons. He asked for the prioress; she was at church; when service was over, he summoned all the nuns; one, old and very paralytic, was missing. "Let her be brought," said M. d'Argenson. "His Majesty's orders are," he continued, "that you break up this assemblage, never to meet again. It is your general dispersal that I announce to you; you are allowed but three hours to break up." "We are ready to obey, sir," said the mother-prioress; "half-an-hour is more than sufficient for us to say our last good-bye, and take with us a breviary, a Bible and our regulations." And when he asked her whither she meant to go: "Sir, the moment our community is broken up and dispersed, it is indifferent to me in what place I may be personally, since I hope to find God wherever I shall be." They got into carriages, receiving one after another the farewell and blessing of the mother-prioress who was the last to depart, remaining firm to the end; there were two and twenty, the youngest fifty years old; they all died in the convents to which they were taken. A seizure was at once made of all papers and books left in the cells; Cardinal Noailles did not interfere. M. de St. Cyran had depicted him by anticipation when he said that the weak were more to be feared than the wicked. He was complaining one day of his differences with his bishops. "What can you expect, Monsignor?" laughingly said a lady well disposed to the Jansenists, "God is just, it is the stones of Port-Royal tumbling upon your head." The tombs were destroyed; some coffins were carried to a distance, others left and profaned; the plough passed over the ruins; the hatred of the enemies of Port-Royal was satiated. A few of the faithful, preserving in their hearts the ardent faith of M. de St. Cyran, narrowed, however, and absorbed by obstinate resistance, a few theologians dying in exile and leaving in Holland a succession of bishops detached from the Roman Church—this was all that remained of one of the noblest attempts ever made by the human soul to rise here below above that which is permitted by human nature. Virtues of the utmost force, Christianity zealously pushed to its extremest limits and the most invincible courage sustained the Jansenists in a conscientious struggle against spiritual oppression; its life died out little by little amongst the dispersed members. The Catholic Church suffered therefrom in its innermost sanctuary. "The catholic religion would only be more neglected if there were no more religionists," said Vauban in his *Mémoire* in favor of the Protestants. It was the same as regarded the Jansenists. The Jesuits and Louis XIV. in their ignorant passion for unity and uniformity, had not comprehended that great principle of healthy freedom and sound justice of which the scientific soldier had a glimmering.

The insurrection of the Camisards in the Cévennes had been entirely of a popular character; the Jansenists had penitents amongst the great of this world, though none properly belonged to them or retired to their convents or their solitudes; it was the great French burgessdom, issue for the most part of the magistracy, which supplied their most fervent associates. Fénelon and Madame Guyon founded their little church at court and amongst the great lords; and many remained faithful to them till death. The spiritual letters of Fénelon, models of wisdom, pious tact, moderation and knowledge of the human heart, are nearly all addressed to persons engaged in the life and the offices of the court, exposed to all the temptations of the world. It is no longer the desert of the penitents of Port Royal, or the strict cloister of Mother Angelica; Fénelon is for only inward restrictions and an abstention purely spiritual; from afar and in his retreat at Cambrai, he watches over his faithful flock with a tender preoccupation which does not make him overlook the duties of their position. "Take as penance for your sins," he wrote, "the disagreeable liabilities of the position you are in: the very hindrances which seem injurious to our advancement in piety turn to our profit, provided that we do what depends on ourselves. Fail not in any of your duties towards the court, as regards your office and the proprieties, but be not anxious for posts which awaken ambition." Such are, with their discreet tolerance, the teachings of Fénelon, adapted for the guidance of the dukes of Beauvilliers and Chevreuse, and of the duke of Burgundy himself. He went much further and on less safe a road when he was living at court, under the influence of Madame Guyon. A widow and still young, gifted with an ardent spirit and a lofty and subtile mind, Madame Guyon had imagined in her mystical enthusiasm a theory of *pure love*, very analogous fundamentally if not in its practical consequences to the doctrines taught shortly before by a Spanish priest named Molinos, condemned by the court of Rome in 1687. It was about the same time that Madame Guyon went to Paris, with her book on the *Moyen court et facile de faire l'Oraison du Cœur* (*Short and easy Method of making Orison with the Heart*). Prayer, according to this wholly mystical teaching, loses the character of supplication or intercession, to become the simple silence of a soul absorbed in God. "Why are not simple folks so taught?" she said: "Shepherds keeping their flocks would have the spirit of the old anchorites; and laborers, whilst driving the plough, would talk happily with God: all vice would be banished in a little while and the kingdom of God would be realized on earth."

It was a far cry from the sanguinary struggle against sin and the armed Christianity of the Jansenists; the sublime and specious visions of Madame Guyon fascinated lofty and gentle souls: the duchess of Charost, daughter of Fouquet, Mesdames de Beauvilliers, de Chevreuse, de Mortemart, daughters of Colbert, and their pious husbands were the first to be chained to her feet. Fénelon, at that time preceptor to the children of France (royal family), saw her, admired her, and became imbued with her doctrines. She was for a while admitted to the intimacy of Madame de Maintenon. It was for this little nucleus of faithful friends that she wrote her book of *Torrents.* The human soul is a torrent which returns to its source, in God who lives in perfect repose and who would fain give it to those who are His. The Christian soul has nothing more that is its, neither will nor desire. It has God for soul, He is its principle of life. "In this way, there is nothing extraordinary. No visions, no ecstasies, no entrancements. The way is simple, pure and plain; there the soul sees nothing but in God, as God sees Himself and with His eyes." With less vagueness and quite as mystically, Fénelon defined the sublime love taught by Madame Guyon in the following maxim, afterwards condemned at Rome: "There is an habitual state of love of God which is pure charity without any taint of the motive of self-interest. Neither fear of punishment nor desire of reward have any longer part in this love; God is loved not for the merit or the perfection or the happiness to be found in loving Him." What singular seductiveness in those theories of pure love which were taught at the court of Louis XIV. by his grandchildren's perceptor, at a woman's instigation, and zealously preached fifty years afterwards by President (of New Jersey College) Jonathan Edwards in the cold and austere atmosphere of New England!

Led away by the generous enthusiasm of his soul, Fénelon had not probed the dangers of his new doctrine. The Gospel and Church of Christ, whilst preaching the love of God, had strongly maintained the fact of human individuality and responsibility. The theory of *mere* (*pure*) love absorbing the soul in God put an end to repentance, effort to withstand evil and the need of a Redeemer. Bossuet was not deceived. The elevation of his mind, combined with strong common-sense, caused him to see through all the veils of the mysticism. Madame Guyon had submitted her books to him; he disapproved of them, at first quietly, then formally, after a thorough examination in conjunction with two other doctors. Madame Guyon retired to a monastery of Meaux; she soon returned to Paris, and her believers rallied round her. Bossuet, in his anger, no longer held his hand. Madame Guyon was shut up first at Vincennes, and then in the Bastille; she remained seven years in prison, and ended by retiring to near Blois, where she died in 1717, still absorbed in her holy and vague reveries praying no more, inasmuch as she possessed God, "a submissive daughter, however, of the Catholic, Apostolic and Roman Church, having and desiring to admit no other opinions but its," as she says in her will. Bourdaloue calls mere (pure) love "a bare faith which has for its object no verity of the Gospel's, no mystery of Jesus Christ's, no attribute of God's, nothing whatever, unless it be, in a word, God." In presence of death, on the approach of the awful realities of eternity, Madame Guyon no doubt felt the want of a more simple faith in the mighty and living God. Fénelon had not waited so long to surrender.

The instinct of the pious and vigorous souls of the seventeenth century had not allowed them to go astray: there was little talk of pantheism, which had spread considerably in the sixteenth century; but there had been a presentiment of the dangers lurking behind the doctrines of Madame Guyon. Bossuet, that great and noble type of the finest period of the Catholic Church in France, made the mistake of pushing his victory too far. Fénelon, a young priest when the great bishop of Meaux was already in his zenith, had preserved towards him a profound affection and a deep respect: "We are, by anticipation, agreed, however you may decide," he wrote to him on the 28th of July, 1694: "it will be no specious submission, but a sincere conviction. Though that which I suppose myself to have read should appear to me clearer than that two and two make four, I should consider it still less clear than my obligation to mistrust all my lights, and to prefer before them those of a bishop such as you. You have only to give me my lesson in writing; provided that you wrote me precisely what is the doctrine of the Church and what are the articles in which I have slipped, I would tie myself down inviolably to that rule." Bossuet required more; he wanted Fénelon, recently promoted to the archbishopric of Cambrai, to approve of the book he was preparing on *États d'Oraison* (*States of Orison*), and explicitly to condemn the works of Madame Guyon. Fénelon refused with generous indignation: "So it is to secure my own reputation," he writes to Madame de Maintenon in 1696, "that I am wanted to subscribe that a lady, my friend, would plainly deserve to be burned with all her writings for an execrable form of spirituality, which is the only bond of our friendship? I tell you, madame, I would burn my friend with my own hands, and I would burn myself joyfully rather than let the Church be imperilled. But here is a poor captive woman, overwhelmed with sorrows; there is none to defend her, none to excuse her;

they are always afraid to do so. I maintain that this stroke of the pen, given by me against my conscience, from a cowardly policy, would render me forever infamous and unworthy of my ministry and my position." Fénelon no longer submitted his reason and his conduct, then, to the judgment of Bossuet; he recognized in him an adversary, but he still spoke of him with profound veneration. "Fear not," he writes to Madame de Maintenon, "that I should gainsay M. de Meaux; I shall never speak of him but as of my master and of his propositions but as the rule of faith." Fénelon was at Cambrai, being regular in the residence which removed him for nine months in the year from the court and the children of France, when there appeared his *Explication des maximes des saints sur la Vie Intérieure* (*Exposition of the Maxims of the Saints touching the Inner Life*), almost at the same moment as Bossuet's *Instruction sur les États d'Oraison* (*Lessons on States of Orison*). Fénelon's book appeared as dangerous as those of Madame Guyon; he himself submitted it to the pope, and was getting ready to repair to Rome to defend his cause, when the king wrote to him: "I do not think proper to allow you to go to Rome; you must on the contrary repair to your diocese, whence I forbid you to go away; you can send to Rome your pleas in justification of your book."

Fénelon departed to an exile which was to last as long as his life; on his departure, he wrote to Madame de Maintenon: "I shall depart hence, madame, to-morrow, Friday, in obedience to the king. My greatest sorrow is to have wearied him and to displease him. I shall not cease all the days of my life to pray God to pour his graces upon him. I consent to be crushed more and more. The only thing I ask of his Majesty is that the diocese of Cambrai, which is guiltless, may not suffer for the errors imputed to me. I ask protection only for the sake of the Church, and even that protection I limit to not being disturbed in those few good works which my present position permits me to do in order to fulfil a pastor's duties. It remains for me, madame, only to ask your pardon for all the trouble I have caused you. I shall all my life be as deeply sensible of your former kindnesses as if I had not forfeited them, and my respectful attachment to yourself, madame, will never diminish."

Fénelon made no mistake in addressing to Madame de Maintenon his farewell and his regrets; she had acted against him with the uneasiness of a person led away for a moment by an irresistible attraction and returning, quite affrighted, to rule and the beaten paths. The *mere love* theory had no power to fascinate her for long. The archbishop of Cambrai did not drop out of that pleasant dignity. The pious councillors of the king were working against him at Rome, bringing all the influence of France to weigh upon Innocent XII. Fénelon had taken no part in the declarations of the Gallican Church, in 1682, which had been drawn up by Bossuet; the court of Rome was inclined towards him; the strife became bitter and personal; pamphlets succeeded pamphlets, letters letters; Bossuet published a *Relation du Quietisme* (*an Account of Quietism*) and remarks upon the reply of M. de Cambrai. "I write this for the people," he said, "in order that, the character of M. de Cambrai being known, his eloquence may, with God's permission, no more impose upon anybody." Fénelon replied with a vigor, a fulness and a moderation which brought men's minds over to him. "You do more for me by the excess of your accusations," said he to Bossuet, "than I could do myself. But what a melancholy consolation when we look at the scandal which troubles the house of God and which causes so many heretics and libertines (free-thinkers) to triumph! Whatever end may be put by a holy pontiff to this matter, I await it with impatience, having no wish but to obey, no fear but to be in the wrong, no object but peace. I hope that it will be seen from my silence, my unreserved submission, my constant horror of illusion, my isolation from any book and any person of a suspicious sort, that the evil you would fain have caused to be apprehended is as chimerical as the scandal has been real, and that violent measures taken against imaginary evils turn to poison."

Fénelon was condemned on the 12th of March, 1699; the sentence of Rome was mild and hinted no suspicion of heresy; it had been wrested from the pope by the urgency of Louis XIV. "It would be painful to his Majesty," wrote the bishop of Meaux in the king's name, "to see a new schism growing up amongst his subjects at the very time that he is applying himself with all his might to the task of extirpating that of Calvin, and if he saw the prolongation, by manœuvres which are incomprehensible, of a matter which appeared to be at an end. He will know what he has to do and will take suitable resolutions, still hoping, nevertheless, that his Holiness will not be pleased to reduce him to such disagreeable extremities." When the threat reached Rome Innocent XII. had already yielded.

Fénelon submitted to the pope's decision, completely and unreservedly. "God gives me grace to be at peace amidst bitterness and sorrow," he wrote to the Duke of Beauvilliers on the 29th of March, 1699: "amongst so many troubles I have one consolation little fitted to be known in the world, but solid enough for those who seek God in good faith, and that is, that my conduct is quite decided upon and that I have no longer to deliberate. It only remains for me to submit and hold my peace; that is what I have always desired. I have now but to choose the terms of my submission; the shortest, the simplest, the most absolute, the most devoid of any restriction, are those that I rather prefer. My conscience is disburdened in that of my superior: in all this, far from having an eye to my advantage, I have no eye to any man, I see but God, and I am content with what He does."

Bossuet had triumphed: his vaster mind, his more sagacious insight, his stronger judgment had unravelled the dangerous errors in which Fénelon had allowed himself to be entangled; the archbishop of Cambrai, however, had grown in the estimation of good men on account of his moderation, his gentle and high-spirited independence during the struggle, his submission, full of dignity, after the papal decision. The mind of Bossuet was the greater; the spirit of Fénelon was the nobler and more deeply pious. "I cannot consent to have my book defended even indirectly," he wrote to one of his friends on the 21st of July, 1699: "in God's name, speak not of me but to God only, and leave men to think as they please; as for me I have no object but silence and peace after my unreserved submission."

Fénelon was not detached from the world and his hopes to quite such an extent as he would have had it appear. He had educated the duke of Burgundy, who remained passionately attached to him, and might hope for a return of prosperity. He remained in the silence and retirement of his diocese, with the character of an able and saintly bishop, keeping open house, grandly and simply, careful of the welfare of the soldiery who passed through Cambrai, adored by his clergy and the people. "Never a word about the court, or about public affairs of any sort that could be found fault with, or any that smacked the least in the world of baseness, regret or flattery," writes St. Simon; "never anything that could give a bare hint of what he had been or might be again. He was a tall, thin man, well made, pale, with a large nose, eyes from which fire and intellect streamed like a torrent, and a physiognomy such that I have never seen any like it, and there was no forgetting it when it had been seen but once. It combined everything, and there was no conflict of opposites in it. There was gravity and gallantry, the serious and the gay; it savored equally of the learned doctor, the bishop and the great lord; that which appeared on its surface, as well as in his whole person, was refinement, intellect, grace, propriety and, above all, nobility. It required an effort to cease looking at him. His manners corresponded therewith in the same proportion, with an ease which communicated it to others; with all this, a man who never desired to show more wits than they with whom he conversed, who put himself within everybody's range without ever letting it be perceived, in such wise that nobody could drop him, or fight shy of him, or not want to see him again. It was this rare talent, which he possessed to the highest degree, that kept his friends so completely attached to him all his life, in spite of his downfall, and that, in their dispersion, brought them together to speak of him, to sorrow after him, to yearn for him, to bind themselves more and more to him, as the Jews to Jerusalem, and to sigh after his return and hope continually for it, just as that unfortunate people still expects and sighs after the Messiah."

Those faithful friends were dropping one after another: the death of the duke of Burgundy and the duke of Chevreuse, in 1712, and that of the duke of Beauvilliers, in 1714, were a fatal blow to the affections as well as to the ambitious hopes of Fénelon. Of delicate health, worn out by the manifold duties of the episcopate, inwardly wearied by long and vain expectation, he succumbed on the 7th of January, 1715, at the moment when the attraction shown by the duke of Orleans towards him and "the king's declining state" were once more renewing his chances of power; "he was already consulted in private and courted again in public," says St. Simon," because the inclination of the rising sun had already shown through." He died, however, without letting any sign of yearning for life appear, "regardless of all that he was leaving and occupied solely with that which he was going to meet, with a tranquillity, a peace, which excluded nothing but disquietude and which included penitence, despoilment and a unique care for the spiritual affairs of his diocese." The Christian soul was detaching itself from the world to go before God with sweet and simple confidence. "O how great is God: how all in all! How as nothing are we when we are so near Him, and when the veil which conceals Him from us is about to lift!" [Œuvres de Fénelon, *Lettres Spirituelles*, xxv. 128.]

So many fires smouldering in the hearts, so many different struggles going on in the souls that sought to manifest their personal and independent life have often caused forgetfulness of the great mass of the faithful who were neither Jansenists nor Quietists. Bossuet was the real head and the pride of the great catholic Church of France in the seventeenth century; what he approved of was approved of by the immense majority of the French clergy, what he condemned was condemned by them. Moderate and prudent in conduct as well as in his opinions, pious without being fervent, holding discreetly aloof from all excesses, he was a Gallican without fear and without estrangement as regarded the papal power to which he steadfastly paid homage. It was with pain and not without having sought to escape therefrom that he found himself obliged, at the assembly of the clergy in 1682, to draw up the solemn declarations of the Gallican Church. The meeting of the clergy had been called forth by the eternal discussions of the civil power with the court of Rome on the question of the rights of *régale*, that is to say, the rights of the sovereign to receive the revenues of vacant bishoprics and to appoint to benefices belonging to them. The French bishops were of independent spirit; the archbishop of Paris, Francis de Harlay, was on bad terms with Pope Innocent XI.; Bossuet managed to moderate the discussions and kept within suitable bounds the declaration which he could not avoid. He had always taught and maintained what was proclaimed by the assembly of the clergy of France, "that St. Peter and his successors, vicars of Jesus Christ, and the whole Church itself received from God authority over only spiritual matters and such as appertain to salvation, and not over temporal and civil matters, in such sort that kings and sovereigns are not subject to any ecclesiastical power, by order of God, in temporal matters, and cannot be deposed directly or indirectly by authority of the keys of the Church; finally that, though the pope has the principal part in questions of faith, and though his decrees concern all the churches and each church severally, his judgment is, nevertheless, not irrefragable, unless the consent of the Church intervene." Old doctrines in the Church of

France, but never before so solemnly declared and made incumbent upon the teaching of all the faculties of theology in the kingdom.

Constantly occupied in the dogmatic struggle against Protestantism, Bossuet had imported into it a moderation in form which, however, did not keep out injustice. Without any inclination towards persecution, he, with almost unanimity on the part of the bishops of France, approved of the king's piety in the revocation of the Edict of Nantes. "Take up your sacred pens," says he in his funeral oration over Michael Le Tellier, "ye who compose the annals of the Church; haste ye to place Louis amongst the peers of Constantine and Theodosius. Our fathers saw not as we have seen an inveterate heresy falling at a single blow, scattered flocks returning in a mass and our churches too narrow to receive them, their false shepherds leaving them without even awaiting the order and happy to have their banishment to allege as excuse; all tranquillity amidst so great a movement; the universe astounded to see in so novel an event the most certain sign as well as the most noble use of authority, and the prince's merit more recognized and more revered than even his authority. Moved by so many marvels, say ye to this new Constantine, this new Theodosius, this new Marcian, this new Charlemagne, what the six hundred and thirty Fathers said aforetime in the council of Chalcedon: you have confirmed the faith; you have exterminated the heretics; that is the worthy achievement of your reign, that is its own characteristic. Through you heresy is no more. God alone could have wrought this marvel. King of heaven, preserve the king of earth; that is the prayer of the churches, that is the prayer of the bishops." Bossuet, like Louis XIV., believed Protestantism to be destroyed; "Heresy is no more," he said: it was the same feeling that prompted Louis XIV., when dying, to the edict of March 8, 1715. "We learn," said he, "that, abjurations being frequently made in provinces distant from those in which our newly converted subjects die, our judges to whom those who die *relapsed* are denounced find a difficulty in condemning them, for want of proof of their abjuration. The stay which those who were of the religion styled reformed have made in our kingdom since we abolished therein all exercise of the said religion is a more than sufficient proof that they have embraced the catholic religion, without which they would have been neither suffered nor tolerated." There did not exist, there could not exist, any more Protestants in France; all who died without sacraments were *relapsed* and as such dragged on the hurdle. Those who were not married at a catholic church were not married. M. Guizot was born at Nîmes on the 4th of October, 1787, before Protestants possessed any civil rights in France.

Bossuet had died on the 12th of April, 1704. When troubles began again in the Church, the enemies of the Jansenists obtained from the king a decree interdicting the *Réflexions morales sur le Nouveau Testament*, an old and highly esteemed work by Father Quesnel, some time an Oratorian, who had become head of the Jansenists on the death of the great Arnauld. Its condemnation at Rome was demanded. Cardinal de Noailles, archbishop of Paris, had but lately, as bishop of Châlons, approved of the book; he refused to retract his approbation; the Jesuits made urgent representations to the pope; Clement XI. launched the bull, *Unigenitus*, condemning *a hundred and one* propositions extracted from the *Réflexions morales.* Eight prelates, with Cardinal de Noailles at their head, protested against the bull; it was, nevertheless, enregistered at the parliament, but not without difficulty. The archbishop still held out, supported by the greater part of the religious orders and the majority of the doctors of Sorbonne. The king's confessor, Letellier, pressed him to prosecute the cardinal and get him deposed by a national council; the affair dragged its slow length along at Rome; the archbishop had suspended from the sacred functions all the Jesuits of his diocese; the struggle had commenced under the name of Jansenism against the whole Gallican Church; the king was about to bring the matter before his bed of justice, when he fell ill; he saw no more of Cardinal de Noailles, and this rupture vexed him: "I am sorry to leave the affairs of the Church in the state in which they are," he said to his councillors; "I am perfectly ignorant in the matter; you know and I call you to witness that I have done nothing therein but what you wanted and that I have done all you wanted; it is you who will answer before God for all that has been done, whether too much or too little; I charge you with it before Him, and I have a clear conscience; I am but a know-nothing who have left myself to your guidance." An awful appeal from a dying king to the guides of his conscience; he had dispeopled his kingdom, reduced to exile, despair or falsehood fifteen hundred thousand of his subjects, but the memory of the persecutions inflicted upon the Protestants did not trouble him; they were, for him, rather a pledge of his salvation and of his acceptance before God; he was thinking of the Catholic Church, the holy priests exiled or imprisoned, the nuns driven from their convent, the division among the bishops, the scandal amongst the faithful; the great burden of absolute power was evident to his eyes; he sought to let it fall back upon the shoulders of those who had enticed him or urged him upon that fatal path. A vain attempt in the eyes of men, whatever may be the judgment of God's sovereign mercy; history has left weighing upon Louis XIV. the crushing weight of the religious persecutions ordered under his reign.

CHAPTER XLVIII.

LOUIS XIV., LITERATURE AND ART.

It has been said in this history that Louis XIV. had the fortune to find himself at the culminating point of absolute monarchy and to profit by the labors of his predecessors, reaping a portion of their glory; he had likewise the honor of enriching himself with the labors of his contemporaries and attracting to himself a share of their lustre; the honor, be it said, not the fortune, for he managed to remain the centre of intellectual movement as well as of the court, of literature and art as well as affairs of State. Only the abrupt and solitary genius of Pascal or the prankish and ingenuous geniality of La Fontaine held aloof from king and court; Racine and Molière, Bossuet and Fénelon, La Bruyère and Boileau lived frequently in the circle of Louis XIV. and enjoyed in different degrees his favor; M. de la Rochefoucauld and Madame de Sévigné were of the court; Lebrun, Rigaud, Mignard painted for the king; Perrault and Mansard constructed the Louvre and Versailles; the learned of all countries considered it an honor to correspond with the new academies founded in France. Louis XIV. was even less a man of letters or an artist than an administrator or a soldier, but literature and art as well as the superintendents and the generals found in him the *king*. The puissant unity of the reign is everywhere the same. The king and the nation are in harmony.

Pascal, had he been born later, would have remained independent and proud, from the nature of his mind and of his character as well as from the connection he had full early with Port-Royal, where they did not rear courtiers; he died, however, at thirty-nine, in 1661, the very year in which Louis XIV. began to govern. Born at Clermont in Auvergne, educated at his father's and by his father, though it was not thought desirable to let him study mathematics, he had already discovered by himself the first thirty-two propositions of Euclid, when Cardinal Richelieu, holding on his knee little Jacqueline Pascal and looking at her brother, said to M. Pascal, the two children's father, who had come to thank him for a favor, "Take care of them; I mean to make something great of them." This was the native and powerful instinct of genius divining genius; Richelieu, however, died three years later, without having done anything for the children who had impressed him beyond giving their father a share in the superintendence of Rouen; he thus put them in the way of the great Corneille, who was affectionately kind to Jacqueline, but took no particular notice of Blaise Pascal. The latter was seventeen; he had already written his *Traité des Coniques* (*Treatise on Conics*) and begun to occupy himself with his "arithmetical machine," as his sister, Madame Périer, calls it. At twenty-three he had ceased to apply his mind to human sciences; "when he afterwards discovered the *roulette* (*cycloid*), it was without thinking," says Madame Périer, "and to distract his attention from a severe tooth-ache he had." He was not twenty-four when anxiety for his salvation and for the glory of God had taken complete possession of his soul. It was to the same end that he composed the *Lettres Provinciales*, the first of which was written in six days, and the style of which, clear, lively, precise, far removed from the somewhat solemn gravity of Port-Royal, formed French prose as Malherbe and Boileau formed poetry. This was the impression of his contemporaries, the most hard of them to please in the art of writing. "That is excellent, that will be relished," said the recluses of Port-Royal, in spite of the misgivings of M. Singlin. More than thirty years after Pascal's death, Madame de Sévigné, in 1689, wrote to Madame de Grignan; "Sometimes, to divert ourselves, we read the little Letters (to a provincial). Good heavens, how charming! And how my son reads them! I always think of my daughter, and how that excess of correctness of reasoning would suit her; but your brother says that you consider that it is always the same thing over again. Ah! my goodness, so much the better! Could any one have a more perfect style, a raillery more refined, more natural, more delicate, worthier offspring of those dialogues of Plato which are so fine? And when, after the first ten letters, he addresses himself to the reverend Jesuit fathers, what earnestness, what solidity, what force! What eloquence! What love for God and for the truth! What a way of maintaining it and making it understood! I am sure that you have never read them but in a hurry, pitching on the pleasant places; but it is not so, when they are read at leisure." Lord Macaulay once said to M. Guizot: "Amongst modern works I know only two perfect ones, to which there is no exception to be taken, and they are Pascal's Provincials and the Letters of Madame de Sévigné.

Boileau was of Lord Macaulay's opinion; at least as regarded Pascal. "Corbinelli wrote to me the other day," says Madame de Sévigné on the 15th of January, 1690: "he gave me an account of a conversation and a dinner at M. de Lamoignon's: the persons were the master and mistress of the house, M. de Troyes, M. de Toulon, Father Bourdaloue, a comrade of his, Despréaux and Corbinelli. The talk was of ancient and modern works. Despréaux supported the ancient with the exception of one single modern which surpassed in his opinion both old and new. Bourdaloue's comrade, who assumed the well-read air and who had fastened on to Despréaux and Corbinelli, asked him what in the world this book could be that was so remarkably clever. Despréaux would not give the name. Corbinelli said to him, 'Sir, I conjure you to tell me, that I may read it all night,' Despréaux answered laughing, 'Ah! sir, you have read it more than once, I am sure.' The Jesuit joins in with a disdainful air and presses Despréaux to name this marvellous writer. 'Do not press me, father,' says Despréaux. The father persists. At last Despréaux takes hold of his arm and squeezing it very hard says: 'You will have it, father; well then, egad! it is Pascal.' 'Pascal,' says the father, all blushes and astonishment; 'Pascal is as beautiful as the false can be.' 'False,' replied Despréaux: 'false! Let me tell you that he is as true as he is inimitable: he has just been translated in three languages.' The father rejoined 'he is none the more true for that.' Despréaux grew warm and shouted like a madman: 'Well! father, will you say that one of yours did not have it printed in one of his books that a Christian was not obliged to love God? Dare you say that that is false?' 'Sir,' said the father in a fury, 'we must distinguish.' 'Distinguish!' cried Despréaux: 'distinguish, egad, distinguish! Distinguish whether we are obliged to love God!' And, taking Corbinelli by the arm, he flew off to the other end of the room, coming back again and rushing about like a lunatic; but he would not go near the father any more, and went off to join the rest of the company. Here endeth the story; the curtain falls." Literary taste and religious sympathies combined in the case of Boileau to exalt Pascal.

The Provincials could not satisfy for long the pious ardor of Pascal's soul; he took in hand his great work on the *Vérité de la religion.* He had taken a vigorous part in the discussions of Port-Royal as to subscription of the formulary; his opinion was decidedly in favor of resistance. It was the moment when MM. Arnauld and Nicole had discovered a *restriction*, as it was then called, which allowed of subscribing with a safe conscience. "M. Pascal, who loved truth above all things," writes his niece Marguerite Périer; "who, moreover, was pulled down by a pain in the head, which never left him; who had exerted himself to make them feel as he himself felt; and who had expressed himself very vigorously in spite of his weakness, was so grief-stricken that he had a fit and lost speech and consciousness. Everybody was alarmed. Exertions were made to bring him round, and then those gentlemen withdrew. When he was quite recovered, Madame Périer asked him what had caused this incident. He answered: 'When I saw all those persons that I looked upon as being those whom God had made to know the truth and who ought to be its defenders, wavering and falling, I declare to you that I was so overcome with grief that I was unable to support it, and could not help breaking down.'" Blaise Pascal was the worthy brother of Jacqueline; in the former as well as the latter the soul was too ardent and too strong for its covering of body. Nearly all his relatives died young. "I alone am left," wrote Mdlle. Périer, when she had become, exceptionally, very aged: "I might say like Simon Maccabeus, the last of all his brethren: All my relatives and all my brethren are dead in the service of God and in the love of truth. I alone am left, please God I may never have a thought of backsliding!"

Pascal was unable to finish his work. "God, who had inspired my brother with this design and with all his thoughts," writes his sister, "did not permit him to bring it to its completion, for reasons to us unknown." The last years of Pascal's life, invalid as he had been from the age of eighteen, were one long and continual torture, accepted and supported with an austere disdain of suffering. Incapable of any application, he gave his attention solely to his salvation and the care of the poor. "I have taken it into my head," says he, "to have in the house a sick pauper, to whom the same service shall be rendered as to myself; particular attention to be paid to him, and, in fact, no difference to be made between him and me, in order that I may have the consolation of knowing that there is one pauper as well treated as myself, in the perplexity I suffer from finding myself in the great affluence of every sort in which I do find myself." The spirit of M. de St. Cyran is there, and also the spirit of the Gospel, which caused Pascal, when he was dying, to say, "I love poverty, because Jesus Christ loved it. I love wealth, because it gives the means of assisting the needy." A genius unique in the extent and variety of his faculties, which were applied with the same splendid results to mathematics and physics, to philosophy and polemics, disdaining all preconceived ideas, going unerringly and straightforwardly to the bottom of things with admirable force and profundity, independent and free even in his voluntary submission to the Christian faith, which he accepts with his eyes open after having weighed it, measured it and sounded it to its uttermost depths, too steadfast and too simple not to bow his head before mysteries, all the while acknowledging his ignorance. "If there were no darkness," says he, "man would not feel his corruption; if there were no light, man would have no hope of remedy. Thus, it is not only quite right but useful for us that God should be concealed in part, and revealed in part, since it is equally dangerous for man to know God without knowing his own misery, and to know his own misery without knowing God." The lights of this great intellect had led him to acquiesce in his own fogs: "One can be quite sure that there is a God, without knowing what He is," says he.

In 1627, four years after Pascal and, like him, in a family of the long robe, was born, at Dijon, his only rival in that great art of writing prose which established the superiority of the French language. At sixteen, Bossuet preached his first sermon in the drawing-room of Madame de Rambouillet, and the great Condé was pleased to attend his theological examinations. He was already famous at court as a preacher and a polemist when the king gave him the title of bishop of Condom, almost immediately inviting him to become preceptor to the Dauphin. A difficult and an irksome task for him who had already written for Turenne an exposition of the catholic faith and had delivered the funeral orations over Madame Henriette and the queen of England. "The king has greatly at heart the Dauphin's education," wrote Father Lacoüe to Colbert: "he regards it as one of his grand state-strokes in respect of the future." The Dauphin was not devoid of intelligence. "Monseigneur has plenty of wits," said Councillor Le Goût de Saint-Seine in his private journal, "but his wits are under a bushel." The boy was indolent, with little inclination for work, roughly treated by his governor, the duke of Montausier, who was endowed with more virtue than ability in the superintendence of a prince's education. "Oh!" cried Monseigneur, when official announcement was made to him of the project of marriage which the king was conducting for him with the Princess Christine of Bavaria, "we shall see whether M. Huet (afterwards bishop of Avranches) will want to make me learn ancient geography any more!" Bossuet had better understood what ought to be the aim of a king's education. "Remember, Monseigneur," he constantly repeated to him, "that, destined as you are to reign some day over this great kingdom, you are bound to make it happy." He was in despair at his pupil's inattention. "There is a great deal to endure with a mind so destitute of application," he wrote to Marshal Bellefonds: "there is no perceptible relief and we go on, as St. Paul says, hoping against hope." He had written a little treatise on inattention, *De Incogitantia*, in the vain hope of thus rousing his pupil to work. "I dread nothing in the world so much," Louis XIV. would say, "as to have a sluggard (*fainéant*) dauphin; I would much prefer to have no son at all!" Bossuet foresaw the innumerable obstacles in the way of his labors. "I perceive, as I think," he wrote to his friends, "in the Dauphin the beginnings of great graces, a simplicity, a straightforwardness, a principle of goodness, an attention, amidst all his flightiness, to the mysteries, a something or other which comes with a flash in the middle of his distractions to call him back to God. You would be charmed if I were to tell you the questions he puts to me and the desire he shows to be a good servant of God. But the world! the world! the world! pleasures, evil counsels, evil examples! Save us, Lord, save us! Thou didst verily preserve the children from the furnace, but Thou didst send Thine angel, and, as for me, alas! what am I? Humility, trepidation, absorption into one's own nothingness!"

It was not for Bossuet that the honor was reserved of succeeding in the difficult task of a royal education. Fénelon encountered in the duke of Burgundy a more undisciplined nature, a more violent character and more dangerous tendencies than Bossuet had to fight against in the grand-dauphin; but there was a richer mind and a warmer heart: the preceptor, too, was more proper for the work. Bossuet, nevertheless, labored conscientiously to instruct his little prince, studying for him and with him the classical authors, preparing grammatical expositions, and, lastly, writing for his edification the *Traité de la Connaissance de Dieu et de soimême* (*Treatise on the Knowledge of God and of Self*), the *Discours sur l'histoire universelle* (*Discourse on Universal History*), and the *Politique tirée de l'Écriture sainte* (*Polity derived from Holy Writ*). The labor was in vain; the very loftiness of his genius, the extent and profundity of his views rendered Bossuet unfit to get at the heart and mind of a boy who was timid, idle and kept in fear by the king as well as by his governor. The Dauphin was nineteen when his marriage restored Bossuet to the Church and to the world; the king appointed him almoner to the dauphiness and, before long, Bishop of Meaux.

Neither the assembly of the clergy and the part he played therein, nor his frequent preachings at court diverted Bossuet from his duties as bishop; he habitually resided at Meaux in the midst of his priests. The greater number of his sermons, written at first in fragments, collected from memory in their aggregate, and repeated frequently with divergences in wording and development, were preached in the cathedral of Meaux. The Dauphin sometimes went thither to see him. "Pray, sir," he had said to him in his childhood, "take great care of me whilst I am little; I will of you when I am big." Assured of his righteousness as a priest and his fine tact as a man, the king appealed to Bossuet in the delicate conjunctures of his life. It is related that it was the bishop of Meaux who dissuaded him from making public his marriage with Madame de Maintenon. She, more anxious for power than splendor, did not bear him any ill-will for it; amidst the various leanings of the court, divided as it was between Jansenism and Quietism, it was to the simple teaching of the Catholic Church, represented by Bossuet, that she remained practically attached. Right-minded and strong-minded, but a little cold-hearted, Madame de Maintenon could not suffer herself to be led away by the sublime excesses of the Jansenists or the pious reveries of Madame Guyon; the Jesuits had influence over her, without her being a slave to them; and that influence increased after the death of Bossuet. The guidance of the bishop of Meaux, in fact, answered the requirements of spirits that were pious and earnest without enthusiasm; less ardent in faith and less absolute in religious practice than M. de St. Cyran and Port Royal, less exacting in his demands than Father Bourdaloue, susceptible now and then of mystic ideas, as is proved by his letters to Sister Cornuau, he did not let himself be won by the vague ecstasies of absolute (pure) love; he had a mind large enough to say, like Mother Angelica Arnauld: "I am of all saints' order and all saints are of my order;" but his preferences always inclined towards those saints and learned doctors who had not carried any religious tendency to excess and who had known how to rest content with the spirit of a rule and a faith that were practical. A wonderful genius, discovering by flashes and as if by instinct the most profound truths of human nature and giving them expression in an incomparable style, forcing, straining the language to make it render his idea, darting at one bound to the sublimest height by use of the simplest terms, which he, so to speak, bore away with him, wresting them from their natural and proper signification. "There, in spite of that great heart of hers, is that princess so admired and so beloved: there, such as Death has made her for us!" Bossuet alone could speak like that.

He was writing incessantly, all the while that he was preaching at Meaux and at Paris, making funeral orations over the queen, Maria Theresa, over the Princess Palatine, Michael Le Tellier and the prince of Condé; the edict of Nantes had just been revoked; controversy with the Protestant ministers, headed by Claude and Jurieu, occupied a great space in the life of the bishop of Meaux; he at that time wrote his *Histoire des variations*, often unjust and violent, always able in its attacks upon the Reformation; he did not import any zeal into persecution, though all the while admitting unreservedly the doctrines universally propagated amongst Catholics: "I declare," he wrote to M. de Bâville, "that I am and have always been of opinion, first, that princes may by penal laws constrain all heretics to conform to the profession and practices of the Catholic Church; secondly, that this doctrine ought to be held invariable in the Church, which has not only conformed to but has even demanded similar ordinances from princes." He at the same time opposed the constraint put upon the new converts to oblige them to go to mass, without requiring from them any other act of religion. "When the emperors imposed a like obligation on the Donatists," he wrote to the bishop of Mirepoix, "it was on the supposition that they were converted or would be; but the heretics at the present time, who declare themselves by not fulfilling their Easter (communicating), ought to be rather hindered from assisting at the mysteries than constrained thereto, and the more so in that it appears to be a consequence thereof to constrain them likewise to fulfil their Easter, which is expressly to give occasion for frightful sacrilege. They might be constrained to undergo instruction, but, so far as I can learn, that would hardly advance matters, and I think that we must be reduced to three things; one is to oblige them to send their children to the schools, or, in default, to find means of taking them out of their hands; another is to be firm as regards marriages; and the last is to take great pains to become privately acquainted with those of whom there are good hopes, and to procure for them solid instruction and veritable enlightenment: the rest must be left to time and to the grace of God; I know of nothing else." About the same time Fénelon, engaged upon the missions in Poitou, being as much convinced as the bishop of Meaux of a sovereign's rights over the conscience of the faithful as well as of the terrible danger of hypocrisy, wrote to Bossuet telling him that he had demanded the withdrawal of the troops in all the districts he was visiting: "It is no light matter to change the sentiments of a whole people. What difficulty must the apostles have found in changing the face of the universe, overcoming all passions and establishing a doctrine till then unheard of, seeing that we cannot persuade the ignorant by clear and express passages which they read every day in favor of the religion of their ancestors, and that the king's own authority stirs up every passion to render persuasion more easy for us! The remnants of this sect go on sinking little by little, as regards all exterior observance, into a religious indifference which cannot but cause fear and trembling. If one wanted to make them abjure Christianity and follow the Koran, there would be nothing required but to show them the dragoons; provided that they assemble by night and withstand all instruction, they consider that they have done enough." Cardinal Noailles was of the same mind as Bossuet and Fénelon. "The king will be pained to decide against your opinion as regards the new converts," says a letter to him from Madame de Maintenon: "meanwhile the most general is to force them to attend at mass. Your opinion seems to be a condemnation of all that has been hitherto done against these poor creatures; it is not pleasant to hark back so far, and it has always been supposed that, in any case, they must have a religion." In vain were liberty of conscience and its inviolable rights still misunderstood by the noblest spirits, the sincerity and high-mindedness of the great bishops instinctively revolted against the hypocrisy engendered of persecution. The tacit assuagement of the severities against the Reformers, between 1688 and 1700, was the fruit of the representations of Bossuet, Fénelon and Cardinal Noailles. Madame de Maintenon wrote at that date to one of her relatives: "You are converted; do not meddle in the conversion of others. I confess to you that I do not like the idea of answering before God and the king for all those conversions."

At the same time with the controversial treatises, the *Élévations sur les mystères* and the *Méditations sur l' Évangile* were written at Meaux, drawing the bishop away to the serener regions of supreme faith. There might he have chanced to meet those reformers, as determined as he in the strife, as attached, at bottom, as he, for life and death, to the mysteries and to the lights of a common hope. "When God shall give us grace to enter Paradise," St. Bernard used to say, "we shall be above all astonished at not finding some of those whom we had thought to meet there and at finding others whom we did not expect." Bossuet had a moment's glimpse of this higher truth; in concert with Leibnitz, a great intellect of more range in knowledge and less steadfastness than he in religious faith, he tried to reconcile the Catholic and Protestant communions in one and the same creed. There were insurmountable difficulties on both sides; the attempt remained unsuccessful.

The bishop of Meaux had lately triumphed in the matter of Quietism, breaking the ties of old friendship with Fénelon and more concerned about defending sound doctrine in the Church than fearful of hurting his friend, who was sincere and modest in his relations with him and humbly submissive to the decrees of the court of Rome. The archbishop of Cambrai was in exile at his own diocese; Bossuet was ill at Meaux, still, however, at work, going deeper every day into that profound study of Holy Writ and of the Fathers of the Church which shines forth in all his writings. He had stone and suffered agonies, but would not permit an operation. On his deathbed, surrounded by his nephews and his vicars, he rejected with disdain all eulogies on his episcopal life: "Speak to me of necessary truths," said he, preserving to the last the simplicity of a great and strong mind, accustomed to turn from appearances and secondary doctrines to embrace the mighty realities of time and of eternity. He died at Paris on the 12th of April, 1704, just when the troubles of the Church were springing up again. Great was the consternation amongst the bishops of France, wont as they were to shape themselves by his counsels. "Men were astounded at this mortal's mortality." Bossuet was seventy-three.

A month later, on the 13th of May, Father Bourdaloue in his turn died: a model of close logic and moral austerity, with a stiff and manly eloquence, so impressed with the miserable insufficiency of human efforts, that he said as he was dying, "My God, I have wasted life, it is just that Thou recall it." There remained only Fénelon in the first rank, which Massillon did not as yet dispute with him. Malebranche was living retired in his cell at the Oratory, seldom speaking, writing his *Recherches sur la vérité* (*Researches into Truth*), and his *Entretiens sur la métaphysique* (*Discourses on Metaphysics*), bolder in thought than he was aware of or wished, sincere and natural in his meditations as well as in his style. In spite of Fléchier's eloquence in certain funeral orations, posterity has decided against the modesty of the archbishop of Cambrai, who said at the death of the bishop of Nîmes, in 1710, "We have lost our master." In his retirement or his exile, after Bossuet's death, it was around Fénelon that was concentrated all the lustre of the French episcopate, long since restored to the respect and admiration it deserved.

Fénelon was born in Périgord at the castle of Fénelon on the 6th of August, 1651. Like Cardinal Retz he belonged to an ancient and noble house and was destined from his youth for the Church. Brought up at the seminary of St. Sulpice, lately founded by M. Olier, he for a short time conceived the idea of devoting himself to foreign missions; his weak health and his family's opposition turned him ere long from his purpose, but preaching of the gospel amongst the heathen continued to have for him an attraction which is perfectly depicted in one of the rare sermons of his which have been preserved. He had held himself modestly aloof, occupied with confirming *new Catholics* in their conversion or with preaching to the Protestants of Poitou; he had written nothing but his *Traité de l'éducation des filles*, intended for the family of the duke of Beauvilliers, and a book on the *ministère du pasteur*. He was in bad odor with

Harlay, archbishop of Paris, who had said to him curtly one day: "You want to escape notice, M. Abbé, and you will;" nevertheless, when Louis XIV. chose the duke of Beauvilliers as governor to his grandson, the duke of Burgundy, the duke at once called Fénelon, then thirty-eight years of age, to the important post of preceptor.

Whereas the grand-dauphin, endowed with ordinary intelligence, was indolent and feeble, his son was, in the same proportion, violent, fiery, indomitable. "The duke of Burgundy," says St. Simon, "was a born demon (*naquit terrible*), and in his early youth caused fear and trembling. Harsh, passionate, even to the last degree of rage against inanimate things, madly impetuous, unable to bear the least opposition, even from the hours and the elements, without flying into furies enough to make you fear that everything inside him would burst; obstinate to excess, passionately fond of all pleasures, of good living, of the chase madly, of music with a sort of transport and of play too, in which he could not bear to lose; often ferocious, naturally inclined to cruelty, savage in raillery, taking off absurdities with a patness which was killing; from the height of the clouds he regarded men as but atoms to whom he bore no resemblance, whoever they might be. Barely did the princes his brothers appear to him intermediary between himself and the human race, although there had always been an affectation of bringing them all three up in perfect equality; wits, penetration, flashed from every part of him, even in his transports; his repartees were astounding, his replies always went to the point and deep down, even in his mad fits; he made child's play of the most abstract sciences; the extent and vivacity of his wits were prodigious, and hindered him from applying himself to one thing at a time, so far as to render him incapable of it."

As a sincere Christian and a priest, Fénelon saw from the first that religion alone could triumph over this terrible nature; the duke of Beauvilliers, as sincere and as christianly as he, without much wits, modestly allowed himself to be led; all the motives that act most powerfully on a generous spirit, honor, confidence, fear and love of God, were employed one after the other to bring the prince into self-subjection. He was but eight years old and Fénelon had been only a few months with him, when the child put into his hands one day the following engagement:

"I promise M. l'abbé de Fénelon, on the honor of a prince, to do at once whatever he bids me, and to obey him the instant he orders me anything, and, if I fail to, I will submit to any kind of punishment or disgrace.

"Done at Versailles the 29th of November, 1689.

"*Signed:* LOUIS."

The child, however, would forget himself and relapse into his mad fits. When his preceptor was chiding him one day for a grave fault, he went so far as to say: "No, no, sir; I know who I am and what you are." Fénelon made no reply; coldly and gravely he allowed the day to close and the night to pass without showing his pupil any sign of either resentment or affection. Next day the duke of Burgundy was scarcely awake when his preceptor entered the room: "I do not know, sir," said he, "whether you remember what you said to me yesterday, that you know what you are and what I am. It is my duty to teach you that you do not know either one or the other. You fancy yourself, sir, to be more than I; some lacqueys, no doubt, have told you so, but I am not afraid to tell you, since you force me to it, that I am more than you. You have sense enough to understand that there is no question here of birth. You would consider anybody out of his wits who pretended to make a merit of it that the rain of heaven had fertilized his crops without moistening his neighbor's. You would be no wiser if you were disposed to be vain of your birth, which adds nothing to your personal merit. You cannot doubt that I am above you in lights and knowledge. You know nothing but what I have taught you; and what I have taught you is nothing compared with what I might still teach you. As for authority you have none over me; and I, on the contrary, have it fully and entirely over you; the king and Monseigneur have told you so often enough. You fancy, perhaps, that I think myself very fortunate to hold the office I discharge towards you; disabuse yourself once more, sir: I only took it in order to obey the king and give pleasure to Monseigneur, and not at all for the painful privilege of being your preceptor; and, that you may have no doubt about it, I am going to take you to his Majesty and beg him to get you another one, whose pains I hope may be more successful than mine." The duke of Burgundy's passion was past, and he burst into sobs: "Ah! sir," he cried, "I am in despair at what took place yesterday; if you speak to the king, you will lose me his affection; if you leave me, what will be thought of me? I promise you . . . I promise you . . . that you shall be satisfied with me, but promise me . . . "

Fénelon promised nothing: he remained, and the foundation of his authority was laid forever in the soul of his pupil. The young prince did not forget what he was, but he had felt the superiority of his master. "I leave the duke of Burgundy behind the door," he was accustomed to say, "and with you I am only little Louis."

God, at the same time with Fénelon, had taken possession of the duke of Burgundy's soul. "After his first communion, we saw disappearing little by little all the faults which, in his infancy, caused us great misgivings as to the future," writes Madame de Maintenon. "His piety has caused such a metamorphosis that, from the passionate thing he was, he has become self-restrained, gentle, complaisant; one would say that that was his character and that virtue was natural to him." "All his mad fits and spites yielded at the bare name of God," Fénelon used to say: "one day when he was in a very bad temper and wanted to hide in his passion what he had done in his disobedience, I pressed him to tell me the truth before God: then he put himself into a great rage and bawled, 'Why ask me before God? Very well, then, as you ask me in that way, I cannot deny that I committed that fault.' He was as it were beside himself with excess of rage, and yet religion had such dominion over him that it wrung from him so painful an avowal." "From this abyss," writes the duke of St. Simon, "came forth a prince, affable, gentle, humane, self-restrained, patient, modest, humble and austere towards himself, wholly devoted to his obligations and feeling them to be immense; he thought of nothing but combining the duties of a son and a subject with those to which he saw himself destined."

"From this abyss" came forth also a prince, singularly well-informed, fond of study, with a refined taste in literature, with a passion for science; for his instruction Fénelon made use of the great works composed for his father's education by Bossuet, adding thereto writings more suitable for his age; for him he composed the *Fables* and the *Dialogues des Morts*, and a *Histoire de Charlemagne* which has perished. In his stories, even those that were imaginary, he paid attention before everything to truth. "Better leave a history in all its dryness than enliven it at the expense of truth," he would say. The suppleness and richness of his mind sufficed to save him from wearisomeness; the liveliness of his literary impressions communicated itself to his pupil. "I have seen," says Fénelon in his letter to the French Academy, "I have seen a young prince, but eight years old, overcome with grief at sight of the peril of little Joash; I have seen him lose patience with the chief priest for concealing from Joash his name and his birth; I have seen him weeping bitterly as he listened to these verses:—

"Oh! miseram Euridicen anima fugiente vocabat;
Euridicen toto referebant flumine ripæ."

The soul and mind of Fénelon were sympathetic; Bossuet, in writing for the grand-dauphin, was responsive to the requirements of his own mind, never to those of the boy's with whose education he had been entrusted.

Fénelon also wrote *Télémaque.* "It is a fabulous narrative," he himself says, "in the form of a heroic poem, like Homer's or Virgil's, wherein I have set forth the principal actions that are meet for a prince whose birth points him out as destined to reign. I did it at a time when I was charmed with the marks of confidence and kindness showered upon me by the king; I must have been not only the most ungrateful but the most insensate of men to have intended to put into it satirical and insolent portraits; I shrink from the bare idea of such a design. It is true that I have inserted in these adventures all the verities necessary for government and all the defects that one can show in the exercise of sovereign power, but I have not stamped any of them with a peculiarity which would point to any portrait or caricature. The more the work is read, the more it will be seen that I wished to express everything without depicting anybody consecutively; it is, in fact, a narrative done in haste, in detached pieces and at different intervals; all I thought of was to amuse the duke of Burgundy and, whilst amusing, to instruct him, without ever meaning to give the work to the public."

Télémaque was published, without any author's name and by an indiscretion of the copyist's on the 6th of April, 1699. Fénelon was in exile at his diocese; public rumor before long attributed the work to him; the *Maximes des saints* had just been condemned, *Télémaque* was seized, the printers were punished; some copies had escaped the police: the book was reprinted in Holland; all Europe read it, finding therein the allusions and undermeanings against which Fénelon defended himself. Louis XIV. was more than ever angry with the archbishop. "I cannot forgive M. de Cambrai for having composed the *Télémaque*," Madame de Maintenon would say. Fénelon's disgrace, begun by the *Maximes des saints* touching *absolute* (pure) *love*, was confirmed by his ideal picture of kingly power. Chimerical in his theories of government, high-flown in his pious doctrines, Fénelon, in the conduct of his life as well as in his practical directions to his friends, showed a wisdom, a prudence, a tact which singularly belied the free speculations of his mind or his heart. He preserved silence amid the commendations and criticisms of the *Télémaque*. "I have no need and no desire to change my position," he would say: "I am beginning to be old and I am infirm; there is no occasion for my friends to ever commit themselves or to take any doubtful step on my account. I never sought out the court, I was sent for thither. I stayed there nearly ten years without obtruding myself, without taking a single step on my own behalf, without asking the smallest favor, without meddling in any matter and confining myself to answering conscientiously in all matters about which I was spoken to. I was dismissed; all I have to do is to remain at peace in my own place. I doubt not that, besides the matter of my condemned work, the policy of *Télémaque* was employed against me upon the king's mind, but I must suffer and hold my tongue."

Every tongue was held within range of King Louis XIV. It was only on the 22nd of December, 1701, four years after Fénelon's departure, that the duke of Burgundy thought he might write to him in the greatest secresy: "At last, my dear archbishop, I find a favorable opportunity of breaking the silence I have kept for four years. I have suffered many troubles since, but one of the greatest has been that of being unable to show you what my feelings towards you were during that time and that my affection increased with your misfortunes instead of being chilled by them. I think with real pleasure on the time when I shall be able to see you again, but I fear that this time is still a long way off. It must be left to the will of God, from whose mercy I am always receiving new graces. I have been many times unfaithful to Him since I saw you, but He has always done me the grace of recalling me to Him, and I have not, thank God, been deaf to His voice. I continue to study all alone, although I have not been doing so in the regular way for the last two years, and I like it more than ever. But nothing gives me more pleasure than metaphysics and ethics, and I am never tired of working at them. I have done some little pieces myself, which I should very much like to be in a position to send you, that you might correct them as you used to do my themes in old times. I shall not tell you here how my feelings revolted against all that has been done in your case, but we must submit to the will of God and believe that all has happened for our good. Farewell, my dear archbishop, I embrace you with all my heart; I ask your prayers and your blessing.—LOUIS."

"I speak to you of God and yourself only," answered Fénelon in a letter full of wise and tender counsels; "It is no question of me. Thank God, I have a heart at ease: my heaviest cross is that I do not see you, but I constantly present you before God in closer presence than that of the senses. I would give a thousand lives like a drop of water to see you such as God would have you."

Next year, in 1702, the king gave the duke of Burgundy the command of the army in Flanders. He wrote to Fénelon: "I cannot feel myself so near you without testifying my joy thereat, and, at the same time, that which is caused by the king's permission to call upon you on my way: he has, however, imposed the condition that I must not see you in private. I shall obey this order, and yet I shall be able to talk to you as much as I please, for I shall have with me Saumery, who will make the third at our first interview after five years' separation." The archbishop was preparing to leave Cambrai so as not to be in the prince's way; he now remained, only seeing the duke of Burgundy, however, in the presence of several witnesses; when he presented him with his table-napkin at supper, the prince raised his voice, and, turning to his old master, said, with a touching reminiscence of his childhood's passions: "I know what I owe you; you know what I am to you."

The correspondence continued, with confidence and deference on the part of the prince, with tender, sympathetic, far-sighted, paternal interest on the part of the archbishop, more and more concerned for the perils and temptations to which the prince was exposed in proportion as he saw him nearer to the throne and more exposed to the incense of the world. "The right thing is to become the counsel of his Majesty," he wrote to him on the death of the grand-dauphin, "the father of the people, the comfort of the afflicted, the defender of the

Church; the right thing is to keep flatterers aloof and distrust them, to distinguish merit, seek it out and anticipate it, to listen to everything, believe nothing without proof and, being placed above all, to rise superior to every one. The right thing is to desire to be father and not master. The right thing is not that all should be for one, but that one should be for all, to secure their happiness." A solemn and touching picture of an absolute monarch, submitting to God and seeking His will alone. Fénelon had early imbued his pupil with the spirit of it; and the pupil appeared on the point of realizing it; but God at a single blow destroyed all these fair hopes. "All my ties are broken," said Fénelon: "I live but on affection and of affection I shall die; we shall recover ere long that which we have not lost; we approach it every day with rapid strides; yet a little while, and there will be no more cause for tears." A week later he was dead, leaving amongst his friends, so diminished already by death, an immeasurable gap, and amongst his adversaries themselves the feeling of a great loss. "I am sorry for the death of M. de Cambrai," wrote Madame de Maintenon on the 10th of January, 1715: "he was a friend I lost through Quietism, but it is asserted that he might have done good service in the council, if things should be pushed so far." Fénelon had not been mistaken, when he wrote once upon a time to Madame de Maintenon, who consulted him about her defects: "You are good towards those for whom you have liking and esteem, but you are cold so soon as the liking leaves you; when you are frigid your frigidity is carried rather far, and, when you begin to feel mistrust, your heart is withdrawn too brusquely from those to whom you had shown confidence."

Fénelon had never shown any literary prepossessions. He wrote for his friends or for the duke of Burgundy, lavishing the treasures of his mind and spirit upon his letters of spiritual guidance, composing, in order to convince the duke of Orleans, his *Traité de l'existence de Dieu*, indifferent as to the preservation of the sermons he preached every Sunday, paying more attention to the plans of government he addressed to the young dauphin than to the publication of his works. Several were not collected until after his death. In delivering their eulogy of him at the French Academy, neither M. de Boze, who succeeded him, nor M. Dacier, director of the Academy, dared to mention the name of *Télémaque*. Clever (*spirituel*) "to an alarming extent" (*à faire peur*) in the minutest detail of his writings, rich, copious, harmonious, but not without tendencies to lengthiness, the style of Fénelon is the reflex of his character; sometimes, a little subtle and covert, like the prelate's mind, it hits and penetrates without any flash (*éclat*) and without dealing heavy blows. "Graces flowed from his lips," said Chancellor d'Aguesseau, "and he seemed to treat the greatest subjects as if, so to speak, they were child's play to him; the smallest grew to nobleness beneath his pen, and he would have made flowers grow in the midst of thorns. A noble singularity, pervading his whole person, and a something sublime in his very simplicity, added to his characteristics a certain prophet-like air. Always original, always creative, he imitated nobody, and himself appeared inimitable." His last act was to write a letter to Father Le Tellier, to be communicated to the king: "I have just received extreme unction; that is the state, reverend father, when I am preparing to appear before God, in which I pray you with instance to represent to the king my true sentiments. I have never felt anything but docility towards the Church and horror at the innovations which have been imputed to me. I accepted the condemnation of my book in the most absolute simplicity. I have never been a single moment in my life without feeling towards the king personally the most lively gratitude, the most genuine zeal, the most profound respect and the most inviolable attachment. I take the liberty of asking of his Majesty two favors which do not concern either my own person or anybody belonging to me. The first is that he will have the goodness to give me a pious and methodical successor, sound and firm against Jansenism, which is in prodigious credit on this frontier. The other favor is that he will have the goodness to complete with my successor that which could not be completed with me on behalf of the gentlemen of St. Sulpice. I wish his Majesty a long life, of which the Church as well as the State has infinite need. If peradventure I go into the presence of God, I shall often ask these favors of Him."

How dread is the power of sovereign majesty, operative even at the deathbed of the greatest and noblest spirits, causing Fénelon in his dying hour to be anxious about the good graces of a monarch ere long, like him, a-dying!

Our thoughts may well linger over those three great minds: Pascal, Bossuet and Fénelon, one layman and two bishops, all equally absorbed by the great problems of human life and immortality; with different degrees of greatness and fruitfulness they all serve the same cause; whether as defenders or assailants of Jansenism and Quietism, the solitary philosopher or the prelates engaged in the court or in the guidance of men, all three of them serving God on behalf of the soul's highest interests, remained unique in their generation and without successors as they had been without predecessors.

Leaving the desert and the Church and once more entering the world we immediately encounter, amongst women, one and one only in the first rank—Marie de Rabutin-Chantal, marchioness of Sévigné, born at Paris on the 5th of February, 1627, five months before Bossuet. Like a considerable number of women in Italy in the sixteenth century and in France in the seventeenth, she had received a careful education: she knew Italian, Latin and Spanish; she had for masters Ménage and Chapelain; and she early imbibed a real taste for solid reading, which she owed to her leaning towards the Jansenists and Port-Royal. She was left a widow at five and twenty by the death of a very indifferent husband; and she was not disposed to make a second venture. Before getting killed in a duel, M. de Sévigné had made a considerable gap in the property of his wife, who, however, had brought him more than five hundred thousand livres. Madame de Sévigné had two children: she made up her mind to devote herself to their education, to restore their fortune and to keep her love for them and for her friends. Of them she had many, often very deeply smitten with her; all remained faithful to her and she deserted none of them, though they might be put on trial and condemned like Fouquet, or perfidious and cruel like her cousin M. de Bussy-Rabutin. The safest and most agreeable of acquaintances, ever ready to take part in the joys as well as the anxieties of those whom she honored with her friendship, without permitting this somewhat superficial sympathy to agitate the depths of her heart, she had during her life but one veritable passion, which she admitted nobody to share with her. Her daughter, Madame de Grignan, the *prettiest girl in France*, clever, virtuous, business-like, appears in her mother's letters fitful, cross-grained and sometimes rather cold; Madame de Sévigné is a friend whom we read over and over again, whose emotions we share, to whom we go for an hour's distraction and delightful chat; we have no desire to chat with Madame de Grignan, we gladly leave her to her mother's exclusive affection, feeling infinitely obliged to her, however, for having existed, inasmuch as her mother wrote letters to her. Madame de Sévigné's letters to her daughter are superior to all her other letters, charming as they are; when she writes to M. de Pomponne, to M. de Coulanges, to M. de Bussy, the style is less familiar, the heart less open, the soul less stirred; she writes to her daughter as she would speak to her; it is not letters, it is an animated and charming conversation, touching upon everything, embellishing everything with an inimitable grace. She gave her daughter in marriage to Count de Grignan in January, 1669; next year her son-in-law was appointed lieutenant-general of the king in Provence; he was to fill the place there of the duke of Vendôme, too young to discharge his functions as governor. In the month of January, 1671, M. de Grignan removed his wife to Aix: he was a Provençal, he was fond of his province, his castle of Grignan and his wife; Madame de Sévigné found herself condemned to separation from the daughter whom she loved exclusively. "In vain I seek my darling daughter, I can no longer find her, and every step she takes removes her farther from me. I went to St. Mary's, still weeping and still dying of grief; it seemed as if my heart and my soul were being wrenched from me; and in truth, what a cruel separation! I asked leave to be alone; I was taken into Madame du Housset's room, and they made me up a fire. Agnes sat looking at me without speaking; that was our bargain; I stayed there till five o'clock without ceasing to sob; all my thoughts were mortal wounds to me. I wrote to M. de Grignan, you can imagine in what key. Then I went to Madame de La Fayette's, who redoubled my griefs by the interest she took in them; she was alone, ill and distressed at the death of one of the nuns; she was just as I could have desired. I returned hither at eight; but, when I came in, oh! can you conceive what I felt as I mounted these stairs? That room into which I used always to go, alas! I found the doors of it open, but I saw everything disfurnished, everything disarranged, and your little daughter, who reminded me of mine. The wakenings of the night were dreadful; I think of you continuously, it is what devotees call an habitual thought, such as one should have of God, if one did one's duty. Nothing gives me any distruction; I see that carriage which is forever going on and will never come near me; I am forever on the highways; it seems as if I were afraid sometimes that the carriage will upset with me; the rains there have been for the last three days reduced me to despair; the Rhone causes me strange alarm. I have a map before my eyes,

I know all the places where you sleep. This evening you are at Nevers, on Sunday you will be at Lyons, where you will receive this letter. I have received only two of yours, perhaps the third will come, that is the only comfort I desire; as for others, I seek for none." During five and twenty years Madame de Sévigné could never become accustomed to her daughter's absence. She set out for the Rochers, near Vitry, a family-estate of M. de Sévigné's; her friend the duke of Chaulnes was governor of Brittany. "You shall now have news of our States as your penalty for being a Breton. M. de Chaulnes arrived on Sunday evening, to the sound of everything that can make any in Vitry; on Monday morning he sent me a letter, I wrote back to say that I would go and dine with him. There are two dining-tables in the same room; fourteen covers at each table. Monsieur presides at one, Madame at the other. The good cheer is prodigious; joints are carried away quite untouched, and as for the pyramids of fruit, the doors require to be heightened. Our fathers did not foresee this sort of machine, indeed they did not even foresee that a door required to be higher than themselves. Well, a pyramid wants to come in, one of those pyramids which make everybody exclaim from one end of the table to the other; but so far from that boding damage, people are often, on the contrary, very glad not to see any more of what they contain; this pyramid, then, with twenty or thirty porcelain dishes, was so completely upset at the door that the noise it made put to silence the violins, hautbois and trumpets. After dinnor M. de Locmaria and M. de Coëtlogon danced with two fair Bretons some marvellous jigs (*passe-pieds*) and some minuets in a style that the court-people cannot approach; wherein they do the Bohemian and Breton step with a neatness and correctness which are charming. I was thinking all the while of you, and I had such tender recollections of your dancing and of what I had seen you dance, that this pleasure became a pain to me. The States are sure not to be long; there is nothing to do but to ask for what the king wants; nobody says a word, and it is all done. As for the governor, he finds, somehow or other, more than forty thousand crowns coming in to him. An infinity of presents, pensions, repairs of roads and towns, fifteen or twenty grand dinner-parties, incessant play, eternal balls, comedies three times a week, a great show of dress, that is the States. I am forgetting three or four hundred pipes of wine which are drunk; but, if I did not reckon this little item, the others do not forget it, and put it first. This is what is called the sort of twaddle to make one go to sleep on one's feet; but it is what comes to the tip of your pen when you are in Brittany and have nothing else to say."

Even in Brittany and at the Rochers, Madame de Sévigné always has something to say. The weather is frightful, she is occupied a good deal in reading the romances of La Calprenède and the *Grand Cyrus* as well as the *Ethics* of Nicole. "For four days it has been one continuous tempest; all our walks are drowned, there is no getting out any more. Our masons, our carpenters keep their rooms; in short, I hate this country and I yearn every moment for your sun; perhaps you yearn for my rain; we do well, both of us. I am going on with the *Ethics* of Nicole which I find delightful; it has not yet given me any lesson against the rain, but I am expecting it, for I find everything there, and conformity to the will of God might answer my purpose if I did not want a specific remedy. In fact, I consider this an admirable book; nobody has written as these gentlemen have, for I put down to Pascal half of all that is beautiful. It is so nice to have one's self and one's feelings talked about, that, though it be in bad part, one is charmed by it. What is called searching the depths of the heart with a lantern is exactly what he does; he discloses to us that which we feel every day, but have not the wit to discern or the sincerity to avow. I have even forgiven the *swelling in the heart* (*l' enflure du cœur*) for the sake of the rest, and I maintain that there is no other word to express vanity and pride, which are really wind: try and find another word; I shall complete the reading of this with pleasure."

Here we have the real Madame de Sévigné, whom we love, on whom we rely, who is as earnest as she is amiable and gay, who goes to the very core of things, and who tells the truth of herself as well as of others. "You ask me, my dear child, whether I continue to be really fond of life; I confess to you that I find poignant sorrows in it, but I am even more disgusted with death; I feel so wretched at having to end all this thereby that, if I could turn back again, I would ask for nothing better. I find myself under an obligation which perplexes me; I embarked upon life without my consent, and I must go out of it; that overwhelms me. And how shall I go? Which way? By what door? When will it be? In what condition? Shall I suffer a thousand, thousand pains, which will make me die desperate? Shall I have brain-fever? Shall I die of an accident? How shall I be with God? What shall I have to show Him? Shall fear, shall necessity bring me back to Him? Shall I have no sentiment but that of dread? What can I hope? Am I worthy of Heaven? Am I worthy of Hell? Nothing is such madness as to leave one's salvation in uncertainty, but nothing is so natural; and the stupid life I lead is the easiest thing in the world to understand; I bury myself in these thoughts and I find death so terrible that I hate life more because it leads me thereto than because of the thorns with which it is planted. You will say that I want to live forever then: not at all; but, if my opinion had been asked, I should have preferred to die in my nurse's arms; that would have removed me from vexations of spirit and would have given me Heaven full surely and easily."

Madame de Sévigné would have very much scandalized *those gentlemen* of Port-Royal, if she had let them see into the bottom of her heart as she showed it to her daughter. Pascal used to say: "There are but three sorts of persons: those who serve God, having found Him; those who employ themselves in seeking Him, not having found Him; and those who live without seeking Him or having found Him. The first are reasonable and happy; the last are mad and miserable; the intermediate are miserable and reasonable." Without ever having sought and found God in the absolute sense intended by Pascal, Madame de Sévigné kept approaching Him by gentle degrees. "We are reading a treatise by M. Hamon of Port-Royal on *continuous prayer;* though he is a hundred feet above my head, he nevertheless pleases and charms us. One is very glad to see that there have been and still are in the world people to whom God communicates His Holy Spirit in such abundance; but, oh God! when shall we have some spark, some degree of it? How sad to find one's self so far from it and so near to something else! Oh fie! Let us not speak of such plight as that: it calls for sighs and groans and humiliations a hundred times a day."

After having suffered so much from separation and so often traversed France to visit her daughter in Provence, Madame de Sévigné had the happiness to die in her house at Grignan. She was sixty-nine and she had been ill for some time; she was subject to rheumatism; her son's wildness had for a long while retarded the arrangement of her affairs; at last he had turned over a new leaf, he was married, he was a devotee; Madame de Grignan had likewise found a wife for her son, whom the king had made a colonel at a very early age, and a husband for her daughter, little Pauline, now Madame de Simiane. "All this together is extremely nice and too nice," wrote Madame de Sévigné to M. de Bussy, "for I find the days going so fast and the months and the years that, for my part, my dear cousin, I can no longer hold them. Time flies and carries me along in spite of me; it is all very fine for me to wish to stay it, it bears me away with it, and the idea of this causes me great fear; you will make a pretty shrewd guess why." Death came at last, and Madame de Sévigné lost all her terrors: she was attacked by small-pox whilst her sick daughter was confined to her bed, and died on the 19th of April, 1696, thanking God that she was the first to go after having so often trembled for her daughter's health. "What calls far more for our admiration than for our regrets," writes M. de Grignan to M. de Coulanges, "is the spectacle of a brave woman facing death, of which she had no doubt from the first days of her illness, with astounding firmness and submission. This person, so tender and so weak towards all that she loved, showed nothing but courage and piety when she believed that her hour was come, and we could not but remark of what utility and of what importance it is to have the mind stocked with good matter and holy reading, for the which Madame de Sévigné had a liking, not to say a wonderful hungering, from the use she managed to make of that good store in the last moments of her life." She had often taken her daughter to task for not being fond of books. "There is a certain person who undoubtedly has plenty of wits, but of so nice and so fastidious a sort that she cannot read anything but five or six sublime works, which is a sign of distinguished taste. She cannot bear historical books, a great deprivation this and of that which is a subsistence to everybody else; she has another misfortune, which is that she cannot read twice over those choice books which she esteems exclusively. This person says that she is insulted when she is told that she is not fond of reading; another bone to pick." Madame de Sévigné's liking for good books accompanied her to the last, and helped her to make a good end.

All the women who had been writers in her time died before Madame de Sévigné. Madame de Motteville, a judicious and sensible woman, more independent at the bottom of her heart than in externals, had died in 1689, exclusively occupied, from the time that she lost Queen Anne of Austria, in works of piety and in drawing up her *Mémoires.* Mdlle. de Montpensier, "my great Mademoiselle," as Madame de Sévigné used to call her, had died at Paris on the 5th of April, 1693, after a violent illness, as feverish as her life. Impassioned and haughty, with her head so full of her greatness that she did not marry in her youth, thinking nobody worthy of her except the king and the emperor who had no fancy for her, and ending by a private marriage with the duke of Lauzun, "a cadet of Gascony," whom the king would not permit her to espouse publicly, clever, courageous, hare-brained, generous, she has herself sketched her own portrait. "I am tall, neither fat nor thin, of a very fine and easy figure. I have a good mien, arms and hands not beautiful, but a beautiful skin and throat too. I have a straight leg and a well-shaped foot; my hair is light and of a beautiful auburn; my face is long, its contour is handsome, nose large and aquiline; mouth neither large nor small, but chiselled and with a very pleasing expression, lips vermilion; teeth not fine, but not frightful either, my eyes are blue, neither large nor small, but sparkling, soft and proud like my mien. I talk a great deal without saying silly things or using bad words. I am a very vicious enemy, being very choleric and passionate, and that, added to my birth, may well make my enemies tremble, but I have also a noble and a kindly soul. I am incapable of any base and black deed; and so I am more disposed to mercy than to justice. I am melancholic, I like reading good and solid books; trifles bore me, except verses, and them I like of whatever sort they may be, and undoubtedly I am as good a judge of such things as if I were a scholar."

A few days after *Mademoiselle,* died, likewise at Paris, Madelaine de la Vergne, marchioness of La Fayette, the most intimate friend of Madame de Sévigné. "Never did we have the smallest cloud upon our friendship," the latter would say: "long habit had not made her merit stale to me, the flavor of it was always fresh and new; I paid her many attentions from the mere prompting of my heart without the propriety to which we are bound by friendship having anything to do with it; I was assured too that I constituted her dearest consolation, and for forty years past it had always been the same thing." Sensible, clever, a sweet and safe acquaintance, Madame de La Fayette was as simple and as true in her relations with her confidantes as in her writings. *La Princesse de Clèves* alone has outlived the times and the friends of Madame de La Fayette. Following upon the "great sword-thrusts" of

La Calprenède or Mdlle. de Scudéry, this delicate, elegant and virtuous tale, with its pure and refined style, enchanted the court, which recognized itself at its best and painted under its brightest aspect; it was farewell forever to the "Pays de Tendre." Madame de La Fayette had very bad health; she wrote to Madame de Sévigné on the 14th of July, 1693, "Here is what I have done since I wrote to you last. I have had two attacks of fever; for six months I had not been purged; I am purged once, I am purged twice; the day after the second time, I sit down to table: oh! dear! I feel a pain in my heart, I do not want any soup. Have a little meat then. No, I do not want any. Well, you will have some fruit. I think I will. Very well, then, have some. I don't know, I think I will have something by and by; let me have some soup and a chicken this evening. Here is the evening, and there are the soup and the chicken: I don't want them. I am nauseated; I will go to bed, I prefer sleeping to eating. I go to bed, I turn round, I turn back, I have no pain, but I have no sleep either. I call, I take a book, I shut it up. Day comes, I get up, I go to the window: it strikes four, five, six; I go to bed again, I doze till seven, I get up at eight, I sit down to table at twelve, to no purpose, as yesterday; I lay myself down in my bed again in the evening, to no purpose, as the night before. Are you ill? Nay. I am in this state for three days and three nights. At present I am getting some sleep again, but I still eat merely mechanically, horse-wise, rubbing my mouth with vinegar; otherwise, I am very well, and I haven't even so much pain in the head." Fault was found with Madame de La Fayette for not going out. "She had a mortal melancholy. What absurdity again! Is she not the most fortunate woman in the world? That is what people said," writes Madame de Sévigné: "it needed that she should be dead to prove that she had good reason for not going out and for being melancholy: her reins and her heart were all gone, was not that enough to cause those fits of despondency of which she complained? And so, during her life she showed reason, and after death she showed reason, and never was she without that divine reason which was her principal gift."

Madame de La Fayette had in her life one great sorrow which had completed the ruin of her health. On the 16th of March, 1680, after the closest and longest of intimacies, she had lost her best friend, the duke of La Rochefoucauld. Carried away in his youth by party-strife and an ardent passion for Madame de Longueville, he had at a later period sought refuge in the friendship of Madame de La Fayette. "When women have well-formed minds," he would say, "I like their conversation better than that of men; you find with them a certain gentleness which is not met with amongst us, and it seems to me, besides, that they express themselves with greater clearness and that they give a more pleasant turn to the things they say." A meddler and intriguer during the Fronde, sceptical and bitter in his *Maximes*, the duke of La Rochefoucauld was amiable and kindly in his private life. Factions and the court had taught him a great deal about human nature, he had seen it and judged of it from its bad side; witty, shrewd, and often profound, he was too severe to be just: the bitterness of his spirit breathed itself out completely in his writings, he kept for his friends that kindliness and that sensitiveness of which he made sport. "He gave me wit," Madame de La Fayette would say, "but I reformed his heart." He had lost his son at the passage of the Rhine, in 1672. He was ill, suffering cruelly. "I was yesterday at M. de La Rochefoucauld's," writes Madame de Sévigné in 1680; "I found him uttering loud shrieks; his pain was such that his endurance was quite overcome without a single scrap remaining; the excessive pain upset him to such a degree that he was sitting out in the open air with a violent fever upon him. He begged me to send you word and to assure you that the wheel-broken do not suffer during a single moment what he suffers one half of his life, and so he wishes for death as a happy release." He died with Bossuet at his pillow. "Very well prepared as regards his conscience," says Madame de Sévigné again: "that is all settled; but, in other respects, it might be the illness and death of his neighbor which is in question, he is not flurried about it, he is not troubled about it. Believe me, my daughter, it is not to no purpose that he has been making reflections all his life; he has approached his last moments in such wise that they have had nothing that was novel or strange for him." M. de La Rochefoucauld, thought worse of men than of life. "I have scarcely any fear of things," he had said: "I am not at all afraid of death." With all his rare qualities and great opportunities, he had done nothing but frequently embroil matters in which he had meddled, and had never been anything but a great lord with a good deal of wit. Actionless penetration and sceptical severity may sometimes clear the judgment and the thoughts, but they give no force or influence that has power over men. "There was always a *something* (*je ne sais quoi*) about M. de La Rochefoucauld," writes Cardinal de Retz, who did not like him: "he was for meddling in intrigues from his childhood and at a time when he had no notion of petty interests, which were never his foible, and when he did not understand great ones, which, on the other hand, were never his strength. He was never capable of doing anything in public affairs, and I am sure I don't know why; his views were not sufficiently broad and he did not even see comprehensively all that was within his range, but his good sense, very good speculatively, added to his suavity, his insinuating style and his easy manners, which are admirable, ought to have compensated more than it did for his lack of penetration. He always showed habitual irresolution, but I really do not know to what to attribute this irresolution; it could not, with him, have come from the fertility of his imagination, which is anything but lively. He was never a warrior, though he was very much the soldier. He was never a good party-man, though he was engaged in it all his life. That air of bashfulness and timidity which you see about him in private life was turned in public life into an air of apology. He always considered himself to need one, which fact, added to his maxims, which do not show sufficient belief in virtue, and to his practice, which was always to get out of affairs with as much impatience as he had shown to get into them, leads me to conclude that he would have done far better to know his own place and reduce himself to passing, as he might have passed, for the most polite of courtiers and the worthiest (*le plus honnête*) man, as regards ordinary life, that ever appeared in his century."

Cardinal de Retz had more wits, more courage and more resolution than the duke of La Rochefoucault; he was more ambitious and more bold; he was, like him, meddlesome, powerless and dangerous to the State. He thought himself capable of superseding Cardinal Mazarin and far more worthy than he of being premier minister; but every time he found himself opposed to the able Italian, he was beaten. All that he displayed, during the Fronde, of address, combination, intrigue and resolution would barely have sufficed to preserve his name in history, if he had not devoted his leisure in his retirement to writing his *Mémoires*. Vigorous, animated, always striking, often amusing, sometimes showing rare nobleness and high-mindedness, his stories and his portraits transport us to the very midst of the scenes he desires to describe and the personages he makes the actors in them. His rapid, nervous, picturesque style, is the very image of that little dark, quick, agile man, more soldier than bishop, and more intriguer than soldier, faithfully and affectionately beloved by his friends, detested by his very numerous enemies and dreaded by many people, for the causticity of his tongue, long after the troubles of the Fronde had ceased and he was reduced to be a wanderer in foreign lands, still archbishop of Paris without being able to set foot in it. Having retired to Commercy, he fell under Louis XIV.'s suspicion. Madame de Sévigné, who was one of his best friends, was anxious about him. "As to our cardinal, I have often thought as you," she wrote to her daughter: "but, whether it be that the enemies are not in a condition to cause fear, or that the friends are not subject to take alarm, it is certain that there is no commotion. You show a very proper spirit in being anxious about the welfare of a person who is so distinguished and to whom you owe so much affection." "Can I forget him whom I see everywhere in the story of our misfortunes," exclaimed Bossuet in his funeral oration over Michael Le Tellier, "that man so faithful to individuals, so formidable to the State, of a character so high that he could not be esteemed or feared or hated by halves, that steady genius whom, the while he shook the universe, we saw attracting to himself a dignity which in the end he determined to relinquish as having been too dearly bought, as he had the courage to recognize in the place that is the most eminent in Christendom, and as being after all quite incapable of satisfying his desires, so conscious was he of his mistake and of the emptiness of human greatness? But, so long as he was bent upon obtaining what he was one day to despise, he kept everything moving by means of powerful and secret springs, and, after that all parties were overthrown, he seemed still to uphold himself alone, and alone to still threaten the victorious favorite with his sad but fearless gaze." When Bossuet sketched this magnificent portrait of Mazarin's rival, Cardinal de Retz had been six years dead, in 1679.

Mesdames de Sévigné and de La Fayette were of the court, as were the duke of La Rochefoucauld and Cardinal de Retz; La Bruyère lived all his life rubbing shoulders with the court; he knew it, he described it, but he was not of it and could not be of it. Nothing is known of his family. He was born at Dourdan, in 1639, and had just bought a post in the Treasury (*trésorier de France*) at Caen, when Bossuet, who knew him, induced him to remove to Paris as teacher of history to the duke, grandson of the great Condé. He remained forever attached to the person of the prince, who gave him a thousand crowns a year, and he lived to the day of his death at Condé's house. "He was a philosopher," says Abbé d'Olivet in his *Histoire de l'Académie Française;* "all he dreamt of was a quiet life. with his friends and his books, making a good choice of both, not courting or avoiding pleasure, ever inclined for moderate fun and with a talent for setting it going, polished in manners and discreet in conversation; dreading every sort of ambition, even that of displaying wit." This was not quite the opinion formed by Boileau of La Bruyère. "Maximilian came to see me at Auteuil," writes Boileau to Racine on the 19th of May, 1687, the very year in which the *Caractères* was published: "he read me some of his Theophrastus. He is a very worthy (*honnête*) man and one who would lack nothing, if nature had created him as agreeable as he is anxious to be. However, he has wit, learning and merit." Amidst his many and various portraits La Bruyère has drawn his own with an amiable pride. "I go to your door, Ctesiphon; the need I have of you hurries me from my bed and from my room. Would to heaven I were neither your client nor your bore! Your slaves tell me that you are engaged and cannot see me for a full hour yet; I return before the time they appointed, and they tell me that you have gone out. What can you be doing, Ctesiphon, in that remotest part of your rooms, of so laborious a kind as to prevent you from seeing me? You are filing some bills, you are comparing a register; you are signing your name, you are putting the flourish. I had but one thing to ask you and you had but one word to reply: *yes* or *no.* Do you want to be singular? Render service to those who are dependent upon you, you will be more so by that behavior than by not letting yourself be seen. O man of importance and overwhelmed with business, who in your turn have need of my offices, come into the solitude of my closet; the philosopher is accessible; I shall not put you off to another day. You will find me over those works of Plato, which treat of the immortality of the soul and its distinctness from the body; or with pen in hand to calculate the distances of Saturn and Jupiter. I admire God in His works, and I seek by knowledge of the truth to regulate my mind and become better. Come in, all doors are open to you; my antechamber is not made to wear you out with waiting for me; come right in to me without giving me notice. You bring me something more precious than silver and gold, if it be an opportunity of obliging you. Tell me, what can I do for you? Must I leave my books, my study, my work, this line I have just begun? What a fortunate interruption for me is that which is of service to you!"

From the solitude of that closet went forth a book unique of its sort, full of sagacity, penetration and severity without bitterness; a picture of the manners of the court and of the world, traced by the hand of a spectator who had not essayed its temptations, but who guessed them and passed judgment on them all, "a book," as M. de Malézieux said to La Bruyère, "which was sure to bring its author many readers and many enemies." Its success was great from the first, and it excited lively curiosity. The courtiers liked the portraits; attempts were made to name them; the good sense, shrewdness and truth of the observations struck everybody; people had met a hundred times those whom La Bruyère had described. The form appeared of a rarer order than even the matter; it was a brilliant, uncommon style, as varied as human nature, always elegant and pure, original and animated, rising sometimes to the height of the noblest thoughts, gay and grave, pointed and serious. Avoiding, by richness in turns and expression, the uniformity native to the subject, La Bruyère rivetted attention by a succession of touches making a masterly picture, a terrible one sometimes, as in his description of the peasants' misery: "To be seen are certain ferocious animals, male and female, scattered over the country, dark, livid and all scorched by the sun, affixed to the soil which they rummage and throw up with indomitable pertinacity; they have a sort of articulate voice, and, when they rise to their feet, they show a human face; they are, in fact, men; at night they withdraw to the caves, where they live on black bread, water and roots; they spare other men the trouble of sowing, tilling and reaping for their livelihood, and deserve, therefore, not to go in want of the very bread they have sown." Few people at the court, and in La Bruyère's day, would have thought about the sufferings of the country-folks and conceived the idea of contrasting them with the sketch of a court-ninny: "Gold glitters," say you, "upon the clothes of Philemon; it glitters as well at the tradesman's. He is dressed in the finest stuffs; are they a whit the less so when displayed in the shops and by the piece? Nay, but the embroidery and the ornaments add magnificence thereto; then I give the workman credit for his work. If you ask him the time, he pulls out a watch which is a masterpiece; his sword-guard is an onyx; he has on his finger a large diamond which he flashes into all eyes and which is perfection; he lacks none of those curious trifles which are worn about one as much for show as for use; and he does not stint himself either of all sorts of adornment befitting a young man who has married an old millionaire. You really pique my curiosity: I positively must see such precious articles as those. Send me that coat and those jewels of Philemon's; you can keep the person. Thou'rt wrong, Philemon, if with that splendid carriage and that large number of rascals behind thee and those six animals to draw thee thou thinkest thou art thought more of. We take off all those appendages which are extraneous to thee to get at thyself, who art but a ninny."

More earnest and less bitter than La Rochefoucauld, and as brilliant and as firm as Cardinal de Retz, La Bruyère was a more sincere believer than either. "I feel that there is a God, and I do not feel that there is none; that is enough for me; the reasoning of the world is useless to me; I conclude that God exists; are men good enough, faithful enough, equitable enough to deserve all our confidence, and not make us wish at least for the existence of God to whom we may appeal from their judgments and have recourse when we are persecuted or betrayed?" A very strong reason and of potent logic, naturally imprinted upon an upright spirit and a sensible mind, irresistibly convinced, both of them, that justice alone can govern the world.

La Bruyère had just been admitted into the French Academy, in 1693: in his admission-speech he spoke in praise of the living, Bossuet, Fénelon, Racine, La Fontaine; it was not as yet the practice; those who were not praised felt angry, and the journals of the time bitterly attacked the new Academician; he was hurt, and withdrew almost entirely from the world; four days before his death, however, "he was in company; all at once he perceived that he was becoming deaf, yes stone deaf. He returned to Versailles, where he had apartments at Condé's house; apoplexy carried him off in a quarter of an hour on the 11th of May, 1696," leaving behind him an incomparable book wherein, according to his own maxim, the excellent writer shows himself to be an excellent painter, and *four dialogues against Quietism*, still unfinished, full of lively and good-humored hostility to the doctrines of Madame Guyon: they were published after his death.

We pass from prose to poetry, from La Bruyère to Corneille, who had died in 1684, too late for his fame, in spite of the vigorous returns of genius which still flash forth sometimes in his feeblest works. Throughout the Regency and the Fronde, Corneille had continued to occupy almost alone the great French stage; Rotrou, his sometime rival with his piece of *Venceslas* and ever tenderly attached to him, had died, in 1650, at Dreux, of which he was civil magistrate. An epidemic was ravaging the town, and he was urged to go away: "I am the only one who can maintain good order, and I shall remain," he replied: "at the moment of my writing to you the bells are tolling for the twenty-second person to-day; perhaps, to-morrow it will be for me, but my conscience has marked out my duty; God's will be done!" Two days later he was dead.

Corneille had dedicated *Polyeucte* to the regent Anne of Austria; he published in a single year *Rodogune* and the *Mort de Pompée*, dedicating this latter piece to Mazarin, in gratitude, he said, for an act of generosity with which His Eminence had surprised him. At the same time he borrowed from the Spanish drama the canvas of the *Menteur*, the first really French comedy which appeared on the boards, and which Molière showed that he could appreciate at its proper value. After this attempt, due perhaps to the desire felt by Corneille to triumph over his rivals in the style in which he had walked abreast with them, he let tragedy resume its legitimate empire over a genius formed by it; he wrote *Héraclius* and *Nicomède*, which are equal in parts to his finest master-pieces. But by this time the great genius no longer soared with equal flight; *Théodore* and *Pertharite* had been failures. "I don't mention them," Corneille would say, "in order to avoid the vexation of remembering them." He was still living at Rouen, in a house adjoining that occupied by his brother, Thomas Corneille, younger than he, already known by some comedies which had met with success. The two brothers had married two sisters:

"Their houses twain were made in one;
With keys and purse the same was done;
Their wives can never have been two.
Their wishes tallied at all times;
No games distinct their children knew;
The fathers lent each other rhymes;
Same wine for both the drawers drew."—[Ducis.]

It is said that when Peter Corneille was puzzled to end a verse he would undo a trap that opened into his brother's room, shouting: "*Sans-souci*, a rhyme!"

Corneille had announced his renunciation of the stage; he was translating into verse the *Imitation of Christ.* "It were better," he had written in his preface to *Pertharite*, "that I took leave myself instead of waiting till it is taken of me altogether; it is quite right that after twenty years' work I should begin to perceive that I am becoming too old to be still in the fashion. This resolution is not so strong but that it may be broken; there is every appearance, however, of my abiding by it."

Fouquet was then in his glory, "no less superintendent of literature than of finance," and he undertook to recall to the stage the genius of Corneille. At his voice, the poet and the tragedian rose up at a single bound:

> "I feel the selfsame fire, the selfsame nerve I feel,
> That roused th' indignant Cid, drove home Horatius' steel;
> As cunning as of yore this hand of mine I find,
> That sketch'd great Pompey's soul, depicted Cinna's mind"—

wrote Corneille in his thanks to Fouquet. He had some months before said to Mdlle. du Parc, who was an actress in Molière's company, which had come to Rouen, and who was, from her grand airs, nicknamed by the others the *Marchioness*,—

> "Marchioness, if Age hath set
> On my brow his ugly die;
> At my years, pray don't forget,
> You will be as—old as I.
>
> Yet do I possess of charms
> One or two, so slow to fade,
> That I feel but scant alarms
> At the havoc Time hath made.
>
> You have such as men adore,
> But these that you scorn to-day
> May, perchance be to the fore,
> When your own are worn away.
>
> These can from decay reprieve
> Eyes I take a fancy to;
> Make a thousand years believe
> Whatsoe'er I please of you.
>
> With that new, that coming race,
> Who will take my word for it,
> All the warrant for your face
> Will be what I may have writ."

Corneille reappeared upon the boards with a tragedy called *Œdipe*, more admired by his contemporaries than by posterity; on the occasion of Louis XIV.'s marriage, he wrote for the king's comedians the *Toison d'or*, and put into the mouth of France those prophetie words:—

> "My natural force abates, from long success alone;
> Triumphant blooms the State, the wretched peoples groan:
> Their shrunken bodies bend beneath my high emprise;
> Whilst glory gilds the throne, the subject sinks and dies."

Sertorius appeared at the commencement of the year 1662. "Pray where did Corneille learn politics and war?" asked Turenne when he saw this piece played. "You are the true and faithful interpreter of the mind and courage of Rome," Balzac wrote to him: "I say further, sir, you are often her teacher, and the reformer of olden times, if they have need of embellishment and support. In the spots where Rome is of brick, you rebuild it of marble; where you find a gap, you fill it with a master-piece, and I take it that what you lend to history is always better than what you borrow from it. . . ." "They are grander and more Roman in his verses than in their history," said La Bruyère. "Once only, in the *Cid*, Corneille had abandoned himself unreservedly to the reality of passion; scared at what he might find in the weaknesses of the heart, he would no longer see aught but its strength; he sought in man that which resists and not that which yields, thus giving his times the sublime pleasure of an enjoyment that can belong to nought but the human soul, a cherished proof of its noble origin and its glorious destiny, the pleasure of admiration, the appreciation of the beautiful and the great, the enthusiasm aroused by virtue. He moves us at sight of a master-piece, thrills us at the sound of a noble deed, enchants us at the bare idea of a virtue which three thousand years have forever separated from us" (*Corneille et son temps*, by M. Guizot). Every other thought, every other prepossession are strangers to the poet: his personages represent heroic passions which they follow out without swerving and without suffering themselves to be shackled by the notions of a morality which is still far from fixed and often in conflict with the interests and obligations of parties, thus remaining perfectly of his own time and his own country, all the while that he is describing Greeks or Romans or Spaniards.

There is no pleasure in tracing the decadence of a great genius. Corneille wrote for a long while without success, attributing his repeated rebuffs to his old age, the influence of fashion, the capricious taste of the generation for young people; he thought himself neglected, appealing to the king himself, who had ordered *Cinna* and *Pompée* to be played at court:—

"Go on; the latest born have naught degenerate,
Naught have they which would stamp them illegitimate:
They, miserable fate! were smother'd at the birth,
And one kind glance of yours would bring them back to earth;
The people and the court, I grant you, cry them down;
I have, or else they think I have, too feeble grown;
I've written far too long to write so well again;
The wrinkles on the brow reach even to the brain;
But counter to this vote how many could I raise,
If to my latest works you should vouchsafe your praise!
How soon so kind a grace, so potent to constrain,
Would court and people both win back to me again!
'So Sophocles of yore at Athens was the rage;
So boil'd his ancient blood at five-score years of age,'
Would they to Envy cry, 'when Œdipus at bay
Before his judges stood, and bore the votes away.'"

Posterity has done for Corneille more than Louis XIV. could have done; it has left in oblivion *Agésilas*, *Attila*, *Titus* and *Pulchérie*, it has preserved the memory of the triumphs only. The poet was accustomed to say with a smile, when he was reproached with his slowness and emptiness in conversation: "I am Peter Corneille all the same." The world has passed similar judgment on his works; in spite of the rebuffs of his latter years, he has remained "the great Corneille."

When he died, in 1684, Racine, elected by the Academy in 1673, found himself on the point of becoming its director: he claimed the honor of presiding at the obsequies of Corneille. The latter had not been admitted to the body until 1641, after having undergone two rebuffs. Corneille had died in the night. The Academy decided in favor of Abbé de Lavau, the outgoing director. "Nobody but you could pretend to bury Corneille," said Benserade to Racine, "yet you have not been able to obtain the chance." It was only when he received into the Academy Thomas Corneille, in his brother's place, that Racine could praise to his heart's content the master and rival who, in old age, had done him the honor to dread him. "My father had not been happy in his speech at his own admission," says Louis Racine ingenuously: "he was in this, because he spoke out of the abundance of his heart, being inwardly convinced that Corneille was worth much more than he." Louis XIV. had come in for as great a share as Corneille in Racine's praises. He, informed of the success of the speech, desired to hear it. The author had the honor of reading it to him, after which the king said to him: "I am very pleased; I would praise you more, if you had praised me less." It was on this occasion that the great Arnauld, still in disgrace and carefully concealed, wrote to Racine: "I have to thank you, sir, for the speech which was sent me from you. There certainly was never anything so eloquent, and the hero whom you praise is so much the more worthy of your praises in that he considered them too great. I have many things that I would say to you about that if I had the pleasure of seeing you, but it would need the dispersal of a cloud which I dare to say is a spot upon this sun. I assure you that the ideas I have thereupon are not interested and that what may concern myself affects me very little. A chat with you and your companion would give me much pleasure, but I would not purchase that pleasure by the least poltroonery. You know what I mean by that; and so I abide in peace and wait patiently for God to make known to this perfect prince that he has not in his kingdom a subject more loyal, more zealous for his true glory, and, if I dare say so, loving him with a love more pure and more free from all interest. That is why I could not bring myself to take a single step to obtain liberty to see my friends, unless it were to my prince alone that I should be indebted for it." Fénelon and the great Arnauld held the same language, independent and submissive, proud and modest, at the same time. Only their conscience spoke louder than their respect for the king.

At the time when Racine was thus praising at the Academy the king and the great Corneille, his own dramatic career was already ended. He was born, in 1639, at La Ferté-Milon; he had made his first appearance on the stage in 1664 with the *Frères ennemis*, and had taken leave of it in 1673 with *Phèdre*, *Esther* and *Athalie*, played in 1689 and in 1691 by the young ladies of St Cyr, were not regarded by their author and his austere friends as any derogation from the pious engagements he had entered into. Racine, left an orphan at four years of age and brought up at Port-Royal under the influence and the personal care of M. Le Maître, who called him *his* son, did not at first answer the expectations of his master. The glowing fancy of which he already gave signs caused dismay to Lancelot, who threw into the fire one after the other two copies of the Greek tale *Théagène et Chariclée* which the young man was reading. The third time the latter learnt it off by heart and, taking the book to his severe censor, "Here," said he, "you can burn this volume too as well as the others."

Racine's pious friends had fine work to no purpose: nature carried the day, and he wrote verses. "Being unable to consult you, I was prepared, like Malherbe, to consult an old servant at our place," he wrote to one of his friends, "if I had not discovered that she was a Jansenist like her master, and that she might betray me, which would be my utter ruin, considering that I receive every day letter upon letter or rather excommunication upon excommunication, all because of a poor sonnet." To deter the young man from poetry, he was led to expect a benefice and was sent away to Uzès to his uncle's, Father Sconin, who set him to study theology. "I pass my time with my uncle, St. Thomas and Virgil," he wrote on the 17th of January, 1662, to M. Vitard, steward to the duke of Luynes: "I make lots of extracts from theology and some from poetry. My uncle has kind intentions towards me, he hopes to get me something; then I shall try to pay my debts. I do not forget the obligations I am under to you. I blush as I write; *Erubuit puer, salva res est* (the lad has blushed; it is all right). But that conclusion is all wrong; my affairs do not mend."

Racine had composed at Uzès the *Frères ennemis*, which was played on his return to Paris, in 1664, not without a certain success; *Alexandre* met with a great deal, in 1665; the author had at first entrusted it to Molière's company, but he was not satisfied and gave his piece to the comedians of the Hôtel de Bourgogne; Molière was displeased and quarrelled with Racine, towards whom he had up to that time testified much good will. The disagreement was not destined to disturb the equity of their judgments upon one another. When Racine brought out *Les Plaideurs*, which was not successful at first, Molière, as he left, said out aloud, "The comedy is excellent, and they who deride it deserve to be derided." One of Racine's friends, thinking to do him a pleasure, went to him in all haste to tell him of the failure of the *Misanthrope* at its first representation. "The piece has fallen flat," said he, "never was there anything so dull; you can believe what I say, for I was there." "You were there, and I was not," replied Racine, "and yet I don't believe it, because it is impossible that Moliere should have written a bad piece. Go again and pay more attention to it."

Racine had just brought out *Alexandre* when he became connected with Boileau, who was three years his senior and who had already published several of his satires. "I have a surprising facility in writing my verses," said the young tragic author ingenuously. "I want to teach you to write them with difficulty," answered Boileau, "and you have talent enough to learn before long." *Andromaque* was the result of this novel effort and was Racine's real commencement.

He was henceforth irrevocably committed to the theatrical cause. Nicole attacking Desmarets, who had turned prophet after the failure of his *Clovis*, alluded to the author's comedies and exclaimed with all the severity of Port-Royal: "a romance-writer and a scenic poet is a public poisoner not of bodies but of souls." Racine took these words to himself, and he wrote in defence of the dramatic art two letters so bitter, biting and insulting towards Port-Royal and the protectors of his youth that Boileau dissuaded him from publishing the second and that remorse before long took possession of his soul, never to be entirely appeased. He had just brought out *les Plaideurs*, which had been requested of him by his friends and partly composed during the dinners they frequently had together. "I put into it only a few barbarous law-terms which I might have picked up during a law-suit and which neither I nor my judges ever really heard or understood." After the first failure of the piece, the king's comedians one day risked playing it before him. "Louis XIV. was struck by it and did not think it a breach of his dignity or taste to utter shouts of laughter so loud that the courtiers were astounded." The delighted comedians, on leaving Versailles, returned straight to Paris and went to awaken Racine. "Three carriages during the night in a street where it was unusual to see a single one during the day woke up the neighborhood. There was a rush to the windows, and, as it was known that a councillor of requests (law-officer) had made a great uproar against the comedy of the *Plaideurs*, nobody had a doubt of punishment befalling the poet who had dared to take off the judges in the open theatre. Next day all Paris believed that he was in prison." He had a triumph, on the contrary, with *Britannicus*, after which the king gave up dancing in the court-ballets, for fear of resembling Nero; *Bérénice* was a duel between Corneille and Racine for the amusement of Madame Henriette; Racine bore away the bell from his illustrious rival, without much glory; *Bajazet* soon followed. "Here is Racine's piece," wrote Madame de Sévigné to her daughter in Jan., 1672; "if I could send you La Champmeslé, you would think it good, but without her it loses half its worth. The character of Bajazet is cold as ice, the manners of the Turks are ill observed in it, they do not make so much fuss about getting married; the catastrophe is not well led up to, there are no reasons given for that great butchery. There are some pretty things, however, but nothing perfectly beautiful, nothing which carries by storm, none of those bursts of Corneille's which make one creep. My dear, let us be careful never to compare Racine with him, let us always feel the difference; never will the former rise any higher than *Andromaque.* Long live our old friend Corneille!" Let us forgive his bad verses for the sake of those divine and sublime beauties which transport us. They are master-strokes which are inimitable." Corneille had seen *Bajazet*: "I would take great care not to say so to anybody else," he whispered in the ear of Segrais, who was sitting beside him, "because they would say that I said so from jealousy; but, mind you, there is not in *Bajazet* a single character with the sentiments which should and do prevail at Constantinople; they have all, beneath a Turkish dress, the sentiments that prevail in the midst of France." The impassioned loyalty of Madame de Sévigné and the clear-sighted jealously of Corneille were not mistaken; Bajazet is no Turk, but he is none the less very human. "There are points by which men recognize themselves though there is no resemblance; there are others in which there is resemblance without any recognition. Certain sentiments belong to nature in all countries; they are characteristic of man only and everywhere man will see his own image in them." [*Corneille et son temps*, by M. Guizot.] Racine's reputation went on continually increasing; he had brought out *Mithridate* and *Iphigénie; Phèdre* appeared in 1677. A cabal of great lords caused its failure at first. When the public, for a moment led astray after the *Phèdre* of Pradon, returned to the master-work of Racine, vexation and wounded pride had done their office in the poet's soul. Pious sentiments ever smouldering in his heart, the horror felt for the theatre by Port-Royal and penitence for the sins he had been guilty of against his friends there revived within him; and Racine gave up profane poetry forever. "The applause I have met with has often flattered me a great deal," said he at a later period to his son, "but the smallest critical censure, bad as it may have been, always caused me more of vexation than all the praises had given me of pleasure." Racine wanted to turn Carthusian; his confessor dissuaded him, and his friends induced him to marry. Madame Racine was an excellent person, modest and devout, who never went to the theatre and scarcely knew her husband's plays by name; she brought him some fortune; the king had given the great poet a pension, and Colbert had appointed him to the treasury (*trésorier*) at Moulins; Louis XIV., moreover, granted frequent donations to men of letters; Racine received from him nearly fifty thousand livres; he was appointed historiographer to the king; Boileau received the same title; the latter was not married; but Racine before long had seven children. "Why did not I turn Carthusian!" he would sometimes exclaim in the disquietude of his paternal affection when his children were ill. He devoted his life to them with pious solicitude, constantly occupied with their welfare, their good education and the salvation of their souls. Several of his daughters became nuns; he feared above everything to see his eldest son devote himself to poetry, dreading for him the dangers he considered he himself had run. "As for your epigram, I wish you had not written it," he wrote to him: "independently of its being commonplace, I cannot too earnestly recommend you not to let yourself give way to the temptation of writing French verses which would serve no purpose but to distract your mind; above all you should not write against anybody." This son, the object of so much care, to whom his father wrote such modest, grave, paternal and sagacious letters, never wrote verses, lived in retirement and died young without ever having married. Little Louis or *Lionval*, Racine's last child, was the only one who ever dreamt of being a writer. "You must be very bold," said Boileau to him, "to dare write verses with the name you bear! It is not that I consider it impossible for you to become capable some day of writing good ones, but I mistrust what is without precedent, and never, since the world was world, has there been seen a great poet son of a great poet." Louis Racine never was a great poet, in spite of the fine verses which are to be met with in his poems *la Religion* and *la Grâce*. His *Mémoires* of his father, written for his son, describe Racine in all the simple charm of his domestic life. "He would leave all to come and see us," writes Louis Racine: "an equerry of the duke's came one day to say that he was expected to dinner at Condé's house. 'I shall not have the honor of going,' said he: 'it is more than a week since I have seen my wife and children who are making holiday to-day to feast with me on a very fine carp; I cannot give up dining with them.' And, when the equerry persisted, he sent for the carp, which was worth about a crown. 'Judge for yourself,' said he, 'whether I can disappoint these poor children who have made up their minds to regale me, and would not enjoy it if they were to eat this dish without me.' He was loving by nature," adds Louis Racine: "he was loving towards God when he returned to Him; and, from the day of his return to those who, from his infancy, had taught him to know Him, he was so towards them without any reserve; he was so all his life towards his friends, towards his wife and towards his children."

Boileau had undertaken the task of reconciling his friend with Port-Royal. Nicole had made no opposition, "not knowing what war was." M. Arnauld was intractable. Boileau one day made up his mind to take him a copy of *Phèdre*, pondering on the way as to what he should say to him. "Shall this man," said he, "be always right, and shall I never be able to prove him wrong? I am quite sure that I shall be right to-day; if he is not of my opinion, he will be wrong." And going to M. Arnauld's, where he found a large company, he set about developing his thesis, pulling out *Phèdre* and maintaining that if tragedy were dangerous it was the fault of the poets. The younger theologians listened to him disdainfully, but at last M. Arnauld said out loud: "If things are as he says, he is right and such tragedy is harmless." Boileau declared that he had never felt so pleased in his life. M. Arnauld being reconciled to *Phèdre*, the principal step was made; next day the author of the tragedy presented himself. The culprit entered, humility and confusion depicted on his face; he threw himself at the feet of M. Arnauld, who took him in his arms; Racine was thenceforth received into favor by Port-Royal. The two friends were preparing to set out with the king for the campaign of 1677. The besieged towns opened their gates before the poets had left Paris. "How is it that you had not the curiosity to see a siege?" the king asked them on his return: "it was not a long trip." "True, sir," answered Racine, always the greater courtier of the two, "but our tailors were too slow. We had ordered travelling suits; and when they were brought home, the places which your Majesty was besieging were taken." Louis XIV. was not displeased. Racine thenceforth accompanied him in all his campaigns; Boileau, who ailed a great deal and was of shy disposition, remained at Paris. His friend wrote to him constantly, at one time from the camp and at another from Versailles, whither he returned with the king. "Madame de Maintenon told me this morning," writes Racine, "that the king had fixed our pensions at four thousand francs for me and two thousand for you; that is, not including our literary pensions. I have just come from thanking the king. I laid more stress upon your case than even my own; I said in as many words: 'Sir, he has more wit than ever, more zeal for your Majesty and more desire to work for your glory than ever he had.' I am nevertheless really pained at the idea of my getting more than you. But, independently of the expenses and fatigue of the journeys from which I am glad that you are delivered, I know that you are so noble-minded and so friendly that I am sure you would be heartily glad that I were even better treated. I shall be very pleased if you are." Boileau answered at once: "Are you mad, with your compliments? Do not you know perfectly well that it was I who suggested the way in which things have been done? And can you doubt of my being perfectly well pleased with a matter in which I am accorded all I ask? Nothing in the world could be better, and I am even more rejoiced on your account than on my own." The two friends consulted one another mutually about their verses; Racine sent Boileau his spiritual songs. The king heard the *Combat du Chrétien* sung, set to music by Moreau:

"O God, my God, what deadly strife!
Two men within myself I see:
One would that, full of love to Thee,
My heart were leal, in death and life;
The other, with rebellion rife,
Against Thy laws inciteth me."

He turned to Madame de Maintenon, and, "Madame," said he, "I know those two men well." Boileau sends Racine his ode on the capture of Namur. "I have risked some very new things," he says, "even to speaking of the white plume which the king has in his hat; but, in my opinion, if you are to have novel expressions in verse, you must speak of things which have not been said in verse. You shall be judge, with permission to alter the whole, if you do not like it." Boileau's generous confidence was the more touching, in that Racine was sarcastic and bitter in discussion. "Did you mean to hurt me?" Boileau said to him one day. "God forbid!" was the answer. "Well, then, you made a mistake, for you did hurt me."

Racine had just brought out *Esther* at the theatre of St. Cyr:

Madame de Brinon, lady-superior of the establishment which was founded by Madame de Maintenon for the daughters of poor noblemen, had given her pupils a taste for theatricals. "Our little girls have just been playing your *Andromaque*," wrote Madame de Maintenon to Racine, "and they played it so well that they never shall play it again in their lives, or any other of your pieces." She at the same time asked him to write, in his leisure hours, some sort of moral and historical poem from which love should be altogether banished. This letter threw Racine into a great state of commotion. He was anxious to please Madame de Maintenon and yet it was a delicate commission for a man who had a great reputation to sustain. Boileau was for refusing. "That was not in the calculations of Racine," says Madame de Caylus in her *Souvenirs*. He wrote *Esther*. "Madame de Maintenon was charmed with the conception and the execution," says Madame de La Fayette; "the play represented in some sort the fall of Madame de Montespan and her own elevation; all the difference was that Esther was a little younger and less particular in the matter of piety. The way in which the characters were applied was the reason why Madame de Maintenon was not sorry to make public a piece which had been composed for the community only and for some of her private friends. There was exhibited a degree of excitement about it which is incomprehensible; not one of the small or the great but would go to see it, and that which ought to have been looked upon as merely a convent-play became the most serious matter in the world. The ministers, to pay their court by going to this play, left their most pressing business. At the first representation at which the king was present, he took none but the principal officers of his hunt. The second was reserved for pious personages, such as Father La Chaise, and a dozen or fifteen Jesuits, with many other devotees of both sexes; afterwards it extended to the courtiers." "I paid my court at St. Cyr the other day more agreeably than I had expected," writes Madame de Sévigné to her daughter: "we listened, Marshal Bellefonds and I, with an attention that was remarked and with certain discreet commendations which were not perhaps to be found beneath the head-dresses of all the ladies present. I cannot tell you how exceedingly delightful this piece is; it is a unison of music, verse, songs, persons, so perfect that there is nothing left to desire. The girls who act the kings and other characters were made expressly for it. Everything is simple, everything innocent, everything sublime and affecting. I was charmed and so was the marshal, who left his place to go and tell the king how pleased he was, and that he sat beside a lady well worthy of having seen *Esther*. The king came over to our seats: 'Madame,' he said to me, 'I am assured that you have been pleased.' I, without any confusion, replied, 'Sir, I am charmed; what I feel is beyond expression.' The king said to me, 'Racine is very clever.' I said to him, 'Very, Sir; but really these young people are very clever too, they throw themselves into the subject as if they had never done aught else.' 'Ah! as to that,' he replied; 'it is quite true.' And then his Majesty went away and left me the object of envy. The prince and princess came and gave me a word, Madame de Maintenon a glance; she went away with the king. I replied to all, for I was in luck."

Athalie had not the same brilliant success as *Esther*. The devotees and the envious had affrighted Madame de Maintenon, who had requested Racine to write it. The young ladies of St. Cyr, in the uniform of the house, played the piece quite simply at Versailles before Louis XIV. and Madame de Maintenon in a room without a stage. When the players gave a representation of it at Paris, it was considered heavy, it did not succeed. Racine imagined that he was doomed to another failure like that of *Phèdre*, which he preferred before all his other pieces. "I am a pretty good judge," Boileau kept repeating to him: "it is about the best you have done; the public will come round to it." Racine died before success was achieved by the only perfect piece which the French stage possesses, worthy both of the subject and of the sources whence Racine drew his inspiration. He had with an excess of scrupulousness abandoned the display of all the fire that burned within him, but beauty never ceased to rouse him to irresistible enthusiasm. Whilst reading the Psalms to M. de Seignelay when lying ill, he could not refrain from paraphrasing them aloud. He admired Sophocles so much, that he never dared touch the subjects of his tragedies. "One day," says M. de Valicour, "when he was at Auteuil, at Boileau's, with M. Nicole and some distinguished friends, he took up a Sophocles in Greek and read the tragedy of *Œdipus* translating it as he went. He read so feelingly that all his auditors experienced the sensations of terror and pity with which this piece abounds. I have seen our best pieces played by our best actors, but nothing ever came near the commotion into which I was thrown by this reading, and, at this moment of writing, I fancy I still see Racine book in hand and all of us awe-stricken around him." Thus it was that, whilst repeating, but a short time before, the verses of *Mithridate*, as he was walking in the Tuileries, he had seen the workmen leaving their work and coming up to him, convinced as they were that he was mad and was going to throw himself into the basin.

Racine for a long while enjoyed the favors of the king, who went so far as to tolerate the attachment the poet had always testified towards Port-Royal. Racine, moreover, showed tact in humoring the susceptibilities of Louis XIV. and his counsellors. "Father Bouhours and Father Rapin (Jesuits) were in my study when I received your letter," he writes to Boileau: "I read it to them, on breaking the seal, and I gave them very great pleasure. I kept looking ahead, however, as I was reading, in case there was anything too Jansenistical in it. I saw towards the end the name of M. Nicole and I skipped boldly or rather mean-spiritedly over it. I dared not expose myself to the chance of interfering with the great delight and even shouts of laughter caused them by many very amusing things you sent me. They are both of them, I assure you, very friendly towards you and indeed very good fellows." All this caution did not prevent Racine, however, from displeasing the king. After a conversation he had held with Madame de Maintenon about the miseries of the people, she asked him for a memorandum on the subject. The king demanded the name of the author and flew out at him. "Because he is a perfect master of verse," said he, "does he think he knows everything? And, because he is a great poet, does he want to be minister?" Madame de Maintenon was more discreet in her relations with the king than bold in the defence of her friends; she sent Racine word not to come and see her until further orders. "Let this cloud pass," she said: "I will bring the fine weather back." Racine was ill; his naturally melancholy disposition had become sombre. "I know, Madame," he wrote to Madame de Maintenon, "what influence you have; but in the house of Port-Royal I have an aunt who shows her affection for me in quite a different way. This holy woman is always praying God to send me disgraces, humiliations and subjects for penitence; she will have more success than you." At bottom, his soul was not sturdy enough to endure the rough doctrines of Port-Royal; his health got worse and worse; he returned to court; he was readmitted by the king who received him graciously. Racine continued uneasy; he had an abscess of the liver and was a long while ill. "When he was convinced that he was going to die, he ordered a letter to be written to the superintendent of finances asking for payment which was due of his pension. His son brought him the letter. 'Why,' said he, 'did not you ask for payment of Boileau's pension too? We must not be made distinct. Write the letter over again and let Boileau know that I was his friend even to death.' When the latter came to wish him farewell, he raised himself up in bed with an effort: 'I regard it as a happiness for me to die before you,' he said to his friend. An operation appeared necessary. His son would have given him hopes. 'And you too!' said Racine, 'you would do as the doctors and mock me? God is the Master and can restore me to life, but Death has sent in his bill.'"

He was not mistaken: on the 21st of April, 1699, the great poet, the scrupulous Christian, the noble and delicate painter of the purest passions of the soul expired at Paris at fifty-nine years of age, leaving life without regret, spite of all the successes with which he had been crowned. Unlike Corneille with the *Cid*, he did not take tragedy and glory by assault, he conquered them both by degrees, raising himself at each new effort and gaining over little by little the most passionate admirers of his great rival; at the pinnacle of this reputation and this victory, at thirty-eight years of age, he had voluntarily shut the door against the intoxications and pride of success, he had mutilated his life, buried his genius in penitence, obeying simply the calls of his conscience, and, with singular moderation in the very midst of exaggeration, becoming a father of a family and remaining a courtier, at the same time that he gave up the stage and glory. Racine was gentle and sensible even in his repentance and his sacrifice. Boileau gave religion the credit for this very moderation: "Reason commonly brings others to faith, it was faith which brought M. Racine to reason."

Boileau had more to do with his friend's reason than he probably knew. Racine never acted without consulting him. With Racine Boileau lost half his life. He survived him twelve years without ever setting foot again within the court after his first interview with the king. "I have been at Versailles," he writes to his publisher, M. Brossette, "where I saw Madame de Maintenon and afterwards the king, who overcame me with kind words; so, here I am more historiographer than ever. His Majesty spoke to me of M. Racine in a manner to make courtiers desire death, if they thought he would speak of them in the same way afterwards. Meanwhile, that has been but very small consolation to me for the loss of that illustrious friend, who is none the less dead though regretted by the greatest king in the universe." "Remember," Louis XIV. had said, "that I have always an hour a week to give you when you like to come." Boileau did not go again. "What should I go to court for?" he would say: "I cannot sing praises any more."

At Racine's death Boileau did not write any longer. He had entered the arena of letters at three and twenty, after a sickly and melancholy childhood. The *Art Poétique* and the *Lutrin* appeared in 1674; the first nine Satires and several of the Epistle had preceded them. Rather a witty, shrewd and able versifier than a great poet, Boileau displayed in the *Lutrin* a richness and suppleness of fancy which his other works had not foreshadowed. The broad and cynical buffoonery of Scarron's burlesques had always shocked his severe and pure taste. "Your father was weak enough to read *Virgile travesti* and laugh over it," he would say to Louis Racine, "but he kept it dark from me." In the *Lutrin*, Boileau sought the gay and the laughable under noble and polished forms: the gay lost by it, the laughable remained stamped with an ineffaceable seal. "M. Despréaux," wrote Racine to his son, "has not only received from Heaven a marvellous genius for satire, but he has also, together with that, an excellent judgment which makes him discern what needs praise and what needs blame." This marvellous genius for satire did not spoil Boileau's natural good feeling. "He is cruel in verse only," Madame de Sévigné used to say. Racine was tart, bitter in discussion; Boileau always preserved his coolness: his judgments frequently anticipated those of posterity. The king asked him one day who was the greatest poet of his reign. "Molière, Sir," answered Boileau, without hesitation. "I shouldn't have thought it," rejoined the king somewhat astonished, "but you know more about it than I do." Molière, in his turn, defending La Fontaine against the pleasantries of his friends, said to his neighbor at one of those social meals in which the illustrious friends delighted: "Let us not laugh at the good soul (*bonhomme*), he will probably live longer than the whole of us." In the noble and touching brotherhood of these great minds, Boileau continued invariably to be the bond between the rivals; intimate friend as he was of Racine, he never quarrelled with Molière, and he hurried to the king to beg that he would pass on the pension with which he honored him to the aged Corneille, groundlessly deprived of the royal favors. He entered the Academy on the 3rd of July, 1684, immediately after La Fontaine. His satires had retarded his election. "He praised without flattery, he humbled himself nobly," says Louis Racine, "and, when he said that admission to the Academy was sure to be closed against him for so many reasons, he set a-thinking all the Academicians he had spoken ill of in his works." He was no longer writing verses when Perrault published his *Parallèle des anciens et des modernes.* "If Boileau do not reply," said the prince of Conti, "you may assure him that I will go to the Academy and write on his chair, 'Brutus, thou sleepest.'" The ode on the capture of Namur, intended to crush Perrault whilst celebrating Pindar, not being sufficient, Boileau wrote his *Reflexions sur Longin,* bitter and often unjust toward Perrault, who was far more equitably treated and more effectually refuted in Fénelon's letter to the French Academy.

Boileau was by this time old; he had sold his house at Auteuil, which was so dear, but he did not give up literature, continuing to revise his verses carefully, pre-occupied with new editions, and reproaching himself for this preoccupation. "It is very shameful," he would say, "to be still busying myself with rhymes and all those Parnassian trifles, when I ought to be thinking of nothing but the account I am prepared to go and render to God." He died on the 13th of March, 1711, leaving nearly all he had to the poor; he was followed to the tomb by a great throng. "He had many friends," was the remark amongst the people: "and yet we are assured that he spoke evil of everybody." No writer ever contributed more than Boileau to the formation of poetry; no more correct or shrewd judgment ever assessed the merits of authors, no loftier spirit ever guided a stronger and a juster mind. Through all the vicissitudes undergone by literature and spite of the sometimes excessive severity of his decrees, Boileau has left an ineffaceable impression upon the French language; his talent was less effective than his understanding; his judgment and his character have had more influence than his verses.

Boileau had survived all his friends; La Fontaine, born in 1621 at Château-Thierry, had died in 1695. He had entered in his youth the brotherhood of the Oratory, which he had soon quitted, being unable, he used to say, to accustom himself to theology; he went and came between town and town, amusing himself everywhere, and already writing a little:

> "For me the whole round world was laden with delights;
> My heart was touch'd by flower, sweet sound and sunny day,
> I was the sought of friends and eke of lady gay."

Fontaine was married, without caring much for his wife, whom he left to live alone at Château-Thierry. He was in great favor with Fouquet. When his patron was disgraced, in danger of his life, La Fontaine put into the mouth of the nymphs of Vaux his touching appeal to the king's clemency:

> "May he, then, o'er the life of high-soul'd Henry pore,
> Who, with the power to take, for vengeance yearn'd no more:
> Oh! into Louis' soul this gentle spirit breathe."

Later on, during Fouquet's imprisonment at Pignerol, La Fontaine wrote further:

> "I sigh to think upon the object of my prayers;
> You take my sense, Ariste; your generous nature shares
> The plaints I make for him who so unkindly fares.
> He did displease the king; and lo! his friends were gone;
> Forthwith a thousand throats roar'd out at him like one:
> I wept for him, despite the torrent of his foes,
> I taught the world to have some pity for his woes."

La Fontaine has been described as a solitary being, without wit and without external charm of any kind. La Bruyère has said: "A certain man appears loutish, heavy, stupid; he can neither talk nor relate what he has just seen: he sets himself to writing, and it is a model of story-telling; he makes speakers of animals, trees, stones, everything that cannot speak; there is nothing but lightness and elegance, nothing but natural beauty and delicacy in his works." "He says nothing, or will talk of nothing but Plato," Racine's daughters used to say. All his contemporaries, however, of fashion and good breeding did not form the same opinion of him: the dowager-duchess of Orleans, Marguerite of Lorraine, had taken him as one of her gentlemen-in-waiting; the duchess of Bouillon had him in her retinue in the country; Madame de Montespan and her sister, Madame de Thianges, liked to have a visit from him; he lived at the house of Madame de La Sablière, a beauty and a wit, who received a great deal of company; he said of her:

> "Warm is her heart and knit with tenderest ties
> To those she loves, and, elsewise, otherwise;
> For such a sprite, whose birth-place is the skies,
> Of manly beauty blent with woman's grace,
> No mortal pen, though fain, can fitly trace."

"I have only kept by me," she would say, "my three pets (*animaux*): my dog, my cat, and La Fontaine." When she died, M. and Madame d'Hervart received into their house the now old and somewhat isolated poet. As D'Hervart was on his way to go and make the proposal to La Fontaine he met him in the street. "I was coming to ask you to put up at our house," said he. "I was just going thither," answered La Fontaine with the most touching confidence. There he remained to his death, contenting himself with going now and then to Château-Thierry, as long as his wife lived, to sell, with her consent, some strip of ground; the property was going, old age was coming:

"John did no better than he had begun,
Spent property and income both as one:
Of treasure saw small use in any way;
Knew very well how to get through his day;
Split it in two: one part, as he thought best,
He passed in sleep, did nothing all the rest."

He did not sleep, he dreamt. One day dinner was kept waiting for him: "I have just come," said he as he entered, "from the funeral of an ant; I followed the procession to the cemetery, and I escorted the family home." It has been said that La Fontaine knew nothing of natural history; he knew and loved animals; up to his time, fable-writers had been merely philosophers or satirists; he was the first who was a poet, unique not only in France but in Europe, discovering the deep and secret charm of nature, animating it with his inexhaustible and graceful genius, giving lessons to men from the example of animals, without making the latter speak like man, ever supple and natural, sometimes elegant and noble, with penetration beneath the cloak of his simplicity, inimitable in the line which he had chosen from taste, from instinct, and not from want of power to transport his genius elsewhither; he himself has said:

"Yes, call me truly, if it must be said,
Parnassian butterfly and like the bees
Wherein old Plato found our similes:
Light rover I, forever on the wing,
Flutter from flower to flower, from thing to thing,
With much of pleasure mix a little fame."

And in *Psyché*:

"Music and books, and junkettings and love,
And town and country—all to me is bliss;
There nothing is that comes amiss:
In melancholy's self grim joy I prove."

The grace, the naturalness, the original independence of the mind and the works of La Fontaine had not the luck to please Louis XIV., who never accorded him any favor, and La Fontaine did not ask for any:

> "All dumb I shrink once more within my shell,
> Where unobtrusive pleasures dwell;
> True, I shall here by Fortune be forgot:
> Her favors with my verse agree not well;
> To importune the gods beseems me not."

Once only, from the time of Fouquet's trial, the poet demanded a favor: Louis XIV. having misgivings about the propriety of the *Contes* of La Fontaine, had not yet given the assent required for his election to the French Academy, when he set out for the campaign in Luxembourg. La Fontaine addressed to him a ballad:

> "Just as, in Homer, Jupiter we see
> Alone o'er all the other gods prevail;
> You, one against a hundred though it be,
> Balance all Europe in the other scale.
> Them liken I to those who, in the tale,
> Mountain on mountain piled, presumptuously
> Warring with Heaven and Jove. The earth clave he,
> And hurl'd them down beneath huge rocks to wail:
> So take you up your bolt with energy;
> A happy consummation cannot fail.
>
> Sweet thought! that doth this month or two avail
> To somewhat soothe my Muse's anxious care.
> For certain minds at certain stories rail,
> Certain poor jests, which naught but trifles are.
> If I with deference their lessons hail,
> What would they more? Be you more prone to spare,
> More kind than they; less sheathed in rigorous mail;
> Prince, in a word, your real self declare:
> A happy consummation cannot fail."

The election of Boileau to the Academy appeased the king's humor, who preferred the other's intellect to that of La Fontaine. "The choice you have made of M. Despréaux is very gratifying to me," he said to the board of the Academy: "it will be approved of by everybody; you can admit La Fontaine at once: he has promised to be good." It was a rash promise, which the poet did not always keep.

The friends of La Fontaine had but lately wanted to reconcile him to his wife; they had with that view sent him to Château-Thierry; he returned without having seen her whom he went to visit. "My wife was not at home," said he: "she had gone to the sacrament (*au salut*)." He was becoming old; those same faithful friends, Racine, Boileau and Maucroix were trying to bring him home to God. Racine took him to church with him; a Testament was given him: "That is a very good book," said he: "I assure you it is a very good book." Then all at once addressing Abbé Boileau, "Doctor, do you think that St. Augustin was as clever as Rabelais?" He was ill, however, and began to turn towards eternity his dreamy and erratic thoughts; he had set about composing pious hymns. "The best of thy friends has not a fortnight to live," he wrote to Maucroix; "for two months I have not been out, unless to go to the Academy for amusement. Yesterday, as I was returning, I was seized in the middle of Rue du Chantre with a fit of such great weakness that I really thought I was dying. O my dear friend, to die is nothing, but thinkest thou that I am about to appear before God? Thou knowest how I have lived. Before thou hast this letter, the gates of eternity will perchance be opened for me." "He is as simple as a child," said the woman who took care of him in his last illness: "if he has done amiss, it was from ignorance rather than wickedness." A charming and a curious being, serious and simple, profound and childlike, winning by reason of his very vagaries, his good-natured originality, his helplessness in common life, La Fontaine knew how to estimate the literary merits as well as the moral qualities of his illustrious friends. "When they happened to be together," says he in his tale of *Psyché*, "and had talked to their heart's content of their diversions, if they chanced to stumble upon any point of science or literature, they profited by the occasion, without, however, lingering too long over one and the same subject, but flitting from one topic to another like bees that meet as they go with different sorts of flowers. Envy, malignity or cabal had no voice amongst them; they adored the works of the ancients, refused not the moderns the praises which were their due, spoke of their own with modesty and gave one another honest advice, when any one of them fell ill of the malady of the age and wrote a book, which happened now and then. In this case, Acanthus (Racine) did not fail to propose a walk in some place outside the town, in order to hear the reading with less noise and more pleasure. He was extremely fond of gardens, flowers, foliage. Polyphile (La Fontaine) resembled him in this, but then Polyphile might be said to love all things. Both of them were lyrically inclined, with this difference, that Acanthus was rather the more pathetic, Polyphile the more ornate."

When La Fontaine died on the 13th of April, 1695, of the four friends lately assembled at Versailles to read the tale of *Psyché*, Molière alone had disappeared. La Fontaine had admired at Vaux the young comic poet, who had just written the *Fâcheux* for the entertainment given by Fouquet to Louis XIV.:

> "It is a work by Molière;
> This writer, of a style so rare,
> Is now-a-days the court's delight.
> His fame, so rapid is its flight,
> Beyond the bounds of Rome must be:
> Amen! For he's the man for me."

In his old age he gave vent to his grief and his regret at Molière's death in this touching epitaph:

> "Beneath this stone Plautus and Terence lie,
> Though lieth here but Molière alone:
> Their threefold gifts of mind made up but one,
> That witch'd all France with noble comedy.
> Now are they gone: and little hope have I
> That we again shall look upon the three:
> Dead men, methinks, while countless years roll by,
> Terentius, Plautus, Molière will be."

Molière and French comedy had no need to take shelter beneath the mantle of the ancients; they, together, had shed upon the world incomparable lustre; Shakspeare might dispute with Corneille and Racine the sceptre of tragedy, he had succeeded in showing himself as full of power, with more truth, as the one, and as full of tenderness, with more profundity, as the other; Molière is superior to him in originality, abundance and perfection of characters; he yields to him neither in range, nor penetration, nor complete knowledge of human nature. The lives of these two great geniuses, authors and actors both together, present in other respects certain features of resemblance. Both were intended for another career than that of the stage; both, carried away by an irresistible passion, assembled about them a few actors, leading at first a roving life, to end by becoming the delight of the court and of the world. John Baptist Poquelin, who before long assumed the name of Molière, was born at Paris, in 1622; his father, upholstery-groom-of-the-chamber (*valet de chambre tapissier*) to Louis XIV., had him educated with some care at Clermont (afterwards Louis-le-Grand) College, then in the hands of the Jesuits. He attended, by favor, the lessons which the philosopher Gassendi, for a long time the opponent of Descartes, gave young Chapelle. He imbibed at these lessons, together with a more extensive course of instruction, a certain freedom of thinking which frequently cropped out in his plays and contributed later on to bring upon him an accusation of irreligion. In 1645 (? 1643), Molière had formed, with the ambitious title of *illustre théâtre,* a small company of actors who, being unable to maintain themselves at Paris, for a long while tramped the provinces, through all the troubles of the Fronde. It was in 1653 that Molière brought out at Lyons his comedy *l'Étourdi,* the first regular piece he had ever composed, The *Dépit amoureux* was played at Béziers, in 1656, at the opening of the session of the States of Languedoc; the company returned to Paris in 1658; in 1659, Molière, who had obtained a licence from the king, gave at his own theatre *les Précieuses ridicules.* He broke with all imitation of the Italians and the Spaniards, and, taking off to the life the manners of his own times, he boldly attacked the affected exaggeration and absurd pretensions of the vulgar imitators of the Hôtel de Rambouillet. "Bravo! Molière," cried an old man from the middle of the pit: "this is real comedy." When he published his piece, Molière, anxious not to give umbrage to a powerful clique, took care to say in his preface that he was not attacking real *précieuses* but only the bad imitations.

Just as he had recalled Corneille to the stage, Fouquet was for protecting Molière upon it. The *École des Maris* and the *Fâcheux* were played at Vaux. Amongst the ridiculous characters in this latter, Molière had not described the huntsman. Louis XIV. himself indicated to him the marquis of Soyecour; "There's one you have forgotten," he said. Twenty-four hours later, the bore of a huntsman, with all his jargon of venery, had a place forever amongst the *Fâcheux* of Molière. The *École des Femmes* the *Impromptu de Versailles,* the *Critque de l'École des Femmes,* began the bellicose period in the great comic poet's life. Accused of impiety, attacked in the honor of his private life, Molière, returning insult for insult, delivered over those amongst his enemies who offered a butt for ridicule to the derision of the court and of posterity. The *Festin de Pierre* and the signal punishment of the libertine (free-thinker) were intended to clear the author from the reproach of impiety; *la Princesse d'Élide* and *l'Amour médecin* were but charming interludes in the great struggle henceforth instituted between reality and appearance; in 1666, Molière produced *le Misanthrope,* a frank and noble spirit's sublime invective against the frivolity, perfidious and showy semblances of court. "This misanthrope's despitefulness against bad verses was copied from me; Molière himself confessed as much to me many a time," wrote Boileau one day; the indignation of Alceste is deeper and more universal than that of Boileau against bad poets; he is disgusted with the court and the world because he is honest, virtuous and sincere, and sees corruption triumphant around him; he is wroth to feel the effects of it in his life and almost in his own soul. He is a victim to the eternal struggle between good and evil without the strength and the unquenchable hope of Christianity. The *Misanthrope* is a shriek of despair uttered by virtue, excited and almost distraught at the defeat she forbodes. The *Tartuffe* was a new effort in the same direction, and bolder in that it attacked religious hypocrisy and seemed to aim its blows even at religion itself. Molière was a long time working at it; the first acts had been played in 1664 at court under the title of *l'Hypocrite*, at the same time as *la Princesse d'Élide.* "The king," says the account of the entertainment in the Gazette de Loret, "saw so much analogy of form between those whom true devotion sets in the way of heaven and those whom an empty ostentation of good deeds does not hinder from committing bad, that his extreme delicacy in respect of religious matters could with difficulty brook this resemblance of vice to virtue, and though there might be no doubt of the author's good intentions, he prohibited the playing of this comedy before the public until it should be quite finished and examined by persons qualified to judge of it, so as not to let advantage be taken of it by others, less capable, of just discernment in the matter." Though played once publicly, in 1667, under the title of *l'Imposteur*, the piece did not appear definitively on the stage until 1669, having undoubtedly excited more scandal by interdiction than it would have done by representation. The king's good sense and judgment at last prevailed over the terrors of the truly devout and the resentment of hypocrites. He had just seen an impious piece of buffoonery played. "I should very much like to know," said he to the prince of Condé, who stood up for Molière, an old fellow-student of his brother's, the prince of Conti's, "why people who are so greatly scandalized at Molière's comedy say nothing about *Scaramouche?*" "The reason of that," answered the prince, "is that *Scaramouche* makes fun of heaven and religion, about which those gentry do not care, and that Molière makes fun of their own selves, which they cannot brook." The prince might have added that all the blows in *Tartuffe*, a masterpiece of shrewdness, force and fearless and deep wrath, struck home at hypocrisy.

Whilst waiting for permission to have *Tartuffe* played; Moliére had brought out *le Médecin malgré lui*, *Amphitryon*, *Georges Dandin* and *l' Avare*, lavishing freely upon them the inexhaustible resources of his genius, which was ever ready to supply the wants of kingly and princely entertainments. *Monsieur de Pourceaugnac* was played for the first time at Chambord on the 6th of October, 1669; a year afterwards, on the same stage, appeared *le Bourgeois gentilhomme*, with the interludes and music of Lulli. The piece was a direct attack upon one of the most frequent absurdities of his day; many of the courtiers felt in their hearts that they were attacked; there was a burst of wrath at the first representation, by which the king had not appeared to be struck. Molière thought it was all over with him. Louis XIV. desired to see the piece a second time; "You have never written anything yet which has amused me so much; your comedy is excellent," said he to the poet; the court was at once seized with a fit of admiration.

The king had lavished his benefits upon Molière, who had an hereditary post near him as groom-of-the-chamber; he had given him a pension of seven thousand livres and the licence of the king's theatre; he had been pleased to stand godfather to one of his children, to whom the duchess of Orleans was godmother; he had protected him against the superciliousness of certain servants of his bedchamber, but all the monarch's puissance and constant favors could not obliterate public prejudice and give the comedian whom they saw every day on the boards the position and rank which his genius deserved. Molière's friends urged him to give up the stage. "Your health is going," Boileau would say to him, "because the duties of a comedian exhaust you. Why not give it up?" "Alas!" replied Molière with a sigh, "it is a point of honor that prevents me." "A what?" rejoined Boileau; "what! to smear your face with a moustache as Sganarelle and come on the stage to be thrashed with a stick? That is a pretty point of honor for a philosopher like you!"

Molière might probably have followed the advice of Boileau, he might probably have listened to the silent warnings of his failing powers, if he had not been unfortunate and sad. Unhappy in his marriage, justly jealous and yet passionately fond of his wife, without any consolation within him against the bitterness and vexations of his life, he sought in work and incessant activity the only distractions which had any charm for a high spirit, constantly wounded in its affections and its legitimate pride: *Psyché*, *Les Fourberies de Scapin*, *La Comtesse d'Escarbagnas*, betrayed nothing of their author's increasing sadness or suffering. *Les Femmes savantes* had at first but little success; the piece was considered heavy; the marvellous nicety of the portraits, the correctness of the judgments, the delicacy and elegance of the dialogue were not appreciated until later on. Molière had just composed *Le Malade imaginaire*, the last of that succession of blows which he had so often dealt the doctors; he was more ailing than ever; his friends, even his actors themselves pressed him not to have any play. "What would you have me do?" he replied: "there are fifty poor workmen who have but their day's pay to live upon; what will they do if we have no play? I should reproach myself with having neglected to give them bread for one single day, if I could really help it." Molière had a bad voice, a disagreeable hiccouch and harsh inflexions: "He was, nevertheless," say his contemporaries, "a comedian from head to foot; he seemed to have several voices, everything about him spoke, and, by a caper, by a smile, by a wink of the eye and a shake of the head, he conveyed more than the greatest speaker could have done by talking in an hour." He played as usual on the 17th of February, 1673; the curtain had risen exactly at four o'clock; Molière could hardly stand, and he had a fit during the burlesque ceremony (at the end of the play) whilst pronouncing the word *Juro*. He was icy-cold when he went back to Baron's box, who was waiting for him, who saw him home to Rue Richelieu, and who at the same time sent for his wife and two Sisters of Charity. When he went up again, with Madame Molière, into the room, the great comedian was dead. He was only fifty-one.

It has been a labor of love to go into some detail over the lives, works and characters of the great writers during the age of Louis XIV. They did too much honor to their time and their country, they had too great and too deep and effect in France and in Europe upon the successive developments of the human intellect to refuse then an important place in the history of that France to whose influence and glory they so powerfully contributed.

Molière did not belong to the French Academy; his profession had shut the doors against him. It was nearly a hundred years after his death, in 1778, that the Academy raised to him a bust, beneath which was engraved:

> "His glory lacks naught, ours did lack him."

It was by instinct and of its own free choice that the French Academy had refused to elect a comedian; it had grown and its liberty had increased under the sway of Louis XIV. In 1672, at the death of Chancellor Séguier, who became its protector after Richelieu, "it was so honored that the king was graciously pleased to take upon himself this office: the body had gone to thank him; his Majesty desired that the dauphin should be witness of what passed on an occasion so honorable to literature; after the speech of M. Harlay, archbishop of Paris and the man in France with most inborn talent for speaking, the king appearing somewhat touched, gave the Academicians very great marks of esteem, inquired the names, one after another, of those whose faces were not familiar to him, and said aside to M. Colbert, who was there in his capacity of simple Academician: 'You will let me know what I must do for these gentlemen.' Perhaps M. Colbert, that minister who was so zealous for the fine arts, never received an order more in conformity with his own inclinations." From that time, the French Academy held its sittings at the Louvre. and, as regarded complimentary addresses to the king on state occasions, it took rank with the sovereign bodies.

For thirty-five years the Academy had been working at its *Dictionnaire.* From the first the work had appeared interminable:

> "These six years past they toil at letter F,
> And I'd be much obliged if Destiny
> Would whisper to me: Thou shalt live to G,"—

wrote Boise-Robert to Balzac. The Academy had entrusted Vaugelas with the preparatory labor. "It was," says Pellisson, "the only way of coming quickly to an end." A pension, which he had not been paid for a long time past, was revived in his favor. Vaugelas took his plan to Cardinal Richelieu. "Well, sir," said the minister, smiling with a somewhat contemptuous air of kindness, "you will not forget the word *pension* in this dictionary." "No, Monsignor," replied M. de Vaugelas with a profound bow, "and still less *reconnaissance* (*gratitude*)." Vaugelas had finished the first volume of his *Remarques sur la langue Française*, which has ever since remained the basis of all works on grammar. "He had imported into the body of the work a something or other so estimable (*d'honnête homme*) and so much frankness that one could scarcely help loving its author." He was working at the second volume when he died, in 1649, so poor that his creditors, siezed his papers, making it very difficult for the Academy to recover his *Mémoires.* The dictionary, having lost its principal author, went on so slowly that Colbert curious to know whether the Academicians honestly earned their modest *medals for attendance* (*jetons de présence*) which he had assigned to them, came one day unexpectedly to a sitting: he was present at the whole discussion, "after which, having seen the attention and care which the Academy was bestowing upon the composition of its dictionary, he said, as he rose, that he was convinced that it could not get on any faster, and his evidence ought to be of so much the more weight in that never man in his position was more laborious or more diligent."

The Academicians, who were men of letters, worked at the dictionary; the Academicians, who were men of fashion, had become pretty numerous; Arnauld d'Andilly and M. de Lamoignon, whom the body had honored by election, declined to join, and the Academy resolved to never elect anybody without a previously expressed desire and request. At the same time when M. de Lamoignon declined, the king, fearing that it might bring the Academy into some disfavor, procured the appointment, in his stead, of the coadjutor of Strasbourg, Armand de Rohan-Soubise. "Splendid as your triumph may be," wrote Boileau to M. de Lamoignon, "I am persuaded, sir, from what I know of your noble and modest character, that you are very sorry to have caused this displeasure to a body which is after all very illustrious, and that you will attempt to make it manifest to all the earth. I am quite willing to believe that you had good reasons for acting as you have done." The Academy from that moment regarded the title it conferred as irrevocable: it did not fill up the place of the Abbé de St. Pierre when it found itself obliged to exclude him from its sittings by order of Louis XV.; it did not fill up the place of Mgr. Dupanloup when he thought proper to send in his resignation. In spite of court-intrigues it from that moment maintained its independence and its dignity. "M. Despréaux," writes the banker Leverrier to the duke of Noailles, "represented to the Academy with a great deal of heat that all was rack and ruin, since it was nothing more but a cabel of women that put Academicians in the place of those who died. Then he read out loud some verses by M. de St. Aulaire. . . . This M. Despréaux before the eyes of everybody, gave M. de St. Aulaire a black ball and nominated, all by himself, M. de Mimeure. Here, Monseigneur, is proof that there are Romans still in the world, and for the future, I will trouble you to call M. Despréaux no longer your dear poet, but your dear Cato."

With his extreme deafness, Boileau had great difficulty in fulfilling his Academic duties. He was a member of the Academy of medals and inscriptions, founded by Colbert in 1662, "in order to render the acts of the king immortal by deciding the legends of the medals struck in his honor." Pontchartrain raised to forty the number of the members of the *petite académie*, extended its functions, and entrusted it thenceforth with the charge of publishing curious documents relating to the history of France. "We had read to us to-day a very learned work, but rather tiresome," says Boileau to M. Pontchartrain, "and we were bored right eruditely; but afterwards there was an examination of another which was much more agreeable, and the reading of which attracted considerable attention. As the reader was put quite close to me, I was in a position to hear and to speak of it. All I ask you, to complete the measure of your kindnesses, is to be kind enough to let everybody know that, if I am of so little use at the Academy of Medals, it is equally true that I do not and do not wish to obtain any pecuniary advantage from it.

The Academy of Sciences had already for many years had sittings in one of the rooms of the king's library. Like the French Academy, it had owed its origin to private meetings at which Descartes, Gassendi and young Pascal were accustomed to be present. "There are in the world scholars of two sorts," said a note sent to Colbert about the formation of the new Academy. "One give themselves up to science because it is a pleasure to them: they are content, as the fruit of their labors, with the knowledge they acquire, and if they are known, it is only amongst those with whom they converse unambitiously and for mutual instruction; these are *bonâ fide* scholars, whom it is impossible to do without in a design so great as that of the *Académie royale.* There are others who cultivate science only as a field which is to give them sustenance, and, as they see by experience that great rewards fall only to those who make the most noise in the world, they apply themselves especially, not to making new discoveries, for hitherto that has not been recompensed, but to whatever may bring them into notice; these are scholars of the fashionable world, and such as one knows best." Colbert had the true scholar's taste; he had brought Cassini from Italy to take the direction of the new Observatory; he had ordered surveys for a general map of France; he had founded the *Journal des Savants;* literary men, whether Frenchmen or foreigners, enjoyed the king's bounties; Colbert had even conceived the plan of a universal Academy, a veritable forerunner of the Institute. The arts were not forgotten in this grand project; the academy of painting and sculpture dated from the regency of Anne of Austria; the pretensions of the Masters of Arts (*maitres ès arts*), who placed an interdict upon artists not belonging to their corporation, had driven Charles Lebrun, himself the son of a Master, to agitate for its foundation; Colbert added to it the academy of music and the academy of architecture, and created the French school of painting at Rome. Beside the palace for a long time past dedicated to this establishment, lived for more than thirty-five years, Le Poussin, the first and the greatest of all the painters of that French school which was beginning to spring up, whilst the Italian school, though blooming still in talent and strength, was forgetting more and more every day the nobleness, the purity, and the severity of taste which had carried to the highest pitch the art of the fifteenth century. The tradition of the masters in vogue in Italy, of the Caracci, of Guido, of Paul Veronese, had reached Paris with Simon Vouët, who had long lived at Rome. He was succeeded there by a Frenchman "whom, from his grave and thoughtful air, you would have taken for a father of Sorbonne," says M. Vitet in his charming *Vie de Lesueur:* "his black eye beneath his thick eyebrow nevertheless flashed forth a glance full of poesy and youth. His manner of living was not less surprising than his personal appearance. He might be seen walking in the streets of Rome, tablets in hand, hitting off by a stroke or two of his pencil at one time the antique fragments he came upon, at another the gestures, the attitudes, the faces of the persons who presented themselves in his path. Sometimes, in the morning, he would sit on the terrace of Trinità del Monte, beside another Frenchman five or six years younger, but already known for rendering landscapes with such fidelity, such fresh and marvellous beauty, that all the Italian masters gave place to him, and that, after two centuries, he has not yet met his rival."

"Of these two artists, the older evidently exercised over the other the superiority which genius has over talent. The smallest hints of Le Poussin were received by Claude Lorrain with deference and respect; and yet, to judge from the prices at which they severally sold their pictures, the landscape-painter had for the time an indisputable superiority."

Claude Gelée, called Lorrain, had fled when quite young from the shop of the confectioner with whom his parents had placed him; he had found means of getting to Rome; there he worked, there he lived, and there he died, returning but once to France, in the height of his renown, for just a few months, without even enriching his own land with any great number of his works; nearly all of them remained on foreign soil. Le Poussin, born at the Andelys in 1593, made his way with great difficulty to Italy; he was by that time thirty years old and had no more desire than Claude to return to France, where painting was with difficulty beginning to obtain a standing. His reputation, however, had penetrated thither; King Louis XIII. was growing weary of Simon Vouët's factitious lustre; he wanted Le Poussin to go to Paris; the painter for a long while held out; the king insisted: "I shall go," said Le Poussin, "like one sentenced to be sawn in halves and severed in twain." He passed eighteen months in France, welcomed enthusiastically, lodged at the Tuileries, magnificently paid, but exposed to the jealousies of Simon Vouët and his pupils; worried, thwarted, frozen to death by the hoarfrosts of Paris; he took the road back to Rome in November, 1642, on the pretext of going to fetch his wife, and did not return any more. He had left in France some of his masterpieces, models of that new, independent and conscientious art, faithfully studied from nature in all its Italian grandeur and from the treasures of the antique. "How did you arrive at such perfection?" people would ask Le Poussin. "By neglecting nothing," the painter would reply. In the same way Newton was soon to discover the great laws of the physical world "by always thinking thereon."

During Le Poussin's stay at Paris, he had taken as a pupil Eustache Lesueur, who had been trained in the studio of Simon Vouët, but had been struck from the first with the incomparable genius and proud independence of the master sent to him by fate. Alone he had supported Le Poussin in his struggle against the envious, alone he entered upon the road which revealed itself to him whilst he studied under Le Poussin. He was poor, he had great difficulty in managing to live. The delicacy, the purity, the suavity of his genius could shine forth in their entirety nowhere but in the convent of the Carthusians, whose cloister he was commissioned to decorate. There he painted the life of St. Bruno, breathing into this almost mystical work all the religious poetry of his soul and of his talent, ever delicate and chaste even in the allegorical figures of mythology with which he before long adorned the Hôtel Lambert. He had returned to his favorite pursuits, embellishing the churches of Paris with incomparable works, when, overwhelmed by the loss of his wife, and exhausted by the painful efforts of his genius, he died at thirty-seven in that convent of the Carthusians which he glorified with his talent, at the same time that he edified the monks with his religious zeal. Lesueur succumbed in a struggle too rude and too rough for his pure and delicate nature. Lebrun had returned from that Italy which Lesueur had never been able to reach; the old rivalry, fostered in the studio of Simon Vouët, was already being renewed between the two artists; the angelic art gave place to the worldly and the earthly. Lesueur died; Lebrun found himself master of the positon, assured by anticipation, and as it were by instinct, of sovereign dominion under the sway of the young king for whom he had been created.

Old Philip of Champagne alone might have disputed with him the foremost rank. He had passionately admired Le Poussin, he had attached himself to Lesueur. "Never," says M. Vitet, "had he sacrificed to fashion; never had he fallen into the vagaries of the degenerate Italian style." This upright, simple, painstaking soul, this inflexible conscience, looking continually into the human face, had preserved in his admirable portraits the life and the expression of nature which he was incessantly trying to seize and reproduce. Lebrun was preferred to him as first painter to the king by Louis XIV. himself; Philip of Champagne was delighted thereat; he lived in retirement, in fidelity to his friends of Port-Royal, whose austere and vigorous lineaments he loved to trace, beginning with M. de St. Cyran and ending with his own daughter, Sister Suzanne, who was restored to health by the prayers of Mother Agnes Arnauld.

Lebrun was as able a courtier as he was a good painter: the clever arrangement of his pictures, the richness and brilliancy of his talent, his faculty for applying art to industry, secured him with Louis XIV. a sway which lasted as long as his life. He was first painter to the king, he was director of the Gobelins and of the academy of painting: "He let nothing be done by the other artists but according to his own designs and suggestions. The worker in tapestry, the decorative painter, the statuary, the goldsmith took their models from him: all came from him, all flowed from his brain, all bore his imprint." The painter followed the king's ideas, being entirely after his own heart; for fourteen years he worked for Louis XIV., representing his life and his conquests, at Versailles; painting for the Louvre the victories of Alexander, which were engraved almost immediately by Audran and Édelinck. He was jealous of the royal favor, sensitive and haughty towards artists, honestly concerned for the king's glory and for the tasks confided to himself. The growing reputation of Mignard, whom Louvois had brought back from Rome, troubled and disquieted Lebrun. In vain did the king encourage him. Lebrun, already ill, said in the presence of Louis XIV. that fine pictures seem to become finer after the painter's death. "Do not you be in a hurry to die, M. Lebrun," said the king: "we esteem your pictures now quite as highly as posterity can." The small gallery at Versailles had been entrusted to Mignard; Lebrun withdrew to Montmorency, where he died in 1690, jealous of Mignard at the end as he had been of Lesueur at the outset of his life. Mignard became first painter to the king. He painted the ceiling of Val-de-Grâce, which was celebrated by Molière, but it was as a painter of portraits that he excelled in France: "M. Mignard does them best," said Le Poussin not long before, with lofty good nature, "though his heads are all paint, without force or character." To Mignard succeeded Rigaud as portrait-painter, worthy to preserve the features of Bossuet and Fénelon. The unity of organization, the brilliancy of style, the imposing majesty which the king's taste had everywhere stamped about him upon art as well as upon literature, were by this time beginning to decay simultaneously with the old age of Louis XIV., with the reverses of his arms and the increasing gloominess of his court; the artists who had illustrated his reign were dying one after another as well as the orators and the poets; the sculptor James Sarazin had been gone some time; Puget and the Anguiers were dead, as well as Mansard, Perrault and Le Nôtre; Girardon had but a few months to live; only Coysevox was destined to survive the king whose statue he had many a time moulded. The great age was disappearing slowly and sadly, throwing out to the last some noble gleams, like the aged king who had constantly served as its centre and guide, like olden France which he had crowned with its last and its most splendid wreath.

CHAPTER XLIX.

LOUIS XIV. AND HIS COURT.

LOUIS XIV. reigned everywhere, over his people, over his age, often over Europe; but nowhere did he reign so completely as over his court. Never were the wishes, the defects and the vices of a man so completely a law to other men as at the court of Louis XIV. during the whole period of his long life. When near to him, in the palace of Versailles, men lived and hoped and trembled; everywhere else in France, even at Paris, men vegetated. The existence of the great lords was concentrated in the court, about the person of the king. Scarcely could the most important duties bring them to absent themselves for any time. They returned quickly, with alacrity, with ardor; only poverty or a certain rustic pride kept gentlemen in their provinces. "The court does not make one happy," says La Bruyère, "it prevents one from being so anywhere else."

At the outset of his reign, and when, on the death of Cardinal Mazarin, he took the reins of power in hand, Louis XIV. had resolved to establish about him, in his dominions and at his court, "that humble obedience on the part of subjects to those who are set over them," which he regarded as "one of the most fundamental maxims of Christianity." "As the principal hope for the reforms I contemplated establishing in my kingdom lay in my own will," says he in his *Mémoires*, "the first step towards their foundation was to render my will quite absolute by a line of conduct which should induce submission and respect, rendering justice scrupulously to any to whom I owed it, but, as for favors, granting them freely and without constraint to any I pleased and when I pleased, provided that the sequel of my acts showed that, for all my giving no reason to anybody, I was none the less guided by reason."

The principle of absolute power, firmly fixed in the young king's mind, began to pervade his court from the time that he disgraced Fouquet and ceased to dissemble his affection for Mdlle. de La Vallière. She was young, charming and modest. Of all the king's favorites she alone loved him sincerely. "What a pity he is a king!" she would say. Louis XIV. made her a duchess; but all she cared about was to see him and please him. When Madame de Montespan began to supplant her in the king's favor, the grief of Madame de La Vallière was so great that she thought she should die of it. Then she turned to God, in penitence and despair. Twice she sought refuge in a convent at Chaillot. "I should have left the court sooner," she sent word to the king on leaving, "after having lost the honor of your good graces, if I could have prevailed upon myself never to see you again; that weakness was so strong in me that hardly now am I capable of making a sacrifice of it to God: after having given you all my youth, the rest of my life is not too much for the care of my salvation." The king still clung to her. "He sent M. Colbert to beg her earnestly to come to Versailles and that he might speak with her. M. Colbert escorted her thither; the king conversed for an hour with her and wept bitterly. Madame de Montespan was there to meet her with open arms and tears in her eyes." "It is all incomprehensible," adds Madame de Sévigné: "some say that she will remain at Versailles and at court, others that she will return to Chaillot; we shall see." Madame de La Vallière remained three years at court, "half penitent," she said humbly, detained there by the king's express wish, in consequence of the tempers and jealousies of Madame de Montespan, who felt herself judged and condemned by her rival's repentance. Attempts were made to turn Madame de La Vallière from her inclination for the Carmelites': "Madame," said Madame Scarron to her one day, "here are you one blaze of gold: have you really considered that at the Carmelites', before long, you will have to wear serge?" She, however, persisted. She was already practising in secret the austerities of the convent. "God has laid in this heart the foundation of great things," said Bossuet, who supported her in her conflict: "the world puts great hindrances in her way and God great mercies; I have hopes that God will prevail; the uprightness of her heart will carry everything."

"When I am in trouble at the Carmelites'," said Madame de La Vallière, as at last she quitted the court, "I will think of what those people have made me suffer." "The world itself makes us sick of the world," said Bossuet in the sermon he preached on the day of her taking the dress: "its attractions have enough of illusion, its favors enough of inconstancy, its rebuffs enough of bitterness, there is enough of injustice and perfidy in the dealings of men, enough of unevenness and capriciousness in their intractable and contradictory humors—

there is enough of it all, without doubt, to disgust us." "She was dead to me the day she entered the Carmelites'," said the king thirty-five years later, when the modest and fervent nun expired at last, in 1710, at her convent, without having ever relaxed the severities of her penance. He had married the daughter she had given him to the prince of Conti. "Everybody has been to pay compliments to this saintly Carmelite," says Madame de Sévigné, without appearing to perceive the singularity of the alliance between words and ideas: "I was there too with Mademoiselle. The prince of Conti detained her in the parlor. What an angel appeared to me at last! She had to my eyes all the charms we had seen heretofore. I did not find her either puffy or sallow; she is less thin, though, and more happy-looking. She has those same eyes of hers and the same expression; austerity, bad living and little sleep have not made them hollow or dull; that singular dress takes away nothing of the easy grace and easy bearing. As for modesty, she is no grander than when she presented to the world a princess of Conti, but that is enough for a Carmelite. In real truth, this dress and this retirement are a great dignity for her." The king never saw her again, but it was at her side that Madame de Montespan, in her turn forced to quit the court, went to seek advice and pious consolation. "This soul will be a miracle of grace," Bossuet had said.

It was no longer the time of "this tiny violet that hides itself in the grass," as Madame de Sévigné used to remark. Madame de Montespan was haughty, passionate, "with hair dressed in a thousand ringlets, a majestic beauty to show off to the ambassadors:" she openly paraded the favor she was in, accepting and angling for the graces the king was pleased to do her and hers, having the superintendence of the household of the queen whom she insulted without disguise, to the extent of wounding the king himself: "Pray consider that she is your mistress," he said one day to his favorite. The scandal was great; Bossuet attempted the task of stopping it. It was the time of the Jubilee: neither the king nor Madame de Montespan had lost all religious feeling; the wrath of God and the refusal of the sacraments had terrors for them still. Madame de Montespan left the court after some stormy scenes; the king set out for Flanders. "Pluck this sin from your heart, Sir," Bossuet wrote to him: "and not only this sin, but the cause of it; go even to the root. In your triumphant march amongst people whom you constrain to recognize your might, would you consider yourself secure of a rebel fortress if your enemy still had influence there? We hear of nothing but the magnificence of your troops, of what they are capable under your leadership! And as for me, Sir, I think in my secret heart of a war far more important, of a far more difficult victory which God holds out before you. What would it avail you to be dreaded and victorious without, when you are vanquished and captive within?" "Pray God for me," wrote the bishop at the same time to Marshal Bellefonds, "pray Him to deliver me from the greatest burden man can have to bear or to quench all that is man in me that I may act for Him only. Thank God, I have never yet thought, during the whole course of this business, of my belonging to the world; but that is not all, what is wanted is to be a St. Ambrose, a true man of God, a man of that other life, a man in whom everything should speak, with whom all his words should be oracles of the Holy Spirit, all his conduct celestial; pray, pray, I do beseech you."

At the bottom of his soul and in the innermost sanctuary of his conscience Bossuet felt his weakness; he saw the apostolic severance from the world, the apostolic zeal and fervor required for the holy crusade he had undertaken. "Your Majesty has given your promise to God and the world," he wrote to Louis XIV. in ignorance of the secret correspondence still kept up between the king and Madame de Montespan. "I have been to see her," added the prelate: "I find her pretty calm: she occupies herself a great deal in good works. I spoke to her as well as to you the words in which God commands us to give Him our whole heart; they caused her to shed many tears; may it please God to fix these truths in the bottom of both your hearts and accomplish His work, in order that so many tears, so much violence, so many strains that you have put upon yourselves may not be fruitless."

The king was on the road back to Versailles; Madame de Montespan was to return thither also, her duties required her to do so, it was said; Bossuet heard of it; he did not for a single instant delude himself as to the emptiness of the king's promises and of his own hopes. He determined, however, to visit the king at Luzarches. Louis XIV. gave him no time to speak. "Do not say a word to me, sir," said he, not without blushing, "do not say a word; I have given my orders, they will have to be executed." Bossuet held his tongue. "He had tried every thrust; had acted like a pontiff of the earliest times, with a freedom worthy of the earliest ages and the earliest bishops of the Church," says St. Simon. He saw the inutility of his efforts; henceforth, prudence and courtly behavior put a seal upon his lips. It was the time of the great king's omnipotence and highest splendor, the time when nobody withstood his wishes. The great Mademoiselle had just attempted to show her independence: tired of not being married,

With a curse on the greatness which kept her astrand,

she had made up her mind to a love-match. "Guess it in four, guess it in ten, guess it in a hundred," wrote Madame de Sévigné to Madame de Coulanges: "you are not near it; well, then, you must be told. M. de Lauzun is to marry on Sunday at the Louvre, with the king's permission, mademoiselle . . . mademoiselle de . . . mademoiselle, guess the name . . . he is to marry Mademoiselle, my word! upon my word! my sacred word! Mademoiselle, the great Mademoiselle, Mademoiselle daughter of the late Monsieur, Mademoiselle grand-daughter of Henry IV., Mademoiselle d'Eu, Mademoiselle de Dombes, Mademoiselle de Montpensier, Mademoiselle d'Orléans, Mademoiselle, cousin-german to the king, Mademoiselle destined to the throne, Mademoiselle, the only match in France who would have been worthy of Monsieur!" The astonishment was somewhat premature; Mademoiselle did not espouse Lauzun just then, the king broke off the marriage. "I will make you so great," he said to Lauzun, "that you shall have no cause to regret what I am taking from you; meanwhile, I make you duke and peer and marshal of France." "Sir," broke in Lauzun, insolently, "you have made so many dukes that it is no longer an honor to be one, and, as for the bâton of marshal of France, your Majesty can give it me when I have earned it by my services." He was before long sent to Pignerol, where he passed ten years. There he met Fouquet and that mysterious personage called the Iron Mask, whose name has not yet been discovered to a certainty by means of all the most ingenious conjectures. It was only by settling all her property on the duke of Maine after herself that Mademoiselle purchased Lauzun's release. The king had given his posts to the prince of Marcillac, son of La Rochefoucauld. He at the same time overwhelmed Marshal Bellefonds with kindnesses. "He sent for him into his study," says Madame de Sévigné, "and said to him: 'Marshal, I want to know why you are anxious to leave me; is it a devout feeling? Is it a desire for retirement?

Is it the pressure of your debts? If the last, I shall be glad to set it right and enter into the details of your affairs.' The marshal was sensibly touched by this kindness: 'Sir,' said he, 'it is my debts; I am over head and ears. I cannot see the consequences borne by some of my friends who have assisted me and whom I cannot pay.' 'Well,' said the king; 'they must have security for what is owing to them. I will give you a hundred thousand francs on your house at Versailles, and a patent of retainder (*brevet de retenue*—whereby the emoluments of a post were not lost to the holder's estate by his death) for four hundred thousand francs, which will serve as a policy of assurance if you should die; that being so, you will stay in my service.' In truth, one must have a very hard heart not to obey a master who enters with so much kindness into the interests of one of his domestics; accordingly, the marshal made no objection, and here he is in his place again and loaded with benefits."

The king entered benevolently into the affairs of a marshal of France; he paid his debts, and the marshal was his *domestic;* all the court had come to that; the duties which brought servants in proximity to the king's person were eagerly sought after by the greatest lords. Bontemps, his chief valet, and Fagon, his physician, as well as his surgeon Maréchal, very excellent men too, were all-powerful amongst the courtiers. Louis XIV. had possessed the art of making his slightest favors prized; to hold the candlestick at bedtime (*au petit coucher*), to make one in the trips to Marly, to play in the king's own game, such was the ambition of the most distinguished; the possessors of grand historic castles, of fine houses at Paris, crowded together in attics at Versailles, too happy to obtain a lodging in the palace. The whole mind of the greatest personages, his favorites at the head, was set upon devising means of pleasing the king; Madame de Montespan had pictures painted in miniature of all the towns he had taken in Holland; they were made into a book which was worth four thousand pistoles, and of which Racine and Boileau wrote the text; people of tact, like M. de Langlée, paid court to the master through those whom he loved. "M. de Langlée has given Madame de Montespan a dress of the most divine material ever imagined; the fairies did this work in secret, no living soul had any notion of it; and it seemed good to present it as mysteriously as it had been fashioned. Madame de Montespan's dressmaker brought her the dress she had ordered of him; he had made the body a ridiculous fit; there was shrieking and scolding as you may suppose. The dressmaker said, all in a tremble: 'As time presses, madame, see if this other dress that I have here might not suit you for lack of anything else.' 'Ah! what material! Does it come from heaven? There is none such on earth.' The body is tried on; it is a picture. The king comes in. The dressmaker says, 'Madame, it is made for you.' Everybody sees that it is a piece of gallantry: but on whose part? 'It is Langlée,' says the king: 'it is Langlée.' 'Of course,' says Madame de Montespan, 'none but he could have devised such a device, it is Langlée, it is Langlée.' Everybody repeats, 'it is Langlée;' the echoes are agreed and say, 'it is Langlée;' and as for me, my child, I tell you, to be in the fashion, 'it is Langlée.'"

All the style of living at court was in accordance with the magnificence of the king and his courtiers; Colbert was beside himself at the sums the queen lavished on play; Madame de Montespan lost and won back four millions in one night at bassette; Mdlle. de Fontanges gave away twenty thousand crowns' worth of New Year's gifts; the king had just accomplished the dauphin's marriage: "He made immense presents on this occasion; there is certainly no need to despair," said Madame de Sévigné; "though one does not happen to be his valet, it may happen that, whilst paying one's court, one will find one's self underneath what he showers around. One thing is certain, and that is, that away from him all services go for nothing; it used to be the contrary." All the court were of the same opinion as Madame de Sévigné.

A new power was beginning to appear on the horizon, with such modesty and backwardness that none could as yet discern it, least of all could the king. Madame de Montespan had looked out for some one to take care of and educate her children. She had thought of Madame Scarron; she considered her clever; she was so herself, "in that unique style which was peculiar to the Montemarts," said the duke of St. Simon; she was fond of conversation; Madame Scarron had a reputation for being rather a blue-stocking; this the king did not like; Madame de Montespan had her way; Madame Scarron took charge of the children secretly and in an isolated house. She was attentive, careful, sensible. The king was struck with her devotion to the children entrusted to her. "She can love," he said; "it would be a pleasure to be loved by her." The confidence of Madame de Montespan went on increasing.

"The person of quality (Madame de Montespan) has no partnership with the person who has a cold (Madame Scarron), for she regards her as the confidential person; the lady who is at the head of all (the queen) does the same; she is, therefore, the soul of this court," writes Madame de Sévigné in 1680. There were, however, frequent storms; Madame de Montespan was jealous and haughty, and she grew uneasy at the nascent liking she observed in the king for the correct and shrewd judgment, the equable and firm temper of his children's governess. The favor of which she was the object did not come from Madame de Montespan. The king had made the Parliament legitimatize the duke of Maine, Mdlle. de Nantes and the count of Vexin; they were now formally installed at Versailles. Louis XIV. often chatted with Madame Scarron. She had bought the estate of Maintenon out of the king's bounty. He made her take the title. The recollection of Scarron was displeasing to him. "It is supposed that I am indebted for this present to Madame de Montespan," she wrote to Madame de St. Géran; "I owe it to my little prince. The king was amusing himself with him one day, and, being pleased with the manner in which he answered his questions, told him that he was a very sensible little fellow. 'I can't help being,' said the child, 'I have by me a lady who is sense itself.' 'Go and tell her,' replied the king, 'that you will give her this evening a hundred thousand francs for your sugar-plums.' The mother gets me into trouble with the king, the son makes my peace with him; I am never for two days together in the same situation, and I do not get accustomed to this sort of life, I who thought I could make myself used to anything." She often spoke of leaving the court. "As I tell you everything honestly," she wrote in 1675 to her confessor, Abbé Gobelin, "I will not tell you that it is to serve God that I should like to leave the place where I am; I believe that I might work out my salvation here and elsewhere, but I see nothing to forbid us from thinking of our repose and withdrawing from a position which vexes us every moment. I explained myself badly if you understood me to mean that I am thinking of being a nun; I am too old for a change of condition, and according to the property I shall have, I shall look out for securing one full of tranquillity. In the world, all reaction is towards God; in a convent, all reaction is towards the world; there is one great reason; that of age comes next." She did not, however, leave the court except to take to the waters the little duke of Maine, who had become a cripple after a series of violent convulsions. "Never was anything more agreeable than the surprise which Madame de Maintenon gave the king," writes Madame de Sévigné to her daughter. "He had not expected the duke of Maine till the next day, when he saw him come walking into his room and only holding by the hand of his governess; he was transported with joy. M. de Louvois on her arrival went to call upon Madame de Maintenon; she supped at Madame de Richelieu's, some kissing her hand, others her gown, and she making fun of them all, if she is not much changed; but they say that she is." The king's pleasure in conversing with the governess became more marked every day: Madame de Montespan frequently burst out into bitter complaints. "She reproaches me with her kindnesses, with her presents, with those of the king, and has told me that she fed me and that I am strangling her; you know what the fact is; it is a strange thing that we cannot live together and that we cannot separate. I love her and I cannot persuade myself that she hates me." They found themselves alone together in one of the court-carriages. "Let us not be duped by such a thing as this," said Madame de Montespan rudely; "let us talk as if we had no entanglements between us to arrange; it being understood of course," added she, "that we resume our entanglements when we get back." "Madame de Maintenon accepted the proposal," says Madame de Caylus, who tells the story, "and they kept their word to the letter." Madame de Maintenon had taken a turn for preaching virtue. "The king passed two hours in my closet," she wrote to Madame de St. Géran; "he is the most amiable man in his kingdom. I spoke to him of Father Bourdaloue. He listened to me attentively. Perhaps he is not so far from thinking of his salvation as the court suppose. He has good sentiments and frequent reactions towards God." "The star of Quanto (Madame de Montespan) is paling," writes Madame de Sévigné to her daughter: "there are tears, natural pets, affected gayeties, poutings—in fact, my dear, all is coming to an end. People look, observe, imagine, believe there are to be seen as it were rays of light upon faces which, a month ago, were thought to be unworthy of comparison with others. If Quanto had hidden her face with her cap at Easter in the year she returned to Paris, she would not be in the agitated state in which she now is. The spirit indeed was willing, but great is human weakness; one likes to make the most of a remnant of beauty. This is an economy which ruins rather than enriches."

"Madame de Montespan asks advice of me," said Madame de Maintenon; "I speak to her of God, and she thinks I have some understanding with the king; I was present yesterday at a very animated conversation between them. I wondered at the king's patience, and at the rage of that vain creature. It all ended with these terrible words: 'I have told you already, Madame; I will not be interfered with.'"

Henceforth, Madame de Montespan "interfered with" the king. He gave the new dauphiness Madame de Maintenon as her mistress of the robes. "I am told," writes Madame de Sévigné, "that the king's conversations do nothing but increase and improve, and that they last from six to ten o'clock, that the daughter-in-law goes occasionally to pay them a shortish visit, that they are found each in a big chair, and that, when the visit is over, the talk is resumed. The lady is no longer accosted without awe and respect, and the ministers pay her the court which the rest do. No friend was ever so careful and attentive as the king is to her; she makes him acquainted with a perfectly new line of country—I mean the intercourse of friendship and conversation, without chicanery and without constraint; he appears to be charmed with it."

Discreet and adroit as she was, and artificial without being false, Madame de Maintenon gloried in bringing back the king and the court to the ways of goodness. "There is nothing so able as irreproachable conduct," she used to say. The king often went to see the queen; the latter heaped attentions upon Madame de Maintenon. "The king never treated me more affectionately than he has since she had his ear," the poor princess would say. The dauphiness had just had a son. The joy at court was excessive. "The king let anybody who pleased embrace him," says the Abbé de Croisy: "he gave everybody his hand to kiss. Spinola, in the warmth of his zeal, bit his finger; the king began to exclaim: 'Sir,' interrupted the other, 'I ask your Majesty's pardon; but, if I hadn't bitten you, you would not have noticed me.' The lower orders seemed beside themselves, they made bonfires of everything. The porters and the Swiss burned the poles of the chairs and even the floorings and wainscots intended for the great gallery. Bontemps, in wrath, ran and told the king, who burst out laughing and said, 'Let them be, we will have other floorings.'"

The least clearsighted were beginning to discern the modest beams of a rising sun. Madame de Montespan, who had a taste for intellectual things, had not long since recommended Racine and Boileau to the king to write a history of his reign. They had been appointed historiographers. "When they had done some interesting piece," says Louis Racine in his *Mémoires*, "they used to go and read it to the king at Madame de Montespan's. Madame de Maintenon was generally present at the reading. She, according to Boileau's account, liked my father better than him, and Madame de Montespan, on the contrary, liked Boileau better than my father, but they always paid their court jointly, without any jealousy between them. When Madame de Montespan would let fall some rather tart expressions, my father and Boileau, though by no means sharpsighted, observed that the king, without answering her, looked with a smile at Madame de Maintenon, who was seated opposite to him on a stool, and who finally disappeared all at once from these meetings. They met her in the gallery and asked her why she did not come any more to hear their readings. She answered very coldly: 'I am no longer admitted to those mysteries.' As they found a great deal of cleverness in her, they were mortified and astonished at this. Their astonishment was very much greater, then, when the king, being obliged to keep his bed, sent for them with orders to bring what they had newly written of history, and they saw as they went in Madame de Maintenon sitting in an arm-chair near the king's pillow, chatting familiarly with his Majesty. They were just going to begin their reading, when Madame de Montespan, who had not been expected, came in, and, after a few compliments to the king, paid such long ones to Madame de Maintenon, that the king, to stop them, told her to sit down: 'As it would not be fair,' he added, 'to read without you a work which you yourself ordered.' From this day, the two historians paid their court to Madame de Maintenon as far as they knew how to do so."

The queen had died on the 30th of July, 1683, piously and gently, as she had lived. "This is the first sorrow she ever caused me," said the king, thus rendering homage, in his superb and unconscious egotism, to the patient virtue of the wife he had put to such cruel trials. Madame de Maintenon was agitated but resolute. "Madame de Montespan has plunged into the deepest devoutness," she wrote, two months after the queen's death: "it is quite time she edified us; as for me, I no longer think of retiring." Her strong common-sense and her far-sighted ambition, far more than her virtue, had secured her against rocks ahead; henceforth she saw the goal, she was close upon it, she moved towards it with an even step. The king still looked in upon Madame de Montespan of an evening on his way to the gaming-table; he only stayed an instant, to pass on to Madame de Maintenon's; the latter had modestly refused to become lady in attendance upon the dauphiness. She, however, accompanied the king on all his expeditions, "sending him away always afflicted but never disheartened." Madame de Montespan, piqued to see that the king no longer thought of anybody but Madame de Maintenon, "said to him one day at Marly," writes Dangeau, "that she had a favor to ask of him, which was to let her have the duty of entertaining the second-carriage people and of amusing the antechamber." It required more than seven years of wrath and humiliation to make her resolve upon quitting the court, in 1691.

The date has never been ascertained exactly of the king's private marriage with Madame de Maintenon. It took place probably eighteen months or two years after the queen's death; the king was forty-seven, Madame de Maintenon fifty. "She had great remains of beauty, bright and sprightly eyes, an incomparable grace," says St. Simon, who detested her, "an air of ease and yet of restraint and respect, and a great deal of cleverness, with a speech that was sweet, correct, in good terms and naturally eloquent and brief."

Madame de La Vallière had held sway over the young and passionate heart of the prince, Madame de Montespan over the court, Madame de Maintenon alone established her empire over the man and the king. "Whilst giving up our heart, we must remain absolute master of our mind," Louis XIV. had written, "separate our affections from our resolves as a sovereign, that she who enchants us may never have liberty to speak to us of our business or of the people who serve us, and that they be two things absolutely distinct." The king had scrupulously applied this maxim; Mdlle. de La Vallière had never given a thought to business; Madame de Montespan had sought only to shine, disputing the influence of Colbert when he would have put a limit upon her ruinous fancies, leaning for support at the last upon Louvois, in order to counterbalance the growing power of Madame de Maintenon; the latter alone had any part in affairs, a smaller part than has frequently been made out, but important, nevertheless, and sometimes decisive. Ministers went occasionally to do their work in her presence with the king, who would turn to her when the questions were embarassing, and ask, "What does your

Solidity think?" The opinions she gave were generally moderate and discreet. "I did not manage to please in my conversation about the buildings," she wrote to Cardinal Noailles, "and what grieves me is to have caused vexation to no purpose. Another block of chambers is being built here at a cost of a hundred thousand francs; Marly will soon be a second Versailles. The people, what will become of them?" And later on: "Would you think proper, monsignor, to make out a list of good bishops? You could send it me, so that, on the occasions which are constantly occurring, I might support their interests, and they might have the business referred to them in which they ought to have a hand and for which they are the proper persons; I am always spoken to when the question is of them; and, if I were better informed, I should be bolder." "It is said that you meddle too little with business," Fénelon wrote to her in 1694: "your mind is better calculated for it than you suppose. You ought to direct your whole endeavors to giving the king views tending to peace and especially to the relief of the people, to moderation, to equity, to mistrust of harsh and violent measures, to horror for acts of arbitrary authority, and finally to love of the Church and to assiduity in seeking good pastors for it." Neither Fénelon nor Madame de Maintenon had seen in the revocation of the edict of Nantes "an act of arbitrary authority or a harsh and violent measure." She was not inclined towards persecution, but she feared lest her moderation should be imputed to a remnant of prejudice in favor of her former religion, "and this it is," she would say, "which makes me approve of things quite opposed to my sentiments." An egotistical and cowardly prudence, which caused people to attribute to Madame de Maintenon, in the severities against the Huguenots, a share which she had not voluntarily or entirely assumed.

Whatever the apparent reserve and modesty with which it was cloaked, the real power of Madame de Maintenon over the king's mind peeped out more and more into broad daylight. She promoted it dexterously by her extreme anxiety to please him as well as by her natural and sincere attachment to the children whom she had brought up and who had a place near the heart of Louis XIV. Already the young duke of Maine had been sent to the army at the dauphin's side; the king was about to have him married [August 29, 1692] to Mdlle. de Charolais; carefully seeking for his natural children alliances amongst the princes of his blood, he had recently given Mdlle.

de Nantes, daughter of Madame de Montespan, to the duke, grandson of the great Condé. "For a long time past," says St. Simon, "Madame de Maintenon, even more than the king, had been thinking of marrying Mdlle. de Blois, Madame de Montespan's second daughter, to the duke of Chartres; he was the king's own and only nephew, and the first moves towards this marriage were the more difficult in that Monsieur was immensely attached to all that appertained to his greatness, and Madame was of a nation which abhorred misalliances and of a character which gave no promise of ever making this marriage agreeable to her." The king considered himself sure of his brother; he had set his favorites to work and employed underhand intrigues. "He sent for the young duke of Chartres, paid him attention, told him he wanted to have him settled in life, that the war which was kindled on all sides put out of his reach the princesses who might have suited him, that there were no princesses of the blood of his own age, that he could not better testify his affection towards him than by offering him his daughter whose two sisters had married princes of the same blood; but that, however eager he might be for this marriage, he did not want to put any constraint upon him and would leave him full liberty in the matter. This language, addressed with the awful majesty so natural to the king to a prince who was timid and had not a word to say for himself, put him at his wits' end." He fell back upon the wishes of his father and mother. "That is very proper in you," replied the king: "but, as you consent, your father and mother will make no objection;" and, turning to Monsieur, who was present, "Is it not so, brother?" he asked. Monsieur had promised: a messenger was sent for Madame, who cast two furious glances at her husband and her son, saying that, as they were quite willing, she had nothing to say, made a curt obeisance and went her way home. Thither the court thronged next day; the marriage was announced. "Madame was walking in the gallery with her favorite, Mdlle. de Château-Thiers, taking long steps, handkerchief in hand, weeping unrestrainedly, speaking somewhat loud, gesticulating and making a good picture of Ceres after the rape of her daughter Proserpine, seeking her in a frenzy and demanding her back from Jupiter. Everybody saluted, and stood aside out of respect. Monsieur had taken refuge in lansquenet; never was anything so shame-faced as his look or so disconcerted as his whole appearance, and this first condition lasted more than a month with him. The duke of Chartres came into the gallery, going up to his mother as he did every day to kiss her hand. At that moment Madame gave him a box o' the ear so loud that it was heard some paces off, and, given as it was before the whole court, covered the poor prince with confusion and overwhelmed the countless spectators with prodigious astonishment." That did not prevent or hamper the marriage, which took place with great pomp at Versailles on the 18th of February, 1692. The king was and continued to the last the absolute and dread master of all his family to its remotest branches.

He lost through this obedience a great deal that is charming and sweet in daily intercourse. For him and for Madame de Maintenon the great and inexhaustible attraction of the duchess of Burgundy was her gaiety and unconstrained ease, tempered by the most delicate respect, which this young princess, on coming as quite a child to France from the court of Savoy, had tact enough to introduce and always maintain amidst the most intimate familiarity. "In public, demure, respectful with the king, and on terms of timid propriety with Madame de Maintenon, whom she never called anything but *aunt*, thus prettily blending rank and affection. In private, chattering, frisking, fluttering around them, at one time perched on the arm of one or the other's chairs, at another playfully sitting on their knee, she would throw herself upon their necks, embrace them, kiss them, fondle them, pull them to pieces, chuck them under the chin, tease them, rummage their tables, their papers, their letters, reading them sometimes against their will, according as she saw that they were in the humor to laugh at it, and occasionally speaking thereon. Admitted to everything, even at the reception of couriers bringing the most important news, going into the king at any hour, even at the time the council was sitting, useful and also fatal to ministers themselves, but always inclined to help, to excuse, to benefit, unless she were violently set against any body. The king could not do without her; when, rarely, she was absent from his supper in public, it was plainly shown by a cloud of more than usual gravity and taciturnity over the king's whole person; and so, when it happened that some ball in winter or some party in summer made her break into the night, she arranged matters so well that she was there to kiss the king the moment he was awake and to amuse him with an account of the affair" [*Mémoires de St. Simon*, t. x. p. 186].

The dauphiness had died in 1690; the duchess of Burgundy

was, therefore, almost from childhood queen of the court and before long the idol of the courtiers; it was around her that pleasure sprang up; it was for her that the king gave the entertainments to which he had habituated Versailles, not that for her sake or to take care of her health he would ever consent to modify his habits or make the least change in his plans. "Thank God, it is over," he exclaimed one day, after an accident to the princess; "I shall no longer be thwarted in my trips and in all I desire to do by the representations of physicians. I shall come and go as I fancy; and I shall be left in peace." Even in his court and amongst his most devoted servants, this monstrous egotism astounded and scandalized everybody. "A silence in which you might have heard an ant move succeeded this sally," says St. Simon, who relates the scene: "we looked down; we hardly dared draw breath. Everybody stood aghast. To the very builder's-men and gardeners everybody was motionless. This silence lasted more than a quarter of an hour. The king broke it, as he leaned against a balustrade of the great basin, to speak about a carp. Nobody made any answer. He afterwards addressed his remarks about these carp to some builder's-men who did not keep up the conversation in the regular way; it was but a question of carp with them. Everything was at a low ebb, and the king went away some little time after. As soon as we dared look at one another out of his sight, our eyes meeting told all." There was no venturing beyond looks. Fénelon had said with severe charity, "God will have compassion upon a prince beset from his youth up by flatterers."

Flattery ran a risk of becoming hypocrisy. On returning to a regular life, the king was for imposing the same upon his whole court; the instinct of order and regularity, smothered for a while in the hey-day of passion, had resumed all its sway over the naturally proper and steady mind of Louis XIV. His dignity and his authority were equally involved in the cause of propriety and regularity at his court; he imposed this yoke as well as all the others; there appeared to be entire obedience; only some princes or princesses escaped it sometimes, getting about them a few free-thinkers or boon-companions; good, honest folks showed ingenuous joy; the virtuous and far-sighted were secretly uneasy at the falsehood and deplored the pressure put on so many consciences and so many lives. The king was sincere in his repentance for the past, many persons in his court were as sincere as he; others, who were not, affected, in order to please him, the externals of austerity; absolute power oppressed all spirits, extorting from them that hypocritical complaisance which it is liable to engender; corruption was already brooding beneath appearances of piety; the reign of Louis XV. was to see its deplorable fruits displayed with a haste and a scandal which are to be explained only by the oppression exercised in the last years of King Louis XIV.

Madame de Maintenon was like the genius of this reaction towards regularity, propriety, order; all the responsibility for it has been thrown upon her; the good she did has disappeared beneath the evil she allowed or encouraged; the regard lavished upon her by the king has caused illusions as to the discreet care she was continually taking to please him. She was faithful to her friends, so long as they were in favor with the king; if they had the misfortune to displease him, she, at the very least, gave up seeing them; without courage or hardihood to withstand the caprices and wishes of Louis XIV., she had gained and preserved her empire by dint of dexterity and far-sighted suppleness beneath the externals of dignity.

She never forgot her origin. "I am not a grandee," she would say: "I am a mushroom." Her life, entirely devoted to the king, had become a veritable slavery; she said as much to Mdlle. d'Aumale at St. Cyr. "I have to take for my prayers and for mass the time when everybody else is still sleeping. For, when once they begin coming into my room, at half-past seven, I haven't another moment to myself. They come filing in and nobody goes out without being relieved by somebody higher. At last comes the king; then of course they all have to go out: he remains with me up to mass. I am still in my night-cap. The king comes back after mass; then the duchess of Burgundy with her ladies. They remain whilst I dine. I have to keep up the conversation, which flags every moment, and to manage so as to harmonize minds and reconcile hearts which are as far as possible asunder. The circle is all round me, and I cannot ask for anything to drink; I sometimes say to them (aside), 'It is a great honor, but really I should prefer a footman.' At last they all go away to dinner. I should be free during that time, if Monseigneur did not generally choose it for coming to see me, for he often dines earlier in order to go hunting. He is very difficult to entertain, having very little to say and finding himself a bore and running away from himself continually: so I have to talk for two. Immediately after the king has dined, he comes into my room with all the royal family, princes and princesses: then I must be prepared for the gayest of conversation and wear a smiling face amidst so much distressing news. When this company disperses, some lady has always something particular to say to me; the duchess of Burgundy also wants to have a chat. The king returns from hunting. He comes to me. The door is shut and nobody else is admitted. Then I have to share his secret troubles, which are no small number. Arrives a minister; and the king sets himself to work. If I am not wanted at this consultation, which seldom happens, I withdraw to some further distance and write or pray. I sup, whilst the king is still at work. I am restless, whether he is alone or not. The king says to me, 'You are tired, madame; go to bed.' My women come. But I feel that they interfere with the king, who would chat with me and who does not like to chat before them; or, perhaps, there are some ministers still there, whom he is afraid they may overhear. Wherefore I make haste to undress, so much so that I often feel quite ill from it. At last I am in bed. The king comes up and remains by my pillow until he goes to supper. But a quarter of an hour before supper, the dauphin and the duke and duchess of Burgundy come in to me again. At ten, everybody goes out. At last I am alone, but very often the fatigues of the day prevent me from sleeping."

She was at that time seventy. She was often ailing; but the duchess of Burdundy was still very young, and the burthen of the most private matters of court-diplomacy fell entirely upon Madame de Maintenon. "The princess des Ursins is about to return to Spain," she said: "if I do not take her in hand, if I do not repair by my attentions the coldness of the duchess of Burgundy, the indifference of the king, and the curtness of the other princes, she will go away displeased with our court, and it is expedient that she should praise it and speak well of it in Spain."

It was, in fact, through Madame de Maintenon and her correspondence with the princess des Ursins that the private business between the two courts of France and Spain was often carried on. At Madrid, far more than at Versailles, the influence of women was all-powerful. The queen ruled her husband, who was honest and courageous but without wit or daring; and the princess des Ursins ruled the queen, as intelligent and as amiable as her sister the duchess of Burgundy, but more ambitious and more haughty. Louis XIV. had several times conceived some misgiving of the camarera major's influence over his grandson; she had been disgraced and then recalled; she had finally established her sway by her fidelity, ability, dexterity, and indomitable courage. She served France habitually, Spain and her own influence in Spain always; she had been charming, with an air of nobility, grace, elegance and majesty all together, and accustomed to the highest society and the most delicate intrigues, during her sojourn at Rome and Madrid; she was full of foresight and calculation, but impassioned, ambitious, implacable, pushing to extremes her amity as well as her hatred, faithful to her master and mistress in their most cruel trials, and then hampering and retarding peace for the sake of securing for herself a principality in the Low Countries. Without having risen from the ranks, like Madame de Maintenon, she had reached a less high and less safe elevation; she had been more absolutely and more daringly supeme during the time of her power, and at last she fell with the rudest shock, without any support from Madame de Maintenon. The pretensions of Madame des Ursins during the negotiations had offended France; "this was the stone of stumbling between the two supreme directresses," says St. Simon; after this attempt at sovereignty, there was no longer the same accord between Madame de Maintenon and Madame des Ursins, but this latter had reached in Spain a point at which she more easily supposed that she could dispense with it. The queen of Spain had died at the age of twenty-six, in 1714; did the princess for a moment conceive the hope of marrying Philip V. in spite of the disproportion in rank and age? Nobody knows; she had already been reigning as sovereign mistress for some months, when she received from the king this stunning command: "Look me out a wife." She obeyed; she looked out. Alberoni, an Italian priest, brought into Spain by the duke of Vendôme, drew her attention to the princess of Parma, Elizabeth Farnese. The principality was small, the princess young; Alberoni laid stress upon her sweetness and modesty: "Nothing will be more easy," he said, "than for you to fashion her to Spanish gravity, by keeping her retired; in the capacity of her camerera major, entrusted with her education, you will easily be able to acquire complete sway over her mind." The princess des Ursins believed him and settled the marriage. "Cardonne has surrendered at last, madame," she wrote on the 20th of September, 1714, to Madame de Maintenon; "there is nothing left in Catalonia that is not reduced. The new queen, at her coming into this kingdom, is very fortunate to find no more war there. She whom we have lost would have been beside herself with delight at enjoying peace after having experienced such cruel sufferings of all kinds. The longer I live, the more I see that we are never so near a reverse of Fortune as when she is favorable or so near receiving favors as when she is maltreating us. For that reason, madame, if one were wise, one would take her inconstancy graciously."

The time had come for Madame des Ursins to make definitive trial of Fortune's inconstancy. She had gone to meet the new queen, in full dress and with her ornaments; Elizabeth received her coldly; they were left alone; the queen reproached the princess with negligence in her costume; Madame des Ursins, strangely surprised, would have apologized, "but, all at once, there was the queen at offensive words, and screaming, summoning, demanding officers, guards, and imperiously ordering Madame des Ursins out of her presence. She would have spoken; but the queen, with redoubled rage and threats, began to scream out for the removal of this mad woman from her presence and her apartments, she had her put out by the shoulders and on the instant into a carriage with one of her women, to be taken at once to St. Jean-de- Luz. It was seven o'clock at night, the day but one before Christmas, the ground all covered with ice and snow; Madame des Ursins had no time to change gown or head-dress, to take any measures against the cold, to get any money or anything else at all." Thus she was conducted almost without a mouthful of food to the frontier of France. She hoped for aid from the king of Spain; but none came: it got known that the queen had been abetted in everything and beforehand by Philip V. On arriving at St. Jean-de-Luz, she wrote to the king and to Madame de Maintenon: "Can you possibly conceive, madame, the situation in which I find myself? Treated, in the face of all Europe, with more contempt by the queen of Spain than if I were the lowest of wretches? They want to persuade me that the king acted in concert with a princess who had me treated with such cruelty. I shall await his orders at St. Jean-de-Luz, where I am in a small house close by the sea. I see it often stormy and sometimes calm; a picture of courts. I shall have no difficulty in agreeing with you that it is of no use looking for stability but in God. Certainly it cannot be found in the human heart, for who was ever more sure than I was of the heart of the king of Spain?"

The king did not reply at all and Madame de Maintenon but

coldly, begging the princess, however, to go to Versailles. There she passed but a short time, and received notice to leave the kingdom. With great difficulty she obtained an asylum at Rome, where she lived seven years longer, preserving all her health, strength, mind and easy grace until she died, in 1722, at more than eighty-four years of age, in obscurity and sadness, notwithstanding her opulence, but avenged of her Spanish foes, Cardinals della Giudice and Alberoni, whom she met again at Rome, disgraced and fugitive like herself. "I do not know where I may die," she wrote to Madame de Maintenon, at that time in retirement at St. Cyr. Both had survived their power; the princess des Ursins had not long since wanted to secure for herself a dominion; Madame de Maintenon, more far-sighted and more modest, had aspired to no more than repose in the convent which she had founded and endowed. Discreet in her retirement as well as in her life, she had not left to chance the selection of a place where she might die.

CHAPTER L.

LOUIS XIV. AND DEATH (1711—1715).

"ONE has no more luck at our age," Louis XIV. had said to his old friend Marshal Villars returning from his most disastrous campaign. It was a bitter reflection upon himself which had put these words into the king's mouth. After the most brilliant, the most continually and invariably triumphant of reigns, he began to see fortune slipping away from him and the grievous consequences of his errors successively overwhelming the State. "God is punishing me, I have richly deserved it," he said to Marshal Villars, who was on the point of setting out for the battle of Denain. The aged king, dispirited and beaten, could not set down to men his misfortunes and his reverses; the hand of God Himself was raised against his house; Death was knocking double knocks all round him. The grand-dauphin had for some days been ill of small-pox. The king had gone to be with him at Meudon, forbidding the court to come near the castle. The small court of Monseigneur were huddled together in the lofts. The king was amused with delusive hopes: his chief physician, Fagon, would answer for the invalid. The king continued to hold his councils as usual, and the deputation of *market-women* (*dames de la Halle*), came from Paris to have news of Monseigneur, went away, declaring that they would go and sing a *Te Deum*, as he was nearly well. "It is not time yet, my good women," said Monseigneur who had given them a reception. That very evening he was dead, without there having been time to send for his confessor in ordinary. "The parish priest of Meudon, who used to look in every evening before he went home, had found all the doors open, the valets distracted, Fagon heaping remedy upon remedy without waiting for them to take effect. He entered the room and hurrying to Monseigneur's bedside, took his hand and spoke to him of God. The poor prince was fully conscious, but almost speechless. He repeated distinctly a few words, others inarticulately, smote his breast, pressed the priest's hand, appeared to have the most excellent sentiments and received absolution with an air of contrition and wistfulness" [*Mémoires de St. Simon*, ix.]. Meanwhile word had been sent to the king, who arrived quite distracted. The princess of Conti, his daughter, who was deeply attached to Monseigneur, repulsed him gently: "You must think only of yourself now, Sir," she said. The king let himself sink down upon a sofa, asking news of all that came out of the room, without any one's daring to give him an answer. Madame de Maintenon, who had hurried to the king, and was agitated without being affected, tried to get him away: she did not succeed, however, until Monseigneur had breathed his last. He passed along to his carriage between two rows of officers and valets, all kneeling and conjuring him to have pity upon them who had lost all and were like to starve.

The excitement and confusion at Versailles were tremendous. From the moment that small-pox was declared, the princes had not been admitted to Meudon. The duchess of Burgundy alone had occasionally seen the king. All were living in confident expectation of a speedy convalescence; the news of the death came upon them like a thunderclap. All the courtiers thronged together at once, the women half-dressed, the men anxious and concerned, some to conceal their extreme sorrow, others their joy, according as they were mixed up in the different cabals of the court. "It was all, however, nothing but a transparent veil," says St. Simon, "which did not prevent good eyes from observing and discerning all the features. The two princes and the two princesses, seated beside them, taking care of them, were most exposed to view. The duke of Burgundy wept, from feeling and in good faith, with an air of gentleness, tears of nature, of piety and of patience. The duke of Berry, in quite as good faith, shed abundance, but tears, so to speak, of blood, so great appeared to be their bitterness; he gave forth not sobs but shrieks, howls. The duchess of Berry (daughter of the duke of Orleans) was beside herself. The bitterest despair was depicted on her face. She saw her sister-in-law, who was so hateful to her, all at once raised to that title, that rank of dauphiness, which were about to place so great a distance between them. Her frenzy of grief was not from affection, but from interest; she would wrench herself from it to sustain her husband, to embrace him, to console him, then she would become absorbed in herself again with a torrent of tears which helped her to stifle her shrieks. The duke of Orleans wept in his own corner, actually sobbing, a thing which, had I not seen it, I should never have believed," adds St. Simon, who detested Monseigneur and had as great a dread of his reigning as the duke of Orleans had: "Madame, re-dressed in full dress, in the middle of the night, arrived regularly howling, not quite knowing why either one or the other; inundating them all with her tears as she embraced them and making the castle resound with a renewal of shrieks, when the king's carriages were announced, on his return to Marly." The duchess of Burgundy was awaiting him on the road. She stepped down and went to the carriage-window. "What are you about, madame?" exclaimed Madame de Maintenon: "do not come near us, we are infectious." The king did not embrace her, and she went back to the palace but only to be at Marly next morning before the king was awake.

The king's tears were as short as they had been abundant. He lost a son who was fifty years old, the most submissive and most respectful creature in the world, ever in awe of him and obedient to him, gentle and good natured, a proper man amid all his indolence and stupidity, brave and even brilliant at the head of an army. In 1688, in front of Philipsburg, the soldiers had given him the name of "Louis the Bold." He was full of spirits and always ready, "revelling in the trenches," says Vauban. The duke of Montausier, his boyhood's strict governor, had written to him: "Monseigneur, I do not make you my compliments on the capture of Philipsburg; you had a fine army, shells, cannon and Vauban. I do not make them to you either on your bravery; it is an hereditary virtue in your house; but I congratulate you on being open-handed, humane, generous, and appreciative of the services of those who do well; that is what I make you my compliments upon." "Did not I tell you so?" proudly exclaimed the chevalier de Grignan, formerly attached (as *menin*) to the person of Monseigneur, on hearing his master's exploits lauded: "for my part, I am not surprised." Racine had exaggerated the virtues of Monseigneur in the charming verses of the prologue to *Esther:*

Thou givest him a son, an ever ready aid,
Apt or to woo or fight, obey or be obey'd;
A son who, like his sire, drags vict'ry in his train,
Yet boasts but one desire, that father's heart to gain;
A son, who to his will submits with loving air,
Who brings upon his foes perpetual despair.
As the swift spirit flies, stern Equity's envoy,
So, when the king says "Go," down rusheth he in joy,
With vengeful thunderbolt red ruin doth complete,
Then tranquilly return to lay it at his feet.

In 1690 and in 1694 he had gained distinction as well as in 1688. "The dauphin has begun as others would think it an honor to leave off," the prince of Orange had said, "and, for my part, I should consider that I had worthily capped anything great I may have done in war if, under similar circumstances, I had made so fine a march." Whether it were owing to indolence or court-cabal, Monseigneur had no more commands; he had no taste for politics and always sat in perfect silence at the council, to which the king had formally admitted him at thirty years of age, "instructing him," says the marquis of Sourches, "with so much vigor and affection that Monseigneur could not help falling at his feet to testify his respect and gratitude." Twice, at grave conjunctures, the grand-dauphin allowed his voice to be heard; in 1685, to offer a timid opposition to the edict of Nantes, and, in 1700, to urge very vigorously the acceptance of the king of Spain's will: "I should be enchanted," he cried, as if with a prophetic instinct of his own destiny, "to be able to say all my life, 'The king my father and the king my son.'" Heavy in body as well as mind, living on terms of familiarity with a petty court, probably married to Mdlle. Choin, who had been for a long time installed in his establishment at Meudon, Monseigneur, often embarrassed and made uncomfortable by the austere virtue of the duke of Burgundy, and finding more attraction in the duke of Berry's frank geniality, had surrendered himself, without intending it, to the plots which were woven about him. "His eldest son behaved to him rather as a courtier than as a son, gliding over the coldness shown him with a respect and a gentleness which, together, would have won over any father less a victim to intrigue. The duchess of Burgundy, in spite of her address and her winning grace, shared her husband's disfavor." The duchess of Berry had counted upon this to establish her sway in a reign which the king's great age seemed to render imminent; already, it was said, the chief amusement at Monseigneur's was to examine engravings of the coronation-ceremony, when death carried him off suddenly on the 14th of April, 1711, to the consternation of the lower orders, who loved him because of his reputation for geniality. The severity of the new dauphin caused some little dread.

"Here is a prince who will succeed me before long," said the king on presenting his grandson to the assembly of the clergy: "by his virtue and piety he will render the Church still more flourishing and the kingdom more happy." That was the hope of all good men. Fénelon, in his exile at Cambrai, and the dukes of Beauvilliers and Chevreuse, at court, began to feel themselves all at once transported to the heights with the prince whom they had educated and who had constantly remained faithful to them. The delicate foresight and prudent sagacity of Fénelon had a long while ago sought to prepare his pupil for the part which he was about to play. It was piety alone that had been able to triumph over the dangerous tendencies of a violent and impassioned temperament. Fénelon, who had felt this, saw also the danger of devoutness carried too far. "Religion does not consist in a scrupulous observance of petty formalities," he wrote to the duke of Burgundy; "it consists, for everybody, in the virtues proper to one's condition. A great prince ought not to serve God in the same way as a hermit or a simple individual." "The prince thinks too much and acts too little," he said to the duke of Chevreuse: "his most solid occupations are confined to vague applications of his mind and barren resolutions; he must see society, study it, mix in it, without becoming a slave to it, learn to express himself forcibly and acquire a gentle authority. If he do not feel the need of possessing firmness and nerve, he will not make any real progress: it is time for him to be a man. The life of the region in which he lives is a life of effeminacy, indolence, timidity and amusement. He will never be so true a servant to the king and to Monseigneur as when he makes them see that they have in him a man matured, full of application, firm, impressed with their true interests and fitted to aid them by the wisdom of his counsels and the vigor of his conduct. Let him be more and more little in the hands of God, but let him become great in the eyes of men; it is his duty to make virtue, combined with authority, loved, feared and respected."

Court-perfidy dogged the duke of Burgundy to the very head of the army over which the king had set him; Fénelon, always correctly informed, had often warned him of it. The duke wrote to him, in 1708, on the occasion of his dissensions with Vendôme: "It is true that I have experienced a trial within the last fortnight, and I am far from having taken it as I ought, allowing myself to give way to an oppression of the heart caused by the blackenings, the contradictions and the pains of irresolution and the fear of doing something untoward in a matter of extreme importance to the State. As for what you say to me about my indecision, it is true that I myself reproach myself for it, and I pray God every day to give me, together with wisdom and prudence, strength and courage to carry out what I believe to be my duty." He had no more commands, in spite of his entreaties to obtain, in 1709, permission to march against the enemy. "If money is short, I will go without any train," he said: "I will live like a simple officer; I will eat, if need be, the bread of a common soldier, and none will complain of lacking superfluities when I have scarcely necessaries." It was at the very time when the archbishop of Cambrai was urgent for peace to be made at any price. "The people no longer live like human beings," he said in a memorial sent to the duke of Beauvilliers; "there is no counting any longer on their patience, they are reduced to such outrageous trials. As they have nothing more to hope, they have nothing more to fear. The king has no right to risk France in order to save Spain; he received his kingdom from God, not that he should expose it to invasion by the enemy, as if it were a thing with which he can do anything he pleases, but that he should rule it as a father and transmit it as a precious heirloom to his posterity." He demanded at the same time the convocation of the assembly of notables.

It was this kingdom, harassed on all sides by its enemies, bleeding, exhausted, but stronger, nevertheless, and more bravely faithful than was made out by Fénelon, that the new dauphin found himself suddenly called upon to govern by the death of Monseigneur, and by the unexpected confidence testified in him before long by the king. "The prince should try more than ever to appear open, winning, accessible and sociable," wrote Fénelon: "he must undeceive the public about the scruples imputed to him; keep his strictness to himself, and not set the court apprehending a severe reform of which society is not capable, and which would have to be introduced imperceptibly, even if it were possible. He cannot be too careful to please the king, avoid giving him the slightest umbrage, make him feel a dependence founded on confidence and affection, relieve him in his work, and speak to him with a gentle and respectful force which will grow by little and little. He should say no more than can be borne; it requires to have the heart prepared for the utterance of painful truths which are not wont to be heard. For the rest, no puerilities or pettinesses in the practice of devotion; government is learnt better from studying men than from studying books."

The young dauphin was wise enough to profit by these sage and able counsels. "Seconded to his heart's content by his adroit young wife, herself in complete possession of the king's private ear and of the heart of Madame de Maintenon, he redoubled his attentions to the latter, who, in her transport at finding a dauphin on whom she might rely securely instead of one who did not like her, put herself in his hands and, by that very act, put the king in his hands. The first fortnight made perceptible to all at Marly this extraordinary change in the king, who was so reserved towards his legitimate children, so very much the king with them. Breathing more freely after so great a step had been made, the dauphin showed a bold front to society, which he dreaded during the lifetime of Monseigneur, because, great as he was, he was often the victim of its best received jests. The king having come round to him; the insolent cabal having been dispersed by the death of a father, almost an enemy, whose place he took; society in a state of respect, attention, alacrity; the most prominent personages with an air of slavishness; the gay and frivolous, no insignificant portion of a large court, at his feet through his wife, it was observed that this timid, shy, self-concentrated prince, this precise (piece of) virtue this (bit of) misplaced learning, this gawky man, a stranger in his own house, constrained in everything—it was observed, I say, that he was showing himself by degrees, unfolding himself little by little, presenting himself to society in moderation, and that he was unembarrassed, majestic, gay, and agreeable in it. A style of conversation, easy but instructive, and happily and aptly directed, charmed the sensible courtier and made the rest wonder. There was all at once an opening of eyes and ears and hearts. There was a taste of the consolation, which was so necessary and so longed for, of seeing one's future master so well fitted to be from his capacity and from the use that he showed he could make of it."

The king had ordered ministers to go and do their work at the prince's. The latter conversed modestly and discreetly with the men he thought capable of enlightening him; the duke of St. Simon had this honor, which he owed to the friendship of the duke of Beauvilliers, and of which he showed himself sensible in his *Mémoires*. Fénelon was still at Cambrai, "which all at once turned out to be the only road from all the different parts of Flanders. The archbishop had such and so eager a court there that for all his delight he was pained by it, from apprehension of the noise it would make and the bad effect he feared it might have on the king's mind." He, however, kept writing to the dauphin, sending him plans of government prepared long before: some wise, bold, liberal, worthy of a mind that was broad and without prejudices; others chimerical and impossible of application. The prince examined them with care: "He had comprehended what it is to leave God for God's sake, and had set about applying himself almost entirely to things which might make him acquainted with government, having a sort of foretaste already of reigning, and being more and more the hope of the nation, which was at last beginning to appreciate him."

God had in former times given France a St. Louis: He did not deem her worthy of possessing such an ornament a second time. The comfort and hope which were just appearing in the midst of so many troubles vanished suddenly like lightning: the dauphiness fell ill on the 5th of February; she had a burning fever and suffered from violent pains in the head; it was believed to be scarlet-fever (*rougeole*), with whispers, at the same time, of ugly symptoms; the malady went on increasing; the dauphin was attacked in his turn; sacraments were mentioned; the princess, taken by surprise, hesitated without daring to speak. Her Jesuit confessor, Father La Rue, himself proposed to go and fetch another priest. A *Récollet* (*Raptionist*) was brought; when he arrived she was dying. A few hours later she expired, at the age of twenty-six, on the 12th of February, 1712. "With her there was a total eclipse of joys, pleasures, amusements even, and every sort of grace; darkness covered the whole face of the court; she was the soul of it all, she filled it all, she pervaded all the interior of it." The king loved her as much as he was capable of loving; she amused him and charmed him in the sombre moments of his life; he, like the dauphin, had always been ignorant of the giddinesses of which she had been guilty; Madame de Maintenon, who knew of them and who held them as a rod over her, was only concerned to keep them secret; all the court, with the exception of a few perfidious intriguers, made common cause to serve her and please her. "Regularly ugly, pendent cheeks, forehead too prominent, a nose that said nothing; of eyes the most speaking and most beautiful in the world; a carriage of the head gallant, majestic, graceful, and a look the same; smile the most expressive, waist long, rounded, slight, supple; the gait of a goddess on the clouds; her youthful, vivacious, energetic gayety, carried all before it, and her nymph-like agility wafted her everywhere like a whirlwind that fills many places at once and gives to them movement and life. If the court existed after her it was but to languish away" [*Mémoires de St. Simon*, xi.]. There was only one blow more fatal for death to deal; and there was not long to wait for it.

"I have prayed and I will pray," writes Fénelon: "God knows whether the prince is for one instant forgotten. I fancy I see him in the state in which St. Augustin depicts himself: "My heart is obscured by grief. All that I see reflects for me but the image of death. All that was sweet to me, when I could share it with her whom I loved, becomes a torment to me since I lost her. My eyes seek for her everywhere and find her nowhere. When she was alive, wherever I might be without her, everything said to me, You are going to see her. Nothing says so now. I find no solace but in my tears. I cannot bear the weight of my wounded and bleeding heart, and yet I know not where to rest it. I am wretched; for so it is when the heart is set on the love of things that pass away." "The days of this affliction were soon shortened," says St. Simon: "from the first moment I saw him, I was scared at his fixed, haggard look, with a something of ferocity, at the change in his countenance and the livid marks I noticed upon it. He was waiting at Marly for the king to awake; they came to tell him he could go in; he turned without speaking a word, without replying to his gentlemen (*menins*) who pressed him to go; I went up to him, taking the liberty of giving him a gentle push; he gave me a look that pierced right to the heart and went away. I never looked on him again. Please God in His mercy I may look on him forever there where his goodness, no doubt, has placed him!"

It was a desperate but a short struggle. Disease and grief were victorious over the most sublime courage. "It was the spectacle of a man beside himself, who was forcing himself to keep the surface smooth, and who succumbed in the attempt." The dauphin took to his bed on the 14th of February; he believed himself to be poisoned, and said, from the first, that he should never recover. His piety alone, through the most prodigious efforts, still kept up; he spoke no more, save to God, continually lifting up his soul to Him in fervent aspirations. "What tender, but tranquil views! What lively motions towards thanksgiving for being preserved from the sceptre and the account that must be rendered thereof! What submission and how complete! What ardent love of God! What a magnificent idea of infinite mercy! What pious and humble awe! What invincible patience! What sweetness! What constant kindness towards all that approached him! What pure charity which urged him forward to God! France at length succumbed beneath this last chastisement; God gave her a glimpse of a prince whom she did nor deserve. Earth was not worthy of him; he was already ripe for a blessed eternity!"

"For some time past I have feared that a fatality hung over the dauphin," Fénelon had written at the first news of his illness: "I have at the bottom of my heart a lurking apprehension that God is not yet appeased towards France. For a long while He has been striking, as the prophet says, and His anger is not yet worn out. God has taken from us all our hope for the Church and for the State."

Fénelon and his friends had expected too much and hoped for too much; they relied upon the dauphin to accomplish a work above human strength; he might have checked the evil, retarded for a while the march of events, but France carried simultaneously in her womb germs of decay and hopes of progress, both as yet concealed and confused, but too potent and too intimately connected with the very sources of her history and her existence for the hand of the most virtuous and most capable of princes to have the power of plucking them out or keeping them down.

There was universal and sincere mourning in France and in Europe. The death of the little duke of Brittany, which took place a few days after that of his parents, completed the consternation into which the court was thrown. The most sinister rumors circulated darkly; a base intrigue caused the duke of Orleans to be accused; people called to mind his taste for chemistry and even magic, his flagrant impiety, his scandalous debauchery; beside himself with grief and anger, he demanded of the king to be sent to the Bastille; the king refused curtly, coldly, not unmoved in his secret heart by the perfidious insinuations which made their way even to him, but too just and too sensible to entertain a hateful lie, which, nevertheless, lay heavy on the duke of Orleans to the end of his days.

Darkly, but to more effect, the same rumors were renewed before long. The duke of Berry died at the age of twenty-seven on the 4th of May, 1714, of a disease which presented the same features as the scarlet fever (*rougeole pourprée*) to which his brother and sister-in-law had succumbed. The king was old and sad: the state of his kingdom preyed upon his mind; he was surrounded by influences hostile to his nephew, whom he himself called "a vaunter of crimes." A child who was not five years old remained sole heir to the throne. Madame de Maintenon, as sad as the king, "naturally mistrustful, addicted to jealousies, susceptibilities, suspicions, aversions, spites, and woman's wiles" [*Lettres de Fénelon au duc de Chevreuse*], being, moreover, sincerely attached to the king's natural children, was constantly active on their behalf. On the 19th of July, 1714, the king announced to the premier president and the attorney-general of the parliament of Paris that it was his pleasure to grant to the duke of Maine and to the count of Toulouse, for themselves and their decendants, the rank of princes of the blood, in its full extent, and that he desired that the deed should be enregistered in the parliament. Soon after, still under the same influence, he made a will which was kept a profound secret and which he sent to be deposited in the strong-room (*greffe*) of the parliament, committing the guardianship of the future king to the duke of Maine, and placing him, as well as his brother, on the council of regency, with close restrictions as to the duke of Orleans, who would be naturally called to the government of the kingdom during the minority. The will was darkly talked about: the effect of the elevation of the bastards to the rank of princes of the blood had been terrible. "There was no longer any son of France:

the Spanish branch had renounced; the duke of Orleans had been carefully placed in such a position as not to dare say a word or show the least dissatisfaction; his only son was a child; neither the duke (of Berry), his brothers, nor the prince of Conti, were of an age or of standing, in the king's eyes, to make the least trouble in the world about it. The bombshell dropped all at once when nobody could have expected it, and everybody fell on his stomach as is done when a shell drops: everybody was gloomy and almost wild; the king himself appeared as if exhausted by so great an effort of will and power." He had only just signed his will, when he met, at Madame de Maintenon's, the Ex-Queen of England. "I have made my will, Madame," said he: "I have purchased repose; I know the impotence and uselessness of it; we can do all we please as long as we are here; after we are gone, we can do less than private persons; we have only to look at what became of my father's, and immediately after his death too, and of those of so many other kings. I am quite aware of that; but, in spite of all that, it was desired; and so, Madame, you see it has been done; come of it what may, at any rate I shall not be worried about it any more." It was the old man yielding to the entreaties and intrigues of his domestic circle; the judgment of the king remained steady and true, without illusions and without prejudices.

Death was coming, however, after a reign which had been so long and had occupied so much room in the world that it caused mistakes as to the very age of the king. He was seventy-seven, he continued to work with his ministers; the order so long and so firmly established was not disturbed by illness any more than it had been by the reverses and sorrows of late; meanwhile, the appetite was diminishing, the thinness went on increasing, a sore on the legs appeared, the king suffered a great deal. On the 24th of August he dined in bed, surrounded as usual by his courtiers; he had a difficulty in swallowing; for the first time, publicity was burdensome to him; he could not get on, and said to those who were there that he begged them to withdraw. Meanwhile the drums and hautboys still went on playing beneath his window, and the twenty-four violins at his dinner. In the evening, he was so ill that he asked for the sacraments. There had been wrung from him a codicil which made the will still worse. He, nevertheless, received the duke of Orleans, to whom he commended the young king. On the 26th he called to his bedside all those of the court who had the entry. "Gentlemen," he said to them, "I ask your pardon for the bad example I have set you. I have to thank you much for the way in which you have served me and for the attachment and fidelity you have always shown me. I am very sorry not to have done for you what I should have liked to do. The bad times are the cause of that. I request of you on my great-grandson's behalf the same attention and fidelity that you have shown me. It is a child who will possibly have many crosses to bear. Follow the instructions my nephew gives you; he is about to govern the kingdom, and I hope that he will do it well; I hope also that you will all contribute to preserve unity. I feel that I am becoming unmanned and that I am unmanning you also; I ask your pardon. Farewell, gentlemen, I feel sure that you will think of me sometimes."

The princesses had entered the king's closet; they were weeping and making a noise; "You must not cry so," said the king who asked for them to bid them farewell. He sent for the little dauphin. His governess, the duchess of Ventadour, brought him on to the bed. "My child," said the king to him, "you are going to be a great king. Render to God that which you owe to Him; recognize the obligations you have towards Him; cause Him to be honored by your subjects; try to preserve peace with your neighbors. I have been too fond of war; do not imitate me in that, any more than in the too great expenses I have incurred. Take counsel in all matters, and seek to discern which is the best in order to follow it. Try to relieve your people, which I have been so unfortunate as not to have been able to do." He kissed the child, and said," Darling, I give you my blessing with all my heart." He was taken away; the king asked for him once more and kissed him again, lifting hands and eyes to heaven in blessings upon him. Everybody wept. The king caught sight in a glass of two grooms of the chamber who were sobbing: "What are you crying for?" he said to them: "did you think that I was immortal?" He was left alone with Madame de Maintenon: "I have always heard say that it was difficult to make up one's mind to die," said he: "I do not find it so hard." "Ah, Sir," she replied; "it may be very much so, when there are earthly attachments, hatred in the heart or restitutions to make!" "Ah!" replied the king, "as for restitutions to make, I owe nobody any individually; as for those that I owe the kingdom, I have hope in the mercy of God."

The duke of Orleans came back again; the king had sent for him. "When I am dead," he said: "you will have the young king taken to Vincennes; the air there is good; he will remain there until all the ceremonies are over at Versailles and the castle well cleaned afterwards; you will then bring him back again." He at the same time gave orders for going and furnishing Vincennes, and directed a casket to be opened in which the plan of the castle was kept, because, as the court had not been there for fifty years, Cavoye, grand chamberlain of his household, had never prepared apartments there. "When I was king . . . ," he said several times.

A quack had brought a remedy which would cure gangrene, he said. The sore on the leg was hopeless, but they gave the king a dose of this elixir in a glass of Alicante. "To life and to death," said he as he took the glass: "just as it shall please God." The remedy appeared to act; the king recovered a little strength. The throng of courtiers, which, the day before, had been crowding to suffocation in the rooms of the duke of Orleans, withdrew at once. Louis XIV. did not delude himself about this apparant rally. "Prayers are offered in all the churches for your Majesty's life," said the parish-priest of Versailles. "That is not the question," said the king: "it is my salvation that much needs praying for."

Madame de Maintenon had hitherto remained in the back-rooms, though constantly in the king's chamber when he was alone. He said to her once, "What consoles me for leaving you, is that it will not be long before we meet again." She made no reply. "What will become of you?" he added: "you have nothing." "Do not think of me," said she: "I am nobody; think only of God." He said farewell to her: she still remained a little while in his room and went out when he was no longer conscious. She had given away here and there the few movables that belonged to her, and now took the road to St. Cyr. On the steps she met Marshal Villeroi: "Good-bye, marshal," she said curtly and covered up her face in her coifs. He it was who sent her news of the king to the last moment. The duke of Orleans, on becoming regent, went to see her and took her the patent (*brevet*) for a pension of sixty thousand livres, "which her disinterestedness had made necessary for her," said the preamble. It was paid her up to the last day of her life. History makes no further mention of her name; she never left St. Cyr. Thither the czar Peter the Great, when he visited Paris and France, went to see her;

she was confined to her bed; he sat a little while beside her. "What is your malady?" he asked her through his interpreter. "A great age," answered Madame de Maintenon, smiling. He looked at her a moment longer in silence; then, closing the curtains, he went out abruptly. The memory he would have called up had vanished. The woman on whom the great king had, for thirty years, heaped confidence and affection was old, forgotten, dying; she expired at St. Cyr on the 15th of April, 1719, at the age of eighty-three.

She had left the king to die alone. He was in the agonies; the prayers in extremity were being repeated around him; the ceremonial recalled him to consciousness. He joined his voice with the voices of those present, repeating the prayers with them. Already the court was hurrying to the duke of Orleans'; some of the more confident had repaired to the duke of Maine's; the king's servants were left almost alone around his bed; the tones of the dying man were distinctly heard above the great number of priests. He several times repeated: *Nunc et in hora mortis.* Then he said quite loud: "O my God, come Thou to help me, haste Thee to succor me." Those were his last words. He expired on Sunday, the 1st of September, 1715, at eight a.m. Next day, he would have been seventy-seven years of age, and he had reigned seventy-two of them.

In spite of his faults and his numerous and culpable errors, Louis XIV. had lived and died like a king. The slow and grievous agony of olden France was about to begin.

END OF THE FOURTH VOLUME.

www.ingramcontent.com/pod-product-compliance
Lightning Source LLC
LaVergne TN
LVHW020933110826
845150LV00004B/851

9781425552367